Intelligent Networks and Intelligence in Networks

IFIP – The International Federation for Information Processing

IFIP was founded in 1960 under the auspices of UNESCO, following the First World Computer Congress held in Paris the previous year. An umbrella organization for societies working in information processing, IFIP's aim is two-fold: to support information processing within its member countries and to encourage technology transfer to developing nations. As its mission statement clearly states,

> IFIP's mission is to be the leading, truly international, apolitical organization which encourages and assists in the development, exploitation and application of information technology for the benefit of all people.

IFIP is a non-profitmaking organization, run almost solely by 2500 volunteers. It operates through a number of technical committees, which organize events and publications. IFIP's events range from an international congress to local seminars, but the most important are:

- the IFIP World Computer Congress, held every second year;
- open conferences;
- working conferences.

The flagship event is the IFIP World Computer Congress, at which both invited and contributed papers are presented. Contributed papers are rigorously refereed and the rejection rate is high.

As with the Congress, participation in the open conferences is open to all and papers may be invited or submitted. Again, submitted papers are stringently refereed.

The working conferences are structured differently. They are usually run by a working group and attendance is small and by invitation only. Their purpose is to create an atmosphere conducive to innovation and development. Refereeing is less rigorous and papers are subjected to extensive group discussion.

Publications arising from IFIP events vary. The papers presented at the IFIP World Computer Congress and at open conferences are published as conference proceedings, while the results of the working conferences are often published as collections of selected and edited papers.

Any national society whose primary activity is in information may apply to become a full member of IFIP, although full membership is restricted to one society per country. Full members are entitled to vote at the annual General Assembly, National societies preferring a less committed involvement may apply for associate or corresponding membership. Associate members enjoy the same benefits as full members, but without voting rights. Corresponding members are not represented in IFIP bodies. Affiliated membership is open to non-national societies, and individual and honorary membership schemes are also offered.

Intelligent Networks and Intelligence in Networks

IFIP TC6 WG6.7 International Conference on Intelligent Networks and Intelligence in Networks, 2–5 September 1997, Paris, France

Edited by

Dominique Gaïti

University Pierre and Marie Curie - Paris
and University of Technology - Troyes
France

SPRINGER SCIENCE+BUSINESS MEDIA, LLC

First edition 1997

Originally published by International Federation for Information Processing in 1997
MyCopy version of the original edition 1997

DOI 10.1007/978-0-387-35323-4

A catalogue record for this book is available from the British Library

Printed on permanent acid-free text paper, manufactured in accordance with ANSI/NISO Z39.48-1992 and ANSI/NISO Z39.48-1984 (Permanence of Paper).
www.springer.com/mycopy

CONTENTS

Preface

International Conference
Intelligent Network and Intelligence in Networks (2IN97)

French Ministry of Telecommunication, 20 Avenue de Segur, Paris - France
September 2-5, 1997

Organizer: IFIP WG 6.7 - Intelligent Networks

Sponsorship: IEEE, Alcatel, Ericsson, France Telecom, Nokia, Nordic Teleoperators, Siemens, Telecom Finland, Lab. PRiSM

Aim of the conference

To identify and study current issues related to the development of intelligent capabilities in networks. These issues include the development and distribution of services in broadband and mobile networks.

This conference belongs to a series of IFIP conference on Intelligent Network. The first one took place in Lappeeranta August 94, the second one in Copenhagen, August 95. The proceedings of both events have been published by Chapman&Hall.

IFIP Working Group 6.7 on IN has concentrated with the research and development of Intelligent Networks architectures. First the activities have concentrated in service creation, service management, database issues, feature interaction, IN performance and advanced signalling for broadband services. Later on the research activities have turned towards the distribution of intelligence in networks and IN applications to multimedia and mobility. The market issues of new services have also been studied. From the system development point of view, topics from OMG and TINA-C have been considered.

Conference chair:

Olli Martikainen FIN and Guy Pujolle F

Program committee chair:

Dominique Gaïti F

Program committee members:

James Aitken UK
Almeida Maria J.B. BR
Andy Bihain USA
Gilles Brégant F
Carla Capellmann, GER
Christian Chabernaud F
Peter Delgado UK
Heinz Dibold GER

Jacques Ferber F
Frank Gallivan USA
Philip Ginzboorg FIN
Shri Goyal USA
Serge Haddad F
Heikki Hammainen FIN
Villy Baek Iversen DK
Bijan Jabbari USA
Jorma Jormakka FIN
Koos Koen RSA
Ulf Körner S
Paul Kühn GER
Roberto Kung F
Jacques Labetoulle F
Xuejia Lai CH
Martine Lapierre F
Kari Lautanala FIN
Aurel A. Lazar USA
Valeri A. Naoumov RF
Karl W. Neunast GER
Jorgen Norgaard DK
Hervé Precioso F
Kimmo Raatikainen FIN
Konstantin E. Samouylov RF
Manfred Schneps-Schneppe RUS
Lennart Söderberg S
Haitao Tang CN

Organizing committee chair:

Nadia Boukhatem F

Organizing committee members:

André-Luc Beylot
Selma Boumerdassi
Thierry Hua
Ali Marefat
Jian-Ping Zhang

PART ONE

Research on IN Intelligence

A Distributed Intelligent Computer/Telephony Network Integration Architecture for Unified Media Communication

Plamen L. Simeonov⁺, Peter Hofmann*
⁺Siemens AG: Plamen.Simeonov@sietec.de
*Technical University Berlin, FSP-PV/PRZ: peterh@prz.tu-berlin.de

Abstract - This paper presents a distributed IN architecture called *@INGate* [1], [2], that elaborates a Unified Media Communications Service (UMCS) providing both messaging and telephony services between circuit switching and packet networks. It represents an InterWorking Unit (IWU) in CTI networks allowing the user access to a Unified Message Store-Line (UMSL) via traditional PSTN/ISDN equipment such as telephones and fax machines on the one side and networked computers equipped with mail readers and Web browsers on the other side to enable both online and off-line communication.

The core of this new architecture is the Network-Bridge Service Node (NB-SN), a distributed intelligent network (IN) element consisting of a Channel Matrix Switch (CMS) to connect to the PSTN/ISDN, several Ressource Platforms (RP) containing Media Conversion Processors (MCP) to perform the media translation in the required interchange formats, an Internet Gateway (IG) to hold the subscribers' mailboxes and provide the Internet connectivity, and a Service Node Controller (SNC) to manage the overall service logic and the above NB-SN components. The Service Node itself is managed along with other nodes in a distributed IN by a TMN-compliant Operation, Administration and Maintenance (OAM) center.

The @INGate system was jointly developed by Siemens AG and the Technical University Berlin.

Keywords: CTI, IWU, PSTN/Internet-Gateway

I. Introduction

The @INGate project designed an InterWorking Unit (IWU) between ISDN/PSTN (TE2) and Internet Terminals (IT), cf. fig. 1, [3], which hosts a generic Unified Media Communication Service (UMCS). This architecture addresses three basic elements:

- *protected network links:* Channel Matrix Switch (CMS) facing PSTN/ISDN (incl. connections to mobile radio networks) and Internet Gateway (IG);
- *enhanced media contents*: Resource Platforms (RP) using Media Conversion Processors (MCP);
- *reliable service and resource control:* Service Node Controller (SNC).

II. @INGate Reference Model

The @INGate Reference Model contains the following network elements (cf. fig. 2):

- Network-Bridge Service Node (NB-SN)
- Service Data Server (SDS)
- Operation, Administration and Maintenance Center (OAMC)
- WWW Server
- Firewall

The Network-Bridge Service Node (NB-SN) consists of the following modules:

- Service Node Controller (SNC)
- Resource Platforms (RP)
- Media Conversion Processors (MCP)
- Channel Matrix Switch (CMS)

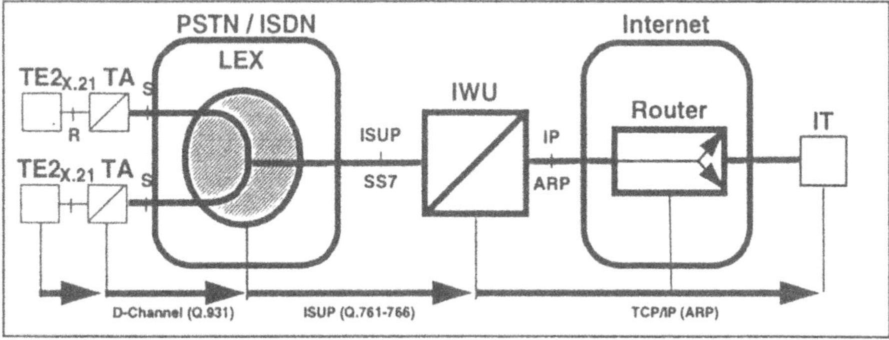

Fig. 1 @INGate as IWU

Intelligent Networks and Intelligence in Networks D. Gaiti (Ed.)
Published by Chapman & Hall

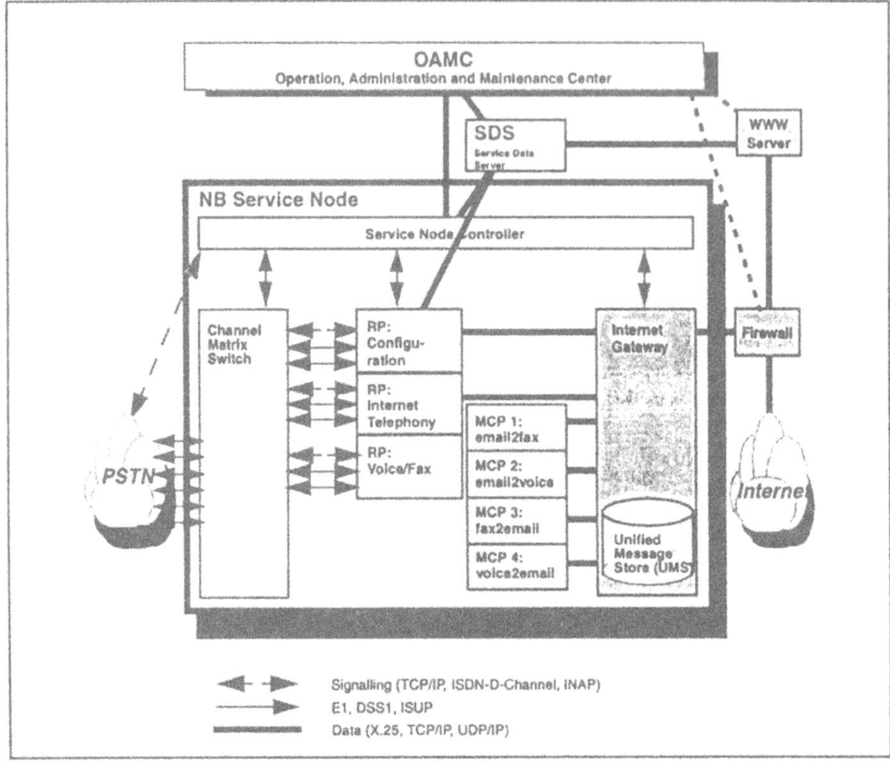

Fig. 2 @INGate Reference Model

•Internet Gateway (IG)

The Service Date Server (SDS) holds all service- and subscriber relevant information such as configuration data, user profile information and Automated Message Acount (AMA) records in a database.

The OAM center allows access to all the components of the @INGate Service Node, e.g. via telnet sessions to UNIX hosts or SNMP-based management.

The WWW Server supports WWW-based management of all NB-SN components in addition to the TMN-conformant OAM workstation, as well as Customer Service Control (CSC) such as configuration of service specific parameters through the Internet by using security-enhanced Web browsers.

Currently, the UMCS logic in the SN Controller guarantees the secure service access from the telephony network, whereas a dedicated firewall computer connects the Network-Bridge Service Node to the Internet.

III. Network-Bridge Service Node (NB-SN)

The Network-Bridge Service Node represents the core of the Interworking Unit between PSTN/ ISDN and Internet. In the following sections we describe its components.

A *Service Node Controller (SNC)*

The Service Node Controller controls the allocation and deallocation of resources in the Resource Platforms and the overall play-out of the service. Services offered by the NB-SN are implemented in the SNC by Service Logic Programs (SLPs) interfacing to their subparts and resources in the RPs directly or via the matrix switch.

B *Resource Platform (RP)*

The Resource Platforms implement specific resource functions such as voice/fax reception, DTMF/voice recognition, storage, play of announcements, etc.

Appropriate RPs are assigned to incoming and outgoing calls, as well as to service logic by the SNC. There are four different RP types in @INGate: one for recording/sending fax and voice messages, one for storage (mailbox, UMS), one for the interface to Internet Telephony, and one for configuration of user profiles via DTMF/VR.

C *Media Conversion Processors (MCP)*

The Media Conversion Processors have the task to convert media messages

1. between RP-specific and Internet formats, and
2. between two different RP-specific formats.

D *Channel Matrix Switch (CMS)*

The Channel Matrix Switch is controlled by the SNC and routes calls from the PSTN/ISDN to the appropriate resource platforms via circuit and call related signalling (CCS7 interface of ISUP).

E *Internet Gateway (IG)*

The Internet Gateway basically consists of a Unified Media Storage (UMS) and telephony software. The UMCS logic is located at the SNC. The software consists of a standard Internet Telephony (IT) client modified for use as a gateway, and an interface to a special ressource hardware handler. Since most IT applications today support half-duplex operation, only half-duplex communication is implemented at the moment. This coincides with the fact that the selected resource hardware (voice modem) also performs only a half-duplex voice recording and playback.

Note: The Internet Telephony Gateway logically belongs to the Internet Gateway. However, because of real-time constraints it will be located on the Ressource Platform. This may be a special Internet Telephony RP (IT-RP), if special hardware/operating systems are necessary.

IV. Unified Media Communication Service (UMCS)

The @INGate project aims at implementing a generic Unified Media Communication Service that can be accessed from both the switching telephone network and the packet-driven Internet. This service imposes some constraints on the message format that is intended to support both worlds:

- The identity of the subscriber (i.e. owner of the message) must be verifyable.
- The unified message format must accommodate both telephony (e.g. G3 fax) and Internet data formats (e.g. JPEG, ASCII text).
- The format must handle multi-part messages that occur in the Internet world (MIME-format emails).
- The message format must identify the type of the content data it encapsulates.
- The message format must be efficiently accessible from both Internet e-mail software and telephony services residing in the RPs.

There are several choices for the implementation of such a Unified Message Format (UMF), especially if timing and performance of necessary conversion procedures are taken into account. The messages might be stored either in a proprietary format (e.g. involving a multimedia database or special file formats) or in a standard format (e.g. standard UNIX mailbox format). The proprietary format has the advantage that it can be implemented in a very efficient manner compared to ordinary UNIX mailboxes that store all data (even long audio files) in one mailbox file. The drawback is, however, that standard Internet daemons such as POP3 daemons have to be rewritten to use this new format. This would also make running a POP daemon computationally more expensive. There are two strategies to solve the conversion problem:

- *"Lazy" Conversion* of media types on demand, e.g. when a user accesses her mailbox using her Internet MUA and the mailbox contains voice messages enter using a telephone the POP daemon converts these voice messages into MIME audio/basic.
- All incoming messages are converted to/from a canonical format (CF) as soon as they come in. If the CF is the standard UNIX mailbox with MIME types at least for the Internet access, no conversion on-the-fly is required.

The standard UNIX mailbox with a canonical format was chosen. In a later revision the proprietary format with lazy conversion should be favoured because of better performance.

Currently, from the PSTN/ISDN side only the UMCS subscriber can reach Internet Telephony users from an analog telephone. She can then select the desired party using DTMF tones (either from a shortlist or by entering the IP number). The Internet side is not limited to subscribers: everyone can call a PSTN/ISDN number from the Internet, provided that she is willing to pay by credit card or using digital cash for using UMCS.

V. Operation, Administration, and Maintenance (OAM)

The OAM workstation allows access to all the components of the Network-Bridge Service Node (NB-SN). The structure of the @INGate architecture is oriented on IN Standards. TMN standards such as [5] and [6] are used to support management within the IN. The management information is processed by distributed SNMP agents inside the different NB-SN components.

One of the main challenges of TMN integration in Intelligent Networks is the lack of usable standards. We used the ETSI Baseline documents [7] and the ITU-T Recommendations to map the TMN Functional Model to the @INGate physical architecture (fig. 3).

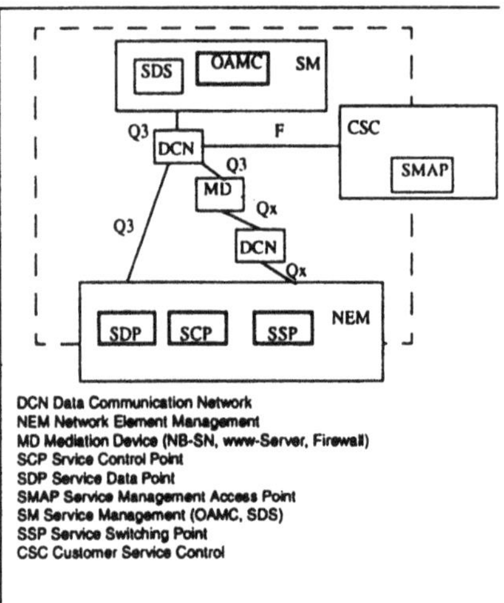

Fig. 3 Mapping of TMN to @INGate

The implementation of the management platform is based on HP OpenCall, which is used to control the IN management aspects of the service node. The Customer Service Control (CSC) management is supported over the Internet by HP OpenView as part of the OpenCall platform, with additional modules implemented by the PRZ lab at the TU Berlin. Some management information is accessible via a Web interface, mainly to support service subscribers to access and change their profiles using the Internet .

The @INGate management defines three main services:

A Service & Subscriber Administration

This management service includes the needed functions for the administration of user profiles. The operator has total access to this data. The service subscriber can modify certain data in the user profile to get the service fitted to her needs.

B Operation & Maintenance

This management service offers the functions for management of the service node operation. Typical functions are load-control, reachability, availability and statistics for billing and control purposes.

C Element Management

This management service offers the functions needed by the SNC to control the modules inside the NB-SN. It behaves to upper TMN instances as a single Network Element, representing the Network Elements inside it.

VI. Service Data Server (SDS)

The Service Data Server (SDS) is a common data repository for all components of the @INGate system. It holds information about

- configuration of resources
  - available conversion functions
  - PSTN/ISDN ports
- configuration of services
  - distribution of processes
  - configuration of recovery functions
- subscriber profile data
  - personal data
  - billing information (bank account, special usage plans etc.)
  - available conversion functions
  - PSTN/ISDN port preferences (fax number for email digests etc.)

Resource and service configuration can be accessed and manipulated by the OAM component. Subscriber profile data can also be accessed by OAM, the subscriber herself can also change parts of the profile using the Web-based interface (e.g. email-to-fax number). The Charging and Billing component uses the billing information in the subscriber profile.

The SDS holds for each subscriber a certain amount of profile information some of which can be changed by the subscriber using the Web or the telephony (DTMF) based interface. The following list gives some of the profile attributes and their description:

- *User Identifier*: a unique integer number for each user stored in the Subscriber Database.
- *User Name*: the full user name (e.g. "Erika Musterfrau").
- *Login Name:* a short unique user handle (e.g. "erikam");
- *Account Activation Time*: the time when the user account becomes valid.
- *Account Deactivation Time:* the time of the automatic expiration of the account.
- *Billing Policy:* the billing policy to be applied by the Billing Subsystem.
- *Security Identifier:* an identifier specific to the underlying security system.
- *Security Data*: information specific to the underlying security system.
- *Address:* the user/subscriber address used by the Billing System to send the accounts/bills.

- *Privilege Attributes:* indication of the invocation privileges for the different end-user roles.
- *Telephone Number:* the telephone number of the user/subscriber.
- *Mailing Address:* the mailing address of the user/subscriber.
- *Language Preference:* the language preference of the user; this data can be used by the system to determine the the user interface.
- *Account Balance:* the current account balance of the user.
- *Fax Number*: the default fax number to be used for the email-to-fax service.
- *Auto Fax Times:* an array of time specifications; at each of these times the email-to-fax system sends all new messages to the fax number in the Fax Number field.

VII. WWW Server

The WWW-Server serves a dual purpose in the architecture of the @INGate system:

- it allows remote WWW-based management of @INGate services as an alternative to the centralized OAM concepts.
- it allows the subscribers to modify parts of their personal profiles that are held in the SDS.

There are several NB-SN components to be managed using the WWW-Interface. Since not all of them directly support the configuration via HTML, some database conversions were implemented:

- SNMP MIBs into HTML
- database tables (especially in the SDS) into HTML

The following components can be managed with the WWW-server:

- Mail Server in the Internet Gateway (native HTML-Interface)
- Service Node Controller (MIB-to-HTML)
- Ressource Platforms (MIB to HTML)
- SDS (forms-based access to subscriber profile database: self-subscibtion, CSC)

The @INGate Service Node will distribute its services securely through a SSL-enabled [4] server (SNC, cf. fig. 2) which requires the usage of a certificate-based authentication scheme.

VIII. Charging and Billing (C&B)

The UMC service will be accessible from both PSTN/ISDN and Internet. It should be able to handle service requests from POTS subscribers and from anonymous users originating from the Internet /8-11/.

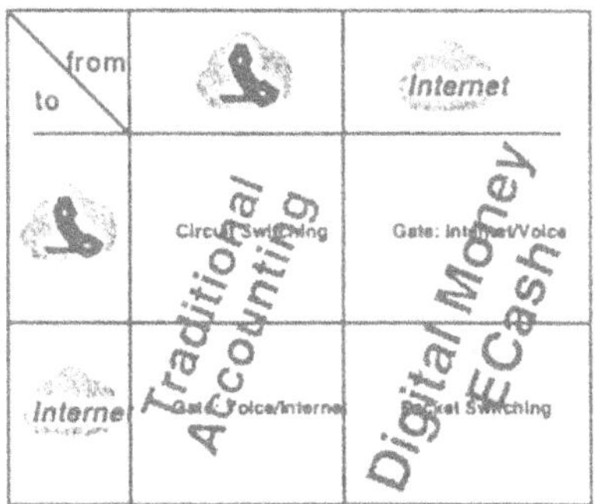

Fig. 4 Billing Areas Internet/IN

IX. Related Work

We look upon every approach of combining internet services to a telecommerce platform as related work. Regarding our activities on billing for anonymous customers the closest relationship exists to ecash shops [8], [9]. We cover the activities and movements of other billing or secure transaction initiatives like SET [10] but our main concern in @INGate is the evolution of digital money [11] which supports the distributed NB-SN architecture.

X. Conclusions and Outlook

This paper has shown an exciting new way to integrate two worlds that have evolved very differently - the ubiquitous plain old telephone system (POTS) on the one hand and the rapidly developing packet-data Internet on the other hand.

Personal Cordless Telephony (PCT) /13/ is a service that Siemens currently implements for one of its international customers with the Service Node architecture. The service allows the access to a distinct subscriber from a group of persons via mobile telephony while calling a known fixed network number.

This service is the first step towards a complete PSTN, ISDN, DECT and GSM integration. In this manner, PCT is a basic service towards PCS that will build up the skeleton of much more complex communications services, such as routing of multimedia data throughout diverse networks.

The Personal Cordless Telephony and the Unified Media Communication Service (UMCS) presented in this paper build up together the base for the next generation telecommunications services. Whereas the PCT service introduces Distributed Intelligent Network Elements (DINE), Service Nodes, in the IN routing techniques of the PCS world, the @INGate architecture and the UMC service provide a practical approach to Enhanced Media Contents Provisioning (EMCP) in the CTNI area.

Both services are mutually complementary and build the ground pillars of a layered service model (LSM) in an integrated media communications architecture (IMCA). These two basic services are enhanced with additional components and functionalities spread out throughout all media and network types in a similar way that the layers of an OSI protocol stack implement particular characteristics of the communication process.

Whereas the first pillar of services will grow horizontally, thus including new network types and routing mechanisms, the second one will grow vertically in order to develop complex applications with different (possibly hierarchically structured) media types such as video-telephony, conferencing, teleworking, teleoffice, telefactory, virtual enterprise, etc.)

Both services will be developed, justified and tested in an interplay relation in order to be finally merged in a configurable CTNI service. The evolution of the Network-Bridge Service Node is characterized by the following features:

- •NB-SN as multimedia platform represents a mirroring (extension) of the data networks concerning news and data transfer, as well as tele-(co)operation services;
- •NB-SN as network bride (CTNI) allows the access to other networks, resources and services: radio and satellite networks, electronical and optical broadband networks, etc.;
- •NB-SN as a glue element (mediation function) in access networks and thus to closed loop interactive services in the business and entertainment areas;
- •NB-SN as first step towards the realisation of true active intellient networks and thus towards the complete integration of autonomous data, programs, services and functionalities (mindware) within the global telecommunications network of all physical carriers.

Regarding the new developments in the packet network technology such as seamless ATM networks, new flexible addressing types, intelligent switches, agent routing and management methods, it is marked out that the network bridge service node will obtain the same characteristics and functionalities in order to guarantee its mediation function among the communications networks.

There is one distict trend that can be clearly discerned: the Distributed Intelligent Network Element (DINE) Service Node will continue to grow.

XI. Acknowledgements

The work discussed in this paper was performed in the context of a project grant by Siemens AG. We would like to acknowledge the support of Prof. Carl, director of IN development at Siemens AG - Berlin who initiated the @INGate project. Many thanks to Hewlett Packard for the donation of the HP OpenView management platform as part of their HP-OUA activities [12].

XII. References

[1] P. L. Simeonov, *MediaWeb - Product Definition*, Doc. Nr. P30308-A7957-A000-04-7618, Siemens AG, OEN TI PSI1, 1996.

[2] P. L. Simeonov, *Add-On IN Gateway Services for Service Node in Distributed Telecom Networks*, Internal Paper, Siemens AG, Oct. 1996.

[3] Peter Bocker; ISDN - Digitale Netze für Sprach-, Text-, Daten-, Video- und Multimediakommunikation; Springer; 1997; ISBN 3-540-57431-X

[4] Alan O. Freier and Philip Karlton and Paul C. Kocher, The SSL Protocol Version 3.0: ftp://ftp.iesd.auc.dk/pub/ietf/internet-drafts/draft-freier-ssl-version3-01.txt

[5] ITU-T, *ITU-T Recommendation Series X.7xx Data Communication Networks Management*

[6] ITU-T, *ITU-T Recommendation Series M.3xxx Maintenance Telecommunications Management Network*

[7] ETSI, *ETR 067, „Baseline Document on the Integration of IN and TMN"*, Sept. 1992

[8] DigiCash; *DigiCash ecash - cybershops home page*; http://www.digicash.com/shops/cybershop.html

[9] Mark Twain Bank; *Alphabetical list - Mark Twain Bank Ecash Accepting Shops*; http://www.marktwain.com/shops.html

[10] Mastercard; *Secure Electronic Transactions*; http://www.mastercard.com/set/; 1997

[11] Daniel C. Lynch and Leslie Lundquist, *digital money*, John Wiley & Sons, Inc, NY, ISBN 0-471-14178-X.

[12] HP OUA; Homepage; http://www.ovoua.org

[13] Personal Cordless Telephony: Description, Siemens A, OEN TI, Doc. Nr. P30308-A7671-T000-01-7618, 18.06.1996, A. Vogel

2
Quality of Service questions of stream objects built on CORBA

J. Jormakka
Helsinki Telephone Company, Research
P.O.Box 138, 00381 Helsinki, Finland,
E-mail:jorma.jormakka@hpy.fi
tel:+358 9 6064721, fax:+358 9 6064839

Abstract

Helsinki Telephone Company Research is currently involved in a project evaluating suitability of CORBA as a presentation layer distribution technology for streams.

One application of CORBA is connection management of streams, that is basically as a replacement of signalling for communicating objects transferring voice and video, for instance for video-on-demand or videotelephony. Another application is service management, like ordering videotelephony or video-on-demand service.

These kind of scenarios can be build using the ideas from TINA-C so that the operational and stream interfaces of TINA DCE are realised by CORBA and the stream transport by IP. The role of TINA is to clarify the relations of customers, retailers and third party content providers by mapping the relations to TINA reference points.

Quality aspects of the streams in this kind of solution are essential from many points of view. Firstly, a solution replacing signalling for streams must meet sufficient delay and blocking requirements similar to those of SS7. Secondly, passing QoS requirements to the underlying GIOP has to be investigated. Thirdly, reliability/robustness issues are very relevant in a transparent distribution method such as CORBA - how does the solution react to unavailability of a remote object and so on.

This paper does not present ready solutions but explains initial ideas and problematic.

Keywords

CORBA, QoS, GOS, Performance.

This paper is based on work done in the EURESCOM project "EURESCOM Services Platform". The project has the following participants: KPN Research , Finnet-group, British Telecom, Deutch Telecom, France Telecom and Telecom Ireland. The views presented are author's personal opinions.

Intelligent Networks and Intelligence in Networks D. Gaiti (Ed.)
Published by Chapman & Hall

1. WHY CORBA, WHY DISTRIBUTION ON PRESENTATION LAYER?

Loosely speaking a stream is a connection which carries video or voice and consequently has some real time performance requirements. One of the reasons why operators are interested in CORBA is that the choice of a network for carrying streams is not easy. Granted that the solution is a broadband network there are several alternatives:

- native ATM end-to-end: ATM with UNI 3.1/Q.2931 or UNI 4.0
- IP over ATM: some form of IP switching, MARS for multicast?
- Internet with QoS, implying RSVP, maybe also IPv6, NHRP?
- IP directly on SDH ? (though SDH hardly is sufficiently flexible for end-to-end connections)
- some other solution.

When the future solution or solutions are not known it is natural to separate application software from the network by a common interface situated somewhere between the layers 4 and the lower part of 7 in the OSI model. CORBA is one serious alternative. It corresponds rather well to the OSI presentation layer and the COSS services correspond to certain extent to the Common Application Service Elements of OSI. Many of the arguments in favour of CORBA as an improvement to the TCP/UDP socket interface are equally valid for the OSI presentation and belong to the normal reasons for using a presentation layer. While these are good arguments one must remember that OSI presentation layer did not become popular, therefore it is important to think what were the experiences learned from the OSI presentation when considering CORBA.

One of the reasons for the failure of the OSI presentation's popularity was that the OSI applications did not gain acceptance which depended on the difficulty of interworking and on the high cost, vendors also seemed to prefer to develop either proprietary solutions or solutions based on de-facto standards. CORBA has better chances since it is not a competitor but complementary to Internet protocols and relates to application distribution as a part of software development procedure rather than to multi-vendor interworking which is mainly in the interest of operators.

On the lower layers of OSI protocols there were problems in addresses. In many implementations simply setting a selected mode of X.25 addressing was too difficult for the user. Furthermore, X.25 was seen expensive and often OSI implementors decided also to support TCP/IP sockets as an alternative to X.25. With CORBA using IIOP should not have these problems but what about other GIOPs ?

Setting correctly the presentation address (NSAP, TSAP, SSAP, PSAP) in OSI implementations often took some time in interworking trials. Furthermore, in some OSI implementations optional parameters of ACSE, such as AE Titles and Access Controls were used as mandatory parameters in the meaning that interworking was not possible unless these parameters were used - causing interworking problems with implementations which lacked them. In CORBA these addressing related issues include GIOP addresses and representation of interoperable object references (IOR) and do not yet seem to contain major interworking problems (which is odd since IORs look both long and strange and they change often).

In OSI protocols there were many options which the implementations only partially supported. Even though functional profiles were created for agreeing on the options they remained an interworking problem. With CORBA it is possible that partial support of COSS services is a similar future problem.

The general impression given by OSI implementations was that the software was transferring data from one layer / one data structure to another too many times. Raw data could be passed as pointers but still the result was a large and possibly ineffective software. This problem appeared especially when considering the OSI presentation layer. It can be seen as a logical problem: coding and decoding from ASN.1 does not always fit in the 6th layer but partially could be done better on the 7th layer. When decoding from transfer syntax the presentation layer can only create some structures and decode data from the transfer syntax to these structures since it has no knowledge what to do with the application data. Later these structures usually are changed to other internal structures suitable for the application software. For instance in a CMISE implementations using XOM/XMP data from GDMO-defined MIBs could be taken to some internal structures which then are converted to the (rather clumsy) data structures passed to XOM/XMP and then the data is finally put to the transfer syntax. For performance and memory reasons it can be more tempting to code partially the transfer syntax in the application rather than to pass the data in internal structures to the presentation layer for coding to the transfer syntax, some X.500 implementations did so.

The above mentioned situation with OSI implementations is basically the same with CORBA but since there are less protocol layers the problem should be less apparent. Application development with CORBA does not look like if it would result to this large number of conversions between data structures typical to OSI applications.

In OSI presentation ASN.1 with BER coding rules is the transfer syntax and has been seen as a performance bottleneck. In CORBA IDL is closer to C++ and coding can be faster in principle. Still it is good to notice that the problem was not ASN.1 which is a good language, nor BER, but the complicated structures specified for the applications that caused the performance problems in OSI, with IDL performance also depends on the structures used.

The design procedure in OSI applications is made by ITU and ISO standardisation and is based on state automatons, message sequence charts, description languages ASN.1, ASN macros, GDMO. CORBA based applications may use the OMG proposal of Object Oriented Analysis and Design using the Unified Modelling Language (UML). Concerning the design procedure, both methods produce an application that can (?) be implemented. It is difficult to say if implementation of CORBA based applications is easier than implementation of OSI applications. The comparison is difficult since thinking of OSI the writer has in mind some past development of large OSI applications following complicated standards whereas with CORBA implementation procedure only can think of some simple examples. Some comparison can be made between OSI management application implementation procedure and implementing a distributed application using CORBA, both being object based approaches - in fact, OSI TMN may change CMISE to CORBA in near future.

A development environment for OSI management applications can for instance include compilers for ASN.1 and GDMO, a ready OSI-stack up to TLI, session, presentation or even application - one possibility being the XOM/XMP interface. A user writes GDMO and ASN.1 definitions and compiles in principle automatically the MIBs. In practise a programmer most probably has to have knowledge of the structures and functions produced. This procedure in OSI management is untypical for development of OSI software which is structured around implementations of service elements as automatons. Object based implementation procedures with OSI are therefore connected with object based applications (CMISE, X.500) and there is no general procedure of this kind.

A CORBA application is usually developed with the IDL approach. Alternative ways are DII for the client and DSI for the server. There is also ORB interface for client and server but it has only some operations. Implementation of CORBA determines the actual development procedures, in IONA's Orbix the CORBA software basically consists of client and server libraries and orbixd daemon. In the IDL approach IDL definitions are first written and the IDL is compiled to the chosen programming language (e.g., C++). This compilation produces for a client an IDL stub and for a server object an IDL skeleton. The server object can inherit from a Base Object Adapter, BOA Approach, or is made with the TIE Approach. The server is registered to the ImplementationRepository and then can be used by clients. The daemon orbixd reads the ImplementationRepository database to see which object implementation is activated.

A main difference in CORBA and OSI is the philosophy of distribution. OSI applications are built on the concepts of an agent and a server and the distribution is on the application layer. CORBA makes the distribution more transparently using stubs. The method used by CORBA is occasionally given as a major improvement but many styles of distribution have their own advantages. Other distribution methods include calling interfaces like the TCP/UDP socket interface or TLI, transparent distribution of files by remote calls being made by the application invoking normal local operating system calls if a file is remote (like in NFS). Finally there is distribution made on the user interface level like in X. These are all good methods of distribution but object-oriented distribution on presentation layer is currently more interesting than the other solutions because of the strong support to distributed processing from ISO/ODP, TINA and naturally OMG.

Another difference in CORBA is emphasis on stateless operation. However, there are applications which can gain from automatons and very possibly all future applications based on CORBA will not be stateless.

As a conclusion, distributing applications using a presentation layer is advantageous especially since there are many network alternatives. Distribution using object-oriented approach can apply ideas from ISO/ODP and TINA and CORBA is a practical way for implementing those ideas, yet OMG CORBA has MicroSoft OLE as a strong competitor. However, concerning multi-vendor interoperability problems CORBA uses similar ideas as the OSI presentation and the (inter)working problems appeared with applications.

Because of the transparent way of distribution performance and reliability aspects in CORBA are more important than in non-transparent distribution methods. Four questions can be posed:

- What is the impact of the CORBA layer between application and GIOP to delays?
- How to pass QoS parameters from application to stream transmission protocol through CORBA?
- What are the reliability/robustness issues?
- What about traffic/congestion controls?

Since streams and streams connection management are the interesting applications of CORBA in this paper, the discussion will be limited to such usage.

2. APPLICATION OF CORBA TO VOICE AND VIDEOTELEPHONY

CORBA suits well to cases when a large application should be distributed transparently. It seems unnecessarily complicated for basic communication tasks like sending voice or video from one place to another, why not simply use RSVP for signalling and IP for streams. However, applications tend to become more complicated in time and there is need for something like CORBA. In the project described here the goal is to gain some experience on CORBA with streams and the simple application must be seen in this light, it is only a simple case which could be done easier but we are interested in applying CORBA.

One possible solution using CORBA with streams is to implement videotelephony directly on an ATM network using CORBA for signalling. A solution of this kind is xbind [10] which calls directly UNI. Since the future popularity of native ATM solutions is a question mark, this type of solution was not selected.

Another possibility is that signalling goes through CORBA and IP carries streams. Unspecified quality using IPv4 is probably not sufficient in future but a suitable QoS can be reserved with RSVP and the streams carried by IPv6. This alternative is also being investigated but in another project.

The selected solution is loosely based on TINA. In the TINA concept CORBA plays the role of KTN (Kernel Transport Network). TINA-C has defined stream interfaces and one possibility was to interpret this so that the streams would actually go through CORBA. Knowing that present implementations of CORBA actually bring a considerable overhead to streams over simple socket based transmission, it is a more practical solution to use directly Internet protocols for the streams omitting CORBA even though the concepts are expressed as far as possible in TINA-C terminology, so in this way the solution is only loosely TINA. Connection management (signalling) is made through CORBA and corresponds to TINA operational interfaces.

Structuring the problem in TINA way had as a first step identification of TINA reference points. It turned out that it was possible to formulate the question in this way, the following figure shows the reference points in an application where third party (3pty) video-on-demand service is subscribed by a customer from a retailer. A stream interface is between the customer and the 3Pty. It realises TINA reference points TCon and ConS.

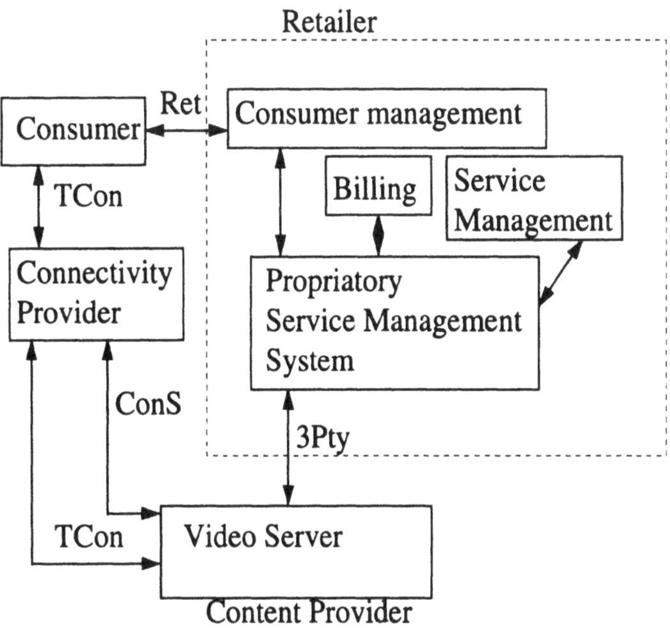

Figure 1. Initial assignment of TINA Reference points to a practical implementation.

Under CORBA, actually between two ORBs, is GIOP which now contains an operational interface for transporting signalling messages and a stream interface for transporting video and audio. These protocols must be selected. In literature there are some proposals, e.g., [9] proposes using CORBA either on SS7 or on TCP/IP where TCP/IP is on top of ATM. For mapping of CORBA to SS7 [9] gives two proposals: GIOP over TCAP and GIOP over SCCP. However, the selected solution was more practical: for signalling is used IIOP since it exists in CORBA 2.0. For streams is used a socket interface which is wrapped into objects in order to make something resembling TINA stream objects. So, both stream and operational protocols use IP.

One possibility is that the IP runs on the public Internet. This solution was tried and the delays obtained from Orbix grid example server were on the range of 1 second from Finland to Germany.

One alternative is that IP actually runs on N-ISDN in the following configuration:

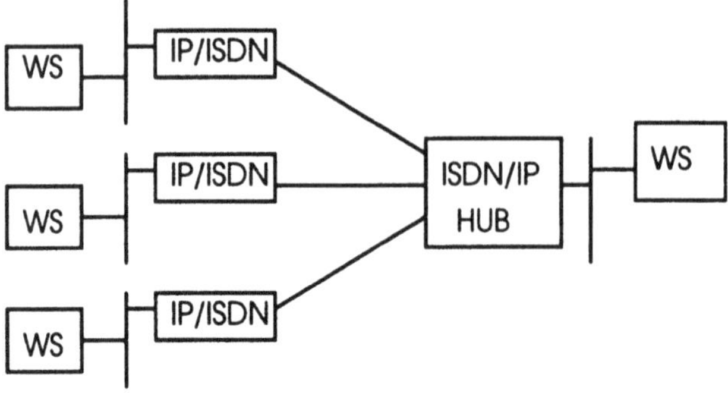

Figure 2. Stream objects managed by CORBA based IDL-defined interface and the stream is on ISDN and for the workstation ORB-software it looks like the stream is transmitted on IP (IP/ISDN router is used).

It is also possible to support several networks and have a decision point which selects the network to be used during a connection.

3. PASSING QOS REQUIREMENTS THROUGH CORBA

In this section QoS does not have the usual meaning from E.800 where QoS contains the engineering aspects of QoS, largely covered by GOS, reliability concepts and nonengineering related concepts of goodness of the service (time to repair, customer service, etc.). Instead QoS here means stream quality as in ATM when ATM cells are used to carry video and voice. This QoS concept is related to the PSTN concept of transmission quality (attenuation, jitter etc.). It is also related to the QoS parameters in many data communication protocols, e.g., OSI-session.

Inside ORB QoS can be assumed to be good but between ORBs it is determined by the stream transmission protocol. Here it is unnecessary to decide if the streams are transmitted using CORBA implying that between ORBs the streams go through GIOP or if a special protocol is transmitting the streams. It is known that the CORBA alternative has a considerable overhead and the likely choice is that the streams do not go through GIOP. Four our purposes this makes little difference since it is a question of passing the QoS parameters.

OMG has not done much work on this issue. TINA-C has treated QoS, referred to as flowQoS in [7], means the quality of streams in terms of bandwidth, jitter and errors and it is quite analogous to the QoS in ATM. The simplest solution is to use the flowQoS concept from TINA-C but the problematic is more difficult since the realistic network alternatives for carrying streams do not use QoS in a similar way.

In ATM QoS is the quality of the connection in terms of cell losses and cell delays (CLR, CDV, CTD). It is requested by the initiator of the connection.

The concept of QoS in the Internet draft protocol RSVP is in some respect different, like the QoS is requested by the receiver and the state is soft, i.e., if the state of the sender is not refreshed regularly it is not kept.

There are also ways where QoS requirements are not passed to the stream transmission protocol but instead this lost information of needed QoS is recovered in the network/ link layer, like in different forms of IP switching.

Here we come to the same problem which the CORBA interface seemed to remove, we would need to know the underlying network in order to give a suitable QoS descriptor. Two solutions seem possible. The first is to use a QoS descriptor of undefined type (Any) and have the content the specific QoS description method of the network. This solution is easy for CORBA but makes the application network dependent. The better possibility is to classify the traffic sources by a simple integer, like {normal videophone, good video-on-demand, . . . , other} and collect statistics by a suitable statistics object which is on CORBA level. This statistics is used for mapping the traffic characteristics to QoS and traffic parameters. In this case the application only gives the classifying integer which is reserved for this purpose and not for instance a TCP-port number which has other usage.

4. IMPACT OF THE CORBA LAYER ON PERFORMANCE

As the streams are used to carry video and audio one natural reference point is PSTN where circuit-switched network is used to carry the voice and the SS7 network makes the signalling. This network has evolved to ISDN and to IN. In PSTN performance questions contain as an essential part GOS (Grade of Service) which originally meant call blocking but also contains different forms of signalling delays and blocking.

The performance impact of CORBA in a usage where the connection management of stream objects is made with CORBA should contain these GOS related matters:

identification of GOS parameters,

setting target values, the target values can be compared to those of SS7, like 100 ms packet delays,

measuring the delays, the measurement types could be described as in E.502,

breaking the delays to components, the delay components caused by CORBA being interesting here,
maybe also implementing and trying performance improvements.

Another aspect of performance impact of CORBA is the load on network elements. It this case the relevant matters are identification of:
workloads in the workstations (CPU load), throughput,
other resources in the workstations (memory usage, number of processes, number of sockets, etc.),
workloads in the network (message lengths, number of messages).

Delays in CORBA originate from several sources. The following delays also mean workloads to the workstation:
additional remote invocations for naming,
marshalling/demarshalling overhead, in OSI terminology this is encoding/decoding to transfer syntax,
demultiplexing, in OSI terminology this is address resolution,
and naturally also data copying and memory management.

Some delays in CORBA do not involve a workload. An example is invoking blocking operations which stops the invoker until there comes an answer. There are ways to avoid these delays: a nonblocking invocation can be defined in IDL by the keyword *oneway*. Also Event service enables asynchronous communication between objects.

Blocking problems can be caused in CORBA by invoking a remote object which cannot be started since there are too many process invocations or is a server supports only one thread.

5. RELIABILITY/ROBUSTNESS ISSUES

CORBA objects appear as local objects because the client's IDL stub acts as a local proxy. In reality the application is distributed, therefore reliability problems are caused by network failures. What happens in this kind of situation is that a CORBA object (a client or an server object) should receive an exception.

Robustness issues include also load balancing in case of server failure and mirrowing objects.

CORBA leaves reliability/robustness issues mostly on the responsibility of the application developer. Measurement of the reliability/robustness issues in the measurement set-up in Figure 2 is not possible in the sense that any failure probabilities could be obtained. Instead a list of reliability/robustness issues can be composed and solutions can be implemented and tried.

6. TRAFFIC AND CONGESTION CONTROLS

There seems to be a potential problem that in CORBA architecture there can appear focused overload if a large number of clients try to use the same server object. Focused overload can appear in :

Naming, if locator of objects becomes congested since too many clients try to access objects in the same ORB. The objects need not be the same,

LifeLong, if in creating an object a loader becomes congested. Loader is involved in starting an instance of an object,

Event, if too many operations are made to an object from several clients

Solving the problem of focused overloads involves:
identification of workloads,
modelling of network elements,
defining congestion control mechanisms.

CORBA architecture does not contain traffic and congestion controls. Since there are no traffic and congestion controls, there is no reason to investigate the typical problems of such methods: fairness and possible break down of the control e.g., by spreading of overloads. Below are some suggestions.

Focused overload can arise either in the object or in the locator trying to find the object. One way to solve this is by inserting congestion control filter to the server object. Orbix CORBA software provides hooks called filters which give the implementor eight places where to insert congestion control filter code. This solution will still be sensitive to focused overloads as the server object is a centralised element. Another possibility is to insert congestion control to a local part of the server, in this case a smart proxy in Orbix terminology, However, setting parameters of the congestion control would involve asking the congestion state of the server.

Focused overloads could be considered in situations analogous to IN: overload arising from many calls passing a central element, e.g., in number translation service, overload caused by mass calls, overload caused by number portability.

7. SUGGESTED GOS/QOS PARAMETERS

QoS parameters are set for a service. In the application of CORBA to voice/video telephony there are three natural levels that could be investigated.

- On the highest level there is the TINA stream object, this object can in some way be compared to DSS1 service and the GOS parameters can be similar to call set-up time, disconnection time, call blocking.
- On the next level, this TINA stream object is made using CORBA services. Delays of the relevant CORBA services can be taken as QoS parameters.
- Below CORBA there is GIOP. The incremental delays created by GIOP can be taken as QoS parameters.

Directly using the two latter choices would involve selecting some benchmarking applications implemented on top of CORBA. There are such measurements in [1]-[6]. Using the first alternative sets already as the benchmark the implementation of the TINA stream object. The two lower levels can be treated by breaking the measured delay to actions, for instance in invocation of a remote object there are parts such as locating the server, creating an instance of the object involving memory allocation, binding to the object etc. It is also relevant to identify in each case if the delay is of latency type, like latency in a buffer, or if it presents a workload to some processing element.

7.1 GOS/QoS and NP parameters for a TINA stream computational object

In this case the interface which is considered sees the stream objects.

We cannot measure call blocking in the measurement set-up. The following GOS parameters are proposed:

ConnectionSet-upDelay

This from a user of the client side stream object initiating a video connection to the time that the there is a one-way or two-way video established between the client and the server.

DisconnectionDelay

This from a user of the client side stream object closing a video connection to the time that the client and the server are in the final stage of disconnection.

MessageResponseTimes

These are response times of messages sent during the connection. The messages are not decided but could contain for example the following.

PauseResponseTime

Time from sending a pause to the time the stream stops.

For Network Performance (NP) the following elements can be measured:

Message load

Separately on the stream and operational networks. In Figure 2 both networks are IP. This means that the port numbers have to be identified.

Calls per hour, transactions per hour

Maximum throughput in terms of video calls or messages.

7.2 GOS parameters for CORBA services

The CORBA services of interest for performance measurements are:

LifeLong LifeLong includes creation, moving and deletion of objects.
Naming Naming involves locating the object and binding to it.
Event Event includes RPC calls and exceptions in case of failure.

Other COSS services can be included in case they are implemented by many of used ORBs.

GOS parameters for LifeLong:

ObjectCreationTime

The time to create an object.
This operation is announced to take 650 ms in Orbix [1].

ObjectDeletionTime

The time to delete an object.

ObjectMoveTime

The time to move an object.

GOS parameters for Naming:

(Notice that _bind() is Orbix-specific, CORBA 2.0 uses factory for this purpose.)

ObjectActivationDelay

The time for remotely activating a server when the locator is not used.
In Orbix remotely activating a server when the locator service is not used has been announced in [1] to take 4 s. Activation involves that the daemon orbixd forks up a new server process and the new server makes initialisation and a call impl_is_ready.

ObjectBindDelay

The time for returning an object reference from the start of name binding.

Measurement of the Bind delay

The delay of this operation can be measured by calculating the time how long _bind() takes. _bind() can accept a server name or it can also locate the object. In [1] binding is announced to take 960 ms provided that the server is already activated.

BindException Delay

The time from sending a try of bind to receiving the exception to the CATCH in the client assuming that the server is not available.

GOS parameters for Event

EventResponseTime

The time from sending a try to getting a response (CATCH) for a selected benchmarking event.

EventExceptionTime

The time from sending a try of an event to receiving the exception to the CATCH in the client assuming that the event fails.

7.3 GOS parameters for GIOP

The measurement of delays is made between two different OBRs using IIOP where the TCP/IP actually is replaced by ISDN in the following configuration from Figure 2:

WS - LAN-IP/ISDN router - HUB - IP/ISDN router - LAN -WS

The time is measured by calling time stamps of the operating system and by a sniffer in the local LAN.

Incremental DII delay

DII presents an API that can be called from a programming language. DII can be made using Any class which can potentially lead to long delays. In this measurement the incremental delay of a benchmark implementation of a client with DII and a similar client with IDL is evaluated. What is being measured includes the delay caused by serialisation of data in IIOP (in CORBA parlance marshalling/ demarshalling). A separate measurement of this data serialisation delay is probably not feasible.

Measurement set-up for measurement of the Incremental delay of DII

Client uses DII, server object uses DSI. Client requests an attribute defined as Any. It is necessary to agree on an implementation for benchmarking.

IONA Orbix performance measurements in [1] contain some results with the following set-up:
- two lightly loaded Spark stations
- IIOP they use TCP/IP and XDR encoding.

In request/reply the delays are 8-191 ms and with one-way calls 3-140 ms.

Incremental connection set-up delay of IIOP:

Time for setting up the TCP/IP connection in the measurement set-up (Figure 2). A similar connection set-up time using directly TCP/IP through the socket interface is measured and the incremental time is attributed to CORBA.

Measurement set-up for the delay of IIOP

Client uses IDL stub, server uses IDL skeleton.

Measurement set-up for the acceptable delay of IIOP

Client uses IDL stub, server uses IDL skeleton. Introduce additional delays using a measurement set-up in order to set target QoS parameter values (maximum acceptable delays, ignorable delays).

ImplementationRepositoryResponseTime

The operation get implementation returns object implementation from the ImplementationRepository. This delay is measured by selecting a suitable benchmark implementation and measuring the response time.

InterfaceRepositoryResponseTime

The operation get interface returns interface from the InterfaceRepository. This delay is measured by selecting a suitable benchmark implementation and measuring the response time.

8. POSSIBLE METHODS FOR PERFORMANCE IMPROVEMENTS

Several performance improvement alternatives for CORBA applications have been proposed in the literature. The following list gives a few possibilities which can be or have been implemented:

- Using IIOP performance gives worse performance than using directly TCP/UDP-sockets because of CORBA overhead. CORBA can have better performance than a socket based solution if both client and server are local and ORB can dispense with interprocess communication. In [1] there is a measurement of this kind. If the server and the client share a common library is used, i.e., C-structures are passed by pointer in the same address space, the delay is 2.7 ms. It can be noted that author's solution achieving a similar performance gain in one OSI application (in VTT's X.500 a DUA communicated with a local DSA through shared memory skipping the OSI-stack) required code writing and resulted to minor differences in behaviour when using the stack and when using the shared memory. This is clearly much easier to do with CORBA.
- Another way of improving performance is caching data in a smart proxy.
- In ORBline CORBA request reuse improves performance of DII.
- Using improved elements (loader, locator, Basic Object Adaptor/ Object Oriented Object Adaptor, etc.).
- If a server object in CORBA has only one thread, only one call can be processing at a time. This can create a performance problem. Multi-thread support in servers is one solution. CORBA v2.0 does not require multi-threading. However, HP ORB plus and Multi-Threaded Orbix support this.
- Some ORB implementations contain some performance bottlenecks, e.g., Orbix using IIOP opens a new TCP/IP connection and thus a new socket for every object reference in the server side. In some other ORBs this is solved in a better way.
- There are a number of improvements to reliability, e.g., a smart proxy binds to another server if a server fails.
- ORBs can regularly bing each other and measure response times for GIOP but such method has to be built on top of CORBA.

9. RELATED WORK

In CORBA performance measurements the emphasis has been on throughput and latency, the latter term actually refers to response times. References [1]-[5] contain some results of performance measurements of CORBA. The performance studies of CORBA are similar to performance studies of distributed databases in the sense that they try to set benchmarks.

OMG has considered defining QoS for streams for CORBA [8]. These ideas are influenced by TINA-C.

10. REFERENCES:

[1] Orbix: The Orbix Architecture, IONA Technologies Ltd. August 1993. ARCH.DOC, info@iona.ie

[2] D.C.Schmidt, T.Harrison, E.Al-Shaer: Object-Oriented Components for High-speed Network Programming, USENIX, Monterey, June 1995.

[3] A.Gokhale, D.C.Schmidt: Measuring the Performance of Communication Middleware on High-Speed Networks, SIGCOMM, Stanford Univ, August, 1996.

[4] A.Gokhale, D.C.Schmidt: Evaluating CORBA Latency and Scalability Over High-Speed ATM Networks, ICDCS 97, Baltimore, May 27-30, 1997.

[5] A.Gokhale, D.C.Schmidt: The Performance of the CORBA Dynamic Invocation Interface and Dynamic Skeleton Interface over High-Speed ATM Networks, GLOBECOM, London, November 18-22, 1996.

[6] I.Pyarali, T.Harrison, D.C.Schmidt: Design and Performance of an Object-Oriented Framework for High-Speed Electronic Mefical Imaging, USENIX COOTS, Toronto, June 1996.

[7] P.Leydekkers, M.Jorgensen (ed.): Unification of Connection/Session Graphs, Stream Interfaces, and Channel Models, TINA-C Report, version 1.3, 16. April 1996.

[8] Streams and QoS: White Paper, OMG, at //www.omg.org/

[9] EURESCOM project P508, project information, available for EURESCOM partners.

[10] A.A.Lazar, S. Bhonsle, K.S.Lim: A Binding Architecture for Multimedia Networks, J. Parallel and Distributed Systems, Vol. 30, No 2, Nov. 1995, pp. 204-216, http://www.ctr.columbia.edu/comet/xbind/

PART TWO

Control

3

Towards seamless control and management systems

F. J-P. Dupuy

France Télécom BD/CNET

2 Avenue de Pierre Marzin
Technopole Anticipa
22300 Lannion
FRANCE
tel: 33 2 96 05 36 65
fax: 33 2 96 05 37 84
e-mail: dupuy@lannion.cnet.fr

Abstract

The control and management services add new value to the telecommunications networks. As these services evolve, due to various factors like an increasing network technology diversity, increasing processing capabilities at the public periphery and reglementary acts, two trends can be observed : an externalization of the intelligence and the absence of a common technical approach between the public and private control and management systems.
The objectives of this paper are to give a short state of the art of the control and management systems (intelligent networks, computer-telephony integration servers, Internet) and to highlight the benefits that would be gained by interconnecting them (i.e. providing more 'seamlessness' and building a global information network). Once the advantages explained, the paper lists the requirements that can be anticipated on this global and seamless control and management system : fine identification of the information flows, independence of the platform providers, deployment flexibility, system reusability. In order to solve most of these requirements, the telecommunication community should now agree upon a single, generic enough, software architecture.
As explained brievely in this paper, TINA proves to be a good candidate, provided that more global effort is spent on its assessment and validation.

Keywords

Distributed network control systems, intelligent networks, TINA

Intelligent Networks and Intelligence in Networks D. Gaiti (Ed.)
Published by Chapman & Hall

1 INTRODUCTION

Control and management represent indeniably very crucial functions in telecommunications networks. Controlling a telecommunication resource aims at using it, immediately or lately, for a limited period of time or not, whereas managing a resource corresponds to operations ensuring its availability, configuration validity, performance, accounting, etc.

Three elements, at least, that impel the current control and management systems to evolve can be identified. The first one is that the telecommunication resources keep on increasing and varying both in the public and private networks : wireless access networks, multiplexing systems and hubs, cell or frame switching systems, external processing servers, etc. This steady diversification suggests to rationalize and harmonize the way to control and manage all these resources in order to lower the global network cost (and to get economies of scale).

The second element is the increase of processing capabilities at the public network periphery and consequently the emergence of control and management functions 'outside' these public networks. Not surprisingly, but still regrettably, the solutions chosen for providing control and management systems in the public or private networks rely on the same principles - intelligent processing units external to the tranport network - but are technically different. The evolution of the public networks is mainly taken over by the telecommunications standard bodies (ANSI, ETSI, UIT-T) or by consortia like TINA-C[1], whereas that of the private networks is taken over by the computer and private telecommunications equipment manufacturers (ECTF[2], ECMA[3], Novell, Microsoft). Thus very similar control and management functions, like call processing, signal processing, network management, service control, are now available both in the public networks (Intelligent Networks, Telecommunication Management Networks) and in the customer premises equipments (Microsoft TAPI, JTAPI to-be, PABX and CTI[4] servers, Intranet). And no continuity (neither logical nor physical) exists between the two kinds.

---

[1]. Telecommunication Information Networking Architecture Consortium

[2]. Enterprise Computer Telephony Forum

[3]. European Computer Manufacture's Association

[4]. Computer Telephony Integration

There is actually no seam at all - in the proper sense - between the two types of control and management systems, no direct interworking, although, as shown in this paper, it would provide new service features.

Lastly, the third element of evolution could be the reglementary decisions, like the ones aiming at opening the networks amd having them interconnected. Since the control and management systems are more and more externalized, openness is likely to be required at two interface levels, at the resource control and management interface between the processing servers and the transport network equipments on one hand, at the interoperability interface between the various control and management systems[5] on the other hand.
This paper describes why an evolvement of the actual control and management systems towards more open and distributed processing systems (e.g. TINA-like systems) is necessary and what it actually means and implies.

2 THE TELECOMMUNICATIONS RESOURCES TO CONTROL AND MANAGE

In order to illustrate the constant increase of the telecommunication resource diversity, the usual layer model is used. The first telecommunication resource layer corresponds to the transmission infrastructures, subdivided into the access networks and the transmission networks. The resources of this layer provide the support for transporting informations, this support being either a cupper pair, a cable, an optical fiber or an electromagnetic field. New transmission techniques have emerged these last years, like the Synchronous Digital Hierarchical transmission for the transmission networks, FDMA/TDMA , Asynchronous Digital Subscriber Lines, or Digital European Cordless Telephony for the access networks.
The second telecommunication resource layer is called the transport layer and relies on the transmission infrastructures. It provides OSI level 2 links and OSI level 3 network channels and includes 64 kbit/s telephony circuits, X.25 virtual circuits, IP datagrams, frame relay, cell switching, etc. The newness here is embodied by new IP routing protocols (I-PNNI), frame or tag switching in the local networks, packet radio services (GPRS) over GSM networks, ATM, etc.
The third layer is characterized by information storage and processing servers, connected to the (private or public) telecommunications networks as end-points : (domain) naming servers, vocal or electronic mail boxes, intelligent peripherals

---

[5]. Needless to say that the second level is more acceptable, because more secure.

(DTMF detection, interactive voice response, voice processing), information caching servers, information servers (WWW, VoD).
There is no sense, of course, in aiming at a single control and management system for all theses resources. There are nevertheless reasons for targetting more interworking between the different (control and management) systems : it can help to provide new control and management services and consequently to satisfy end-users , to optimize the transport network usage, to reduce its load, and possibly to reduce the network and service development costs.

2. TOWARDS SEAMLESS CONTROL AND MANAGEMENT SYSTEMS

2.1 Control and management systems, as information networks

Control and management of network resources or end-user telecommunications services can be called telecommunications global intelligence: they necessitate information processing and storage at various computing nodes (e.g. Service Control Points, Operations Systems, ...) and information transmission between these nodes (inband, outband on SS7 or X.25 networks). Therefore, control and management systems are real information networks, as TINA-C is actually considering them (Dupuy, 1995) (Rubin, 1994).

Compared to the protocol reference model (ITU-T I.320 Recommendation), a perception inversion has nevertheless to be operated : these control and management systems should be considered less and less as logical resources associated with the switching systems, but as value-added networks served by switching or transmission equipments. The same analogy, as that suggested in (Buckley, 1995) for the universal signalling network concept, can apply : control and management systems are comparable with computers and the transport networks with peripheral devices.

2.2 Private and public information networks

The control and management systems deployed until now by the public telecommunications operators are different in nature and rarely interconnected one to the others : a IN service control point interconnected to a service data server or to a service management point by SS7 networks represents an example of a control-oriented information network; the future CAMEL systems or the SS7 network interconnection of Home Location Repositories and Mobile Service Centers represent other control-oriented information networks.

Telecommunication Management Networks are obviously management-oriented information networks. As a matter of fact, the current trend, as embodied by the information networks referred to above, is to more and more externalize the control and management services, out of the transport network equipments, in order to shorten the service development cycle and to unbind these services from the equipment technology: the information networks tend to be logically and physically separated from the transport networks.

Internet represents another public control-oriented and management-oriented information network: it allows to control the delivery of a service (by means of HTTP for HTML page retrieval services or SMTP / POP3 for electronic mail services), to control flow reservations (by means of RSVP) or to manage routing tables and routers (SNMP).

The WAN interconnections of local corporate networks, in which CTI ("Computer Telephony Integration") servers control the corporate PABX, represent another kind of full-fledged information networks. Incoming and outgoing calls can be processed, controlled, negotiated on a separate kernel network (TCP/IP), before the actual connection establishment.

Thus an important phenomenon is currently occuring : control-oriented or management-oriented information networks are emerging both in private and public networks, with unfortunately very few attempts to provide interworking between them.

2.3 Drivers for an interworking of the information networks

One possible driver for such an interworking between the various control-oriented and management-oriented information systems could be a regulatory act, requiring more openness at the control and management level (Kung, 1995), in the same vein of the one requiring the interconnection of the transport networks (i.e. access and transmission networks).

Another driver for such an interconnection is new service provisioning. Internetworking between customer premises equipements and public networks was the first step, interworking between the corresponding control and management systems is now the challenge to meet: it will enable new service offers that will benefit to all actors and will be more cost-effective.

For example, freephone services offered by public operators and corporate call center services do not currently interwork directly : if a client dials the freephone number of company C that has three call centers, the client call termination is not garanteed if the first proposed routing ends at a busy call center. As another example, Internet access services and intelligent call control services do not interwork neither : if a client is using a phone line to access the Web and a caller is trying to reach her, there is no means for the time being to notify the callee that she can suspend her PPP session for an incoming telephone call and no means to re-activate her PPP session after the call is terminated. One can easily find other services that would become possible if the control (or management) systems could interwork better, if they were 'seamless'.

3. REQUIREMENTS ON THESE SEAMLESS CONTROL AND MANAGEMENT SYSTEMS

Further more, if the advantages and drivers for interconnecting the control and management systems are taken in, the requirements upon these systems in order to garantee seamlessness and workability are straightly put up.

3.1 Requirement 1 : Identify the various information flows and their constraints

The semantics of the some control-oriented or management-oriented flows depends heavily upon the end-users, the telecommunications services, whereas for others it tends to become stable. For example, the information related to telephony call control is expected to keep on evolving in the near future, in order to integrate new service features like call presentation, incoming call screening, personal user mobility. On the other hand, bi-point or multi-point connection control information is likely to be stabilized.

Consequently, all information flows cannot (any more) be supported by a single application level protocol, let this application level protocol be broadband and specified for service integration (e.g. B-ISUP). This statement implies two requirements : i) the control-oriented and management-oriented information flows need to be finely identified and specified; ii) generic communication protocols such as remote procedure calls (DCE RPC, IN TCAP, OMG IIOP) should be used as a basis for supporting the various flows.

TINA-C worked out a control-oriented and management-oriented flow identification that is worth being illustrated here : a separation of concern has been proposed and specified between access control, service control, communication control, connection control, access management, service management, network resource management.

Access control includes user/terminal identification and authentification, access session management, customization of the service portfolio presentation, service directory, ... Service control corresponds to instantiating a specific service usage for the user (e.g. a conference call with maximum three parties, an information retrieval service which screens all java applets). Communication control corresponds to establishing 1-1, 1-n or m-n communications (binding objects in RM-ODP) between logical end-points, regardless of the actual physical end-point addresses and the transport network technology. Access management corresponds for example to managing one's profile, authentication data or access control policy, etc.
This work enables to better analyze the requirements and constraints upon each flow and to design the information systems accordingly.

3.2 Requirement 2 : Reuse control and management systems when possible

This requirement can be put in other words : the specification, design and development of a control and management system for each flow that a transport network needs to support is definitely not cost-efficient. Network designers should look for reuse, even partial. Of course, a system supporting for example connection control for an access network (e.g. DCS1800, DECT, GSM, RTC, FTTx) is so specific and tailor-made for a given technology that one cannot expect to reuse it for another access network[6]. By reuse here, it is meant the ability to use the services of a control or management system supporting a particular flow when designing the support system for another information flow; for example, a communication control system can be built upon another system supporting connection control.

To do so, all control and management protocols need to be specified according to the same model and language (e.g., the Interface Definition Language of OMG plus a formal language), in order for the designer to really compare the advantages and drawbacks of each and to choose one adequately.

---

[6]. Recent studies seem to prove that a single software system, well designed, could very well provide control (and management) to different kinds of transmission networks (RTC, SDH, ATM) (Nakamura, 1995)

One can understand that the exercise is far from being simple, after a glance at the candidate list : Q.931, Q.932 , Q.2931 or DSS2, GSM9.2, ISUP, ECMA QSIG, CMIP, SNMP, CMOP, DSM-CC, TCP/IP, INAP/TCAP, etc. This would nevertheless result in specifications like the following one :

```
interface SocketControl {

  void SocketRequest (
        in SHORT domain,
        in SHORT type,
        in SHORT protocol,
        out SHORT socket_id
  );
  void SocketConnection (
        in SHORT socket_id,
        in SOCK_ADR ptr_adr
        in SHORT adress_length,
  );
  };
```

3.3 Requirement 3: Provide better flexibility for the control and management service deployment

The basic software infrastructure of the control-oriented and management-oriented global system needs to be well balanced : an identical kernel of functionalities has to be present on each computing node, in order for the system engineer to deploy the control or management services conditionally to the quality of service he looks after, rather than to the basic processing functionalities requested by the services.

Currently, for example, signaling services are deployed according to a hierarchical algorithm : the signalling messages are processed first by local switches first, then by transit switches if it is a long-distance call, by a service control point if the service is 'intelligent', eventually by an international switch if it is an international call. This engineering architecture meets well the current signalling requirements and the E.164 numbering plan. On the opposite, communication control based on logical addresses (e.g., universal personal number) might require a different network engineering architecture, consisting in processing the address translation as soon as possible, for example in the local switches or in the service control points attached to them.

TINA-C proposes to base the processing environment of each information network nodes on the same core functionalities, encapsulated by a single API.

3.4 Requirement 4 : Provide more flexibility in the choice of the kernel transport network

The current kernel transport network deployment and the information network constraint diversity in terms of quality of service (jitter, bandwidth, delay) require to base the interconnection of all the information network computing nodes upon various kernel transport network technologies : quasi-associated signaling networks, IP networks, ATM VC/VPs, X.25 virtual circuits, etc.

The flexibility that will be looked for can be illustrated as follows : a freephone service mixed with a call center service. An incoming call for a corporate employee is currently routed by the public network to the corporate PABX, and processed in more and more cases by a CTI server. If the callee initially dials a corporate freephone number, the call can be processed by a service control point of the public network. This call is thus processed by two external servers, interconnected by two different kernel transport networks : SS7 and a line between the PABX and the CTI server. More flexibility could consist here in enabling direct and connection-less interworking, between the SCP and the CTI server.

3.5 Requirement 5 : Control and management independent of the platform providers

Since control and management services are mostly externalized from the transport network equipments, in order precisely to provide independence from the equipement technology, and to reduce the service life cycle, developing these now external services on monolithic and proprietary software platforms would be a really bad decision. The control and management services should rather be deployed and run on open distributed processing systems : OMG CORBA 2.0 request brokers and standard operating systems (X/Open, COSE, ...).

4. SOFTWARE ARCHITECTURES

The best way to satisfy the requirements given above is first to consider the control-oriented and management-oriented information networks like open distributed systems, second to specify the concepts, principles and rules - a software architecture - that these control and management systems should comply with.

A few software architectures exist now, like the Windows Object Service Architecture from Microsoft, The Intelligent Network Conceptual Model from ITU-T, The Computer Supported Telephony Application from ECMA, the DAVIC architecture, TINA from TINA-C (Dupuy, 1995), the Reference Model of Open Distributed Processing from ITU-T (Stéfani, 1995), the W3C architecture, the Java development kit, etc.

TINA seems to have a good ground : it is open to various technologies (IN, Java, DSM-CC, HTTP, SNMP, ORB, etc), it is non-prioprietary since jointly designed by a consortium, it is telecommunication-oriented. Nevertheless, it currently lacks greater publicity and support, in order to enlarge the user community to non public network actors (e.g., ECTF, ECMA). It also lacks large scale experimentation, as of the World Wide Web, in order to test its scalability and to measure its performance.

5. CONCLUSION

Control and management are adding value to the private or public telecommunicatons networks. They are currently evolving due to three major factors : the increase of the network technology diversity, the increase of processing capabilities at the public periphery, and reglementary acts. Quite surprinsingly, no attempt to interconnect the various - private and public - control and management systems has been made, excepted by military institutions and universities (Internet). A global, seamless control and management system, made of Internet, intelligent networks and computer telephony integration systems, should be targetted at, as it would really burst the service offers. TINA-C is on the way of specifying and standardizing the software architecture required for such a seamless control and management system. Nevertheless, more effort should be devoted to the task, in order to turn the vision now into reality.

6. REFERENCE

F. Dupuy, G. Nilsson, Y. Inoue, "The TINA Consortium: Towards Networking Telecomunications Information Services", ISS'95, Berlin, avril 1995.

H. Rubin, N. Natarajan, «A Distributed Software Architecture for Telecommunication Networks», IEEE Network, January/February 1994.

Buckley, "Evolution of intelligence and signalling in the far future", ISS'95, Berlin, avril 1995.

R. Kung, "Open Networking : is it technically feasible ?", ISS'95, Berlin, avril 1995.

H. Nakamura, T. Kai, H. Tanaka, "Software Architecture of the All Band Switching Node System for Efficient Processing of N/BISDN Calls", ISS'95, Berlin, avril 1995.

Jean-Bernard Stéfani, «Open Distributed processing: an architectural basis for information networks», Computer communications, volume 18, number 11, November 1995.

7 BIOGRAPHY

The author graduated from Ecole Polytechnique in 1988 and specialized in telecommunications at Telecom Paris in 1990. Joining CNET at Lannion in 1990, his first studies related to object-orientation and distributed systems applied to on-line services, e.g. Videotex. He worked for an internal CNET project on Intelligent Networks, before joining the TINA-C core team in 1993 for almost 2 years. Back in CNET Lannion since end 1994, he led a team in charge of experimenting TINA. Since January 1997, he is responsible for a R&D department on network software architecture and platforms.

4

Session Management and Control for Intelligent Multimedia Networks

O. Schreyer, St. Abramowski, T. Helbig, U. Konrads, K. Neunast

Philips Research Laboratories
P.O. Box 1980, D-52021 Aachen, Germany
Tel.: +49.241.6003.573, Fax: +49.241.6003.518
e-mail: schreyer@pfa.research.philips.com

Abstract

State-of-the-art in implementing multimedia applications is their development "from scratch". Application programmers have to re-implement common functions, such as communication control, anew for each multimedia application. To overcome the inefficiency, functions common to different networked multimedia applications (the so-called middleware) should be provided via application-oriented programming abstractions. Based on our Multimedia Reference Model as an overall conceptual framework we focus on an important middleware part, called session management and control (SMC). It realizes functions to unify and simplify the usage of data processing and data transfer capabilities of the basic communication and operating systems. We explain concepts and motivation of the basic SMC functionality and illustrate them by an example scenario.

Keywords

Multimedia, middleware, session management and control, application programming interface, stream control, quality of service

Intelligent Networks and Intelligence in Networks D. Gaiti (Ed.)
Published by Chapman & Hall

1 INTRODUCTION

Advances in computer and communication technology have enabled the integration of digital audio and video in various fields of applications, leading to the emergence of so-called multimedia applications. Current multimedia applications are either local, single-user systems like computer games and CD-i applications or, if networked, restricted to a certain class of applications like video-on-demand, or tele-shopping. In the future, networked multi-user multimedia applications with a high degree of interactivity will emerge. Examples for such applications are networked tele-diagnosis, tele-teaching or tele-collaboration applications, as well as distributed multi-user games, or news editing tools for digital TV studios with distributed components like journalist workstations, video servers, and special effect rendering machines.

State-of-the-art in implementing multimedia applications is their development "from scratch", i.e. directly on top of basic communication and operating system functions. Application programmers have to re-implement common functions, such as communication control or quality of service handling, anew for each multimedia application instead of being able to concentrate on the core application logic itself. This is time consuming and inefficient. The solution is obvious: Functions common to different networked multimedia applications should be provided via application-oriented programming abstractions.

These application-oriented functions (often referred to as middleware) close the gap between the functionality offered by basic communication and operating systems and the requirements of interactive, distributed multi-user multimedia applications. The following generic functions are among the essential ones needed for networked multi-user multimedia applications:

- configuring of multimedia communication and processing topologies,
- communication and coordination of multiple concurrent application entities,
- negotiating quality of service requirements and reserving resources,
- controlling and synchronizing data streams.

For complex systems, such as networked multimedia systems, an overall conceptual framework is strongly needed that allows to offer different views to end users, application designers, providers, and operators. In chapter 2 we shortly discuss our *Multimedia Reference Model.*

Session management and control is an important middleware part in this model covering the usage of *data processing and data transfer* capabilities of basic communication and operating systems. In chapter 3 we explain the basic terminology to embed SMC into the context of multimedia systems.

For the cooperation with applications we developed a *session management and control application programming interface* focused on in this paper. In the main part we explain motivation and concepts of the different groups of SMC operations. Finally we show the usage by an example scenario.

2 THE MULTIMEDIA REFERENCE MODEL: A FRAMEWORK

For complex systems, such as networked multimedia systems, an overall conceptual framework is strongly needed. Different views have to be offered to end users, application designers, providers, and operators. In [3] we introduced the *Multimedia Reference Model* (see figure 1) by applying the modelling technique of the Intelligent Network Conceptual Model (INCM) based on our experiences with the realization of IN concepts (as shown e.g. for the service creation environment PHIDES [1] and the Open Switching platform [2]).

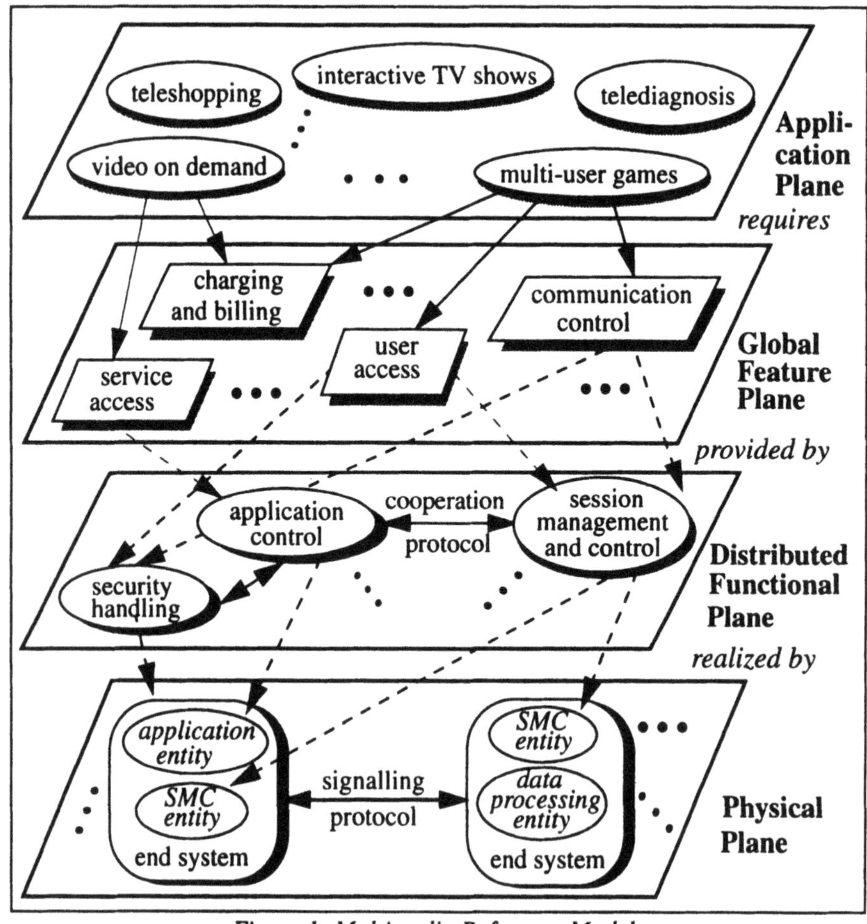

Figure 1: Multimedia Reference Model

The **Application Plane** describes the end user's view to the offered applications. Examples for such applications are tele-diagnosis, tele-shopping, interactive TV shows, video on demand, or multi-user games.

The **Global Feature Plane** defines the application building blocks (ABB) necessary to construct the networked, interactive, multi-user, multimedia applications described on the Application Plane. Those ABBs are combined to construct the application logic. The basic ABB for underlying multimedia communication is the communication control ABB.

The **Distributed Functional Plane** (DFP) describes a functional architecture constructed of functional entities and their cooperation protocols, which are needed to provide the functionality for the application building blocks of the global feature plane. Session management and control is a basic functional entity.

The **Physical Plane** describes possible distribution scenarios that can reach from centralized realization of single-vendor solutions to the maximum distribution where every functional entity of the DFP is realized on one physical end-system.

3 BASIC TERMS OF SESSION MANAGEMENT AND CONTROL

As mentioned above, application-oriented (middleware) functions offered via a generic application programming interface enable application programmers to efficiently use the basic capabilities of the physical network in their applications without detailed knowledge of the implementation or of the intrinsics of the underlying communication infrastructure.

Session management and control (SMC) is an important middleware function on the DFP in our model. It covers the functionality to unify and simplify the usage of *data processing and data transfer* capabilities of the physical network components ("physical layer"). That means, the SMC is a distributed software on top of the basic communication and operating systems forming the physical layer. The *management* part of SMC refers to functions to configure data processing and data transfer entities in the sense of making them known to SMC, defining their attributes, or removing them from the control of SMC. The *control* part of SMC is concerned with functions provided to unify and simplify the runtime control of these entities.

The term **application** denotes software in the overall system that invokes SMC (middleware) functions during run-time to trigger and control the required data processing and data transfer actions in the physical network components. In the DFP, applications are represented by **application control functions (ACFs)** that are application parts realizing the interaction with the middleware. An ACF is considered to be an addresseable piece of software allocated on a single, well-defined end-system (see below). Each ACF may act on behalf of a **user**. However, in view of SMC, a user is (only) represented by a unique identity in relation to the ACF

The total amount of SMC functions provided to ACFs is collected in the **session management and control application programming interface (SMC-API)**. The interaction between SMC and ACFs, consisting of SMC function invocations from the applications and their corresponding responses as well as possible notifications from the SMC, is defined by the **session management and control application protocol (SMCAP)**.

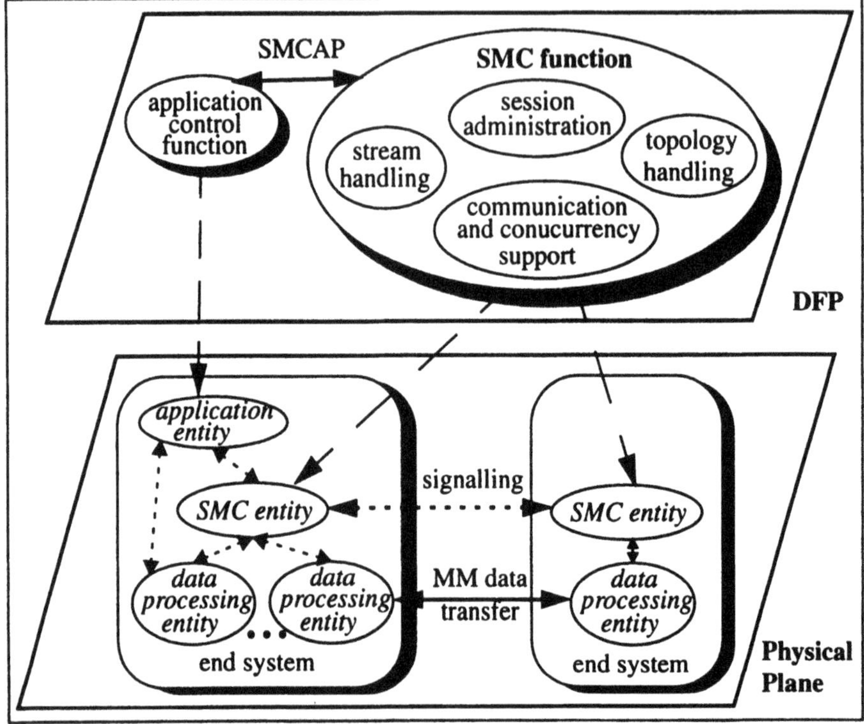

Figure 2: Placement of the SMC-API in Multimedia Reference Model

To keep the relationship between ACF/SMC interactions, the **session** concept as administrative wrapper for an (application) context is introduced. For this, the SMC-API contains functions to create, protect, modify, and release - i.e. to administrate - sessions (see chapter 4.1). For each session, a set of data called **session profile** is stored and maintained by SMC.

In figure 2 the embedding of the SMCAP in the DFP is shown. In the physical plane, we consider networks consisting of interconnected **end-systems**. End-systems are well-defined, separated, and addresseable pieces of hardware where both the software realizing the data processing and data transfer functions and the SMC software is running and/or the software realizing the ACFs. Examples for end-systems can be a PC connected to the network as well as a set-top box. An application entity should normally communicate with a local (or at least a well-defined) SMC entity.

4 SMC-API OPERATIONS

In the following, we explain motivation and concepts of the different groups of SMC-API operations. These are:

- functions to administrate (i.e. create, inquire, etc.) sessions (chapter 4.1),
- functions to handle multimedia processing topologies (chapter 4.2),
- functions to negotiate quality of service contracts (chapter 4.3),
- stream handling functions to control data transfer and processing during run-time (chapter 4.4),
- further, only shortly considered function groups are (chapter 4.5)
  - functions for application concurrency and coordination support,
  - functions to support communication among application entities,
  - functions to access the operational interfaces of processing entities,
  - functions for session event handling,
  - SMC management.

An example scenario (chapter 5) concludes this overview.

4.1 Session Administration Operations

A basic SMC task is storing and maintaining the context in which its functions are called. For this, the **session** concept as administrative wrapper for the relationship between all interactions concerning this context is introduced. Based on this concept, the following SMC functionality has to be provided:

- *Creating a session*

A session is created after a corresponding request from an ACF. In response, the SMC sends back the **unique session identifier** to be the common identification means for all interactions between ACFs and SMC belonging to the same (session) context. The ACF may *optionally* provide a **session name** by which the session can be identified by other ACFs without knowing the session identifier. The ACF creating a session becomes its **session master**. The role of the session master (and the related rights) may be passed and shared among ACFs. There *must always* be at least one session master. A session without any session master (e.g. if the (last) session master leaves the session by error) is automatically shut down by SMC.

- *Adding, removing, and authenticating participants of sessions*

An ACF is a **participant** of a session if it has been explicitly registered. Multiple ACFs can participate in a session. As soon as the session is created by the session master ACF (this is the first participant) and as long as the session exists, other ACFs may enter the session. The actual list of participants of a session is maintained in the session profile. An *end-system* is considered to be participating in a session as soon as one ACF located on the end-system is participating in the session. Removing an end-system from a session means to remove all ACFs located on this end-system from the session.

- *Inquiring sessions*

In general, an ACF can query SMC concerning information about sessions and their attributes with or without being registered in any session. Inquiries may concern all sessions in progress (session directory), sessions on a specific end-system or sessions where a specific ACF is participating in etc. The SMC-API may offer inquiry functions. Another solution could be read-only interface to the session profile database.

- *Protecting sessions*

The execution of an SMC function (requested by an ACF) may be protected depending on the status of the calling ACF/user and the status of the session. Protection procedures (as password authentication or check of global rights or credit limits) are performed by a **security handling function** that is an function *outside SMC.* If SMC is requested to perform a protected function then it invokes the security controller to check or authenticate the user which the requesting ACF acts on behalf of. Only if the security handler responds that the check or authentication has been successful, the SMC function will be invoked.

- *Merging and splitting of sessions*

If two different sessions are merged then the lists of participants are merged and all previous session masters share the session mastership of the new session.

If an existing session shall be split into two new sessions the session master has to provide the two new lists of session participants and the new session masters, and both processing topologies of the new sessions (see chapter 4.2).

- *Releasing a session*

A session is pulled down by SMC if
- a session master sends a corresponding request,
- timer conditions are met (e.g. concerning the last ACF request), or
- the only session master leaves the session (e.g. by a system fault).

SMC then releases all existing processing topologies in the session (see chapter 4.2), broadcasts a shut-down notification to all session participants, and deletes the session profile.

4.2 Processing Topology Handling Functions

The basic target of SMC is to unify and simplify the usage of multimedia data processing and data transfer capabilities. For this, SMC-API functions are provided to define and manage processing topologies for multimedia data in terms of creating, changing or removing processing entities and their interconnecting communication paths in the context of sessions. The definition of these functions is based on abstractions of the physical layer given in chapter 4.2.1 extending the work introduced in [3].

An ACF defining a processing topology and one or more data processing entities of this topology may run on the same end-system (PC or workstation). The difference between them is that the ACF only *controls* the data processing (via SMC) while at the data processing entity the *processing* of the multimedia data is performed. So for example, the ACF could look like a console/icon-bar for originating (SMC-API) commands (e.g. by pressing buttons), while the processing entity (functional node) is the software receiving video data and presenting them in a window.

4.2.1 Network Abstractions for Session Management and Control

A **data processing entity (DPE)** is a piece of hard- and/or software that generates, transforms or consumes multimedia data and is involved in multimedia communication (data transfer) with other DPEs. DPEs are located on end-systems. Examples are video server, microphone or telephone. At the SMC-API, a DPE is abstracted by a **functional node (FN).** An FN is either a **source**, a **sink**, or a **relator**. A **source** only generates data units. A **sink** only consumes data units. A **relator** both consumes and generates data units. Examples are a microphone as source, a loudspeaker as sink of audio data, and an audio mixer as relator.

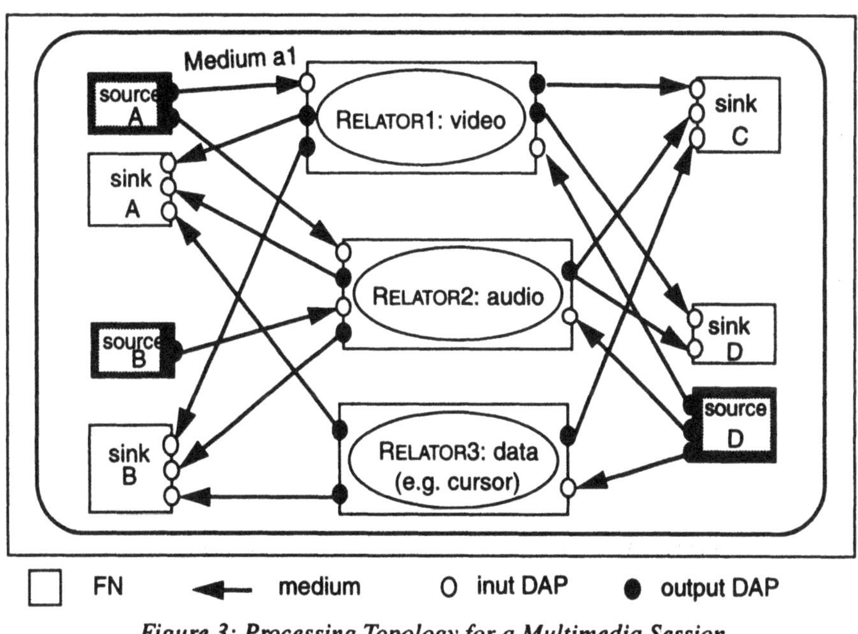

Figure 3: Processing Topology for a Multimedia Session

Each FN has a number of **data access points (DAP)** to access the data. Depending on the direction of data movement, there exist **input DAPs** and **output DAPs**. FNs consume data units by reading them from input DAPs and produce data units by writing them to output DAPs. DAPs are typed with the type of data they are able to convey (e.g. audio or video). DAPs may support a single or multiple types.

A **medium** is the abstract representation of the data transfer functionality for moving data from one DAP of an FN to another DAP of another FN. The data movement is uni-directional. Multiple media may originate from a single output DAP, while only exactly one medium may end at an input DAP. Multiple media may connect two FNs, e.g. audio and video.

Based on these abstractions, a **processing topology** is a directed graph given by the directed interconnection of DAPs of functional nodes with media. An example is shown in figure 3. A **data path** is a path in a processing topology. Data paths always start at output DAPs, may go through relator nodes, and do always ends at an input DAP. A **data flow** is then the sequential chain of data units that is processed and transferred on data paths.

4.2.2 Defining and Realizing a Processing Topology

Each ACF participating in a session can define any number of processing topologies for the session by executing the following steps:

1. create or join a session (see chapter 4.1).
2. announce the new topology to SMC (that returns a unique *processing topology identifier* to be used as common identification means for all subsequent interactions concerning this topology).
3. define the desired structure of the processing topology, i.e. the nodes and media of the topology, as well as stream control and synchronization relationships and QoS requirements.
4. build up the topology in the actual session.
5. activate and manage controlled streams in the processing topology.

During life-time of a session an ACF can inquire the status of a processing topology (see chapter 4.1), change a topology by adding or removing FNs, re-negotiate QoS parameters (see chapter 4.3), or release a topology.

All FNs and media being available for instantiation are stored in a SMC data base. The maintenance of this data base, e.g. if new data processing and transfer functions are introduced in the overall system (i.e. in the physical layer) is done by corresponding management actions (see chapter 4.5.5).

- *Defining functional nodes for the topology graph*

Defining a node of a processing topology means to identify

- the **type** of desired (data) processing function to be realized by the FN

  To get the unique type name of a processing function, an ACF may interact with a **trader** function. Trading is a typical middleware functionality *outside* SMC.

- optionally, a **name** of the functional node

  A functional node name (unique within the session) can be used by (other) ACFs to get the unique identifier of this node from SMC and to avoid duplicate creation of the same node instance.

- optionally, the **location** (end-system) of the processing function
  The ACF can optionally define the end-system on which the processing function (represented by the FN) shall be executed. If the ACF does not define a location, then SMC determines an appropriate end-system for the FN.

According to this information, an *instance* of the processing function will be started up by SMC on the determined end-system when building up the processing topology (see below).

- *Defining media for the topology*

A medium is defined to get an identifier for a data path between two functional nodes and to provide quality of service (QoS) parameters, if no end-to-end QoS handling is realized for a complete data path (see chapter 4.3).

- *Defining the linkage of nodes with media*

In this definition step the nodes are interconnected by media. Data movement is directed, so for each medium the source node and the sink node are defined. Each input or output functionality of a node is addressed by a DAP. The actual instantiation of the communication paths abstracted by the media is performed during the build up of the topology.

- *Defining streams*

In the context of an application, the control of data processing and transfer functionality by ACFs may also be required during runtime, e.g. to interactively start/stop a data flow, to alter the speed of a data flow, to play it backwards, or to realize synchronization relationships between data flows. The SMC-API includes *stream handling functions* for such purposes. To prepare the usage of stream handling functions an ACF has to define the topology or relevant parts of it as **stream**. The details of SMC stream handling are described in chapter 4.4.

- *Building up processing topologies*

Having defined the structure of the desired processing topology, an ACF can request SMC to build up the topology, i.e. to actually instantiate the logical description in the physical network. In that phase SMC starts up the processing functions represented by FNs, instantiates the DAPs, and establishes a network connection for each medium between FNs (this includes QoS negotiation and resource reservation - see chapter 4.3). If there are no streams defined in the processing topology, SMC *automatically* lifts the blocking of the data generating or consuming functionality of the nodes, such that data transfer becomes active (it then cannot be further influenced via SMC for the complete life-time of the topology, typical application examples are telephone or videophone connections). If there are streams defined in the processing topology, then the stream control code at the FNs (for the desired stream control protocol used by SMC) is instantiated as needed (see chapter 4.4).

- *Changing processing topologies*

To react on dynamic changes in the communication and processing settings of the related applications an ACF can add/remove nodes and/or media to/from a topology, or may re-negotiate QoS parameters. This is done in the same order as for the initial build up of the topology, i.e. the ACF first defines the changes (resulting in SMC database entries) and can then request to actually change the topology.

There can also be automatic topology changes if an ACF leaves a session (by an explicit deregistration or by an erroneous crash). Then SMC automatically shuts down all topology parts belonging to this ACF.

- *Releasing processing topologies*

A processing topology is pulled down by SMC if an ACF participating in the session sends a corresponding request, or the session the processing topology belongs to is released. To release a processing topology, SMC first blocks the data generating or consuming functionality of the functional nodes, pulls down the network connections and releases the corresponding network resources. Then the functional nodes are shut down and, finally, the processing topology profile is deleted. SMC notifies the topology shut down to all session participants.

4.3 QoS Negotiation and Resource Reservation Functions

Quality of Service (QoS) determines the degree of satisfaction experienced by users of a (multimedia communication) service ([5]). On the highest level of abstraction, QoS may be described in terms of "audio in CD quality" or "video in VHS quality". At the application-middleware interface (i.e. at the SMC-API), generic QoS parameters will be negotiated like "sample rate" for audio or "colour resolution" for video. These parameters then have to be mapped in SMC onto requirements to the physical components like "bandwidth", "processing time", or "buffer size".

In the definition phase for a processing topology (see chapter 4.2.2) the requesting ACF provides **end-to-end QoS** requirements referring to data paths or streams of the topology. Examples for possible QoS parameters that can be sent by an ACF are given below. In the build up phase of the topology SMC maps the QoS parameters received from the ACF to corresponding resource parameter and tries to reserve the required resources. End-to-end requirements influence both the data transfer on the related data paths and the data processing at the FNs. If the initial reservation fails, or in case of system performance degradation, or by an explicit ACF request, QoS (re-)negotiation between SMC and the ACF may be required.

Note, QoS handling in general (including QoS specification, resource reservation, and QoS negotiation) is a field of great importance and effort both in the academical and the technical world. However, comprehensive concepts and solutions are not yet available. So some parts of this area still remain for further study.

4.3.1 Media Types and QoS Parameters

Figure 4 shows media types[1] with QoS parameters to be negotiated between ACF and SMC. The table is mainly taken from [6]. The ACF provides the required QoS parameters to SMC. There are three cases possible:

- QoS parameters may be defined by *range*. SMC tries to reserve the resources necessary to guarantee the maximum value. Re-negotiation with the ACF is initiated (on runtime) if the minimum value can be no longer guaranteed.
- QoS parameters may also be defined *minimum* value. SMC tries to reserve the resources necessary to guarantee this minimum. Re-negotiation with the ACF is initiated by SMC (on runtime) if the minimum can be no longer guaranteed.
- If an ACF does not define any value for a QoS parameter then a default value is used that is defined for each QoS parameter. SMC applies the default value as if the ACF had defined the QoS parameter only by a minimum value (see above).

Media type	QoS parameter	Example values	Quality characterization
video	frame rate	25 fps	PAL
		60 fps	HDTV
	frame size	>176*144 pixel	MMCF QoS class 1 ("basic multimedia applications" - [5])
	colour resolution	1 bit/pixel	black/white
		24 bits/pixel	16 million possible colours
	end-to-end delay	<250ms	MMCF QoS class 2 ([5])
audio	sample size	8 bit	telephone voice quality
		16 bit	CD quality
	sample rate	44.1 kHz	(for 16 bit sample size)
	end-to-end delay	<150ms	MMCF QoS class 3 ([5])
data	bandwidth	2 Mbps	e.g. for file transfer
	end-to-end delay	<100ms	interactive data applications

Figure 4: Medium types and QoS parameters

Note, at a higher level of abstraction QoS could be defined by more intuitive terms like "low quality black/white video for browsing". Such a requirement could then be translated into the medium type "video" with e.g. "352*288 pixel, 1 bit/pixel colour, <1s delay, MPEG-1 compression". However, we see the definition of such higher level (user) QoS types and the translation of them in the application layer, i.e. outside SMC.

1. Note, we use the term "medium type" although the end-to-end QoS parameters in general refer to a data flow on a data path possibly via several media (with the same type).

4.3.2 Resource Reservation in the Physical Components

In the build up phase of a processing topology SMC maps the QoS parameters received from the ACF to the corresponding resource parameter in the physical network and tries to reserve the required resources. Such network resource parameters are according to [6] bandwidth of the communication channels, buffer spaces, and CPU processing power. Before QoS parameters can be translated in such resource parameters there may be an intermediate translation within SMC into something like *network QoS parameter* and *device QoS parameter*, e.g. latency, bandwidth, delay, and jitter for any relevant data path as well as timing and throughput demands for the FNs.

As a result of the negotiation the elements in the physical layer concerned with processing and communicating real-time critical data have reserved the required resources. This is notified to the ACF. If the reservation fails, then this is notified to the ACF in order to start a re-negotiation.

Resource reservation in the physical components layer is for further study.

4.3.3 QoS (Re-)Negotiation

A (re-)negotiation of the QoS arrangements for a topology can be performed between SMC and ACF if the initial reservation fails, if the degradation of system performance makes it impossible to keep the guaranteed QoS, or after an explicit ACF request, if the QoS requirements on the application side have changed. In the former two cases SMC informs the ACF that re-negotiation is necessary by a session event notification (see chapter 4.5.4).

The field of QoS re-negotiation is for further study.

4.4 Stream Control and Synchronization Functions

The SMC-API *stream handling functions* enable an ACF to control the data processing and transfer functionality of (parts of) a processing topology during runtime, e.g. to interactively start/stop a data flow, to alter speed/direction of a data flow, or to realize synchronization relationships between data flows and processing entities. Examples are the presentation/processing of data originating from any (digital) storage (e.g. to realize a video playback) or a synchronized video presentation on several end-systems.

Stream control functions concern parts (i.e. subgraphs) of topologies. We call such a subgraph **stream**. To realize stream handling functions, SMC orchestrates and monitors the processing and transfer of data at all relevant FNs (e.g. by starting the output of a video server and the input of a video window). This requires SMC to control the *timing* of FN activations by using a **stream control protocols**.

Stream handling requires advanced SMC-API concepts which we explain in the following. The concepts are partly taken from [7].

4.4.1 Stream Control Concepts

- *Stream Control Identifier (SCI)*

When invoking an SMC-API stream handling function the requesting ACF has to identify the stream concerned by the function. For this, we introduce the **stream control identifier (SCI)** as generic identification means for stream handling functions. An SCI can have two semantics:

- A **sink SCI** is defined by *an input DAP* identifier and refers to the topology part covering all data paths between output DAPs of source nodes and the input DAP used as SCI, i.e. a sink SCI concerns all FNs reached in upstream direction from the input DAP used as SCI.
- A **group SCI** groups other (sink or group) SCIs in an SCI hierarchy. Such an SCI is used to control all related data paths (determined by the sink SCIs on the lowest hierarchy level) by single function calls (see chapter 4.4.2) and provides the means to define synchronization relationships among data flows on the related data paths (see below).

SCIs are defined during the topology definition phase. Note, some stream handling functions require further rules to complete their invocation semantics. For example, to stop a stream identified by a sink SCI requires to stop just those of the relevant *active output* DAPs that are not active as source for other streams, such that a multicast stream (from one source, e.g. a video server, to several sink nodes) can be stopped at one specific sink node, but kept at all other sink nodes.

- *Dimension Attributes of a Stream Content*

Basically, SMC controls the timing of functional nodes in streams. For this, an ACF has to define the temporal dimension of a controlled stream **content** (e.g. a file or a data flow captured from a camera). The dimension attributes of a controlled stream are described in the following.

A stream content consists of a sequence of data units. Each data unit is associated with a time-stamp defining its positioning at a time axis. The succession of time-stamps describes the **stream time** (given as sequence numbers, e.g. video frame number, or time units relative to real-time, e.g. SMPTE time-stamps). For periodic streams the **difference between succeeding time-stamps (ΔST)** is fixed. For each stream a "normalized" presentation rate is defined that corresponds to the presentation of the data flow with a speed of 1. The specification is given by the **real-time duration ΔRT** of the data units. This duration corresponds to the stream time difference ΔST (see figure 5). The quotient between stream time and real time, i.e. ΔST/ΔRT is called **ratio.** If the stream content is a stored file then it is bounded, i.e. it has a first and a last data unit, called **LB (lower bound)** and **UB (upper bound).**

Note, the dimension parameters refer to one stream content (e.g. a stored file) presented at a sink FN. If the content changes (e.g. to another file), then it can be necessary to re-define the dimension parameters.

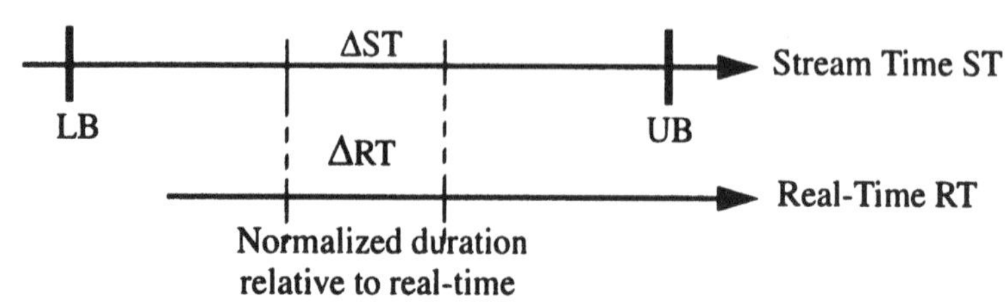

Figure 5: Attributes of a Stored Data Flow

- *The Normalized Real-Time-Line (nRT)*

The basic means to enable synchronization of streams (e.g. audio/video synchronization or synchronized play-out of the same content at different sinks) is the **normalized real-time-line (nRT)**. This is a real-time-line with the default start point '0'. Each SCI has a normalized time-line.

In the first step, the contents of a stream are aligned to the nRT of the sink SCI where they shall be presented (aligning a sequence of contents is the basics for play-lists). The alignment of contents is done by **reference points**, i.e. a point in the content's stream time referring to a point on the nRT. With the content's ratio, for each point in stream time the belonging point on the nRT can be calculated by

$$m_{nRT} = (m_{ST} - P_{ST}) \cdot \frac{\Delta RT}{\Delta ST} + P_{nRT} \qquad \text{(E1)}$$

where P_{ST} and P_{nRT} define reference points and m_{ST} is a point in stream time for which the point m_{nRT} on the nRT shall be calculated.

The play-out at different sinks can be synchronized (e.g. audio and video, or video for cooperative viewing). For this, the nRTs of the sink SCIs are synchronized via nRT of a group SCI grouping the sink SCIs, i.e. sync relationships are *implicitly* defined. If e.g. audio and video contents are synchronized, *both nRTs* of the two sink SCIs are synchronized to nRT of the SCI grouping these sink SCIs by reference points.

- *Presentation Attributes of a Stream*

When presenting a stream, the content's stream-time-line or the nRT to which the content is aligned and the time axis of global real-time are fixed with each other ("start on 12h00 with frame 1"). This is defined by the reference points between stream-time/nRT and global real-time, describing the presentation start point.

To describe the temporal dimension of the stream presentation moreover the **speed factor** S of the presentation is needed. It describes the mapping between nRT and global real-time. A negative value defines a presentation in reverse direction. How speed values other than "1" are either achieved (e.g. by changing the data rate or by dropping/duplicating of data units) depends on the stream control protocol.

4.4.2 Stream Handling Functions

- *Controlling Stream Presentation*

SMC-API stream handling functions enable to control data flows during runtime by providing VCR like operations, e.g. to interactively start/stop a data flow, to seek in a stream content, or to change the speed of a data flow.

If one of the corresponding stream handling function is invoked with an sink SCI as stream identifier then the related data path is determined as described above. If an SCI grouping other SCIs is used then the function is propagated through the complete (sub)hierarchy of this SCI and, therefore, executed for every data flow on a data path related to an sink SCI being a leaf of this hierarchy. In the simplest case (without a synchronization relationship) the propagation of such an invocation means to execute this function in parallel for all these data flows without any synchronization between the executions.

- *Synchronization of Data Flows*

To control different data paths in a synchronized manner, e.g. a video and an audio data flow basically means that at more than one input DAP data, transferred on the data paths, shall arrive synchronized to each other. For this, SMC supports the definition of so called 'sync relationships' for sink SCIs. The definition of such relationships is done as follows:

- First, all related contents have to be aligned to their sink SCI's nRTs.
- A group SCI for the related group of sink SCIs has to be introduced.
- Then each of the sink SCI nRTs must be synchronized to the group SCI's nRT, i.e. one sync definition per sink SCI (for the related streaming concepts see chapter 4.4.1).

SMC uses these attributes on runtime to propagate the related function invocations in an appropriate manner to guarantee the required synchronization parameters.

- *Handling of Composed Streams*

Processing continuous data, such as in news studio environments, require runtime capabilities to concatenate and combine stream contents from different sources (files) to form a resulting data flow. We call the content parts **clips** and the resulting data flow **composed stream**. The latter is represented by a meta definition (also called 'Edit Decision List') which defines the temporal relationships between the clips, i.e. the order in which the clips are concatenated (and possibly special transition effects between clips like overlaying). Furthermore, the meta definition contains the locations (servers) where the source files of the clips are stored. Note, in many cases, the meta definition is the only representation of a composed stream, i.e. this data flow is not actually stored as (new) data material, but has to be established on runtime. SMC provides the means to handle such meta definitions on runtime in a way that an ACF can control a composed stream via the SMC-API as if it were a single physical data flow.

4.5 Further SMC Function Groups

4.5.1 ACF Concurrency and Coordination Support Functions

In distributed applications, ACFs need means to coordinate and synchronize their concurrent actions. Examples are the synchronization of ACF states and the coordination of access to resources. SMC offers *concurrency and coordination support functions* to provide powerful means for these purposes. The underlying concepts are mainly taken from the multipoint communication service specification in the T.120 standard series ([4]). The basic one is the concept of **tokens**. A token represents an information item (e.g. an access right) in the context of an application. Tokens are created and specified by ACFs during runtime and can be grabbed, given back, or checked by ACFs. The possession of a token can be exclusive or non-exclusive. The semantics of a token is **not visible** to SMC. SMC only maintains the existing tokens according to their specification and provides the functions enabling ACFs to *create, request, take, pass, delete*, ... tokens.

4.5.2 ACF-ACF Communication Support Functions

Application control functions are located on different end-systems. In the context of distributed applications, the ACFs need to be able to exchange information. This ACF-ACF communication is facilitated by the *communication support functions* of SMC enabling ACFs to send information items (e.g. a message string) *via SMC* to other ACFs.

Before such a request both ACFs must be participants of the same session. The exception is sending information to a **permanent application control function (PACF)**. A PACF is a specific ACF *permanently* waiting for SMC notifications. PACFs are necessary since, in general, ACFs are not permanently running on their end-systems. In the course of an application, it may be required for ACFs to invoke or inform other ACFs that are not yet running. At most one PACF exists on an end-system. A PACF is uniquely identified by its globally unique end-system address. Depending on the specific end-system a PACF belongs to, it has the capability to appropriately react on requests, e.g. to cause an ACF to join a session.

SMC enables to address individual ACFs, the PACF of an end-system, all ACFs participating in a session, as well as predefined groups of ACFs. Speedy and ordered information delivery is supported by various transfer semantics, such as 'unreliable delivery' and 'reliable FIFO delivery'.

Note, the communication support functions are provided in addition to the processing topology handling functions as described in chapter 4.2. A separation of the ACF-ACF communication from the concepts for processing and transfer of multimedia data mainly results from the different layers of abstractions. ACF-ACF communication is among entities layered on top of SMC. In contrast, the multimedia data are transferred between the data processing entities (see figure 2).

4.5.3 ACF-FN Communication Support Functions

Communication among ACFs and functional nodes may be required, e.g. for directly controlling FN settings (e.g. to change window settings of a video sink, or to define parameters for a relator node performing overlaying effects). To enable ACF-FN communication, SMC provides the necessary address information to ACFs. The exchange of information between ACFs and FNs is outside SMC. It can be realized e.g. via CORBA mechanisms ([8]).

4.5.4 Session Event Handling Functions

In the context of an application, it might be important for an ACF to get informed about the occurrence of events concerning the status of a session. The SMC-API contains functions that enable an ACF to define events it wants to be informed about and corresponding notifications sent by SMC when such an event occurs. Session event handling can be based on an abstract model of state transitions within a session (by a finite state machine like the IN-Basic Call State Model) including a definition of all events that trigger a runtime notification by SMC. Examples are:

- *QoS degradation*, i.e. if QoS descends below the guaranteed limiting value (e.g. the lower margin of the guaranteed QoS range).
- *Session administra*tion notifications, like changing the session master.
- *Stream events*, like reaching the end of a file.
- *Error events*, like the crash of a processing entity. Error events may be automatically notified to the session master ACF.

4.5.5 Functions for SMC Management

In an overall multimedia system, configuration management functionality is required to setup, configure, or delete entities both in the application and in the physical layer. This basically means to maintain the corresponding data bases, used e.g. by SMC, when new processing entities are installed or users are subscribed. The SMC management should include functions to define or remove *data processing entities* in the SMC environment, i.e. store/delete the corresponding data (like address information) in/from the relevant SMC data bases. Furthermore, it should enable introducing or removing *ACFs* in the SMC environment.

5 EXAMPLE SCENARIO

The example describes cooperative and synchronous viewing of a video. The same video is played out to two users at two different end-systems. Figure 6 shows the processing topology. The video is played out by a video server and transferred to two video sinks that are located on the end-systems of the users. The stream has an 1:n-multicast structure. Both users are enabled to manipulate the presentation of the video. Between the two data flows a sync relationship is defined to make sure both users view the same data at the same time. Figure 7 reflects the basic information flows. Of course, not all details of the example scenario can be shown.

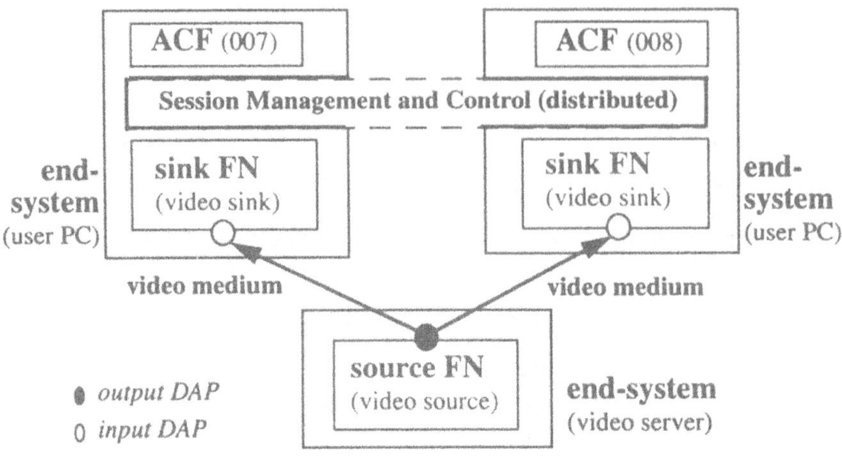

Figure 6: Example Scenario - Cooperative Viewing of a Video

The actions listed below refer to the boxes in figure 7.

1. A user starts an application (represented by ACF '007') to view video files from a server. In the initial step a session is created. The only user interaction may happen to identify the desired video server. All the following steps (till action 8) are then done automatically by the ACF.
2. SMC sets up the session, i.e. a session profile is created, the requesting ACF is stored as session master and first participant, and the initial attributes (e.g. 'masterShare' is "true" to allow later cooperation) are stored. SMC generates a new session identifier and returns it to the ACF.
3. The processing topology definitions for ACF '007' are done, i.e. the definition of the source functional node and the sink node on the end-system (PC) of ACF '007' linked by a medium defined for video. SMC creates a topology profile and a new processing topology identifier. It checks the functional node and medium definitions and stores it in the topology profile.
4. The stream (SCI) definitions for ACF '007' are done. First, the basic sink SCI is defined (i.e. requested by the ACF and generated by SMC). Then, *a group SCI is defined in advance* to be the common SCI for all ACFs joining the session. An alternative solution would be the second ACF participating in the session defines the group SCI when it joins the session and sends the necessary information to the first ACF via ACF-ACF communication (see action 12).

   After the definition phase the ACF requests for the actual instantiation of the processing topology. This may be done automatically by the ACF, i.e. without interaction between user and application.
5. SMC performs the necessary steps to instantiate the processing topology, i.e. it starts up the functional nodes (i.e. the processing functions they represent), instantiates the DAPs, establishes a connection for the medium between the nodes. Since the defined topology represents a "controlled streams", the nodes

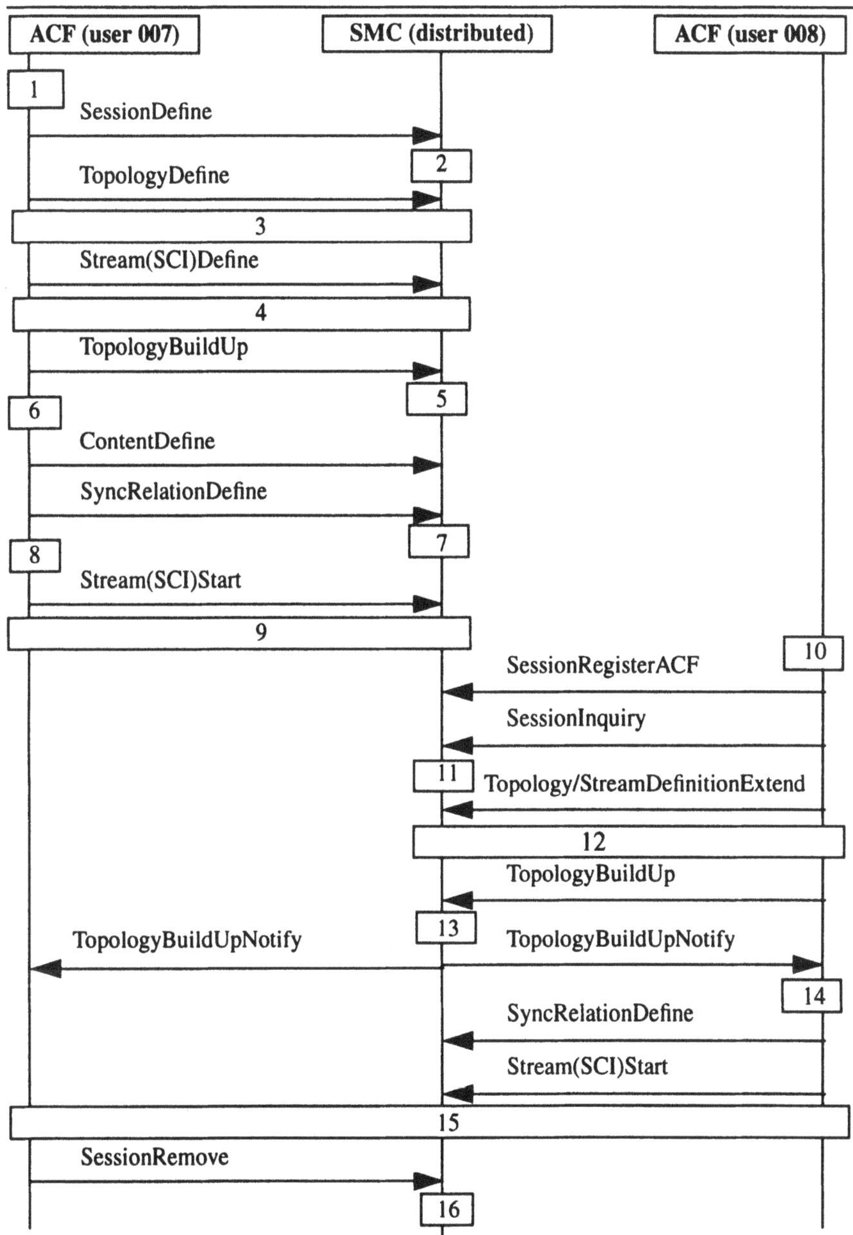

Figure 7: Basic Information Flows for the Example Scenario

keep initially blocked (see chapter 4.4.1). After these steps SMC *notifies* the success of the topology realization to the ACF.

6. The ACF defines the content to be played out, e.g. after the application logic performed a dialogue with a user to manually select a file. The ACF aligns the

content to the sink SCI's nRT and defines the sync relation between the nRTs of sink and group SCI (see chapter 4.4.1).

7. SMC stores the dimension parameter (ratio, lower and upper bound) for the (video) content, the alignment to the sink's nRT, and the reference point between the video sink SCI's nRT and the group SCI's nRT (to prepare for later synchronization with other sinks).
8. After having finished the definitions, the ACF can request the activation of the play-out (e.g. after the user pressed the start button). A technical opportunity is to request an explicit content pre-load first.
9. Having received the start request for the stream SMC lifts the blocking of the nodes, such that the data transfer becomes active and the video presentation at the sink node is started. In the following the user (represented by ACF '007') works with the video (start, stop, seek, etc.).
10. Another user starts an application (represented by ACF '008') to cooperatively work with the first user, i.e. to view the video files together. The ACF registers for the session and queries about the existing topology to be able to define the appropriate extensions. Note, SMC is a *distributed* function, such that the new ACF does not communicate with the same SMC entity as the first ACF. However, the SMC distribution is not visible to the ACFs.
11. SMC stores ACF '008' as new participant and additional master for the session and returns the complete topology profile as response to the query.
12. The topology extensions for ACF '008' are defined. This includes the definition of the sink node on the end-system (PC) of ACF '008' and the linkage to the source node by a medium defined for video. Furthermore, the second sink SCI is defined. Then, the instantiation of the extended topology is requested.
13. SMC starts up the new sink functional node, instantiate its input DAP, and establishes a connection for the medium between the source and the new sink node. The multicast from the source node to the new sink keeps initially blocked. After these steps SMC confirms the actions to *both* ACFs.
14. To enable synchronized played-out between the sinks, the new sink SCI's nRT must be synchronized to the group SCI's nRT in exactly the same way as it was done for the other sink (see action 7). After all definitions are successfully completed the ACF requests for the activation of the stream. For the start command the group SCI is used with a special start time value ("current") such that the data actually played out at the source are multicasted also to the new sink node. Since the first sink node is already active nothing happens for it.
15. SMC now lifts the blocking of the multicast from the source node to the new sink and the blocking of this sink, such that the data transfer becomes active and the video presentation at the new sink node is started.

    In the following, the cooperative work of the users happens. They may select further videos, start/stop the presentation, seek in a file, etc. At the end, the users decide to close the session. In this scenario, ACF '007' sends the release request. ACF '008' does not need to explicitly deregister from the session.

16. SMC releases the session and deletes the session profile. This includes an automatic shut-down and remove of the *complete* topology.

6 CONCLUSIONS

To close the gap between the functionality offered by basic communication and operating systems and the requirements of interactive, distributed multi-user multimedia applications, generic middleware functions should be provided via application-oriented programming abstractions. Based on our Multimedia Reference Model as an overall conceptual framework we introduced session management and control (SMC) as a special middleware part to unify and simplify the usage of data processing and data transfer capabilities in the physical layer. We explained motivation and concepts of the basic groups of SMC functionality reflecting many areas currently under consideration in the academical and the technical world, like quality of service and stream handling. For illustration, we gave an example scenario. On the basis of our concepts a detailed SMC protocol specification is possible.

7 REFERENCES

[1] Abramowski, St., Elixmann, M., Gappisch, H., Heister, U., Heuter, U., Klabunde, K., "*A Service Creation Environment for Intelligent Networks*", Proceedings of the Int. Zurich Seminar on Digital Communication, March 16 - 19, 1992, Zurich, Switzerland

[2] Elixmann, M., de Greef, B.L., Lelkens, A.M.M., Neunast, K.W., Tjabben, H., "*Open Switching — Extending Control Architectures to Facilitate Applications*", Proceedings of the ISS '95, Berlin, Germany, April 23 - 28, 1995

[3] Abramowski, St., Klabunde, K., Konrads, U., Neunast, K.W., Tjabben, H., "*The Multimedia Reference Model: A Framework Facilitating the Creation of Multi-User, Multimedia Applications*", IFIP-TC6 Working Conf. on Intelligent Networks, Copenhagen, Aug. 30-31, 1995

[4] ITU-T Study Group 8, "Multipoint Communication Service for Audiographics and Audiovisual Conferencing - Service Definition, Recommendation T.122"

[5] Multimedia Communications Forum "Multimedia Communications Quality of Service - Framework - Multimedia Desktop Collaboration Requirements", MMCF/95-010

[6] Nahrstadt, K., "An Architecture for End-To-End Quality of Service Provision and its Experimental Validation", PhD thesis, Univ. of Pennsylvania, 1995

[7] Rothermel, K., Helbig, T., "Clock Hierarchies: An Abstraction for Grouping and Controlling Media Streams", IEEE Journal on Selected Areas in Communications, Special Issue on Synchronization Issues in Multimedia Communications Vol. 14, No. 1, January 1996

[8] Object Management Group, "CORBA services: Common Object Services Specification", OMG Document No 95-3-31, March 1995

5

Customer Control of IN Services

O. Færgemand, A. Jensen
Tele Danmark
R&D Telephony Services
Telegade 2, DK-2630 Tåstrup, Denmark
tel: + 45 43 34 43 34
fax: + 45 43 71 88 64
e-mail: of@tdk.dk, alljn@tdk.dk

Abstract

Customer control is becoming an important part of IN-services. Customer control allows the customer to control the setting of his service profile and other data associated with his services. The paper categorises IN-customer into three categories: residential, Small Office and Home Office and business, and discusses their needs for customer control. The paper discusses different ways of implementing customer control: IVR, WWW, proprietary tools and direct access solutions. The paper presents some recent implementations of customer control at Tele Danmark. Finally some future possibilities for customer control are presented.

Keywords

Customer control, IN-service, IVR, DTMF, WWW, VPN.

Intelligent Networks and Intelligence in Networks D. Gaiti (Ed.)
Published by Chapman & Hall

1 INTRODUCTION

In this paper we use "Customer Control" as the ability of the user to control the set-up of his services. Telecommunication services can be implemented in the telecommunications network in various ways. Implementation by IN (Intelligent Network) allows fast and flexible service provisioning. Because speed and flexibility in service offering is a main driver for the use of IN services, customer control of IN services is becoming an important topic for service operators.

Customer control is a subset of Service Management. Strictly defined it excludes the handling of services by the service operator staff. The service operator staff must off course be able to provide the part of service management included in customer control on behalf of the customers - when required.

Customer control includes controlled changes to the service data, i.e. the database of the IN, whereas it does not - for the time being - include changes to the service logic itself. This distinction is not strict and may depend on the type of IN-platform being used, but it focuses our present concerns about offering customer control.

Customer control is seen as beneficial by the service operator for at least two reasons:

- Do-it-yourself by the customer frees operational staff at the service operator from setting up service data for the customer.
- Customer control lets the customer experience more control of his services and more flexible service maintenance, thereby increasing the customer satisfaction.

In the following we characterise the various segments of IN service customers, the various technologies available for their customer control and the resulting possibilities.

2 ACTORS IN CUSTOMER CONTROL AND THEIR NEEDS

2.1 Customer segments

The customers of IN services can be categorised like the customers of telecommunication services in general. In practice, this categorisation is useful:

- Residential customers
- Small Office and Home Office customers
- Business customers.

Residential customers mainly use IN-services like premium rate calling as service users and call diversion schemes as service customers. For customer control of premium rate calling they may want to change the access rights from their telephone and for call diversion they may want to change the routing scheme. The need for customer control is therefore mainly in the area of setting parameters (e.g. time and day and c-number) for call diversion. Attractive pricing and a simple user interface are important for the residential customer. The possibility of assistance from an operator (operator fall-back) is also important.

Small Office and Home Office (SOHO) customers are mainly using the same IN-services as residential customers and some of the cheaper services for business customers (e.g. freephone within a restricted geographical area). Attractive pricing and a simple user interface are important parameters for the SOHO customer as well, but quality parameters such as reliability and availability of the service are becoming important.

Business customers are mainly using national services (e.g. freephone and a universal number for all branches) and international services (e.g. international freephone and VPN - Virtual Private Network). The quality of the service becomes crucial, because many people will depend on the service for the efficiency of their work. Availability of qualified on-line help from experts of the service operator is also important.

Customer control must be accompanied by the ability of the customer to verify his complete "service profile" with the service operator. This implies that efficient feedback must be given on any changes performed by customer control.

2.2 Technologies available

Interactive Voice Response (IVR) The push button telephone (DTMF - Dual Tone Multi Frequency) can be used for setting up IN-services as it is also done for subscriber services implemented in local switches by stimulus procedures (combinations of *, # and figures). This interface is anticipated by vendors by offering IVR systems, intelligent peripherals (IP) to build voice-response systems as parts of the IN-platforms. The penetration of push button telephones is almost 100% in the Danish network and in practice it is assumed that any customer has access to at least one push button telephone.

The lack of a display on ordinary (fixed network) telephones poses some limitations to the use of DTMF for Customer Control, and the penetration of display telephones (fixed network) is still very low. Even when ISDN-access (Integrated Services Digital Network) is well accepted by the customers, it is mainly used for PC's (Personal Computer) in connection with Internet access and not for ISDN-telephones with display.

The advantage of IVR for customer control is that the authenticity of the calling terminal can be assumed from the originating number and that DTMF can be assumed to be available to all our residential customers. The drawback is the complexity of entering large amounts of data via a telephone keypad without a display possibility. The user interface can somehow be improved e.g. by means of Speech Technology (see "Push Self Guide" below) but has its limitations, because it was not built for entering series of data, and because of the lack of a display.

Internet The penetration of WWW-technology (World Wide Web) and the availability of tools for building interactive homepages makes the Internet a very interesting user interface for customer control. It is appealing for services with customer control of bigger complexity than what can be handled by IVR. The security problems are bigger than for IVR, because Internet transmission in principle is unsecured and because the authenticity of the user cannot be assumed by the usage of a fixed, dedicated connection.

Proprietary vendor solutions Until recently all servicing of IN-services by network operator staff was done via a proprietary interface supplied by the IN-vendor. It allows to design form-based interfaces for entering data to IN-services. The design of the form as a service specific maintenance tool is part of the IN-service design. This interface resembles the Internet-interface but because it is part of the IN-platform and operated by IN-platform staff, there are no special security problems. For customer control this interface is so far used on an off-line basis. Today network operator staff receives data from the customer and check the data before they are loaded on the network. The kind of customer controls which are handled this way resembles those which can be handled via Internet. This interface is used for customer control by utilising that each form defines a file format for entering data. This is utilised to format files of customer control data on e.g. a PC, and then load these data on the IN-network.

Direct access The optimal customer control for complex service data is a direct link between the customers' IT-system and the database of the IN-system. This link can today be set-up in different ways, e.g. by using FTP (File Transfer Protocol), RPC (Remote Procedure Call) or ODBC (Open DataBase Connectivity). Emerging technology in this area is covered later in the paper.

2.3 Resulting Possibilities

With the available technology, the needs of the customers can be met in the following ways for various types of service data (simple, complex):

IVR is appealing for services with relatively simple customer control targeted at residential customers. IVR may both be used from a customers own telephone or from another telephone, in which case an authenticaion procedure including the use of a PIN (Personal Identification Number) is used.

WWW is required for more complex services and mainly for the business segment, where Internet access can be assumed. The main benefit of using the WWW is that the user interface is widely known, it allows the customer to connect from different machines and the tools for building specific user interfaces are easy to use.

Proprietary solutions cover the same area as WWW does. The advantages of the proprietary solutions are currently a better security, but as WWW eventually will include more secure access (such as those developed for electronic commerce and banking) the wider availability of tools for WWW will probably decrease the role of the proprietary solutions.

Direct access solutions to IN-databases will eventually be a demand from business customers in order to allow a smooth integration of their IN-services into other aspects of their organisation. These solutions must be seen together with the service operator's attempts to offer maximum control to the customers own services and network (Customer Premises Management).

3 RECENT WORK AT TELE DANMARK

3.1 Remotely controlled call forwarding

Call forwarding is implemented in the local switches in the Danish network. Changing the call forwarding from another telephone than the one being diverted is not available from the switch vendors. Therefore an IN-service has been developed which allows remotely changing the call forwarding. The IN-service prompts for the telephone number involved and the PIN used for authentication of the caller. After validating these data on the IN-platform a series of commands (MML, Man Machine Language) are sent via the management system to the switch involved and the call forwarding is changed.

IVR is used for this customer control because the data entry is a telephone number and a PIN. The customers are used to supply this information via push buttons. The data may in principle be tapped on the network access, but the risk is comparable to other kind of data transmissions done via the telephone network.

3.2 Do-it-yourself Guide

A fully automated Help Desk, a 'Do-it-yourself Guide', has been developed for assisting the residential subscribers in the use of supplementary PSTN-services (Public Service Telephone Network). A problem in using supplementary services has been the user interface, where the customer controls the service by stimulus procedures. Instead the user is guided through a dialogue for setting up the services, eliminating the need for the user to remember service codes and formats for controlling the services. In addition, the help desk allows the customer to activate commands by speech. The system is connected to the O&M-systems of the network and is able to support customer control of services which are implemented on IN or in the local switches. So far, the only IN-service utilising the system is the remotely controlled call forwarding.

3.3 Virtual Private Network (VPN)

VPN is a typical IN-service targeted at big business customers. Ideally the customer, who has subscribed to a VPN by this service have to define the subscribers belonging to the network and the private numbering plan used with the network. Maintaining this service profile is beyond what is feasible by means of IVR. For the time being, the preferred solution is to receive data from the customer via a PC, and check the data before they are entered via the proprietary interface of the IN platform.

3.4 Televoting

Televoting is a service that makes it possible for e.g. broadcasting companies to initiate a vote when and where they please. The customer can define when the voting is to take place, and whether only selected users can participate (based on the participants phone number). It is also possible to put a selected call through to the studio. It is an IN-service whose customer control addresses business users. Customer data is at the moment received via IVR, but a later version with more features will use a WWW interface.

4 ISSUES IN CUSTOMER CONTROL

4.1 Access control

Access to customer control must be implemented in a way which ensures that the data belonging to one customer cannot be inspected or modified by another customer. Because the vendors' proprietary maintenance tool has been designed for operator use, it cannot be offered directly to the customers. In IVR-based customer control privacy can be achieved based on calling line identificaiton which is available throughout the Danish network. In cases where IVR is used from other telephones than the one of the customer, an identification procedure can be used. A central PIN server has been established in connection with our IN-platform.

4.2 Security

Customer control must be implemented in a way which secures the communication between the customer and the operator. Tapping of DTMF signalling is possible by intruding into the customer installation, but DTMF is usually not stored on non-secured machines outside the network operator premises. DTMF is sufficiently secure for customer control, as it is already assumed sufficiently secure for call-set-up. Internet solutions usually lack the desired security, but with software appearing for e.g. electronic banking in connection with certification centres, WWW interfaces can be built, which will be superior to DTMF in terms of security.

4.3 Validation of data

When data are no longer entered via the service operator staff there is obviously a big need for validation before the data are allowed into the IN-platform. The service operator will be held responsible if a customer manages to tamper with his service profiles by unintended customer control. Some work is therefore needed in order to perform validation of customer data, keep a log of subscriber commands and to maintain a help desk which - even pro-actively - can assist customers who experience problems with customer control.

5 FUTURE POSSIBILITIES

5.1 Direct Database Access

Eventually customer control must be seen as the customers ability to access and update a private view of the IN-database associated with the customers services. Emerging technologies for open distributed databases will allow the customer to host and maintain the part of the IN-database associated with the customers services, in a safe way. Initiatives like ODP (Open Distributed Processing) and CORBA (Common Object Request Broker Architecture of the Obj. Mgt. Group consortium) are paving the way for this future.

5.2 Agent Based customer control

Agent technology is a broad term covering intelligent information retrieval and handling across a network. Agent technology could be important when designing more advanced control mechanisms for the customer. One could think of:

- conditional control: a certain parameter shall only be set, if another one has been defined or set to a certain value
- loops: certain parameters should be set for a number of parameters
- transforming high level goals into series of how and when. E.g. "One hour department meeting" into diversion of a number of telephones in one hour. .

Obviously there are a lot of possibilities in this technology and it may gradually lead us in the direction of customer design.

5.3 Towards customer design

The overall goal of a service operator is not to develop advanced services for the customers, but rather to offer an advanced service platform, which meets the customers needs for advanced services. Eventually technology in the shape of some safe, high-level service description language ("IN-Java") will allow for this. Services written in such a language could then be given a better performance by being ported to a more efficient traditional platform. A first step to this could be logic for combining service elements and their profiles (e.g. using agent technology).

There will still be a need for a service operator to develop more advanced services and service elements, but a number of services can be developed/composed by the customers themselves. Service operators may then be measured by the richness of their service element library and flexibility in service composition and customer control..

6 ACKNOWLEDGEMENTS

The authors acknowledge the valuable assistance from their colleagues Bent Banke, Finn Svejstrup, Henrik Thymann and Astrid Wilcken in finalising this paper.

7 REFERENCES

Ericsson (1996) TMOS User Guide, *Generic Service Adapter SCP/SDP*
Ericsson (1994) TMOS Operators Manual, *SMAS 2.1 User Manual*

7 BIOGRAPHY

Ove Færgemand graduated from the Technical University of Denmark 1975. Teaching at the University until 1983. 1983-92 head of group on "Software Techniques" at the Danish Telecom. Research Laboratory. 1992-95, project supervisor at the European Telecom Research Institute (EURESCOM) in Heidelberg. 1988-92 rapporteur in ITU-T SG 10, 1992-96 chairman of the SG. Currently head of the section Telephony Services at Tele Danmark R&D. The work of section includes development of IN-services and speech technology. Publications include papers and books about SDL (ITU-T Specification and Description Language).

Allan Jensen, graduated from the Technical University of Denmark 1985. 1985-95 at the Danish Telecom. Research Laboratory managing the participation of the lab to a number of EU and EURESCOM projects related to Openness and Object-orientation in Telecommunications Systems architechtures. Currently developing IN-services in Tele Danmark R&D Telephony Services.

PART THREE

Services

6

Calypso Service Architecture for Broadband Networks

Petteri Koponen, Juhana Räsänen and Olli Martikainen
Helsinki University of Technology
Laboratory of Telecommunications Software and Multimedia
Otakaari 1, 02150 Espoo, Finland
Telephone: 358 9 4514739, Fax: 358 9 4513293
{Petteri.Koponen,Juhana.Rasanen,Olli.Martikainen}@hut.fi

Abstract

The Calypso project aims at developing an extremely flexible control and service architecture for ATM-based broadband networks. This architecture provides various alternatives to distribute the network and service control functions among clients, servers and different network nodes. This means that a control or service function can reside not only in a network node, but in the customer's workstation or in the service provider's dedicated server. Instead of the traditional ATM or IN signalling, the Calypso architecture uses the TCP/IP protocol suite for the management and control of the network and services. The management, control and user data is transferred by means of IP switching. In addition to IP switching, the architecture will support end-to-end native ATM streams with guaranteed Quality of Service. In this paper we compare the Calypso architecture with the traditional B-ISDN and IN architectures. We focus on describing the Java-based Service Execution Environment that provides a flexible platform for the management and execution of both services and control functions.

Keywords

Intelligent Networks, ATM, Access Networks, Broadband Services, Multimedia Streams, Open Signalling

1 INTRODUCTION

It is expected that broadband media streams will be distributed over fixed and wireless networks to consumer segments within 5–10 years. The consumer media distribution has been delayed mainly due to the cost of transmission capacity. This cost is assumed to come down because of both the creation of the open, ATM (Asynchronous Transfer Mode) -based telecommunications infrastructure and the growing role of service and content providers.

New telecommunications technologies such as IP (Internet Protocol) switch-

Intelligent Networks and Intelligence in Networks D. Gaiti (Ed.)
Published by Chapman & Hall

ing, wireless access techniques and Digital Subscriber Line (xDSL) -based access technologies will accelerate the creation of a cost-efficient and flexible telecommunications infrastructure. IP switching increases the performance of IP-based networks, e.g. intranets and the Internet, by combining the traditional IP routing with ATM switching, while wireless and xDSL technologies, especially Asymmetric Digital Subscriber Line (ADSL), will provide affordable broadband access for consumers.

The Internet and the liberalization of the telecommunications market in Europe in 1998 are the major reasons for the growing role of service and content providers. The question of how to build services that utilize distributed data and applications belonging to other service and content providers leads to further questions: how to manage the interaction between the services; how to build service creation, management and accounting subsystems; and how to introduce security and payment methods in the subsystems. To achieve this, the service functions have to be separated from the network control functions. Also, the service and network architectures have to become considerably simpler and more cost-effective.

In this paper we present the *Calypso* architecture as a cost-effective and flexible alternative for distributing broadband services. The Calypso architecture provides various alternatives to divide the network and service control functions among clients, servers and network nodes. This means that a control or service function can reside not only in a network node, but in the customer's workstation or in the service provider's dedicated server. Instead of the traditional ATM or Intelligent Network (IN) signalling, the Calypso architecture uses the TCP/IP (Transport Control Protocol / Internet Protocol) protocol suite for the management and control of the network and services. The management, control and user data is transferred by means of IP switching. In addition to IP switching, the architecture will provide end-to-end native ATM streams with guaranteed Quality of Service (QoS).

2 MOTIVATION

We believe that the current ATM and IN standards do not meet all the heterogeneous networking requirements of the future. This opinion is not unique – we share it with several academic and non-academic research groups (Lazar, Lim and Marconcini 1996, Leslie, Crosby and Rooney n.d., Newman, Minshall, Lyon and Huston 1997). Below we have listed what we believe are the most vital issues for future broadband networking architecture and some of the problems that ATM faces when addressing these issues.

- The networking requirements will remain *heterogeneous*, i.e. networks of different types will provide different services and the services will require different control functions from the underlying network. This implies that the broadband networks should support a wide – possibly configurable –

variety of control functions for different needs, and that services that use these control functions should be easy to implement, deploy and manage. At present, ATM's control functions, e.g. signalling, are relatively fixed, and the services, e.g. IN service, are assumed to support different networking requirements. For example, support for mobility could be added to ATM networks by implementing the mobile specific features as IN services. However, it has proved to be very difficult to add efficient support for e.g. mobility (Mitts 1996) to ATM networks. This is mainly due to the somewhat heavyweight and rigid UNI/NNI and IN signalling standards.

- The success of the World Wide Web (WWW) and the Internet has made the TCP/IP protocol suite dominant, which implies that also the ATM networks should support the TCP/IP protocols. Doing this in a practical way has proved to be very hard. This is mainly due to some fundamental differences between the ATM and IP protocols; for example, ATM is connection oriented while IP is connectionless (Comer 1995, Cole, Shur and Villamizar 1996).
- It is expected that the distribution of both broadband and narrowband media streams such as TV and radio broadcasts, Video on Demand (VoD), video conferencing and telephony, is becoming an increasingly important service. Because of ATM's short, fixed-length cells and light-weight flow control and error handling functionality, it is possible to transfer streams of all these types over a single ATM link and to benefit from statistical multiplexing. ATM networks are also expected to guarantee streams end-to-end *Quality of Service* (QoS). However, interoperability problems between switches of different vendors have reduced the benefits gained from the ATM technology. The problems are usually related to the complexity of the standardized QoS mechanisms and the corresponding control functions.

To summarize, the broadband network architecture should support heterogeneous networking requirements; provide an efficient implementation of IP transmission; and implement end-to-end point-to-point and point-to-multipoint (and broadcast) streams with QoS guarantees. We – and e.g. (Newman et al. 1997) – believe that the ATM hardware is flexible and cost-efficient enough to be used to implement these features. However, the ATM control functions and the IN service model make this very hard and cause most of the problems in the current ATM networks. This suggests that a more flexible alternative should be studied, which is the aim of the Calypso project.

3 RELATED WORK

The Internet Engineering Task Force's (IETF's) IP over ATM working group discusses several proposals for routing and forwarding IP packets over ATM subnetworks in (Cole et al. 1996). The proposals require two logically separate networks – the IP and the ATM network. For example, all the proposals, excluding the Integrated Models that are planned to use extended Private Network-Network Interface (PNNI) (ATM Forum 1996) routing, implement both IP and ATM routing protocols. In addition, each proposal uses both IP and ATM addresses. We believe that all the architectures discussed in (Cole et al. 1996) are very hard to manage in practise due to their complexity. Also, the proposals are relatively hard to implement because they include several complex protocols. This may cause further interoperability problems.

There are a number of proprietary solutions that use ATM as a backplane- or bus-replacement within a router itself. These include e.g. Ipsilon Networks' *IP switching* (Newman et al. 1997) and Cisco Systems' Tag Switching (Rekhter, Davie, Katz, Rosen and Swallow 1997). Of these, we find IP switching a very innovative and practical solution for running IP over ATM (or, according to Ipsilon Networks, "ATM under IP").

An IP switch consists of an efficient workstation and a simple ATM switch. The workstation – also called the *switch controller* – is connected to the switch via an ATM link, and it manages the switch with *General Switch Management Protocol* (GSMP) (Newman, Edwards, Hinden, Hoffman, Liaw, Lyon and Minshall 1996). GSMP enables the external switch controller to e.g. establish and release ATM Virtual Channels (VCs), query status information and receive asynchronous notifications from the switch. GSMP is not specific to IP switching but it can be used also with other techniques such as the traditional ATM signalling. GSMP is an interesting concept as such, and we have experimented with it in the TOVE project (Puro, Koponen, Räsänen, Nummisalo and Martikainen 1996).

IP switching integrates ATM hardware directly with IP, not requiring logically separate ATM and IP networks. Instead, the switch controller acts as a normal IP router with one exception: in addition to GSMP, it implements a few relatively simple IP switching specific functions that enable it to switch IP packets belonging to long-lasting flows instead of routing them. Ipsilon estimates that this increases the routing performance about 4.5 times (Newman et al. 1997). Although IP switching can provide IP-based media streams with QoS guarantees (this requires careful configuration of the IP switched subnetwork, so that all the IP switches decide to switch the streams instead of routing them and that they establish VCs with the same QoS parameters) and it does not require ATM signalling or routing protocols, we find it too focused on IP as such. For example, connecting an IP switched network to a traditional ATM network requires complex gateway arrangements. Furthermore, IP switching does not guarantee end-to-end QoS for media streams because the decisions that IP switches make are *local in scope*.

The OPENSIG (OPEN SIGnalling) working group is an interesting opening towards open and programmable network architectures. The working group aims to "do research towards understanding open network control issues as they arise in signalling, middleware and service creation on ATM-, Internet- and Mobile-multimedia networking platforms." The Calypso architecture has

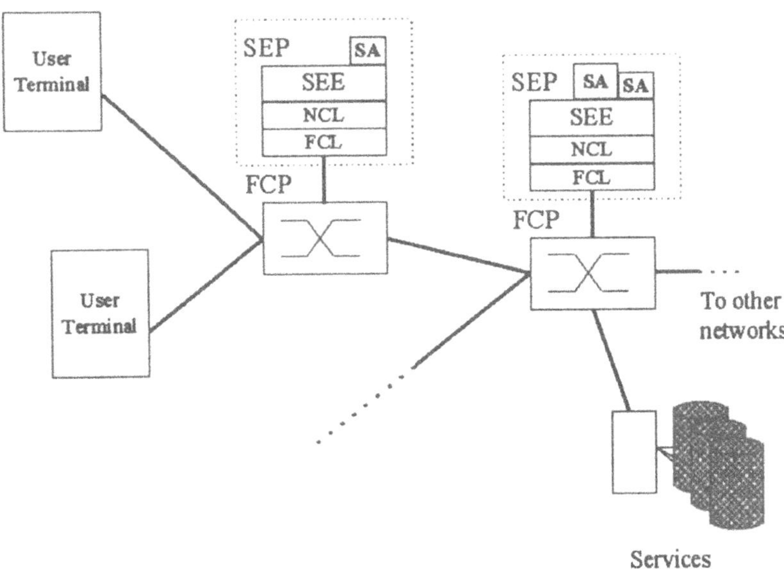

Figure 1 Calypso architecture.

somewhat similar objectives as the two OPENSIG projects: xbind (Lazar et al. 1996) at Columbia University and the Distributed Control of ATM Networks (DCAN) project at University of Cambridge (Leslie et al. n.d.). Both projects propose an open architecture where the control and management functions can reside on external workstations. The xbind project is focused on representing resources such as switches and multimedia devices as Common Object Request Broker Architecture (OMG 1995) (CORBA) objects that are manipulated in order to generate network services. In the DCAN project, the control and management functions are extracted from the network nodes (and end systems) to an external distributed processing platform.

4 CALYPSO ARCHITECTURE

One of the main principles in the Calypso architecture is the separation of the service functions, including the traditional control functions such as signalling, and the switching functions. Figure 1 illustrates this situation; the *Service Execution Point* (SEP) is both logically and physically separated from the *Fabric Control Point* (FCP). In Ipsilon Network's IP switching system and in the TOVE project (Puro et al. 1996) at Helsinki University of Technology, the *switch controller* is a close equivalent to the SEP.

Amongst other areas, the TOVE project has studied the benefits of separating the switch controller (SEP) from the switching fabric (FCP). In addition to the increased flexibility in updating the software and the hardware of the SEP, the approach enables a single SEP to manage a number of FCPs. This is a cost-efficient and practical solution in case the signalling load is relatively small compared to the amount of the data transmitted. A situation like this could occur in broadband access networks where a large portion of data consists of long-lasting audio and video streams. Also, if the SEP cannot handle the current signalling load, a new SEP can easily be introduced and the FCPs can be split into two groups.

The SEP contains the *Service Execution Environment* (SEE) and two layers: the *Fabric Control Layer* (FCL) and the *Network Control Layer* (NCL). The FCL provides means to manage the FCP. It can implement e.g. GSMP or some proprietary switch management protocol as long as it supports the basic functionality of an ATM switch. The NCL implements the TCP/IP protocols needed, including IP routing (or in this case, IP switching), and the basic connection mechanisms of the Calypso architecture. The SEE wraps these layers inside Java objects with well-defined interfaces. Both the SEE and the SAs use these interfaces.

4.1 Service Execution Environment

The SEE is a platform for the management and execution of *Service Agents* (SAs).

We adopt here the broad definition of a service by Magedanz and Popescu-Zeletin (Magedanz and Popescu-Zeletin 1996). They identify in the IN architecture services offered by the underlying network platform (i.e. *bearer services* such as audio, video, or data transmission and signalling services) and services offered by the IN platform to the end users (i.e. *supplementary services* or value-added services). Compared to the IN Service Control Function (SCF) (ITU-T 1995), the SEE contains more functionality because it supports not only the traditional service applications, but also control applications such as signalling. Hence, the above definition of a service is proper for the SEE.

SAs are *Java* programs that the SEE both manages and executes. The management includes e.g. providing means to safely distribute the SAs over the network, and allowing SAs access some of the resources the SEE manages. Also, the SEE executes the SAs and monitors their execution. The management and execution functions are strongly interconnected; for example, the SEE checks at run-time whether an SA is allowed to access a resource depending on the security level the management functions have given to the SA.

According to our definition of services, almost all the SEP's functionality is implemented by SAs that are either *fixed* or *mobile*. The fixed SAs cannot be transferred over the network and they can include native, i.e. non-Java, code because of e.g. efficiency reasons or existing implementations that are to be reused. However, the fixed SAs have to implement the necessary interfaces for management and monitoring purproses, i.e the native code must be wrapped in the corresponding Java classes. The mobile SAs are more flexible in the sense that they can be dynamically injected into an SEE , although this requires quite advanced security mechanisms. How these mechanisms will be implemented is still open.

4.2 Relation to IN and ATM Architectures

Implementing services as SAs and separating the SEP from FCP enables the use of the same hardware and SEE in a very wide range of networking domains. We believe that the most important differences between the Calypso architecture and traditional IN and ATM architectures are due to the additional flexibility that this approach introduces. Among the differences are the following:

- Both services and control functions are implemented as SAs. This differs fundamentally from the IN and ATM architecture where control functions, i.e. signalling, are more or less fixed and services communicate with these by sending IN Application Part (INAP) messages. INAP is not needed in the Calypso architecture because the SAs can communicate with each other using domain or service specific means, e.g. Java Remote Method Invocation (RMI), CORBA or some customized ATM- or IP-based protocol. In the Calypso architecture, thus, fixed INAP messages are replaced with service-specific messages or e.g. RMI or CORBA method calls. Of course, an INAP agent can be implemented as a gateway to IN services if necessary.
- In Calypso architecture, the authorized services can directly control the network by ordering the FCL and NCL to establish end-to-end or local ATM streams. This means that there is no clear separation between services and control functions. Also, the management functions can be implemented as SAs, which opens interesting opportunities to experiment with different management architectures.

We believe that the Calypso architecture is more programmable than the traditional IN and ATM architectures, which reduces the time to create the services and also allows more advanced services to be implemented. However, we must emphasize that we have not planned the Calypso architecture to be a global replacement for the IN and ATM architectures. Instead, it is a cost-effective and flexible alternative to implement subnetworks providing innovative IP and ATM stream-based services.

4.3 Implementation Issues

The implementation of the prototype Calypso SEP platform is based on the results of the TOVE project. The TOVE platform is a standard ATM switch controller which is connected to switching fabric via a 155-Mbps ATM link and is able to control the fabric with GSMP or similar protocol. The operating system used is Linux with ATM extensions and the hardware is common PC/Intel technology. The platform and signalling protocols developed have been tested with the Frame Synchronized Ring (FSR) switch (Raatikainen 1996) developed by the Technical Research Centre of Finland (VTT). The TOVE platform readily implements the FCL functionality of the Calypso SEP, on top of which the NCL and SEE can be implemented.

The NCL will use the TCP/IP stack and ATM extensions of it (such as Classical IP over ATM) for transporting control data between network nodes. The NCL also contains an interface to open end-to-end ATM streams and management of the connections.

The SEE will be implemented as a Java environment that provides a class framework, object repository, authentication and security functions etc. for the Service Agents to use. Java has been selected because it provides a wide selection of tools, TCP/IP support and easy code mobility accross network.

5 FUTURE WORK

The Calypso platform will be applied in the service development in the MediaPoli environment. The MediaPoli consists of a broadband access network in Otaniemi (Helsinki University of Technology) campus area with 1000–3000 customers and digital multimedia services on top of the network. Typical services include ATM telephony, electronic commerce in the WWW and digital media stream distribution. Some service scenarios are given below. The services are developed in research projects and also commercial pilots are allowed. The MediaPoli environment will be open for both domestic and foreign partners.

A scenario of a basic stream service (e.g. a TV channel broadcast) is presented in Figure 2. A TV channel is broadcasted from the server as an ATM point-to-multipoint stream. When User 1 wants to watch the channel, she clicks a Service Icon (SI) (e.g. a Java applet) that represents the service in her browser. The icon connects (1) to the corresponding SA in the SEE that controls this particular service. The icon and agent exchange authentication data and verify that the user has access to the service, e.g. that she has purchased subscription to the channel. In the next phase the SEE uses NCL (2) to establish a new branch (4) to the existing multipoint stream (3), and when the user is informed of the established stream, the icon can launch a viewer application in the user's workstation.

We would like to emphasize that in this architecture the multimedia stream

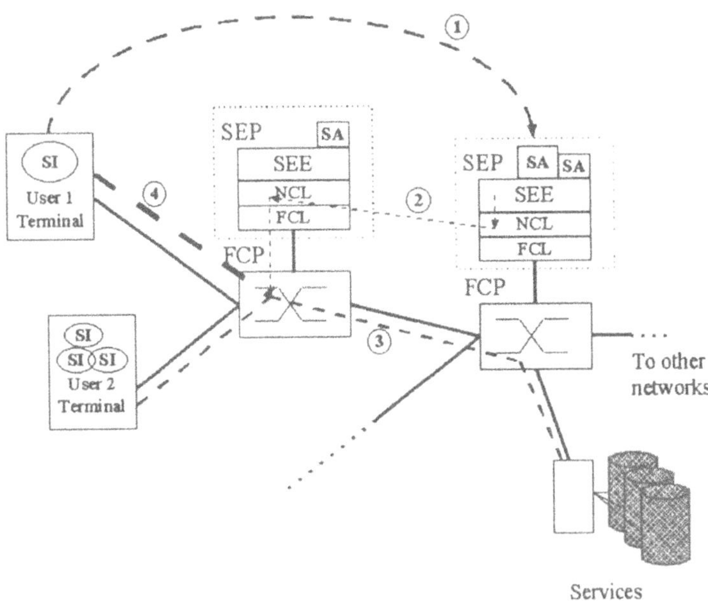

Figure 2 Service scenario.

distribution service can be much richer than the current broadcast TV. It is easy to incorporate auxiliary data into the broadcast, including Universal Resource Locators (URLs), transcript for people with impaired hearing or multilingual translations as subtitles etc. This would make a TV program a true multimedia application.

The ability to move service agents from a network node to another opens interesting possibilities to implement mobile network functions, e.g. location updates. A location update is implemented in the current GSM network as a MAP (Mobile Application Part) protocol dialogue that performs necessary database updates in Home and Visitor Location Registers. The Calypso architecture enables the Mobile Terminal (MT) to inject an agent into the network, and the agent would be responsible for updating the location of the MT.

REFERENCES

ATM Forum (1996). *Private Network-Network Interface Specification Version 1.0.*

Cole, R., Shur, D. and Villamizar, C. (1996). IP over ATM: A Framework Document, IETF RFC 1932.

Comer, D. E. (1995). *Internetworking with TCP/IP - Volume 1*, 3. edn, Prentige-Hall.

ITU-T (1995). *ITU Draft Recommendation Q.1224: Distributed functional plane for intelligent network CS-2*, Berlin.

Lazar, A. A., Lim, K.-S. and Marconcini, F. (1996). Realizing a Foundation for Programmability of ATM Networks with the Binding Architecture, *IEEE Journal of Selected Areas in Communications* **14**(7): 1214–1277.

Leslie, I., Crosby, S. and Rooney, S. (n.d.). The Distributed Control of ATM Network Project, `http://www.cl.cam.ac.uk/Research/SRG/dcan/`.

Magedanz, T. and Popescu-Zeletin, R. (1996). *Intelligent Networks – Basic Technology, Standards and Evolution*, International Thomson Publishing.

Mitts, H. (1996). *Architecture for wireless ATM*, Licentiate's thesis, Helsinki University of Technology.

Newman, P., Edwards, W., Hinden, R., Hoffman, E., Liaw, F. C., Lyon, T. and Minshall, G. (1996). Ipsilon's General Switch Management Protocol – Version 1.1, IETF RFC 1987.

Newman, P., Minshall, G., Lyon, T. and Huston, L. (1997). IP Switching and Gigabit Routers, *IEEE Communications Magazine* **35**(1): 64–69.

OMG (1995). *The Common Object Request Broker: Architecture and Specification Revision 2.0.*

Puro, V.-M., Koponen, P., Räsänen, J., Nummisalo, P. and Martikainen, O. (1996). TOVE in Universal Mobile Telecommunications System, *Proceedings of the 2nd Workshop on Personal Wireless Communications*, Frankfurt.

Raatikainen, P. (1996). *Analysis and Implementation of a High-Speed Packet Switching Architecture – the Frame Synchronized Ring*, PhD thesis, Helsinki University of technology, Espoo.

Rekhter, Y., Davie, B., Katz, D., Rosen, E. and Swallow, G. (1997). Cisco System's Tag Switching Architecture Overview, IETF RFC 2105.

7

Engineering of a broadband connectivity service: the TINA approach

N. Charton, Y. Hervé, N. Mercouroff
Alcatel Telecom Research Division
Route de Nozay
F-91460 Marcoussis, France
Tel: +33 (0)1 69 63 12 70
Fax: +33 (0)1 69 63 17 89
mercouroff@aar.alcatel-alsthom.fr

Abstract

The Telecommunications Information Networking Architecture Consortium, TINA-C, has defined a business model identifying domains for the future telecom industry. One of these domains is the connectivity provider domain, in which stakeholders will support the connectivity requirements of the services within the retailer domain.

The network provider offers the connectivity service to the retailer, that is, through the network to the service, via an interface. The interface supports the specifications of a reference point called the Connectivity Service Reference Point, ConS-RP. The ConS-RP allows for the request of connectivity in the form of a connection graph, independently of the implemented underlying infrastructure (ATM, PSTN, IP, etc.).

The ReTINA ACTS project aims at developing an industrial-quality distributed processing environment (DPE) for telecommunication applications. The ReTINA DPE thus offers a number of services targeted for this type of telecommunication application. Whereas some of these services offer extensions to traditional CORBA services, such as trading and notification services, others support

Intelligent Networks and Intelligence in Networks D. Gaiti (Ed.)
Published by Chapman & Hall

specific requirements from TINA applications, connectivity requirements in particular.

In 1996, a TINA connectivity service implementation was provided for the ReTINA DPE, based on connection management applied to ATM networks. The ReTINA activities include several trials (BVPN service, information service) experimenting the ReTINA DPE implementation, in particular its DPE connectivity service. Feedback from this experimentation allows preliminary observations to be drawn on the service requirements. In particular, it has been shown that performance is a key component for a usage not limited to the sole support of network planning and configuration.

Several solutions for exhibiting sufficient performance of the connectivity service are envisioned. Among these solutions, careful engineering of distributing the connectivity service over CORBA is a key issue. One of the engineering angles covers the definition of the API through which telecommunication services request connectivity. The API takes the form of IDL specifications, and needs to follow the TINA specifications for the ConS-RP. Building a connectivity graph potentially demands several interactions between telecommunication services and a connectivity service. To reduce the number of interactions, which may be related to operation invocations across international networks, it is proposed to factor repetitive invocations into a single, multi-parameter operation invocation.

Regarding the implementation of the connection management itself, it is proposed to tune its engineering to allow for parallelism and concurrency. With parallelism, simultaneous routing can be established in subnetworks belonging to a same network. Concurrency allows for the treatment of simultaneous requests to the connectivity service. While the former decreases the overall response time in connectivity establishment, the latter minimizes the blocking of requests to the connectivity service.

A final aspect of connection management engineering is related to the general deployment of the service over the network. Implementing connection management implies inherent distribution of intelligence. One part of this intelligence is dedicated to the support of connectivity provision to telecommunication services through the ConS-RP interface. Cautious engineering practices advise putting this intelligence as close as possible to the telecommunication service components requesting the connectivity. Other parts of this intelligence are dedicated to the control and management of resources belonging to the network, such as subnetworks and network elements. Once again, a good engineering practice entails locating these parts as close as possible to the resources of concern. This implies contradicting requirements on the implementation which should be handled with care.

The article concludes with the need to support the approaches presented by current trials to find an efficient balance between intelligence distribution over the network and overall performance.

Keywords
TINA, ATM, connectivity service, interfaces, engineering, performance, distribution, reference points

1 TINA CONNECTIVITY SERVICE

TINA provides a common telecommunication software architecture to be used in a multi-stakeholder, multi-domain environment. It provides TINA system implementors with a consistent specification of the prescriptive parts of the architecture that meet the conformance requirements of TINA. These specifications are defined in the form of a set of architectural principles, a business model, and specifications of Reference Points (RPs). A reference point comprises a set of interfaces describing the interactions that take place between the various TINA entities identified in the TINA business model, responsible for performing a given task.

1.1 TINA business model and reference points (RPs)

The TINA Business Model identifies the types of "businesses" in which TINA stakeholders are involved (TINA-C, 1996). It includes the definition of the consumer, the retailer, the broker, the third-party (3Pty) service provider, and the connectivity provider (see Figure 1). In particular, a stakeholder in the business of connectivity provider is the owner (manager) of a transport network (switches, cross-connects, bridges, routers, and trunks), controlled by the TINA connectivity service.

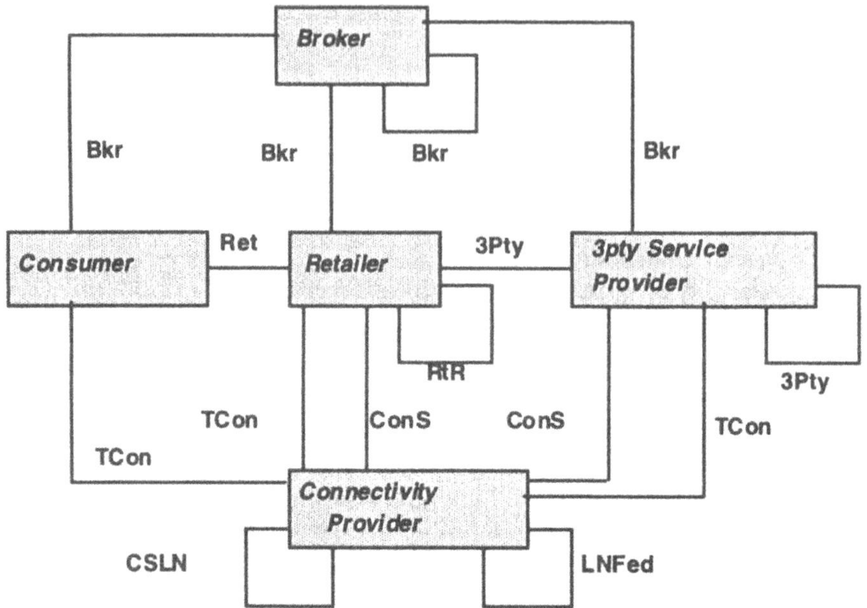

Figure 1 TINA business model and inter-domain RPs.

The *ConS Reference Point* specifies the relationship between those stakeholders providing TINA connectivity services and the stakeholders using those services on behalf of their customers. These specifications structure the usage-part interactions in terms of service sessions, called connectivity-service sessions, which allow for the setup, modification, and release of connectivity sessions and connection graphs. Operations are provided for creating a connection graph associated with the connectivity session, and for adding, removing, modifying, activating, and deactivating one or more branches (possibly all branches) of the connection graph.

1.2 TINA ConS reference point

The TINA Connectivity Service, as specified by the ConS-RP, supports two main services (TINA-C, 1997-b):

- A Connectivity Control Service (CCS): It allows the clients to set up, modify, and release connectivity sessions and the corresponding flow connections; it supports event reports on operational state changes of a flow connection and the management of these event reports.

- A Contract Profile Management (CPM) service: It retrieves and modifies the contract profile associated with each client.

TINA Network Resource Architecture (TINA-C, 1997-a) defines a session as the temporary relation among a group of resources that are assigned to collectively fulfill a task for a period of time. Thus, a connectivity session serves as an environment for establishing and managing network flow connections. TINA handles these connections through the concept of Physical Connection Graph, defined as a set of network flow connections transporting information across the network between flow endpoints.

A network flow connection is characterized by a number of parameters such as an identifier, its topology (either point-to-point bi-/uni-directional or point-to-multipoint uni-directional), the list of endpoints (source and leaves), the traffic type (Constant Bit Rate, Variable Bit Rate, ...), routing constraints, etc. The endpoints of a network flow connection can also be associated to characteristic information, such as the endpoint type (root or leaf), a name, the maximum or average transmission rates, and so on.

1.3 TINA connection management architecture

For implementing a connectivity service over an ATM network, TINA has developed specifications, derived from existing standards such as ITU-T Recommendation M.3100 (ITU-T, 1992-a) and G.803 (ITU-T, 1992-b), under the name of *TINA Connection Management Architecture* (CMA). From a computational viewpoint, CMA is defined by a set of operational interfaces, which specify the operations supported by the Connection Management (CM) objects deployed and interacting over the DPE. Operations are grouped in interfaces according to functional considerations, and independently of distribution aspects of the objects that will support the interfaces (TINA-C, 1995). Interfaces are supported by the following objects (see Figure 2):

- The Connection Coordinator (CC) which coordinates various networks. It offers its clients an interface in compliance with the ConS-RP for specifying end-to-end connectivity in the form of a connection graph.
- The Layer Network Coordinator (LNC) provides connectivity in a layer network by offering an interface to clients to create and manipulate trails.
- The Network Management Layer-Connection Performer (NML-CP) and Element Management Layer-Connection Performer (EML-CP) provide their clients (usually LNC objects or an NML-CP) with a usage interface for the control of Subnetwork Connections. The interfaces defined for the CP is expressed in terms of Subnetwork Connections.

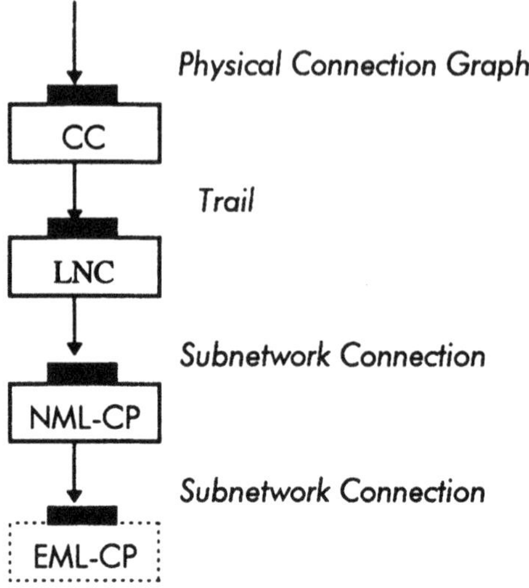

Figure 2 Global connection management architecture.

2 RETINA ACTS PROJECT

The success of the TINA approach to large-scale information networking is predicated, among other things, upon the availability of flexible and scalable DPE technology, and on its seamless deployment in different, heterogeneous network equipment. The ReTINA project is a three-year R&D project launched in September 1995 under the auspices of the European ACTS program. Its main goal is the development of DPE specifications and associated software technology that meet the above requirements. The project has three related objectives:

1. Develop an industrially sound, TINA-compliant Distributed Processing Environment, together with its specifications and an associated set of development tools.
2. Demonstrate and experiment with information network services implemented using the project's DPE.
3. Use the project's DPE specifications as a basis for information networking standards.

The ReTINA project implements:

- The ReTINA TORB (Telecom Object Request Broker) as a combination of software tools and libraries providing abstractions for the management and control of resources made available by the underlying operating systems.
- The ReTINA real-time profile, consisting of an implementation of the ReTINA TORB on a distributed real-time operating system microkernel (CHORUS) with full support for real-time programming, resource management, and temporal quality of service guarantees.
- The ReTINA general-purpose profile, consisting of an implementation of the ReTINA TORB on standard operating systems (UNIX).
- Generic computing and telecommunications services, including the implementation, based on the ReTINA TORB, of object-based data management services (with transactions, queries, and persistence) and generic connection-management services.
- A set of associated application development tools, targeted at the ReTINA TORB, and providing support for information and computational notations used within TINA.
- A set of service demonstrators, built on the ReTINA TORB, using the ReTINA profiles and generic services.

The partners in the project are Alcatel Telecom, Chorus Systems, Siemens, Hewlett-Packard, CSELT, France Telecom, British Telecom, Telenor, O2 Technology, Broadcom, and Lancaster University. In Figure 3 below, the overall workpackage structure, as well as a rough estimate of the distribution of effort among the partners is shown. In the figure, v0, v1, and v2 refer to the main iterations of the basic cycle (requirements - specifications - prototyping) which are planned for the workpackages.

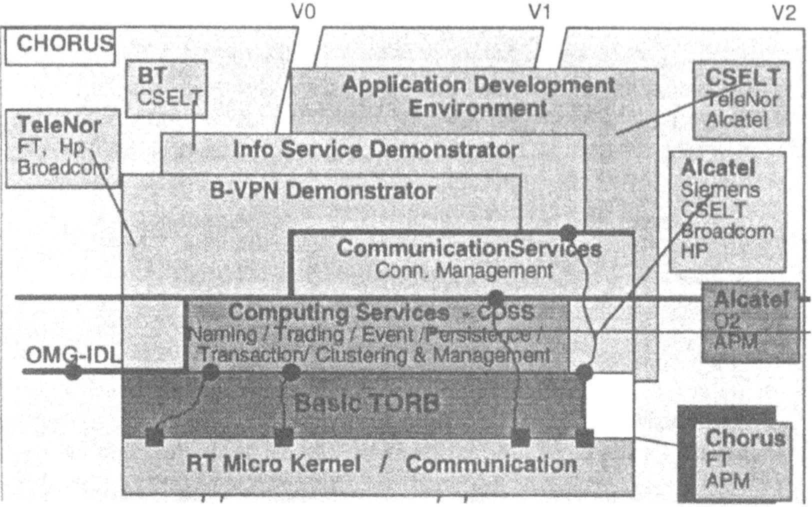

Figure 3 ReTINA DPE structure.

The focus here is on generic telecommunications services in the DPE. The telecommunications industry has expectations from ReTINA DPE to provide a solution to support large, distributed, interactive multimedia applications. Therefore, one of the activities of the project focuses on DPE telecommunications services with particular emphasis on TINA connectivity services (such as Connection Management functions necessary to set up, maintain, and release connections). The objective of this activity is to provide a **ReTINA Connectivity Service** implementation as a core component of the DPE.

An initial implementation of this DPE connectivity service, taking advantage of ongoing work and existing software packages from several partners and from TINA, has been developed with ReTINA. Some conclusions on its specifications can already be drawn.

3 LESSONS LEARNED FROM THE INITIAL IMPLEMENTATION

The prototype of the ReTINA Connectivity Service complies with the first release of TINA-C Connection Management Architecture (TINA-C, 1995), and hence follows the computational specifications described as interface IDL specifications. The prototype was implemented using a commercial Object

Request Broker (ORB) as DPE kernel. No specific effort was made to optimize performance and scalability.

An important issue at the design stage is the granularity of objects. CORBA Object model makes a clear distinction between:

- Objects which are only described by their interfaces and cannot be passed on the network as request parameters, and
- Data structure that flows over the network as request or reply parameters.

For these reasons people sometimes qualify CORBA as Object-Based instead of Object-Oriented.

Furthermore, to cope efficiently with marshalling problems, complex structures such as graphs cannot be directly and simply described as IDL structures (this problem is somewhat similar to the problem of representing complex data structure in relational databases).

Thus, although ORBs define interactions between distributed components in a language-neutral platform, independent of the transport layer, experiments have shown that interfaces must be written with great care: A "naive" design of IDL interfaces can lead to a functionally correct system yet with poor performance.

In the initial implementation of the ReTINA Connectivity Service prototype, clients interact with the connectivity service through the ConS-RP to define a connectivity graph representing the parties involved in point-to-point or point-to-multipoint connections. More precisely, a client requests some factory interface of the connectivity service to instantiate a connection graph. The reference of the graph object is returned to the client who then sends several requests to define the graph (see Figure 4). Several aspects have made this approach appealing:

- Only interactions with the graph objects are specified, which gives more flexibility for the implementation.
- The graph object itself never flows over the network. Instead, simple operations are invoked to define, modify, and control the graph. These operations have simple parameters (for example, adding a port).

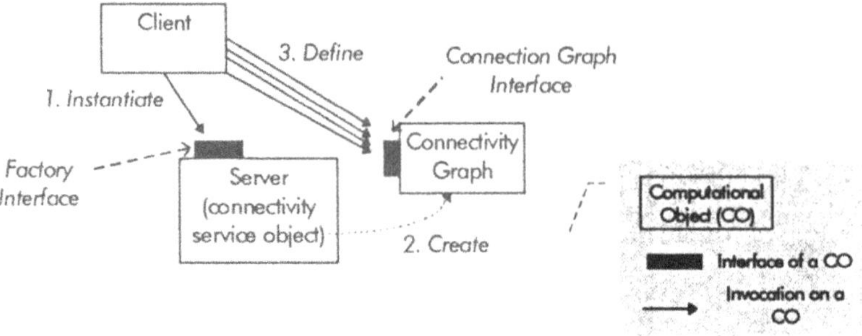

Figure 4 The ReTINA connectivity service (first release).

A solution of this type is suited and performs well when the client and the server are co-localized. Unfortunately, in the general case (distributed remote objects), the solution has turned out to be inefficient.

Indeed in the ReTINA first release, nine remote operation invocations are required between the client and server objects to establish one end-to-end connection. Note that other interactions are required between objects (client and server) within the connectivity service itself. Experimental measures showed that each remote invocation was consuming an "incompressible" amount of time, and that several small requests between remote objects were more costly than a single complex request between them.

Note that better performance would be achieved if the client could instantiate and construct the graph object locally and eventually move it to the connectivity service. Two services are defined in CORBA specifications for this purpose: Externalization and Object LifeCycle. Externalization service enables objects to export their state on a stream, thus giving the opportunity to rebuild the object somewhere else. LifeCycle service permits objects to be migrated across the network. However, neither of these services is currently on the market.

In addition to the design of object interfaces, other implementation issues limit the efficiency of the ReTINA Connectivity Service. In particular, requests are processed sequentially which prevents the current release from being scalable. The main consequence is that the duration of a connection establishment increases with the number of involved network elements.

Finally, experimental results showed that two factors were limiting performance. The first factor deals with the design of computational object interfaces, while the second is related to implementation issues.

4 SPECIFICATIONS OF TINA CONNECTIVITY SERVICE INTERFACES

One of the solutions for exhibiting sufficient performance of the connectivity service is the re-design of object interfaces. The main idea is to reduce the number of required invocations between remote objects. Indeed, as described in the previous section, a CORBA application spends an incompressible part of its processing time on the kernel transport network (DPE network), transporting messages between remote objects. Therefore, interfaces of remote objects should be designed to allow minimal interactions while providing the required service.

It is proposed to replace sequential and repetitive, simple-operation invocations (those with one parameter) by a single, multi-parameter operation invocation.

Telecommunication applications (or Retailers) request the establishment of a connection graph, that is, they use the connectivity service, interacting with a Connectivity Provider. From the computational viewpoint, such interactions correspond to operation invocations from a client object (in the Retailer domain) on server objects (in the Connectivity Provider domain), through interfaces. TINA proposes that the clients interact with the CC (Connection Coordinator) computational object through its Conn_Session_Control interface.

Although building a connection graph might potentially demand several interactions between clients and the connectivity service, TINA proposes a single, rather complex operation, namely the Setup_Flow_Connections operation. This operation is used by the clients to establish a connection graph (one or more flow connections) passing the required information attached to each flow connection as input parameters of the operation. Then the reference of the graph object is returned to the client who may access it to modify or control it (see Figure 5).

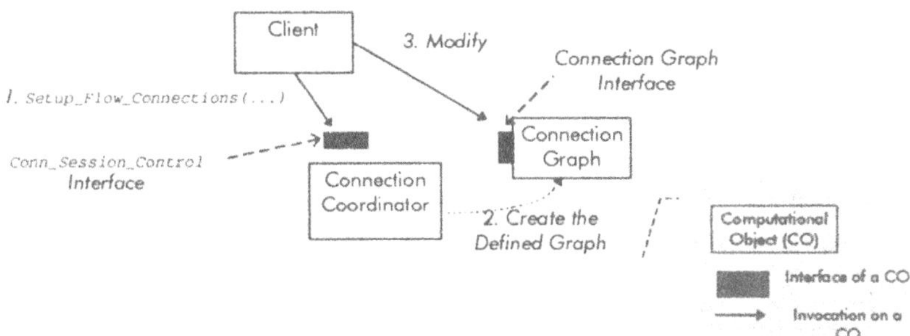

Figure 5 The connectivity service as defined by ConS-RP.

The graph is built by the client object and is described using data structures that flatten the graph. This solution may seem less elegant than the one applied in the first release of ReTINA Connectivity Service. However, it is more pragmatic since a connection graph can be built with a single invocation (instead of nine) between the client and the connectivity service. This approach should eventually improve the connectivity service performance.

5 PARALLELISM AND CONCURRENCY OF TINA CONNECTIVITY SERVICE

The choices of the first prototype were to keep non-functional features as simple as possible. However, several aspects related to performance could be improved at the expense of a more complex implementation. More precisely, performance could be improved by:

- processing multiple requests concurrently;
- processing the establishment of subconnection in parallel.

The first aspect is expected to increase the throughput of the whole connectivity service, while the second would both decrease the perceived latency of each individual client and increase the scalability of the service. Indeed when subconnections are processed in parallel, the expected time needed to set up the whole connection is about equal to the time needed to set up the slowest subconnection, instead of being equal to the sum of the subconnection times (as in the current implementation).

The next paragraph briefly presents the connection establishment algorithm. Then technical issues and possible trade-offs to implement concurrency and parallelism inside a CORBA architecture are discussed.

Figure 6 illustrates the connection establishment algorithm. A connection is basically created in three steps:

- Step 1 consists of a routing algorithm (a variant of Djikstra) that finds a route for the connection. Routing decisions are made according to resource status (for example, available bandwidth) locally cached for efficiency. Consistency of cached information is ensured by the hierarchical nature of the architecture. During this step no I/O operations are performed and only shared resources status can be read.
- Step 2 consists of actual reservation of the resources. Write locks must be acquired for all resources along the route and a local copy of resources be updated.

Note that separating route computation (Step 1) from resource reservation (Step 2) may simplify the backtrack of the routing algorithm, since only resources are read during the first step.

- Step 3 consists of sending CORBA requests over the network to the inferior connectivity layer. This scheme is recursive until single network elements are reached. The thread processing the current request is blocked until every subconnection is established.

On reception of a "create connection" request:

1. Find an admissible route based on available resources.
2. Reserve necessary resources for the establishment of this route.
3. Ask each subnetwork chosen by the routing algorithm to create its own subconnection.

Figure 6 Connection establishment algorithm.

Concurrency

Processing several requests simultaneously requires a multi-threaded Object Request Broker (ORB). This feature is not prescribed by CORBA specifications, but several ORB providers do offer this functionality. Some systems even offer the choice between different threading models (thread per object, thread per request, pool of threads) allowing fine tuning according to the application's needs. Note that the threading model considered here is preemptive.

Locking issues

Locking is not only fundamental for correctness of the program but also for achieving acceptable performance. A misconception of locks can even result in a degradation of performance compared to the same single-threaded application. Basically there is a subtle trade-off between the overhead imposed by fine-grain locks and expected benefit from concurrency.

Several approaches are proposed to control the access to shared resources (for example, endpoints with a given amount of available bandwidth) in the connectivity service. Among them are the transaction-like two-phase locking and the optimistic locking approaches.

∇ *Transaction-like two-phase locking*

A solution is to enclose Step 1 and Step 2 (see Figure 6) into a single subtransaction. Subtransaction here means that the Atomicity, Consistency and Isolation properties—from the usual ACID properties—are respected (Gray, 1993) whatever the actual implementation. Read locks are acquired during Step 1 and Write locks during Step 2. All locks are released after Step 2 has been completed. Granularity of the locks can differ, as follows:

- Coarse grain. All resources are protected by a single lock. This approach is expected to perform well in a single-processor host, because there is at most one thread (for the purposes of this article, called *T*) at a time executing the code of Step 1 and Step 2. The other clients are blocked until the subtransaction has completed for *T*. Doing this limits the number of unnecessary thread-context swappings. Only threads in Step 3 that have received all their replies can preempt *T* to terminate their job.
- Fine grain. Single resources have their own locks. Doing this increases concurrency and allows several processors to calculate routes simultaneously. This solution has the drawback of potentially giving rise to deadlock situations.

∇ *Optimistic locking*

Traditional locking policies are sometimes called pessimistic. This means that the application carefully acquires locks before manipulating shared resources. Optimistic locking makes the assumption that conflicts are rare, and that it is more efficient to execute the operations without acquiring locks and verifying at commit-time that no conflict has occurred. In case of conflict, the transaction must be undone and can be restarted.

The same kind of reasoning can be applied for the connectivity service: No locks are acquired in Step 1, and the resource status is potentially stale. For instance, an endpoint may have less bandwidth left than indicated by its status. When a route has been determined, the thread enters Step 2 and acquires exclusive Write lock, checks that the up-to-date amount of resources is sufficient for establishing the route, and reserves the resources. If the actual capacity of the resources is not sufficient, the thread would have to execute Step 1 once again to find a new admissible route.

6 TINA CONNECTIVITY SERVICE DEPLOYMENT OVER THE NETWORK

A final aspect of the connectivity service engineering is related to the deployment of the service over the network. Indeed the connectivity service controls (with respect to the setup, modification, and release of connections) the whole network, with its set of subnetworks and network elements (for example, ATM switches). Therefore it is by essence a distributed application.

Telecommunication applications uses the connectivity service through the ConS Reference Point, interacting with connectivity service objects. Therefore cautious engineering practices advise putting these objects (namely the CC object) as close as possible to their client.

Simultaneously, other connectivity service objects (namely the EML-CP objects) directly control network elements. The interactions between the EML-CP object and the controlled switch usually requests adaptation functions (since switches do not provide IDL interfaces) and specific communication technology (such as the SNMP protocol). Again, good engineering practice entails locating these objects as close as possible to the resources of concern.

Then engineering decisions should consider the above contradicting requirements: the need to co-localize client and server objects for better performance; the need to localize some connectivity service objects near the applications and other objects near the switches. Other elements may also be considered, such as the characteristics and capacity of the available physical equipment (such as the CPU, microprocessor type of computers and switches). Note that if a switch features an efficient control station, it would be interesting to implement the EML-CP object on it. Furthermore, different administrative domains may co-exist implying a given distribution of objects according to their controlling authority. Finally, engineering decisions should also follow the global objective of the designers who may choose to focus on performance aspects or on other aspects such as security. Thus implementing a connectivity service implies inherent distribution of intelligence. However, to handle this distribution and engineer the connectivity service, there is no strict rule, only a set of requirements, constraints, and objectives.

7 CONCLUSION

After one year of development and trials within ReTINA, it is already possible to gain some experience on TINA connectivity service implementation, and through it, on CORBA application design. Indeed, as an application requiring distribution of intelligence over the network, the TINA Connectivity Service proves to be a good case study for requirements over CORBA-based DPEs. Potential pitfalls, needs for careful design, and possible approaches have been highlighted, which could be applied to many CORBA applications. Such experience is currently under analysis within ReTINA for improving DPE kernel, services, and support tools to telecommunication services.

Similarly, the development of design practices for tuning the computational and the engineering specifications of a key TINA component, the connectivity service, has been initiated. In the domain of computational models, results have already been fed back to TINA-C, and improvement of some of its specifications have already been taken into account (TINA-C, 1997-b). The on-going experimentation within ReTINA now focuses on developing and implementing solutions to tackle the challenge of finding the right balance between intelligence distribution over the network, and application performance and scalability.

8 REFERENCES

Gray, Jim and Reuter, Andreas (1993) Transaction Processing: Concepts and Techniques. Morgan Kaufmann Publishers.

ITU-T (1992-a) Generic Network Information Model. ITU-T Recommendation M.3100.

ITU-T (1992-b) Architectures of Transport Networks Based on the Synchronous Digital Hierarchy (SDH). ITU-T Recommendation G.803.

TINA-C (1995) Connection Management Architecture. TN_JJB.005_1.0_94.

TINA-C (1996) TINA Business Model and Reference Points. EN_RCJ.030_3.1_96.

TINA-C (1997-a) Network Resource Architecture v3.0. NRA_v3.0_97_02_10.

TINA-C (1997-b) The ConS Reference Point v1.0. Draft document.

9 ABBREVIATIONS USED IN THIS ARTICLE

ACID	Atomicity, Consistency, Isolation, Durability
API	Application Programmer Interface
ATM	Asynchronous Transfer Mode
BVPN	Broadband Virtual Private Network
CC	Connection Coordinator
CCS	Connectivity Control Service
CM	Connection Management
CMA	Connection Management Architecture
CO	Computational Object
ConS-RP	Connectivity Service Reference Point
CORBA	Common Object Request Broker Architecture
CP	Connection Performer
CPM	Contract Profile Management
CPU	Central Processing Unit
DPE	Distributed Processing Environment
EML	Element Management Layer
IDL	Interface Definition Language
IP	Internet Protocol
LNC	Layer Network Coordinator
NML	Network Management Layer
NRA	Network Resource Architecture
ORB	Object Request Broker
RP	Reference Point
SNMP	Simple Network Management Protocol
PSTN	Public Switched Telephone Network
TINA	Telecommunications Information Networking Architecture
TINA-C	Telecommunications Information Networking Architecture Consortium
TORB	Telecom Object Request Broker

10 BIOGRAPHIES

N. Charton

Nathalie Charton is a 1992 graduate of the Ecole Nationale Supérieure des Télécommunications (ENST), Paris, France. From 1992 to 1995, she worked as a researcher in the ENST networks department; in 1995, she completed her PhD entitled "Definition of manageable components of services".

In 1996, she joined Alcatel Telecom Research Division in France. She is currently working on the definition and assessment of architectures for future advanced networks, in particular for TINA-based networks. She is also active in the European ACTS project ReTINA, for which she is defining and developing connectivity services.

Y. Hervé

Yann Hervé is a 1994 graduate of the Université Pierre et Marie Curie (Université de Paris VI), France.

He worked for one year at the Institut National de Recherche en Informatique et Automatique (INRIA), the French national institute for research in computer and control sciences, in the area of distributed shared memories applied to distributed domestic-waste collection.

In 1995, he joined Protectic Ingénierie, a French company specializing in CORBA and Distributed Object Technology. He works there today as a technical assistant for Alcatel Telecom Research Division.

N. Mercouroff

In 1986, Nicolas Mercouroff graduated from the Ecole Polytechnique, France. From 1986 to 1991, he worked at the Laboratoire d'Informatique de l'Ecole Polytechnique (LIX), France, and at Brandeis University, Massachusetts, U.S.A. on program validation. He completed his PhD there in 1990.

In 1991, Nicolas Mercouroff joined Alcatel Telecom Research Division. Since then, he has been involved in many projects related to the fields of information technology and telecommunications integration. In 1994 and 1995, as member of the core team of the TINA Consortium, he was in charge of the group working on computing environment specifications. Today he is responsible for TINA and multimedia within Alcatel Telecom Research Division in France, and is the work-package leader in the European ACTS project ReTINA.

8
The Three Level Approach for service creation within Intelligent Networks

Mikko Kolehmainen
Nokia Telecommunications
Hiomotie 5, FIN-00045 Nokia Group, Finland,
Phone: +358-9-511 23959
Fax: +358-9-511 23339
Email: Mikko.Kolehmainen@ntc.nokia.com

Abstract

Conceptually, the task of service creation can be divided into three separate major levels that together provide the full set of functionality needed for efficient service creation. Each one of the major levels can be implemented as a stand-alone solution or they can be integrated together. This paper introduces the main points of the Three Level Approach that is applied by Nokia as the conceptual framework in the area of IN service creation. The paper does not take a stand on how components of the approach can be implemented, instead the emphasis is on the identification of the basic requirements and capabilities.

Keywords

Intelligent Networks (IN), Service Creation, Service Creation Environment (SCE).

Intelligent Networks and Intelligence in Networks D. Gaiti (Ed.)
Published by Chapman & Hall

1 INTRODUCTION

. One of the main goals of the concept of Intelligent Networks (IN) is to reduce the time needed for introducing new telephony services (Thörner 1994) (Capellmann 1996). Therefore, it is quite important that an efficient approach for tasks related to service creation is identified. However, even though the process of service creation contains several phases and requires many tasks both consecutive and parallel to each other, one basic division should be made. The service creation can be conceptually divided into two major parts: development of service logic and development of service management applications.

Both of these parts are of significance to the service implementation and to the usability of the actual service. Usually the interfaces of the logic part of the service are defined quite well by circumstance, since the context of the logic is always tied to the physical implementation of the chosen SCP (Service Control Point) platform. From the SCE (Service Creation Environment) vendor's point of view, the SCP platform is always accurately specified. The role of the management application is a more complicated issue, since the possible execution environments are usually quite heterogeneous.

In this paper, the focus is on the definition of the logic part of the service implementation. The aim of the paper is to introduce the concept of dividing service logic creation into three levels. The paper does not take a stand with regard to different architecture options that could be chosen when implementing tools for service creation. However, in (Kolehmainen 1996) there is one example of how an instance of Service construction level can be implemented. The issues related to the provisioning of services within the approach are only briefly described.

2 RATIONALE AND CORE CAPABILITY REQUIREMENTS

When considering the requirements set for the capabilities of the service creation process, a clear trend of diversity can be identified. This is mostly due to the variety of the positions of telecom operators in their operational regions as well as their business models. In practice this means that different operators need different properties from the tools they are using for the task of service creation. The rationale of diversity in operators' requirements is the fact that resources allocated for and therefore also expectations of the service creation vary greatly.

If the issue is studied from the service creation tool vendor's point of view, the first choice to make is to decide whether the tools the vendor is going to provide are intended to be used by all operators or by some specified group with common characteristics. For example, private second and third operators have different service creation needs and resources than established PPT's. After this decision, the second task for the vendor is to identify what service creation functionalities are needed and of use within the chosen target group. When these strategic decisions have been made, the next step is to identify the actual service creation portfolio within the IN product line.

The process of identifying a product portfolio is understandably a complicated and demanding process that is closely tied to overall strategic guidelines. However, there are certain basic capabilities that can be considered essential in specific tasks related to IN service creation. The ideal approach in defining the service creation tools would then cater for these capabilities and be included in the service creation tool portfolio.

The necessary capabilities identified are presented in Figure 1.

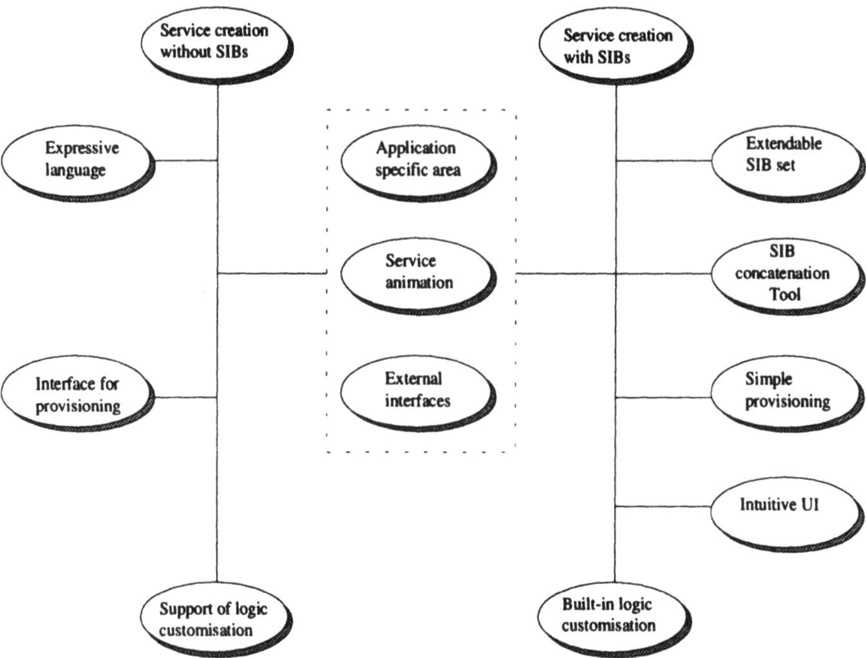

Figure 1 Core requirements set for service creation approach

There are two main lines that differ by their basic presumption. In the first line, the service creation is based on the solution that does not contain the notion of SIBs (Service Independet Building Block). Strictly speaking, this means that services are then constructed with a manner that is not aligned with guidelines presented in Q.1213 (ITU-T 1993). The actual implementation language can then be almost any procedural or object oriented programming language, a common or proprietary one. However, it is always possible, and naturally even recommended, to apply structural programming principles during the service development phase (Kinnunen 1997), (Laakso 1995).

In this context, the more interesting line and the one this paper concentrates on is the one that applies the concept of the SIB within the service creation process. In this approach the core capabilities are more intricate, since the service creation process must then fulfil basic requirements that are not present in the non-SIB approach. The differentiation in the requirements suggested in Figure 1 is mostly due to the differences in the service creation process. The main difference in the process is that before SIBs can be utilised, they have to be implemented in a method specific to the SCP platform.

3 OVERVIEW OF THE THREE LEVEL APPROACH

In the Three Level Approach the main idea is to identify different levels of service creation within the whole concept. The two factors which may be used as varying parameters between different levels are the ease of use and the rapidity of the actual task of service logic definition. As both of these factors are by nature hard to use as a basis for some metrics, it is not reasonable to define accurate identifiers for each of the levels. The more rational approach is to identify the different roles that are then represented by the levels. Figure 2 illuminates the basic idea of the approach.

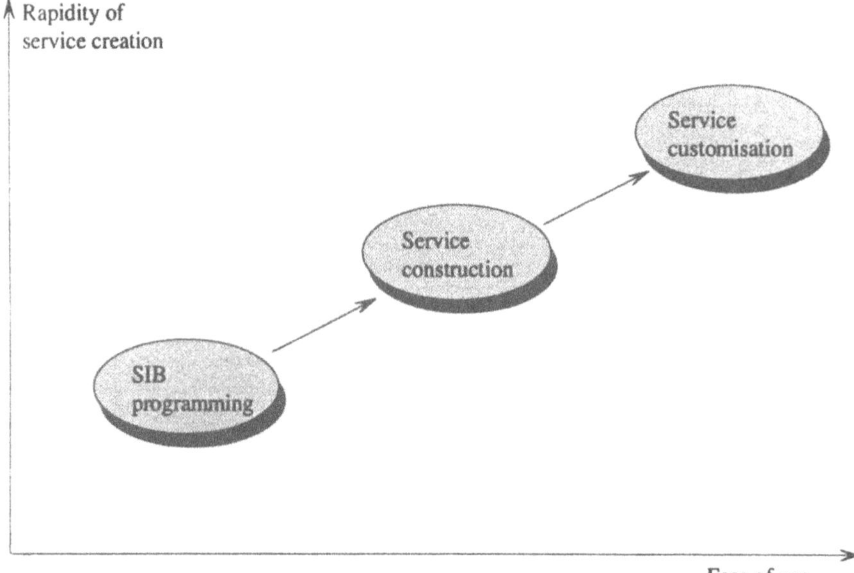

Figure 2 The three level approach

As Figure 2 suggests, the Three Level Approach consists of adjacent levels that can be hierarchically positioned in relation to each other. Each of the levels is targeted towards one specific task in the continuous activity of service creation. From each level there is a possibility for continuation to the upper adjacent level. In practice, this means that the outcome of the lower level in order can be utilised by the upper level in order. However, the levels can be considered independent so that one level can exist without support from tools positioned in some other level. In this case, it simply means that the functional capabilities provided by the nonexistent level are just missing. In any case, the tools of any single level can thus be considered stand-alone by nature.

Each of the levels represent a certain task, not specific tools. Thus, the approach does not bind or require any specific implementation to one single level. Furthermore, since only tasks are represented, it is possible that some tool implementation can provide the capabilities of all levels. On the other hand, the instantiation of the approach can be implemented so that one level can be mapped to one independent tool, which then has a well-defined interface to the neighbouring levels. The important thing is that in order to be independent, each of the levels must be able to provide some means for the service animation, albeit a modest one.

Every level requires specific core expertese from the personnel that are using the tools for their work. At the SIB programming level the core capability required is that of software engineering and programming. The net result of tasks carried out during SIB programming is an increase in the functionality of the platform that is available at the Service construction level. Service construction then requires expertese and understanding related to telecom networks. The outcome of this level is the actual service that can be utilised in the SCP platform. Finally the Customisation level requires expertese and understanding of subscriber needs. The subscriber specific and customisable parts of the service are stored in the service database that is accessed by the service. The data in the database is then used for guiding the behaviour of the service.

In the approach presented, the emphasis is on the definition of the service logic, except of course for the Customisation level that is by definition oriented towards service provisioning. The reason for this is that the relationship of service logic definition as well as service management and provisioning is not bijective by nature. Service management and provisioning must always be integrated with the operator's management and operation support system applications. From the service creation tools' point of view, this requirement is difficult to meet, since the interfaces of those systems are usually unknown to the SCE implementators. Therefore, adaptation work is nearly always needed and thus a generic and functionally adequate method for automatic management application generation is difficult to define.

This approach does not consider physical network configuration as part of the service creation process as (Turner 1995) suggests. The assumption is that the network platform is already defined in the network design phase, which then can be seen as a prior phase before application-oriented IN service creation. In any case, it is important to realise that the network platform capabilities must be considered during some phase of service creation. In fact, in the Three Level Approach the most natural place to do this is the SIB programming level that conceptually provides the interface to the INAP (Intelligent Network Application Protocol) protocol.

4 THE SIB PROGRAMMING LEVEL

The lowest level of the Three Level Approach is responsible of the task of SIB creation. In this level, the idea is that the components being part of the service logic and considered reusable are implemented in a modularised manner so that they have a well-defined interface, when utilised in the next upper level. Basically the idea is that the SIBs are implemented in a programming language that is SCP platform specific. The service defined in the Service construction level is then generated as a program of this language. Therefore, there is always a linguistic mapping between SIBs at the SIB programming level and their representation at the Service construction level. Since the SIBs are the building blocks of the service, it is essential that their role within the service is understood and modelled correctly. Also, the SIBs being the nearest component to the SCP platform and INAP protocol interface towards the SSP (Service Switching Point), the possibilities for defining the SIB behaviour are in principle those provided by the actual SCP platform. In theory, the functionality of the largest possible SIB set that can be implemented at the SIB programming level should be equal to that provided by the actual SCP platform. However, in practise the case may not be so, since this requires that the SCP specific programming language supports modularised modelling and implementation of software components, e.g. SIBs. Of course, on platforms in which the service software is inherently defined with some object oriented language (e.g. Java) the mapping is quite bijective.

As suggested earlier in Figure 1, it is possible to omit the concept of SIBs in the service definition. In this case, the requirement is obviously that the programming language of the SCP platform or the implementation of the SCE does not compel the service designer to follow paradigms of software layering, so that the service could not be implemented without dividing the service software into modules. Of course, a separate issue is, whether unstructured programming is a desirable practice or not.

One of the goals of the IN concept is to reduce the time needed for introduction of new services. Implicitly this means that, in some stage of the process, the service implementation should be, if not an easy task, at least one that requires only limited skills in the area of software engineering. However, it cannot be denied that the complexity of software engineering is present in some of the parts of service implementation. The complexity can be hidden behind automated tools, or it can be located in some defined place in the cycle of service creation.

The SIB programming level can be considered consisting of three separate fields of interest as Figure 3 suggests. The first of them is the task of SIB logic implementation, the second is the deployment of the SIB, and the third one is the support for SIB set administration with specific administrative application. In this context the deployment of a SIB should be understood to contain all the tasks that are required in order to get the SIB available in the SIB library.

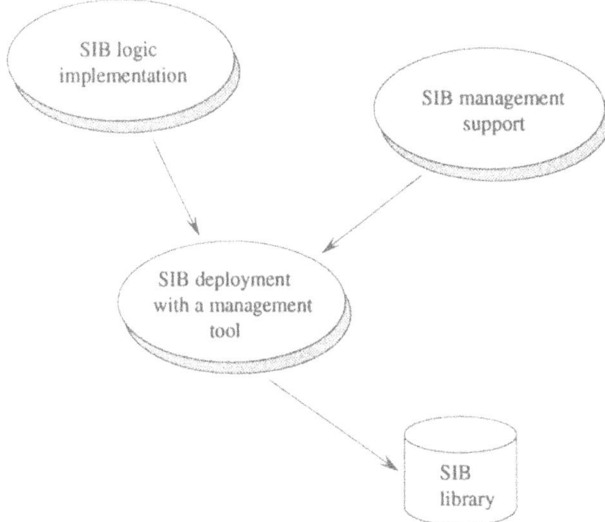

Figure 3 The task areas of SIB programming level

In the Three Level Approach, the SIB programming is the task that is considered to require the most expertise. This is mostly due to the fact that the SIBs access the platform components directly. Also, the concept of reusability proposes that it pays off to invest effort in the optimisation of SIB components. Since SIBs are software modules applying basic engineering paradigms depending on the execution platform, it is quite reasonable to require that people with software background are allocated to this task.

The tools used in this level must definitely provide a possibility for SIB execution, animation, and debugging. Implicitly this requires that there must exist a certain kind of test environment that makes it possible to test the SIBs with the principles of both white-box and black-box testing. This requirement does not preclude that simulation and testing environments could be the same both in SIB programming and Service construction level. However, since different components of the Three Level Approach are conceptually separate, the environments may well be independent level-specific implementations.

After the SIB component has been implemented, it needs to be introduced to the upper level. One applicable approach is to use a specific administration tool for the task of creating a library entry. Since one SIB can be seen to consist of several components, the administration tool must be able to gather the required components together and provide a defined access interface for the tools of the next upper level.

Another issue is the way the management of SIB components is arranged in the SLP (Service Logic Program) context. There are two basic alternatives. One possibility is to ignore the SIB management and provisioning at the SIB programming level. This means that these tasks are left as the responsibility of the service designer. The approach is reasonable, since from usability issues' point of view, the service management and provisioning applications should be considered one entity. Now, if the service management application is drawn together from several independent SIB specific components, it is not likely that the result is optimal.

On the other hand, the task of implementing a management application requires quite a lot of effort. Therefore, there can be an economical motivation, for the management part of the service to be implemented from pre-existing component specific modules. Again, it is reasonable to assume that at the SIB programming level the context and the environment of the management application is already known.

5 SERVICE CONSTRUCTION LEVEL

The actual service definition and implementation takes place at the Service construction level. This level is intended to be aimed at design personnel who are not very familiar with software engineering paradigms, but instead have knowledge about service ideas and network capabilities. In any case, it is required that the personnel whose responsibility it is to design, specify, and implement services must be familiar with relevant protocols, network capabilities, and some basic concepts of programming. Lots of complexity can be hidden behind automated functionalities provided by the service creation tools, but it is mandatory that the user understands the basics of the application area and how the hidden part is functionally positioned within the concept and, of course, the reasons for this positioning.

At the SIB programming level discussed earlier, the main emphasis is on the programming capabilities of the tools, i.e. that the tools intended for SIB implementation provide a complete instruction set that provides access to required SCP and network platform resources. In contrast, at the Service construction level one significant capability is that the tool used for defining the SLPs is easy, intuitive, and efficient to use. In fact, the solution at this level contains the user interface and the functionality that is normally provided by what is usually understood by the concept of an SCE, cnf (Bihain 1994), (Knight 1994), (Locher 1997).

The Service construction level is based fully on the concept of SIBs. As in most SCEs, the service is defined graphically by concatenating SIBs together to form the service logic program. The main idea is that all the services that are constructed according to the three level approach utilise the SIB components implemented in the SIB programming level. In this phase, the key interface is the one provided by the SIB library. In effect, the SIB library must be administrated in a manner that makes it possible to specify different views of the contents of the available SIB set. For this purpose, an administration tool, either separate from or integrated to some already existing tools, is needed. The most important capability of the administration application is the possibility to configure the tools used in the Service construction level. The minimum requirement for configurability is that the available SIB set can be dynamically changed, possibly with or without recompilation of service editing tools.

The task of service testing at this level can be divided into two parts, the first being the simulation and testing of that part to be executed in the SCP platform. The second part is the task of modelling of the kind of behaviour the service execution generates in the network. The difference in emphasis when compared to the SIB programming level is that, when SIBs are tested and simulated, SIBs can be seen only as modules whose interaction to the calling context can be modelled only via careful design and well-chosen test cases within an existing test bed. In the Service construction level testing the SIBs and their functionality can be seen only via SIB interfaces and only as a functional part of the service implementation. Of course, the SIB's interaction with the world outside must be modelled with network simulation, probably with the same implementation as in the construction level.

Conceptually, there is a logical separation between Service construction and SIB programming levels so that the lower level is always tied to some specific SCP platform. In contrast, the Service construction level could be independent from the target platform. For example, one possible net result of this separation is that in a multivendor environment the SLPs need to be implemented only once. The approach makes this possible, if the target SCP platform provides a programming interface that is open enough and a programming language that can be used both as a source format and as a target format for linguistic compilation. This precondition is essential, otherwise the SCP platform remains closed as far as the Three Level Approach is concerned. In Figure 4, there is an illustration of how the separation of levels has an effect in cases where the tools should support this diversity.

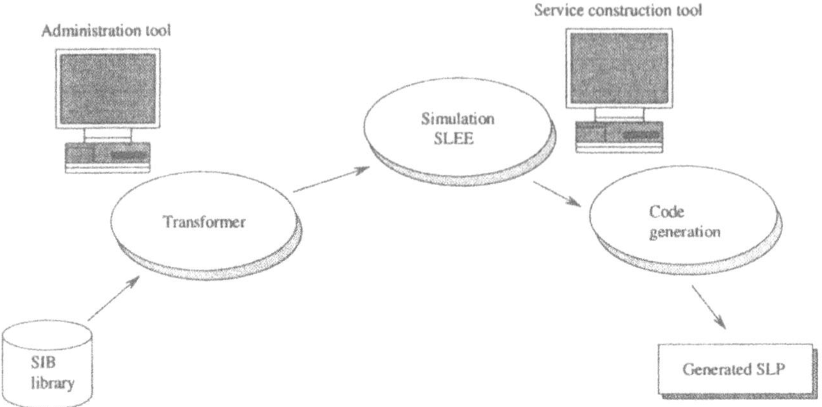

Figure 4 Different language transformations needed between separate levels when component diversion is applied

In Figure 4, the SIB library acts as an interface between SIB programming and Service construction levels. The administration tool can be positioned as a wrapper around the library and thus be seen as a part of the inter-level interface. In order to get the functionality of the SIB available in the SLEE (Service Logic Execution Environment) of the simulation environment, the SIB must be translated into the implementation representation of the Service construction tool. The transformation can be e.g. from an SCP specific language to C++. After the service has been implemented and simulated, it can be generated into the source representation for the target SCP platform. The reason why linguistic transformations of SIB implementations between SIB programming and Service construction levels are needed is the requirement that level implementations are independent of each other. In order to utilise Service construction level tools for generating services for several SCP platforms a generic service simulation SLEE must be used. This then means that the SLEE of the Construction level cannot be tied to the SLEE of some specific SCP platform.

The result of the service logic definition related tasks carried out in the Service creation level is a service logic program that consists of SIB invocations and commands that are needed for representation of a logic flow between those invocations. However, the produced service can hardly be considered as tested, since service logic animation and network behaviour simulation in a workstation is not enough. Therefore, a thorough testing phase in a laboratory environment must take place.

Service provisioning and management is an issue that should be considered at this level. This is because at this stage the service can be seen as an entity and the functional requirements set to the provisioning can be evaluated. When the service consists of SIBs, there are two possibilities: if those SIBs that require provisioning data have necessary provisioning interfaces defined, the combination of these existing routines can be used. If the service constructed requires optimised provisioning and management screens or the operator's service management system has proprietary interfaces, the best solution is to implement the management part as a separate software project.

6 SERVICE CUSTOMISATION LEVEL

Strictly speaking, service customisation is not actually a part of service creation. Rather, it relates more to the service provisioning. However, the difference is quite vague, since in some approaches the logic which is the outcome of customisation can be quite freely defined. This is strongly dependent on the implementation, though.

The purpose of the service customisation is to provide a possibility to attach some parts of the logic of the service after the actual service has been implemented and deployed. It is worth noting that service customisation is always subscriber or subscriber group specific. The idea is therefore that the runtime database is used as a storage of subscriber or subscriber group specific parameterisable data that is used for guiding the behaviour of the executed service. As Figure 5 suggests, there are two main approaches in the service customisation. The first one bases on the concept of storing logic scripts into the database. These scripts are then accessed and executed by a specific script interpreter. The second approach utilises the idea of providing values for predefined database objects, which are then accessed directly by the service.

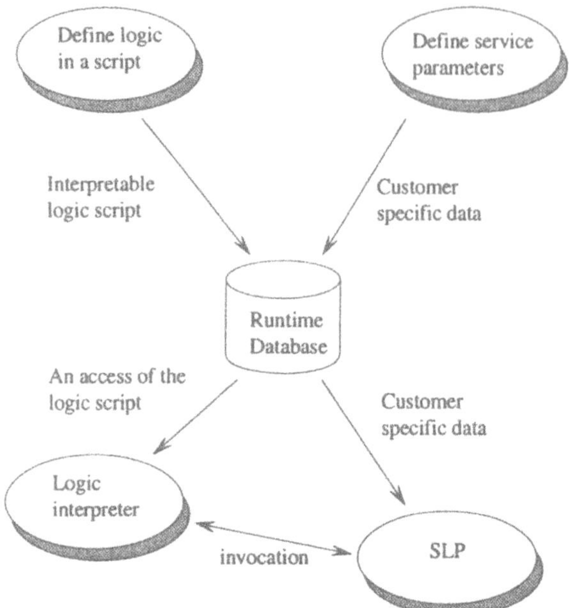

Figure 5 The two possible approaches for service customisation

The two parts of the Customisation level are targeted to two different roles. Since the first approach, script based logic definition, is more demanding than the other, service parameter based customisation, it should be used by personnel whose expertise is close to that of service designer's. Since the scripts can be defined by e.g. graphical editor or as ASCII scripts, their structure cannot be verified as an online task during the editing session. This then suggests that the customisation tools must provide a possibility for simulation of the script logic produced. Therefore, this approach can be seen as a direct extension of Service construction level.

The second part of the Customisation level is utilised according to a different scenario. In this approach, the service customisation data is given through a separate screen, e.g. a decision table that provides only a limited set of combinations all of which can be verified before service deployment, during the implementation of the management application. This approach is then clearly aimed to be used by sales personnel during or immediately after the sales situation.

The important feature of service customisation is that it can be used to extend the life cycle of the actual service logic program. For example, if the service consists of certain basic functionalities and invocation of the logic script interpreter, the service behaviour can be tailored afterwards with capabilities that weren't identified during service requirement analysis. The obvious implementation method for this extension is to define the new functionalities as subscriber or subscriber group specific logic scripts.

7 CONCLUSIONS

In this paper we discussed how the tools used for service creation can be divided into three levels according to their functional capabilities. Each of the levels is essential if the IN service creation is to be utilised in full scale. However, each of the levels can be implemented so that they are instantiated as a stand-alone tool with the support of lower levels as ready-made or tailored solutions.

The SIB programming level is intended to provide the basic framework for creating the SIB components which are then utilised at the Service construction level. As the task of SIB implementation is the critical part of service creation, it is probable that most of the effort needed for introducing services is spent during SIB requirement analysis, design, and implementation. Furthermore, it is important to realise that SIBs must not be seen as single, indvidual components. Instead, they should be considered together as an integral library that then can be used as modules for service logic program implementation.

The Service construction level is intended to provide the editing functionalities of tools that are normally considered as "traditional" SCEs. The service implementation bases directly on the concept of SIBs and their functionalities defined in the SIB programming level. It is anticipated that in this level key factors are the ease of use and how much service introduction time can be speeded up, if all the required SIB components have already been deployed into the SIB library.

With the service customisation, the basic idea is to tailor the behaviour of the service after the actual deployment. There are two basic approaches: in the first one the customisation can be based on scripts that are interpreted by the service logic program. The other possibility is to define dedicated screens that then are used for defining the input parameters for the service. The former approach is suitable for subscribers or subscriber groups that require flexible behaviour and the requirements cannot be determined accurately during service implementation. The latter approach provides only a finite set of different possibilities and therefore testing of customised behaviour can be carried out during service implementation tests.

9 REFERENCES

Bihain, A., White, J. (1994) Service Creation Environment as a software development platform, in *Intelligent Networks* (ed. Harju, J., Karttunen, T.), Proceedings of the IFIP workshop on intelligent networks 1994, IFIP, Chapmann & Hall, Padstow.

Capellmann, C. et al (1996) The P103 Service Creation Environment Model, in *Intelligent Networks and New Technologies* (ed. J. Nørgaard, V. B. Iversen), IFIP, Chapman & Hall, London.

ITU-T (1993) Q.12xx- Series Intelligent Networks Recommendations, ITU-T.

Knight, C. (1994) Service creation from IN to mobile and broadband, in *Intelligent Networks* (ed. Harju, J., Karttunen, T.), Proceedings of the IFIP workshop on intelligent networks 1994, IFIP, Chapmann & Hall, Padstow.
Kinnunen, J. (1997) Intelligent Networks (IN) Service Creation Language, M.Sc. Thesis, Lappeenranta University of Technology, 1997.
Kolehmainen, M. (1996) Nokia SCE - An Architecture for a Lightweight SCE, in *Intelligent Networks and New Technologies* (ed. J. Nørgaard, V. B. Iversen), IFIP, Chapman & Hall, London.
Laakso, R. (1995) Object Oriented Implementation of Intelligent Network Service Logic Programs, M.Sc. Thesis, University of Helsinki, Dept. of Computer Science, 1995.
Locher, M. (1997) Total Service Creation within IN, Intelligent Networks Summit 14th - 16th May 1997, London.
Thörner, J. (1994) Intelligent Networks, Artech House, Norwood .
Turner, G., D. (1995) Service Creation, *BT Technology Journal*, Vol. 13, No. 2, Ipswich, April 1995.

10 BIOGRAPHY

Mikko Kolehmainen was born in 1966. He received his M.Sc. in CS from the University of Helsinki, Department of Computer Science in 1992. He joined Nokia Research Center in 1993 and Nokia Telecommunications in 1996. During his time with Nokia he has been working with issues related to IN and especially to the service creation. Currently he is also a Ph.D. student with the University of Helsinki, Department of Computer Science.

9

A framework of service components modelling for multimedia distribution over broadband network

[a] *O. Martikainen,* [b] *V. Naoumov,* [c] *K. Samouylov,*
[c] *M. Zhidovinov*

[a] *Helsinki University of Technology*
Otakaari 1 room Y228C, FIN-02150 Espoo, FINLAND,
Tel. +358 9451 2174, Telefax +358 9451 3293,
E-mail Olli.Martiakinen@hut.fi

[b] *Lappeenranta University of Technology*
P.O. Box 20, FIN-53851 Lappeenranta, FINLAND,
Tel. +358 5 621 2828, Telefax +358 5 621 2899,
E-mail Valeri.Naoumov@lut.fi

[c] *Peoples' Friendship University of Russia*
P.O Box 9, 117419 Moscow, RUSSIA,
Tel./Telefax +7 095 952 2823,
E-mail Konstantin.Samouylov@mx.pfu.edu.ru,
Michael.Zhidovinov@mx.pfu.edu.ru

Abstract

The paper focuses on the middleware design issues for multimedia applications on top of IP switching environment over ATM networks. It describes the JVOPS Framework and the corresponding JVOPS System Architecture.

Keywords

Media distribution, service modelling, service architecture, broadband network

Intelligent Networks and Intelligence in Networks D. Gaiti (Ed.)
Published by Chapman & Hall

1 INTRODUCTION

With rapid growth of the information industries it seems to be clear that new bridging technologies between different actors of multimedia services provision over broadband networks will be developed and piloted up to the end of the century. These technologies will reflect major shifts at the telecommunications market, which now can be defined as follows

- *shift in the networks infrastructure* towards broadband backbone and access networks;
- *shift in the service value creation* first from the mobile and Internet services;
- *shift in the content industry* where content and/or brokerage service providers will play a significant role in value creation.

One of the enabling factors of these changes is the Internet becoming a basis for service and content creation, and another is the liberalization of telecommunication markets where all main players should join efforts in the creation of network architectures considerably flexible and simpler than today.

The key issue for future networks is to provide a wide range of multimedia services by means of distributed intelligence over user terminals and different service control and provider nodes. The basic idea is presented in the Principles of Intelligent Network Architecture [1] and means that the operation and provision of new services should be independent of core network functions. It is well assumed [2] that modern service architecture must satisfy to the following requirements:

- *support for wide range of services* – support for telecommunication, information and management services;
- *rapid service deployment and provision* – reduce development and deployment cost by components reuse;
- *support for multi-player environment* – open environment for interoperability among multiply providers/operators;
- *universal service access* – access to service independently of physical location and terminal used;
- *independence from the network infrastructure* – service evolution independently of underlying transport and computing technologies.

A number of research and development projects have been already started to support multimedia telecommunication systems implementation. The TOVE (Transparent Object-oriented Virtual Exchange) project [3,4] aims at developing network architecture that would satisfy mentioned above requirements. The research in the Calypso project [5] will focus on how service control should be implemented for media distribution over TOVE broadband network architecture.

In this paper we propose an object-oriented framework architecture for Service Logic Execution Environment modeling and Service Components prototyping in the media distribution control environment.

2 MULTIMEDIA SERVICES DISTRIBUTION MODEL

The service architecture proposed by TINA-C consortium [2] demonstrate three generic aspects of the system:

- *generic User/Provider paradigm* to govern access between stakeholders;
- *flexible session ("call") model* supporting multimedia/multiparty services;
- *open interfaces* to allow for third party development applications, interoperability among stakeholders, global personal and terminal mobility.

User/Provider paradigm is universally applicable to any situation where a User makes use of service offered by a Provider and defines roles of actors and relationship between them in business scenario.

The User/Provider relationship is separated into "Access part", concerning the establishment and maintaining of interaction and "Usage part", concerning the actual use of the capabilities associated with interaction. The separation of Access and Usage parts of service is illustrated at Figure 1.

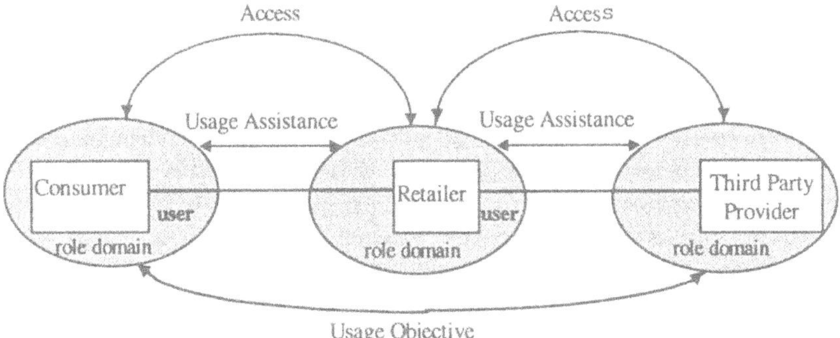

Figure 1 Separation of Access and Usage part of User/Provider interaction in multi-player environment

The Access part concerns to the following activities:

- initiate dialogue between User and Provider;
- exchange of domain and equipment information to facilitate service provision;
- establish and maintain a secure, trusted association between User and Provider.

The Usage part is divided into Usage Assistance – use of services to assist the User/Provider association (such as customization of settings, subscription services, accounting and billing, etc.) and Usage Objective - use of services concerning the primary aim of User/Provider association (such as Media on Demand, Video Conferencing, etc.).

We describe relationship between parties in service provision and their evolution over time by terms of sessions, which are defines as context for relating service provision activities between stakeholders and related to the allocation of resources which are necessary to perform these activities. Three types of sessions are shown in Figure 2.

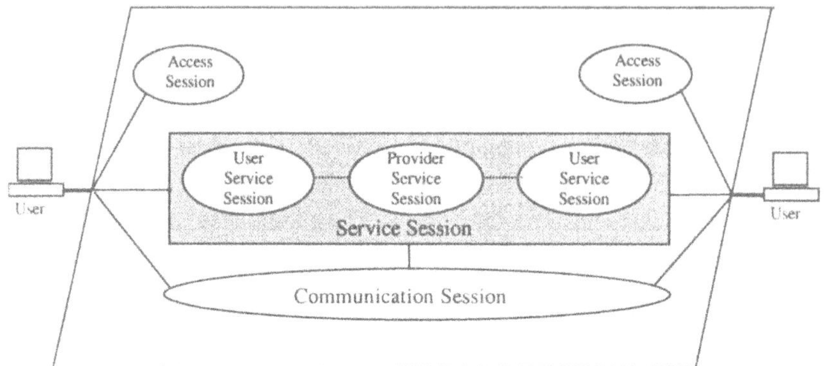

Figure 2 Sessions of User/Provider interactions

Access session, related to Access part of User/Provider relationship, identifies a secure, accountable, manageable association between Users and provides a context for a User to access services offered by Provider.
Service sessions, related to Usage part of User/Provider relationship, provides context for one or more Users to support execution of services. Services session provides the concept of "call" and allows to Users possibility of negotiation through services session, e.g. negotiate what parties are involved, which specific communication configuration are selected, what QoS parameters are required, etc. It is composed of User Service Session part, which represents local view for each user and Provider Service Session part, which represents global view.
Communication session, related to Usage part of User/Provider relationship, provides context for one or more Users to support the telecommunication capabilities necessary for service sessions. The mapping of service sessions onto communication sessions is fully flexible (Call/Connection separation).
From computational viewpoint this architecture can be described by means of interacting service architecture components - entities in computational viewpoint that can be mapped to computational objects or to sets of interacting computation objects. These components are forming a framework for service development and provision, providing abilities for deriving new service components by existing via specialization (adding new features) and composition (putting together several components).
So, in the scope of service architecture in broadband multimedia distribution network it is important to define both refined architecture model based primary on principles of TINA-C service architecture and generic *Service Components Framework,* that can be used by designers for rapid development of wide range of multimedia provision services through specialization and composition of reusable components.

In next section we consider an example of multimedia distribution scenario for TOVE-based network architecture which will also clarify our vision of the model described above.

3 MULTIMEDIA DISTRIBUTION SCENARIO

ATM based networks, such as B-ISDN, is going to be dominant transmission technology on which the information infrastructure will be build. Therefore integrated solutions, where IP routing and switched connections are provided will be needed in future broadband multimedia capable networks. The TOVE network architecture satisfies the requirements listed in the previous sections and provides all necessary facilities to separate control from switching as it shown in Figure 3. Switch controllers (SwC) are used to execute specific Control Functions, e.g. Call Control Function (CCF) and Service Switching Function (SSF) needed in establishing ATM virtual circuits, IP Gateway Function (IPGWF) and IP Switching Functions (IPSF) needed in IP routing.

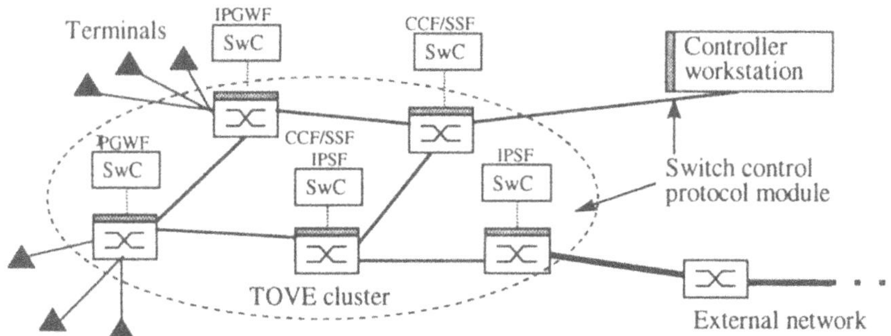

Figure 3 TOVE architecture

Using the TOVE underlying architecture a multimedia distribution scenario can be proposed where main actors are:

- Service Client;
- Content Provider;
- Icon Server;
- Service Server.

The scenario is based on principles of multimedia service provision model proposed in [6]. The model is described in Figures 4 and 5. The service provision mechanism is illustrated as an example for Multimedia on Demand type services.

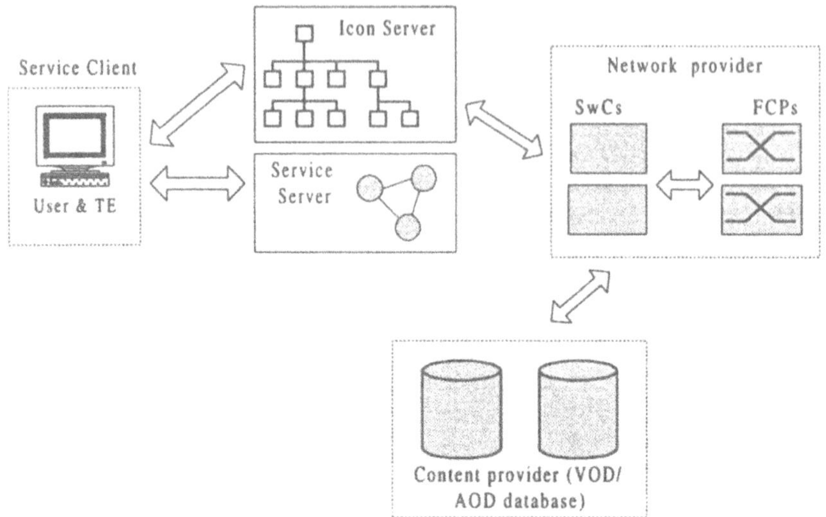

Figure 4 Multimedia service provision system architecture

- The Service Client is represented by User and Terminal Equipment (TE), where the last one is a device with different multimedia capabilities. The TE can be available for the use by many users and provides a level of service that customized to the User.
- The Icon Server represents available services such as AOD/VOD or different multimedia documents.
- The Service Server is a distributed computer controlled system, which provides to Service Client a concrete service with guaranteed QoS parameters.
- The Content Provider is responsible for service content provision on the basis of corresponding databases and for regular renovation of information at the Icon Server environment.
- The Network Provider provides standardized network services as it described in [4].

More details of negotiating between main actors of scenario are shown by means of arrow-type diagram in Figure 5.

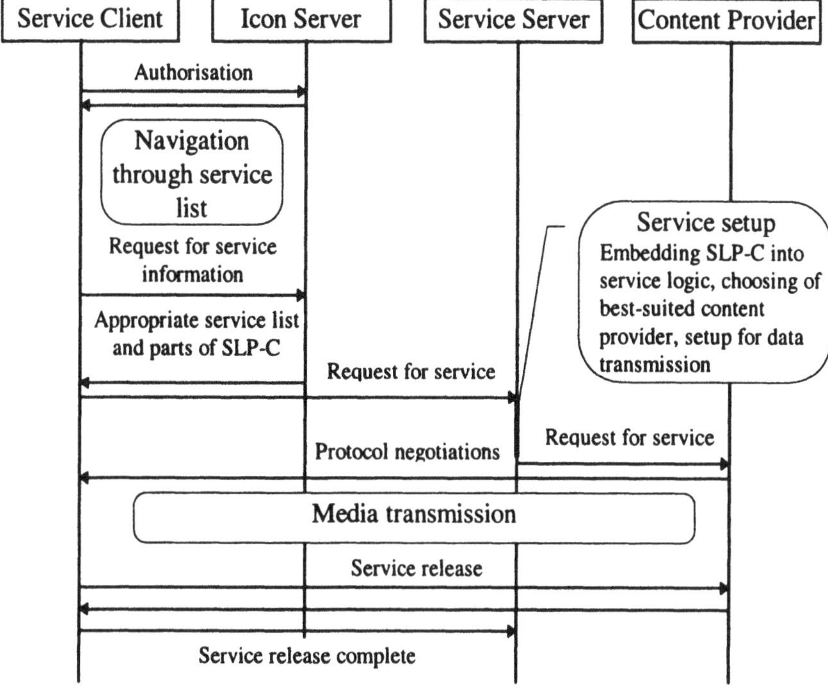

Figure 5 Multimedia service provision scenario example

4 SERVICE COMPONENTS FRAMEWORK IMPLEMENTATION ASPECTS

The Service Components Framework development is based on TINA-C generic principles. However we will not follow strictly the architecture and interfaces solutions provided by the TINA-C and the OMG CORBA. Our approach is based also on the solutions available in Java Platform which at the moment is presented by JavaBeans component architecture [7], Java RMI [8] and JDBC [9] APIs as forthcoming Java Electronic Commerce Framework and Java Media Framework [10]. Our contribution on top of the Java Platform is the development of the middleware for Service Components Framework.
The middleware for Service Components Framework is called JVOPS (JavaVOPS Framework), by analogy with CVOPS [11] and OVOPS [12] Virtual Operations Systems known as sophisticated frameworks for telecommunication applications programming.

4.1 JVOPS Basic Concepts

Distributed systems are hard to build. They require careful thinking about problems that do not occur in local computation. The primary problems are those of partial failure, greatly increased latency, and language compatibility. The Java Platform provides a number of tools (e.g. Java RMI, Java IDL, etc.) that support a general approach for distributed computation using techniques natural to the Java language and environment.

These tools, powerful as they are, do not make distributed computation systems easy to design - they merely make them possible to approach. JVOPS is intended to be an environment with fundamental possibilities for Java-based applications in distributed reliable computing system [14 - 16]. JVOPS supports the development of distributed applications, providing transparent communication mechanism, process migration, load balancing and different degree of reliability to application. It can be used by designers for rapid development of wide range of distributed application through specialization and composition of reusable components.

An interactive distributed application is represented in JVOPS as a family of interacting components called jTasks by analogy with vtasks and otasks in CVOPS and OVOPS, respectively. The jTasks interact with each other with one way synchronous or asynchronous transporters representing method calls or messages. The transporters are routed through communication channels representing the jTask connections. The following abstract classes and principles are used:

- jTask with subclasses jAdapter, jMux, jBus, jProtocol and jFactory representing active components,
- jTransporter with subclasses synchTransporter and asyncTransporter representing synchronous and asynchronous interactions between components,
- jScheduler which manages threads and the execution of jTasks,
- jArch for System Architecture specification and instantiation of jSchedulers, jTasks and their interconnections in each given subsystem.

Different underlying technologies such as RMI, transactional RMI, CORBA IIOP or are encapsulated in jAdapter instances.

The jProtocol class may contain an Extended Finite State Machine (EFSM) abstraction and is characterized by the current states of its instance variables set, behavior function and input/output channels. The jTask and jTransporter classes have been introduced from the OVOPS++ extension of OVOPS [3 - 4]. JavaBeans component architecture can be applied in the implementation of jTask subclasses.

4.2 JVOPS System Architecture

JVOPS System Architecture is shown at Figure 6 and consists of the following subsystems:

- Network Management System (NMS);
- Persistent Store System (PSS);
- Execution Environment (EE);

- Development Environment (DE);
- Processing Units (PU);
- Management Workstation (MW).

Each subsystem in the JVOPS System Architecture contains at least one jArch and jScheduler and the required number of jTasks.

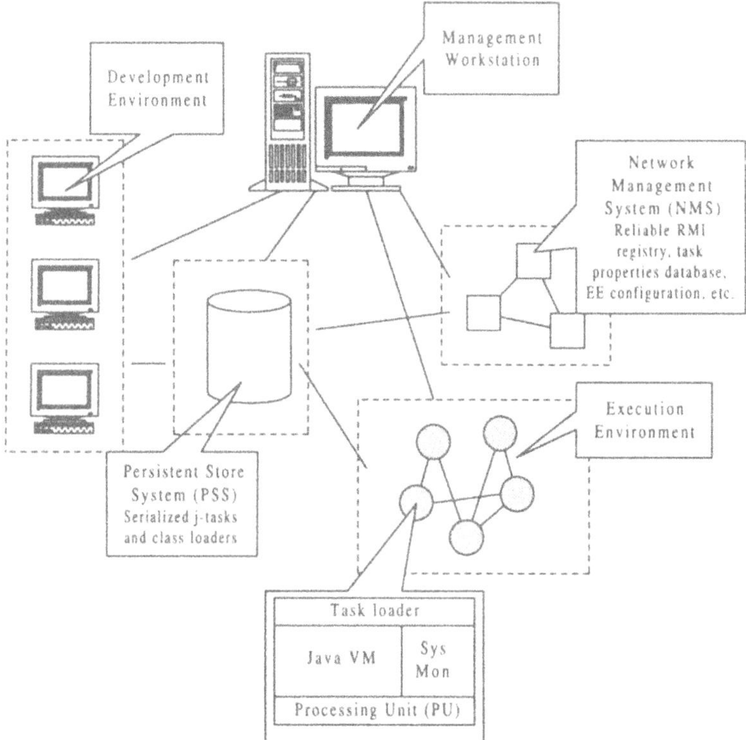

Figure 6 JVOPS System Architecture

The Execution Environment is represented as a set of PUs which are active at the moment over network of nodes in DRC environment [13].

The PU is a basic computing element of the JVOPS application and is described as a Java Virtual Machine with components depicted in Figure 6.

The Network Management System provides the control of j-task functioning and communicating, load balancing, reliability control, task migration between nodes etc.

The Persistent Store System supports the data storage necessary for all kind of EE system needs.

The Development Environment provides the possibility of j-task programming and its integration into application software. After verification and testing j-tasks are to be passed to PSS system and becomes ready for loading into EE system.

4.3 JavaSLEE and JavaSCE

An important part of JVOPS concept is a modern way for service creation and execution over DRC environment.
For intelligent applications Service Component Framework should provide Service Logic Execution Environment (SLEE) for service application and Service Creation Environment (SCE) for service modeling and creation. The SLEE and the SCE are forming a basis for Service Component Framework which is built on top of JavaVOPS Framework.
A general architecture of services application in Java SLEE environment is illustrated in Figure 7. The JavaSLEE provides Service Logic Programs (SLP) entities with all means for normal functioning in JVOPS environment , e.g. load balancing , request dispatching etc. Every SLP in JavaSLEE is a set of jTasks with its internal logic and external interfaces. The structure resembles the IN SIBs logic with Points of Initiation and Points of Return as external interfaces.

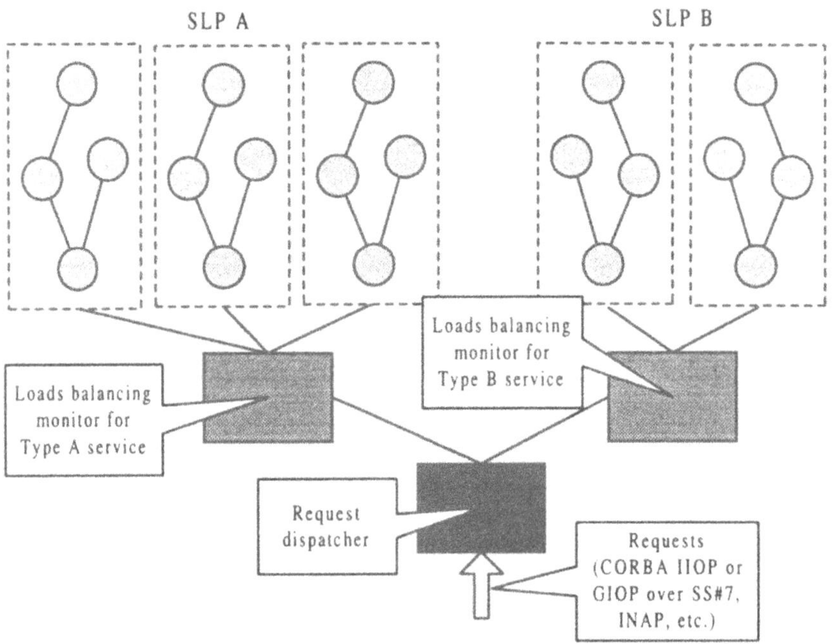

Figure 7 Services application in JavaSLEE

5 EXAMPLE

As an example let us consider the problem of IN integration with new object-oriented platforms. To solve this problem three basic approaches have been proposed in EUROSCOM P508C project [16]. They are

- encapsulation of IN software into CORBA objects;
- the use of external gateway;
- use of SS#7 as transport for interORB communication.

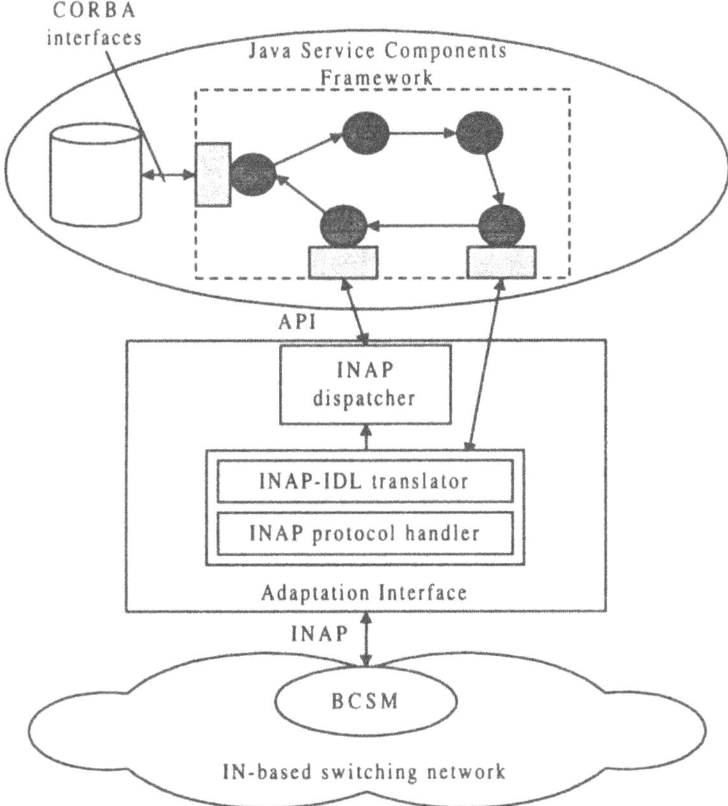

Figure 8 Example of external gateway architecture in Service Component Framework

Figure 8 shows the Service Component Framework application to the second approach and illustrates the Service Component Framework service architecture on top of IN based-switched network. Such kind of solution can allow to Public Network Operators to keep the existing BCSM and INAP interfaces in operation as long as possible/ required, therefore saving investments into previous technologies.

6 REFERENCES

1. ITU-T Recommendation I.312/Q.1201, Principles of Intelligent Network Architecture, 1992, Geneva.
2. TINA-C Deliverable. Service Architecture. Version 4.0. 1996
3. Puro V-M., Koponen P., Rasanen J., Nummisalo P., Martikainen O. (1996) TOVE in Universal Mobile Telecommunications System, Proc. *2nd Workshop on Personal Wireless Communications (Wireless Local Access).* Frankfurt am Main.
4. Puro V-M., Koponen P., Rasanen J., Nummisalo P., Martikainen O.(1996), TOVE in Broadband Multimedia. *TOVE report, Helsinki Univ. of Tech.* Helsinki.
5. Martikainen O. et al. (1997) CALYPSO - System Components and Tools for Media Distribution over Broadband Networks. *Project description, Helsinki University of Technology.* Helsinki
6. Martikainen O., Naoumov V., Samouylov K. (1996) Call Processing Model for Multimedia Services, *Intelligent Networks and New Technologies (V.B.Iversen and J.Nørgaard eds), Chapman & Hall,* London.
7. JavaBeans™ API Specification. Version 1.0-A. *Sun Microsystems Inc.*, 1996.
8. Java™ Remote Method Invocation Specification. Revision 1.4, *Sun Microsystems Inc.*, 1997.
9. The JDBC™ API Version 1.10. Part 1 - Interfaces, Part 2 - Classes and Exceptions. *Sun Microsystems Inc.*, 1996.
10. Java™ API Overview. URL: http://www.javasoft.com/products/api-overview.html
11. Malka J., Ojanpera E. Reference Manual for CVOPS 4.0 (1992). *Technical Research Centre of Finland, Telecommunications Laboratory.* Helsinki
12. Martikainen O., Puro P., Sonninen J. (1995) OVOPS, Object Virtual Operations System for Distributed Application Development. *Proc. INDC 94*, Funchal, Portugal.
13. DRC Project Home Page. URL: http://mds.jpl.nasa.gov/drc
14. Anderson T. E., Culler D. E., Patterson D. A., and the NOW Team (1995) A Case for NOW (Networks of Workstations). *IEEE Micro*, Vol. 15, No. 1, February 1995.
15. Ingham D. B., Caughey S. J., and Little M. C. (1997). Supporting Highly Manageable Web Services. *Proceedings of the Sixth International WWW Conference*, Santa Clara, USA..
16. CORBA as an Enabling Factor for Migration from IN to TINA: A EURESCOM P508 Perspective. Final Draft, Version 4.1, *EURESCOM*, 24 December 1996.

7 BIOGRAPHY

Olli Martikainen, PhD from Helsinki University and MS from Helsinki University of Technology. He has been doing research in several positions in Helsinki University of Technology (1976 - 1982, 1991 - 1997), Oxford University (1980 - 1981), Technical Research Centre of Finland (1982 - 1985, 1989 - 1991), Nokia Electronics (1985 - 1986), Nokia Research Centre (1986 - 1988), Lappeenranta University of Technology (1988 -1989). In 1991 - 1996 he has been research director and vice president at Telecom Finland. Currently he is professor at Helsinki University of Technology. His main areas of interest are telecommunication software methods and tools, network architectures, performance analysis and new industrial and economic structures in telecommunications.

Valeri Naoumov, PhD from Computer Centre of Russian Academy of Sciences (1979) and MS from Peoples' Friendship University (1972). He has been doing research in several positions in Peoples' Friendship University (1973 - 1996), Helsinki University of Technology (1984 - 1985), Institute for Problem of Information Transmission of Russian Academy of Sciences (1992 - 1994), Deutsche Bundespost Telekom (1994 - 1995). Since 1996 he is professor at Department of Information Technology of Lappeenranta University of Technology. Areas of expertise: queuing theory, traffic models, programming, computational algorithms, intelligent network, telecommunication protocols implementation. He has written many technical articles and two books.

Konstantin Samouylov received the MS degree from Peoples' Friendship University of Russia and the PhD degree from Moscow State University in mathematics in 1978 and 1985 respectively. From 1986 to 1992 he taught courses in queuing theory and conducted research in CCS network, teletraffic and performance analysis. Since 1993 he began work in broadband and intelligent networks. Dr. Konstantin Samouylov currently is a head of Telecommunication Systems Laboratory in PFU, Moscow. He has written a number of journal and conference papers in the areas of queuing theory, performance of CCS network and IN software development.

Michael Zhidovinov received his MS degree from Moscow State University in mathematics in 1994. Since 1993 he has been doing research in several positions in Peoples' Friendship University, Moscow. His main areas of interest are telecommunication software methods and tools, network architectures, software engineering.

PART FOUR

Distributed Intelligence

10

Chronicle Learning and Agent oriented techniques for network management and supervision

Joël Quinqueton, Babak Esfandiari, Richard Nock
LIRMM and INRIA
161 rue Ada 34392 Montpellier Cedex 5, France, +33(4)67418532, Fax +33(4)67418500 {jq,nock}@lirmm.fr

Abstract

This paper presents some aspects of the "Réseau futé (Smart Net)" project, whose aim is to introduce Artificial Intelligence techniques (such as machine learning and multi-agent systems) in network management and supervision, in order to help the processing of the large volume of events notifications received by network management operators. We provide experimental and theoretical results on learning patterns called chronicles in order to design a machine assistant to network operators. Theoretical results investigate different levels of help that could be brought by the operator to the assistant. The tests were performed in two distinct realworld situations. They showed the circumstances under which chronicle learning is possible without the help of the operator or another assistant.

Keywords

Interface agents, Chronicles, Machine Learning, Network management, Learnability

1 INTRODUCTION

The aim of the "Réseau Futé (Smart Net)" (Esfandiari, Nock & Quinqueton 1996) project is to introduce Artificial Intelligence techniques (such as machine learning and multi-agent systems) in network management and supervision in order to help the processing of the large volume of alarms and various event notifications received by network management platforms. Actually, many of these alarms prove to have a user-depending utility and have to be filtered. Other events become meaningful when associated to their context, which partly consists in the previous and following events, which dates of detection may vary depending on the traffic. Therefore time has to be explicitly taken into account. We have chosen the Chronicle model (Ghallab 1994) in order to incorporate temporal reasoning in our experimental platform. Thus some of the tasks (alarm filtering, log recording, fault detection...) can be automated via a chronicle recognition system (Dousson 1994), letting the supervision operator focus on more important tasks. Although it is possible to have a

Intelligent Networks and Intelligence in Networks D. Gaiti (Ed.)
Published by Chapman & Hall

model-based approach, we will assume that we do not have a complete knowledge of the network, and that the model can evolve quickly.

Therefore "on-line" knowledge acquisition seems to be a good solution. We have been mainly inspired by Pattie Maes's Interface Agents (Maes & Kozierok 1993), where an agent learns by "looking over the shoulder" of the human operator. The association of the chronicle recognition system and the chronicle acquisition system can eventually provide us a true intelligent assistant to network management and supervision. But chronicle learning can raise theoretical problems, and we have to know under which assumptions it is reasonable to build such a system. For example, (Dousson 1994) advocates for the dialog between the learner and the experts. This paper brings some theoretical results showing how much such a dialog can be useful, and provide some algorithms which have been tested so far. We have implemented a simplified simulation of a network management platform which respects network management standards (GDMO and CMIS) and encloses our assistant. The algorithms present in some cases the desirable properties (Dousson 1994) to provide neither too specific, nor too general chronicles.
Section §2 presents some definitions refering to chronicles; section §3 presents the assistant's structure. Positive and negative results for chronicle learning are investigated in section §4, followed in section §5 by the algorithms and the practical results that were obtained.

2 DEFINITIONS

Temporal knowledge is required for reasoning on events, actions and change (Ghallab 1994), in order to model facts such as : precedence, overlapping, simultaneity between events. While "numerical" approaches based on Operations Research are not adequate for symbolic reasoning, classical and modal logic approaches have problems in finding a good balance between expressiveness and algorithmic complexity. The *chronicle model* proposed by Ghallab is based on two elementary types of formulaes taken from the reified temporal logic : *events* and *holds*.

- a "hold" expresses that some ground domain attribute holds over some interval, for instance : *Hold (position (robot1, docking-site), (t5, t6))*
- an "event" specifies a discrete change of the value of an attribute, for instance : *Event (state (switch): (off, on), t8)*

A chronicle model is a set of *event patterns* and temporal constraints between them and with respect to a context specified by *hold* assertions. If some observed events match the event patterns, and if their occurence dates meet the specified constraints within its context, then an instance of this chronicle occurs. Here is an example of a chronicle taken from (Ghallab 1994) :

```
Chronicle RobotLoadMachine {
event (Robot: (outRoom, inRoom), e1);
```

```
event (Robot: (inRoom, outRoom), e4);
event (MachineInput: (UnLoaded, Loaded), e2);
event (Machine: (Stopped, Running), e3);
e1 < e2;
1' ≤ e3 - e2 ≤ 6';
3' ≤ e4 - e2 ≤ 5';
hold (Machine: Running, (e2, e2));
hold (SafetyConditions: True, (e1, e4));
when recognized {report ''Successful load''; }}
```

Realtime (and therefore with low complexity) chronicle recognition (Dousson 1994) is processed in several steps :

- Transform "holds" into "forbidden events", *i.e.* an event should not change the value of the "held" attribute within the duration of the "hold".
- Possibly create a new instance of a possible chronicle and update (in fact this is always a restriction as time goes by) the *window of relevance* (acceptable time intervals for the expected events in order to complete a chronicle pattern) of all possible chronicles when a new event has been observed.
- Detect "deadlines" and occurence of "forbidden events". In these cases, the corresponding chronicle will be removed from the list of the possible chronicles.
- Trigger off the action corresponding to the completed chronicle.

3 THE ASSISTANT'S STRUCTURE

Our machine assistant is mainly inspired by Pattie Maes's Interface Agents (Maes & Kozierok 1993). An Interface Agent is "a computer program that employs Artificial Intelligence techniques in order to provide assistance to a user dealing with a particular computer application. Such agents learn by 'watching over the shoulder' of the user and detecting patterns and regularities in the user's behaviour". Since we had to deal with realtime aspects and time was a very important parameter, we chose to manipulate chronicles. As shown in figure 1, our assistant has two main components :

- The Chronicle Recognition System (RS), which goal is to receive dated event notifications (such as alarms) and try to match them with chronicles stored in the so-called Confirmed Chronicle Base. Whenever a chronicle has been recognized, the RS processes the corresponding action (such as filtering, fault diagnosis...). If the received events do not match any chronicle, it is up to the supervision operator to take a decision. For more details about the Recognition System, see (Dousson 1994).
- The Learning System (LS), which goal is to watch "over the shoulder" of the supervision operator when he takes a decision, in order to feed the Recognition

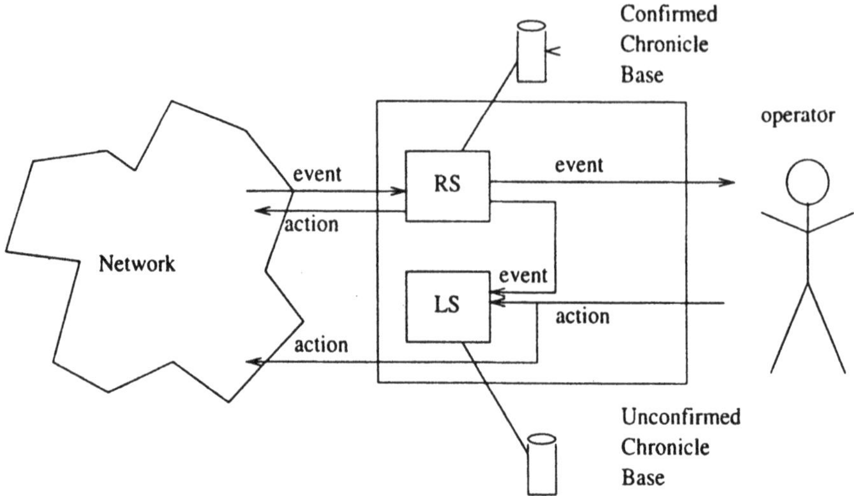

Figure 1 The assistant's structure

System with new chronicles. New chronicles are stored in a so-called Unconfirmed Chronicle Base before being "mature" enough in order to be confirmed (*i.e.* transferred to the Confirmed Chronicle Base). In this paper, we shall describe more precisely this component.

4 LEARNABILITY AND CHRONICLES

Above all, we shall use in all that follows a simpler notation for chronicles: *e.g.* the chronicle

Chronicle X {
event (a_{t_1}, t_1) ; $\cdots$
event (a_{t_i}, t_i) ;
$t_2 - t_1 = \delta_1$; $\cdots$
$t_i - t_{i-1} = \delta_{i-1}$
when recognized {**report** ''α_j''; }}

is rewritten as $\{(a_{t_1}, t_1), ..., (a_{t_i}, t_i); \delta_1 = t_2 - t_1, ..., \delta_{i-1}\} \Rightarrow \alpha_j$, where $a = \{a_1, ..., a_n\}$ is a set of events, and α_j belongs to a set of actions $\alpha = \{\alpha_1, ..., \alpha_{M_1}\}$ which depend on a. As the reader shall remark, we perform some limitations on chronicles, that shall not disturb our study: first of all, *we remove the "holds" on chronicles*. Indeed, they are not that more complicated to manage than "events" or time constraints. Our modelling takes into account that any action is triggered off by some events (i) given some ordering of them, (ii) given some time constraints, and (iii) provided each event can appear many times.

In the discussion of some of the results we give later on learning chronicles, we take into account a type of limitations that are framework dependant. We emphasize on them, since they can be very useful to accelerate the learning task on our main problem: network supervision. In particular, they include the human operator limitations: chronicles are supposed to help him along, simulating, why not, his actions on the network. Any human operator, be him as efficient as possible, cannot recall (i) events that are too spaced out, (ii) the number of times some event has appeared, beyond some threshold, (iii) neither the exact time, nor sufficiently good approximations, that separates two events triggering off an action. And these remarks are all the more valid as the operator generally receives a treamount of events. The first two approximations we shall make are therefore the following:

1. Time is discretized. Any two consecutive events triggering off an action are spaced out by a time measured in the set $\{0, 1, ..., M_3\}$, for some constant M_3.
2. In order to trigger off an action, any event needs at most multiple appearances bounded by some constant M_2.

Therefore, we can rewrite any chronicle involving action α_j as a formula $(m, t) \Rightarrow \alpha_j$, where $m \in \{1, *\}^{nM_2}$ and $t \in \{-M_3, ..., M_3, *\}^{2C^2_{nM_2}}$, where "*" means no value specified, and $C^2_{nM_2}$ is the binomial coefficient $C^k_n = n!/(k!(n-k)!)$. The first part, m, is a monotonous Boolean formula, showing whether an event has to appear for triggering off α_j, taking in account of the fact that there are n distinct events, each one being able to appear M_2 times. The second part, t, is a vector representing the time constraints δ's, be they equality or inequalities. We can even model a chronicle as a complete monotonous Boolean formula, by replacing in t any δ by a word of constant size on the alphabet $\{1; *\}$. Therefore it becomes possible to look for the translation of any positive result concerning Boolean formulas into positive results for learning chronicles.
What follows is composed of three parts. The first one presents models for learning chronicles; it is followed by positive results for chronicle learning. The last section presents negative results.

4.1 Learning chronicles

We suppose that the assistant has access to *oracles*, that supply events, actions and/or messages ("Yes", "No") according to some fixed protocol. We present them from the most passive of them, to the most active ones, for which there can be interactions between assistant and oracles. We have on purpose searched to make the oracles behave as simply as possible. In particular, we did not search to adapt the complex behaviour of experts recommended by (Dousson 1994).

• The most simple of these oracles is entirely passive, and simply supplies on-line streams of events from a and actions from α, according to their appearance on the network. We refer to him as PASSIVE(α).

• The second oracle behaves as PASSIVE(α), except that its output does not present overlapping. PASSIVE$^S(\alpha)$ supplies "examples", that is, couples (stream of events, action) that can be viewed as chronicles subsumed by the chronicles to model. The learner knows that the events provided are exactly those that have triggered off α; PASSIVE$^S(\alpha)$ therefore can be viewed as providing a "one-way help", from the operator to the assistant (the assistant knowing that there is no overlapping). From this point of view, PASSIVE$^S(\alpha)$ is an interesting intermediate between PASSIVE(α), where no explicit help exists between the assistant and the operator, and the following oracles, that represent "two-way helps".

• ACTIVE$_{MQ}(\alpha)$ takes for parameter some set of events from a and some action from α, and is answered "Yes" or "No", depending on the action can be triggered off by this set of events.

• ACTIVE$_{EQ}(\alpha)$ takes for parameter a chronicle (or a set of chronicles) involving an action from α, and is answered (by the operator) either "Yes" if it is judged as correct (and the chronicle is added to the Confirmed Base), or "No", and in that latter case, a stream of events is provided by the operator, for which the chronicle fails.

• ACTIVE$_{GQ}(\alpha)$ takes for parameter a chronicle (or a set of chronicles) involving an action from α, and is answered (by the operator) "Yes" iff any stream of events triggering off the action from α would be triggered off by the chronicle (or one of the set). Otherwise, a stream of events is returned, that can trigger off the action, for which the chronicle fails. This can be viewed as a "generality" query.

Concerning the two passive oracles, we suppose that events (or the examples) are provided according to some unknown, but fixed probability distribution D. In the end of this section we examine a relaxation on the main flaw of this strong hypothesis, which is to take into account the evolution of D through time. The assistant is therefore supplied with streams of type $s_{i_1}, \alpha_{i_1}, s_{i_2}, \alpha_{i_2}, ...$ indexed by time points. s_{i_k} is a stream of events, having a certain probability to appear, that triggers off α_{i_k}. The aim of the assistant is to guarantee, with a certain confidence, that, from a fixed and reasonable time, he shall trigger off the actions from α approximatively "at the same time" they are triggered off in the stream he receives from the passive oracle(s). This means that, if the operator is removed (when we can consider that the learning task for α has ended, see figure 1), and if, say, the assistant re! ceives a stream $s_{i_t}, s_{i_{t+1}}, ...$, then its "failure" probability will be no more than, say $0 < \epsilon < 1$. Which means that, with probability $1 - \epsilon$, α_{i_t} will be triggered off after the appearance of the last event of s_{i_t}, but not after the appearance of the first event of $s_{i_{t+1}}$.

We define two models of learnability, using passive and active oracles, that can be related to the classical PAC-model and to the Exact-Identification-model. In order not to laden our notations, we keep these two names. We note as $c(\alpha)$ the set of chronicles to learn, that trigger off the actions from α, $|c(\alpha)|$ the size of the writing of $c(\alpha)$, and Ω some oracle(s) belonging to the previously enumerated set.

Definition 1 *Let $a = \{a_1, ..., a_n\}$ some set of events, and $\alpha = \{\alpha_1, ..., \alpha_{M_1}\}$ some set of actions to learn, depending on a. We shall say that α is PAC-learnable using Ω if there exists a learning algorithm L using Ω and a polynomial $p(.,.,.,.)$ such that, for any $0 < \epsilon, \delta < 1$ (resp. accuracy and confidence parameters), for any D, after a time bounded by $p(n, \frac{1}{\epsilon}, \frac{1}{\delta}, |c(\alpha)|)$, L puts a set of chronicles $c'(\alpha)$ in the confirmed chronicle base such that*

$$P(P_D(c'(\alpha)\, fails) > \epsilon) < \delta$$

Definition 2 *Let $a = \{a_1, ..., a_n\}$ some set of events, and $\alpha = \{\alpha_1, ..., \alpha_{M_1}\}$ some set of actions to learn, depending on a. We shall say that α is Exactly-Identifiable using Ω if there exists a learning algorithm L using Ω and a polynomial $p(.,.)$ such that, after a time bounded by $p(n, |c(\alpha)|)$, L puts a set of chronicles $c'(\alpha)$ in the confirmed chronicle base equivalent to $c(\alpha)$.*

In the case of the PAC-model, we always have PASSIVE(α)$\subseteq \Omega$ or PASSIVE$^S(\alpha)\subseteq \Omega$; in the case of the Exact-Identification-model, we always have ACTIVE$_{MQ}(\alpha)\subseteq \Omega$. As the reader shall remark (§5), the algorithm proposed for the assistant uses a threshold to put the learnt chronicles in the confirmed base, corresponding to a number of times the actions of the corresponding chronicle were triggered off. Under some assumptions, the algorithm can be viewed as learning monotonous monomials from positive examples only ((Kearns 1989, Kearns & Vazirani 1994)). For the sake of clarity, if we suppose that $|\alpha| = 1$, the threshold t_α for putting α in the confirmed base can be calculated in the same way as (Rivest 1987), theorem 4. If α is triggered by k (constant) chronicles, depending on the fact that the size of a chronicle can be considered as unfixed or constant, the dependance on n in t_α comes from $\mathcal{O}(n)$ to $\mathcal{O}(ln(n))$. The logarithmic dependance in n is important, as n can be very large, and therefore the human factor can be of great help for the threshold calculation.
If we consider D, the main problem it raises is that many set of events might have a probability of appearing varying through time, because of the evolution of the network characteristics. In the other hand, this is not the case for all events: some of them (such as natural events, or unpredictable accidents) may be considered as having a constant appearing probability. Thus, a better framework would allow such variations of D. For example, an unoptimal model would allow the "weight" of any event e at time t, $w_t(e)$, to behave as $w_t(e) \leq \frac{1}{\beta} w_{t'}(e), \forall t' \leq t$. In that case, the learning model remains the same, except that L is required to learn for any such fixed β, and the alloted time is required to have polynomial dependence in $\frac{1}{\beta}$. The fixation of β as small as desired allows to keep closer to reality. The drawback of

fixing β as small as desired is of course that the threshold for any chronicle will be much higher: in the case of PASSIVE$^S(\alpha)$,its dependance in β is $\mathcal{O}\left(\frac{1}{\beta}\right)$ (Proof similar as (Rivest 1987), theorem 4).

4.2 Positive results for learning chronicles

Proposition 1 *If any action from the set α can be supposed to appear in a single chronicle, then*

1. *α is PAC-learnable using PASSIVE$^S(\alpha)$.*
2. *α is PAC-learnable using ACTIVE$_{MQ}(\alpha)$ and PASSIVE(α), and the chronicles built are at least as accurate as those of 1.*
3. *α is Exactly-Identifiable using ACTIVE$_{MQ}(\alpha)$ and ACTIVE$_{GQ}(\alpha)$.*

Parts 1–2 of the previous property raise the problem of learning without ACTIVE$_{MQ}(\alpha)$ or PASSIVE$^S(\alpha)$, thus using only PASSIVE(α), when there exists overlapping between chronicles. Such a problem seems hardly manageable since, provided there are only two disjoint chronicles, we can create some distribution over the events that forces the two chronicles to trigger off almost at the same time, and that forces nealry all their events to appear before any triggering off of one of the two actions. By this, we force at least one chronicle to appear to the assistant much bigger than it should be; this tends to show the usefulness of PASSIVE$^S(\alpha)$ or ACTIVE$_{MQ}(\alpha)$. It is worthwile remarking that even if PAC-learning is not manageable, we could find heuristics in some particular cases, satisfying from an algorithmic point of view. Denote as a "size-k"-overlapping an overlapping where for any two consecutive actions α_i and α_j (triggered off in this order), at most k events happening between the two actions do not participate to the triggering off of α_j. In that case, without learning the chronicles according to definition 1, we could come close to good chronicles, in a satisfying way (possibly closer than $2k$ from the chronicles we would have learnt without overlapping). Such a procedure would be all the more satisfying if the chronicles could be considered as having a large size.
Concerning the cases where an action can be triggered off by multiple chronicles, the learning problem is at least as difficult as for k-term-DNF. It seems that ACTIVE$_{MQ}(\alpha)$ and ACTIVE$_{GQ}(\alpha)$ are not sufficient to Exactly-Identify such multiple chronicles, particularly for the exact-identification of the time constraints. The exact identification apparently needs another oracle quite similar to ACTIVE$_{GQ}(\alpha)$, and is therefore very costly with respect to the operator.

4.3 Hardness results for learning chronicles

The purpose of this section is to show how useful is the operator (in the form of ACTIVE$_{MQ}(\alpha)$) for the learning task. Namely, even if the chronicles are simple,

and already under simple situations, even using different types of oracles, we show that trying to identify them as exactly as possible, or even sometimes learning them, can be very hard. As the reader might have remarked before, some results turn out to be positive when the operator can help by $\text{ACTIVE}_{MQ}(\alpha)$. Exact identification is a stronger task than learning; however, this can be useful to achieve better understanding of the actions; furthermore, the application algorithms are generally implicitly constructed quite as optimization algorithms than learning algorithms.
In order to prove negative results already in simple cases, the propositions of this section make the following assumptions on the learning framework:

1. The events concern only a single action, that is, $|\alpha| = 1$.
2. Calls to $\text{PASSIVE}^S(\alpha)$, $\text{ACTIVE}_{EQ}(\alpha)$ and $\text{ACTIVE}_{GQ}(\alpha)$ are authorized.

In order to formulate our optimization result, we fix as $k-$chronicles the set of chronicles having size not bigger than k. RP denotes the class of polynomial-time randomized algorithms as defined by (Balcazar, Diaz & Gabarro 1988).

Proposition 2 *Under the learning framework of assumptions 1-2, if α only belongs to one chronicle, unless $RP = NP$, no PAC-learning algorithm can learn $c(\alpha)$ by $|c(\alpha)|$-chronicle.*

(Proof made by reduction from the Set-Cover problem (Garey & Johnson 1979)).

Proposition 3 *Under the learning framework of assumptions 1-2, even if the events appear at different times each, with constant time between events and actions, if α is triggered off by only three sets of events, α is not PAC-learnable unless $RP = NP$.*

(Proof made by reduction from Graph-3-Colorability (Garey & Johnson 1979)).

5 PRACTICAL RESULTS: THE LEARNING SYSTEM

Before beginning the description of our system, let us assume that the set of events and actions is finite and "relatively small", in order to generate a reasonable amount of chronicles with enough genericity. We will furthermore consider a particular action called "silence", which does not correspond to any actions of the supervision operator, but which is useful to generate particular chronicles : filters.

Definition 3 *A filter is a chronicle* $\{(a_{t_1}, t_1), (a_{t_2}, t_2)...(a_{t_i}, t_i); \delta_1 = t_2 - t_1, \delta_2, ..., \delta_{i-1}\} \Rightarrow$ $silence$

Filters are used to decrease the sum of the events displayed to the operator: when the corresponding events are received, the system simply ignores them. Given that many different sequences of events can lead to the action "silence", it is hard to learn them without using the operator or the assistants' help (see §4). Learnt chronicles will consist in a set of events terminated by an action. We will see later how we deal with temporal constraints and "holds". As the supervision operator has to interact with the Learning System (for instance to confirm chronicles), it is important for him to understand how our system learns. We believe that incremental learning is easier to follow by a human operator. Furthermore, if the learning algorithm is fast enough, it can be used in realtime, just like the Recognition System, thus enabling better cooperation. The chronicle learning is processed in three steps :

- The chronicle creation
- The chronicle evaluation
- The chronicle confirmation

5.1 The Chronicle Creation

A chronicle is created in two cases:

- When the supervision operator triggers an action: the created chronicle is the set of the received events before the action, plus the action itself.
- When nothing happens during a given time interval: neither received events nor actions. The created chronicle (which will be used as a filter) is the set of the received events since the previous action, followed by the action "silence".

In some cases, the operator triggers several actions in a row, without waiting for the reception of new events. This can have several meanings:

1. these actions all correspond to the whole sequence of the received events;
2. each action corresponds to a subsequence of the received events;
3. a combination of the two previous possibilities.

In the actual system, we have assumed that we only have to face the first possibility. The sequence of actions is therefore considered as one single action which is the concatenation of the sequence. The second possibility corresponds in fact to the more general problem of overlapping chronicles, which is hard to manage. This issue has been discussed in section §4.2. A possible heuristic would be to bufferize the k last received events independently of the triggered actions. When the sum of the received events reaches a certain threshold T which models the memory capacity of the operator, only the T last events are buffered (this also helps to satisfy learnability constraints expressed in section §4.1). Obviously, when the action is triggered by the Recognition System, the corresponding events are deleted, since the corresponding chronicle has already been learnt.

5.2 The Chronicle Evaluation

Now we have to know whether the created chronicle is worth being added to the Unconfirmed Chronicle Base. First we need to define two operators: the inclusion ($\subset$) and the subtraction ($\setminus$) between two chronicles. A chronicle A is included in chronicle B iff their actions are equal and A's sequence of events is a "subword" of B's sequence of events. Dates of occurence of the events are not compared. If $A \subset B$, then we can subtract A from B by removing A's events from B's sequence of events and replacing B's action with the action "silence". The result is what we call a "filter". Of course the result of a subtraction can depend on how to select the subword in B. An easy way is to select the first occurence of each event. For more "realism", it can be interesting to minimize the date differences, but this can be too costly, except if we do not want to obtain necessarily the "best" subword. Another operation is the creation of temporal constraints. By increasing time intervals, we can somehow "generalize" chronicles by accepting chronicles with the same sequence of events and with different time points. Obviously, we only create temporal constraints between two consecutive events, since otherwise trying to create some kind of adequate "constraint-tree" (the root being the first event) would be too costly and not necessarily useful. Remember that we try to preserve a realtime learning algorithm ! Here is the evaluation of a new chronicle C, created following the previous step, given his action a :

```
C is a chronicle with an action a
Begin
    Trust(C) := 1 ;
    For each C' ∈ CB so that C'(action) = a
        Switch C
            Case C ⊆ C' : exit ;
            Case C ⊃ C' : create-and-evaluate-filter
                C'' := C \ C'; exit ;
            Otherwise : continue ;
    For each C' ∈ the UCB so that C'(action) = a
        Switch C
            Case C ⊂ C' add C to the UCB
                Trust(C) := Trust(C') + 1 ;
                remove C' from the UCB ;
                create-and-evaluate-filter C'' := C' \ C ;
            Case C ⊇ C'
                create-and-evaluate-filter C'' := C \ C' ;
                widen C' time interval ;
                Trust(C')++ ;
            Otherwise : continue ;
    add C to the UCB ;
End
```

Filters, like C'', created during the evaluation algorithm must also be evaluated. However, their evaluation is easier, since we do not need to create other chronicles during the evaluation. So far we have favoured the creation of "long" filters, *i.e.* when detecting inclusions between filters, we keep the longer. The opposite point of view can also be considered. It must be noted that the above algorithms may be a valid learning algorithm when no overlapping of events occurs. However, when it is not the case, it becomes a heuristic.

5.3 The Chronicle Confirmation

Now that we have put chronicles in the Unconfirmed Chronicle Base, the question is : when can we put those in the Confirmed Chronicle Base ? We have basically two ways of doing this :

- When the "trust" in a chronicle reaches a certain threshold, it can be automatically confirmed.
- The operator can confirm manually a chronicle by simply "clicking" on it. Here, the operator plays approximatively the role of the ACTIVE_{EQ} oracle. To play it completely, it would be necessary for him to bring the assistant a case where the chronicle fails.

Note that there is a need for a coherence maintenance system in the Confirmed Chronicle base. Indeed, if the system encounters cases where the same sequence of events leads to different actions, it has to detect them. This can be done by comparing each new chronicle to those stored in the Chronicle Base and trying to find inclusions (this time with different actions). Coherence maintenance is not important concerning the Unconfirmed Chronicle base, since those chronicles are not used yet in the recognition system. But this could also help creating "holds": the events obtained by the subtraction of two chronicles with different actions would correspond to "holds".

5.4 Experimentation and First Results

The learning system has been integrated in our experimental and simple network management platform, MAGENTA (Esfandiari, Deflandre, Quinqueton & Dony 1996), which is roughly compatible with ISO and CCITT specifications, namely the Manager-Agent model, GDMO (ISO 1990*b*) and CMIS (ISO 1990*a*). MAGENTA agents can answer queries sent by the MAGENTA manager by browsing network resources. These agents can also spontaneously send notifications to the manager when some specified events occur in the network. These notifications will be considered as events by our assistant. Figure 2 shows MAGENTA's interface for the assistant, which is composed of the following parts:

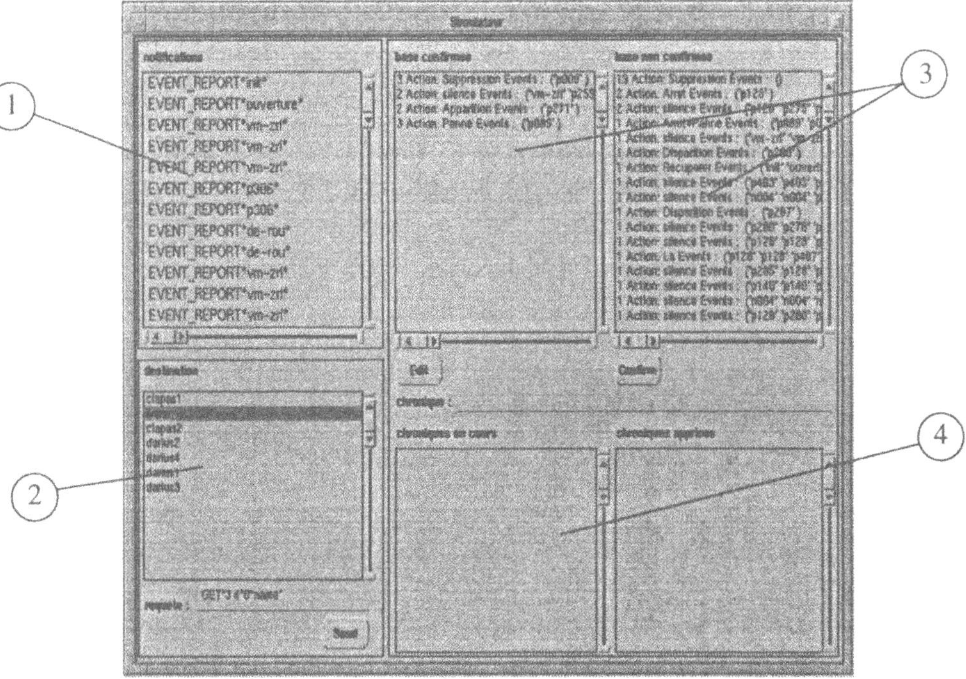

Figure 2 The assistant's interface

1. The "notification" window displays the received events;
2. The "query" window enables the sending of queries to MAGENTA agents by typing the query and designating the agent. These queries can be considered as actions;
3. The "chronicle bases" window displays both the UCB and the CB and therefore shows the Learning System's activity. It is possible to "confirm" a chronicle of the UCB and "edit" any chronicle. The interface should be more ergonomic in the future in order to be easily understood and accepted by the user. For instance, chronicles could be displayed in a graphical way.
4. The lower right part of the interface is dedicated to the Chronicle Recognition System. We have not connected it to our Learning system yet.

The assistant has been tested with data taken from a simulation of a french packet-switched data network. The actions to be triggered off are part of these data (they have been generated by a specific expert system). Results show that with a very small sample of events corresponding to thirty hours of simulation, the assistant behaves quite well, learning five acceptable chronicles out of ten that reached the confirmation threshold. These results are all the more valid as these data contain lots of overlaps, and the actions are not necessarily triggered off by a single sequence of events: these two cases make the algorithm behave only as a heuristic. However, the learnt filters were not satisfying: they did not even reach the confirmation threshold.

We have also tested the assistant on a problem where we could reasonably suppose that there were no overlaps: the data were generated by the behaviour of a user of a programming environment. Some of the generated chronicles were very pertinent and really corresponded to the desire of the user.

6 RELATED WORKS

Building interface agents (sometimes also called software agents) is a very active research field, mostly due to the development of the World Wide Web. The reader shall read for instance (Maes & Kozierok 1993) or (Schlimmer & Hermens 1993). However, we have not so far found papers dealing explicitly with temporal knowledge. Learnability issues are also seldom dealt with.

In network management and supervision, many intelligent architectures, such as expert systems, have been designed to help the operator's tasks, taking in account realtime aspects (Gaïti 1991) (Garijo & Hoffman 1992). The authors only mention the addition of learning mechanisms as a promising perspective.

7 CONCLUSION AND PERSPECTIVES

In this article, we present a chronicle learning system that has been implemented and tested in a realworld domain: network management. We have also studied a learnability model relevant to our framework and raised theoretical results which show the utility of cooperation between the machine assistant and the operator. These results show also that the construction of chronicles is a difficult task. The main difficulty, which is specific to our framework, is the possibility of overlapping between chronicles, that raises the heuristical character of our algorithms. However, without such overlaps, the algorithm behaves quite well, particularly by preventing excessive generalizations, a desirable property (Dousson 1994). In order to improve our system, it would be interesting to better the management of the overlaps, as well as to quantify the loss in performances created in our heuristic. Moreover, the extension of events to first order formalism could increase the semantical value of the learnt chronicles.

But our results, be they theoretical or practical, showed the importance of the help provided by the operator or other assistants. The next important step in our work will be to interconnect assistants in order to accelerate (or to allow !) the learning task. Thus, the assistants would be able to query each other instead of replacing a treamount of events received by the operator by a treamount of questions.

REFERENCES

Balcazar, J. L., Diaz, J. & Gabarro, J. (1988), *Structural Complexity I*, Springer Ver-

lag.
Dousson, C. (1994), Suivi d'évolutions et reconnaissance de chroniques, University thesis, Université Paul Sabatier, Toulouse, LAAS.
Esfandiari, B., Deflandre, G., Quinqueton, J. & Dony, C. (1996), 'Agent-oriented techniques for network supervision', *Annals of Telecommunications* **51**(9-10), 521–529.
Esfandiari, B., Nock, R. & Quinqueton, J. (1996), Réseau futé: Techniques d'intelligence artificielle distribuée pour la supervision-maintenance des réseaux, Progress Report 5, CNRS/CNET 93 1B 142 Proj 5115.
Gaïti, D. (1991), L'utilisation des techniques de l'intelligence artificielle pour la gestion des réseaux, Thèse d'université, Université Paris 6.
Garey, M. & Johnson, D. (1979), *Computers and Intractability, a guide to the theory of NP-Completeness*, Bell Telephone Laboratories.
Garijo, F. J. & Hoffman, D. (1992), A multi-agent architecture for operation and maintenance of telecommunication networks, *in* J. P. Haton, ed., 'Proceedings of the 12th Int. Avignon Conference', EC2 and AFIA, EC2, Paris, pp. 427–436.
Ghallab, M. (1994), Past and future chronicles for supervision and planning, *in* J. P. Haton, ed., 'Proceedings of the 14th Int. Avignon Conference', EC2 and AFIA, EC2, Paris, pp. 23–34.
ISO (1990*a*), *Information Technology - Open Systems Interconnection - Common Management Information Service Definition*. 2nd DP N3070.
ISO (1990*b*), *Information Technology - Structure of Management Information - Part 4. Guidelines for the Definition of Managed Objects*.
Kearns, M. J. (1989), *The Computational Complexity of Machine Learning*, M.I.T. Press.
Kearns, M. J. & Vazirani, U. V. (1994), *An Introduction to Computational Learning Theory*, M.I.T. Press.
Maes, P. & Kozierok, R. (1993), Learning interface agents, *in* 'Proceedings of the 11th Nat Conf on Artificial Intelligence', AAAI, MIT-Press/AAAI-Press.
Rivest, R. (1987), 'Learning decision lists', *Machine Learning* pp. 229–246.
Schlimmer, J. & Hermens, L. (1993), 'Software agents: Completing patterns and constructing user interfaces', *Journal of Applied Intelligence Research* **1**, 61–89.

8 BIOGRAPHY

Joël Quinqueton is graduated from the french Ecole Polytechnique, 1971, and got both PhD thesis (1976) and State Thesis (1981) from the Paris 6 University, in the field of Pattern Recognition and Artificial Intelligence. He is currently Research Director at INRIA and works in the Knowledge Acquisition and Representation Department of LIRMM, in Montpellier, France. His Research fields are Multi agent systems and Machine Learning.
Richard Nock got an Engineer Degree from the Ecole Nationale Superieure Agronomique

de Montpellier, and is now terminating a PhD thesis at LIRMM, in the field of Machine Learning, specially on Computational Learning Theory.
Babak Esfandiari got an Engineer Degree from the Institut des Sciences de l'Ingenieur de Montpellier, and a PhD thesis at LIRMM (January 1997), in the field of Agent Oriented techniques applied to Telecommunication Networks. He participated actively to the the "Réseau futé (Smart Net)" project, and is now at Mitel Corp, Ottawa, Canada.

ACKNOWLEDGMENTS

This work is part of the "Réseau Futé" project, which is supported by France Telecom - CNET under contract no 93 1B 141/142/143 5115.

PART FIVE

Object-oriented

11
DiSC - An Object Oriented Distributed Session Control Implemented with Java

E. Wedlund, C. Johnsson***
Ericsson Telecom AB
Switchlab, Dialoggatan 1, S-126 25 Stockholm Sweden
Phone: +46 8 719 85 96, +46 8 719 4903***
Fax: +46 8 719 66 77
etxelin@kk.ericsson.se, qtxcjo@kk.ericsson.se***

B. J. Olsson
Communicator Teleplan AB
Box 1310, S-171 25 Solna, Sweden
Phone: +46 8 7644500
Fax: +46 8 7644066
bengt.j.olsson@communicator.se

Abstract

Traditional session control is not a sufficient solution in a multimedia services network, it must be renewed in order to handle multimedia and multiuser sessions. In this paper we address this issue and present a proposal for a solution, which we call Distributed Session Control (DiSC). DiSC can be seen both as an overall solution for session control in a network, and simply as a tool for creating complex multimedia sessions. One of the strengths of DiSC is that it does not dictate a new type of network architecture, but will operate on those already existing.

Keywords

signalling, session control, network management, service provisioning, middleware

Intelligent Networks and Intelligence in Networks D. Gaiti (Ed.)
Published by Chapman & Hall

1 INTRODUCTION

This paper describes an object oriented Distributed Session Control (DiSC) for multimedia services networks. The demands placed on a multimedia service network are that it should be flexible, in terms of introducing new services, and that it possibly should support QoS and security, and thereby also billing. Introducing new services can be simplified by moving session and network related issues to a dedicated session control function, such as DiSC, instead of having to deal with it in the applications. Services in the network are expected to be distributed, i.e., a service application can be located so that it is accessible by several/all users in the network. This is supported by e.g. Java and CORBA.

The difference between a multimedia services network and an "old" network, regarding the session control, is that before, a session mainly consisted of two users and one service (POTS). In a multimedia services network, a session can consist of an unlimited number of users and services. In order to support this, a new type of session control is needed. The requirements that can be placed on this session control are:

- Complexity must not grow more than linearly with the number of users and services in a session.
- A user, or an application started by the user, should be able to use an appropriate QoS (if supported by the network).
- It should be possible to charge a user based on different session characteristics.
- It should be possible to use different networks for the same service.

Traditional telecommunication session control implies too much complexity to handle multiuser, multimedia sessions. DiSC solves the complexity problem by using an object oriented view of the session. Distribution of the session control also reduces complexity as well as scaling problems, since each user only keeps information that is relevant for that user.

DiSC is more light-weight than other approaches for multimedia services networks, e.g. TINA (Chapman et al. 1995), in that it only provides a solution for the session handling of the network, which means that it can be used on any existing network. DiSC is not defined for a specific network, which is the case for e.g. the ITU-T H.323 series. In fact, DiSC can interwork with these protocols for creation of connections on various networks, see figure 1 for an example with the H.323 series.

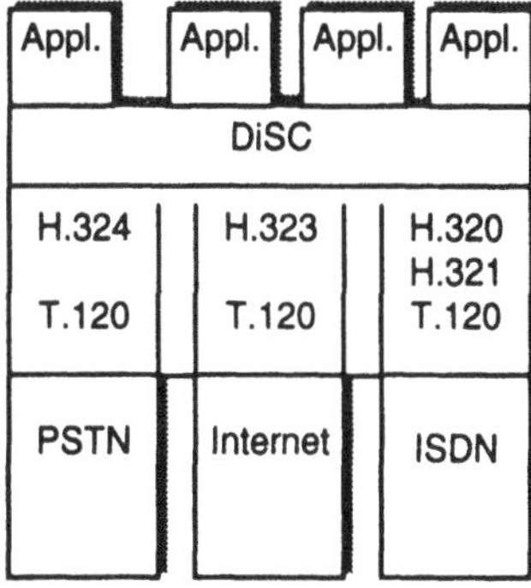

Figure 1. Network Integration through DiSC interworking with the H.323 series.

2 DISTRIBUTED SESSION CONTROL

A project at Bellcore, called the EXPANSE project (Minzer 1991, 1993) introduced an object oriented call model, and a concept of each user having a User Request Manager (URM), which handled negotiation for session establishment. This project was focused on the ISDN, and we have not seen anything from it in the last years. Since we found it to be a useful way of handling the session control, not only for ISDN, we decided to use it in our project.

The Distributed Session Control (DiSC) uses the same call model as the one in the EXPANSE project at Bellcore (Minzer, 1991, 1993). In DiSC, each user also has its own User Request Manager (URM), which handles all negotiation with other URMs for creating and tearing down sessions. The URM can either be placed in the user's computer or in another place in the network.

When discussing DiSC, the term "user" does not necessarily mean a human being, but can also be a distributed application compliant with DiSC, e.g. a media on demand server, or a video conferencing service. This means that there are two ways of using DiSC - as a person to person communication and negotiation, where an application is used for transferring and presenting data between users, and as a tool for a person to utilise distributed applications.

DiSC offers a very flexible and generic model of session control, but one example of its use in a commercial environment is how DiSC can be used by a network operator, which is shown in Figure 2. The service provisioning can be centralised and administered by the network operator, who would benefit from the higher service content. The user would also benefit, since he will be offered compatible services and an easier way to utilise the network(s). In Figure 2, the application server stores applications that can be downloaded when necessary instead of residing at the user's computer. The context server keeps information of what users are possible to contact, and the URM server can have many user's URMs running.

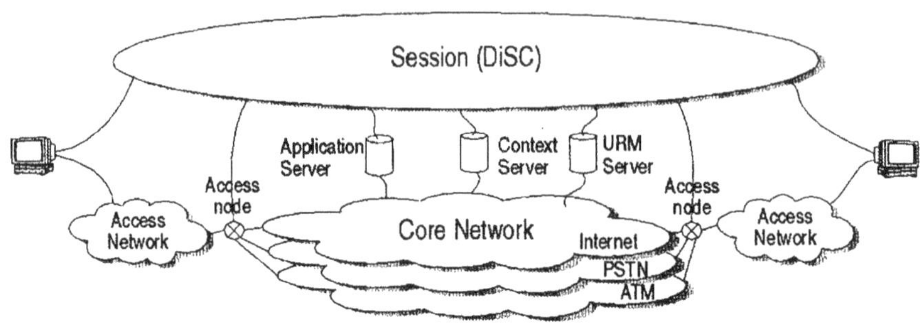

Figure 2.

2.1 A Brief Description of DiSC

Figure 3 shows a network scenario with a user "Claes" who has his URM in his own computer, and a user "Elin" who has her URM in another computer in the network. They are involved in a video conference, where the audio part uses a separate connection. How this session was established will be described further below.

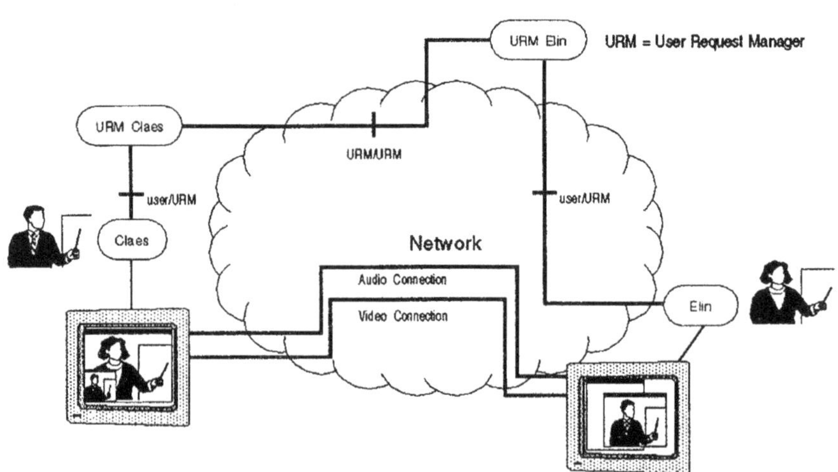

Figure 3. A two-party video conference session.

The User Request Manager (URM) has a LocalView, which describes the session as a tree of objects - DiSCObjects (in EXPANSE denoted call objects). The LocalView only describes the session as viewed from the user, and contains only information that is relevant for the user. Each DiSCObject in the LocalView represents an essential part of the session, e.g. what user is involved, what service is being used, and so on. The signalling for creating, modifying, or tearing down a session is represented as methods for creating or deleting DiSCObjects in the LocalView. The objects in the LocalView, and their relations, are presented in Figure 4, and listed in Table 1.

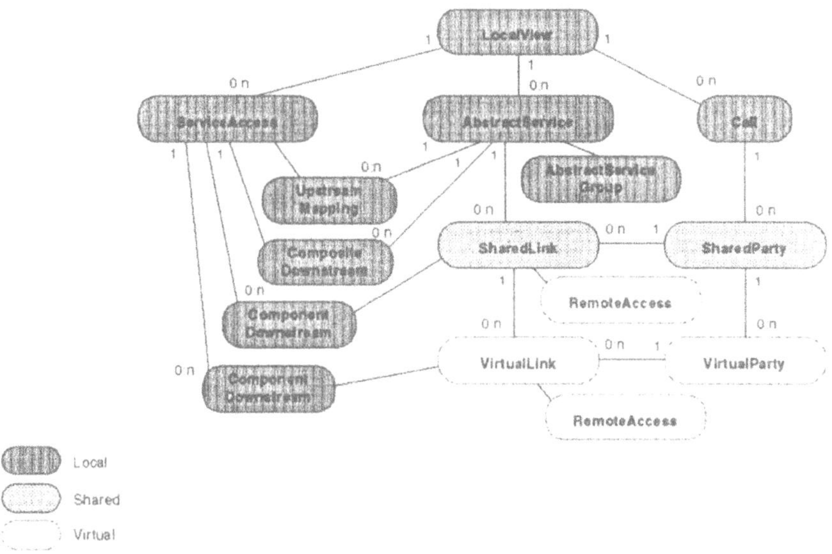

Figure 4. The LocalView.

Table 1.

Object	Explanation
SharedParty	An object representation of a user. Creation of a SharedParty requires confirmation from the remote user which the SharedParty represents. When a SharedParty is created, a corresponding SharedParty is created in the LocalView of the remote user. The SharedParty may contain VirtualParties (see below).
VirtualParty	A reference to a SharedParty in another LocalView.
Call	A call is an association of SharedParties.

SharedLink	Associates a SharedParty with an AbstractService, i.e. defines what service(s) the SharedParty will use for communication.
VirtualLink	A reference to a SharedLink in another LocalView. The user is free to "use" the VirtualLink by creating mapping elements to it. A user can not affect the creation or deletion of a VirtualLink.
AbstractService	Defines a communication service in abstract terms, e.g. video, text, data, etc.
ServiceAccess	An object representation of the network access for the given service. Attributes in the ServiceAccess can be what protocol to be used, if the channel is uni- or bi-directional, a port number etc.
RemoteAccess	An object that describes the ServiceAccess and Mapping at the remote user.
AbstractServiceGroup	AbstractServices may be grouped together in order to enable e.g. synchronisation between different services.
UpstreamMapping	Associates a ServiceAccess with an AbstractService, and makes data produced by the user accessible to the parties in the Call.
CompositeDownstream	A CompositeDownstream mapping element takes data from all the parties associated with that AbstractService and presents it to the user.
ComponentDownstream	The ComponentDownstream mapping element takes data from a specific link (shared or virtual) and presents it to the user.

The DiSCObjects can be divided into three groups: shared, virtual, and local DiSCObjects:

- Shared DiSCObjects can not be created without consent from the remote side. They are always created in pair, e.g., if the user Elin wants to create a SharedParty Claes in her LocalView, she must ask the user Claes to create a

SharedParty Elin in his LocalView. If Claes agrees to that, both objects will be created.

- Virtual DiSCObjects are references to shared DiSCObjects in other LocalViews. For instance, let us say that Elin and Claes have agreed to create the SharedParties as stated above. If Elin later on decides to call another user Bengt in the same call, she will inform Claes of this by telling him to create a VirtualParty hanging under the SharedParty Elin in his LocalView. She will also tell Bengt that there already is one person involved in the call by telling him to create the VirtualParty Claes. A user can not manipulate a virtual object, but it is possible to e.g. create mapping elements to a VirtualLink. The purpose of having shared and virtual objects is to point out who is responsible for that object. Virtual objects are also used for supplying information.
- Local DiSCObjects are objects that only the user has control of. The user may create or delete local objects, although deletion of a local object may cause deletion of shared object, which requires negotiation with other users. For instance, a call is a local object, but in order to delete a call, all SharedParties in it must be deleted. Vice versa - if all the parties in a call have been deleted, there is no use in keeping the call, so it is automatically deleted.

The LocalView in "URM Claes" from Figure 3 is presented in Figure 5. The negotiation needed to create it is presented in Figure 6.

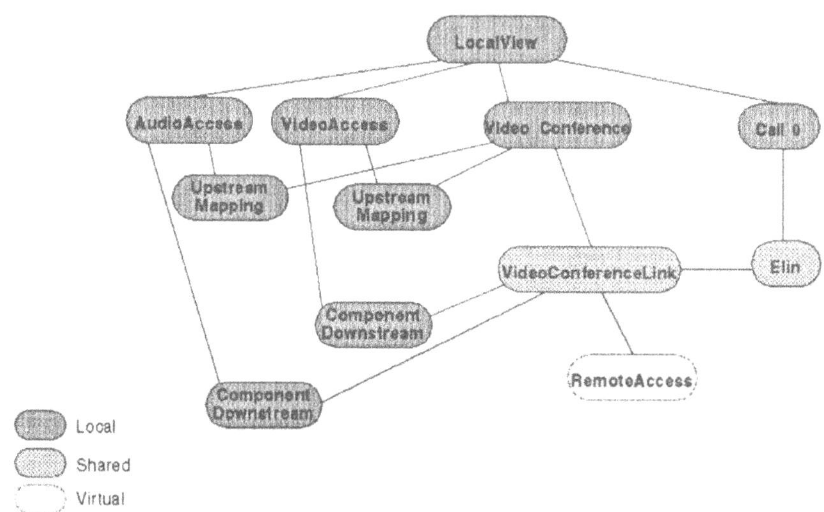

Figure 5.The LocalView for URM Claes.

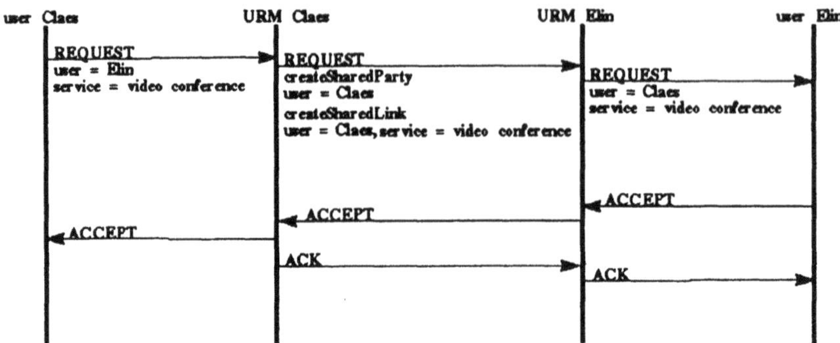

Figure 6. A request.

What is not shown in Figure 6, is the creation of the local objects. Some of them, like a Call or an AbstractService are created automatically by the URM. The mapping can also be created automatically, but the user should be able to change the mapping according to his needs by sending a request to his URM. This is further discussed in section 4.

3 DISC INTERFACE - JAVA VS. CORBA

We have implemented DiSC in Java, and the communication between the URMs is carried out by making Remote Method Invocations (RMIs). This simplifies the implementation of the user/URM, and URM/URM interfaces, but binds DiSC to be implemented in Java. A possibility is to use CORBA for the RMIs, which will allow for any language to be used for the implementation of the user and/or URM. The drawback is that the interfaces will become more complicated to implement. The differences between Java RMI and CORBA are listed in Table 2.

Table 2 Java vs. CORBA

subject	CORBA	Java RMI
Object Types	The code for an object that is passed in a method invocation must exist on both sides of the call. Therefore, objects are passed as the type declared by the interface, even if they are of a derived type.	If the code for an object that is passed in a method invocation does not exist, it is downloaded. Therefore, the object type is preserved, even if the interface has declared a more general type.

Complexity	The objects in the implementation must be mapped onto the object model of the Interface Description Language (IDL) in CORBA.	Since the RMI interface is written in the same language as the rest of the code, this does not imply any difficulties.
Garbage Collection	CORBA supports programming languages that do not have garbage collection. Therefore there is no garbage collector, and the programmer must know when an object should be disposed.	Java has a garbage collector which automatically removes an object if it has no references to it.
Security	No support for security specified.	Support for security.

Another technique for object distribution is Microsoft's DCOM, which like CORBA, is language independent. It has garbage collection, support for security, and can use any available network protocol (not just TCP/IP). However, it has only been available for Windows NT until now, which is one of the reasons why we have not used it.

Our experiences from using Java and Java RMI, are that the RMIs takes a large amount of time, even though this is improving continuously. We also regret that there is no possibility to control the number of TCP connections that are created to carry the RMIs, and that you may not use UDP for this, which probably would improve performance.

We have decided to continue to use Java RMI, mainly to avoid the work implementing a CORBA interface would require. We also anticipate that if the development of Java and Java RMI will continue at the same speed as it is now, it will be a strong competitor to CORBA.

4 ISSUES FOR DISCUSSION

Currently, we have implemented DiSC as a simple conference tool with a few services available on an IP network - since our initial objective simply was to try out how DiSC could be implemented. We have experienced that it is difficult to keep the flexibility of the LocalView when implementing it, since different services can have completely different attributes, and allow different types of session configurations. We have also come to the conclusion that the most likely future for DiSC is to be used as a middleware between an application and the network, and not as a tool itself, and therefore we intend to define an Application Programmer Interface (API). These issues are discussed in the sections below.

4.1 Rules

The LocalView can describe practically all possible and impossible connection scenarios. It is therefore necessary to apply rules to DiSC so that it only describes sessions that are possible to actually create in the real world. For instance, it is theoretically possible to describe a session with one user transmitting voice, and the other user converting it into a video stream before presenting it on the screen. In most cases, we do not want the URM to allow this, since there probably are not many users who have access to a voice to video converter. However, since we do not want to limit the model, the rules should be able to change, both in time and depending on the environment.

Other situations where rules should be applied is e.g.: Should mapping be created automatically when a SharedLink or AbstractService is created? When are network resources reserved? Who is responsible and thus accountable for the call? In these cases, the rules can depend on the type of service, and a user should be able to make personal rules.

The best solution is probably to have a database with rules from which the URM can check what it is supposed to do. The user should be able to update the database with personal rules on e.g. creation of mapping objects, and the network administrator can update it with new network devices etc.

4.2 Network and Application APIs

DiSC introduces an abstract layer of associations between users and services. In order to create the necessary connections, the LocalView must be instantiated in the network. Also allocation of resources for synchronisation, data conversion etc. might need to be done. DiSC currently uses existing APIs to handle e.g. sockets.

As stated before, there are two ways of using DiSC from an applications point of view. From DiSC's point of view, there are three types of applications, which require two different types of interfaces:

- Traditional applications. Already existing applications that handle the creation of connections themselves, for instance through WinSock in a Windows environment. What DiSC can offer to these applications of course depends on how each application sets up connections. DiSC cannot directly interfere with the creation of connections, but in some cases, it might be possible to improve it through DiSC, e.g. by letting DiSC override the WinSock if that is what the application uses (see Figure 7). What DiSC can do here is to know if the connection should be multicast or singlecast, and to let the user decide on some attributes of the connections.

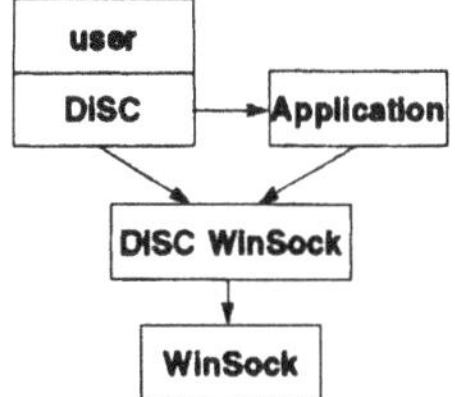

Figure 7 Traditional Application and DiSC

- Collaborative applications. Applications that are used for user to user or group communication, but which expect that the session control and connection creation will be handled by DiSC, see Figure 8. This type of application will replace the DiSC GUI, and use a DiSC API instead of a network interface. DiSC will handle the creation of connections, so that the application does not have to care if the connection is a multi- or singlecast, if the data must be converted etc. Primitives in the DiSC API would be such as "add user", "create mapping", "change attribute", etc. We are currently working on defining an API.

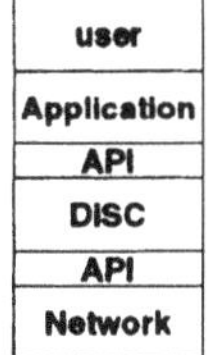

Figure 8 Collaborative Applications and DiSC

- Server applications. Applications that can act as an end user in DiSC. This can be a media on demand server, which users can call through DiSC. Such applications can be written using the DiSC API, so that they can send and receive requests, answer requests etc. (see Figure 9). For instance, if a user calls a service, the service knows what capacity it needs and can respond to the request by demanding the necessary bandwidth.

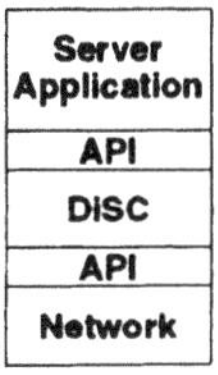

Server Application
API
DiSC
API
Network

Figure 9 Server Applications and DiSC

4.2.1 Creation of Connections

There are mainly two issues that imposes some trouble regarding the creation of connections, and both are introduced by the distribution of the session control. The first one is how to decide whether to create a multicast or unicast connection. If a connection is created when a downstream mapping element is inserted in the LocalView, it is possible to check if the other user(s) have created mapping elements, since this information is kept in the RemoteAccess object. But if none of the others have created downstream mapping elements, there is no possibility to know if the other users in the session are going to create a downstream mapping element. If they will, it would be a good idea to create a multicast connection. This can depend on the type of service being used, e.g. in a video conference, you might not want to see every person you are talking to.

The other problem is: When a session has been established - which URM should create the connection? This also addresses the rule issue: One could have a rule that says that it is the URM who initiated the session who should create the connections. This is not sufficient, though, since a session can be established without anyone wanting to transmit anything yet.

In EXPANSE (Minzer 1993), the network interface is implemented as two levels under the session control level. The first level, called the Transport Resource Manager (TRM) gets a LocalView that has been transformed so that it is easier to identify the network components needed. The URMs communicate so that they do not do overlapping work, and that they can recognise when a connection should be uni- or multicast.

It seems though that it should be possible to make this simpler by always creating mapping elements as soon as a SharedLink is created. This would on the other hand reduce the flexibility of the creation of connections, but again, this can be set by the rules so that a user may choose if he wants a slower but flexible connection setup, or a fast but forcing one.

4.3 Scaling and Complexity

Since DiSC is distributed, scaling problems will not arise just by introducing DiSC to a large network. Perhaps if the URMs are not placed at the users, they might require a lot of memory at the "URM server". This can be solved to some extent by creating semi-centralised URMs that can handle a limited number of users.

If DiSC is to be used for services where a large number of users can be involved in a session, a considerate number of objects will be created and stored. The VirtualParties and VirtualLinks will not use much space, though, since they only are references to SharedParties and SharedLinks in another LocalView. So the one who will take the heavy part is the one with the most SharedParties and SharedLinks, which probably is a part that is responsible for the service somehow. The users (clients) will not have to store large amounts of perhaps irrelevant data.

5 CONCLUSIONS

A key feature of DiSC is that it hides the complexity of the session control from the user and application, which simplifies introduction of new services in a network. An application can be written for DiSC using an API, but already existing applications might also be used with DiSC. Another benefit is that DiSC itself does not require changes on lower levels in the network, since connections can be handled in a traditional way once the session has been created (separation of call and connection control). DiSC supports charging, since it has information about the session on a high level, which can be logged and used for e.g. service based charging.

The main issue when implementing DiSC is how to get the most out of the potential given in the model, without constraining it. As stated in section 4.1, dynamic rules are necessary for customising DiSC, still keeping the flexibility of the model. It is also important, when writing the DiSC API, to make the primitives as general as possible.

Regarding the question if RMI, CORBA, or DCOM should be used, it seems to be a good idea to wait a while before deciding, since RMI still is quite new and unexplored. We will continue our research work using Java for simplicity reasons, but if a commercial system should be created, CORBA might - for the moment - be the best solution.

6 REFERENCES

Chapman, M. and Montesi, S. (1995) Overall Concepts and Principles of TINA, Version 1.0.

Minzer, S. (1991) A Signalling Protocol for Complex Multimedia Services. IEEE Journal on Selected Areas in Communications, Vol. 9, No. 9, 1383-94.

Minzer, S. (1993) EXPANSE Software for Distributed Call and Connection Control. International Journal of Communication Systems, 7, 149-60.

Object Management Group (1997) The Common Object Request Broker: Architecture and Specification.

Weiss, M., Johnsson, A., and Kiniry, J. (1996) Distributed Computing: Java, Corba, and DCE. Open Software Foundation Research Institute.

Sun Microsystems Inc. (1997) Java Remote Method Invocation Specification.

7 BIOGRAPHY

Elin Wedlund received the M. Sc. degree in Electrical Engineering from Lund Institute of Technology in Sweden in 1996. Her master thesis was on the subject of TCP and the ABR service in ATM. Since her graduation she has been working at SwitchLab, which is a lab within Ericsson's applied research organisation, where she studies networking issues.

Claes Jonsson started working at Ericsson in 1995, and has worked on the development of AXE switches before he came to SwitchLab. Alongside his work at Ericsson, he is also a student at the Royal Institute of Technology in Stockholm, where he studies Computer Science. At SwitchLab, he works with implementation issues.

Bengt J. Olsson received the M. Sc. degree in Engineering Physics 1985 and a Ph. D. in Atomic & Molecular Physics 1989 from the Royal Institute of Technology in Stockholm, Sweden, and did his Post doc. at the University of Wisconsin in 1990. He started working at Ericsson in 1991 with system design on SDH systems, and moved to Ellemtel Telecommunication Systems Laboratories in 1994 to become leader of the Network Studies group at SwitchLab. Since April 1997 B.J.O. works as a data/telecom consultant at Communicator Teleplan AB of Stockholm.

12
Realisation Issues for Brokerage

K. Garcha
GPT Limited
New Century Park
Coventry
CV3 1HJ
U.K

Telephone: 01203 665828
Fax: 01203 562638
E-Mail: kul@ncp.gpt.co.uk

Abstract

This paper discusses three important issues related to Information Brokering:

- query processing;
- automated negotiation;
- the integration of external packages into a user's working environment.

The search, retrieval and integration of data from distributed heterogeneous databases for query processing can be very costly. This paper discusses techniques that make query processing more efficient and therefore minimise the cost. The subject of automated negotiation is discussed in terms of self interested brokers, how they can use the negotiation process to work for them (i.e. choosing the stage and level of commitment, adding conditions to decommitment, risk strategy). Technical issues that need to be considered when integrating an external application into a user's collaborative workspace are specified, i.e. communication requirements, interfaces, security, performance, dynamic operation.

Keywords

Information brokering, automated negotiation, electronic trading, query processing

1 INTRODUCTION

The work that contributed to this paper, reference Garcha (1996), was conducted as a small part (3 man months) of the U.K. collaborative project VIRTUOSI, reference Virtuosi (1996). This project was partially funded by the U.K. Department of Trade and Industry, as part of their "LINK" programme. Partners in the project were GPT, BT, BICC, Division, Nottinghamshire County Council, GEC Hirst Research, University of Nottingham, Nottingham Trent University and Manchester University. The three-year project started in November 1993. Part of the project was aimed at supporting the fashion industry by the setting up of a commercial Brokering Service. This would provide information and services for the various interested parties in the fashion and clothing industry (e.g. fabric manufacture, accessories, finance services).

The scope of this paper is: firstly to study the way a Broker can efficiently search, retrieve and integrate data from distributed heterogeneous data sources; secondly how a Broker can successfully negotiate for information and services; and finally the technical issues that need to be considered when integrating external applications into a user's working environment.

There are other related areas of interest not covered by this paper, e.g. other Broker construction issues, Brokers and Agents relationships, Internet support for Brokerage, security of payment mechanisms.

The first section of this document gives some background information on a broker. The second section discusses query processing. The third section shows how external information or services can be negotiated. The final part of this paper considers what issues need to be resolved when integrating an external application into a user's working environment.

2 BROKER

This section gives some background information to the concept of a Broker, further details can be found in reference Foss (1995).

The increase in the number of commercial information services (information, software applications, entertainment, etc.) which are publicly accessible from the world's networks, has brought with it its own problems. Information service providers need to effectively market their products and services in a totally new way. A new automated trading environment is emerging, which requires new management and administration mechanisms. Users are faced with access to an ever increasing mountain of information but do not have the tools capable for efficiently locating, processing and managing this information.

One way of tackling these problems in an integrated manner is by using an intermediary, i.e. an information broker. A broker is not an entity that can be rigidly defined. It could be envisaged as being a freely evolving, self organising entity that would operate in a free market. Brokers would provide personalised information services to the customer by liaising between information service providers and clients. Brokers could be used as marketing entities to target the appropriate audience. The broker is in a good position to mediate the methods of interaction, apportion information rights and revenues and even administer taxes to various parties in a trading model. A broker can be used to search, negotiate, integrate, manipulate and monitor for information and services for clients, saving time and effort. One of the broker's key tasks is to interact in real-time with other brokers belonging to different organisations, buying goods and services for its clients.

It is not practical to build a single system to perform all the functions of a broker, what is required is a modular approach where co-operating specialised autonomous agents find, retrieve, integrate, analyse and present the data. The functionality of agents can vary, some agents will accept queries, and then themselves generate queries to other agents, whereas others will just answer queries (data stores). There is no clear difference between what a broker is and an agent. In our system the broker is the user's intelligent gateway to the particular information services that it provides. The broker itself could be used by other agents and brokers to provide information (i.e. a recursive relationship).

3 QUERY PROCESSING

The broker needs to efficiently process queries from users; retrieving and integrating distributed data can be very costly. Query processing involves developing an ordered set of operations for obtaining a requested set of data, such as selecting the information sources, choosing operations for processing the data, selecting sites where the operations will be performed and the order in which they will be performed. What is required is an automated dynamic system to generate and execute query access plans. This planner needs capabilities such as: executing operations in parallel; re-planning queries that fail while at the same time executing other queries; gathering additional information to aid the query processing and the acceptance of new queries while other queries are being executed.

Further information can be found in reference Knoblock and Ambite (1996).

3.1 Knowledge of a Broker

An important aid to handling query processing is the broker's knowledge base covering its area of expertise (domain), its sources of information and details about its clients. One way of representing the knowledge of a broker is via the use of modelling techniques. These models can be used to determine how to process an information request.

3.1.1 Domain Model

This provides collaborating brokers/agents and any other users with an interface to the broker. The model is a description of the application domain from the point of view of users who may need to obtain information about the application domain. It contains a detailed model of its area of expertise, and the terminology for user communication. This model includes the broker's interest profile - those services that the broker is interested in finding from other brokers and agents. These services would have certain criteria associated with them: quality, credibility etc. .

3.1.2 Source Models

These are the resources available to a broker when information requests cannot be answered internally.

A broker will have models of other agents/brokers and information sources that provide useful information for its domain of expertise.

A source model contains three types of information. Firstly the source model contains a service profile to enable the broker to assess how the services offered by the source match its requirements. The service profile would include an affinity value, giving a measure of to what degree the services required by a broker match the services offered by the source. This value can be used by the broker to decide whether to retain the source and to prioritise the order in which sources are processed. Within the profile there would also be a general description of the services offered by the source together with information on the quality of service, reputation rating, previous customer satisfaction levels etc. Secondly there is a description of the contents of the information source (only of areas of relevance to the domain) and the language that the information source communicates with. Thirdly the relationship between the information source and the domain model is described. This relationship is used to transform domain level queries into a set of queries to the appropriate information sources.

3.1.3 Client Model

The client model provides information specific to customers, e.g. interests, payment rating, satisfaction level etc.

3.2 Steps in Query Processing

Once a query has been received from a user (human/computer) the query can be handled as follows :

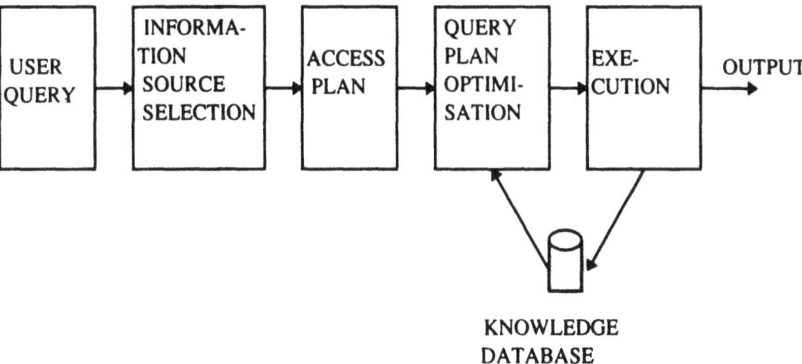

Figure 1 Query Processing.

3.2.1 Information Source Selection

An important and difficult problem is how to efficiently retrieve information from distributed heterogeneous multidatabase systems. Retrieving and integrating distributed data often requires processing and storage of large amounts of intermediate data, which can be costly. This cost can be reduced by using automated algorithms to reformat queries for individual databases and multidatabase systems, making them more cost effective.

The broker firstly needs to reformulate the user's query into one or more queries to specific information sources. The following reformulation operations can be used to achieve this task effectively and efficiently :

Mapping
This maps a domain-level concept to a source-level concept. If a query directly maps onto a single source of information then the mapping is straightforward. However in some cases there may be several information sources that provide access to the same information or no single information source can provide all the required information. The broker will need to choose a solution so as to minimise the cost of the overall query.

Concept Generalisation
Concept Generalisation uses knowledge stored in the domain model, in the form of hierarchical relationships between concepts, to reformulate a query and find an appropriate data source. For example, if in the clothing industry (part of the Virtuosi project), a query requiring information about silk material is not satisfied by the silk concept, then the query could be generalised to the fabrics concept (higher up in the hierarchy), and the information obtained.

Concept Specialisation
This replaces a query specification, with a more specific query request, by checking the constraints of the query. For example if in Virtuosi (part of the project related to the fashion industry) there was a request for all suppliers who stock womens' clothes greater than size 16, then the query could be reformulated using knowledge from the model, that only large-size-clothes suppliers have this size range.

Definition Substitution
This replaces a relation defined between concepts in the domain model with equivalent terms that are available in the source-models.

3.2.2 Query Access Planning

Having selected the sources of information to resolve the query , secondly the broker needs to construct a plan for retrieval of the information requested by the reformulated query by determining the appropriate data manipulation and ordering. This would involve steps such as sending a specific query to some information source, combining results from different information sources and temporarily storing partial results.

The following are some operators that can be used for data manipulation :

- Move: Moves a set of data from one broker/agent to another.
- Join: Combines two sets of data; overlapping data from different sources will need to be combined into one consistent data source.

- Retrieve: Specifies the data to be retrieved from a particular information source.
- Select: Selects a subset of the data using given constraints.
- Construct: Combines existing data to form a new data item.

Data restructuring would be required, where data retrieved from one database must be transformed into the structure specified by a common schema, for integration with data from other sources. Mediation would be required to resolve semantic heterogeneity issues. An example of this would be if data on earnings from multiple sources came in monthly, weekly and hourly salaries but needed integrating into yearly earnings.

To produce a cost-effective query plan the system could use a simple estimation function to calculate the various costs of the operations.

3.2.3 Semantic query-plan optimisation

Knowledge gained about the contents of databases can be used to perform semantic query optimisation to minimise the execution cost of the query. The semantic knowledge can be learnt as a set of rules. Queries can be reformulated by adding, modifying or removing constraints.

E.g. Suppose a query was set-up for the clothing industry (part of Virtuosi) looking for a company who could manufacture 10,000 garments of a particular type a week. However manufacturing capacity in the data source was not indexed. Then a lot of processing would be involved in searching every record. However if the system has a rule stating that medium sized firms have the capacity to handle production of up to 12000 garments and the firm-size field is indexed, then this constraint can be used to speed up processing.

The resulting plan is more efficient and would return the same results as the original one.

3.2.4 Execution

At this stage the optimised query plan is executed. Queries are sent to the appropriate information sources (in parallel where possible), data is transferred, and a response is constructed for the user.

Note - the data coming back will need its metadata and be required to be and formatted so that the receiver understands the information.

3.2.5 Integration

In order to get the lowest cost integration and access plan, reformulation of the queries and generation of the query access plan have to be done at the same time.

Integration of the planning and execution process can also provide many benefits :

- The broker can continuously accept and plan queries while it is executing other queries.
- If a failure occurs, an agent can re-plan the failed portion of the plan while it continues to execute queries that are already in progress. After re-planning the system can redirect the query to a different information source or agent.
- A Broker can issue actions to gather additional information for query processing, e.g. to help to select from a number of potential information sources.

3.2.6 Learning

A broker can improve the performance and accuracy of its query processing operation, by learning over time. Frequently used or difficult to retrieve relatively static information can be stored in cache locally, being referenced as a source directly. Brokers can learn about the contents of information sources in order to minimise the costs of retrieval. Information agents can analyse information sources regularly in order to keep their domain model up-to-date and thus provide a better service. Brokers can learn from other brokers and agents by observing their behaviour and then imitating them. Brokers can learn from activity taking place, such as changing customer interests, customer satisfaction / dissatisfaction, reliability of sources, quality of sources etc. This data can be recorded and maintained in the broker's models and used to make decisions on future activity. Brokers can use feature based (use clients' personal data) or collaborative (use data from other clients with similar interests) techniques to recommend potential useful information or services.

4. AUTOMATED NEGOTIATION

Negotiation is a joint decision making process in which various parties state their requirements, some of which may conflict. Negotiation allows all parties to move towards agreement by a process of concession or the search for new alternatives.

Further information on this subject area can be found in reference Sandholm and Lesser (1995).

4.1 Need for Automated Negotiation

One of the broker's key tasks will be to interact in real-time with other brokers and agents belonging to different organisations, performing monetary transactions in terms of buying goods and services for its clients. The broker will also be interested in forming short term alliances with other brokers and agents in order to respond to more diverse requests from users than it individually could. Through forming these alliances the broker can take advantage of economies of scale without suffering from diseconomies of scale.

Negotiation relies heavily on the ability of agents to communicate and to understand each other. Messages need to be standardised by building common ontologies, message wrappers, etc.

4.2 Types of Multi-Agent Negotiation

There can be various types of multi-agent negotiation depending on the type of environment the broker is dealing with. If the broker is dealing with agents that have only the broker's interests in mind (e g. broker's internal agents) then the broker will be working in a co-operative environment, where the broker should try to minimise costs and maximise revenue of the operation as a whole by sometimes accepting local losses.

When the broker is dealing with agents in a virtual organisation, then the broker will be working in a self-interested environment concerned with maximising its own profit. The brokers and agents within this set-up will only take action for a payment and may not be totally honest whenever it benefits them. They will maintain their own local decision autonomy as they have their own private goals.

The following sections explore automated negotiation among self-interested agents that make negotiation decisions in real-time with limited resources.

4.3 Interaction Protocol

Automated negotiation is currently in its early stages. There is no clearly defined interaction protocol enforced by law (as in traditional negotiation) and when laws are defined there is the potential problem of agents in different countries being governed by different laws. Laws may not be strictly enforced (enforcing them may be impracticably expensive). A computer agent can vanish at any point in time - laws can only be enforced if the terminated agent represented some real world party and the connection between the two can be traced. To address this issue some systems tie each agent to its real world party.

A broker is in an ideal position to enforce an interaction protocol by acting as a trusted intermediary, making sure any laws are adhered to and any other business requirements such as accounts, taxes are also met.

Automated trading can be made to work more effectively by splitting up the delivery of larger goods into smaller deliverables, making it less tempting for each trading partner to defect. Discounts, lateness penalties, deadlines, etc. Can be used to motivate a trading partner to respond in a timely manner.

4.4 Contracting Scenario

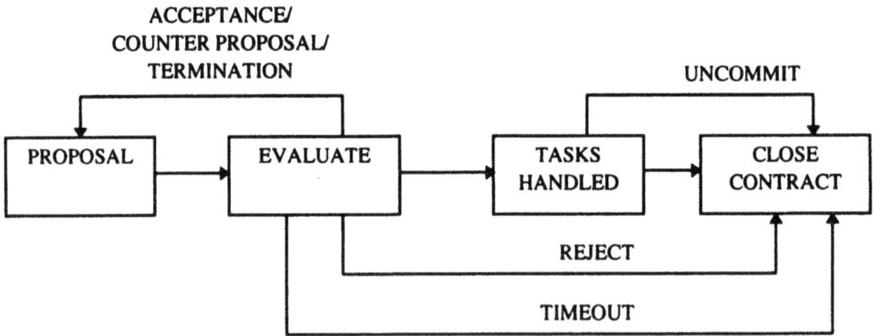

Figure 2 Negotiation Process.

Negotiation can start with either a contractor or a contractee message. For illustration purposes we will assume the contractor sends out the initial message. A contractor's message can specify alternative contracts that the contractor is willing to commit to. Having received the message the contractee can respond in one of the following ways :

A contractee can accept one of the options of the contractor's message by returning a message identifying the negotiation, option and specifying the accepted terms and conditions (tasks, delivery times, quality, payment, commitment, etc.). Once the contractee has accepted, then the contractor is automatically committed to paying the amounts specified and can cancel the deal on a task set only by paying the contractee a penalty. Also once the contractee has accepted an option the contractor becomes decommitted from all the other alternatives it suggested.

If the contractee decides not to accept any of the options and wants to terminate the negotiation, then a terminate message for the specified negotiation should be returned. As a result the contractor becomes decommitted from all of the options it proposed.

The contractee may decide to send a counterproposal that the contractor can either accept, further counterimpose or terminate the negotiation.

4.5 Commitment and Negotiation

Commitment means that one agent binds itself to a potential contract while waiting for the other agent to either accept or reject the offer. If the other party accepts then both parties are bound to the contract.

4.5.1 Stage of Commitment

Traditionally commitment takes place in the bidding phase. If the bidder was awarded the task then the bidder has to take care of it at the price mentioned. Computer agents can be designed so that commitment can take place at any stage of the negotiation process. The choice of commitment can be a static protocol design or it can be decided dynamically.

4.5.2 Levels of Commitment

The level of commitment can also be negotiated over. Commitments can be assigned a level of commitment based on monetary commitment breaking cost. This cost can be made dependent on other variables such as time, events in other negotiations, etc. This enables a broker to take risks. With a low level of commitment the broker would be able to accept a job and later try to contract out parts of the job. With full commitment the broker would have to be able to handle the job itself or have standing offers from agents/brokers that it is able to contract the task to.

Making low commitment offers to multiple agents gives the broker a greater chance of getting its offer accepted quickly while only having to pay a minimal penalty if there is more than one acceptance.

4.6 Conditional Response Time

By adding a condition to the response time, the contractor can motivate the negotiation partner to respond quickly. This can be done by a strict deadline or time-dependent payment scheme. In the strict deadline method the contractor specifies a date that a particular option is available for. If the negotiation partner has not answered by that time the sender of the message gets uncommitted from that option. The time-dependent payment scheme allows a contractor to describe payments that decrease as the acceptance of a contractor message is postponed. In the case of a contractee it allows it to specify payments that increase as the acceptance of a contractee message is postponed.

A time-dependent lateness penalty schedule similar to the above car ; used for delivery of goods and services to a specified time.

4.7 Accepting/Waiting

An agent does not know what offers it will receive in the future but a negotiating agent needs to consider the trade-off between accepting early or waiting for better offers. By waiting an agent may receive better offers later. Having more options available would enable an agent to make a more informed decision. A disadvantage of waiting is that the agent may lose the contract through some other agent accepting the offer, or may be paid less for the same job. If a response deadline is missed the negotiation terminates. The agent can begin a new negotiation on the same issues, but it will not have the other agent's commitment at first.

4.8 Terminating the negotiation

Negotiation can go on indefinitely. Knowing when to terminate is difficult. One way of deciding this is for an agent to stop negotiating once it has made no contracts during a certain fixed number of negotiation iterations. Some agents may use an estimating scheme to decide the feasibility (resources and cost) of handling the operation. Negotiation can be terminated by a "strict deadline" method whereby if the negotiation partner has not responded by a certain date the negotiation ends. In some cases where an agent for some reason cannot achieve the requested task and an important business partner is involved it is in the interest of the agent to send a terminate message.

It is important to take account of overheads likely to be incurred in the negotiating process, as in some cases these may outweigh any benefits gained from the contract.

4.9 Risk strategy

Varying the level of commitment allows a wider variety of negotiation risk management techniques.

High levels of commitment can be used to reduce the risk of failure via adding severe penalties for breaking the contract.

Low levels of commitment allow agents to take the risk of accepting a task without fully knowing how and whether they are going to be able to achieve the task, because the cost of failure is inexpensive.

Using a level of commitment an agent can make the same offer to multiple agents, thereby increasing the chance of acceptance. If there is more than one acceptance the penalty is minimal.

An agent has to decide what level of feasibility checking it should do before accepting, if too much time is spent another agent may win the contract before the reply is sent. If too little time is spent the agent may make an un-beneficial contract.

As agents have limited resources they will need to decide which tasks to work on and in which order. They may want to put more resources on some selective more worthwhile potential contracts and ignore some of their existing obligations.

A group of agents can accomplish a big operation if they take the risk of working together. The level of risk being reduced by adding penalties for any breach of contract.

4.10 Anticipating the future

An intelligent agent should anticipate future negotiation events in its negotiation strategy.

An agent needs to consider during initial negotiations if the cost or feasibility of carrying out a task depends on the carrying out of other future tasks. One single contract may not be beneficial (loss maker) but further potential orders in the future may add up to a large profitable contract. Payments and commitment functions can be set on future events.

In some cases it may be advantageous to work out the feasibility of a task in all possible future scenarios. Where different combinations of to-be-sent and to be received offers have been accepted, different combinations of old and to occur offers have been broken and different domain events have occurred.

4.11 Agent's Knowledge

Agents need knowledge to deal with the negotiation process. A knowledge database can provide information on profiles of its client, information on past dealings, commercial preferences, strategy, constraints, etc., to help make decisions.

For further information reference section 3.1 Knowledge of a Broker.

5 INTEGRATION OF EXTERNAL APPLICATIONS

One of the main functions of a broker will be to integrate external applications into a multi-user virtual environment. This enables applications to be used interactively for remote team based activities enabling real time arbitration, communication and co-operation. Each user can edit the contents with each action being reflected to all the other users. A team of designers of a product, located in different places can meet in their work environment and interactively collaborate on the viability of different designs, in terms of cost and profitability.

Further information on this subject area can be found in references DR. Furness, Dr. Kawahata (1996) and Amselem (1996).

5.1 Requirements

The following are technical issues that need to be considered when integrating external applications into a multi-user Virtual Environment:

Communication
If the application is to run on the same platform as the virtual environment, does the application support that platform? If networking is involved is the required network technology supported?

Interfaces

Are the interfaces and I/O devices (including various types of media) required by the application supported by the virtual environment. Does the environment support open collaborative applications, i.e. the sharing of documents, images etc.

How flexible is the virtual environment in terms of its user interface? For example would it provide translation facilities for an application requiring audio but where the user has no audio facility ? (The virtual environment could convert the audio to text for the user).

Security

Is the required level of security provided by the virtual environment ?, e.g. access only allowed to users specifically granted access to the application.

Performance

Are there enough resources to drive this application at a satisfactory level of performance ?

Distributed Environment

Can the application run on a different machine to the virtual environment and the user without overloading the network with data being passed between users ?

Network Communication Model

Users in a distributed multi-user application sharing the same virtual space interactively require their host machines to communicate with each other using a network. Virtual environments are based on certain types of network models, e.g. Centralised network model, Distributed network model, Broadcast network model. These models define the architecture of the network, e.g. client/server or peer to peer, the way the messages are communicated and to whom. Each approach has its advantages and disadvantages. It needs to be considered how well the network communication model supported by the virtual environment suits your application. For example, if the virtual environment uses a distributed network communication model (peer to peer) it can be difficult to maintain database consistency. In this type of model each peer maintains a local copy of the database, so when changes are made to the database, the peer must communicate these changes to all other peers in the system.

Number of Users

How many users can effectively share the same Virtual Environment compared to what the application is designed for ?

Dynamic loading of applications

Will the system allow dynamic loading and updating of applications as they are required ?

Dynamic connection of users to the system
Does the virtual environment allow users to log in and out of the system as required while running ?

5.2 Tools

Tools that make integration easier are emerging, which enable applications to be run on any platform.

5.3 Administration Issues

Having decided that a particular piece of software can be integrated, a contract needs to be produced for the licensed use of the software, upgrade payment details etc.

5.4 Disintegration

On expiration of the licence, a mechanism is needed to disable the software from the system and clear up any payments due.

6. SUMMARY AND CONCLUSIONS

It can be seen that the broker has an important role to play in the further evolution of the Global Information Infrastructure. This paper has discussed the issues of automated negotiation, integration and query processing that are seen as being crucial to the realisation of Information Brokerage.

GPT are looking at further developing this subject area by developing a prototype with Queen Mary Westfield of London (University) and also carrying out further research as part of an ACTS brokerage programme.

7. REFERENCES

Amselem D. A. (1996) Window on Shared Virtual Environments.

http://www.afit.af.mil/Schools/En/ENG/LABS/GRAPHICS/annobib/writeups/amse95-00.taa.html
Dr. Furness and Dr. Kawahata (1996) GreenSpace project. http://www.hitl.washington.edu/projects/greenspace
Foss J. (1995) Agents in Information Brokering Services, UNICOM Seminar on Business Applications of Intelligent Agent Technology, London.
Garcha K. (1996) Realisation Issues for Brokerage, Virtuosi, GPT Limited.
Knoblock C. and Ambite J. (1996) Agents for Information Gathering, http://www.isi.edu/sims/knoblock/info-agents.html
Sandholm T. and Lesser V. Issues in Automated Negotiation and Electronic Commerce.
http://dis.cs.umass.edu/research/ecommerce.html
Virtuosi Project (1996),
http://www.crg.cs.nott.ac.uk/Virtuosi

Acknowledgements - I would like to thank Jerry Foss of GPT Limited for his help.

8. BIOGRAPHY

Kulwinder Garcha joined GEC in 1987 during the following year GPT was formed from the amalgamation of GEC and Plessey Telecommunications. She has experience at all levels ranging from research to implementation. She has worked on various projects including, systems integration, mobile telecommunications (Telepoint and GSM) and Intelligent Networks.

13

Object Oriented IN service modelling

L. Klostermann, J.A. Kroeze
Ericsson Telecom, the Netherlands
PO Box 8
5120 AA Rijen
the Netherlands
phone +31 161 249911, fax +31 161 249699
e-mail etmlukl@etm.ericsson.se, etmjohk@etm.ericsson.se

Abstract

In this paper we study the possibility to migrate the Intelligent Network Service Model used in standardisation towards an object oriented model. After introducing the current model, we present an initial proposal for an object oriented service model which improves upon the data modelling and service management, while offering migration from the existing model.

Keywords

Intelligent Network, standardisation, service model, object orientation

Intelligent Networks and Intelligence in Networks D. Gaiti (Ed.)
Published by Chapman & Hall

1 INTRODUCTION

This chapter briefly introduces the existing intelligent network service model.

1.1 Intelligent Networks

Intelligent Networks (IN) started a few years ago, when it became clear that switch based hardcoded services have a disadvantage when it comes to service management. As an alternative an architecture was developed with centralised service control, and a communication protocol between the switching layer and the service layer. In this architecture services are executed in a functional entity called Service Control Function (SCF). An implementation of an SCF is referred to as a Service Control Point (SCP).

1.2 Service Independent Building blocks

The purpose of this centralisation was to improve service management. There was a need for better support of the service life cycle. The concept of Service Independent Building block (SIB) was introduced, aiming at easier and faster service development cycles. In this concept each SIB performs a task occurring regularly in services and services are just a concatenation of SIBs, see figure 1. The basic call process is interrupted when the IN service is triggered, such that the service logic program gains control over the call. From a relatively small set of SIBs many services can be composed, using the flexibility offered by parameters. Each SIB in a service has its associated data, the service has its own data which is partly call related data, so-called call instance data. The flow of service execution is apart from the concatenation of SIBs also determined by incoming events from other functional entities like the Service Switching Point (SSP) or Intelligent Peripheral (IP).

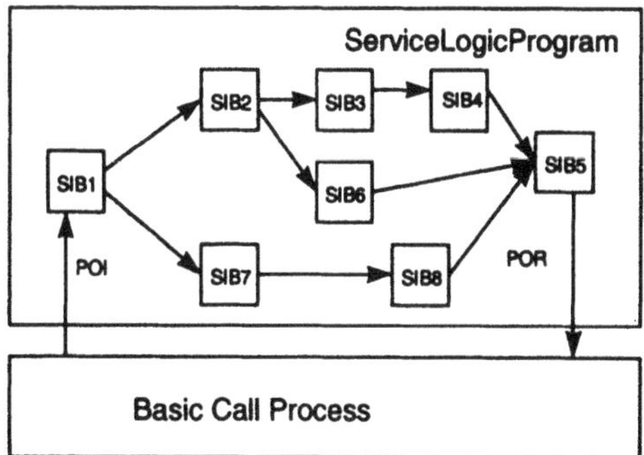

Figure 1 Existing IN service model

1.3 Intelligent network conceptual model

In standardisation of Intelligent Networks, the IN conceptual model is used for protocol development. In this process first some benchmark services are identified. The functionality in these services leads to requirements on the Global Functional Plane (GFP). In turn these requirements may lead to new SIBs.
The functionality of the SIBs is then distributed over the functional entities in the Distributed Functional Plane (DFP), from which a need for a new protocol message between functional entities may be identified.
Finally the protocols are implemented on the physical plane.

2 MOTIVATION FOR A NEW MODEL

This chapter identifies some possibilities for improvement in the existing model.

2.1 Protocol development

With the increased speed of technical developments, growing numbers of protocols and protocol messages are to be supported, having a direct impact on the SIB set. Therefore we see the following improvements related to protocol development:

- from service plane to GFP: The relations between Service Plane and GFP may become more obvious using OO, since the OO model may be derived from a textual specification in a more intuitive way, modelling real-world entities.
- from GFP to DFP: Nowadays there is no methodology to translate the functionality from GFP to DFP. Using OO methodologies supports stepwise refinements, thus distributing functionality at the GFP to functionality over the functional entities of the DFP in a iterative manner.

2.2 Service management

With the current pressure on the service market, service management has again become an issue. Although the GFP service model has currently no direct link to service management and service creation, there are reasons to include it here as well. One such reason is for instance service portability, where a common data model is needed. Possible enhancements we see are:

- Include data modelling aspects in the service model: At present, the context of the SIB modelling is restricted to their functionality in service execution. Data modelling, in particular in the scope of service management, is neglected. Since data modelling is a cornerstone of object orientation, adoptation of OO methodologies will result in a more complete service model.

- Add structure to the SIB set: The set of SIBs presently defined has no structure. On one hand the possibility to make small variations on basic SIBs might be useful, on the other hand a composition of SIBs in units reusable for more services is a valuable addition. The latter aspect is addressed in IN CS2 (Capability Set 2) by so-called high level SIBs. OO inheritance seems a suitable mechanism to support both mechanisms for a SIB set structure.

4 OO SERVICE MODEL

In this chapter we present a proposal for an object oriented service model, which enhances the existing model. We use Object Model Notation (OMT) to represent the models, though we do not always use it in a strictly correct way.

4.1 Service views

The service model supports two views: the execution view and the provisioning/customisation view. The execution view of the service comprises the elementary classes which are active during service execution time, showing classes of different ownership, across levels of subscription and of different temporal character (dynamic or persistent). The provisioning/customisation view on the other hand, represents the perspective of one of the subscribers on the service.

4.2 Service execution view

Meta model

Figure 2 presents the meta model for the service execution view, consisting of the three classes: ServiceSessionManager ServiceLogic and ServiceResource.

The ServiceLogic class represents the flow of control of a service, using the ServiceResource class which models the (physical or logical) resources available in the network for IN services. The ServiceResource class is service independent as opposed to the service specific ServiceLogic class. The ServiceResource class may be looked upon as the OO equivalent of the presently used SIBs.

The ServiceResource class is specialised to the DynamicServiceResource class and the PersistentServiceResource class. The DynamicServiceResource class represents classes of which the instances exist only within the timeframe of one service execution. The PersistentServiceResource class represents the classes of which the instances lifetimes exceed one service execution. Although object lifetime seems a strange criterion for modelling, it separates the objects under control of service management (PersistentServiceResource) from those who are not controlled from service management (DynamicServiceResource).

The ServiceSessionManager keeps a view of the service session and is responsible for (some of the) scheduling, monitoring and event handling. In principle the ServiceSessionManager could be seen as a specialisation of DynamicServiceResource. Because of its central role however, it is modelled as a separate class. ServiceLogic objects may keep private process data.

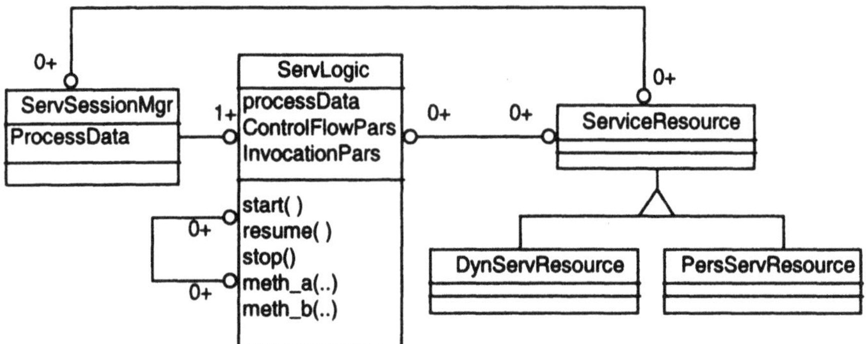

Figure 2 Service execution view meta model

Service creation results in instances of the ServiceLogic class. Service logic processing is started by invoking a method on such an instance. Processing is encapsulated in the ServiceLogic objects. ServiceLogic methods may be invoked synchronous (waiting for the result) or asynchronous (parallel processing).

Refining the meta model

Given the meta model we refine the ServiceResource subclasses. The Call class is a specialisation from DynamicServiceResource, having e.g. Call Instance Data as attributes and methods for call handling.

PersistentServiceResource is specialised to several classes, like announcement, subscriber, queue.

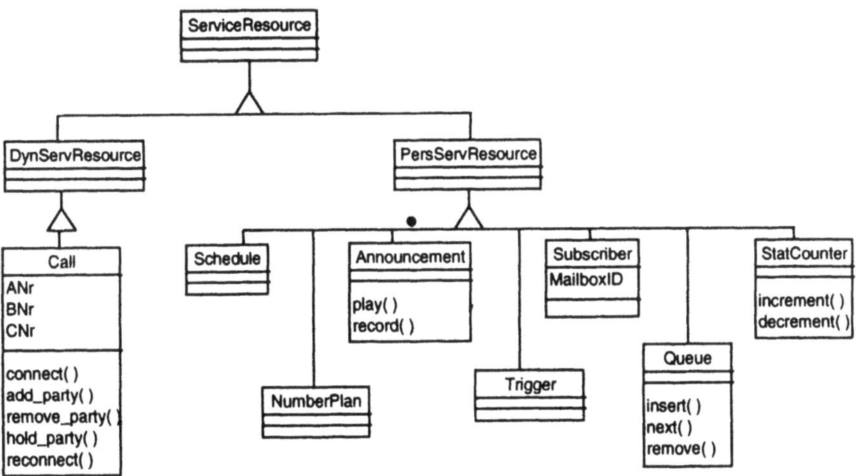

Figure 3 Service execution view, example classes

4.3 Service provisioning/customisation view

The class model of the service provisioning/customisation view is shown in Figure 4. Services are the output of service creation. Services consist of one or more ServiceLogic classes and one or more ServiceTemplate classes.

The ServiceTemplate is used upon subscription, when the subscriber is linked to a service. Subscription may happen on several levels like network provider level, company level, office level or end-user level. For every level there is a template. Once filled out, the ServiceTemplate can be loaded into the network. In this process, several objects are created in the service execution environment. The ProvisioningProfile keeps the bookkeeping of the actual location of the template parameters in the network. During the lifetime of the subscription, the ProvisioningProfile represents the subscription view on the service, for e.g. profile updates by the provider or customer control.

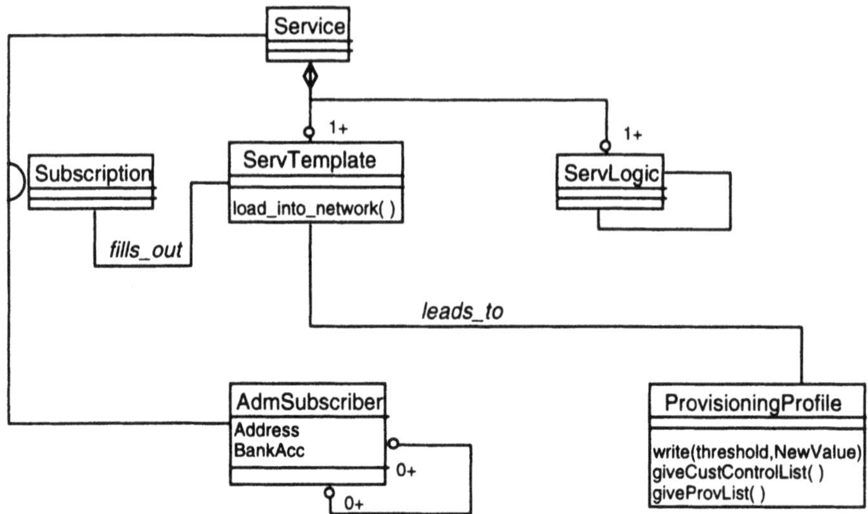

Figure 4 Service provisioning/customisation view

4.4 Combined views

Figure 5 shows the combined service views, illustrating that only the PersistentServiceResource class is linked to the ProvisioningProfile, as opposed to the DynamicServiceResource class.

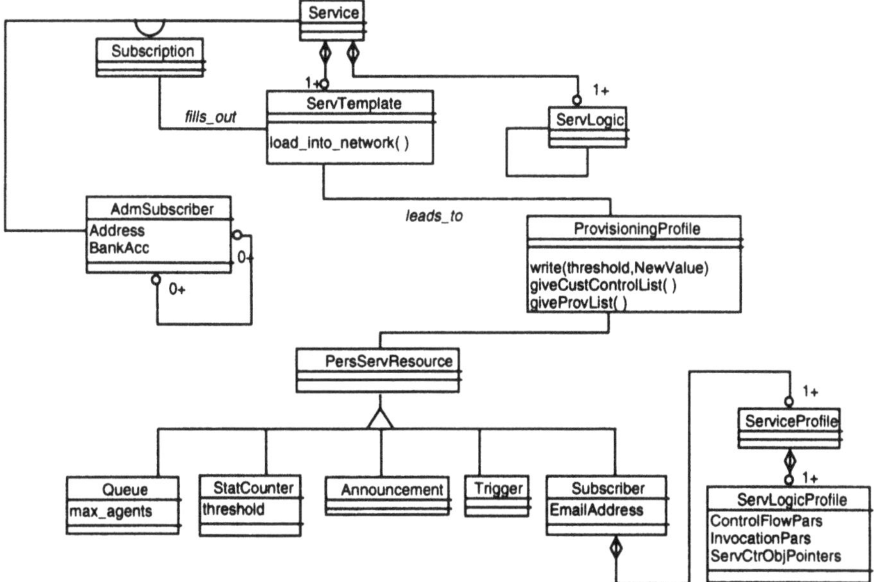

Figure 5 Service combined view

The ServiceProfile and ServiceLogicProfile classes are introduced to represent information which is subscriber specific and thus unknown at service creation time, but still need be linked to the ServiceLogic. In the proposed solution ServiceLogic classes may be reused over many subscribers.

6 CONCLUSION

In this paper we propose an object oriented model for Intelligent Network services. After briefly introducing the current service model we identified two main areas needing improvement, being protocol development in standardisation context, and data modelling, especially important for service management. The proposed model provides improvements in both areas. One of the ways in which this is achieved is by introducing two complementary views. The model is still in a preliminary phase, and further studies are in progress.

7 BIOGRAPHY

Lucas Klostermann (born 1966) obtained a masters degree in physics engineering from Delft University of Technology. After that he worked at CERN in Geneva for four years, doing a PhD in high energy physics. Part of this time he spent developing software for the analysis and interpretation of experimental data from a large experiment. In 1995 he joined Ericsson in the Netherlands, more specifically the IN Application Laboratory of the company. He worked on distributed systems and IN prototyping. Presently he is involved in a TINA validation project and in IN standardisation in ITU.

John Kroeze (born 1965) studied electrical engineering at the University of Twente, resulting in a MSc degree in 1992, after working on his thesis at the Dutch PTT Research laboratory. He worked for three years at the Computing Science Institute of the University of Nijmegen, participating in the European RACE II project R2061 EXPLOIT, where he performed ATM traffic control experiments. In 1995 he joined Ericsson, assigned at the Intelligent Networks Application Laboratory in Rijen, the Netherlands. His current interests include real-time programming, distributed objects, intelligent, broadband and mobile networks (though the intersection of these three seems empty).

PART SIX

Applications

14

Provision of Broadband Video Conference via IN and B-ISDN Integration: Architectural and Modelling Issues

F. Cuomo, M Listanti, F. Pozzi
INFOCOM Dept., University of Rome "La Sapienza"
Via Eudossiana, 18 - 00184 Rome, Italy;
Tel.: +39-6-44585472, Fax.:+39-6-4873300,
e-mail: franci@antares.ing.uniroma1.it

Abstract

This paper deals with the integration between the Intelligent Network (IN) and the B-ISDN for the support of an advanced multimedia service, i.e. the Broadband Video Conference (B-VC). The focus of the paper is the proposal of a new role of the IN that, in a closed interaction with the B-ISDN, furnishes control functionality to handle complex service configuration.

In order to assign such a role, we distinguish different levels of control into the IN architecture and we propose functional models able to represent, at each level, a specific service view, suitable to th IN, and cooperating for a global service provisioning.

Some different options for an IN/B-ISDN interaction are discussed; in particular, the architectural aspects of a solution distributing the IN control logic between the Service Control Function (SCF) and the Service Switching Function (SSF) are described in details.

Finally we consider an actual multimedia service, the Broadband Video Conference, supported with the proposed approach, and we analyse the relevant performance behaviour.

Keywords

IN and B-ISDN, multimedia services, IN architecture.

Intelligent Networks and Intelligence in Networks D. Gaiti (Ed.)
Published by Chapman & Hall

1 INTRODUCTION

The growing user needs and the emerging advanced computer applications require, in addition to networks with high bandwidth capabilities, a powerful signalling system able to manage and to coordinate sophisticated network configuration scenarios.

Up to now the standardisation bodies have defined two B-ISDN signalling protocol releases: the Signalling Capability Set 1 (SCS 1) and Signalling Capability Set 2 (SCS 2) [ITU-T Q.2931, 1994] [ITU-T Q.2971, 1994].

The SCS 1 supports simple switched services consisting of single-connection, bi-directional, point-to-point calls. The objective of SCS 2 was the handling of: multiparty calls, several connections in a single call, correlation among different media, heterogeneous terminals and dynamic change of call topology and connections parameters. This wide objective suggested to split the signalling protocol definition activity in steps. The first step gave rise the SCS 2.1, that is, at present, the unique stable signalling capability set. The main innovation within SCS 2.1 is the point-to-multipoint connection handling.

Unfortunately, there still exists a remarkable gap between the standardised B-ISDN control capabilities and the requirements of new telecommunication services based on multipoint-to-multipoint call configurations, as in the case of the Broadband Video Conference (B-VC). A solution to rapidly fill up this gap is the integration of the B-ISDN and the IN paradigms. This approach has been proposed in previous papers [Maastricht, 1995] [Wakamoto, 1995] [Mukasa, 1995] [Carmagnola, 1996] and is the focus of an European ACTS project, named INSIGNIA [AC068 INSIGNIA deliverables].

As well known, IN allows a flexible introduction of new capabilities, and facilitates and accelerates, in a cost effective manner, service implementation and provisioning in a multi-vendor environment. The flexibility of this paradigm mainly lies in the separation between the control functionality relevant to the transport plane and the ones relevant to the service provisioning.

The classical IN service provisioning is based on a direct interaction between the IN logic, implementing supplementary aspects of the service, and the bearer service furnished at the transport level [ITU Q.1211-Q.1218, 1995]. In the IN/B-ISDN integrated approach, the IN provides a platform to enrich the functionalities furnished by the B-ISDN, in order to realise the handling of several basic calls/connections in a coordinate manner, according to the service logic requirements [Cuomo, 1996].

Figure 1 represents a logical scheme showing how this new functionality, here called *Bearer Connections Coordinator* (BCC), is inserted within the integrated IN/B-ISDN functional architecture.

By considering the present B-ISDN signalling capabilities, the BCC must be entirely located in the IN domain. In the future, the growing of the B-ISDN signalling capabilities could bring a reduction of the functionalities realised in the

IN domain and a migration of some functions within the B-ISDN one. It is also to be noted that we refer to B-ISDN call and connection as a unique entity since, for the time being, they are handled at the B-ISDN level in a monolithic way.

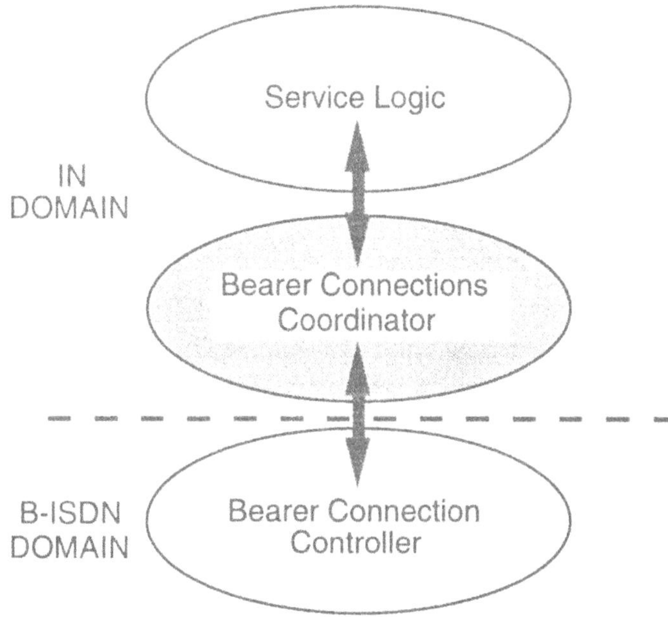

Figure 1 Functional organisation of the integrated IN/B-ISDN paradigm.

In this paper we discuss the functionality of the IN Bearer Connections Coordinator with particular reference to the provisioning of the Broadband Video Conference service. The solution here presented, derived from one of the main outcomes of the INSIGNIA project, foresees that the BCC functionality is shared between the Service Control Function (SCF) entity, located in the Service Control Point (SCP) and the Service Switching Function (SSF) entity, located in the Service Switching Point (SSP).

The coordination between the two entities is carried out by means of two service representation models: the former, named *Global Logic Service Configuration* (GLSC) is resident in the SCF; the latter, named *session*, is resident in the SSF.

This solution establishes a separation between the role of the SSF, that, according to the classical IN paradigm, furnishes functionalities independent of the specific service, and the role of the SCF that realises the service dependent functionalities. Moreover, as it will be described in the following, this solution allows a very efficient SCF/SSF interaction based on a high level service view. The SSF translates such a view into multiple views of lower level (i.e. the Basic

Call State Models - BCSMs), for the interaction with the B-ISDN control functionalities.

As a matter of example, in the second part of the paper, the proposed approach is applied for the provision of the Broadband Video Conference service, which requires very advanced control capabilities to handle the relevant network configuration.

The organisation of the paper is the following: Sec. 2 describes the functional levels in which the BCC is splitted and the relevant service representation models (i.e. the GLSC and the *session*). In Sec. 3 the IN approach is applied for the provision of the B-VC service, showing two architectural solutions. A brief performance evaluation is also carried out.

2 THE BEARER CONNECTIONS COORDINATOR IN THE IN DOMAIN

The fundamental requirement, in the design of an integrated IN/B-ISDN system architecture, is that different basic B-ISDN calls/connections have to be coordinated by the IN, in order to provide the required user plane configuration.

To this aim, in the framework of the INSIGNIA project, a functional architecture structured in four control domains has been developed [AC068 INSIGNIA Deliverable]: i) the *service control domain*, comprising the overall control of the IN service; ii) the *session control domain*, where the association of different B-ISDN calls for the realisation of a single IN service is handled; iii) the *call control domain* where each single B-ISDN call is controlled; iv) the *connection control domain*, where the physical switching resources involved in a B-ISDN call are controlled.

Figure 2 shows the relationships among these four domains and their mapping on the IN functional entities. Moreover, in the same figure, the two functional domains where the BCC functionality is implemented are singled out.

Within the service control domain, the BCC is responsible for the global service control and of the relevant network configuration; this goal is achieved by means of the interaction between the service logic inside the SCF, responsible of the service execution, and a high level representation of all the network components and of their relationships (GLSC).

As far as the session control domain is concerned, the BCC is dedicated to the control and the coordination of all the calls/connections supporting a specific service. By considering a single service instance, two main architectural solutions can be applied: i) a *centralised* approach, the session control function is located in a single SSF; ii) a *distributed* approach, the session control function is distributed among many SSFs.

2.1 The session control domain

The session control domain represents the lower level of coordination of basic B-ISDN calls/connections involved in the provisioning of a single service. As shown in Figure 2, the B-ISDN call/connections are modelled independently by means of the classical BCSM inside *the Call Control Function* (CCF). The connection coordination is obtained by developing, within the *IN Switching Manager* (IN-SM) entity inside the SSF, an enhanced *Switching State Model* (SSM) to be offered to the SCF control [AC068 INSIGNIA Deliverable].

This enhanced model, indicated as *session*, is realised by means of a suitable object modelling, and it is the tool needed to represent the connections, parties and relationships involved in the service in a specific SSF.

The IN Switching Manager handles the call events reported by the BCSMs and correlates them in the context of a session by sending appropriate messages to the SCF. In the other direction, the IN SM receives commands from the SCF and sends appropriate messages to the BCSMs (Figure 2).

In the *centralised* approach, a single session comprises all the B-ISDN calls/connections involved in the service; this means that a single SSP controls the whole set of B-ISDN connections. This solution, especially in multiparty services, where the number of involved connections could be significant, gives rise to an inefficient resource utilisation, both from a transport and a control point of view.

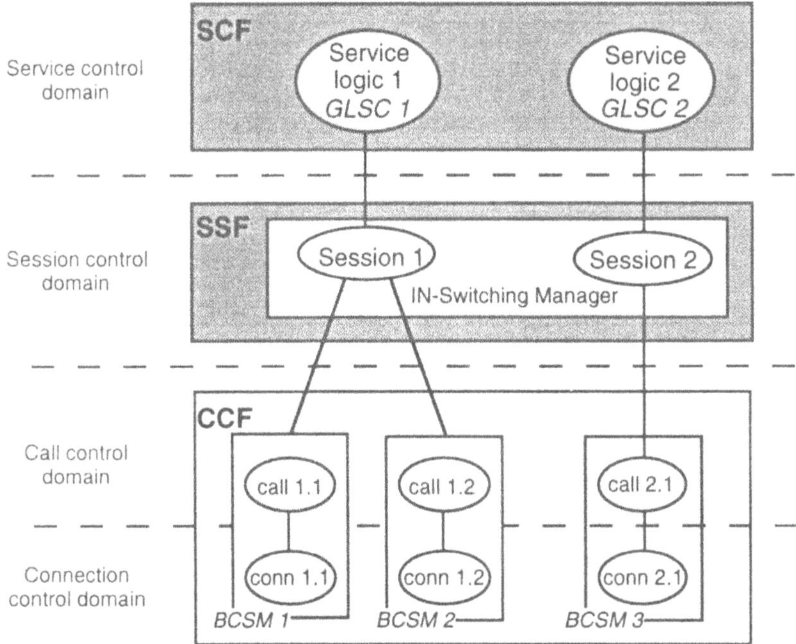

Figure 2 Control domains definition within IN/B-ISDN functional architecture.

A more suitable solution, the *distributed* one, foresees that, if needed, there could be more than one SSF involved in the same service instance. This means that the calls/connections composing the service configuration are controlled by different

SSPs. The controlling SSPs are selected with the aim of minimising the usage of the network resources.

The *distributed* solution implies that the session contained in each SSF represents only a partial view of the service configuration. The merging of these partial views is performed at the service control domain by the SCF.

To fully exploit the potentialities of the session concept, two new control capabilities are introduced within the session control domain:

1. *SCP-initiated call*; the SCP can order the SSP to set-up a call between two users (i.e. a point-to-point connection). This IN functionality supplies the "Third Party Call Initiated" procedure; in this procedure separate paths of a connection towards two remote users are set-up and linked by a third party. This functionality can also be used to set-up a point-to-multipoint connection among a root user and a multiplicity of leaf users. In this case, the root is connected to the SSP by means of a single unidirectional point-to-point connection, while the point-to-multipoint part of the connection starts from the SSP.
2. *SCP-session activation*; this command is used to activate a session (in a generic SSP) on behalf the SCP. This functionality allows the control of the connections involved in a service through a multiplicity of sessions distributed in several SSPs. It is to be noted that this capability differs from that used in the classical IN approach, where the activation of a SSM instance is always due to a user request.

The proposed object model of a session is shown in Figure 3. It contains objects that are abstractions of switching and transmission resources [AC068 INSIGNIA Deliverable].

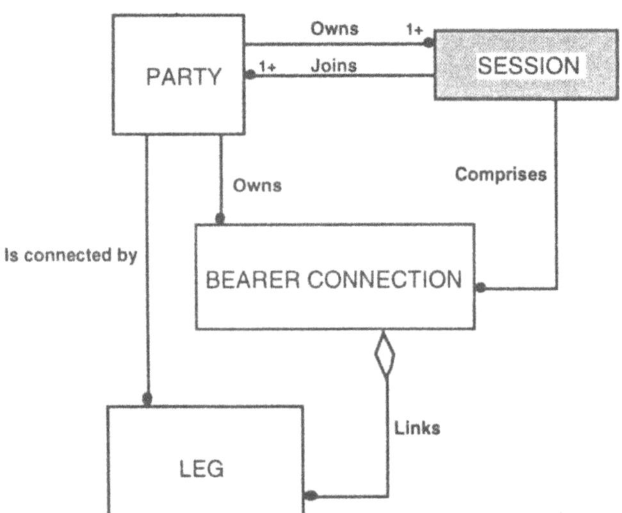

Figure 3 The session object model.

The *session* object represents the session instance. Several parties, represented by the *party* object, can join a session. A party can be either an end user or a network component (e.g. the SCP, when it is necessary to represent SCP-initiated actions). One of the parties joining a session is the session owner. During the service evolution, new parties can be added to a session or joined parties can be removed from a session.

The *bearer connection* object represents the bearer connection processing and is potentially in relationship with several legs. The *leg* object models the processing of the communication path towards a party. The multiplicity of the aggregations between the legs and a bearer connection determines the connection topology: if a bearer connection contains exactly two legs, it is a point-to-point connection; if there are more than two legs per bearer connection, we have a point-to-multipoint connection.

Moreover, each object could also be denoted by one or more attributes regarding some of its specific characteristics. In particular, we can distinguish static attributes and dynamic ones. The static attributes denote fixed characteristics of the object assigned in the active service instance. The dynamic attributes change during the service evolution and are used by the IN logic to follow the dynamic modifications of the service configuration.

The proposed model is a powerful tool to handle the interaction between the service control domain and the B-ISDN control function. It shows each single service component, the state reached by each of them and their relationships. Moreover, this model allows the utilisation of a high level language between the SCF and the SSF (i.e. an enhanced INAP protocol called B-INAP [AC068 INSIGNIA Deliverable]). As a matter of example, the SCF can command in a single interaction the dropping of a party; this implies that, at the SSF level, the object party is removed by the session, together with all its bearers and legs. To this aim, the SSF generates the appropriate messages towards all the BCSMs involved.

2.2 The service control domain

The service control domain realises the global handling of the service. The SCF, interacting with all the SSFs involved in the service, derives the overall network configuration by merging all the partial views represented by the single sessions.

The resultant model, called *Global Logic Service Configuration* is a high level one and it is designed to support the *Service Logic Instance* (SLI). It is worth noting that this model assumes fundamental relevance in case of a service realised adopting the *distributed* approach described above.

The GLSC is composed by four types of objects (Figure 4): i) the *GLSC* object, representing the active service instance; ii) the *session* object, identifying the session instance in each SSF involved in the service provisioning; iii) the *actor* object, representing either users or special resources (intelligent peripheral, bridge audio/video etc.) involved in the service; iv) the *stream* object, representing the information flow among actors.

The actor and the stream objects hold the main parameters needed by the SLI. The actor object contains user specific characteristics, like the E.164 address, and their role in the service (e.g. optional or mandatory). The stream attributes concern the frame structure of the flow (data format and coding, e.g. MPEG1, JPEG), the quality of service and throughput values. The stream direction could be indicated by an attribute assigned to the relationship "is connected to", said attribute assuming the values incoming, outgoing or both.

The GLSC object model allows the SLI to retrieve all the necessary data. Thank to this model, it is possible to identify the session controlling the stream that connects two or more actors; therefore, if an actor has to be excluded from the service, it is straightforward to discriminate the session that the actor has joined and, within the session, the streams to which the actor is connected to.

It is to be noted that the more sophisticated is the service network configuration, the more important is the role played by the GLSC. This happens, for instance, when a great number of special resources are involved or when the service provisioning is carried out by means of the interaction with several SSPs.

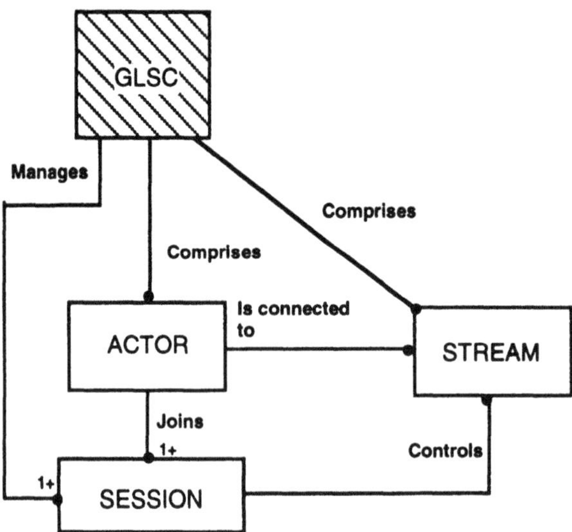

Figure 4 The GLSC object model.

2.3 Interactions between session and service domains

The typical interaction between the session domain and the service one (in the direction that goes from the former to the latter) is the following:

1. each event on the basic bearer connection is driven by the B-ISDN signalling and reported to the IN-SM by means of the *Detection Points* (DP) in the BCSM;

2. the IN-SM modifies, in accordance to the event reported, the state of one or more objects represented in the session instance (for instance, the dynamic attribute representing the state of the bearer connection can be modified from *being set-up* to *set-up*);
3. the new state of the session is reported to the SCF and it is processed by the SLI;
4. according to the state being reported, the SLI updates the GLSC state.

In the opposite direction (from the service domain to the session one), an interaction is needed when, during the service processing, the SLI requires the session domain to execute an operation or when a user asks the SCF to execute a service procedure.

The steps of this interaction are:

1. the SLI retrieves the service network configuration held in the GLSC;
2. according to the information obtained and to the service procedure requested, the SLI commands one or more SSFs to execute the appropriate operation, by means of enhanced INAP messages mentioned above;
3. the IN-SMs add new objects or modify the state of those already present in their session instances, and the SSFs command the underlying CCFs to carry out the requested operations.

3 THE BROADBAND-VIDEO CONFERENCE SERVICE

In this section we apply the IN approach to support a multimedia-multiparty service, the Broadband Video Conference (B-VC).

The B-VC is a telecommunication service which allows end-to-end information transfers between two or more service subscribers [EURESCOM P506,1995]. This service provides the necessary arrangements for a real-time conferencing in which audio, video, and other media types can be exchanged among single individuals (single workstations) or group of individuals (located in conference rooms) via the B-ISDN.

The provision of this service requires very powerful signalling capability to obtain and manage a fully meshed audio/video interconnection among all the subscribers, making the B-VC one of the more complex services to be offered by the B-ISDN.

3.1 Service description

The B-VC service is provided by means of an "on demand" mode. The service consists of the following classes of procedures [AC068 INSIGNIA Deliverable]:

- procedures applicable to a not yet existing conference: conference creation;
- procedures applicable to an inactive conference: inactive conference modification, conference establishment;

- procedures applicable to an active conference: addition of new conferee(s), disconnection of conferee(s), active conference modification, conference closing down.

The conference creation consists of a phase during which the user requiring the service, called hereafter *conference coordinator*, defines the conference profile: the media required, the list of users that could be involved and their profiles (e.g. role in the conference, procedures access rights, etc.). After the creation phase the conference can be activated immediately or later on.

During the inactive phase, the conference profile can be modified by the conference coordinator by means of the *inactive conference modification* procedure.

The *conference establishment* procedure allows the coordinator to start the active phase of the conference service; this procedure consist mainly in inviting the users and then in interconnecting them.

During the active phase of the conference a new conferee can be added to the service; this happens as a consequence of a request coming from an authorised conferee or directly from the new user. The coordinator can or can not accept this request. Of course, a conferee can leave an active conference anytime with the *disconnection of conferee* procedure (also, an authorised conferee can request the disconnection of another conferee).

The *active conference modification* procedure allows a user to request the coordinator to modify his/her profile; in addition the coordinator can use this procedure to indicate a possible new coordinator. Finally the conference closing can be obtained by means of the *conference closing down* procedure.

It is worth noting that the interaction between the users and the service logic can be supported by a *Specialised Resource Function* (SRF) located in a *Broadband Intelligent Peripheral* (B-IP); all the users are connected to this special resource via a data bearer and the B-IP interacts with the SLI by using the INAP protocol.

3.2 Service analysis

In this section we analyse the conference establishment procedure, realised both with the *centralised* architectural solution and with the *distributed* one, and compare the performance of the two approaches; we also study the resulting service representation models at the session domain and at the service domain.

The *centralised* approach is based on a relationship between a SCF and a single SSF. The latter is the SSF in which the conference coordinator has invoked the service logic.

The main steps to realise the service establishment are the following:

- the coordinator invokes, through a data bearer connected to the B-IP previously activated, the establishment procedure;
- the SCF sends to the SSP subsequent "SCP-initiated call" commands to realise a fully meshed interconnection of all the invited users;
- the SSF modifies the session view, orders the CCF to set-up the desired connections (bi-directional point-to-point or unidirectional point-to-multipoint) and reports the results to the SCF;

• the SCF updates the GLSC according to the reported results.

Figure 5 represents the network configuration in the centralised approach for a three users conference.

The connections of the users to the B-IP are not shown; for the sake of neatness only one type of connection (for example the video one) is represented. As depicted in this figure, all the connections have to cross a fixed SSP, where are coordinated in a single session instance. The grey arrows represent the interactions between each independent BCSM and the IN-SM handling that BCSM. This solution can be applied for both the SCS 1 (Figure 5a) and the SCS 2.1 (Figure 5b).

This approach can lead to a very inefficient use of the network resources when the users involved are spread in a wide geographic area and thus can be very distant from the SSP of the conference coordinator.

To overcome this impairment the *distributed* approach can be used (Figure 6). The *distributed* approach leads to a multiple interaction between the SCF and two or more SSFs. The SSPs are chosen so as to obtain an efficient resource utilisation. The algorithm that optimises the resource utilisation is implemented in the SCP that realises the distribution of the connections among the sessions; the SCP commands the creation of new sessions, in addition to that already present in the SSP where the conference coordinator has required the execution of the service. As shown in Figure 6a, the session 2 is created to handle the connections concerning users B and C.

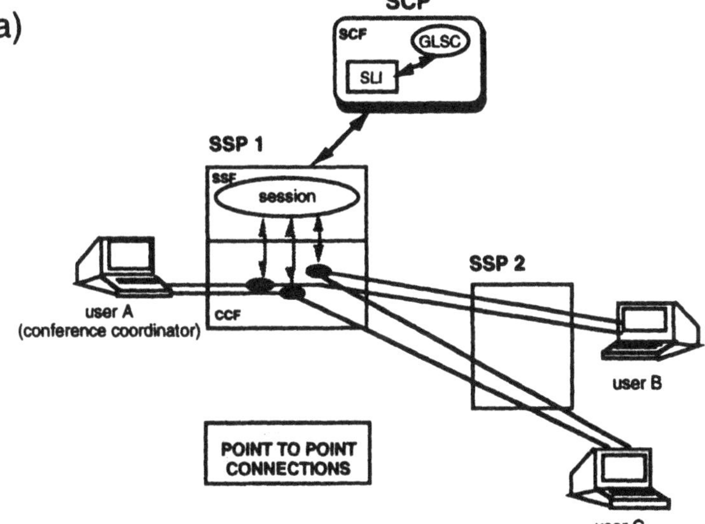

Figure 5a Network configuration in a centralised approach: case of point-to-point connections.

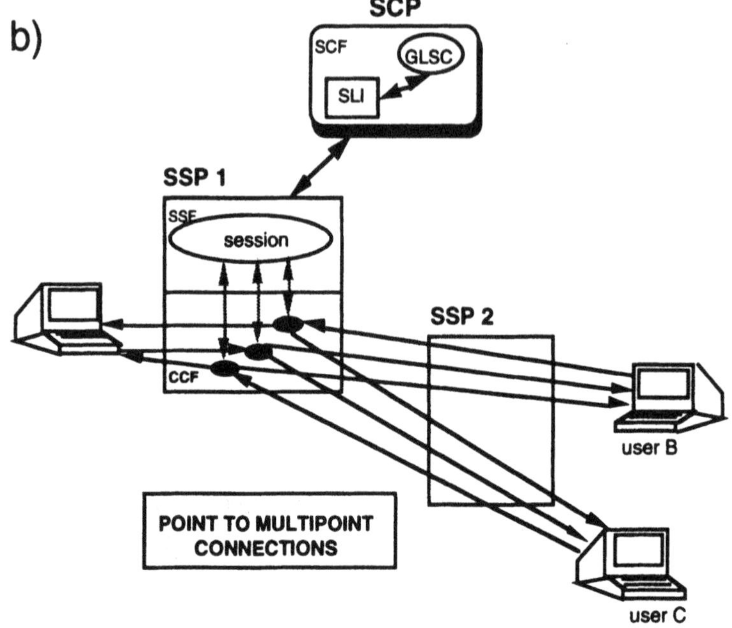

Figure 5b Network configuration in a centralised approach: case of point-to-multipoint connections.

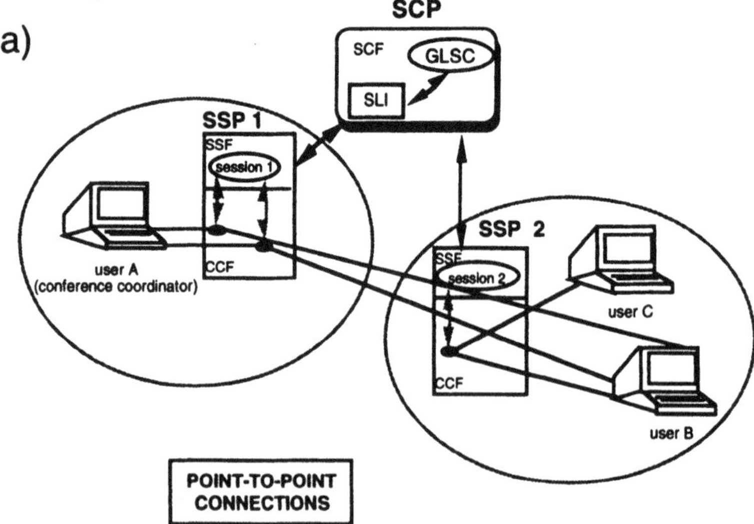

Figure 6a Network configuration in a distributed approach: case of point-to-point connections.

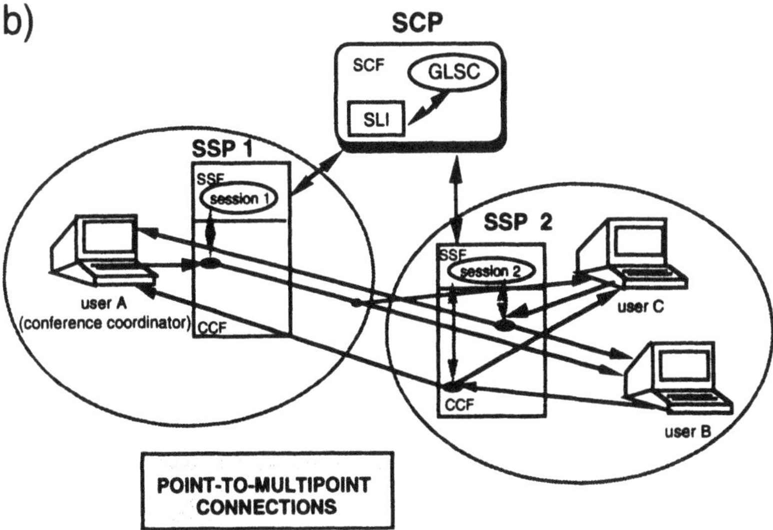

Figure 6b Network configuration in a distributed approach: case point-to-multipoint connections.

In order to compare the two approaches a performance study has been carried out. Two main aspects have been analysed: the signalling load on the network nodes and the transport resource utilisation.

Several network configurations with a variable number of SSPs and conferees have been considered. For a given network configuration we analysed all the possible associations between conferees and SSPs and the presence of a multiplicity of active conferences. Here only a snapshot of results is reported.

As far as the signalling load is concerned, we have analysed both the B-ISDN and the IN one. We have evaluated analytically the number of signalling messages handled by each network element during the realisation of the Video Conference control procedures. Such a number can be taken as a measure of the signalling load at the application level. With respect to the IN signalling load the performance study main results are the following:

- the application of the *distributed* approach does not increase in a significant way the total IN signalling load (just few messages more than the *centralised* approach, the ones required to create new sessions in the SSPs);
- the application of the *distributed* approach allows to reduce the processing load per SSP;
- the utilisation of point-to-multipoint connections implies a significance reduction of the IN messages exchanged (this result can be explained by considering that the number of the B-INAP messages is proportional to the number of connections that must be activated; that is 2*N in the case of

point-to-multipoint connections, N*[N-1] in the case of point-to-point, if N is the number of conferees).

As regards the B-ISDN signalling load, in Figure 7 we report the number of messages as a function of the number of involved conferees. The comparison between distributed approach and centralised one shows that the former is cost effective both for point-to-point and for point-to-multipoint connections.

This vantage is due to the saving of signalling messages exchanged at the Network Node Interface.

Another result is that the adoption of point-to-point-connections determines a better performance behaviour with respect to the point-to-multipoint ones. This can be justified by considering that, even if the number of connections to be set-up in case of PMP is lower than the PP one (2*N vs. N*[N-1], where N is the number of conferees), the signalling messages exchanged for the set-up of a point-to-multipoint connection is proportional to the number of leafs and that one signalling relationship allows to handle a single versus of the communication.

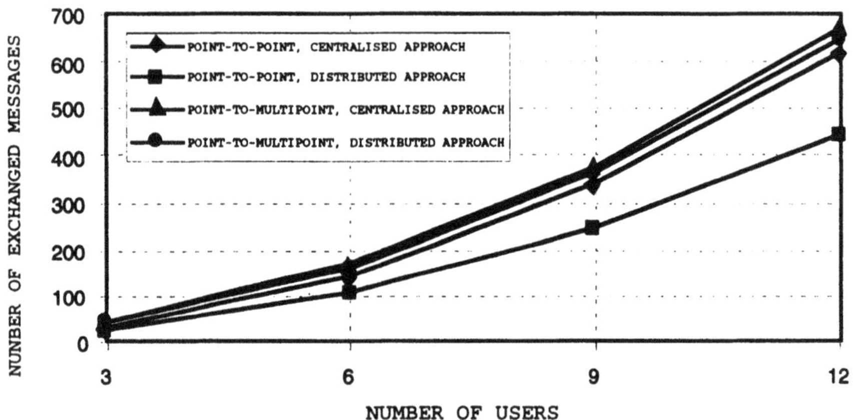

Figure 7 - Total mean B-ISDN load per SSP

To evaluate the transport resource utilisation we assumed a cost function that is linearly dependent on the mutual SSPs distance; in addition, direct connections between each couple of SSPs have been hypothesised.

Figure 8 shows the scheme of a case study network configuration. In this example six SSPs are located at the vertices of two triangles in such a way that the physical distance from a reference point in the centre of the configuration is R1 for the first three SSPs and R2 for the remaining ones. The actual links between the SSPs are not shown.

The rationale behind this choice is to describe a configuration corresponding to a first cluster of SSPs relatively close to each other, surrounded by additional SSPs located at a greater distance. By varying the above introduced parameters R1 and R2, a performance evaluation can be carried out, showing pros and cons of the *centralised* approach versus the *distributed* one, with respect to the transport resources utilisation.

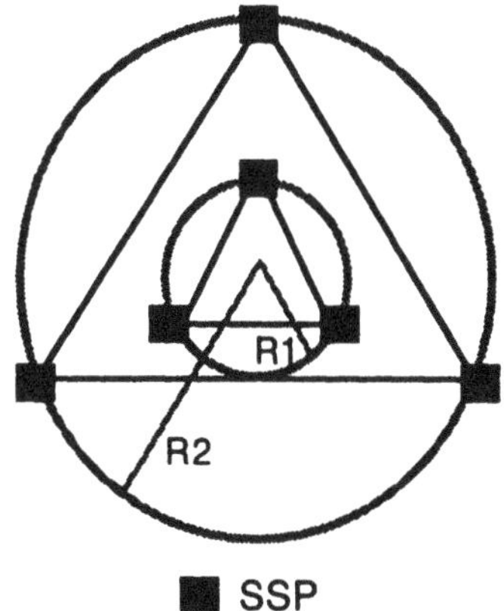

Figure 8 Scheme of the network configuration.

Figures 9 and 10 show the results arising from the analysis of the network configuration depicted in Figure 8, with R2/R1=100. In Figure 9, the SSP relevant to conference coordinator is located on a vertex of the internal triangle, while, in Figure 10, it corresponds to a vertex of the external triangle.

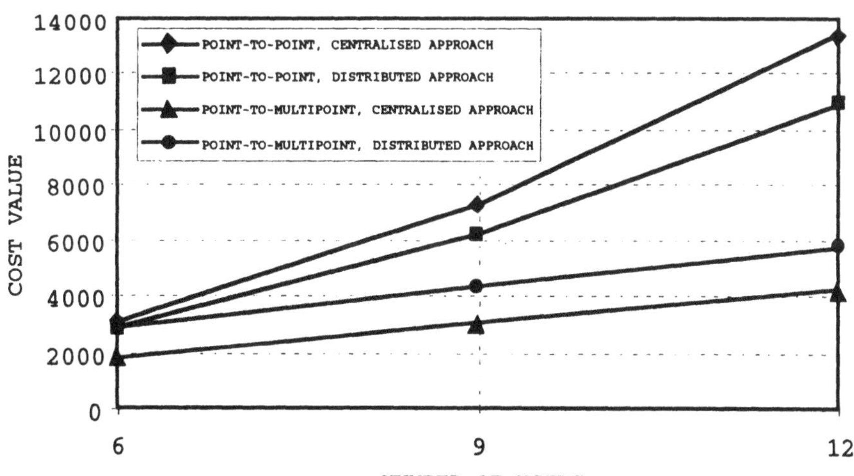

Figure 9 Cost value when the SSP relevant to the conference coordinator is located on the vertex of the internal triangle.

As it can be noted, in the case of point-to-point connections the *distributed* approach is always very cost-effective with respect to the *centralised* approach, whereas if point-to-multipoint connections are used, the *distributed* approach is convenient only if the SSP relevant to the conference coordinator is far away from the "baricentric" position of the network configuration.

Finally, the greater is the number of users, the more convenient is the use of point-to-multipoint connections.

These results can be justified by considering that the *distributed* approach allows the interconnection of users belonging to the same SSP within the SSP itself. Moreover, in the case of point-to-multipoint connections, when a user relevant to a SSP has to be added to an active conference and a leg versus that SSP already exists, no further bandwidth has to be allocated. This is because in this case the cell replication function can be used.

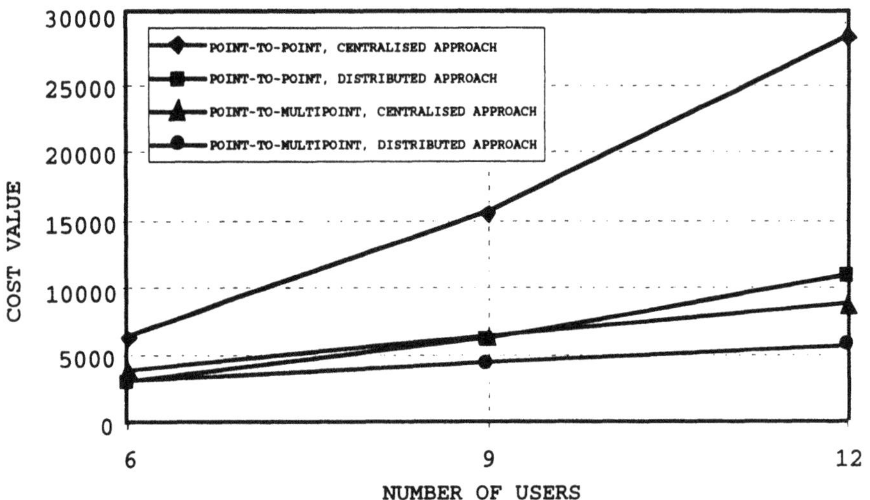

Figure 10 Cost value when the SSP relevant to the conference coordinator is located on the vertex of the external triangle.

3.3 Example of the model instances in the B-VC

In this section, we show an example of instances of the session model and of the service model. These examples refer to the service configuration of Figure 6a in which the *distributed* approach and point-to-point connections are assumed.

The upper part of Figure 11 shows the session instance in the SSP 1 after that the resulting connections are activated; the lower part represents the session 2 in the SSP 2. The session 1 instance models the connections between user A and users B and C, whereas the session 2 instance models the local connection between users B and C.

It is to be noted that the owner of the session 2 is the SCP since this session is the result of an "SCP-activate session" command. In both the sessions the SCP is the owner of the connections activated by "SCP-initiated call" commands. The numbers labelling the objects are assigned in accordance to the temporal activation of the network components.

Figure 12 shows the GLSC instance. This instance represents the overall service configuration, comprising the three service users and the three video information flows. Moreover, the presence of the session object allows actors and streams to be associated to the relevant session. As it can be noted, each actor can belong to one or more sessions, while each stream belongs to one session only.

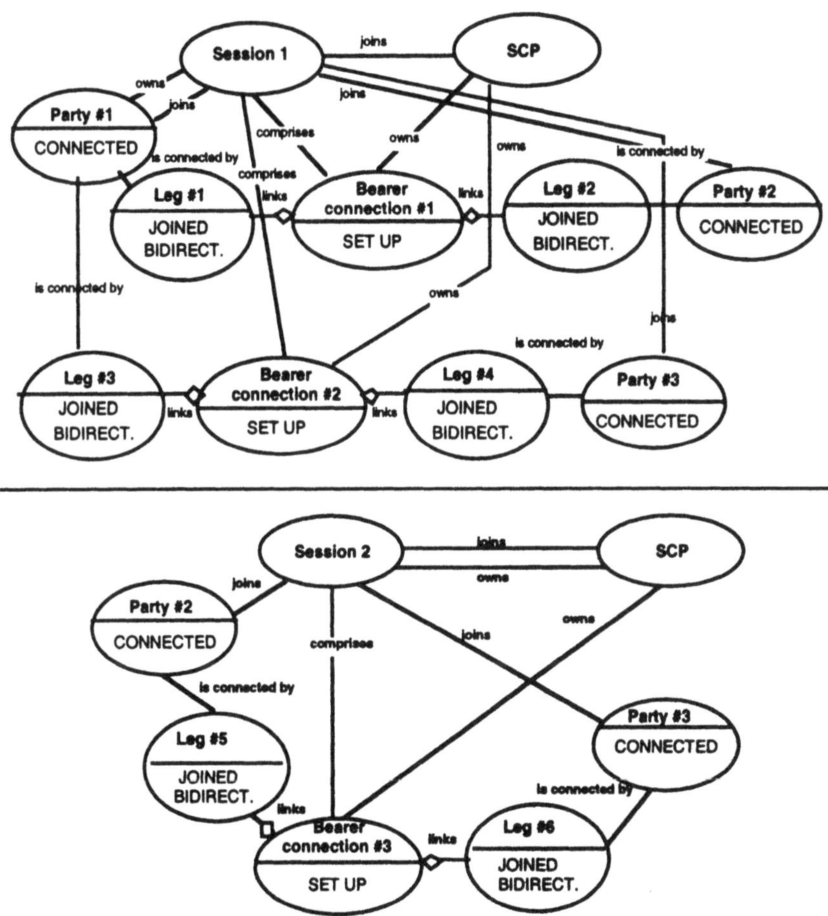

Figure 11 The session instances in SSP 1 and SSP 2.

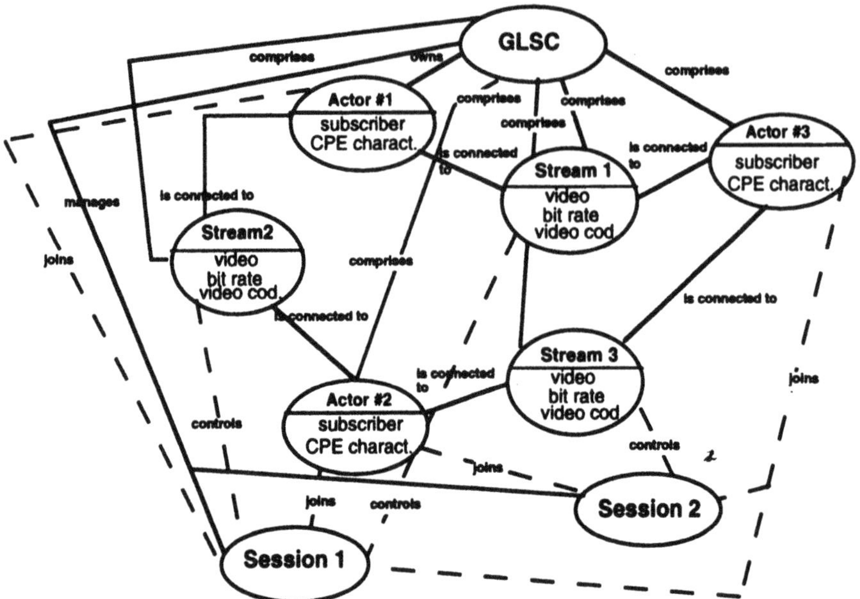

Figure 12 The GLSC instance in the SCP.

4 CONCLUSIONS

In this paper we proposed the introduction of a new functionality in the IN architecture, called Bearer Connections Coordinator and able to realise the provisioning of multimedia-multiparty services in cooperation with the B-ISDN. The solution here presented foresees that the Bearer Connections Coordinator functionality is shared between the Service Control Function and the Service Switching Function entities. Ad hoc object models have been defined for each functional level.

This approach has been applied for the provision of the Broadband Video Conference service, which requires very advanced control capability to handle the relevant network configuration. Finally, some performance results have been discussed in order to single out the main characteristics of the presented architectural solutions.

5 REFERENCES

AC068 INSIGNIA Deliverable (July 1995) Description of selected services.

AC068 INSIGNIA Deliverable (July 1996) First trial: Functions and Architecture Specification.

AC068 INSIGNIA Deliverable (July 1996) First trial: Protocol Specification

Carmagnola, V. Cuomo, F. and Ferretti, M. (June 1996) A layered approach for IN call modeling for the support of multimedia services in a B-ISDN environment, *ICC '96*, Vol. 2, 952-6.

Cuomo, F. Listanti, M. Ronchetti, L. and Salsano, S. (1996) Architectural alternatives for the support of a multipoint service in future B-ISDN, *IIC International Institute of Communications*, 43° international conference of communication.

EURESCOM Project 506 HARMONISATION/INTEGRATION OF B-ISDN AND IN: PIR 1.1 (1995) Scenario for the introduction of Broadband Services and description of selected services.

van Maastricht, C and Schalk, E. (April 1995) Call modeling in a Broadband IN architecture, *ISS'95*, vol. 2, 340-4.

Mukasa, T. Ogino, N. Nakao, K. and Wakahara Y. (November 1995), Proposal for call modeling for Intelligent Network over Broadband ISDN, *Globecom '95*, 1265-71.

ITU-TS WP 1/11, SG 11, Q.2931 (June 1994) B-ISDN User Network Interface Layer 3 specification for Basic Call/Connection Control.

ITU-TS WP 1/11, SG 11, Q.2971 (September 1994), B-ISDN User Network Interface Layer 3 specification for Point-to multipoint Call/Connection Control.

ITU-TS Recommendations Q.1211-Q.1218 (1995), Intelligent Network CS-1.

Wakamoto, M. Fukazawa, M. Kim, M. W. and Murakami, K. (April 1995) Intelligent Network architecture with layered call model for multimedia-on-demand service, *ISS '95*, vol. 1, 201-5.

Francesca Cuomo received her Dr. Eng. degree in Electronics Engineering from the University "La Sapienza" of Roma in 1993. Since the beginning of 1993 she held a scholarship to work with the Telecommunication Networks Group at the INFOCOM Dept. of the University of Roma "La Sapienza". In November 1994 she entered a three years PhD program at the same Department. Since June 1996 she joined the INFOCOM Dept. as a Researcher in Communications, where she currently works in the area of Communications Networks.
Her current research interests focus on modelling and control of broadband networks and support of multimedia communications by means of the IN paradigm.

Marco Listanti received his Dr. Eng. degree in Electronics Engineering from the University "La Sapienza" of Roma in 1980. He joined the Fondazione Ugo Bordoni in 1981, where has been leader of the TLC network architecture group until 1991. In November 1991 he joined the University of Roma, where he is currently an Associate Professor in Switching Systems. He also holds lectures at the University of Roma "Tor Vergata" on Communications Networks. His current research interests focus on multimedia broadband communications, high throughput switching architectures and integration between the Intelligent Network and the B-ISDN.

Fabrizio Pozzi graduated in Telecommunication Engineering at the University of Rome "La Sapienza" in 1996.
In the same year, he got a scholarship offered by Telecom Italia S.p.A. and his graduation thesis was carried out in the context of a collaboration program between the INFOCOM Dept. of the University of Rome "La Sapienza" and Telecom Italia S.p.A.
His research activities concerns the realisation of advanced telecommunication services by means of a B-ISDN/Intelligent Network integration.
He has Joined Telecom Italia S.p.A. since June 1997 as a member of the technical staff in the Business Customers Division.

15

Incoming Call Screening (ICS) service

P. Bleuse, B. Vilain
Alcatel Telecom
Switching Systems Division
Network Systems and Product Management
10, rue Latécoère, B.P. 57
F-78141 Vélizy Cedex, France
Tel: +33 (0)1 30 77 96 65
Fax: +33 (0)1 30 77 98 86
bernard.vilain@vz.cit.alcatel.fr

Abstract

For new telephone companies to position themselves efficiently and cost effectively as long-distance network operators (LDNOs), they need a service to assist them in recognizing and screening local-loop subscribers placing a long-distance or international call.

They must be able to:

- Check that a caller, identified by the calling line identity (CLI) and intending to use their network, is registered.
- Check that they have the information necessary to bill the call.
- Handle calls from unregistered callers and route them selectively towards attendants. Attendants work for operators or telephone companies and are in charge of new and existing subscribers. Attendants in a call center must be able to propose a new intelligent-network (IN) service subscription to these unregistered callers.
- Reroute a call meeting a busy or no-reply condition.
- Restrict calls based on the CLI and the dialed number.
- Generate a Call Detail Record (CDR) for billing purposes.

Intelligent Networks and Intelligence in Networks D. Gaiti (Ed.)
Published by Chapman & Hall

Alcatel proposes the above capabilities to these long-distance network operators (LDNOs) with its new Incoming Call Screening (ICS) service. The ICS service will allow them to check if an incoming call request has been generated by a subscribed user or not, to validate such a request, and to process it accordingly.

The service is invoked whenever a long-distance call attempt is received on incoming trunks, belonging to one or several predefined trunk categories, and when the caller has selected the LDNO as the carrier through equal-access mechanisms.

Thus, the core of Alcatel's ICS service is its ability to check incoming call requests and decide either on further routing or on rejection. Performing a check of this type inside the operator's network makes use of IN architecture, and both the checking and call-handling actions can be fairly sophisticated.

This article contains information on these actions, including the concept of a caller profile, service logics, service triggering, service provision, service subscription, and statistics. The appendix contains a complete glossary and list of abbreviations.

Keywords

Service creation, service triggering, service subscription, call screening, call billing, long-distance network operators

1 ICS SERVICE OVERVIEW

This document describes the Intelligent Network (IN) Incoming Call Screening (ICS) service. The ICS service allows the served network operator or the long-distance network operator (LDNO) to check if an incoming call request has been generated by a subscribed user or not, to validate such a request, and to process it accordingly.

As shown in the figure below, LDNOs do not usually have subscribers connected to them locally. Subscribers place calls through the local-loop operator to the long-distance network operator or international carrier network. The architecture shown below does not include Incoming Call Screening (ICS) or any intelligent-network platform.

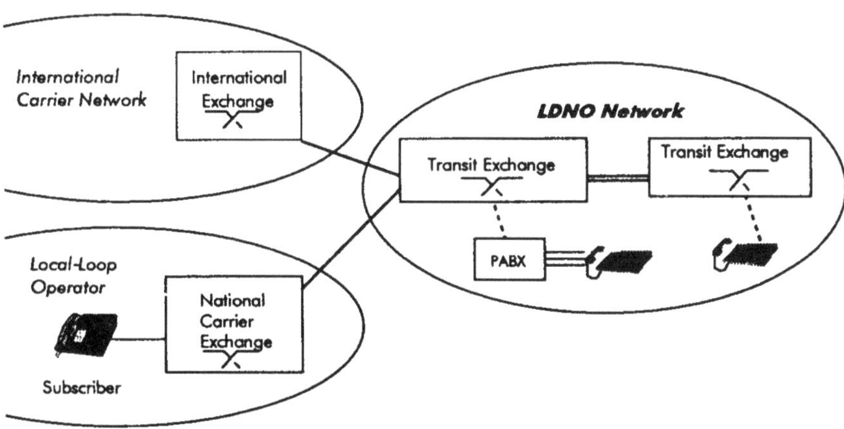

Figure 1 Types of call and network without intelligent network platform.

The next figure shows the same architecture as above, with the difference that it includes an intelligent-network platform supporting IN services, in this case, the ICS service.

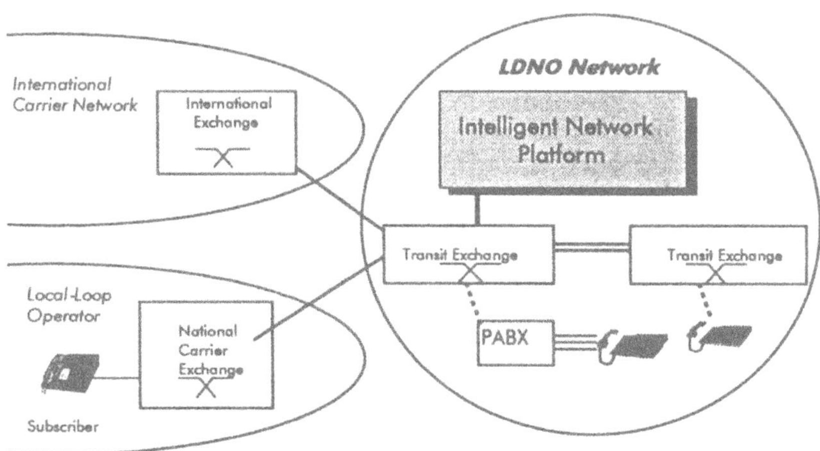

Figure 2 Types of call and network with an intelligent-network platform and Alcatel's Incoming Call Screening (ICS) service.

Alcatel's new Incoming Call Screening service lets LDNOs:

- Check that a caller, identified by the calling line identity (CLI) and intending to use their network, is registered.
- Check that they have the information necessary to bill the call.
- Handle calls from unregistered callers and route them selectively towards attendants. Attendants work for operators or telephone companies and are in charge of new and existing subscribers. Attendants in a call center must be able to propose a new intelligent-network (IN) service subscription to these unregistered callers.
- Reroute a call meeting a busy or no-reply condition.
- Restrict calls based on the CLI and the dialed number.
- Generate a Call Detail Record (CDR) for billing purposes.

According to the agreement with the network operator, the types of call and network of the ICS service are listed below.

- The origin network can be an LDNO or a national carrier.
- The transit network is an LDNO.
- The destination network can be an LDNO, a national carrier, or an international carrier.

Inside the LDNO network, a service user can invoke an IN service. The call is routed to the Service Switching Function (SSF) via PSTN/ISDN/PLMN. The SSF will invoke the service for this particular call at the Service Control Point (SCP). The SCP performs translation and instructs SSF for call completion. The Service Management Point (SMP) is used for the service management. The Information System (IS) enables the service provider to manage all data related to the service.

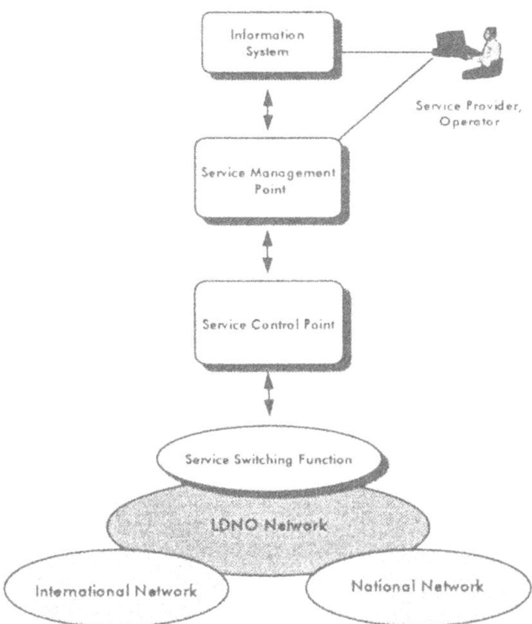

Figure 3 Invoking the ICS service inside the LDNO network.

The Incoming Call Screening service includes the following features:

- Call routing, in which the call is routed to an announcement or to an E164 address.
- Service activation, achieved by specifying the subscription start and expiration dates.
- National-to-national, and national-to-international calling capabilities.
- Service unavailability, which means that if the ICS service is unavailable, whatever the reason, the calls are routed to the dialed number. The call data record includes the information "unchecked call".
- Routing to an interactive voice response server.
- Routing to a voice-mail delivery system.
- Playing an announcement to a party.

- Implementation of a call center overload mechanism to avoid congestion at the attendant's call center.
- Implementation of operator-defined limitation on destination; the list of restricted destinations is common to all caller profiles.
- Implementation of subscriber-defined limitation on destination; the list of restricted destinations applies to a given CallerID; the operator-defined restrictions take precedence over the subscriber-defined restrictions.

The following sections describe the concept of a caller profile, ICS service logic, service triggering, service provision, service subscription, and statistics.

2 CONCEPT OF A CALLER PROFILE

For the ICS service, the interface between the network and the information system is of utmost importance. The Commercial Information System (IS-C) manages the mapping between the caller identification and the caller profile, and, through the Technical Information System (IS-T), passes this information to the network. The network handles each call along the lines of a predefined set of service logics.

2.1 Caller identification, the CallerID

The caller identification, also referred to as the *CallerID*, is composed of:

- the LineID, including the line identities as received in the signaling; the line identities are:
  - the Calling Line Identity (CLI) provided and certified by the network,
  - the User-Provided Identity (UPI);
- the calling party category (CPC) provided by the network;
- the access prefix composed by the caller and transported by the network;
- any additional identity provided by the signaling system along with the calling line identity (CLI); the CLI is provided and certified by the network.

2.2 Caller profile

The caller profile is composed of two information elements:

1. The subscription profile which reflects the situation of the subscriber vis-à-vis the subscription process.
2. The back-office profile which provides additional characterization of the caller.

The subscription profile reflects the situation of the subscriber vis-à-vis the subscription process. Types of subscription status or situation are designated as unknown, undesired, prospect, target, subscriber, nomadic, suspended, and withdrawn.

The back-office profile provides additional characterization of the caller. This information is transparent to the network. The network transmits the information to the IS-T via the Call Detailed Record (CDR).

2.3 Modifying the caller profile

Each modification of the caller profile associated with a CallerID is passed from the IS-C to the IS-T and then to the network. There, it is transformed into a service logic and a group of settings, which are then entered into the network database. Thus, caller profiles are not used as such by the network which can only address the service logic associated with a given caller profile. When a call is processed by the ICS service, the network deduces a service logic from the CallerID. The service logic applied to the caller profile (for example, authorization of routing to a dialed number) is completed with settings applied to the given CallerID.

2.4 Associating CallerIDs to caller profiles

The association of a CallerID to a caller profile is received from the information system. Association with the service logic to be used is determined by the caller profile and by the call character "direct".

With the ICS service, the operator has the ability to specify the CallerID-to-caller profile relationship, either by:

- Specifying a global association with a Calling Party Category (CPC); this would be useful in defining the processing of calls from the lines with the "priority" or "payphone" category, for example. This type of association is managed by the network; or by
- Indicating a complete CallerID; this type of association is managed by the information system.

The figure below shows the principle of determining the caller profile from the CallerID.

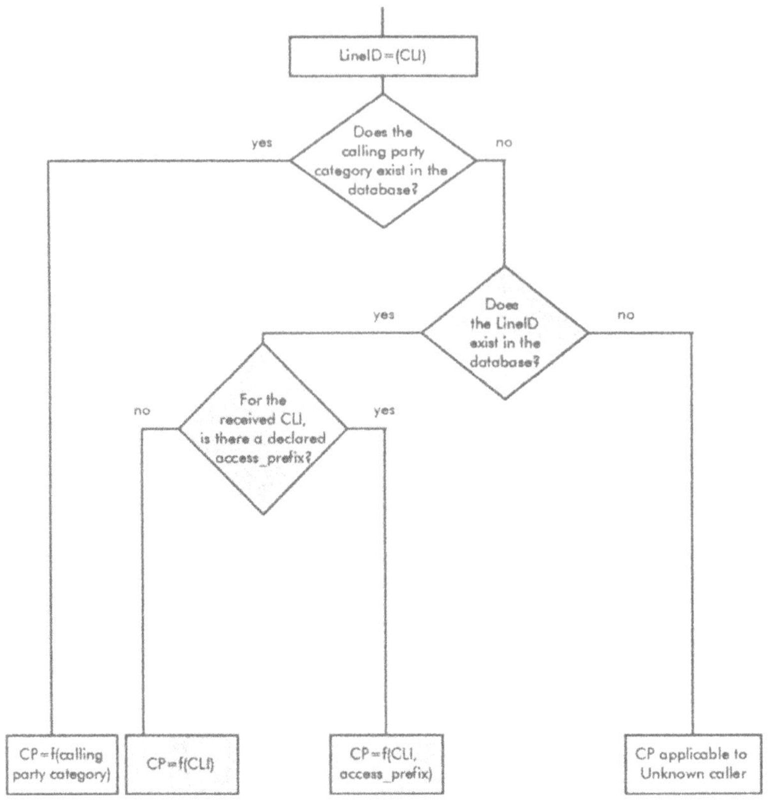

Figure 4 Principle of determining the caller profile from the CallerID.

2.5 Handling caller profiles

The caller profiles are handled as follows:

Neither the IS-C nor the IS-T knows the service logics associated with the caller profile. When an association between a caller profile and a set of CallerIDs is received by the network from the IS-C through the IS-T, the given caller profile is converted into a service logic applicable by the network to the calls from the set of CallerIDs. An example would be the downloading of a prospect's or a target's file.

After processing a call, the related caller profile is conveyed by the network down to the CDR where it is registered. The processing of the CDRs by the IS-C may imply a change in the caller profile. This change is sent back to the network, almost in real time. An example would be the IS-C-managed "restriction on credit overflow". Once the IS-C detects a floor overflow for example, a message requiring the modification of the CallerID is sent to the network.

The "unknown" caller profile is not explicitly declared, and the associated service logic is used when the CallerID is not found in the network database. The network is not allowed to change a caller profile on its own initiative; if such a change is necessary, it is always decided upon and ordered from the IS-C. From a logical point of view, the network is not allowed to create caller-related data on its own initiative. The creation of such data is allowed only if the service logic associated with the caller profile includes this data handling.

3 ICS SERVICE LOGIC

The ICS service offers identified call handling procedures as service logics. A service logic program is associated with a number of calling parties, via the relevant (set of) caller profile(s), and executed in the event of triggering the service by a call placed by one of these calling parties. For a given caller, there will be one given associated caller profile, which in turn determines one given service logic, with a set of given values to be applied to the call.

3.1 Determining the service logic

Each CallerID has a caller profile. The caller profile determines the service logic to be applied. The caller profile determines a group of global settings, applicable to all CallerIDs having that caller profile. The CallerID can also determine a group of specific settings, applicable to the CallerID, when can then override the global settings. The service logic consults the two groups of settings and takes them into account in the service logic.

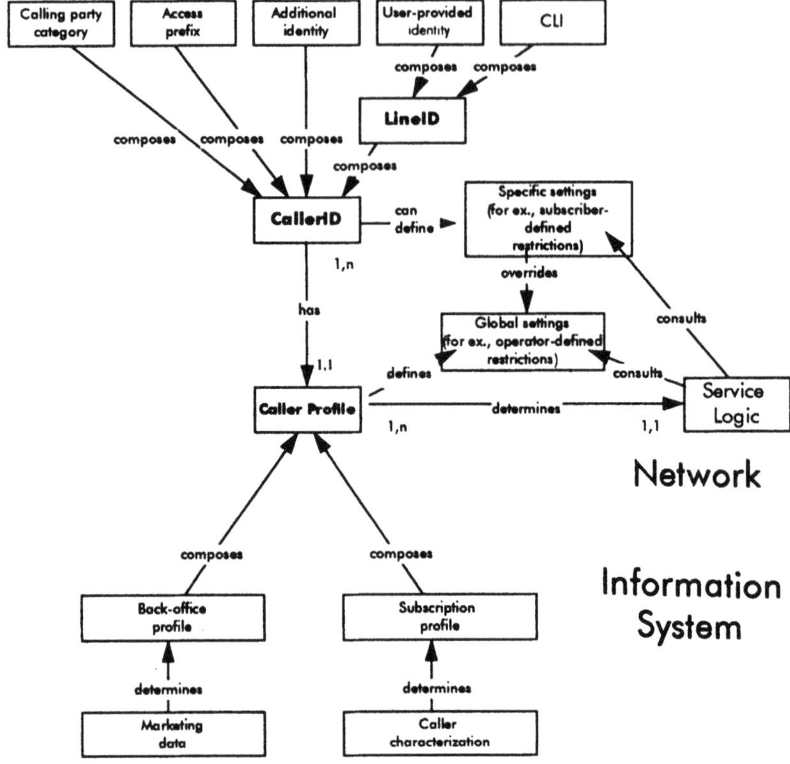

Figure 5 How the CallerID and the caller profile interact to determine the service logic.

To be successful, operators need to apprehend a wider range of caller profiles, beyond the rather simplistic distinction between "registered callers" and "unregistered callers".

Mapping between the CallerIDs and the caller profiles is determined by the Commercial Information System (IC-S) and not by the network. The mapping decision is based on information received from several sources, including market studies (prospect lists), the attendants' system (turning prospects into registered subscribers), and the network.

3.2 Service logic functions

The service logic comprises the following elementary functions, and maximum flexibility is supported as to their sequencing and combination in a more or less complex structure:

- Routing the call to a given destination (this can be the called party, a voice-messaging system, an attendant position).
- Sending a verbal announcement to the caller as a final destination, for example, in the event of failure or a rejected call.
- Creating a Call Detailed Record (CDR), with all the necessary details of the call.
- Checking if a busy or no-reply condition is encountered.
- Checking if operator-defined, originating-call barring restrictions apply to the caller profile.
- Checking if subscriber-defined, originating-call barring restrictions apply to the CallerID.
- Forcing a network-originated call release.
- Sending a subsequent verbal announcement to the caller.
- Checking against call filtering, if applicable to the routing address.

3.3 Service logic routing actions

A service logic identifies a set of actions to be performed in various service logic situations (such as a busy condition). The basic principle consists in using the alternative destination routing of the first determined destination in the event of the busy condition. Thus, the service logic is capable of determining several levels of alternative actions. For example, a call, primarily routed to attendants, can be routed to the dialed number if the attendants are busy, then rerouted to an operator-managed voice-mail delivery system in case the dialed number is busy.

Therefore, the basic principle consists in using alternative destination routing in the event that the first determined destination is busy. The various service logic routing actions are given in the table below.

Table 1 Types of service logic routing actions

Applicable action ➔ ➔Type of routing	Call center overload	Alternative destination on no reply	Alternative destination on busy
To an announcement			
Routing to an announcement	Not applicable	Not applicable	Not applicable
To attendants			
Normal routing to the attendants	Applicable	Applicable	Applicable
Priority routing to the attendants	Not applicable	Applicable	Applicable
To a network address			
Routing to the dialed number	Not applicable	Conditional (subject to caller acceptance)	Applicable
Routing to an operator-managed IVR server	Not applicable	Applicable	Applicable
Routing to an operator-managed voice-mail delivery system (not applicable as initial routing)	Not applicable	Applicable	Applicable
Routing to another network address	Not applicable	Applicable	Applicable

4 SERVICE TRIGGERING

The ICS service is triggered as described below.

- On the user profile, that is, on all calls from a direct-access profile invoke the ICS service.
- On the combination of two call settings:
  - one call settings which is the identity of the incoming trunk, that is, all calls coming from a given trunk marked as an "ICS trunk" invoke the ICS service;
  - one call setting which is the access prefix. For example, all calls dialed with a prefix indicating the operator as the chosen long-distance carrier are triggered, and all calls starting with another prefix for another carrier are not.
- On the reception of a call with a given numbering prefix (for example, 36PQ).

The ICS service is not be triggered if the call demands another IN-provided service. For instance, if a call is received from an ICS trunk but the calling user has dialed one of the 800 prefixes, the relevant 800 service is invoked and not the ICS service.

5 SERVICE PROVISION

The operator or service provider manages the service provision. The operator or service provider will have access to the service management either via the information system or via a PC with a user-friendly graphics interface running under Windows™.

Service information is managed using the object-oriented concept. The operator or service provider can apply management methods to service objects. The main man-to-machine commands are the following: Create, Modify, Display, Remove, List.

The service provider will be able to perform management of configuration, data, statistics, administration, and mail.

6 SERVICE SUBSCRIPTION

ICS service provision requires an arrangement between the service provider and the service subscriber. The service subscriber can request to withdraw from the arrangement, or the service provider can also decide to withdraw.

Once the subscription between the service provider and the service subscriber has been arranged, the service provider registers a CallerID profile in the IN platform. This profile comprises the settings relative to the customer-subscribed functions. The service subscriber can modify these settings via the service provider.

7 STATISTICS

The ICS service provides permanent and on-demand statistical information on:
- call-handling statistics, enabling the operator to measure service usage, such as call type, call time, unsuccessful calls, and so on;
- management statistics, enabling measurement of the Service Management Point (SMP) activity (sessions and commands).

The service offers the following examples of counters for operator statistics:
- number of calls presented to the service;
- number of calls successfully processed by the service;
- number of calls primarily routed to an announcement;
- number of calls primarily routed to an IVR;
- number of calls primarily routed to the called party;
- number of calls primarily routed to an attendant;
- number of calls rejected due to call center overload;
- number of calls with connection to the called party;
- number of calls meeting busy called party or congestion;
- number of calls rerouted to the voice-mail delivery after meeting a busy condition.

8 CONCLUSION

In the context of approaching deregulation, new market players in telecommunications are modifying the value chain. LDNOs need to make money with the traffic they carry for the benefit of end-users who are subscribers of local-loop operators.

The ICS service may become key to allowing LDNOs to check incoming calls and decide to accept or reject the calls. A significant feature of incoming call screening is that it allows new subscriptions to be easily registered, thanks to attendants to whom the calls can be routed. This feature is of utmost importance for newcomers, who might not yet have a fully deployed commercial network. With ICS, they will be able to welcome end-users, especially in the initial phases of launching their network.

ICS may ultimately prove to be a new approach to subscribing an LNDO service, thus allowing LDNOs to capture new subscribers efficiently.

9 GLOSSARY AND ABBREVIATIONS

9.1 Glossary

Access prefix
Prefix dialed by the calling user before the *E.164* number, for example, enabling carrier selection. In France, referred to as *E* or $16\alpha\beta(\gamma)$.

Attendant
Operator's employee working in a call center, in charge of welcoming prospects, targets, and service subscribers.

Back-office profile
Caller's complementary network-transparent characterization, transmitted from the network to the technical information system.

CallerID
Full set of basic and complementary caller identifications applying to a caller, including the LineID.

Caller profile
Information that categorizes a CallerID with respect to the subscription profile, and back-office profile, and which determines the service logic to be applied to the call.

Calling party category
Category applying to the line used by the caller, for example, ordinary line, priority line, payphone, and so on.
LineID
Various line identities received in the relevant signaling fields. Component of the CallerID.
Long-distance call
Calls between two different local areas, or placed to an international destination.
Long-distance network
Network which routes long-distance calls.
Long-Distance Network Operator, LDNO
Network operator which handles long-distance calls for its customers. The long-distance network operator uses the ICS service to control the access to the long-distance network. Also referred to as the operator.
Network operator
Entity which operates network elements and resources.
Nomadic subscriber
Subscriber using the service with identification means which differ from the calling line identity.
Operator
See *Long-Distance Network Operator*.
Prospect
Entity or person known as possibly interested in the long-distance network service.
Remote access
Access reserved to nomadic subscribers, for which the caller identification is not linked to the line identification.
RemoteID
Specific caller identification used in case of nomadic subscribers' remote access.
Service logic
A program which determines how to handle a long-distance call which has triggered the ICS service. For a given caller, there will be one given associated caller profile, which in turn determines one given service logic, with a group of given settings, to be applied to that person's calls.
Service provider
Entity responsible for dealing with the customer. Also called in French *Société de Commercialisation de Services (SCS)*.
Subscriber
Entity or person, which or who has subscribed to the long-distance network, possibly through a service provider.

Subscription profile
Characterization of a caller encompassing subscription status information and refining it through complementary data.
Subscription status
Categorization of a caller with respect to the subscription process.
Target
Prospect with whom a commercial contact has already been established.

9.2 Abbreviations

CDR	Call Detailed Record
CLI	Calling Line Identity
CPC	Calling Party Category
ICS	Incoming Call Screening
IN	Intelligent Network
IS	Information System
IS-C	Commercial Information System
ISDN	Integrated Services Digital Network
IS-T	Technical Information System
IVR	Interactive Voice Response
LDNO	Long-Distance Network Operator
PC	Personal Computer
PLMN	Public Land Mobile Network
PSTN	Public Switched Telephone Network
SCP	Service Control Point
SMP	Service Management Point
SSF	Service Switching Function
UPI	User-Provided Identity

10 BIOGRAPHIES

P. Bleuse

In 1980 Patrice Bleuse graduated in electronics engineering from the Ecole Nationale Supérieure d'Electronique de Caen (ENSEEC/ISMRA), after which he obtained a post-graduate management degree from the Institut d'Administration d'Entreprise (IAE), Paris, France.

He spent the next ten years as R&D director with a French industrial and automotive equipment manufacturer. He was responsible for designing telecommunications equipment such as phonecard boxes and radio terminals, for both industry- and military-class products.

In 1990 he joined Alcatel Telecom as product manager for modems (V/F and baseband) and ISDN-NTs. He then headed the ATM LAN program within the Alcatel Data Networks (ADN) company.

Today, a member of Alcatel Telecom's network systems and product management, Bleuse has worldwide responsibility for Internet-related network solutions for the public switch, the Alcatel E10 system.

B. Vilain

Bernard Vilain is a 1977 graduate of the Ecole Nationale Supérieure des Télécommunications (ENST), Paris, France.

He spent the first seven years of his career at the Centre National d'Etudes des Télécommunications (CNET), the research arm of France Telecom, where he was in charge of product analysis of digital exchanges to prepare the French PSTN for the introduction of ISDN. In 1984, he joined Alcatel Telecom as project manager for pre-intelligent network services on the Alcatel transit node.

At present, his responsibilities cover IN standards activities for Alcatel Telecom. Within the company's network systems and product management organization, he is program manager for intelligent networks and distributed environments; in this capacity he prepares network offerings for IN and mobile product lines worldwide. He was recently nominated chairman for the ITU-T Working Party 2/11 for the 1997-2000 study period, in charge of ISUP, DSS1, and protocol interworking issues.

ARCHITECTURE OF THE MULTI-MODAL ORGANIZATIONAL RESEARCH AND PRODUCTION HETEROGENEOUS NETWORK (MORPHnet)

by

R. J. Aiken (aiken@anl.gov), R. A. Carlson (racarlson@anl.gov), I. T. Foster (itf@mcs.anl.gov), T. C. Kuhfuss (kuhfuss@anl.gov), R. L. Stevens (stevens@mcs.anl.gov), and L. Winkler (lwinkler@anl.gov)

Argonne National Laboratory
9700 South Cass Avenue
Argonne, IL, USA 60439

Electronics and Computing Technologies Division
Phone: 630-252-7155
Fax: 630-252-9689
and
Mathematics and Computer Science Division
Phone: 630-252-6188
Fax: 630-252-6333

January 1997

Argonne National Laboratory, Argonne, Illinois 60439
operated by the University of Chicago for
the United States Department of Energy under
Contract W-31-109-Eng-38

Intelligent Networks and Intelligence in Networks D. Gaiti (Ed.)
Published by Chapman & Hall

Argonne National Laboratory, with facilities in the states of Illinois and Idaho, is owned by the United States government, and operated by The University of Chicago under the provisions of a contract with the Department of Energy.

This technical report is a product of Argonne's Electronics and Computing Technologies and Mathematics and Computer Science Divisions. For information on the divisions' scientific and engineering activities, contact:

Director, Electronics and Computing Technologies Division
Argonne National Laboratory
Argonne, Illinois 60439-4815
Telephone: (630) 252-7586

DISCLAIMER

Available to DOE and DOE contractors from the Office of Scientific and Technical Information, P.O. Box 62, Oak Ridge, TN 37831; prices available from (423) 576-8401.

Available to the public from the National Technical Information Service, U. S. Department of Commerce, 5285 Port Royal Road, Springfield, VA 22151

Available on the World Wide Web at URL
http://www.anl.gov/ECT/Public/research/morphnet.html

Abstract

The research and education (R&E) community requires persistent and scaleable network infrastructure to concurrently support production and research applications as well as network research. In the past, the R&E community has relied on supporting parallel network and end-node infrastructures, which can be very expensive and inefficient for network service managers and application programmers. The grand challenge in networking is to provide support for multiple, concurrent, multi-layer views of the network for the applications and the network researchers, and to satisfy the sometimes conflicting requirements of both while ensuring one type of traffic does not adversely affect the other. Internet and telecommunications service providers will also benefit from a multi-modal infrastructure, which can provide smoother transitions to new technologies and allow for testing of these technologies with real user traffic while they are still in the pre-production mode. Our proposed approach requires the use of as much of the same network and end system infrastructure as possible to reduce the costs needed to support both classes of activities (i.e., production and research). An initial step is to define multiple layers of production services (i.e., at the physical, network media, network bearer, middle, and application layers) that can be made accessible for concurrent use by the network researcher, manager, or application programmer. Breaking the infrastructure into segments and objects (e.g., routers, switches, multiplexors, circuits, paths, etc.) gives us the capability to dynamically construct and configure the virtual active networks to address these requirements. These capabilities must be supported at the campus, regional, and wide-area network levels to allow for collaboration by geographically dispersed groups. The Multi-Modal Organizational Research and Production Heterogeneous Network (MORPHnet) described in this report is an initial architecture and framework designed to identify and support the capabilities needed for the proposed combined infrastructure and to address related research issues.

1 INTRODUCTION

The research and education (R&E) community has a continuing need for persistent and scaleable network infrastructure supporting production and research applications as well as network research. This infrastructure is essential if researchers are to advance the state of the art both in advanced applications (for which reliable "production" network capabilities are required) and in the networking technologies that will provide the infrastructure of the future (for which crashable "research" network capabilities are required). The continually shortening cycle associated with the evolution of network research to production status only fuels the demand for advanced production networking capabilities and further strains the ability to provide it. Historically, the very different requirements of production and research have led to the use of distinct physical infrastructures for these two purposes. Yet, as the demand for increased bandwidth and capabilities continues to increase, the R&E community will have difficulty paying the high costs associated with acquiring and supporting parallel networks. Hence, we propose a new approach that will allow the use of the same physical infrastructure for both research and development purposes. As we explain in this report, this new approach poses significant challenges that will require a major research effort to overcome, but promises substantial benefits in terms of cost savings and enhanced research and production capabilities. In fact, we argue that the economics of network infrastructure associated with this approach are essential if the R&E community is to continue large-scale networking.

The need for integrated production and research infrastructure arises because, while network technologies, bandwidth, and capabilities continue to rapidly improve, enhancements to the resolution and scale of existing multimedia, collaboration, and database applications (and entirely new applications) are increasing demand at an equal or greater rate. So we can expect to see competition for scarce network resources for the foreseeable future. The R&E community cannot financially afford to support both a high-speed production and an extremely high-speed experimental network infrastructure. Neither can it afford to conduct network research at the expense of the scientific application researcher, or favor a plan that stagnates the network research required to meet the constantly increasing applications requirements by funding only production networks. Internet service providers (ISPs)[1] face similar problems: they can ill afford idle bandwidth, even for short

[1] ISPs in the United States include the inter-exchange carriers (IXCs), Regional Bell operating companies (RBOCs), cable companies, alternate access providers, commercial and private providers, and any other entity that provides telecommunications and Internet services to its constituency on a wide-area basis. ISPs in other parts of the world include similar service providers as well as national PT&Ts.

periods, and therefore must seek new and innovative methods to utilize the infrastructure. A successful implementation of an adaptive multi-modal network infrastructure and architecture will not only address the requirement for concurrent production and experimental infrastructure, but also holds promise for quick deployment of research and development (R&D) infrastructure to address national crises[i].

These considerations lead us to conclude that the grand challenge in networking is to implement and concurrently support both advanced production network services (e.g., vBNS[ii], ESnet[iii]), which applications can use with little risk, and a persistent experimental service (e.g., Dartnet, CAIRN[iv]) over as much of the same infrastructure as possible. In building such a shared infrastructure, we must endeavor to ensure that R&D network traffic and experiments do not adversely affect production traffic (and vice versa). This sharing of infrastructure can occur at numerous layers in the network, including the hardware, media, network bearer, transport, and application layers. The efficient sharing of resources will also occur on and within different network scopes, including the local (e.g., Campus), regional (e.g., Gigapop, MREN), and wide area (e.g., vBNS, ESnet, CAIRN) levels.

In addition to increasing networking bandwidth and capabilities, we must become smarter and more efficient users of network technologies because the demand for network capabilities always exceeds the available resource or the user's ability to pay for it. To overcome the physical limitations of traditional supercomputers, we adopted the use of massively parallel machines. Similarly, we need to become more innovative with router, switch, and overall network architecture design to take advantage of parallelism in switches, multiplexors, and routers. Adaptive temporal use and reuse of segmented network infrastructure must also be explored. Some router and Asynchronous Transfer Mode (ATM) switch vendors are already experimenting with such models, as evidenced by dual fabric switches. Active network technologies, as well as quality of service (QoS) support, can also support concurrent virtual networks with radically different technical requirements (e.g., production and R&D networks) and dynamic policies.

The benefits claimed for multi-modal network infrastructure in the R&E community also apply to telecommunication and Internet service providers, who must support concurrent virtual infrastructure for both production and experimental purposes, as well as multiple policy-based virtual networks on the same infrastructure. The benefits are especially applicable if these providers wish to make more efficient use of network resources in addition to being able to strain and test new network capabilities and features in the experimental mode using real applications; even if only on a temporary basis. Telecommunications service providers are currently seeking new and innovative ways to make use of untapped and underutilized infrastructure in the last mile (e.g., local loop) as well as in their own clouds and switching fabrics. ADSL, in fact all nDSL technologies, as well as ATM are perfect examples of these attempts. An adaptive, active infrastructure will greatly enhance the ability of these providers to tap underutilized bandwidth by allowing them to dedicate network resources on a finer granularity in both time and capability. It is important to note that, although the adaptive, multimodal network infrastructure that we propose will support the R&E community by separating production and experimental traffic, this model can easily be adapted to support any number of two or more virtual networks with heterogeneous and sometimes conflicting requirements and policies. For example, these capabilities can be used to separate traffic based on security, business, or acceptable use policies.

2 BENEFITS AND RISKS

Concurrent support for production and experimental network traffic will benefit the research community by providing more convenient access to large-scale testbeds. While small testbeds and localized pilots are useful for laboratory testing and exploration, their small scale does not normally strain and test new network protocols, tools, and architectures in a manner consistent with the demands of large numbers of users or advanced applications. Production applications, as well as a large number of participating end nodes, are required to thoroughly test new protocols and infrastructures. For example, the experimental R&D Dartnet network was used to develop and test new network protocols (e.g., Multicast IP and RTP) with a small number of nodes and participating researchers. Afterwards, the researchers sought out larger-scale networks (e.g., NSFNET and ESnet) to demonstrate and validate these protocols on a larger scale. Modeling and simulation may be of some use in analyzing and testing new protocols and architectures as long as they are not strictly based on Poisson models. Paxton and Floyd[v] have demonstrated that Poisson models, commonly used to design regular telephony services, do not reflect or represent data network traffic accurately. Therefore it is imperative that networking models and simulations be validated via wide-scale implementations and experiments using real user applications.

Concurrent support for both production and experimental network traffic will also have benefits outside the R&E community. Telecommunications and Internet service providers can use a multi-modal network infrastructure to provide "production-level" services concurrently with experimental or evolutionary network services. This will satisfy their requirements for incremental upgrades as well as customer requirements for both production and R&D facilities, large-scale stress testing of targeted infrastructure, and the introduction of new technologies and services as they evolve. Businesses can use a dual-mode environment to run their production applications while simultaneously experimenting with and evolving their use of new network infrastructures and capabilities. The Internet and, generally speaking, most enterprise networks are haunted by the demands and spirits of networks past (e.g., Decnet, SNA, and other proprietary networks), networks present (e.g., IPv4), and networks of the future (e.g., IPv6[vi]). The multi-modal network model provides us with virtual networks, concurrently supported at various layers, that help us cope with this cyclic development and deployment of networks, systems, and applications.

The phased deployment model for new technologies is still valid for initial experimentation (i.e., performing fairly risky experiments such as new protocols that must first be tested in constrained environments). This model subsequently requires that the scope of the experiment be expanded to fully test these new capabilities. The challenge that lies before us is determining how to use as much of the same infrastructure as possible for concurrent and efficient use by both R&D and production traffic after the initial constrained testing is complete; this challenge becomes greater when we seek to stress test new protocols and architectures and benchmark their capabilities under real traffic. Not only is this multi-modal use and support of networks required for supporting the R&E community's combined R&D and production infrastructure requirements, but it is also useful for 1. introducing incremental upgrades (version upgrades or enhancements) to switches and routers in deployed infrastructure, and 2. providing a transition path for applications eager to exploit new network capabilities; e.g., quality of service (QoS) signaling from an application layer. This multi-modal approach does not necessarily invalidate the use of separate network infrastructures, such as separate switches or links, when the concurrent shared use of some or all of the infrastructure cannot be safely achieved.

Some risk is associated with all new technologies, even "pre-production" services offered by ESnet and vBNS, for example. Users and applications need to accept this fact and plan accordingly. One method for dealing with this issue is to perform a risk analysis of the proposed architecture and identify the portions or layers of the infrastructure that lend themselves to shared use. The "comfort levels" associated with this sharing will most likely vary depending on institutional culture and financial factors. However, wise use of adaptive, multi-modal infrastructure is necessary if we are to further enhance our ability to provide for advanced network research and production networks in the face of dwindling financial resources, as well as for more efficient use of infrastructure by the telecommunications and Internet service providers.

3 VIRTUAL PRODUCTION NETWORK SERVICES (VPNS)

A shared infrastructure can use the concept of a variable "bar" of production-level service to facilitate both the smooth introduction of new capabilities and the concurrent support of production and experimental activities. This concept also supports on-demand experimental use and manipulation of network infrastructure, bandwidth, and quality of service. The bar is virtual in that it can be temporal (i.e., exist for short, medium, or long periods of time) or spatial (exist at various levels of network services at the same time), while concurrently providing for multiple levels of production and R&D-level services depending on the requirements and perspectives of the applications and the network R&D experiments.

3.1 VPNS Bar

One issue in providing for both production and R&D experimental network services (the former supports R&D applications) is the definition adopted for the "production layer." A desirable environment would allow for a certain amount of concurrent elasticity where the production layer is perceived on a per application or virtual network basis. For example, when using this approach to support Asynchronous Transfer Mode[vii] (ATM) experimentation over a shared production hardware media, we might see a production ATM service composed of the ATM switch and local loop for the computer scientist experimenting with a network bearer service such as IPv6. Application scientists (e.g., physicists), though, view the IP layer and below as the production layer as they experiment with RSVP[viii] or reliable multicast for their message passing interface (MPI[ix])-based application. Each of these models has been provided separately in the past; i.e., a dedicated network for each scenario, with the possible exception of tunneling, which we will address later. We believe that the challenge is to provide concurrent support of these virtual production networks, as viewed by the applications and network researchers, on the same infrastructure. Each layer would provide the opportunity and concurrent support for network research and production network services at the next layer up. Each layer depends on the production bar of the services below it.

3.2 Hardware Layer

The first level of providing a "production bar" is the hardware level. We can multiplex both production and network R&D traffic on the same hardware by implementing a hardware multiplexing scheme such as Wave Division Multiplexing (WDM) or Sonet block multiplexing. A portion of the service or circuit (i.e., local loop Sonet, or WDM colors) could be physically split off to a set of production switches; the other portion(s) could be physically split out to yet another distinct set of R&D switches. This model allows for the sharing of a local loop while keeping the production and R&D traffic physically separate on the local loop and in the switches. Whether one multiplexes the two types of traffic over the same infrastructure on the local campus or in the carrier cloud (i.e., on either end of the multiplexed local loop) is determined by the entities in control of those infrastructures and any agreements they have come to with the end user. The carrier may indeed carry both the production and R&E traffic over the same set of switches and links or it may provide separate sets inside the cloud so as to separate the two types of traffic inside their cloud. Either solution provides the end user with the view of one access and local loop to the cloud to support both types of traffic.

The hardware layer can be further exploited if it is composed of distinct objects (switches, links, routers, multiplexors) that can be assembled by an application or network manager on either a real-time basis (i.e., milliseconds to seconds) or on a scheduled basis within hours or days in advance of its anticipated use. For example, an OC-12 pipe could be provided by using four OC-3 links and associated multiplexors and switches. The initial allocation can have two OC-3 links dedicated to production use and two OC-3 links used specifically for network research. If the network researchers are not using their portion of the network (i.e., their OC3s) at any given time, it makes sense to allocate those resources to the production traffic. This assumes that the network segments and components in question can easily transition to production-quality status and back to experimental status at the conclusion of use. Conversely, if the network researcher could use three OC3s for a short-term test of new protocols, and the production traffic is not using its share of the infrastructure, the experimental network project could temporarily make use of a specified amount of the production infrastructure for a short time and then restore it to production status after the experiment is completed. The production portion of the infrastructure may choose not to allocate all of its share of the infrastructure to the network R&D experimenter. Even during off-peak hours when the networks can make use of all of the available infrastructure, the production component may choose to keep a small portion of the production infrastructure available for non-real-time production traffic. This temporal, elastic, on-demand control of hardware layer infrastructure can greatly reduce our need for costly redundant services, circuits, switches, and routers.

3.3 The Media Layer

The model that provides a production bar of services at the media layer (e.g., ATM) assumes that the hardware layer is of production quality and takes the model of infrastructure sharing one step further by supporting both R&D and production services over the same physical media. For example, one can provide an ATM virtual path or circuit for the production traffic as well as a separate and distinct ATM permanent path or circuit dedicated to the experimental network research (e.g., implementing both IPv4 and IPv6 in native mode). A single switch, if appropriately designed and implemented, can satisfy both the R&D and production requirements by supporting experimentation with ATM signaling and QoS at the same time production traffic is passing through the same switch. It is important to provide mechanisms in a switch that ensure that one type of traffic (e.g., experimental) does not bring down the switch or trample the other type of traffic (e.g., production). The use of a redundant, yet separate, internal fabric within the switch is an example of such a mechanism.

3.4 IP

The normal mode of operations employed by today's Internet providers relies on IP as the production network bearer service. In this example, the IP bearer service and all the infrastructure underlying it (i.e., the media and hardware layers) are considered production quality for IP-based applications. Applications may experiment with new middleware capabilities and services, such as RSVP for IP based QoS, but they expect that the IP bearer service is of production quality and will not be used for experimentation by network researchers. Any network experimentation at the bearer layer is accomplished by either using a separate infrastructure (e.g., Dartnet for RTP) or by using tunneling. The use of IP as the production bar provides as solid a production bearer network service as IP can deliver while allowing for experimentation with RSVP and other advanced IP-based capabilities.

Tunneling is a powerful tool that can be used to (1) minimize some of the need for duplicative infrastructure on a wide-area IP bearer service basis, and (2) reduce risk to the production bearer service layer. However, because tunneling does not necessarily address the requirement of an application that wishes to test and utilize a new network layer or network to MAC layer capabilities and infrastructure in native end-to-end mode, it should not be viewed as the only tool for concurrently supporting both a production and network R&D infrastructure. Tunneling not only delays the traffic's end-to-end trip, but it also requires the manual configuration of the virtual tunnels; as we saw with the virtual Mbone overlay, this does not easily scale when large numbers of sites become involved. Although tunneling may be useful during the first stage of the experimentation process, it is only a short-term answer for coexistence and may not truly test the routers and switches as they would be tested when they are supported in native (non-tunneled) mode. The model that concurrently supports a native-mode production and non-production bearer service in the routers by no means contradicts the goal of one common bearer service as described in the often-referenced National Academy of Sciences (NAS) publication, "Realizing the Information Future."[x] Rather, it addresses the reality of overlapping time lines for the "network of the past," the "network of the present," and the "network of the future," evidenced today by legacy networks, IPv4 and IPv6 (respectively). These three phases will always be in existence on any given network, although the actual IP versions may change over time, and should be considered a normal state of affairs[xi]. We will always be improving the bearer service (e.g., Multicast in IPv4) as well as introducing new bearer services or versions (e.g., IPv6). Multi-protocol routers implement a version of the concurrent bearer services model when they support concurrent multiple protocols such as IP, IPX, and SNA in native mode.

3.5 Middle Layer

Applications require the existence of many production-quality middleware services to support experiments with new network technologies and to provide the enhanced distributed computing environment capabilities that are required if these experiments are to be tractable. For example, when RSVP makes it to production status, we will see many experiments in which application developers attempt to improve application performance by representing explicitly the varied array of network QoS associated with different application components. In this case, the production bar would be RSVP and it would simultaneously support both production and experimental networking at the application layer. Other middleware production services may include name servers, security key and certificate infrastructure servers and authorities, directories, session managers (e.g., SDR[xii]), advanced IP-based capabilities such as the Mbone, and resource information and scheduling services such as those being developed in the Globus project[xiii].

3.6 Applications

Many applications programmers are constantly in search of new technologies and will use any available technologies to advance their programming environments and capabilities. Many are more than willing to use experimental facilities and will make use of the varied array of production bars previously mentioned, either in a concurrent or temporal mode. Advanced application programmers require the ability to set QoS parameters, monitor infrastructure, and experiment with new network capabilities to support their advanced application and programming environments. One application may require raw access to the SONET or ATM infrastructure via relevant QoS activation and signaling techniques, while another application concurrently requires a production IP layer to support experimentation with RSVP. The infrastructure needs to be able to support both of these requirements simultaneously, on both a short-term (seconds to minutes) and long-term (hours to days) basis.

4 SCOPE OF THE VPNS

In order to deploy an infrastructure that supports both production and experimental network research, telecommunications service providers need to adopt a new customer-supplier model. In this model, the customer and service providers would work together to define the service elements, network management tools, and administrative models and architecture necessary to support the customers' requirements and their view of the network, as well as that of the telecommunication and Internet service providers. This model requires the telecommunications carrier and service providers to work with the customer in the standards arena to define appropriate end user tool and access-to-information capabilities. It also requires the ISPs to be more open with respect to customer non-intrusive access to network and switch state information. This information includes QoS, circuit or access class information, traffic flows, error status, MIB variables and other state information on an end-to-end basis that the end user community requires to monitor and verify its network services. The customer may also require the ability to dynamically configure, reconfigure, and acquire network infrastructure resources based on end user QoS or policy requirements. This will involve the support of active network components (e.g., circuits, switches, routers, multiplexors) in the infrastructure as well as the signaling and op-code capabilities required to dynamically trigger a reconfiguration. In order to fully utilize these capabilities, applications will require state information and appropriate tools for determining what network infrastructure may be available to them at any given time and for reserving the appropriate network resources in a dynamic fashion, whether that be on a millisecond, minute, hourly, or daily reservation basis.

In addition to enhancing non-intrusive access to network state information on an end to end basis, the ISPs also need to work with network research experimenters to define what is necessary to support the network research on their infrastructure without interfering with the production traffic. This might include providing the researcher with the ability to dynamically alter configurations and settings in a dedicated R&D switch and add/drop multiplexors, or providing safe toggles and state changing tools in production switches to affect network management and monitoring tools. All of this is further complicated by the fact that different network management models and tools are required to support the different thresholds and levels of comfort associated with production and experimental traffic. An adaptive network application infrastructure (e.g., active network control over multiplexors, switches, circuits, and routers) programming interface (API) would make it possible for the end user to easily move between production and experimental modes and infrastructures, easing the pain of living in both policy worlds.

The end user may have agreements or contracts with various service providers, each with a different scope, ranging from the campus to the regional area as well as to the wide-area network (WAN). The continuing deregulation of the industry will blur the distinction between regional and wide-area providers, but the location of the actual physical infrastructure still favors regional economies of scale (e.g., major metropolitan areas), so collaboration between close physical or cultural institutions will prevail. In any event, the issue of supporting production and network research on the same infrastructure will need to be addressed on a campus, regional, and wide-area level. A customer's service may be provided by many nested layers of ISPs, some of whom obtain services from other providers. As a result, there is a need to ensure that the end user and network managers have the capabilities and tools necessary for navigating and monitoring the many nested layers of ISPs, as well as peering points, so that the customers can support their applications on an end-to-end basis.

Regardless of the scope, the major focal point of the concurrently supported infrastructure will be at the customers' demarcation point, commonly referred to as the "edge," where the customer's equipment interfaces and peers with that of the service provider–whether it is at the campus, regional, or WAN level. In fact, the end user may be peering with each of these concurrently. The importance of the assumption regarding the provider's cloud demarcation point is that a service provider can support the production and experimental network traffic any way it chooses within its cloud or infrastructure. For example, an ISP may choose to use one switch and a single fabric, or use separate switches and lines as long as the access interface and expected or contracted services to the end user are met. QoS and network management capabilities rely on the ISPs implementing and supporting standards and tools on an end-to-end basis across the campus, regional, and WAN network infrastructures.

4.1 Crash and Burn Test Bed

The local "crash and burn" test bed is the simplest to envision and support because it can be built as a separate small network on a departmental basis. This is the "Bonneville salt flats" model for performing network research and development; it is usually the first choice for the alpha testing of experimental network protocols because if you crash while trying to break the speed record, you do not adversely affect the production applications. This model normally employs a separate, dedicated local network on a room, building, or campus basis whereby the R&D network never connects to or exchanges traffic with the production network. It is easy to manage, provides excellent access to the researcher, and is very flexible, but it does not scale well.

Many organizations also utilize a small number of demonstration or test routers and switches in a separate "sandbox" for the purpose of testing version upgrades and enhancements to network protocols and architectures. However, they normally cannot afford the number of routers or switches necessary to properly test these upgrades and enhancements under expected real-life traffic and stress. Regardless of the amount of testing that is done before deployment, when the upgrades or enhancements are finally enacted in the routers and switches, the production network becomes an experimental network until the modifications are demonstrated to have no ill side effects.

4.2 Shared Campus Infrastructure

The Shared Campus infrastructure is an attempt to share as much of a campus local area network (LAN) infrastructure as possible to support both the production traffic and the network R&D traffic and experiments. This model is attractive because it allows for the easy introduction of "guinea pig" user applications that not only test the new networking capabilities, but also allow the applications to adapt to the new infrastructure on a pre-production basis. These applications normally run on the production network. However, there are a number of users who are willing to test or stress the experimental network even though it may crash. Application programmers are willing to do this because they derive more benefit from the early adoption of the advanced capabilities or bandwidth offered by the experimental network than the cost or pain associated with the conversion of their codes to take advantage of the new capabilities. This model can be implemented with completely separate network segments for the production network and the experimental R&D network, or it can be built of separate segments that share some subset of gateways, routers, and switches. In a shared network, the traffic may "cross in the night" as it passes through the routers or switches (e.g., virtual LANs [VLANs], ATM private virtual paths [PVPs], or shared routers). The campus network manager may choose to support both types of traffic on the same regional or WAN link as described in Sections 4.3 and 4.4. The challenge on the campus level is how to operate and manage the shared gateways and switches, and how to define a campus network operation center (NOC) that is responsive to both the requirements and thresholds for production and research activities.

The campus LAN will continue to be a heterogeneous mixture of LAN technologies providing the "last foot" to the desktop, including ATM and non-ATM technologies, such as 100 Megabit and Gigabit Ethernet. Because of this heterogeneous mixture, applications will require the development and deployment of integrated solutions that map layer-three-based services (e.g., RSVP) to layer-two services (e.g., ATM or switched Ethernet), including those supporting QoS and network management. In order to take advantage of the QoS capabilities available in layer-two services, applications require the capability for some level of cross-layer signaling (e.g., RSVP to ATM). In situations where a high-speed server is located directly on an ATM network, the application will need to be able to directly view and control the layer-two QoS parameters. In addition, there will be situations where a high-speed server is located on a very-high-speed, non-blocking switched Ethernet segment, or it is the only node on a high-speed broadcast segment. Because these latter two scenarios carry no possibility of media collisions or contention, we need to explore ways to extend bona fide layer-two QoS (e.g., ATM) across these traditionally non-QoS supporting media so that the applications can achieve end-to-end QoS in a heterogeneous media environment.

4.3 Shared Regional Infrastructure

Because the local loop usually accounts for approximately 30%-50% of the cost for connecting to either a regional or WAN ISP, major link/access cost savings can be realized by multiplexing a local loop to support both production and network R&D traffic and applications. This approach can generally be achieved in two different ways, depending on the user's level of trust that one type of traffic will not adversely affect the other type of traffic.

The "no trust " scenario, which might be invoked to support very experimental research, would use two sets of switches on either end of the local loop (see Section 3.2) with two switches located on the campus and two switches located at the loop demarcation point where the local loop enters the carrier's cloud. The traffic is separated on the local loop such that the only infrastructure shared by the two types of traffic is the local loop itself, not even the switches. It is important to note that the service access interface and agreements that users have with their carriers will determine whether both sets of traffic could eventually be carried over the same lines and switches inside the carrier cloud or carried on distinct infrastructure. The disadvantage of this approach is that extra switches are required to implement this scheme. On the other hand, the advantage perceived by some for separate infrastructure is that the two types of traffic are kept physically separate, which reduces the risk of any problems that may arise from the inadvertent confluence of the two types of traffic. The support of both the production and R&D environments may be achieved through the aggregation of various network infrastructure segments and components, which may be dynamically combined and configured to produce a temporary production or experimental network.

The "guarded trust" model entails one set of switches on either end of the loop in addition to the sharing of the physical local loop. The separation of R&D and production traffic at this level can be easily accomplished via the use of ATM PVPs or Permanent Virtual Circuits (PVCs), assuming that there are guarantees that no bleed-over from one type of traffic to the other occurs or that no errant application can adversely affect the other type of traffic due to congestion control, buffer management, QoS management, or any other policy enforcing algorithms implemented in the switches. Because the separation of traffic, either based on type or policy, is not accomplished in hardware, users as well as network managers and providers require tools that they can use to monitor the network infrastructure and assure themselves that their requirements are being met.

Either production or R&D networks could make use of segmented network infrastructure, in which switches, routers, and muxs are assumed to be either for production or for experimentation purposes and can be dynamically aggregated into virtual networks on demand. It is also apparent that this capability can be easily adopted by the commercial sector for supporting end-user demands for temporary network requirements for trade shows, demonstrations, proofs of concept, and temporal use of additional bandwidth. This type of capability can be supported through the use of adaptive hardware devices and techniques such as end user on-demand control of Sonet drop/add multiplexors, aggregating/de-aggregating WDM color frequency multiplexors, or real-time manipulation and configuration of switches and routers. In order to support this capability, the telecommunications industry needs to alter its business and technical models to not only provide non-intrusive access to network state information but also to provide the ability for the end user to safely manipulate the network infrastructure to create either production or R&D networks as they need them, even if under special circumstances and for only a short time period.

We can extend the concept of regional sharing of infrastructure one step further by defining a network peering point–where multiple local entities and institutions can connect and peer with each other–and providing a common funnel and peering point with WAN ISPs such as Sprint, MCI, the vBNS and ESnet. The Network Access Points (NAPs)[xiv] were originally designed to support this model, but the implementations failed in this regard because they only provided ISP-to-ISP peering. The Gigapop is the latest iterative concept and attempt to support a communal sharing of infrastructure to peer local institutions with advanced production services and ISPs. We contend that the Multimode Gigapop (M-Gigapop) extends the Gigapop and NAP concept because it can concurrently support both production and R&D traffic on as much of the same infrastructure as possible and hand off the traffic to the appropriate commercial or R&D ISP, depending on the type of traffic. The research challenges again are how to ensure that one type of traffic does not adversely affect the other at the M-Gigapop and how to provide for distributed network management of the peering point(s) (i.e., what end user tools and management capabilities are required in the switches, routers, and multiplexors).

4.4 Shared WAN Infrastructure

When providing shared wide-area infrastructure, the telecommunications service providers (e.g., MCI[xv]) and ISPs (e.g., ESnet and vBNS) will face many of the same issues as the traditional regional carriers (e.g., Ameritech[xvi]) and ISPs (e.g., CICnet[xvii]). The major issues center on what access interface and capabilities are provided to the end user and how experimental traffic, if any, is supported on the same or separate infrastructure as production traffic. For example, all experimental traffic may be provided over physically separate circuits and switches within the WAN ISP's cloud. The ability of the telecommunications carriers to provide multi-modal infrastructure may be hindered by the fact that some of their customers do not like to assume any risk. The federally funded private WAN ISPs (e.g., ESnet, NSI, vBNS, DREN[xviii]) may have a little more latitude in supporting some experimental network traffic and capabilities within their clouds, but they are also reluctant to assume much risk because some members of the application research community they support expect absolute production-level services. However, the challenge still facing all ISPs who expect to be solvent and viable service providers in the future will be how to support multiple varied policy (e.g., production versus experimental or guaranteed versus best-effort services) virtual networks because it is too costly for both the end user and the provider to support duplicative infrastructures (for the reasons already outlined in this report). Small amounts of calculated risk are critical in the evolution of networks and must be assumed by the end user and the service providers. Even when we test router or switch upgrades in a bounded environment prior to deploying these changes into production networks, we still assume some risk when we finally deploy the upgrades because any change to the running system or network in effect changes it from a production to an experimental network, albeit a controlled one. We all can think of many occasions where seemingly small upgrades or modifications have caused far-reaching problems. We need to develop networks that are more resilient and fault tolerant (i.e., can support experimental as well as production traffic and be dynamically configured to compensate for problems) on both a macroscopic and microscopic level. The on-demand use and re-use of network infrastructure components and segments will further enable the service providers to support both the production and experimental requirements, as well as the other varied and sometimes conflicting policy-based network requirements of its customers in a more efficient and cost-effective manner.

Because we can expect to see the use of ATM continue for provision of regional and WAN service, we need to address the issue of ATM QoS support in the ISP clouds as well as access to these capabilities by the end user. One approach is to treat the ATM cloud as only a raw bit pipe and to rely on techniques such as RSVP to provide end-to-end QoS across not only the non-ATM LAN technologies (see Section 4.2), but also the carriers' ATM clouds. This type of approach defeats one of the major reasons an end user would consider deploying ATM on the campus or explicitly request it for WAN services. One can argue that RSVP QoS is not the hard QoS some applications require, and therefore we should utilize ATM QoS whenever possible. In either case, the ability of the end users to use ATM QoS signaling in a dynamic fashion to satisfy their dynamic application requirements is dependent on the availability of standards-based signaling implementations and APIs in the switches and end host systems, as well as admission control capabilities for both ATM and RSVP. The current state of deployment for ATM equipment that can support applications dynamically signaling and managing QoS in regional and WAN networks is fairly poor; this may impede the adoption of native ATM by the end user community. The lack of RSVP admission control tools available for use by the end user and network manager, as well as the lack of admission policies based on the application and campus network manager's perspective, may also impede the adoption of RSVP.

4.5 Impact of Shared Infrastructure on the End System

The concurrent support of production and R&D infrastructure must extend to and include the workstation. The current mode for supporting multiple-network use policies is based on the use of separate workstation and IP network addresses for the production traffic, and a separate workstation and IP address for the experimental R&D traffic. The R&D IP address must be garnered from a Class B, C, or Classless Internet Domain Routing (CIDR[xix]) address block that is different from the one used for the production network. The IPv6 address space is much larger than that utilized by IPv4; however, there is nothing in the IPv6 address or routing specification that will alter the need for using separate addresses from different address spaces in order to support multiple policies on the same end node. Hybrid solutions exist that involve using a workstation with two network interface cards (NICs), each having an address on different networks (e.g., different CIDR blocks). The reason for selecting addresses for the production and R&D NICs from different network address spaces, or for multihoming the two addresses on the same NIC, is to ensure that, when necessary, the production traffic takes a different route over the infrastructure than that taken by the experimental R&D traffic. Given the fact that current IP routing algorithms choose routes for traffic based on the network portion (e.g., top 24 bits of a Class C address) of the destination address, we have no option but to use two separate addresses to enforce the varied policies associated with production and R&D networks. This is an issue that mostly affects the end user, the workstation, and possibly the campus network because the regional and WAN clouds are treated primarily as switching engines at the IP level and will route any packet based only on its destination IP address and the associated routing table entry (which indicates which interface provides the next-best hop for the packet on its way to the destination).

The practice of using two different IP addresses on a workstation from different network address spaces or subnets is referred to as multihoming[2] and gives one workstation the ability to send and receive traffic over two distinct networks or subnets based on policy. Some workstations possess the ability to support two distinct IP addresses on a single NIC, thereby achieving the same result with only one NIC. One can bind the appropriate workstation source IP address when opening a socket for transmission (i.e., binding the production IP address as the source address in packets when the application is doing production work, and the experimental IP address when the application is performing network research). However, there is no way for the application programmer to know which IP address on the destination workstation or server belongs to the production or experimental subnet. Several methods can be used to solve this problem. The first method requires the user to possess a prior knowledge about which host IP addresses of the destination node are on the production or research subnets. The second method uses a local configuration file (i.e., a "hosts.exp.txt" file) that lists the domain names and IP addresses of all the experimental hosts and subnets. This method assumes those host addresses not listed in this file are used for production purposes. The third method involves making modifications to the Domain Name System[xx] (DNS) to identify experimental host addresses. This would allow for a site administrator to define experimental hosts in the DNS and thus leverage off an existing and scaleable infrastructure. The fourth method makes use of VLAN technologies to build experimental R&D subnets that extend across the campus and possibly regional or wide-area networks.

In the effort to reduce the amount of infrastructure required to concurrently support production and R&D environments, we would like to minimize the amount of hardware required by the end user to easily live within both a production and R&D environment. Ideally this would entail using only one workstation, one multihomed NIC, and one physical subnet. It would also allow applications to move between production and R&D environments on their screens simply by moving their mouses from the production window to the R&D window and vice versa. This requires that state information

---

[2] Some administrators propose using separate workstations and network infrastructure to avoid the administrative issues associated with multihoming. However, it may prove to be more efficient to multihome the relatively small number of workstations that require both a production and research address, and to rely on DHCP to dynamically configure IPv4 production hosts and the use of IPv6 link and local address capabilities to dynamically assign addresses to IPv6 end nodes.

associated with that process be handled appropriately as part of a processes' normal context switch. The end user should be able to specify that a particular window and/or environment is either for experimental or production use and the kernel within the node must be able to determine which mode is active so that it may act appropriately (i.e., set the correct source IP address in the outgoing packet). The kernels on both the sending and receiving nodes must verify that only experimental-to-experimental and production-to-production traffic flows occur.

5 R&D CHALLENGES

The need for advanced programming environments for the application and end user domains is driving the need to support network research in the area of network management tools. Application programmers require the ability to monitor, analyze, and debug their applications, including the impact of network traffic conditions. Network managers require the ability to protect, ensure, monitor, analyze, and debug the network services that they are providing. To support concurrent production and experimental activities, the suggested R&D areas of focus are on network management as well as end user tools for utilizing a shared infrastructure that is as efficient and error free as possible. Providing dual-modality network capabilities (i.e., production and research) with sufficient safeguards requires advances for ATM and IP (both IPv4 and IPv6) in the areas of network management, QoS, admission control, cost accounting, and end station dual-modality support. It is important that the application programmer and network researcher be able to utilize network resources to meet their programmatic goals; the campus network manager and other service providers (MAN, WAN) must be able to manage and fully utilize scarce network resources. The adaptive, on-demand configuration and management of lower-layer network infrastructure (e.g., add/drop multiplexors, switches, routers, and network segments) greatly enhances the ability of service providers to support multiple policy and multimode virtual networks on the same infrastructure. Much of the experimentation with protocols, switches, and routers has been initially focused on the campus level. While the network researcher's focus will most likely be initiated on the campus level, it is important to focus on the end-to-end applications performance, which will undoubtedly include the campus to ISP demarcation point. It is imperative that ISPs and carriers support the QoS and non-intrusive end-to-end network management tools and capabilities that are required by the applications and the campus/LAN network managers to determine network performance characteristics. It is also crucial that ISPs and carriers support network research capabilities as part of their infrastructure because they derive direct benefit from the results, regardless of whether it is via dedicated or shared infrastructure.

5.1 Network Management

Applications programmers require real-time network diagnostic and analysis tools that can be utilized for monitoring services and debugging on an end-to-end basis across the multitude of campus, regional, and WAN network infrastructures. They also require tools to utilize QoS to dynamically adapt their application to utilize network services. While the traditional notion of an NOC that monitors network activities remains important, advanced network capabilities call for new weapons in the network management arsenal.

There are some network management tools and capabilities that are commonly required and employed among the WAN, LAN, and campus network managers; however, there are also capabilities that may be unique to each one of these areas. In particular, the tools utilized by the ISPs providing regional and wide-area networking services will most likely intersect but not necessarily be a proper subset of those tools employed by the campus/LAN network manager. Many tools in the ATM environment to date have been proprietary. For ATM to be widely adopted, more interoperable management and debugging tools need to be available. Standards bodies such as the ATM Forum and the IETF need be lobbied to get vendors to adopt interoperable management and debugging tool suites. The following is a non-exclusive, initial list of basic capabilities that the campus/LAN manager will need to support a dual-mode infrastructure and provide for the applications' and network manager's requirements.

- Reference implementations of ATM device discovery, ATM ping and ATM traceroute across heterogeneous vendors' equipment.

- Reference implementation of ATM QoS traceroute that traverses each switch and returns the QoS on a per PVC, SVC, PVP basis.

- The ability to securely (i.e., authentication) manage admission control, cost accounting, and priority policies, as well as QoS support for RSVP, IPv6 and ATM (i.e., fair and efficient tools for allocating network resources, including priority bidding and cost accounting).

- Tools for debugging cross layer signaling, admission control and other QoS capabilities for RSVP, ATM, and any other QoS supporting protocols.

- The ability to support both production and network experimental R&D activities on the same infrastructure with varying degrees of thresholds, alarms, and required responses.

- The ability to debug IP and ATM networks concurrently, including the ability to capture, analyze, and display cells, packets, and flows.

- Distributed inter-NOC capabilities with other regional, WAN, and LAN/campus network NOCs, including the ability to exchange trouble ticket information as well as to remotely view the state of the network from another NOC's point of view or point of presence.

- VLAN and switched Ethernet management and analysis tools that are integrated with or can be run concurrently with IP and debugging tools to promote a coherent multiple-layer view of the network.

- The ability to load beta versions of code into the LAN or WAN experimental infrastructure components to enable the testing and experimentation of new capabilities while concurrently running production traffic.

- Support of the negotiation of end-to-end QoS IP "best effort" services, non-ATM, switched Ethernet, and other broadcast technologies.

- The ability to dynamically configure, use, and re-use network infrastructure segments and components (i.e., Sonet drop/add multiplexors, ATM switches, routers, links, and circuits) from a pool of networking resources and objects to create on-demand virtual production or experimental networks.

Regional and WAN ISP managers require many of the same tools that the campus/LAN managers utilize (listed above); however, they also require the following additional tools and capabilities if they are to support the concurrent multi-modal use of infrastructure:

- Tools and capabilities that allow non-intrusive monitoring, analysis, state and data gathering, querying, and providing QoS support for the application programmer as well as the campus/LAN or regional network manager.

- The capability for the campus/LAN manager to support both a production and experimental network environment across WAN infrastructure with as little risk as possible.

- Capabilities for applications to easily request particular classes of traffic (e.g., UBR and ABR) burn rates as well as manage QoS for ATM and RSVP at the carrier demarcation points.

- Provision of multiple dynamic classes of QoS between endpoints.

- Provision of IP and integrated services protocol support for secure RSVP and IPv6 policy, cost accounting, and admission tools that will provide the end user or campus network manager with the ability to securely control the use and management of their traffic on an end-to-end basis in native mode.

- The capability to support the loading of beta versions of code into the experimental infrastructure components at the request of or via issuance of commands by the campus network researcher to enable the testing and experimentation of new network capabilities.

5.2 Application

Application programmers require network management tools that they can use to determine the state of the network in real time in order to debug their distributed applications, determine whether the network is functioning up to expected levels, dynamically configure and manage virtual production network services, and query and request appropriate QoS. This last requirement includes the ability for cross layer (e.g., RSVP or IPv6 to ATM) signaling to affect the required environment as well as to bid for priority status when resources are scarce. These tools may be used directly by the programmer or accessed automatically by programs running on behalf of the programmer. For example, an adaptive parallel application might be constructed to use a research network when it is available–or the production network when it is not (or vice versa)–or to interact with the research network management system to tune system parameters. In all cases, a key issue will be providing tools that can translate between low-level network constructs (e.g., ATM QoS) to the higher-level tools and concepts used by application programmers.

The environment for the programmers can be greatly enhanced by providing them with the capability for migrating seamlessly between production and experimental status on one workstation with the mere movement of their mouses from the production window to the experimental window and vice versa. The application programmers may also wish to avail themselves of multiple levels of production network infrastructure. For example, they may implement production-quality IPv4 and experimental IPv6 services over a production ATM network while at the same time running both production and experimental applications over the production IPv4 services. Specific tools and capabilities required by the end user for making use of the dual-mode infrastructure include the following:

- Reference implementations of ATM device discovery, ATM ping, ATM traceroute, and other ATM tools across heterogeneous vendors' equipment that the user can invoke to ensure that the ATM pipe is functioning at expected levels.

- Convenient application-level interfaces to information provided by ATM tools, enabling applications to determine and then adapt to changes in both link-level and end-to-end performance.

- Reference implementation of ATM QoS traceroute that traverses each switch and returns the QoS on a per PVC, SVC, PVP basis.

- Application support for cross layer (i.e., IP to ATM and RSVP to ATM) QoS signaling, including querying and invocation.

- Direct view and control of layer-two QoS parameters by applications wishing to use high-speed, QoS-enabled servers.

- The ability for an application to negotiate end-to-end QoS over non-ATM, switched Ethernet, and broadcast network segments when the destination node is either the lone server on a broadcast network or is on its own virtual LAN through switched Ethernet or other VLAN technology.

- Seamless dual modality (i.e., production and R&D) application support on one workstation.

- Ability, when required, to bid securely (i.e., authenticated) for priority use of scarce network resources (assumes some cost accounting and bidding system capabilities).

- Secure (i.e., authenticated) admission control querying and reservation capabilities for RSVP, IPv6, and ATM.

- Session control tools that seamlessly integrate QoS tools, as well as the multimedia, directory, information agents, and labspace environments tools.

- Integrated analysis and debugging tools and capabilities to support the integrated QoS, multimedia, information agents, and labspace environments.

- Versions of application programming tools (e.g., MPI, CORBA) that are enhanced with QoS signaling capabilities and performance tools that can explain observed network performance in application terms.

- Scheduling tools that allow programmers to specify network QoS requirements as well as computing or data requirements when requesting the resources required for a particular computation.

- Distributed computing environments that securely utilize network-based admission control techniques for ATM, RSVP, and other QoS protocols and services.

- The ability, as well as the application programming interface (API), to dynamically configure, use, and re-use network infrastructure segments and components (i.e., SONET drop/add multiplexors, ATM switches, routers, links, and circuits) from a pool of networking resources and objects to create on-demand virtual production or experimental networks. A standard characterization of network infrastructure segments and components from an end user's and application's perspective is required so that the end user can correctly create, configure, and monitor virtual network infrastructure.

The validation and evaluation of these tools and concepts will require access to a suite of interesting applications that can be used to stress various aspects of the multi-modal network infrastructure. Examples of such applications include the following:

- Distributed collaborative engineering applications in which engineers at different sites collaborate on the design and evaluation of complex systems. The Argonne BoilerMaker[xxi] system is an example of such an application; this allows engineers to use virtual reality systems to guide placement of inlets in a simulated industrial boiler.

- Remote I/O applications in which, for example, programs running on a supercomputer access input datasets or create output datasets located on remote file systems. These applications require the ability to manage and monitor network QoS to achieve high supercomputer utilization when streaming data between supercomputer and remote file system. The Argonne RIO project[xxii] is developing infrastructure for such applications.

- Remote visualization applications, in which data produced on a supercomputer by a scientific instrument or read from a file are streamed to a display device at another location. Many such applications were demonstrated as part of the I-WAY project.

- Remote instrument control applications, which may feature multiple data streams with different characteristics, including time-critical control data, high-bandwidth video, and audio.

- Distributed computation applications in which large numerical computations are distributed over multiple distributed computing resources in order to solve larger problems or to solve fixed size problems more quickly. Computational chemistry and astrophysics are two examples of disciplines in which this approach has been applied successfully.

6 CONCLUSION

Application developers are rarely eager to invest a large amount of effort and time to convert their codes to "test drive" new network technologies, especially if the infrastructure is to be short lived. Yet the development and deployment of new architectures and protocols are extremely dependent on applications, without which it is not possible to test and stress the infrastructure or to validate that it works with real applications and can be deployed in production mode. For example, the I-WAY[xxiii] network developed to support Supercomputing 95 succeeded, by virtue of tremendous effort, in demonstrating the benefits associated with an advanced pre-production infrastructure; yet this infrastructure evaporated immediately after the close of Supercomputing 95, making it difficult for many of the principal investigators and institutions to continue their collaborations. Network researchers need real applications and traffic to use and stress their experimental and production networks, and application developers are constantly seeking new network capabilities to enhance their computational environments. Neither group can progress without a persistent high-end, advanced infrastructure and without addressing the daunting cost associated with concurrently supporting both a production and experimental infrastructure. We must endeavor, then, to find the technical, social, and political means necessary to share as much infrastructure as possible at the campus, regional, and wide-area network level to support both production and experimental R&D activities.

7 ACKNOWLEDGMENTS

Special thanks to Jeffrey Kipnis of Ameritech not only for listening to these ideas and acting as a sanity check on what we are proposing, but also for being willing to explore ways to implement these concepts.

Work was supported by Argonne National Laboratory under interagency agreement, through U. S. Department of Energy contract W-31-109-Eng-38.

Argonne employees reporting work performed at Argonne:

Electronics and Computing Technologies Division and Mathematics and Computer Science Division, Argonne National Laboratory, Argonne, Illinois 60439

---

8 REFERENCES

[i] Computer Science and Telecommunications Board, The National Research Council, Computing and Communications in the Extreme, National Academy Press, Washington, D.C., 1996

[ii] http://www.cise.NSF.gov/ncri/nsfnet.htm

[iii] http://www.es.net

[iv] CAIRN is the successor to DARTNET - http://www.fnc.gov/cairn.html

[v] Paxton, V., Floyd, S., Wide-Area Traffic: The Failure of Poisson Modeling, IEEE/ACM Transactions on Networking, Vol. 3., No. 3, pp 226-244, June 1995

[vi] IPv6 is also known as IPNG and is defined in the following Internet Engineering Task Force (IETF) Request for Comments (RFCs); S. Deering, R. Hinden, Internet Protocol, Version 6 (IPv6) Specification, 1/04/1996 (http://ds.internic.net/rfc/rfc1883.txt); Y. Rekhter, T. Li, An Architecture for IPv6 Unicast Address Allocation, 1/04/1996 (http://ds.internic.net/rfc/rfc1887.txt); A. Conti, S. Deering, Internet Control Message Protocol for the Internet Protocol Version 6 (IPv6), 1/04/1996 (http://ds.internic.net/rfc/rfc1885.txt); M. Borden, E. Crawley, B. Davie, S. Bastell, Integration of Real Time Services in an IP-ATM Network Architecture, 8/11/1995 (http://ds.internic.net/rfc/rfc1821.txt); S. Deering, R. Hinden, IP Version 6 Addressing Architecture, 1/04/1996 (http://ds.internic.net/rfc/rfc1884.txt)

[vii] htpp://www.atmforum.com/atmforum/atm_introduction.html

[viii] http://www.ietf.cnri.reston.va.us/html.charters/rsvp-charter.html

[ix] The Message Passing Interface (MPI) - http://www.mcs.anl.gov/mpi/index.html

---

[x] Computer Science and Telecommunications Board, The National Research Council, Realizing the Information Future, National Academy Press, Washington, D.C., 1994

[xi] Aiken, R., Cavallini, J., Standards: When are they too much of a good thing?, ACM StandardView, June 1994, Interop Connexions, August 1994, Harvard NII Standards Workshop Proceedings, MIT Press, May 1995

[xii] http://cs.ucl.ac.uk/mice/sdr

[xiii] Foster, I., Kesselman, C., Globus: A Metacomputing Infrastructure Toolkit, Intl. J. Supercomputing Applications, 1997 (to appear). See also http://www.globus.org/

[xiv] Aiken, R., Braun, H., Ford P., NSF Implementation Plan for the Interagency Interim National Research and Education Network (NREN), General Atomics/San Diego Supercomputer Center, GA-A21174, May 1992

[xv] http://www.mci.com/

[xvi] http://www.ameritech.com/welcome/

[xvii] http://www.cicnet.net/

[xviii] The Defense Research and Engineering Network, http://www.arl.mil/HPCMP/DREN/drenexe3.html

[xix] CIDR is defined in the following IETF RFCs; R. Hinden, Applicability Statement for the Implementation of Classless Interdomain Routing (CIDR) (ftp://ds.internic.net/rfc/rfc1517.txt); Y. Rehkter, T. Li, An Archirecture for IP Address Allocation with CIDR, 9/24/1993 (ftp://ds.internic.net/rfc/rfc1518.txt); V. Fuller, T. Li., J. Yu, K. Varadhan, Classless InterDomain Routing (CIDR): An Address Assignment and Aggregation Strategy, 9/24/1993 (ftp://ds.internic.net/rfc/rfc1519.txt); Y. Rehkter, C. Topolcic, Exchanging Routing Information Across Provider Boundaries in the CIDR Environment, 9/24/1993 (ftp://ds.internic.net/rfc/rfc1520.txt)

[xx] P. Mockpatris, Domain Names - Concepts and Facilities, 11/01/1987, (http://ds.internic.net/rfc/rfc1034.txt); P. Mockapetris, Domain Names - Implementation and Specification, 11/01/1987 (http://ds.internic.net/rfc/rfc1035.txt)

[xxi] Diachin, D., Freitag, L., Heath, D., Herzog, J., Michels, W., Plassmann, P., Remote Engineering Tools for the Design of Pollution Control Systems for Commercial Boilers, Intl. J. Supercomputer Applications, 10(2): 208—218, 1996.

[xxii] Http://www.mcs.anl.gov/globus/RIO/

[xxiii] DeFanti, T., Foster, I., Papka, M., Stevens, R., Kuhfuss, T., Overview of the I-WAY: Wide Area Visual Supercomputing, Intl. J. Supercomputer Applications, 10(2): 123-130, 1996. See also http://www.iway.org/

9 BIOGRAPHY

Bob Aiken is DOE's Network Research and Next Generation Internet program manager. Prior to this current position , he was Network Research Manager at Argonne National Lab (ANL) where he co-authored the MORPHNET paper as a means for focusing ANL's network research program. Bob was both the Network Research and ESnet program manager at various times during his tenure (1990-1996) at DOE where he helped build the U.S High Performance Computing and Communications (HPCC) National Research and Education Network (NREN) program. For one year (1991-1992) Bob was the NREN program manager at the National Science Foundation., where he co-authored the vBNS, Network Access Points (NAPs), and Routing Arbiter (RA) concept and architecture which extracted the US government as the default Internet backbone provider and encouraged the current distributed commercial Internet. Before his detail to DOE (1988-1990), Bob created and managed ESnet's Network Information Services group whose responsibilities included directory services, information services, e-mail, as well as network management, debugging and analysis. Bob's network career is a direct evolution of his work on supercomputers and its requirements for high speed LAN networks (1980-1986).

Richard Carlson is a research scientist in the Network Research section of the Electronics and Computing Technologies Division of Argonne National Laboratory. His main focus is on high speed host-to-host communications over high speed networks. Carlson received his BS in electrical engineering from the Illinois Institute of Technology. He is a member of the IEEE Computer Society and the Fibre Channel Association.

Ian Foster received his PhD in Computer Science from Imperial College, London. He is currently a Scientist in the Mathematics and Computer Science Division at Argonne National Laboratory, and Associate Professor of Computer

Science at the University of Chicago. Dr. Foster has published three books and over a hundred papers on various aspects of parallel and distributed computing. His current research focuses on the techniques required to integrate high-performance computing into large-scale internetworked environments. He coleads the Globus project that is investigating resource management, configuration, and security issues for high-performance distributed computing.

Timothy Kuhfuss is the Director of the Electronics and Computing Technologies Division at Argonne National Laboratory. His responsibilities include leading development, prototyping, and operation of Laboratory telecommunications, networking and computing systems. Tim is a member of the ATM Forum, founding member of the ENR and Past Chair of the ENR User Technical Requirements Working Groups. Tim has been designing advanced systems for over 14 years. Past accomplishments include creating the Laboratory's ATM development program, a campus wide Ethernet, FDDI and Broadband systems for Argonne and the National Institutes of Health. Tim possesses an M.S. in Electrical Engineering from The Johns Hopkins University, a B.S. in Biomedical Engineering from Marquette University and a MBA from the University of Chicago.

Rick Stevens is director of the Mathematics and Computer Science Division and director of the High-Performance Computing and Communications program at Argonne National Laboratory. He is also the leader of the Argonne Computing and Communications Infrastructures Futures Laboratory, an effort to develop multimedia collaborative environments, virtual reality, and advanced networking. Stevens is also a principal investigator in three Grand Challenge projects: in computational chemistry, computational biophysics, and astrophysics. Professional activities include membership on the organizing committee for the 1997 Workshop on PetaFLOPS Software Models; the steering committee for the DOE2000 Collaboratory Pilot Project; the technical advisory board for IBM's Highly Parallel Supercomputing Laboratory; and the Energy Sciences Networking Steering Committee. He regularly serves on conference program committees and site evaluation committees.

Linda Winkler is a research scientist in the Network Research section of the Electronics and Computing Technologies Division of Argonne National Laboratory. She recieved her M.S. in Management and B.S. in Computer Science from Purdue University. She is Technical Director for the Metropolitan Research and Education Network and was the primary Network Architect for I-WAY Demonstration at SuperComputing '95. She has published a book on web based computing. Her primary focus is on high end computing and high speed networking.

PART SEVEN

Databases, Web

17

Database usage and requirements in intelligent networks

J. Taina and K. Raatikainen
University of Helsinki, Department of Computer Science
P.O. Box 26 (Teollisuuskatu 23), FIN-00014 University of Helsinki, Finland.
Telephone: +358 9 7084 {4247,4243}. Fax: +358 9 7084 4441.
E-mail: {juha.taina,kimmo.raatikainen}@cs.Helsinki.FI

Abstract

In this paper we present and analyze IN data managers for dynamic data. We examine database needs for call control, service switching, special resources, service data, and service management. We take a closer study for database requirements for service data in SDF and management data in SMF. The issues addressed in the requirements analysis are needed application interfaces, logical object model, and core database requirements. From the analysis we draw a conclusion that it is possible to fulfill the requirements and that SDF and SMF can share the same database architecture if compromises are made.

Keywords

IN CS-1/2, database interfaces, logical data models, performance, fault-tolerance, data security

Intelligent Networks and Intelligence in Networks D. Gaiti (Ed.)
Published by Chapman & Hall

1 INTRODUCTION

Databases in Intelligent Networks have gained a dominant role in the last few years. Not only service-related data is in databases, but also special resources, management, switching, IN service triggering, and network traffic control have data that can be managed in a database management system.

The nature of the database managers differ drastically. Service management must support fast data access that is tailored for reads while management databases should be tailored for reliable distributed updates. Service switching and IN triggering need very fast data access with little security and transaction control. Special resource functions need multimedia data services. All these classes have different database needs. An open question is: how much the database requirements of different managers have in common?

In this paper we try to answer that question. In order to do that, we need to identify the data managers in Intelligent Networks and analyse their characteristics. After that we can summarise the requirements that are set for the managers, and how they can be met.

The requirements analysis for database architectures in IN is derived from the work that has been done in international standardisation, especially in ITU-T. From database management point of view, most interesting part of IN is the IN Distributed Functional Plane (DFP) ITU-T 1993a, 1996), in particular the recommendations in the Capability Sets 1 and 2 (IN CS-1 and IN CS-2). In the recommendations, the database requirements are given as functional description of the elements. Database requirements for telecommunications based on IN CS-1 have been studied in Eurescom research projects (Eurescom 1993, 1994). Based on the Object Distributed Processing (ODP) engineering viewpoint, the database requirements have also been examined (Kerboul *et al.* 1993).

The rest of this paper is organised as follows. In Section 2 we summarise functional entities in CS-2 Distributed Functional Plane (DFP) that are either clients or servers for database requests. In Section 3 we take a closer study of the requirements of SDF and SMF data managers.

2 DATABASE ASPECTS IN INTELLIGENT NETWORKS

Databases have a dominant role in IN CS-2 Distributed Functional Plane (DFP). Not only the Service Data Function has a data management, but also several other functional entities have either database managers or services that need database management. In the CS-2 architecture, CCF, SSF, SRF, SDF, and SCF has data managers. The SMF architecture is left for further study in CS-2. Since management needs to keep track of managed data, a database management system is needed in the SMF architecture.

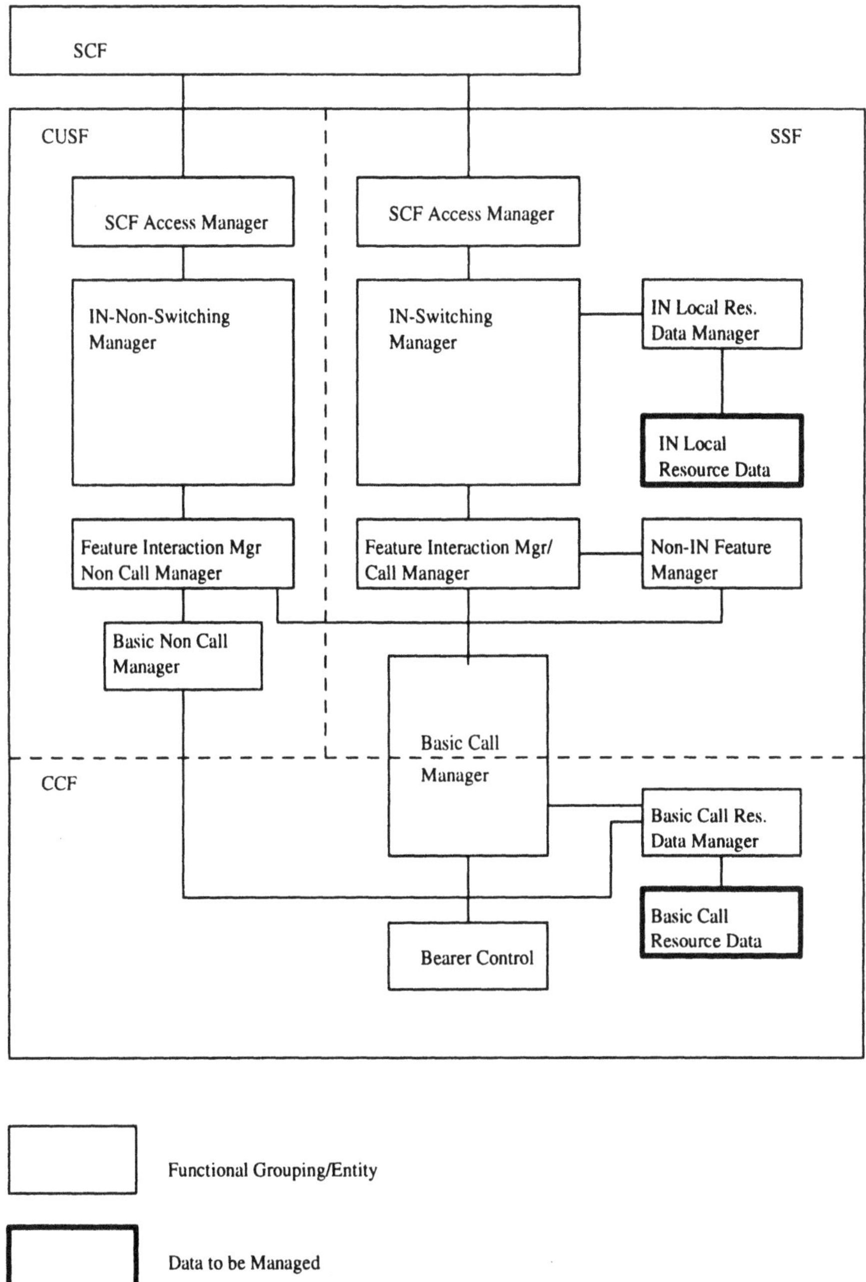

Figure 1 Q.1224/IN CS-2 service switching/call control function architecture.

Most of the data managers are embedded to functional entities. Only data managers in SDF and perhaps SMF are global in the sense that they can accept requests from other functional entities. The managers of other entities service requests from inside the entity.

2.1 Service switching and call control functions

The functional model of SSF/CCF/CUSF is described in Figure 1. The most interesting functional entities in the model are two data managers: IN local resource data manager and Basic call resource data manager. Neither of the managers have been described in CS-1, except that they are assumed to exist (ITU-T 1993a). The CS-2 draft only states that CCF manages basic call resource data which consists of call references (ITU-T 1996). Hence it is difficult to say what are the requirements for the data managers. We assume that the IN local resource data manager is responsible of managing data that is related to triggering IN services. Such data has a simple structure. A manager must be tailored for fast data access with a simple key. As of the Basic Call Resource Data Manager, we assume that it is responsible of managing dynamic call connection data. The managed data is temporal. Static data may be present if routing information is kept in the database.

2.2 Special resource function

The Special Resource Function (SRF) offers specialised resources for IN services that are beyond Service Control Function services. For instance, SRF is responsible of voice recognition, conference bridges, etc. As such, it is a very specialised functional entity with its own database requirements.

The architecture of CS-2 SRF is in Figure 2. The most interesting entity of the architecture is the Data Part (DP). The ITU-T Q.1224 draft states that the DP is composed of Database manager and database which contains recorded voice, sound, image, text (ITU-T 1996).

The SRF Data Part is a multimedia database. As such, it has to offer fast data access for complex data. The database is defined to be a server for internal data requests. The SRF can also be a client for a SDF since it can accept service logic scripts from SCF that can include SDF data requests. The SRF management has been left for further study in CS-2. The recommendations state that SMF is responsible of management of the service specialised resources, such as User Interaction scripts, resource functions, and data. It is also possible that service subscribers can manage their private data in SRF. Together these request types imply that the SRF must offer a database interface for external requests.

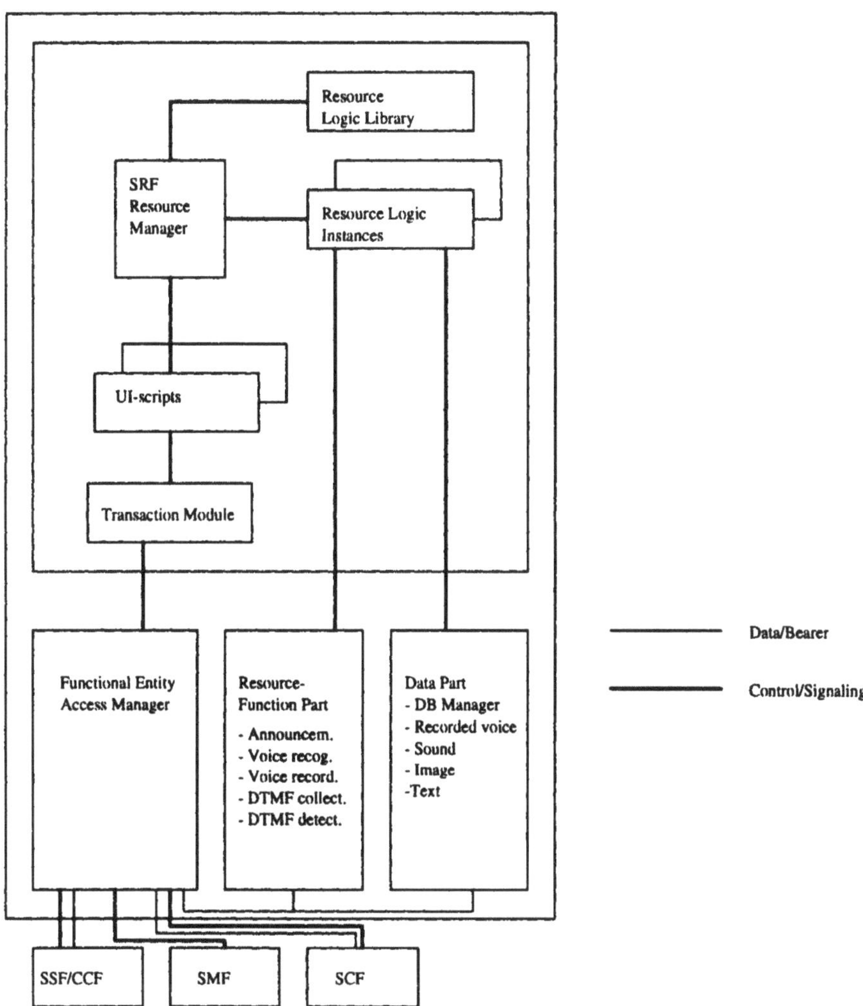

Figure 2 Q.1224/IN CS-2 service resource function architecture.

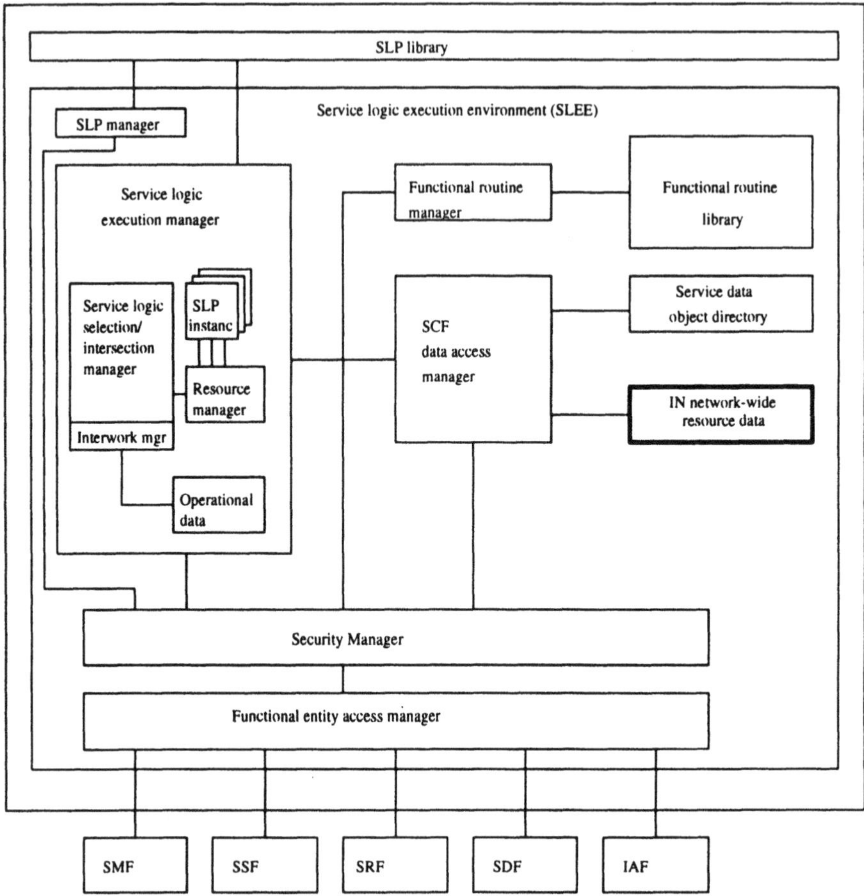

Figure 3 Q.1214/IN CS-1 service control function architecture.

2.3 Service control function

A similar structure than in SSF/CCF/CUSF is present in CS-2 SCF model in Figure 3. The architecture model has two data managers: Resource manager and SCF data access manager. The resource manager controls the local SCF resources and provides access to network resources in support of service logic program execution. The former resources are needed only on SCF execution and can be considered an integrated member of the architecture. The latter resources, while referencing to global network related data, are accessed via the other data manager, SCF data access manager. Thus, the resource manager sets requirements only to the SCF data access manager and not directly to an IN database architecture.

The SCF data access manager provides the functionality needed to provide for storage, management, and access of shared and persistent information in the SCF. The data access manager also provides the functionality needed to access remote information in SDFs (ITU-T 1996). This implies that the data access manager is both a client to one or more SDFs, and a database manager for SCF local data.

The SCF data access manager manages two types of data: the Service data object directory and the IN network-wide resource data. The Service data object directory provides means to address the appropriate SCF for access to a specific data object (ITU-T 1996). This implies that the data object directory is used for SCF interaction instead of SDF data requests. However, the recommendations also state that the service logic element manager, which is responsible of service logic programs, interacts with the data access manager to access service data objects in SDFs. The SCF data access manager uses the service data object directory to locate service data objects from SDFs (ITU-T 1996). This implies that the service data object directory is used for SDF access. We assume that the SCF data access manager is responsible for all remote data access regardless of its location. It can access both SCFs and SDFs.

The other data element, IN network-wide resource data, is defined to be a data base for information about location and capabilities of resources in the network that can be accessed by the executed service logic programs (ITU-T 1996). Furthermore the recommendation states that usually the addressed functional entity is a service resource function SRF. Hence the IN network-wide resource data is location information about useful service resources, mostly SRFs. A SCF requests special services from a SRF which executes the request. The SCF may forward a service script for execution or request a single operation (ITU-T 1996).

Our conclusion is that a SCF is a database client for SDFs and SCFs, and a service client for SRFs. The recommendations do not state what kind of data is stored in SCFs, but it is probably directly related to service execution. All global service-related data should reside in SDFs.

2.4 Service data function

The CS-2 SDF architecture model is in Figure 4. The entity is responsible of real-time access and maintenance of global network related data. The ITU-T recommendations state that the SDF contains and manages data which is related to service logic processing programs and accessed in the execution of the programs (ITU-T 1996). This definition limits SDF for a server of requests from SCFs.

According to the CS-2 recommendations, the SDF contains customer and network data for real time access by the SCF. Its tasks include secured data acquisition and management of data, distributed requests with data location transparency to the requester, inter-networking security, optimal distributed data access depending on the network traffic, data replication and access rights for

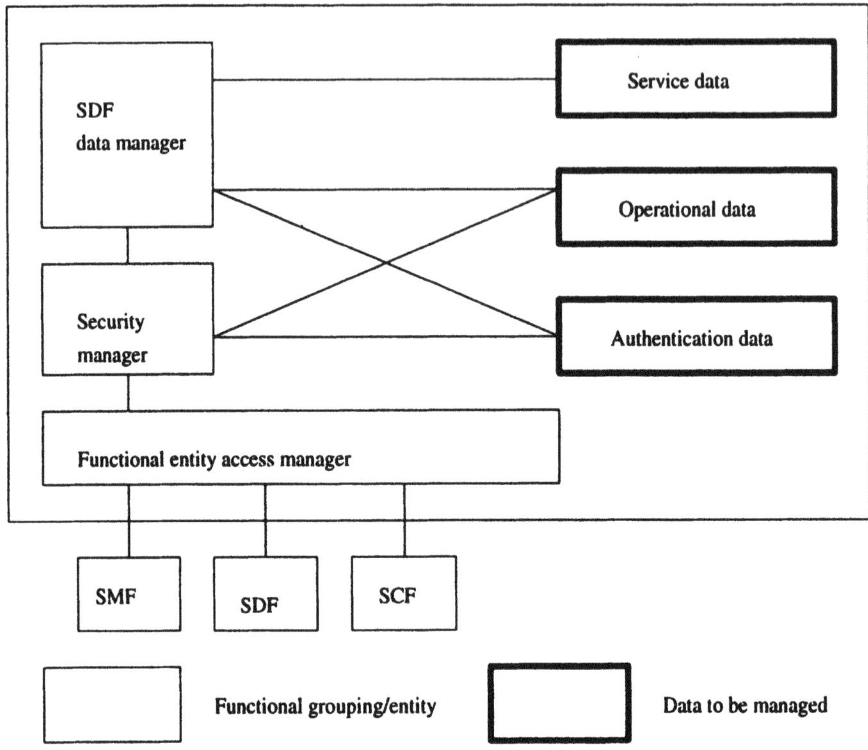

Figure 4 Q.1214/IN CS-1 service data function architecture.

replicated data, authentication and access control for secure access to service data, data support for security services, and fault-tolerance (ITU-T 1996). These tasks are typical to a distributed database management system.

The SDF data types are not as clearly listed. The recommendations state that SDF data types are authenticate data for user authentication and access rights (PIN-codes etc.), private operational data for SDF administration, and service data for the provision of a service. In other words, SDF data can contain anything. We have done a closer study of database use in CS-1 services and service features (Raatikainen 1994). There are five basic types of database operations that are needed in CS-1:

1. **Retrieval of structured objects from persistent subscriber data objects.** Some of the retrievals trigger a later update.
2. **User management actions that modify persistent subscriber data objects.** These actions must be protected against unauthorised use.
3. **Verification of Personal Identification Number** (PIN).
4. **Writing sequential log records.**

5. **Mass calling and Televoting**. The operations need high-volume small updates that must be serialised.

The most common of these operations are retrieving structured objects and writing sequential log records. Security operations, such as PIN verification, are also common. Management updates are not as common as the previous types. And finally, mass calling and televoting occur only on special occasions. They may also need SCFs that are specifically tailored for that use.

For IN CS-2, the third item (PIN verification) must be expanded to support general authentication and security services. Other than that, the list holds true in CS-2 as well.

The relationships between functional entities in IN DFP define how the entities communicate with each other. The Intelligent Network Application Protocol (INAP) that is required to support of Functional entity communication in CS-1 is defined in ITU-T (1993b). The INAP will support any mapping of functional entities into physical network entities. Thus the protocol is defined for maximal distribution, e.g. that every network entity consists of a single functional entity.

The INAP is a collection of Application Service Elements (ASE) that provide the necessary communication capabilities between functional entities. The CS-1 defines ASE for SCF-SDF communication is called "User Data Manipulation". It consists of two operations: Query and UpdateData. In Chatras *et al.* (1994) it is stated that the ASE is oversimplified. It has two problems: service-dependent semantics of operation parameters and authentication. The service-dependent semantics imply that the actions a SDF must perform are also service-dependent. The result of this is that every SDF must be tailored for each service. Authentication problems occur when a SDF is accessed from an external network. The SDF must perform the authentication of users and provide access control. In the ASE specification the only way to carry out authentication is to use attribute value comparison. The ASE does not define when the comparison should take place (Raatikainen 1993). In CS-2, the INAP interface exists for backward compatibility reasons. However, the recommended new SDF interface is based on X.500 Directory Access Protocol (DAP). The new protocol fixes the problems with ASE and tailored SDFs.

The SDF data management is not addressed in CS-2. Since SDF offers database management services, it should manage its own data. Write requests arrive mostly from SCFs and SDFs when service data is changing. In case of larger updates, such as adding new services and customers, the update request should arrive from the SMF. Hence SDF at least serves all types of SCF and SDF requests, and large SMF update requests.

2.5 Service management function

The SMF has been left for further study in CS-2. Here we assume that SMF will be based on Telecommunications Management Network (TMN) since one of the possible long term IN architecture plans is to be compatible with Telecommunications Information Networking Architecture (TINA). One of the goals in TINA consortium is to have a common foundation between IN and TMN (Demounem *et al.* 1995).

TMN (ITU-T Recommendations in M.3000 Series) is a generic architecture to be used for all kinds of management services. It is based on the principles of the OSI Management (ITU-T Recommendations in X.700 Series).

The fundamental idea in the OSI Management is that the knowledge representing the information used for management is separated from the functional modules performing the management actions. OSI Management is based on interactions between management applications that can take the roles of manager and agent. The interactions that take place are abstracted in terms of management operations and notifications. Management activities are effected through the manipulation of managed objects (MOs).

An agent manages the MOs within its local system environment. It performs management operations on MOs as a consequence of management operations issued by a manager. An agent may also forward notifications emitted by MOs to a manager. The agent maintains a part of the Management Information Tree (MIT) that contains instances of MOs organised as a hierarchical database tree. In brief, the principles of OSI Management (and TMN) require that the database system contains the functionality of an OSI Management Agent.

If IN service management is based on TMN, the managed objects are all IN elements, including IN Distributed Functional Plane entities. The manager of a functional entity has knowledge of the management needs of the element. The SMF needs database services for maintaining this information. TMN architecture can be used for all network management, not only for IN element management. The more management is left for TMN, the more database services are needed.

3 REQUIREMENTS ANALYSIS

As we have seen, the CS-2 DFP has several database management systems. We classify them into two groups: embedded systems and external systems. An embedded database management system is an integral part of the functional entity where it is defined. An external database management system has clients at other functional entities, or it offers distributed database operations with other external systems.

The functional entities in CS-2 that have internal database management systems are CCF, SSF, and SRF. A CCF has Basic Call Resource Data manager, a SSF has IN Local Resource Data manager, and a SRF has Data Part. These database managers are so deeply integrated to the appropriate elements that their requirements are beyond the scope of a general analysis. In short, the SSF/CCF requires fast data access from databases because they are related to connecting calls and triggering IN services. The SRF data base is a multimedia database. The requirements of such a system are beyond normal analysis of a database management system. A comprehensive analysis of multimedia databases is in Khoshafian *et al.* (1996).

The IN Distributed Functional Plane has two external database management systems: Service Data Function, which has external clients, and Service Management Function, which must have distributed database features for management. Since CS-2 does not specify the structure of management data, we assume that it is based on the TMN data model.

In the analysis we consider the requirements from both SDF and SMF data management point of views. The issues addressed here are database interfaces and request types, logical data models, and core database issues. We have two goals for the analysis: 1) to identify the requirements and 2) to see how compatible the requirements are. If it turns out that SDF and SMF requirements are compatible, SMF can use SDF database services. In such a case, the SDF database is both a manager and a managed element. Even if SMF and SDF architectures are separated, the same design principles can be used on both architectures, and database management systems can access data from one another.

3.1 Database interfaces and request types

The needed database interfaces depend on the requests sources. A SDF has to answer requests that are related to service interaction. A SMF has to answer requests that are related to service management. These requirements also define the requirements for database interfaces.

A SDF may interact with SCFs, SDFs, and SMFs. Also in CS-2, it is mentioned that a SRF may request data from a SDF, for instance when a customer wants to use a different language in a message than the default one (ITU-T 1996). All these requests are local in a network. In addition, SDF has to answer requests from SDFs and SCFs in external networks, and requests that come from monitor terminals.

In CS-1, the SDF interface is CS-1 INAP. In CS-2, the defined SDF interface is X.500 DAP. Both of the interfaces must be supported in a SDF database. Next to these, a high-level query interface is needed for requests from monitor terminals.

Hence three interface types are needed:

1. An interface for X.500 DAP requests that arrive from other functional elements. These are the main source of requests for a SDF. The requests may be both reads and updates. Even if the SMF model is based on TMN and X.700 CMIP, the SDF database is updated via the X.500 interface. However,

if the SDF element is managed, the management functions will probably use X.700 CMIP. Hence the SDF has two update interfaces depending on the nature of the update. Data is managed via X.500, database functionality (entity-related data) is managed via X.700.
2. An interface for now obsolete CS-1 INAP requests that must be supported for backward compatibility. These requests should be relatively rare since all implementations should use DAP. Nevertheless it must be supported.
3. An interface for high-level query language requests that arrive from monitoring staff. These requests are database management requests that arrive directly from a terminal. This interface is mandatory for management reasons. A SMF is not intended for this kind of database management, although it can be used as such if the SMF is embedded to the same physical element with the SDF.

The listed three interface types are sufficient for CS-2. However, in the future also an interface for Object Distributed Processing (ODP) channel is needed if long term IN architecture plan is to be compatible with TINA. TINA architecture is based on the ODP models and interfaces.

The SMF interfaces are more problematic since they have not been defined in CS-2. It is difficult to exactly state which kind of interfaces are needed for an appropriate SMF database architecture, but TMN interfaces can be given as the first assumption.

The TMN interfaces are based on OSI X.700 Common Management Information Protocol (CMIP). As such, the SMF data management system must support two types of interfaces:

1. TMN management requests that arrive from Management Information System (MIS) Agents. A MIS agent is needed to connect a managed element to a TMN manager.
2. TMN notifications that arrive from managed objects. A managed object can notify its manager that something special has happened. The manager is responsible of responding the request. If TMN notifications are added to the SMF data architecture, the resulting database is an active database. However, this is not a mandatory requirement since the manager can accept notifications and translate them to appropriate database requests. That way the database has to answer only regular TMN requests.
3. High-level query language requests. These are similar to SDF requests.

3.2 Logical data model

The CS-1 and CS-2 recommendations do not specify anything about SDF or SMF database models. In CS-2 it is only stated that SDF may be based on a database management system (ITU-T 1996). Hence no requirements raise from the recommendations. This is a good design policy since it allows the use of different types of database management systems without breaking recommendations. But on the other hand, it does not give much to the system designer.

Some requirements can be derived from the interfaces and from the possible IN long term architecture plan that intends to join TMN and IN under TINA. From these sources we can derive the following candidates for a SDF and SMF logical data model.

ITU-T X.500 model

This is a logical choice for the SDF data model since the interface of SDF is based on X.500. The drawback of it is that it is intended for a global directory model and hence is not necessarily sufficient for a logical data model. The model is somewhat old-fashioned since it is related to the hierarchical model that has not been used in decades.

ITU-T X.700 model

If SMF is based on TMN, X.700 model is a logical choice for the SMF logical data model. The model is intended for data management, so it can be used in a database management system. It is also designed after the X.500 data model which makes it a more developed one. The drawback of the model is its lack of acceptance in database fields. No general commercial databases are based on X.700 data model, although X.700 implementations do exist.

OMG-based model

Once the long-term IN architecture plan comes true, the IN distributed functional plane architecture can be based on TINA object modelling, which in turn is based on Object Management Group (OMG) core object model (OMG 1992). Hence an OMG-based model is a good candidate for both the SDF and the SMF database architecture. In the short term, an OMG-based model is not as attractive as the ITU-T models. We have shown that not all X.500 and X.700 features can be mapped directly to an OMG-based model (Taina 1994). A special layer is needed to implement X.500 and X.700 special features. In the long term, however, this approach is the best one. It allows the use of OMG Object Request Broker (ORB) architectures which is a necessity in a TINA platform.

ODMG-93 model

One interesting candidate for the logical data model is ODMG-93 (Cattel 1994). It is an OMG-compliant data model that is intended for object-oriented databases. The advantage of the model is that several database vendors are going to publish ODMG-93 based object database management systems. It can also be used directly with ORB architecture. Both OMG and ODMG models are widely accepted and research on both models is active.

Choice of model

The chosen model for a database management system can be any of the three models, or it can be something completely different. Currently most database management systems are based on the relational model, which works well in IN database architectures. However, since IN is already mostly object-oriented, and TINA is completely object-oriented, an object-oriented database management system simplifies IN data modelling.

3.3 Core database issues

In the core database issues we deal with the requirements that the IN environment sets to the database architectures and implementations. These requirements raise both from the ITU-T recommendations and from the general telecommunications recommendations.

We consider the requirements from five points of view: 1) request throughput and response time that deals with the issue of how much user requests must be served in a specific time, 2) fault-tolerance that deals with data availability issues, 3) data security that deals with database security issues, 4) data distribution issues that deals with requirements for distributed data management, and 5) relaxing ACID-properties (Atomicity, Consistency, Isolation, and Durability) that deals with database transaction model issues.

Throughput and response time.

The recommendations of CS-1 and CS-2 state that SDF must offer real-time access to data (ITU-T 1993a, 1996). It does not state what the exact real-time requirements are. We assume that real-time in this context does not imply a real-time database, e.g. a database with timing constraints. Instead, the requirements imply a high throughput database.

Nevertheless, exact response times in SDF are often more important than throughput. This is due to the fact that most SDF read requests are for SCF or SRF logic programs that have exact time limits. If the database cannot give a response within a specific time limit, it is better not to waste resources and hence abort the request. As a result of this, SDF request management policy should favour predictable response times with the cost of less throughput. The best alternative is that the database can guarantee that all requests are replied within a specific time interval. Unfortunately this is not possible unless the time interval is very high or the database workload is very low. Otherwise a single overloaded condition ruins the guaranteed policy.

The average time limit for a read request in SDF is around 50 ms. About 90% of all read requests must be served in that time. For updates, the time limits are not as strict. It is better to finish an update even at a later time than abort the request.

In SMF, the roles of throughput and response times are reversed. Since the primary task of SMF is management and management operations should be committed, it is more important to finish as many management requests as possible than finish less requests with predictable times. SMF read requests are either high-level query language commands or requests that are related to management updates. They are more liberal with time limits than SDF reads because the result of the request is valid even after a time period.

The only SMF request that may need predictable time limits is a TMN notification request. Since the notification describes an unusual condition in the managed entity, it must be processed as soon as possible. A regular request processing policy may not be efficient enough for the notification. Instead, the notification can be served better if the request has a specific time limit. In this case it should also be guaranteed that the notification is be served in time.

Fault-Tolerance

The IN functionality is dependent on high availability of SDF data. The total non-access time of data should not exceed seconds in a year and it is allowed to be only fractions of a second at a time. Two things should be noted in case of a system failure: 1) the effect of it for the call (call is dropped), and 2) the effect of it for charging (user calls for free). The first can be acceptable as long as the probability of it is low. The latter is not acceptable. Hence SDF fault-tolerance should be tailored for continuous data access, especially in charging situations.

Also SMF database should be fault-tolerant but since it is for service and network element management, it is not as necessary to service execution than SDF data management. We think that the fault-tolerance level can be relaxed in management. The database should be fault-tolerant, but the allowed down time can be minutes in a year instead of seconds, and the recovery time can be longer than in SDF data management as long as data is available. It is more important to ensure that committed data in SMF will not disappear in a failure than support full fault-tolerance.

Data Security

Security is one of the major issues in CS-2. A SDF must support secure requests, such as PIN identification. Also requests from external networks must be secure. It is not clear from the recommendations how high a security level is needed for the IN database architecture. It is probable that a well-known Bell-LaPadula security model (Bell *et al.* 1976) is sufficient. In the model, a request is allowed to read-access an object only if its clearance is the same or higher than the object's classification. A request is allowed to write-access an object only if its clearance is the same or lower than object's classification. In other words, requests are allowed read data that is less or equal secure than their own security level, and are allowed to update data that is less or equal secure than their own security level.

The SMF security level does not differ from the SDF security level. Although management security issues are not addressed in CS-2, the SMF may receive requests from external networks or external users. The Bell-LaPadula model should be sufficient for the SMF security model.

A simple and often used addition to the Bell-LaPadula security model is to define private security groups. A member of a private security group may access all data that is in her security group. For other data, the Bell-LaPadula model used. This addition allows an user to have private data that only she can access. If user data is at a higher security level than user access level, the users cannot read any other than their own private data. They can still write other data if they are allowed to have a reference to it.

Data distribution and replication

As the name states, IN Distributed Functional Plane is distributed. This definition encloses both the fact that IN DFP has several functional elements, and the fact that the plane can have several instances of the same functional element.

Although the IN DFP defines a distributed model, it does not force the architectures to be distributed. In principle a monolithic SDF could serve all IN data requests in a small network. Such a solution is not practical since the database can easily become a bottleneck. The approach can be used if the workload can be analysed and the network is reliable enough.

If the IN service database architecture is distributed, a logical distribution level is to define each SDF as a node in a distributed database. The CS-2 model supports this approach well since a SDF can interact with other SDFs in the same or in an external network. The X.500 data model supports distribution since it is a distributed directory standard. The recommendations state that SDF architecture must support location transparency (ITU-T 1996).

In SMF, distribution is even a more natural feature than in SDF. The TMN model is naturally hierarchical and distributed. If SMF follows TMN, the SMF model is also distributed. Also most management requests are distributed because they can update several network elements which can be geographically far from each other. Although this can be handled with a single management node, the management system is usually distributed such that it is closer to the elements that are managed.

If SDF and SMF are distributed, also data replication becomes an issue. In principle distribution does not require replication. In practice it does, since otherwise often referenced data has to be requested from an external source. It is better to replicate data closer to the location of the requester. This is especially true in SDF, since most SDF requests are read-requests. If updates dominate, like probably in SMF, the advantages of data replication are lost since all updates must be done to all replicas in the distributed database.

Relaxing ACID-properties

Finally, the ACID-properties summarise how a database management system processes requests. A requests spawns one or more transactions into one or more database nodes in a distributed database. If the database is not distributed, a request spawns one transaction. When a transaction is finished, it commits the changes it has made to the database. Usually only then the changes are visible to other transactions. A transaction has ACID-properties (Atomicity, Consistency, Isolation, and Durability) that describe how it can coexist with other transactions. Some of the properties can be relaxed in order to gain better throughput or response time.

- **Relaxing Atomicity**. Transactions are atomic. The updates a transaction makes to the database are either accepted completely or not accepted at all. There is no reason to relax atomicity in IN databases. The same result can be gained by allowing requests to spawn several transactions all of which are atomic.
- **Relaxing Consistency**. A transaction moves the database from one consistent state to another. If the database is consistent before the transaction execution, it will be consistent after the execution. Consistency should not be relaxed either. If it is relaxed, the database becomes inconsistent in which case the data no longer reflects the real-world situation. The inconsistent database can no longer return right answers.
- **Relaxing Isolation**. In strict isolation transactions should not make their updates visible to the database before commits, and thus transactions do not interfere with each other. This can be relaxed in SDF databases but not in SMF databases. The result of the relaxation is that a transaction may sometimes read wrong data in order to finish in time. This may or may not be tolerable, depending on the type of the transaction. In management it should never be tolerable since read data affects management updates. Reading uncommitted data can lead the database into an inconsistent state.
- **Relaxing Durability**. Once a transaction is committed the changes made in it will not be lost because of subsequent failures. This can be relaxed in SDF databases to certain extent. In busy conditions it is acceptable that committed writes may be lost, as long as the probability of loosing a committed write is small and it goes to zero in time. It should not be relaxed in management databases. If for instance billing information is lost due to relaxed durability, the result of the data loss can become very costly to the charging operator.

We have summarised both the SDF and SMF database manager requirements in Table 1. The requirements for the database managers are mostly similar. If a compromise can be defined in object models, throughput versus response times, and ACID-properties, it is possible to design a database management system that can be used in both SDF and SMF. Since the requirements for data access are stricter in SMF than in SDF (SMF needs full ACID-properties), the combined

SDF/SMF architecture may become too inefficient for IN. On the other hand, since SDF databases should offer estimated response times, long SMF transactions may suffer from update aborts and lack of resources since short high-priority SDF transactions may steal all resources from them.

Table 1 Summary of SDF and SMF database requirements

Requirement type	*SDF*	*SMF*
Interfaces	Multiple application interfaces	Multiple application interfaces
Data model	Object-oriented logical data model	Object-oriented logical data model
Response times vs. Throughput	Predictable response times in favour of throughput	Throughput in favour of predictable response times
Data security	Full data security	Full data security
Fault tolerance	Full fault-tolerance	Relaxed fault-tolerance
Distribution	Data distribution and replication	Data distribution and replication
ACID-properties	Full Atomicity and Consistency, relaxed Isolation and Durability	Full Atomicity and Consistency, Isolation, and Durability

4 DISCUSSION AND CONCLUSIONS

In this paper we have summarised the requirements that an IN database architecture must fulfil both in service execution (SDF) and service management (SMF that uses TMN). The requirements are all derived from user needs. The SDF users are IN DFP functional entities such as SCFs, or external applications from other telecommunication networks that want to access data either via an INAP or X.500 DAP interface. The SMF users are management agents that want to access X.700 management data. If X.500 and X.700 requests access different data, the database management system may support both X.500 and X.700. However, when the requests have a common subset of data the database management system must have a mapping between the two models, plus a mapping to the actual database data model. The actual database model must then be complete enough to support both models and also database-related aspects such as transactions and data integrity. This can cause problems since the models are not 100% compatible. If the mapping becomes too complex, either SDF and SMF data must be stored separately or one of the models must be simplified.

Similarly, when SDF and SMF access common data in a database, the created transactions may conflict with each other. SDF transactions are usually short high priority transactions. SMF management transactions are complex and long, and often they cannot have as high a priority as SDF transactions. In a database that favours predictable execution times this can lead to a situation where SMF transactions cannot meet their deadlines or have to wait forever because higher priority SDF transactions steal the needed resources.

A possible way to implement different database interfaces is to build a set of interpreter processes each of which handles a certain request model. In order to do this an uniform interpreter-database connection is a necessity. The interpreter may either use an embedded database language or a special interpreter language. Both alternatives are equally good and possible to implement. In fact a good interpreter request language is very close to an embedded database language.

As a conclusion, it should be possible to build a database architecture that fulfils the listed requirements as long as the restrictions above are taken into account. It might not be possible to build a database architecture that can best answer both SDF and SMF requests. If the model differences between service use and management may be handled with an efficient model mapping then it should be possible to build a database architecture that can support both SDF service transactions and SMF management transactions. Such a database management system must guarantee that the SMF management transactions have a chance to finish execution in time.

6 REFERENCES

Bell, D.E. and LaPadula, L.J. (1976) *Secure computer systems: Unified exposition and multics interpretation.* Technical report, The Mitre Corporation.

Cattel, R.G.G. (1994) *Object Database Standard: ODMG-93 Release 1.1.* Morgan Kaufman Publishers, San Francisco.

Chatras, B. and Gallant, F. (1994) Protocols for Remote Data Management in Intelligent Networks CS1, in *Intelligent Network'94 Workshop Record*, IEEE Communications Society.

Demounem, L. and Zuidweg, H. (1995) On the Coexistence of IN and TINA, in *Proceedings of TINA'95 conference.* TINA-C, Red Bank, N.J.

Eurescom (1993) *Fact-finding Study on Requirements on Databases for Telecom Services.* Technical report, Eurescom, Heidelberg, Germany.

Eurescom (1994) *TMN Management of Pan-European IN Based Freephone Service*. Technical report, Eurescom, Heidelberg, Germany.

ITU-T Recommendation Q.1214 (1993a) *Distributed Functional Plane for Intelligent Network CS-1*. ITU, Geneva, Switzerland.

ITU-T Recommendation Q.1218 (1993b) *Interface Recommendation for Intelligent Network CS1*. ITU, Geneva, Switzerland.

ITU-T Draft Recommendation Q.1224 (1996) *Distributed Functional Plane for Intelligent Network CS-2*. ITU, Geneva, Switzerland.

Kerboul, R., Pageot, J.-M. and Robin, V. (1993) Database Requirements for Intelligent Network: How to Customize Mechanisms to Implement Policies, in *Proceedings of the 4th TINA Workshop*. TINA-C, Red Bank, N.J.

Khoshafian, S. and Baker, A.B. (1996) *MultiMedia and Imaging Databases*. Morgan Kaufmann, San Francisco.

OMG (1992) *Object Management Architecture Guide* - Revision 2.0 - Second Edition.

Raatikainen, K.E.E. (1993) A Framework for Evaluating the Performance of IN Services, in *Proceedings of Workshop on Intelligent Networks*. Lappeenranta University of Technology, Finland.

Raatikainen, K.E.E. (1994) *Information Aspects of Services and Service Features in Intelligent Network Capability Set 1*. Technical report, University of Helsinki, Department of Computer Science, Finland.

Taina, J. (1994) *Evaluation of OMG, ODMG, X.500, and X.700 Data Models*. Technical report, University of Helsinki, Department of Computer Science, Finland.

7 BIOGRAPHY

Juha Taina received the MSc degree in computer science from the University of Helsinki, in 1992. He is currently a Ph.D. student in computer science at the Univeristy of Helsinki. His research interests include real-time databases, object-oriented real-time database models, and databases in telecommunications.

Kimmo Raatikainen received the Ph.D. degree in computer science from the University of Helsinki, in 1990. He is currently an associate professor in computer science at the University of Helsinki. He is a member of ACM, IEEE (Communications and Computer Societies), and IFIP TC6 Special Interest Group of Intelligent Networks. His research interests include nomadic computing, telecommunications software architectures, and real-time databases.

18

CORBA access to telecommunications databases

P. Porkka and K. Raatikainen
University of Helsinki, Department of Computer Science
P.O. Box 26 (Teollisuuskatu 23), FIN-00014 University of Helsinki, Finland.
Telephone: +358 9 7084 {4677,4243}. Fax: +358 9 7084 4441.
E-mail: {pasi.porkka,kimmo.raatikainen}@cs.Helsinki.FI

Abstract

Distributed object technology, CORBA in particular, will be the basis for the next generation of telecommunications software. Intelligent Networks Long-Term Architecture, Telecommunications Management Network, Telecommunications Information Networking Architecture are all based on object technology. The Telecommunications Task Force of OMG is actively working towards CORBA-based solutions.

In this paper we present how the standard CORBAservices specified by OMG can be used to provide access to telecommunications databases. The challenging task is to introduce database objects into Object Request Broker without registering each database object as an ORB object. The RODAIN Object-Oriented Database Adapter (ROODA) is our solution to bring database objects and services for CORBA clients. The ROODA implements interfaces that will provide essentials parts of Persistent Object Service, Object Transaction Service, and Object Query Service as well as the Dynamic Skeleton Interface.

Keywords

Database Access, CORBA, Object Services, Object Database Adapter

Intelligent Networks and Intelligence in Networks D. Gaiti (Ed.)
Published by Chapman & Hall

1 INTRODUCTION

Databases are important building blocks in modern telecommunications systems. Databases are already used in several areas, such as call connection, number translations, Intelligent Network services, mobility management. Due to the growing use also data value and volume are increasing rapidly. The requirements for database architectures to be used in the telecommunications originate in the following areas: real-time access to data, fault tolerance, distribution, object orientation, efficiency, flexibility, multiple interfaces, and compatibility with other object standards (Taina *et al.* 1996).

Real-time access to data means that transactions usually have deadlines that specify when the transaction must be finished. Fault-tolerance means that the database should, in the practice, be almost always available. The requirement of object orientation is based on the general trend in telecommunications standards: **Intelligent Networks Long-Term Architecture** (IN LTA) (ITU-T 1993), **Telecommunications Management Network** (TMN) (ITU-T 1992), and **Telecommunication Information Networking Architecture** (TINA) (Barr *et al.* 1993) are all based on object technology. In particular, the de facto standards based on the OMG specifications are of crucial importance.

The efficiency requirements that the telecommunications services set to databases are strict. Thousands of short transactions must be answered in a second. At the same time very long transactions must also get resources. The requirement of flexibility arises from the fact that telecommunications databases must support very different kinds of transactions. Multiple interfaces to the database are a necessity. A telecommunications database has different types of users. For example, some of the users want to see the database as an X.500 Directory while others want to see it as an X.700 Management Information Tree. In a near future, TINA object invocation and access based on the OMG CORBA will be required.

In this paper we describe how database access through CORBA can be arranged. In particular, we describe how we will implement a CORBA compliant **Object Database Adapter** (ODA) called **RODAIN Object-Oriented Database Adapter** (ROODA) that provides a CORBA access to the RODAIN Database. In addition to the OMG Object Services called **Object Transaction Service** (OTS) and **Persistent Object Service** (POS), the ROODA provides an IDL interface to an ODMG-93 (Cattell 1994) compliant **Object Query Language** (OQL) as specified in the OMG **Object Query Service** (OQS). The ROODA also allows applications to register their own IDL interfaces to speed-up the database access.

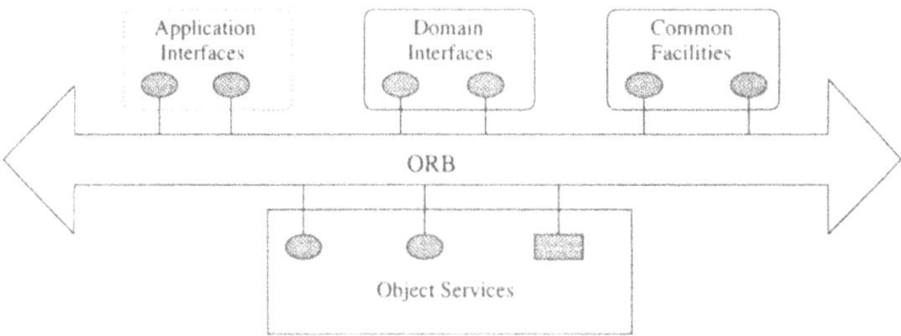

Figure 1 Object Management Architecture.

The rest of the paper is organised as follows. In Section 2 we describe the essentials of the OMG specifications that affect any implementation of ODA: Object Management Architecture (OMA), Object Request Broker (ORB), and Object Adapters. In Section 3 we review two known Object Database Adapters called Sunrise ODA and Orbix+ObjectStore Adapter. Finally, in Section 4 we present the RODAIN OODA and its functionality which includes the Object Transaction Service, the Persistent Object Service, and the Object Query Service as specified by OMG.

2 OBJECT MANAGEMENT ARCHITECTURE

The Object Management Group (OMG) has defined an architecture called Object Management Architecture (OMA) (OMG 1993) that provides the conceptual infrastructure upon which all OMG specifications are based. The OMA has gained the status of the most important de facto standard in the area of distributed computing. In this section we describe the essentials of OMA for database access in distributed computing environments.

2.1 OMA Overview

The key building blocks of the Object Management Architecture are shown in Figure 1. They include Object Request Broker (ORB), Object Services, Common Facilities, Domain Interfaces, and Application Interfaces.

Object Request Broker (ORB) (OMG 1996a), commercially known as CORBA, is the communications backbone of OMA. The ORB transparently provides its clients to make requests and to receive responses using object invocations in a distributed environment. **Object Services** (OMG 1996b) is a collection of services (interfaces and objects) that support basic functions for using and implementing objects. For database access the most important services are the Object Transaction Service (OTS), the Persistent Object Service (POS), and the Object Query Service (OQS).

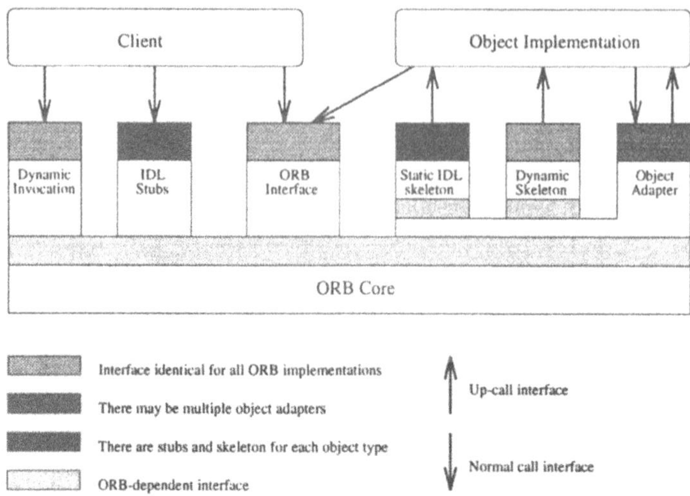

Figure 2 Structure of ORB interfaces [3/CORBA V2.0].

Common Facilities (OMG 1995) is a collection of services that many applications may share but which are not as fundamental as the Object Services. The Common Facilities are divided into two major categories: Horizontal Common Facilities that are used by most systems, and Vertical Market Facilities that are domain-specific. **Domain Interfaces** represent vertical areas that provide functionality of direct interest to end-users in particular application domains. Domain interfaces may combine some common facilities and object services but are designed to perform particular tasks for users within a certain vertical market or industry. **Application Interfaces** while not an actual OMG standardisation activity are critical when considering a comprehensive system architecture. The Application Interfaces represent component-based applications performing particular tasks for a user.

2.2 Essentials in CORBA

The CORBA makes an interface between clients and objects allowing object implementations to be machine and language independent. As Figure 2 depicts, a CORBA client has three primary ways of making a request:

1. The client can use the Dynamic Invocation Interface.
2. The client can use an OMG IDL Stub.
3. The client can directly interact with the ORB through the ORB Interface.

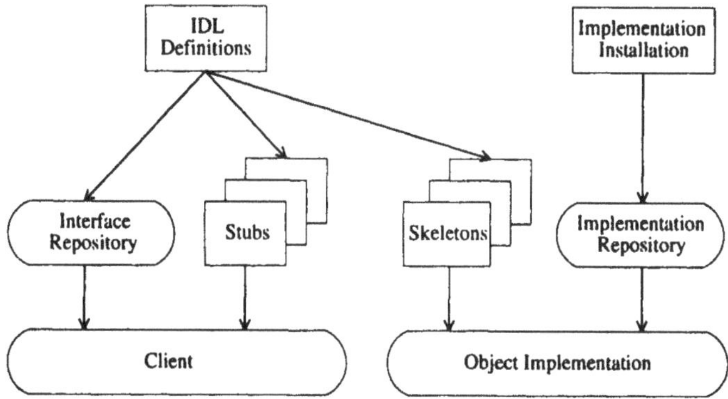

Figure 3 Interface and implementation repositories [6/CORBA V2.0].

Figure 3 shows how an interface and implementation information is made available to clients and object implementations. The interface is defined in OMG IDL and/or in the Interface Repository: The definition is used to generate the Client Stubs and the object Implementation Skeletons. The object implementation information is provided at installation time and is stored in the Implementation Repository for use during the request delivery.

Interface Repository is a service that provides persistent objects that represent the IDL information in a form available at runtime. The Interface Repository information may be used by the ORB to perform requests. Moreover, using the information in the Interface Repository, it is possible for a program to encounter an object whose interface was not known when the program was compiled, yet, be able to determine what operations are valid on the object and make an invocation on it.

Implementation Repository contains information that allows the ORB to locate and activate implementations of objects. Although most of the information in the Implementation Repository is specific to an ORB or operating environment, the Implementation Repository is the conventional place for recording such information. Ordinarily, installation of implementations and control of policies related to the activation and execution of object implementations is done through operations on the Implementation Repository.

In addition to its role in the functioning of the ORB, the Implementation Repository is a common place to store additional information associated with implementations of ORB objects.

Object Implementation is a definition that provides the information needed to create an object and to allow the object to participate in providing an appropriate set of services. An implementation typically includes definitions of the methods that operate upon the state of an object, and information about the intended type of the object.

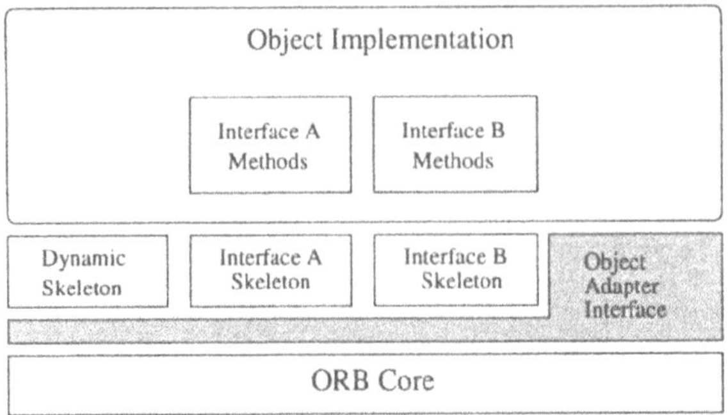

Figure 4 Structure of a typical object adapter [9/CORBA V2.0].

An object implementation provides the semantics of the object, usually by defining data for the object instance and code for the methods of the object. Often the implementation will use other objects or additional software to implement the behaviour of the object. In some cases, the primary function of the object is to have side-effects on other things that are not objects. A variety of object implementations can be supported, including separate servers, libraries, a program per method, an encapsulated application, an object-oriented database. Through the use of additional object adapters, it is possible to support virtually any style of object implementation.

2.3 Object Adapter

Generally, object implementations do not depend on the ORB or how the client invokes the object. Object implementations may select interfaces to ORB-dependent services by the choice of Object Adapter. When an invocation occurs, the ORB Core together with the Object Adapter and The Skeleton arrange that a call is made to the appropriate method of the implementation.

An Object Adapter, a typical structure of which is shown in Figure 4, is the primary way that an object implementation accesses ORB services such as object reference generation. An object adapter exports a public interface to the object implementation, and a private interface to the skeleton.

An object adapter called the **Basic Object Adapter** (BOA) should be available in every ORB implementation. Although the BOA will generally have an ORB-dependent implementation, object implementations that use it should be able to run on any ORB that supports the required language mapping, assuming they have been installed appropriately.

CORBA specification mentions two other Object Adapters: **Library Object Adapter** (LOA) and **Object Database Adapter** (ODA). An LOA is primarily used for objects that have library implementations. It accesses persistent files but does not support activation or authentication because the objects are assumed to be in the clients program. An ODA uses a connection to a Database Management Systems (DBMS) to provide access to the objects stored in the database. Since a DBMS provides the methods and persistent storage, objects may be registered implicitly and no state is required in the object adapter.

3 OBJECT DATABASE ADAPTERS

An Object Database Adapter (ODA) allows object implementations to be written in the database programming language of the ODBMS, that is a language incorporating persistence into the programming environment. The object implementation is still responsible for managing the persistence state of the objects it implements but the task of an object implementor is much simpler in the programming environment provided by ODBMS. Besides persistency other database features like data consistency and crash recovery are available to the object implementation (Reverbel 1996a).

The importance of integrating ORB and ODBMS is widely recognised. Many vendors of ORBs and ODBMSes have announced plans to integrate their products. However, due to the commercial interests involved only a few design and implementation plans have been published: Sunrise ODA (Reverbel 1996a, 1996b, 1996c) and Orbix+ObjectStore Adapter (Iona 1995b).

3.1 The Sunrise ODA

The motivation behind the Sunrise ODA was the fact that object persistence was not sufficiently supported in CORBA-based environments. The initial design of the Sunrise ODA was for Iona's Orbix and Object Design's ObjectStore. Currently there are also releases for Orbix, mSQL, and Sunrise's own object-relational mediator as well as for VisiBroker and ObjectStore.

Rather than replacing the BOA, the Sunrise ODA is an add-on to the BOA (see Figure 5). The Sunrise ODA is implemented as a library that uses and extends the BOA services. It does not maintain any ORB-specific information in the database. Therefore, schema evolution is not needed when the Sunrise ODA is ported to another ORB. It is even possible that a single database is simultaneously accessed through CORBA servers based upon different ORBs.

3.2 Orbix+ObjectStore Adapter

IONA Technologies Ltd. has integrated its Orbix with the ObjectStore OODBMS. The result of this integration is called Orbix+ObjectStore Adapter (OOSA). The OOSA makes Orbix objects persistent by storing them in ObjectStore. On the other hand, ObjectStore objects can be accessed remotely by making them CORBA compliant. Due to commercial interests involved design and implementation information on OOSA is only partially public (Iona 1995a, 1995b).

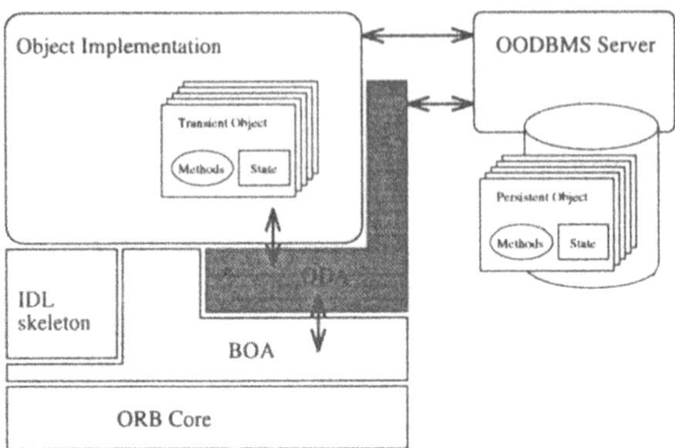

Figure 5 Sunrise ODA.

Orbix and ObjectStore are both object-oriented and based on C++ but their objectives are quite different. ObjectStore provides powerful support for persistence but it supports only a limited form of distribution. Orbix provides a flexible distribution model but has only basic support for persistence.

The integration allows an object to benefit both from persistency available in ObjectStore and from distribution transparency available in Orbix. The integrated system has three different types of processes (see also Figure 6):

1. **ObjectStore servers**: The innermost part in Figure 6 contains a set of ObjectStore servers. They are responsible for saving objects.
2. **Orbix servers**: The middle part contains a set of Orbix servers. These processes serve Orbix clients and are clients of ObjectStore servers.
3. **Orbix clients**: They reside in the outer part and make remote invocations on the objects provided by the Orbix server processes.

Naturally, a process can be both an Orbix client and an Orbix server when the process contains Orbix+ObjectStore objects and makes remote calls to other Orbix+ObjectStore objects. An object can also use ObjectStores distribution support. An object can be loaded into several Orbix server processes. In this case ObjectStore controls the concurrent access to the copies of the object.

Orbix clients do not necessarily be aware whether or not the called object is an object both in Orbix and in ObjectStore. References to both types of objects are transmitted in the same way. If the given reference points to an ObjectStore object, the object will be automatically loaded into the server process.

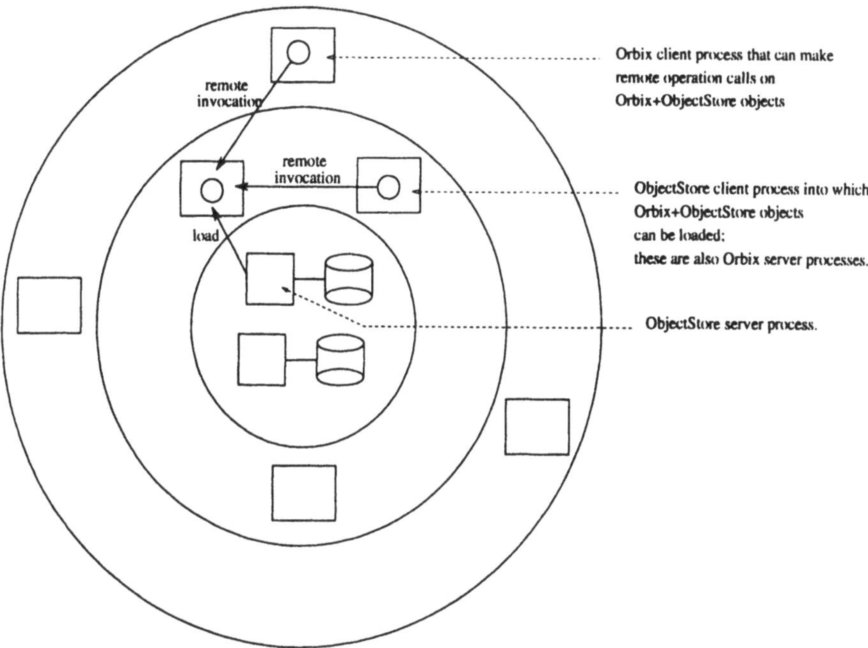

Figure 6 Process types of OOSA.

4 RODAIN OBJECT-ORIENTED DATABASE ADAPTER

The **RODAIN Object-Oriented Database Adapter** (ROODA) is the way how we are going to provide CORBA clients an access to the RODAIN Database (Niklander *et al.* 1997). The ROODA will provide:

1. the OMG Persistent Object Service (POS),
2. the OMG Object Transaction Service (OTS),
3. an IDL interface to an ODMG-93 (Cattell 1994) compliant OQL interface as specified in the OMG Object Query Service (OQS), and
4. an flexible way of registering application specific IDLs to the database based on the OMG Dynamic Skeleton Interface (DSI).

4.1 ROODA Architecture

Figure 7 depicts how the CORBA access to the RODAIN Database will be organised in our prototype implementation. CORBA clients use ORB to obtain services available in our CORBA interface to the RODAIN Database. The ROODA acts as an interpreter between the ORBs and the RODAIN Database.

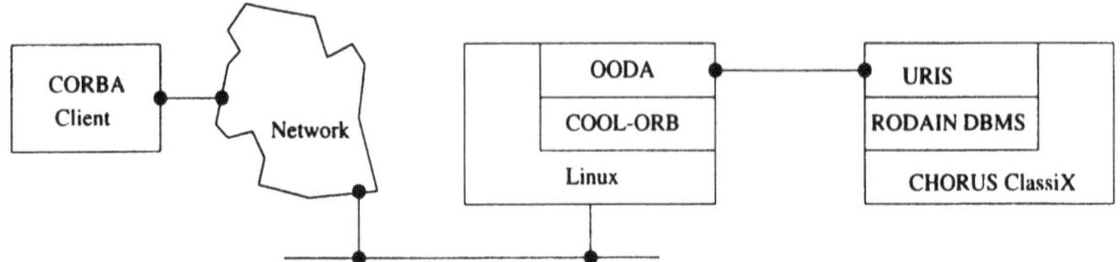

Figure 7 Interactions between CORBA clients, ROODA, and RODAIN database.

There are certain similarities between the OMG and ODMG-93 specifications that help us in building the interfaces:

- The data model used in RODAIN (Kiviniemi *et al.* 1996) is a real-time extension of the object model specified by ODMG-93 (Cattell 1994) which, in turn, is a superset of the object model specified by OMG (OMG 1993).
- The Object Definition Language (ODL) used in ODMG-93 is a superset of Interface Definition Language (IDL) of OMG.
- OMG recommends to use ODMG-93 as a standard interface for Persistent Object Service (POS).

In our prototype we have divided the Object Database Adapter into two parts. The ROODA, which interacts with the CORBA clients, runs on a front-end node. The ROODA use an internal interface of URIS to access the database system.

4.2 Object Mapping

At some level of abstraction there exists only objects in ODMG-93 and OMG. For example, the database is an object and the fetch operation is done by a method call to the database object. Changing the value of an attribute is done by a method call. Actually all of the functionality in the system is modelled by method calls to objects. Therefore, ORBs that access the database need to include information about object classes. However, the all the information should not be revealed outside the database. In particular, problems in distributed updates make it necessary to restrict the access from ORB to the class and type definitions (schema) in the database.

One of the primary advantages of using an OODA instead of POS is the fact that an object reference for every object in the database does not need to be registered with the ORB. Considering the case when the database consists of millions of objects this is a huge advantage. However, knowing only the logical name of the database is not sufficient for making queries. The ORB must have some information available about the contents of the database. Therefore, the ROODA maintains a copy of the database schema. As Figure 8 outlines, the classes defined in schema map CORBA-objects into database objects.

The ROODA also acts as the border between CORBA and RODAIN. There are certain information in RODAIN, for example the complete database schema,

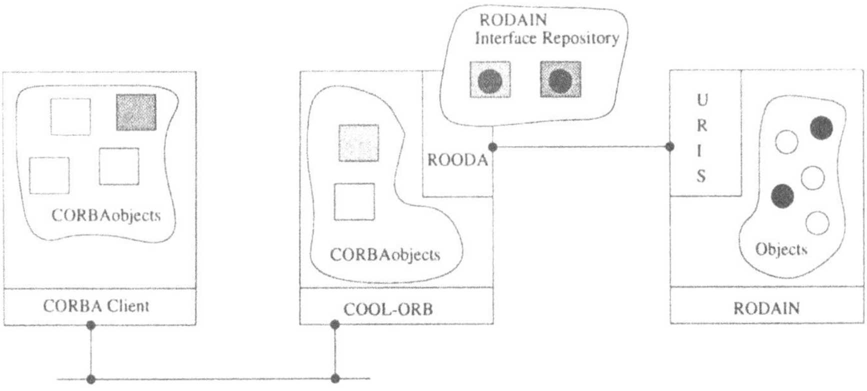

Figure 8 Mapping between CORBA and RODAIN objects.

which is not to be shown outside without strict control. Results of the queries from RODAIN are database objects but results given to the CORBA client are CORBA objects. If the result of a query leads to another query, the ROODA should know how the information from CORBA attaches itself to RODAIN objects. This means that there has to be some way of translating messages in ROODA. This translation is done by using an Interface Repository which includes the database schema that has interface definitions of all classes in the database. The definitions are expressed in OMG IDL. When we restrict the use of the database schema only to ROODA, not other parts of CORBA, we can be sure of the proper use of the schema.

4.3 Functionality

The functionality to be implemented in the ROODA can be semantically separated into two independent parts:

1. The ROODA provides **database access** to the RODAIN system. The CORBA interface is simply a way of using the database. In this role the ROODA provides only those tasks which directly use the database for retrieving, updating, and deleting objects in the database. This functionality is defined in ODMG-93 (Cattell 1994) and in the OMG Object Query Service.
2. The ROODA provides **database services** to CORBA clients. In this role the ROODA provides to CORBA clients the possibility of storing persistent objects in a way defined in POS. The ROODA can also take part in a distributed transaction as specified in OTS. The ROODA can also be the co-ordinator of a distributed transaction that only involves RODAIN Database nodes.

How different semantics these parts have, they use the same basic services of RODAIN. When a RODAIN user wants to change the database schema, schema management functions are to be used. When a CORBA client needs to store an object of a certain class for the first time, the class must be stored into database. In this task the ROODA uses the same schema management functions.

Below we examine the functionality provided by ROODA in terms of the relevant standards; which parts of different standards the ROODA must provide. The RODAIN Database system is based on the ODMG-93 standard. An OODA is introduced but not specified in CORBA references.

The **ODMG-93** standard describes the functionality relevant to use in a database. In order to allow a client fully to exploit the benefits of any database system, most aspects of the ODMG-93 standard must be supported. The RODAIN Data Model (Kiviniemi *et al.* 1996) is a real-time extension of the ODMG-93 object model. The functionality include means of data management: retrieval, modification, and deletion. Inherently, using a database through its own management system, other capabilities of the databases are also available: the so-called ACID properties, recovery, concurrency control, indexing.

An ODA is mentioned in the **CORBA reference** as an interface to databases. In addition, an OODA can be used to implement some of the functionalities described in CORBAservices. The ROODA will implement the functionality described in the Persistent Data Service module of POS (OMG 1996b). The ROODA will also also roles described in Object Transaction Service (OTS). In the OTS context the ROODA can be the co-ordinator of an internal RODAIN transaction or the recoverable server in a normal or nested transaction. In addition, parts of Object Query Service (OQS) are included into the ROODA through the OQL interface.

In order to become a production system in telecommunications, new services and service features must be easily introduced. A generic OQL-based queries with RODAIN Interface Repository service consumes too much resources. Therefore, service specific interfaces are needed. Currently we are examining whether or not the OMG Dynamic Skeleton Interface (DSI) can be used to as the means of deploying service-specific interfaces to the database.

Persistent Object Service

The Persistent Object Service (POS) provides a common interface to the mechanism used for retaining and managing the persistent state of objects. The POS has the primary responsibility for storing the persistent state of objects. Figure 9 shows the main components involved in the Persistent Object Service.

A *Client* is an application that uses a *Persistent Object* (PO). It is common for clients to need to control or to assist in managing persistence. In particular, the timing of when the persistent state is preserved or restored, and the identification of which persistent state is to be used for an object, are two aspects often of interest to clients. However, the client of the object can be completely ignorant of the persistence mechanism, if the object chooses to hide it. *Persistence Identifier*

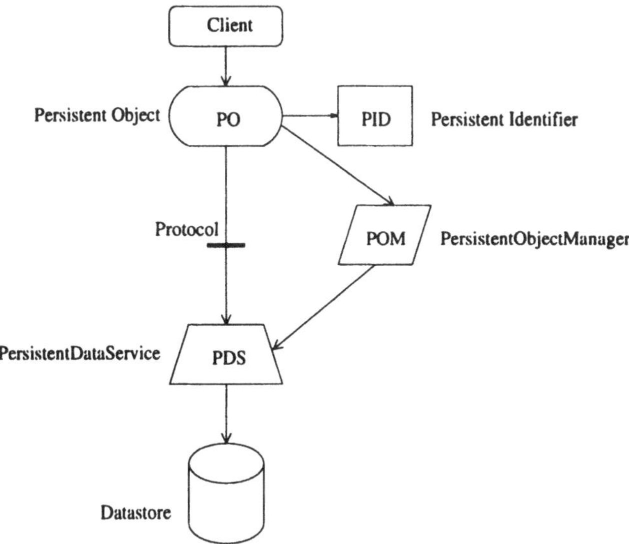

Figure 9 Major components of the POS and their interactions.

(PID) describes the location of persistent data of an object in some *Datastore* and generates a string identifier for that data.

The most crucial part of an *Object Implementation* is often in the definition and manipulation of persistence. The first decision the object makes is what interface to its data it needs. The POS captures that choice in the selection of the *Protocol* used by the object. The Protocol provides one of several ways to get data in and out of an object. The POS also defines a *Persistence Object Manager* (POM) that handles much of the complexity of establishing connections between objects and storage. The POM allows new components to be introduced without affecting the objects or their clients. An object has a single POM to which it routes its high-level persistence operations.

The *Datastore* provides one of several ways to store the data of an object independently of the address space containing the object. By having an interface that is hidden from objects and their clients, a Datastore can provide service to any and all objects that indirectly use the Datastore interface.

Persistent Data Service (PDS) actually implements the mechanism for making data persistent and manipulates it. The PDS provides a uniform interface for any combination of Datastore and Protocol. It co-ordinates the basic persistence operations for a single object. The PDS interacts with the object to get data in and out of the object using a *Protocol.* A protocol may consist of calls from the object to PDS, calls from PDS to the object, implicit operations implemented with hidden interfaces, or some combination. The Persistent Object Service specification defines three Protocols:

1. the *Direct Attribute Protocol* (DA protocol),

2. the *ODMG Protocol*, and
3. the *Dynamic Data Object Protocol* (DDO protocol).

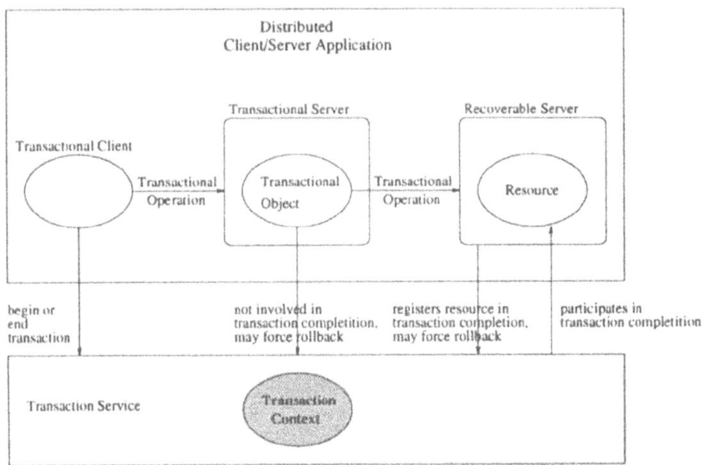

Figure 10 Basic elements of the Transaction Service [10-4/CORBAservices].

Object Transaction Service

The Object Transaction Service (OTS) provides transaction synchronisation across the elements of a distributed client/server application. A transaction can involve multiple objects performing multiple requests. The scope of a transaction is defined by a transaction context that is shared by the participating objects. The OTS places no constraints on the number of objects involved, the topology of the application or the way in which the application is distributed across a network.

Applications supported by the OTS consist of the entities shown in Figure 10:

- *Transactional Client* (TC) is an arbitrary program that can invoke operations of many transactional objects in a single transaction. The program that begins a transaction is called the transaction originator.
- *Transactional Object* (TO) is an object whose behaviour is affected by being invoked within the scope of a transaction. A transactional object typically contains or indirectly refers to persistent data that can be modified by requests. The term non-transactional object refers to an object none of whose operations are affected by being invoked within the scope of a transaction. Transactional objects are used to implement two types of application servers: *Transactional Server* and *Recoverable Server.*
- *Recoverable Objects* are objects whose data is affected by committing or rolling back a transaction. A recoverable object must participate in the Transaction Service protocols by registering an object called a resource with

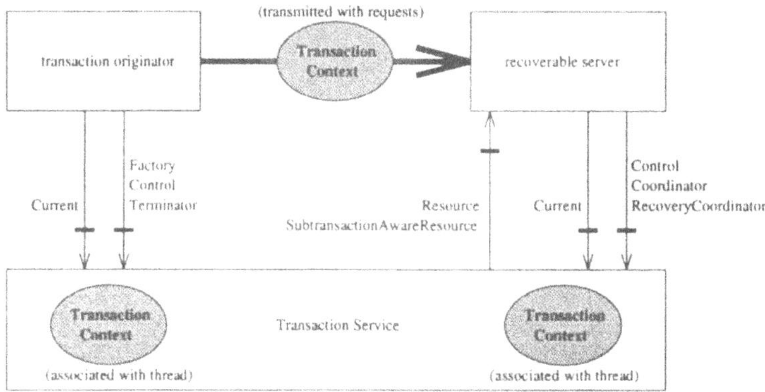

Figure 11 Interfaces of the Transaction Service [10-1/CORBAservices].

the Transaction Service. The Transaction Service drives the commit protocol by issuing requests to the resources registered for the transaction. A recoverable object typically involves itself in a transaction because it is required to retain in stable storage certain information at critical times in its processing. When a recoverable object restarts after a failure, it participates in a recovery protocol based on the contents (or lack of contents) of its stable storage.

- *Transactional Server* is a collection of one or more objects whose behaviour is affected by the transaction but these objects have no recoverable states of their own. A transactional server does not participate in the completion of the transaction but it can force the transaction to be rolled back.
- *Recoverable Server* is a collection of objects, at least one of which is recoverable. It participates in the protocols by registering one or more Resource objects with the Transaction Service. The Transaction Service drives the commit protocol by issuing requests to the resources registered for a transaction.

Figure 11 illustrates the major components and interfaces defined by the Object Transaction Service: **Transaction originator** is an arbitrary program that begins a transaction. **Factory** interface is used by the originator to create a transaction. **Control** interface allows an explicit management or propagation of the transaction context. **Terminator** interface is used by the transaction originator to commit or rollback the transaction. **Coordinator** interface is available to a recoverable server. **Resource** interface, which implements the two-phase commit protocol, is registered by the recoverable server to the Transaction Service. **SubtransactionAwareResource** interface can also be registered by the recoverable server to track the completion of subtransactions. **RecoveryCoordinator** interface can be used in certain failure cases to determine the outcome of transaction and to coordinate the recovery process with the Object

Transaction Service. **Current** interface defines operations that allow a client of the OTS to explicitly manage the association between threads and transactions. The interface also defines operations that simplify the use of the OTS.

Object Query Service

The Object Query Service (OQS) (OMG 1996b) provides selection, insertion, updating, and deletion on collections of objects. These operations are defined as predicate-based queries. Operations are executed to *source* collection and they may return *result* collections of objects. The result collections of objects may be either selected from source collections or produced by query evaluators. The source and result collections may be typed.

The specification of OQS is based on the following design principles:

- The OQS should allow arbitrary user objects to invoke queries on arbitrary collections of other objects. Such queries may specify values of attributes, invoke operations, and invoke arbitrary OMG Object Services.
- The OQS should support the OMG architecture. Therefore, it should allow querying against any objects, with arbitrary attributes and operations.
- The OQS must allow use of performance enhancing mechanisms such as indexing.
- The OQS should smoothly and efficiently co-operate with the internal mechanisms of database systems, especially in specifying collections and in using indexing.
- The OQS must also allow the native systems to contribute in specifying collections and indexing.

The specification of OQS is based on existing standards for query. When necessary to accommodate other design principles the model is extended. In OQS the *query evaluator* can be *nested* and *federated* like the transactions in the Object Transaction Service. Objects may participate in the Query Service in two ways:

- **Any CORBA object is queryable**. The Query Evaluator evaluates the query predicate and query operations. Query operations are performed by invoking operations on that object through its published OMG IDL interface. If an operation is not supported, then an exception is triggered. This mechanism provides generality but prevents optimisation.
- **Objects may participate as members of collections**. The collection has a specific query interface. In other words the collection is a Query Evaluator. This way allows Query Evaluators or any associated native query system to evaluate the query using the internal optimisation.

Table 1 OQS modules and their interfaces

CosQueryCollection

Interface	*Purpose*
CollectionFactory	To create collections
Collection	To represent generic collections
Iterator	To iterate over collections

CosQuery

Interface	*Purpose*
QueryLanguageType	To represent query language types
QueryEvaluator	To evaluate query predicates and execute operations
QueryableCollection	To represent the scope and result of queries
QueryManager	To create query objects and perform query processing
Query	To represent queries

The Query Service provides definitions and interfaces for creating and manipulating collections of objects. The collections are defined as objects with methods for inserting and deleting members. Associated iterators are defined in order to allow manipulation of collections. The members of the same collection may be of different types. The CORBA collections may directly map to collections managed by native query systems. These native collections may include arbitrary CORBA objects. The Query Service is independent of any specific query language. A Query Service provider must support either SQL or OQL-93 query language, that is the Object Query Language defined in the ODMG-93 standard.

The Query Service defines two types of service; see also Table 1:

- Collections include two interfaces to create and manipulate collections of objects. The *Collection* interface includes operations for creating and manipulating collections. The *Iterator* interface defines operations for traversing over and retrieving objects.
- The *Query Framework* interface defines a framework for an object query. The *QueryLanguageType* interface classifies query language types defined in OMG IDL. The *QueryEvaluator* interface defines basic operations for query evaluation. The *QueryableCollection* interface defines the result of the query. The *QueryManager* defines a more powerful QueryEvaluator which can create arbitrary Query objects. Query objects can provide graphical query construction, pre-compilation and optimisation of a query, asynchronous query execution.

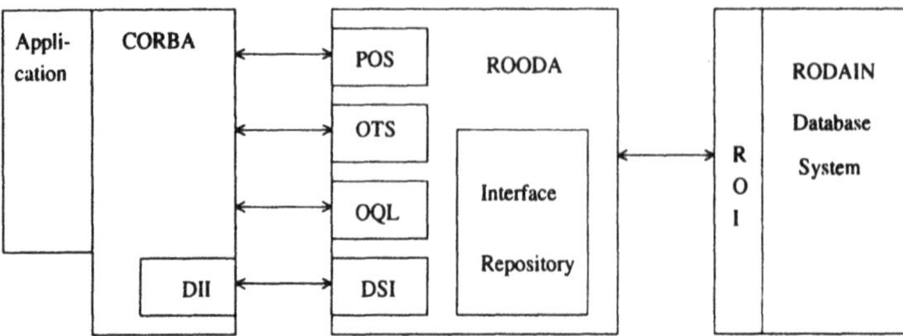

Figure 12 OODA interfaces to CORBA and RODAIN.

4.4 Interfaces to ORB

Since the services provided by any ODA must be transparent, the ORB interfaces must be constructed using existing service interfaces. The interfaces that an ODA should, at least partially, support include POS, OTS, OQS, and DSI. Figure 12 depicts the interfaces to those services the functionality of which the ROODA is designed to support.

The interfaces are:

- In the POS context the ROODA must provide functionality described in Persistent Data Service module. ROODA should interact with the RODAIN Database in order to get data in and out. The ROODA should also interact directly with the object itself in order to get data in and out using protocol. OMG endorses ODMG-93 as a standard interface for storing persistent object state.
- In the OTS context the ROODA must provide functionality described for Recoverable Server. The ROODA must have properties or understand messages of/from objects *Current*, *Control*, *Coordinator*, *RecoveryCoordinator*, *Resource*, and *SubTransactionAwareResource*.
- In the OQS context the ROODA must act as a *Query Evaluator*. Query Evaluator is responsible for evaluating the query predicate and performing all query operations by invoking operations on that object.
- In the DSI context the ROODA offers to a CORBA client a way of dynamic invocation of objects. On the client side the counterpart of DSI is the *Dynamic Invocation Interface* (DII).

4.5 Interface to RODAIN

The interace to RODAIN URIS is built on the ODMG-93 standard data model, which is used in RODAIN. The functions described in the ODMG-93 standard (Cattell 1994) or in our real-time extensions (Kiviniemi *et al.* 1996) offer a low-level interface into RODAIN. The basic idea of this object oriented approach is that RODAIN contains objects for which the CORBA client can make method calls. Or the client can fetch the objects to its own memory, modify them and finally return them into the database. Due to the nature of ODMG-93 data model even the fetches are method calls which are applied to the database-object.

The ODMG-93 model's interface may be too low-level for sophisticated use. Therefore, we have will use an intermediate language between the ROODA and the RODAIN Database based on clauses in relational algebra. Other URISes that interpret other protocols also use algebraic clauses. The intermediate language based on such clauses can, in a rather straightforward manner, be optimised by a single optimiser regardless the used protocol.

5 CONCLUSIONS

Object technology based on the OMG specifications will be the next step in telecommunications software. As introduced in this paper CORBAservices standardised by the OMG provide a sound basis for database access in telecommunications. The Persistent Object Service and Object Transaction Service are the ways in which CORBA objects can be stored and manipulated in a database system. The Object Query Service and Dynamic Skeleton Interface provide the other side of the coin. When CORBA is used as an enabling technology in telecommunications, the databases containing the operational, administrative, and management data must be accessed through CORBA.

An Object Database Adapter is the key component when objects and services available in telecommunications databases are provided to CORBA clients. A typical database includes millions or billions of objects. If all these objects must be registered as CORBA objects, any ORB implementation will not scale to the needs of telecommunications. Therefore, the ODA must provide an interface repository that dynamically provides query results as CORBA objects. Another ability needed in the ODA is dynamic registration of application specific interfaces for database services.

6 REFERENCES

Barr, W.J., Boyd, T. and Inoue, Y. (1993) The TINA initiative. *IEEE Communications Magazine*, **31**, 3, 70-6.

Cattell, R.G.G. (ed.) (1994) *The Object Database Standard: ODMG-93*. Morgan Kauffmann, San Francisco, Calif.

Iona (1995a) *The Orbix Architecture*. Iona Technologies Ltd., Dublin.

Iona (1995b) *The Orbix+ObjectStore Adapter*. Iona Technologies Ltd., Dublin.

ITU-T Recommendation M.3010 (1992) *Principles for a Telecommunications Management Network*. International Telecommunications Union, Geneva.

ITU-T Recommendation Q.1201 (1993) *Principles of Intelligent Network*. International Telecommunications Union, Geneva.

Kiviniemi, J. and Raatikainen, K.E.E. (1996) *Object Oriented Data Model for Telecommunications*. Report C-1996-75, University of Helsinki, Department of Computer Science, Finland.

Niklander, T., Kiviniemi, J. and Raatikainen, K.E.E. (1997) A real-time database for future telecommunication services, in *Proceedings of 2IN'97*, Chapman & Hall, London.

OMG (1993) *Object Management Architecture Guide*. John Wiley & Sons, New York.

OMG (1995) *CORBAfacilities: Common Facility Architecture*. John Wiley & Sons, New York.

OMG (1996a) *CORBA: Common Object Request Broker Architecture and Specification*. John Wiley & Sons, New York.

OMG (1996b) *CORBAservices: Common Object Service Specification*. John Wiley & Sons, New York.

Reverbel, F. (1996a) ORB/ODBMS integration. URL="http://www.acl.lanl.gov/~reverbel/orb_odbms.html".

Reverbel, F. (1996b) ORB/ODBMS integration in the Sunrise project. URL= "http://www.acl.lanl.gov/~reverbel/reverbel_orb_odbms.html".

Reverbel, F. (1996c) *Persistence in Distributed Object Systems: ORB/ODBMS Integration*. Ph.D. Dissertation, University of New Mexico, Computer Science Department.

7 BIOGRAPHY

Pasi Porkka received the B.Sc. degree in computer science from the University of Helsinki, in 1996. He is currently a research assistant in RODAIN research project and completing his M.Sc. thesis about integrating CORBA to object-oriented database. His research interests include real-time databases, CORBA architecture and data mining from relational databases.

Kimmo Raatikainen received the Ph.D. degree in computer science from the University of Helsinki, in 1990. He is currently an associate professor in computer science at the University of Helsinki. He is a member of ACM, IEEE (Communications and Computer Societies), and IFIP TC6 Special Interest Group of Intelligent Networks. His research interests include nomadic computing, telecommunications software architectures, and real-time databases.

19

WEB-Based Enhanced Services

C. Rheinart
Compagnie IBM France
Le Plan du Bois
06610 La Gaude
France
Tel. (+33) 4 92 11 49 29
Fax. (+33) 4 93 24 78 21
E-mail: rheinart@vnet.ibm.com

Abstract

This article describes a prototype of integration of the Telephony and Internet domains for the enabling of new and existing Services for access via WWW protocols by operators, subscribers, or both. The described solution enables telephone subscribers who also have a WWW browser to perform:

- Self-registration for the use of a Telco Multiple Services Platform, and
- Self-registration and service management of single number call forwarding service.

Intelligent Networks and Intelligence in Networks D. Gaiti (Ed.)
Published by Chapman & Hall

1 INTRODUCTION

Web-Based Enhanced Services is a generic term for the enabling of new and existing services for access via WWW protocols by operators, subscribers, or both.
This solution is to be installed by a telephone company and enables telephone subscribers who also have a WWW browser to perform:

- Self-registration for the use of a Telco Multiple Services Platform (MSP) supporting various enhanced services (Voice, Fax, Conferencing,...), and
- Self-registration and service management of an innovative single number call forwarding service (Follow-me), via Java-based and e-commerce technology.

This solution allows the telephone company to offer these two new services with minimal requirement for operator services support. The benefits of this approach are:

- Reduces need for operator provisioning/support of enhanced telephony services, network management services.
- Reduces the subscriber's dependence on operators for provisioning and managing Enhanced Services.
- Remaining operator consoles can also be replaced by more extensive Web interfaces, thus allowing operator support to be provided from any Web browser on the telephone company's intranet, and reducing the need for specialised operator consoles.
- Eliminates touch-tone user interface as an obstacle to Enhanced Services.
- Enables wide range of new services at the intersection of the Internet and telephony.

This Web-based approach may be extended to a wide range of enhances services, which correspond to the implementation of the Computer-Telephone Integration (CTI) on a public network. A new generation of compact, portable devices which operate both as a mobile telephone and as an intelligent data terminal is emerging. The subscriber would then have a portable device which can both manage the Enhanced Services as well as make use of them.

In the following, we will consider some of the issues encountered by both the Telco Operator and the subscriber regarding the introduction of new Enhanced services. Then, we will describe the technical approach which has been selected for the development of the Follow-me application as regards to the self-registration and subscriber data provisioning functions. At least we will mention the difficulties encountered with this approach.

2 POSITIONING

A Multiple Services Platform is an example of a network computing systems which allows a Public Network Operator to flexibly introduce advanced services. Enhanced services, for example, include:

- Voice applications (voice mail, calling cards, voice activated dialling, call forwarding, etc...)
- Fax applications (fax mail, never-busy fax, etc...)
- Data applications providing services accessible via a Personal computer

Moreover, a Multiple Services Platform may act as a Intelligent Peripheral (IP), controlled by an external intelligence (Service Control Point, SCP) within the Intelligent Network Architecture. IBM MSP/6000 is an example of such a multiple services platform.

Enhanced Services are often, but not always, provided by a telephone company, and are then usually closely integrated with the Central Office (C.O.) switches. Figure 1 shows a simple conceptual model of a Multiple Services Platform (MSP), which conforms to European approaches to Enhanced Services. Here the called party number, that is the dialled number, causes the voice channel to be routed by the C.O. switch to a front end switch controlled by the MSP Call Manager. Moreover, the C.O. switch notifies the Call Manager of the call details via a Common Channel Signalling System 7 or other interface. The Call Manager determines which MSP application should handle the call. For example, the MSP allocates voice mailboxes to specific processors, and to deposit a voicemail for a specific subscriber, the voice channel is routed to the processor for that subscriber's mailbox (or to an alternate).

In the same way, if a calling party calls the "single number" for an Enhanced Services subscriber with a single number call forwarding service, the Call Manager recognises the called number as a forwarded number and hands the call off to the forwarding service application, which runs on one of the Enhanced Services (ES) processors. The forwarding service determines where to forward the call, places a call to that number, and connects the incoming call when the subscriber responds.

Enhanced Services platforms thus provide valuable services for subscribers and are quite profitable for the telephone carriers. One of their chief disadvantages is that they are expensive and time-consuming to operate because they demand significant support from telephone operators in provisioning, configuring, managing and updating the service for each subscriber. As a result they are difficult to scale up. In principle, some of this support could be performed by the subscribers; for example, adding or deleting barred numbers in a calling barring service. However, the only interface available to the subscriber is the telephone instrument itself; so these support operations turn into either obscure code sequences, such as *70 (which typically disables call waiting), which subscribers cannot remember, or into frustrating exercises in DTMF menu navigation. More complex services such as configuring single number call forwarding are too complex to manage reliably by this means. The result is that the telephone company must provide operator support for the provisioning, configuration, management and updating of these services.

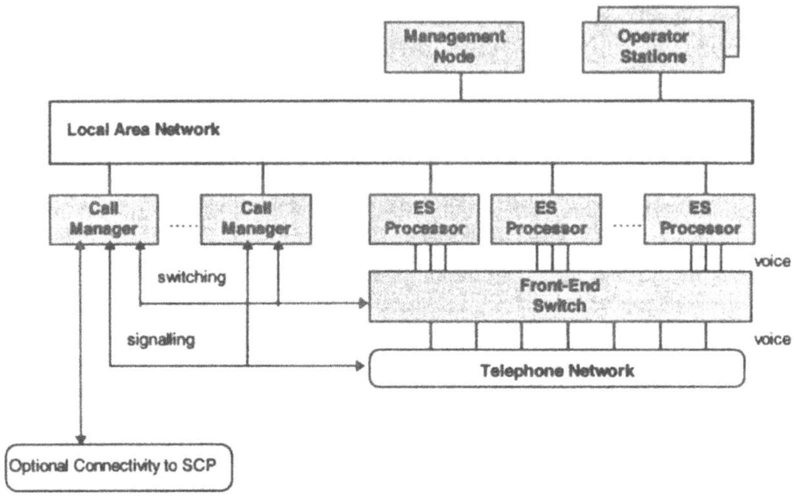

Figure 1 Conceptual model of a Multiple Services Platform (MSP).

Increasingly however, both consumer and business subscribers have access to the Internet and can make use of a Web browser. By some estimates, there are of the order of 100 million Web browsers in existence world-wide (after 3 years). Compare this with of the order of 1 billion telephone lines world-wide (after 125 years). A natural step is therefore to enable at least these subscribers to perform support operations on their Enhanced Services via the Web. Recently mobile telephones incorporating palmtop computers with built-in Web browsers have become available from AT&T and from Nokia, making these natural devices for subscriber management of Enhanced Services.

Figure 2 shows a conceptual extension of the MSP for this purpose. If the Enhanced Services platform is made accessible via the telephone company's own intranet, the subscriber can gain network access to the Enhanced Services platform (modulo security provisions) by one of three paths:

- Dial-up access via the company's own gateway. This points to the close relationship between Enhanced Services and Internet service.
- Access via some other Internet Service Provider and then via the Internet itself.
- Broadband access via a leased, packet-switched connection to an enterprise, or, in the future, via an ADSL or HFC access network.

Here the Enhanced Services platform is supplemented with a WWW server platform. The Web server is provided with an application interface to the subscriber-manageable parts of the Enhanced Services; that is, most of the functions previously performed by the telephone operators, typically using specialised operator consoles. Of course, the operator consoles can also be replaced by more extensive Web-interfaces, thus allowing operator support to be provided from any Web browser on the telephone company's intranet, and reducing the need for specialised operator consoles

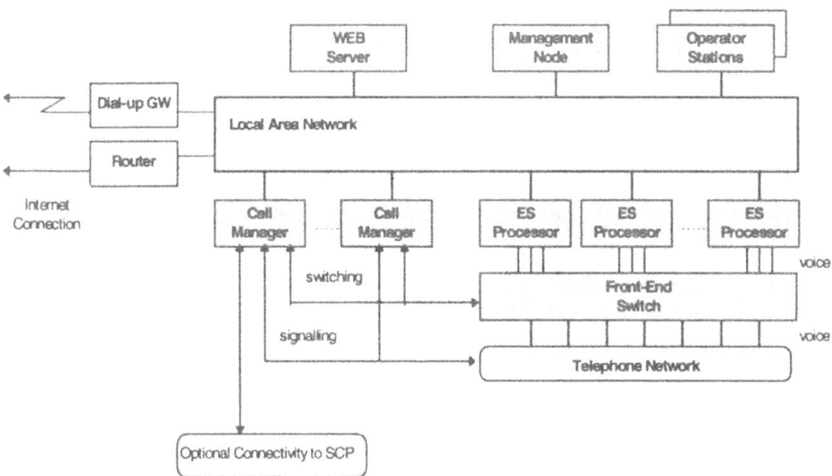

Figure 2 Conceptual model of Web-based Enhanced Services

While this is an interesting first step, this Web-based approach could eventually be extended to a very wide range of Enhanced Services. In essence, this approach is the implementation of Computer-Telephone Integration (CTI) on a public network, as opposed to a PBX, and one could eventually implement many of the advanced services that a PBX-based CTI system provides. For example, one might use a Web browser to access a White Pages telephone directory; clicking on a name in the directory would set up a PSTN call from the subscriber to the selected party. Similarly, an enterprise home page could display an 800 number, which is dialled when clicked. Contemporary CTI client applications are often based on the Microsoft Telephony API (TAPI), but these involve dedicated Windows applications and user interfaces. Today is emerging a range of Java object classes, which will fulfil the same function for a Web browser Java application that TAPI provides for a Windows application.

3 TECHNICAL APPROACH

Figure 3 shows a software structure for the prototyping of a WES application.

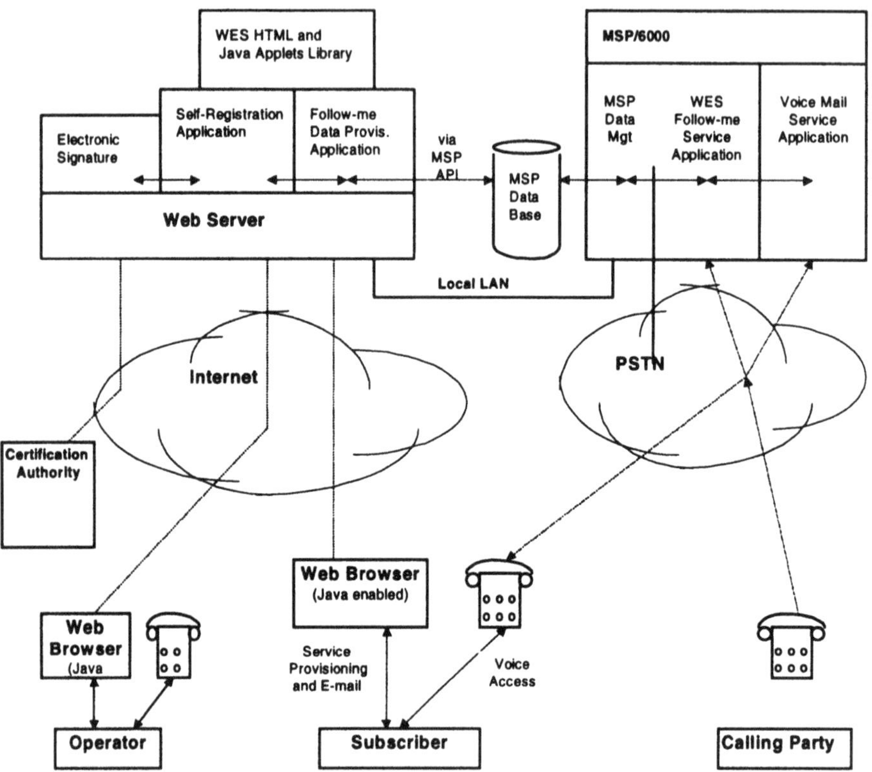

Figure 3. Software structure for the prototyping of a WES application

The client side consists of a standard Java-enabled Web-browser, which is supplemented by Java applets downloaded from the WES server. The client processor is not defined, except that it must have some access to the Internet. The server side runs on an RS/6000, which may be an existing part of the Enhanced Services platform. The WES server communicates with one or more subscriber applications, namely in our case, with the Self-Registration and Follow-me Data provisioning applications. The subscriber applications communicate either with MSP platform which implements the actual Enhanced Services on the MSP, or with external services such as a credit agency for electronic commerce. Associated with the subscriber applications are HTML JavaScript content for the Web pages, and Java applets to provide additional function at the client side.

The user navigates to the home page of the telephone company's Enhanced Services and logs in. The user is identified by his Subscriber Identification associated to his Personal Identification Number (PIN) which is a kind of password. The browser and server establish a session based on Secure Sockets and the server downloads the appropriate set of applets. The user selects the specific Enhanced Service he or she wishes to use and the applets establish the session with the appropriate WES server application. The subscriber may now perform Self-Registration or modify his or her personal single profile, and so forth.

4 SINGLE NUMBER CALL FORWARDING SERVICE

In this service, the user establishes a daily or hourly calendar which defines where his or her telephone calls should be finally delivered. The user gives out a single number to his customers or co-workers or family, but calls to that number are routed according to a schedule established by the user. The user can also specify multiple numbers to be tried in sequence. For example:

- 07:00-08:00 Mobile, Voicemail
- 08:00-09:00 Office, Voicemail
- 10:00-11:00 Voicemail
- 11:00-12:30 Branch office, secretary, voicemail
- 12:30-01:15 Mobile, Voicemail
- 01:15-06:00 Office, Voicemail
- 06:00-07:00 Mobile, Voicemail
- 07:00-08:00 Voicemail

Here the user has defined one or more numbers where he or she may be reached at different times of a particular day.

When the user is called, the Follow-me determines how the call is to be handled. If the call has to be forwarded, the Follow-Me service dials each of the numbers specified for that time of day until the user answers; if the user does not answer, the calls will eventually be forwarded to voicemail. When one of the called numbers is answered, Follow-Me might request the responding person to accept or not the call by prompting for the input by DTMF (Touch-tone) key of a digit. Acceptance or not of the call might be coupled to a call screening function, which would consist in replaying an announcement message recorded from the calling party. The responding party would accept or not the call according the tonality of the voice.

Meanwhile the calling party receives a pre-recorded message that Follow-Me is searching for the called party, and the calling party can at any time opt to be transferred to voicemail. In a first step the out-dialled calls are billed to the called party, but call details are provided in the Call Data Record to fit specific carrier needs. This is a valuable service for mobile workers, even if they have mobile telephones, and is worth of Web-based implementation, because it is too complex to set up via a DTMF UIF.

As far is concerned the definition of the single number, several possibilities exist. This number can be:

- One number among a range of real telephone numbers that would be allocated by the carrier to the MSP. During the self-registration process, MSP would allocate one of these numbers to the subscriber.
- One number among a range of logical telephone numbers that would be rerouted by the carrier to a fixed forwarding number (corresponding to MSP). This rerouting of the call could be done with the assistance of an Intelligent Network Service Control Point. During the self-registration process, MSP would allocate one of these logical numbers to the subscriber.
- The main telephone number of the subscriber, which appears on his business card for instance, and which would be rerouted by the carrier to a fixed forwarding number (corresponding to MSP) in case of no answer. Again the rerouting of the call could be done with the assistance of a Service Control Point. During the self-registration process, the subscriber would specify this single number.

Whatever the chosen alternative, calls to this single number are always delivered by the C. O. switch to the MSP. When the MSP Call Manager receives an incoming call with the associated signalling information (calling party number, called party number, original called party number and call reason), it identifies the call as a Follow-Me call, since it has a registry of the single numbers, and hands the call off to the Follow-Me service application.

The basic definition of the forwarding schedule is via a Web browser form. However, it may also be possible to enter or deduce the forwarding schedule from the subscriber's electronic calendar, for example, Lotus Organizer or the Lotus Notes calendar, if this is maintained on the personal computer.

5 SUBSCRIBER SELF REGISTRATION

We have noted above that a disadvantage of Enhanced Services from the telephone company's point of view is the high cost of operator support. A method of permitting the subscriber to establish the basic subscription to the MSP platform electronically is highly desirable and also original. Provisioning here means establishing the basic information about the subscriber: name, billing method, address, telephone numbers, and so forth. Generally this requires the subscriber to complete some paperwork, mail it to the company and wait a few days for the service to be enabled. Alternatively the subscriber may be able to call an operator number, give a credit card number as surety for the first bill, and establish a billing arrangement with the company. The first method involves a workflow process in the back office. The second method involves both an operator interaction and a workflow process in the back office.

A better method is to allow the subscriber to establish an e-commerce relationship with the company. This requires no human intervention. It also allows "on-demand" subscription to the services, permitting the subscribers to "try it and see". It also allows travellers to establish a local telephone number instantly and to subscribe to Enhanced Services such as voicemail and call forwarding for a few days at a time. Self-Registration thus simultaneously reduces the cost of provisioning and enable greater flexibility for the subscribers.

The service is implemented here as follows. The user indicates via a Web interaction the desire to become an MSP subscriber. The MSP Self-Registration service collects basic information about the subscriber, including a credit card number or other credit identification, which is transmitted securely to the Self-Registration service via the Secure Sockets Layer (SSL) protocol.

Authentication of the credit information is verified via an electronic signature, in case the user has obtained such a signature from a Certification Authority like Verisign. Validation of the credit information can be done by a connection to the pertinent credit organism.

The Self-Registration service then creates the subscriber profile on the MSP and asks the subscriber what service(s) he or she wants to use. Thereafter, whenever an MSP service is activated on behalf of that subscriber, the MSP generates a Call Detail Record which is billed out (in real-time or not) to the subscriber's credit account via a financial switch. Subsequently, the subscriber can re-visit the Self-Registration Web page and add or delete services or terminate the MSP subscription completely.

6 WES OPERATOR

We have seen that this solution allows the telephone company to reduce the need for operator provisioning/support of enhanced telephony services. However in a emergency or if the subscriber is unable to access the WES service via a workstation, the subscriber may call the MSP operator to perform certain actions:

- To become a MSP subscriber,
- To display/modify or cancel a current forwarding request,
- To enter a future forwarding request,
- To change his basic administration information such as his credit card number, his bank account, his e-mail address or even his home address,
- To request his Personal Identification Number, in case he has lost it,
- To cancel the Follow Me service subscription and so forth...

In this solution, the operator console for the enhanced telephony services is also a Web browser. This console is connected to the same Local Area Network as the Web Server. For security reason, communication with the Web server may use an access IP port different from the one used by the subscribers. When an operator on a WEB browser console wants to get access to the system, first of all, he has to authenticate himself as an operator. To each operator is allocated a specific operator-ID and a PIN number. You should consider an operator as a standard subscriber with specific privileges.

When receiving a call from a subscriber, the operator needs to handle two types of situations:

- The subscriber is able to authenticate himself as a real subscriber, that is, he is able to provide his subscriber identification and his PIN number. This is the case when the subscriber does not have access temporary to a Web browser, or simply when he is lost while handling a forwarding request. The operator must be able to act as this subscriber. The implementation solution consists to give the operator the possibility to copy in his own context, the context of the calling subscriber. Some carriers may feel that the updating of some basic information related to the subscriber (credit card number, bank account, e-mail address or even the home address) should be performed via the operator to avoid frequent updates from the subscriber.
- The subscriber is NOT able to authenticate itself as a real subscriber: he has lost his subscriber identification or his PIN number. The operator is able to search in the database and to retrieve the requested information. The problem is how to transmit this information ? The operator can not be sure of the person who is calling. The most secure way is to send it via mail (e-mail in our case), as it is done for any credit card. We know that e-mail is not a secure transport protocol, but the user can changed his PIN number as soon he has received the e-mail message.

As an extension of this solution, we can imagine a customer who does not have access to a WEB browser but who wants to take profit of the follow-me service. He may request the operator to perform the operations on his behalf. Nothing prevents the operator to do this. You should note in this case that the subscriber will receive his Subscriber-ID and PIN number by physical mail rather than by e-mail.

Indeed, the operator will also have to deal with requests coming from the carrier control operations. He needs to be able to perform the following actions:

- To display all information related to a specific subscriber,
- To cancel the registration of a specific subscriber for a specific service,
- To cancel the registration of a user as a MSP subscriber, and so forth...

DIFFICULTIES

User Interface

One of the main motivations of this prototype lied in the fact that the poverty of the user interface via the DTMF keys inhibited any service somewhat sophisticated, if it required a certain number of subscriber data. With a Web browser, a graphical interface allows indeed to simplify the user task. However a telephone user remains still today, in his culture, reluctant to spend a minimum amount time to manage his telephone calls.

With the same goal to minimise the time spent by the subscriber for data provisioning, Java applets allow indeed to save time for the local interactions, but the time spent to download the Java classes may be an inhibitor for the user having a low speed Internet connection, even when these classes are put together and compressed.

Self-Registration

We have noted above that the self-registration process comprises two parts:
- self-register to the MSP platform itself,
- self-register to a new service.

Self-registration to the MSP platform
Via the subscriber-Id and the PIN number, the user is correctly identified and the subscriber data are conveyed in a secure way via the Secure Sockets Layer (SSL) protocol. The issue of the authentication of the subscriber remains. Nothing prevents a malicious user from specifying a credit card number and an address that would not belong to him, and it may apply even when the credit card is valid and has not been stolen. The issue gets even more complex because there is in our case no purchase of any material good which would allow an easier checking later on. However, the system may work like this, as it is the case today with most of the shopping over the Net, the minimum being to validate the credit card.

To go further on and to overcome the fear of many people, especially in some countries, to place their credit card on the Net, the solution is to use an electronic signature which can be obtained from a Certification Authority. The difficulty lies in the broad acceptance and usage of these facilities.

Self-registration to a new service
The introduction of a new service which needs data provisioning from the subscriber requires also often a provisioning action in the switches of the network. Generally speaking, to make automatic this C.O. update function requires a gateway connection with the Telco System Management Service. In the case of our prototype, this constraint is relaxed by selecting the Single Number values among a set of logical telephone numbers provided by the Telco, as described in chapter 'Single Number Call Forwarding service'. This approach did allow to provision the switches of the network in advance.

Billing

Several questions arise concerning the billing:
- How to charge the service ?
  - fee per service
  - fee per service usage
  - monthly fee.
- How often would the Telco want to charge the customer ?
- Would the customer prefer ONE bill for all the services, including services he is using to day ?

The answers to all these questions are Telco specific. However, it appears that a connection with the current Telco billing system is recommended, to get the required flexibility.

CONCLUSION

The technology exists today to allow an Internet user to self-register to Telco enhanced services and to manage his personal data, while reducing to a minimum the role of the Telco service operator.
However, some cultural reluctance from the telephone user exists today:

1. to place his credit card number on the Net,
2. and to spend a certain amount of time to update his personal data.

Concerning the first point, until the electronic signatures facilities are widely deployed and well advertised to the users, the Telco service operator will keep a significant role for the delivery of the subscriber number with an associated password.

Concerning the second point, a Telco company could begin to offer on the Net a list of services which could be quickly activated and exercised by the user, while requiring little amount of user interactions. This would allow the user to get familiar with Internet habits and be prepared to accept more sophisticated applications.

7 BIOGRAPHY

CHARLES RHEINART graduated as engineer of the « Ecole Nationale Supérieure d'Ingénieur de Toulouse » in 1968 in the domain of Applied Mathematics. He has been working for IBM in the areas of networking, transmission protocols and network management for over 20 years. He participated in 1994 in a RACE project targeted to group collaborative working over broadband networks. He has joined in 1996 the IBM European Telecommunications Solution Center (TSC) architecture group located in La Gaude (France). His current area of interest is the integration of the Telephony and Internet domains.

PART EIGHT

Specification

OST - An Object-Oriented Computer Networks System Specification Tool

Claudia Maria Sbardelotto, Lisandro Zambenedetti Granville, Luciano Paschoal Gaspary, Maria Janilce B. Almeida

Federal University of Rio Grande do Sul (UFRGS-CPGCC)

Campus do Vale, Bloco IV - Bento Gonçalves, 9500 - Agronomia – PO 15064, ZIP 91501-970, Brazil – Tel: +55.51.316.6161, Fax: +55.51.319.1576

{claudias, granvile, paschoal, janilce}@inf.ufrgs.br

Abstract

With the purpose of lessening the software production efforts in computer networks area, the use of tools that help the system specification and implementation process is needed. This work presents a development tool based on the NSOMA methodology, intended to help the designers in the formal definition of specifications. It is composed of a graphical editor, an animation module that allows the visualization of specification dynamic behavior and a source code automatic generating module.

Keywords

computer networks, specification tool, NSOMA, object orientation, animation, source code generation

Intelligent Networks and Intelligence in Networks D. Gaiti (Ed.)
Published by Chapman & Hall

1 INTRODUCTION

The use of tools for developing software is currently a fact, due to advantages such as reduced production time and easy system maintenance, documentation and expansion. The use of a number of features available for each tool provides help for the various stages of software developing.

There are many system specification and implementation environments designed for computer networks. Most designers, though, still use primitive, user-unfriendly methodology, as these environments are usually based on complex Formal Description Techniques (FDTs) (Cohen, 1986). An Object Orient Specification Tool (OST) has been developed at Federal University of Rio Grande do Sul bearing this difficulty in mind. OST associates a modeling and developing methodology to a formal specification technique. This tool allows better comprehension and organization of the system components and thus becomes a very efficient way to produce easy-to-use tools regardless of the programming language they are based on, whieh are only a few and mastered by few designers.

OST is based on the Network System Object Modeling Approach (NSOMA) (see item 2 below), integrating object-orientation concepts to SDL (Specification and Description Language). OST is composed of three modules: a graphic editor, which allows creating and editing a specification from NSOMA's graphic grammar, an animation module, which provides instruments to visualize the dynamic behavior of the specifications, and an automatic source code generator. These modules are presented in sections 3, 4 and 5, respectively and section 6 introduces an example.

2 NETWORK SYSTEM OBJECT MODELING APPROACH (NSOMA)

The goal of NSOMA is to make SDL easier to use, associating it to the object-orientation paradigm under the Object Modeling Technique (OMT) method (Almeida, 1994) (Rumbaugh, 1991). As the human mind can see the world as a series of inter-related objects, the use of this concept furthers comprehension. Thus, the real world is brought closer to the computing world. It also allows the possibility of reusing previously developed entities in the creation of new software.

Because NSOMA specifications are hierarchically defined, this approach is broken into three specification levels. These levels allow the designers to start from a more abstract level and then refine their specification, bringing it closer to the implementation.

The following are NSOMA specification levels:

- Abstract structural level: at this level, classes' behavior and relations are determined.
- Detailed structural level: at this level, each class's behavior is determined. Ports, internal signals, attributes and operations are defined.
- Operation level: at this level, each previously defined operation is detailed.

The abstract structural level description is based on OMT concepts. It allows the definition of highly abstract classes that form a network system and the relations between them. Their corresponding objects represent elements of a network system - protocols, functions, services, entities. These classes are described and identified by their type, name, attributes and operations.

A class can be defined from another's definition. In such case, one says the first inherits from the second and calls it a subclass, which may inherit attributes and operations from the parent class totally or partially. In addition, a class can be defined as a combination of other classes, though preventing the latter from inheriting attributes or operations from the former. A class can inherit classes that were defined by combination. In such case, the subclass inherits all classes that compose the parent class.

The detailed structural level is where attributes, operations and internal signals are actually defined for a given class. Every class modeled at the abstract structural level is refined at the detailed structural level. The internal signals allow communication between operations of the same class. They can be synchronous or asynchronous.

Ports and external signals supply communication between elements of different classes. It can also be synchronous or asynchronous. Communication is considered synchronous when the source operation enters a hold state for a response signal, thus being blocked indefinitely, whereas asynchronous communication does not hold and therefore is not blocked. External signals are defined outside classes' behavior, which allows their further individual use.

The operation level allows every previously defined operation to have its behavior diagramed, thus determining the system's control flux. Hierarchically, it is the closest level to implementation and it is strongly based on SDL. Graphically, this level is described by diagrams that represent a state machine of the operations.

3 THE GRAPHIC EDITOR

This editor implements all functions necessary to system specification in NSOMA. The software uses NSOMA's graphic syntax to help the user interact more naturally. Specifications are created through the manipulation of the grammar graphics (Gaspary, 1995) (Granville, 1995). The textual approach is not neglected, though, allowing the user to textually visualize the specifications being

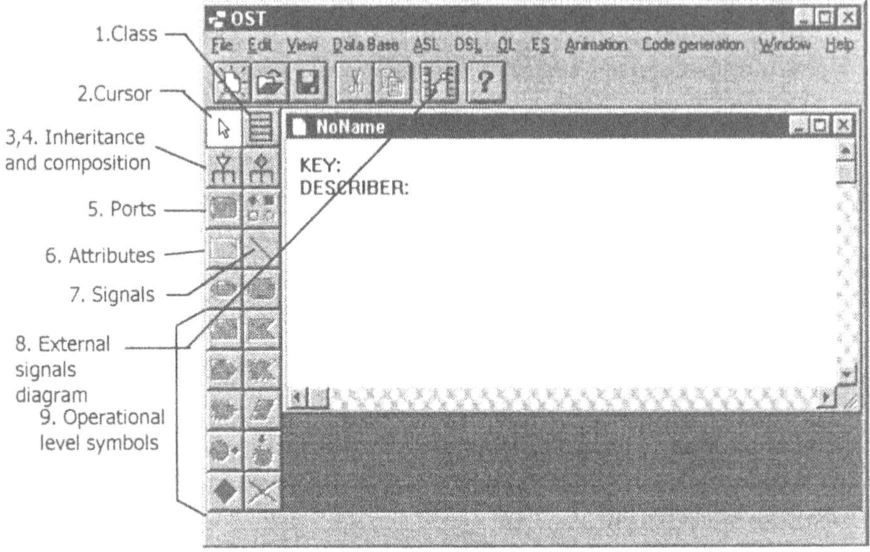

built. Figure 1 shows the tool's main interface.

Figure 1 OST's graphic interface

From the *File* menu, the user can create new specifications, load pre-existent specifications from a database, save specifications onto database as well as retrieve classes from a class library. From the *Edit* menu, objects can be selected from the editor and copied to Windows transfer area, which can prove helpful to documentation using other software. The *ASL*, *DSL*, *OL* and *ES* menus are used to select symbols corresponding to each of NSOMA's levels. *Animation* and *Generate Source Code* start operations from their respective modules, which are presented below. Finally, *Window* and *Help* have window management functions for OST, which are standard to Windows applications.

The upper toolbar provides quick access to the most commonly used functions. It accesses these functions: creation of a new specification, loading and saving an ongoing specification, deletion of selected symbols and their copy to Windows transfer area, reading the external signals diagram and help.

To start a new specification, select *New* from the *File* menu or click on the corresponding icon on the toolbar. That will open a window representing the abstract specification level. On the upper left corner the words *Key* and *Describer* can be seen, without any links to text. Also, four buttons on the left become active. These are the functions that can be used at this level. To create a new class, for instance, click on the class button (1) of figure 1. Next, use the mouse to insert new classes in the window. Initially, the application will automatically generate names and types for the classes in order to avoid repetitions.

To include a class from the library in your specification, select *Load class* from the *File* menu. A dialog box will display all library classes so that one can be picked. The chosen class is then loaded from the database and included in the diagram.

Buttons (3) and (4) on figure 1 allow the representation of class relations. Click on the corresponding button and then on a class graphic to create a line that represents a relation between two classes.

Finally, button (2) brings the user back to selection mode. Using this, the user can move the graphics on the screen by dragging them. Also, many objects can be selected simultaneously and then moved, copied to the transfer area or deleted.

Figure 2 shows the active menu for a class *Class3*. This class can have its name and type changed, as well as some graphic features of inheritance and composition.

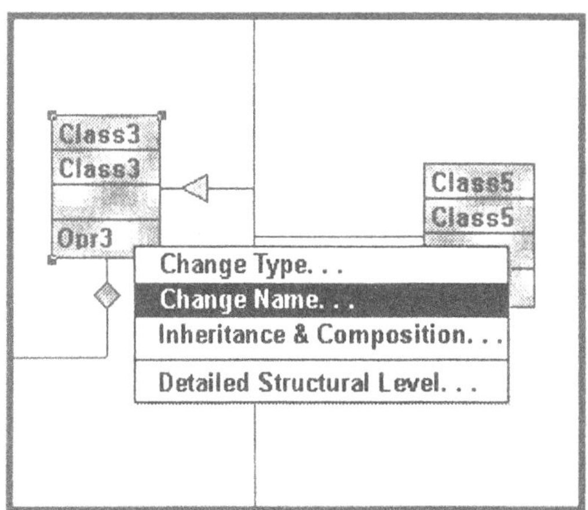

Figure 2 Context-sensitive menus

The last option of the menu starts edition at the detailed structural level. Double clicking on a class also starts this function.

Accessing the detailed structural level opens a new window. New buttons are activated on the left, disabling the buttons for the previous level. This new level enables functions for creating operations, internal signals (7), external signals (8) and attributes (6), shown in figure 1. The manipulation of objects follows the same pattern for manipulation as the abstract level.

NSOMA's last level is accessed by double-clicking an operation, the same pattern used to access the detailed level. Once again, the left-hand toolbar is updated to show the options valid for the current operational level, as shown in figure 1.

At any level, a specification's textual description can be read. To do that, select this option from the menu in the corresponding level. The text is presented in a new dialog box. This cannot be altered, though, in order to assure consistency with the graphic specification.

To include all these functions in the editor, an object-oriented programming approach was used to build it. The basic classes that were implemented can be divided into two separate groups, database class and graphic class (Trainini, 1995). The database classes (*Data_ob*) are responsible for the semantic consistency of a given specification (see figure 3). Each new element added to the diagram is actually a database object. If it cannot be created, some database rule violation can be assumed. Further information on how database elements interrelate to keep specification consistency can be found in (Gaspary, 1995) (Granville, 1995).

On the other hand, the graphic classes are responsible for the implementation of all graphic functionality. There are basically a window class (*TDragDropWindow*) and a graphic object class (*TShape*). These two primitive classes work together to implement drag-and-drop and multiple selection functions, among others. Window classes for each specification level were derived from *TDragDropWindow*. All graphic symbols used in the editor were derived from *TShape*.

The basic classes are divided into two separate groups for the sake of comprehension. Actually, there is high interaction between the two groups. In fact, any graphic element is a database object and a graphic object at the same time. It must be consistent to its specification as well as have all the necessary graphic functionality.

The basic classes, in their turn, are also derived from a library set (OWL, which accompanies Borland C++). OWL contains many of the required features. Figure 3 shows a general map of the classes used by the editor.

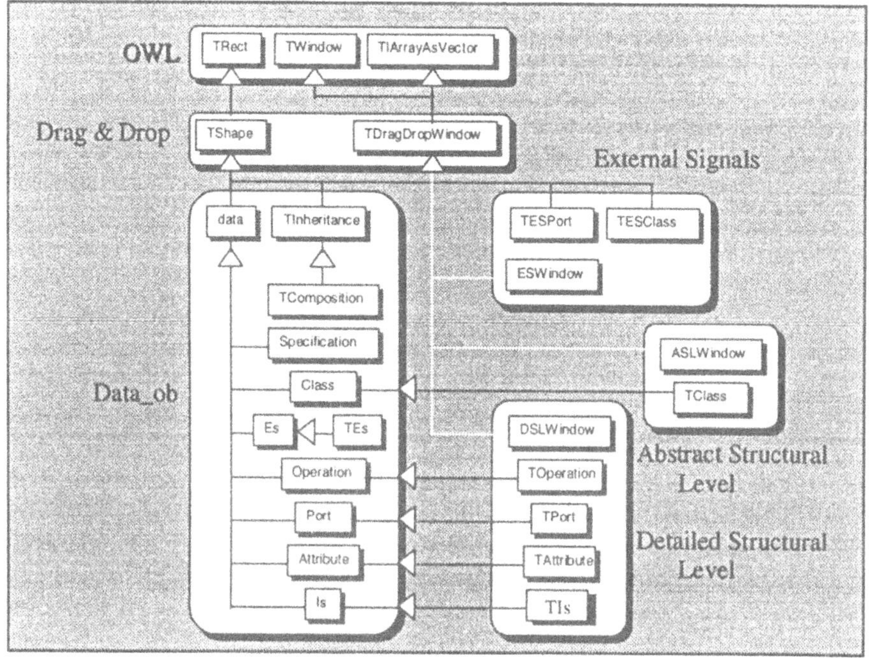

Figure 3 Set of classes for the OST editor

4 ANIMATION MODULE

The animation of a system's dynamic behavior is a basic need to its definition and specification (Allende, 1995). It fosters the understanding of the description being specified, translated as reduced construction cycles since a number of problems can be verified during the early development stages (Verilog, 1994).

OST provides an environment to visualize animation, in addition to plenty of statistic data and some deadlock-detection facilities. This kind of functionality can be found in verification systems.

The animation was implemented using, basically, symbols from the operational level and operation representation structure (Gaspary, 1996). The animation controls were implemented in two new classes called *AnimOL_Sym* and *AnimOperation*, which relate to the editor's structure as seen in figure 4. *AnimOL_Sym* associates every animation-relevant symbol to a count variable, in order to provide statistics on the use of this symbol. Also, it has a drawing method for the symbol being run, so that it can be highlighted. *AnimOperation* implements an input signal queue for each operation, which keeps the signals from being lost. Using the same pattern as for symbols at the operational level, a drawing method for the highlighted operation symbol should follow.

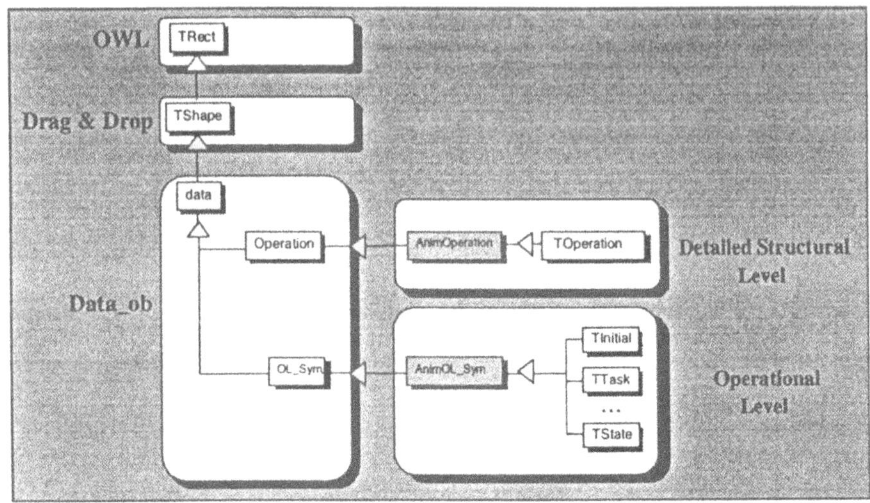

Figure 4 *AnimOL_Sym* and *AnimOperation* classes

Figure 5 shows how the animation works. Every operation of a given specification is pointed by a control entity. The figure shows a semaphore composed of two operations (master and slave) (Verilog, 1994]. This entity points at the initial symbols of each operation, and then to their subsequent operations, according to given navigation options.

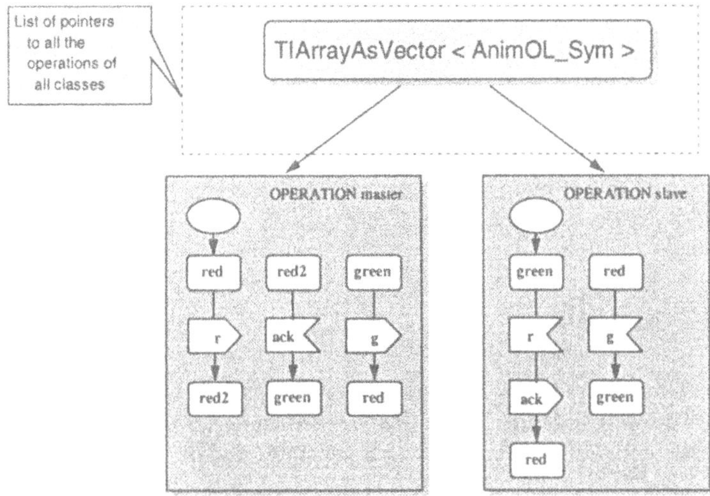

Figure 5 Visiting tree of a given specification

OST's animation provides the following operations: *Start*, *Next Step*, *Previous Step*, *Auto*, *Next Stop* and *Stats* (Eijk, 1988).

1. *Start*: sets the animation environment and enables the *Next Step* operation.
2. *Next Steps Menu*: show actions that can be started. When this menu cannot be enabled, that means, when no operation can offer a transition to be started, the animation will have reached a deadlock state and therefore cannot be run any further. A message will inform the user of any such case.
3. *Next Step*: allows the start of a new transition in the animation. After the menu is built, the user is expected to interact with the system by indicating which transition should be started.
4. *Previous Step*: allows reversing one or more steps of the animation. It gives the opportunity to test many execution alternatives, though preventing the need to restart the whole process repeatedly.
5. *Auto*: runs the animation automatically, with no interaction with the user. Therefore, the system should be informed about the conditions to halt the animation. This conditions are linked to a certain number of iterations over a symbol or to a set run time. Of course, deadlocks will also halt the execution.
6. *Next Stop*: combines interactive and automatic execution. It allows the animation to be automatized to a point where a decision has to be made. Then, the user will choose which action to take.
7. *Stats*: these can be checked during or after the animation, presenting information such as:
   - *Elapsed time*: shows elapsed during animation.
   - *Unvisited symbols*: a very useful option, as it shows dead code in the specification. It can be expanded to show whole-unused paths.

- *Potential livelock points*: extensively visited points can be thought of as livelocks.
- *Total visited symbols*: general overview of the total visitation.

The functions available in the animation module enable a larger and clearer view of the specification being developed. Furthermore, the user can assess specific situations and decide if they perform as expected.

5 CODE GENERATOR

The language hierarchy provides instruments for automatic code generation (Fröberg, 1993). The classes defined at the abstract structural level are mapped to C++ classes. Each defined class is coded in a separate module, containing the definition of the operations and attributes that are converted, respectively, into functions and variables.

When a class is initialized, each operation is run as a process and its descriptor is stored as an internal attribute to the class, like user-defined attributes. The ports, in their turn, become the methods visible externally to the class. Each method receives messages from external operations to the class and forwards them to their corresponding destiny processes.

The *datagram_function* in figure 6 shows the code generation. As we see, each port is mapped to a method that will be used to provide communication with other classes. Similarly, figure 5.2 shows operation *receive* receiving a signal *a*. The class's constructor initializes its operations in separate processes. Finally, each operation is defined from a state machine, in non-structured source code.

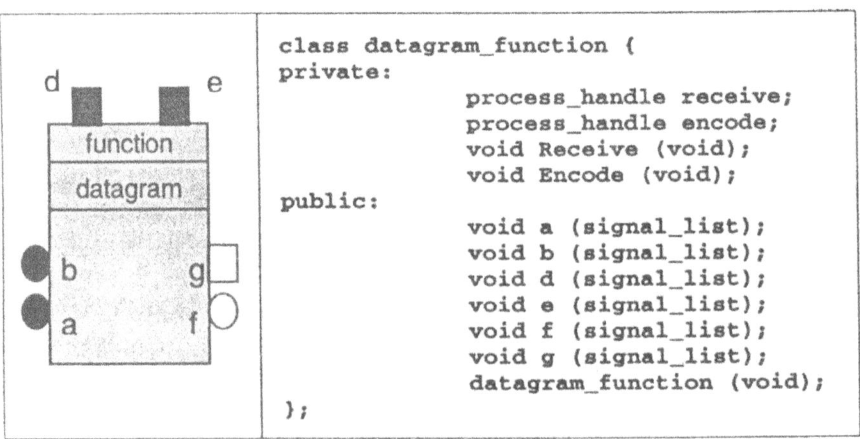

Figure 6 *datagram_function* class

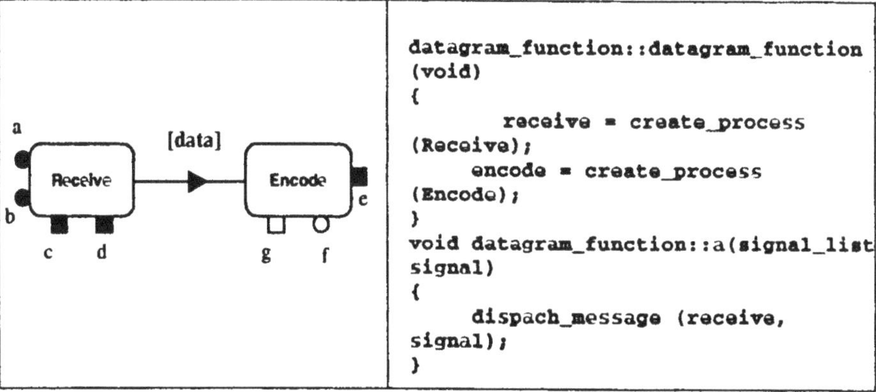

Figure 7 *datagram_function* class's operations

6 EXAMPLE – THE HTTP PROTOCOL

The figure 8 shows the diagrams resulting from the HTTP Protocol Specification. It's an incomplete high level description, where details were neglected in order to have a more didactic example.

The protocol is designed as two distinct classes named *Server* and *Client,* each of them inheriting the classes corresponding to the HTTP previous version. HTTP first versions define just simple requests, which are less complex than the current one. So, inheriting such definition is a fast way to design more complex specifications.

The client class has an operation named *Request*, which creates and sends HTTP messages to the server side and waits for the server response. Messages are sent and received via ports (in the example *In* and *Out).* Such ports are showed in the *Fine Structural Level* diagram and are placed next to the corresponding operation. The behavior of *Request* is defined in the *Operational Level* that is quite similar to an ordinary standard SDL diagram. The messages exchanged by classes are done by means of external ports and the associations of them are defined in the *External Signals* diagram.

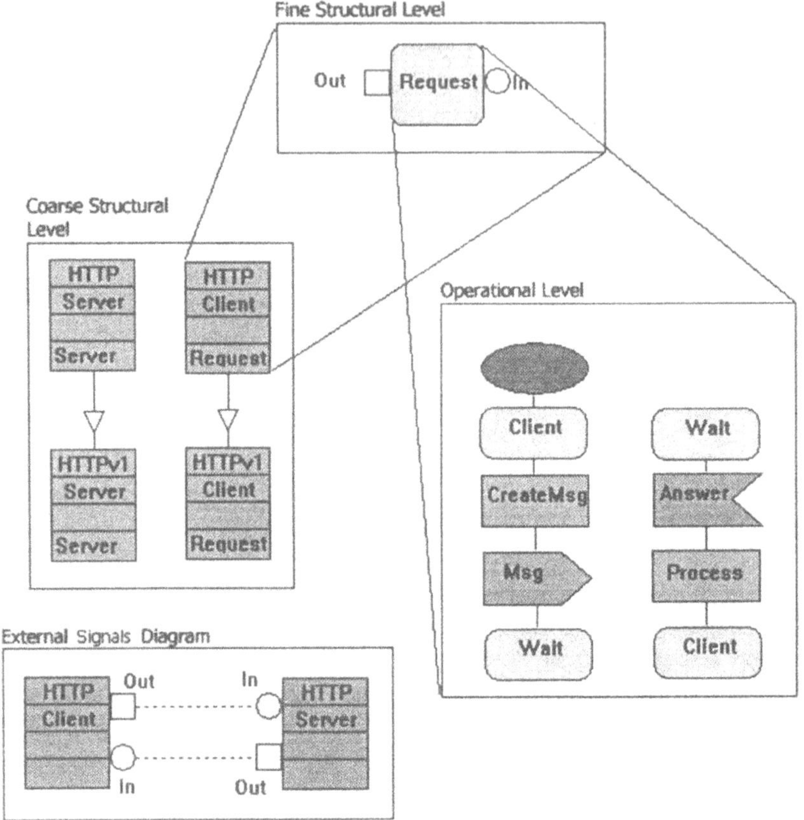

Figure 8 HTTP protocol example diagrams

7 CONCLUSIONS

OST is a very powerful specification tool. It provides any users, either computer networks programmers or information systems designers, with a tool based on a standard FDT, such as SDL, and then improves this tool using an object-oriented paradigm, which is known as a potential productivity booster in software development.

The many modules that form OST offer a more efficient way to specify systems. Its editor allows the creation of a specification using NSOMA's graphic grammar, furthering comprehension and interaction. OST's on-line syntax check avoids user errors. In addition, classes can be reused, which makes the construction process ever evolving, incremental, fast and efficient. Under the computer networks area jargon, classes can represent the basic concepts of model, layer, protocol, service and entity.

OST's animation feature increases comprehension of the systems developed. This is fundamental for a software developing team where a single and clear idea of what is being done is a must. Also, errors associated to the dynamic behavior of the specification (deadlocks and livelocks, for instance) can be detected. Furthermore, automatic code generation avoids the manual codification of a whole system. Consequently, the source code is free of lexical and syntactical errors.

OST can be further expanded, including specification verification and validation mechanisms that will assure even better correctness. Even though the editor is syntax-oriented, no lexical consistency is performed. This reflects on source code generation, which becomes undesirably linked to errors from the specification stage. Such lexical consistency is also to be included in future expansions.

7 REFERENCES

Almeida, Maria Janilce (1994) Especificação de sistemas na área de redes de computadores: uma abordagem orientada a objetos. Porto Alegre: UFRGS (tese de doutorado).

Allende, Jesús Sánchez. (1995) GLAv2.0 - Graphical Animation for LOTOS - Quick reference. Technical University of Madrid. Spain.

Cohen, B. *et al.* (1986) The Specification of Complex Systems. Great Britain: Addyson Wesley.

van Eijk, Peter Herman Johan (1988) Software tools for the specification language LOTOS. Twente University.

Fröberg, M. W. (1993) Automatic Code Generation from SDL to a Declarative Programming Language. Proceedings of SDL Forum.

Gaspary, Luciano Paschoal (1995) Editor gráfico do nível operacional do SDL OO. Porto Alegre: UFRGS (trabalho de diplomação).

Gaspary, Luciano Paschoal (1996) Estudo de Simulação e Animação em Ambientes de Especificação de Redes. PortoAlegre: UFRGS (trabalho individual).

Granville, Lisandro Zambenedetti (1995) Editor gráfico dos níveis estrutural abstrato e estrutural detalhado do SDL OO. Porto Alegre: UFRGS (trabalho de diplomação).

Rumbaugh, James (1991) Object-oriented modeling and design. New Jersey: Prentice-Hall-Englewood Cliffs.

Trainini, Paulo Silveira (1995) Manipulador das estruturas do editor gráfico para SDL OO. Porto Alegre: UFRGS (Trabalho de diplomação).

Verilog Corporation. Geode - Technical Presentation. Preliminary Version. July, 1994.

21

Specification and Design of Interactive Multimedia Services for Broadband Intelligent Networks

G. N. Prezerakos, I. S. Venieris
National Technical University of Athens
Department of Electrical and Computer Engineering
9 Heroon Polytechniou str, 15773 Athens, Greece
tel. + 30 1 772 2551 / fax + 30 1 772 2534
e_mail: ivenieri@cc.ece.ntua.gr

Abstract

We describe a complete methodology for the creation of interactive multimedia services (IMM) over Broadband Intelligent Networks (IN), that covers all phases from verbal description of a service up to the point when the service is ready for deployment. The paper discusses alternatives for the distribution of the service logic in the IN/B-ISDN network elements as well as the specification of the messages flows across interfaces. SDL is used for the production of a formal description of the service which is mapped into a Service Logic Program and simulated with a Service Creation and Simulation Environment. Throughout the paper two services are used as running examples to demonstrate the proposed methodology: a Video on Demand (VoD) service which is a novel IN service and a Broadband Video Conference Service (B-VC) which is based on an existing implementation originally targeted for a TCP/IP network platform.

Keywords

Broadband Intelligent Network, Multimedia Service design.

Intelligent Networks and Intelligence in Networks D. Gaiti (Ed.)
Published by Chapman & Hall

1 INTRODUCTION

In the last few years the area of Intelligent Networks (IN) has been rapidly expanding on a world-wide scale. The resulting need for specification of the target IN architecture has led to the creation of a framework for the description and design of IN services referred to as the IN Conceptual Model (INCM). The INCM sets the guidelines for a set of evolving specifications called capability sets (CS) which define requirements in a variety of IN-related aspects such as service creation, service management, service interaction, network management, service processing and network interworking.

The basic principles of IN service specification have been laid out by ITU-T in (ITU-T I.210) for the narrowband environment. Moreover the IN Conceptual Model is described in detail in (ITU-T Q.1201) as consisting of four planes : the service plane, the global functional plane, the distributed functional plane and the physical plane. *The Service Plane* is primarily used for representing services from the user's point of view. In that context the various services and service features are described independently of the actual implementation. *The Global Functional Plane* (GFP) is primarily used for representing services from the service designer's point of view. Service functionality is assumed to be included in units called Service Independent Building Blocks (SIBs) which are independent of how the functionality is distributed across the network. Thus the network is seen, from that plane, as a single entity. SIBs can be chained together in various combinations in order to realise services and features specified in the Service Plane. The way these SIBs are combined in the process of service creation is called Global Service Logic (GSL) . The implementation of the GSL is called a Service Logic Program (SLP). *The Distributed Functional Plane* (DFP) is primarily used for representing services from the network designer's and service provider's point of view. Service functionality is divided between various network units referred to as "functional entities" while these entities are connected by means of information flows referred to as "relationships". Functional entities are independent of how the functionality is physically implemented in the network. From this plane the network is viewed as being comprised of functional entities connected by information flows. *The Physical Plane* is primarily used for representing services from the network operator's and equipment provider's point of view. The physical architecture of an IN structured network is described in terms of physical components, referred to as "physical entities", and the interfaces between them. One or more functional entities and relationships from the DFP can be mapped to a physical entity or interface respectively in the physical plane.

The definition of such a solid theoretical background meant to address the core problem concerning the introduction of the IN concept that is flexibility in design and deployment of telecom services as well as customisation of the service. The combination of these advantages can lead to reduced development time and cost thus permitting the service providers to keep in pace with market needs. Nevertheless the process of service design and deployment is still in many cases extremely time consuming a fact that also leads to the consumption of significant financial resources. The introduction of interactive multimedia services which in turn demand increased bandwidth and more complex features belonging to the currently non-standardised CS-2 / CS-3 only makes the situation more complicated.

Various interesting aspects of the IN service design process can be found in the literature (Thörner, 1994), (Nyeng, 1993), (Olsen, 1995). Existing research in the field of IN service development proposes the adoption of the Specification and Description Language (SDL) as a key tool during such a process. Several approaches can be distinguished:

a) The use of SDL as a stand-alone description, simulation and verification tool for IN services. Approaches of this kind range from simple ones (Nyeng, 1993), to more sophisticated (Doza, 1990) to quite complicated where several models of IN services are examined (Kelly, 1995).
b) The use of SDL for the production of IN service source code targeted to a software development platform such as CORBA (Olsen, 1995).
c) The use of a Service Creation and Simulation Environment (SCSE) which may also incorporate the specification phase by including an SDL based specification tool (Niitsu, 1992), (Bosco, 1994). An SCSE has the ability of producing the actual Service Logic code that runs on the IN network therefore it is considered by many developers as a crucial element in the service development process.

The use of SDL as a stand-alone tool adopts the object oriented concepts that have become available with SDL-92. The object oriented methodology offers an elegant way of describing a service, incorporating a new service feature into an existing service and incorporating a new service in an existing description. Moreover by the use of SDL compatible validation and simulation tools the resulting system can be checked against errors in design and operation. On the other side describing a service in such a manner makes the transition from the prose to the formal description non-straightforward. This situation arises from the fact that the prose description is based on a telecom based view of the service while the object oriented approach is software engineering oriented. This is also the reason while such a design demands excessive effort from the developer's side in order to be understood. Even in the cases where such a service has been validated and simulated without problems this method does not present the developer with an smooth path towards the actual implementation since a direct mapping from the SDL description towards an SCSE is not provided.

The use of SDL for generating C/C++ code targeted to a platform such as CORBA is a more viable alternative although it presents some drawbacks like : SDL specification of the system following very strict rules, adaptation of the resulting C code to CORBA, involvement with implementation details that would be transparent if an SCSE was used. As a general remark it could be stated that systems designed in that manner require a tedious debugging process before the production of a high-level language code is attempted while the produced code always requires extensive changes in order to be downloaded to the IN network.

ITU-T has already standardised some IN service design elements (i.e. SIBs) which could be used for the specification of an IN service and for its design provided that a relevant design tool exists. Unfortunately SIB based design is not supported by any major commercially available development tool therefore the potential developer still faces the problem of providing a mapping from the SIB based specification to the selected development platform. Moreover it will be demonstrated in this paper that the specification of a telecom service includes aspects from both the Global and the Distributed Functional Planes, a fact which cannot be dealt with by using SIBs which are targeted to the GFP only. On the other hand SDL by offering the capability of mixing features from both functional planes is a more promising candidate for the specification phase of a service.

The approach discussed in this paper attempts to combine SDL service specification with a commercially available IN SCSE. The use of such a software platform renders the remaining INCM planes transparent to the potential service designer who has to bear in mind only the requirements of the GFP. Any enhancement regarding specific service functions or parts of the service logic can be easily accommodated by imposing high-level modifications to the existing design. Another advantage is that the stage of producing C/C++ code and then modifying it to suit the specific system architecture does no longer exist since the platform based service design is directly incorporated into the IN network. The main difference from the (c) approach presented earlier is that SDL specification is treated independently from the SCSE which is used for development. The reason is that a lot of commercial development environments lack a specification - verification module (SDL compatible or not) and the ones that do present the potential developer with an additional level of usage complexity. As it will be shown in this paper treating the specification outside the creation environment does not pose any significant problems during the development phase of the service.

After a detailed presentation of the proposed methodology we proceed with two examples of service creation. The first is a typical IMM service of Video on Demand (VoD) service which serves as a case of an originally non-existent interactive multimedia service which is 100% compliant with the IN environment. The other is the Broadband Video Conferencing Service (B-VC), an existing service with special call and data handling requirements originally targeted for a different network platform which is migrated to the IN environment. The latter example demonstrates the advantages of the IN concept in aspects regarding cost minimisation of incorporating applications developed having in mind varying telecommunication concepts into the IN concept.

This paper is organised as follows: Section 2 presents an overview of the proposed methodology. Section 3 covers the stages of prose description and functional architecture as well as the interface specification in the Distributed Functional Plane. Section 4 discusses the issue of formal service description in SDL. Section 5 covers service design by means of commercial development platforms. Finally, conclusions are presented in Section 6.

2 METHODOLOGY FOR SERVICE DESIGN AND IMPLEMENTATION

It is a well known that telecommunication applications are of a distributed nature. Distribution can be seen in terms of players as well as in terms of systems. From one point of view the service logic is distributed across the various network elements which are actively involved in the life cycle of a service. From a different point of view service capabilities depend upon the various players in the field of design and deployment i.e. service users, service developers, service providers, telecom operators and equipment providers. Thus the problems one faces with the implementation of a telecom service, having in mind the aforementioned objectives, are mainly concerned with the impact of each player on the service, the distribution of service logic across the various systems, the interworking between these systems, the definition of a common description which is both accurate as well as understandable and the evolution of such a service description into a Service Logic Program. Provided that the network infrastructure is quite invariable, thus rendering the telecom operators indifferent, the impact of the rest of the players has to be examined.

The service user group is of course a key player in the sense that it is the ultimate judge of the success or failure of a new service or of a new feature added to an existing service. The user's view of a service should always be considered as the starting point of every service creation effort. Even in the cases where a market demand does not yet exists but its creation is attempted by a service provider, a description of how a potential user might envisage a service should always be provided.

The service developer and the service provider are, if not identical, at least closely cooperating organisations. The service provider is responsible for merging the user's demands with its own preferences and the target IN architecture in order to produce a formal service description. The service developer maps this description to a set of service building blocks that are used to describe the service logic. The current trend is the usage of a Service Creation and Simulation Environment which facilitates the development process by the aid of visual programming tools and object-oriented techniques.

Finally service logic has to be tested, debugged and loaded to the various network nodes. In theory if the development process is conformant to the international standards only minor modifications are required in order for the service to become operational. In practice, since broadband capability sets are currently under standardisation, the existing equipment capabilities (switches, workstations etc.)

have to be taken into account while the development phase is still ongoing. Due to its complex nature this area is left for further research and is out of the scope of the paper.

The proposed methodology is presented in Figure 1 in the form of discrete stages:

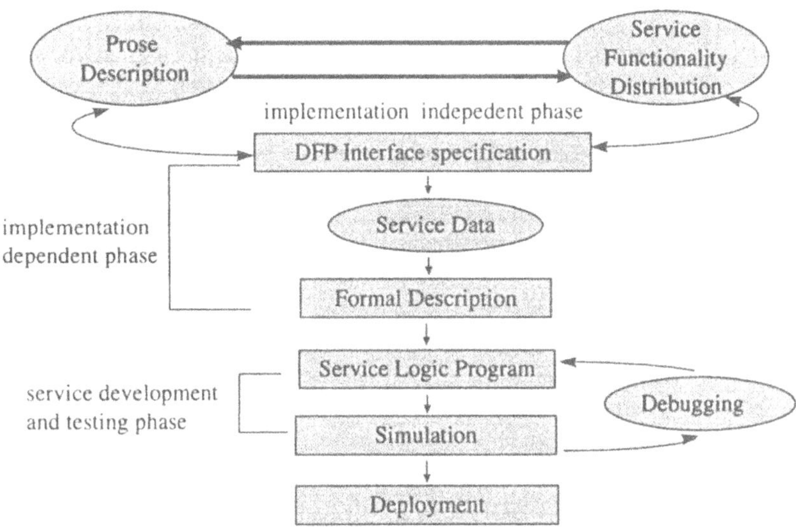

Figure 1 Specification and Design Methodology.

A prose description of the service from the user's point of view is the first stage of service creation. Based on the prose description a definition of how the service functionality will be distributed is carried out. This is an attempt to define which networks elements will be involved in the service and up to what degree and also the parts of service logic that they will host. This stage is followed by the interface specification in the DFP. By aggregating the previously acquired information along with a definition of the data structures required by the service a formal description of the service is produced in SDL. This description is consequently transformed into Service Logic Code and simulated with a SCSE. Finally the service, after being successfully tested and tuned, becomes operational.

The impact of each stage upon IN service creation is also examined from a practical standpoint by using the two real-life IN services already mentioned: the Video on Demand (VoD) and the Broadband Video Conference (B-VC) service. These services have been selected bearing in mind that they are broadband interactive multimedia services, comprehensible within the telecom community with a development process that presents difficulties similar to many telecom services and also that their service logic contains modules that can be reused in other IN based services.

The VoD is a service that enables the user to connect to a video server and view a movie or a television program (or in general any audiovisual information) from home by using a TV set equipped with a set-top box. The assumption will be made that no realisation of this service previously existed therefore the service is directly targeted to the IN architecture. The version of the VoD service examined in this paper is based on (Vezzoli, 1996). The B-VC service facilitates the communication between groups of users by enabling them to setup conferences in which each of the conferees can participate from his own premises. Originally targeted to a TCP/IP network the service is migrated to the IN architecture by trying to retain as many of its existing features as possible while adding IN functionality. The version of the B-VC service examined in this paper is based on (Brandt, 1997). The service logic for both services is presented in detail with emphasis given in the GFP and the DFP. The flow of the service is depicted by means of Broadband Intelligent Network Application Part (B-INAP) messages exchanged between the various network entities from the point of service request until the point where the service logic is terminated.

3 SERVICE DESCRIPTION AND FUNCTIONAL ARCHITECTURE

3.1 Prose description

The prose description of a service from the potential user's point of view can be dealt with various software engineering strategies. The following are considered as key steps in such an approach:

It is better to decompose the life of a service session into consequent discrete stages. Apart from facilitating the description itself, such a decomposition makes the transition to subsequent phases of the development process easier.

A service scenario should be given for each of these service stages. The scenarios are structured on the basis that the service logic prompts the user for input, the user responds and the service reacts accordingly by following one of the possible service logic execution paths. Implementation specific details as well as the functional architecture are not considered at all during this phase. The only fact that is taken into account is that the user possesses a multimedia terminal of some kind connected to an underlying broadband network infrastructure.

In a summarised description of the VoD service in terms of stages, the following stages can be identified: Service Provider Selection, Authentication-Authorisation, Type of Content Selection, Address Translation, Content Selection. In a summarised description of the B-VC service in terms of stages, the following stages can be identified: Conference creation, Static Conference Management, Add user to conference, Conference Establishment, Join conferee, Leave conference, Close conference and Dynamic conference management.

According to (ITU-T, Q.1213) each Service Logic Program is composed by a series of interconnected SIBs. Service execution always commences from the Basic Call Processing (BCP) SIB and proceeds to other SIBs through Points of Initiation (POIs). The service is terminated in a similar fashion when the execution returns to the BCP SIB through Points of Return (PORs). Following along this line, services can initially be represented by diagrams showing the interconnection between the various service stages and the Basic Call State Model (BCSM) through POIs and PORs.

The relevant diagram for the VoD service is given in Figure 2 and for B-VC service in Figure 3:

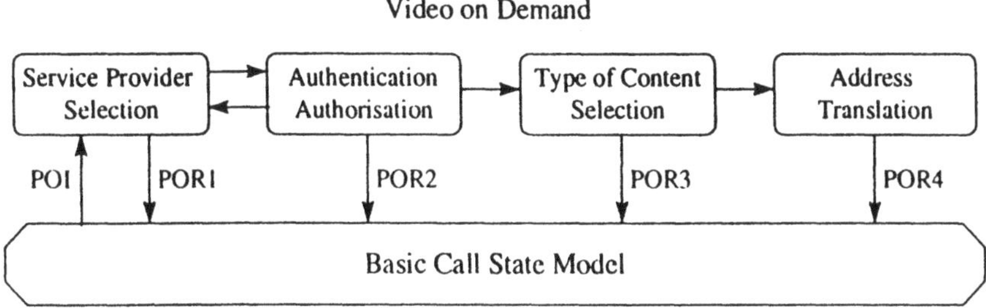

Figure 2 Decomposition of the VoD Service.

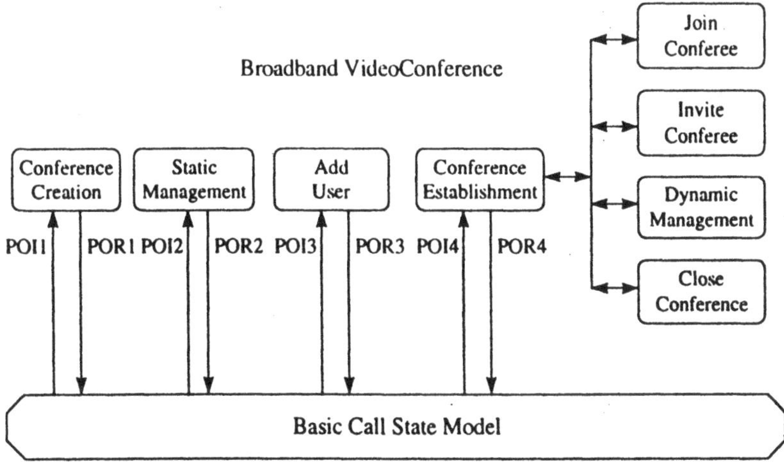

Figure 3 Decomposition of the B-VC service.

These diagrams, since they comprise aspects of both the service plane and the GFP, can serve as the link between the prose description phase of the service and the SDL specification.

3.2 Service functionality distribution

The IN architecture is based on information exchange between the following network elements: the Broadband Service Control Point (B-SCP), the Broadband Service Switching Point (B-SSP), the Service Data Point (SDP), the Broadband Intelligent Peripheral (B-IP) and the Customer Premises Equipment (CPE). In the context of the standardised approach towards IN service development the Service

Logic resides completely inside the B-SCP, the B-SSP realises the service's switching functionality, the SDP is in charge of database transactions, the B-IP provides the resources needed (audiovisual announcements) for communication with the CPE. The CPE functionality is usually restricted to the realisation of a User Network Interface (UNI) signaling stack although the existence of intelligent CPEs is not excluded.

The concept of realising the Service Logic completely inside the B-SCP may be proven vulnerable when one proceeds to real life implementations. In practice the B-SCP is a workstation which depending on the load imposed by service execution may not be able to handle the required number of transactions. A viable alternative, if the involvement of a more powerful machine severely affects the cost curve of the service, is to split the service functionality between the B-SCP and the B-IP by moving significant parts of the service logic there.

Moreover the need for adding service logic functionality to the B-IP arises from the fact that the standardised approach that was mentioned earlier is a heritage from the days of narrow-band services where an audio message was played to the user and the required user response was entered by pressing buttons in the telephone keypad. On the other hand broadband interactive multimedia services are expected to compose several different media in order to interact with the user and acquire a user response of similar nature thus rendering the duties of the B-IP far more complex than the transmission of audio messages. Communication between the user and the IN service can be handled by integrated parts of service logic that reside in the B-IP (nevertheless still activated by the B-SCP). Aware of this situation ITU-T has attempted to standardise such an approach in (ITU-T, Q1228). For the needs of this paper, following ITU terminology, we will be referring to "scripts" and to "scripts functionality". Selected parts of the VoD service will be presented by using the "scripts" approach.

User requests would be best transferred to the B-SCP by the User To Service Interaction (UTSI) feature. Because this feature is not available in the services demonstrated in this paper, an alternate approach which uses the B-IP as a relay for signalling between the CPE and the service logic was chosen. When user input is needed the logic issues a *PromptAndCollectUserInfo* request. All user requests are send to the B-IP over a connection between CPE and B-IP. The request is then send to the B-SCP as the *CollectedUserInfo* message.

The topology of the VOD service, presented in Figure 4, is aligned with the above line of thought.

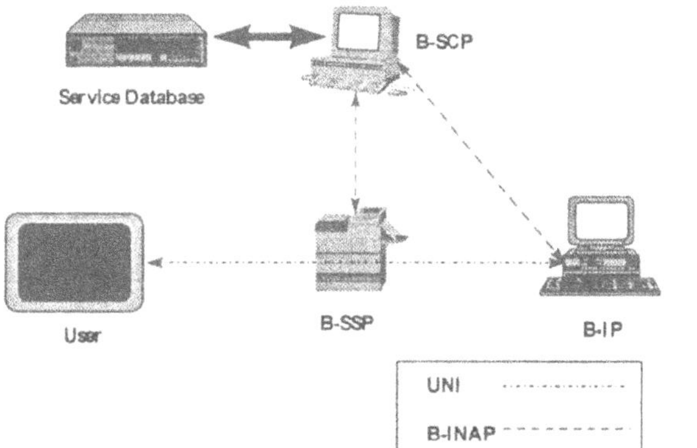

Figure 4 VoD Topology.

The B-SCP/B-IP and B-SCP/B-SSP communication is achieved through the B-INAP layer of the IN protocol stack. The Service Database is contained within the B-SCP. The User/B-IP communication is achieved through UNI signalling and the B-IP handles the User/B-SCP communication by appropriately routing the respective messages.

In cases where an existing service is adapted to the IN architecture (as the B-VC service) the B-IP can undertake an additional role towards the facilitation of the migration process. Since the B-IP is used as a router that conveys the necessary information between the User and the B-SCP, the protocol stack that handles the user to service communication can be retained in the new environment. Moreover several service functions can become B-SCP independent and completely realised within the B-IP. It is easier to port major parts of the original application to the B-IP (which in most cases is a workstation compatible with the original implementation) than to the B-SCP which may operate under a different software / hardware platform.

The B-VC service presents the additional complexity of how it handles conference data and user connections. During certain operations, such as conferee addition, certain database records should remain locked to prevent other users performing the same or different functions from altering them simultaneously. The most effective way to handle such a situation is to use database locking in the record level. Assuming that special facilities such as record locking are not always available within the B-SCP then the only alternative is to duplicate the Service Database Tables (SDTs) in the B-IP. Database synchronisation can be achieved by moving records between the B-SCP and the B-IP only when it is dictated by a B-VC operation. The resulting service topology is presented in Figure 5.

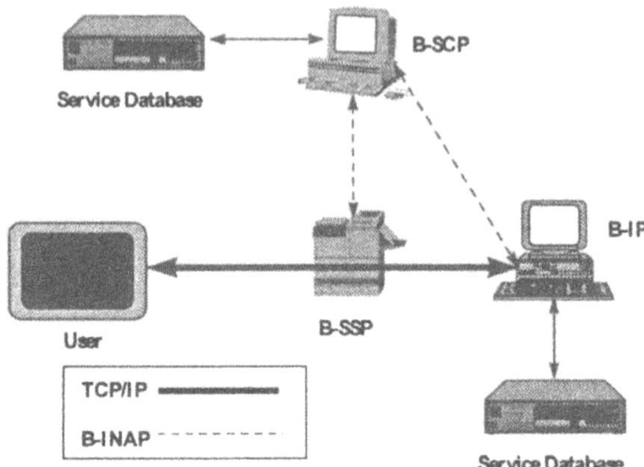

Figure 5 B-VC Topology.

The Service Database is contained in both the B-SCP and the B-IP. The User/B-IP communication is achieved through the initially used TCP/IP protocol and the B-IP handles the User/B-SCP communication by appropriately routing the respective messages.

The need for interaction between Service Logic Program instances arises in operations like 'Join Conferee' where the conferee that wishes to join a running conference activates a Service Logic Instance which consequently should communicate with the Service Logic Instance of the running conference and negotiate the conferee's participation. When the conferee is joined the user initiated Service Logic Instance must be dropped. It is the duty of the B-IP to undertake the correlation of the two instances.

3.3 Interface specification in the Distributed Functional Plane

When the service logic allocation to the various network elements has been completed the interfaces between them must be specified prior to a formal service description. This includes the information flows connecting the various elements consisting of messages, data types and data structures that will be utilised by the B-INAP layer of the IN protocol stack.

Summarising the presentation in section 3.2, the actively involved network elements in any approach are the B-SCP and the B-SSP. The SDP is usually a database engine incorporated in the B-SCP and it is not considered as a separate entity. The service's database design though is an important aspect of the overall development process and a research field of its own right. This paper address only the problem of locating the SDTs, according to the selected IN service functionality distribution. It is obvious that a minimum prerequisite towards a formal service specification is the definition of the SCP/SSP and SCP/IP interfaces along with the corresponding information flows.

The scripts approach to the VoD service demands that the service logic is divided between the B-SCP and the B-IP. Initially the user is first connected to the B-IP, then the B-SCP demands a script execution from the B-IP. The script is executed and finally the result is conveyed to the B-SCP. An evolution of the Information flows for a VoD service, proposed in (Vezzoli, 1996), towards the scripts approach is presented in Figure 6 for the Service Provider Selection stage:

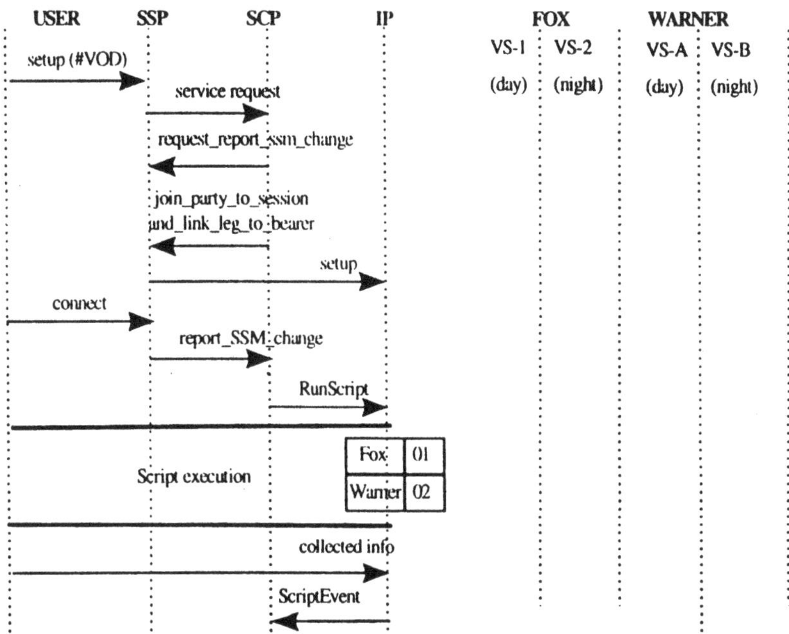

Figure 6 VoD Information flows.

Data structures can have a great influence on IN service design. A properly designed service should allow the potential user to exploit the offered functionality to the greatest extent while bearing in mind that different users usually require different treatment from each IN service. A useful starting point might therefore be to identify Subscriber and user profiles that would determine which parts of the service functionality are to be used. The data handed by the service logic could be subdivided as: (i) service data (e.g. fixed data and announcements), (ii) management and subscription data (e.g. Subscription profiles), (iii) user data (e.g. user profiles), (iv) call instance data (e.g. counts against unauthorised access attempts)

Service data and call instance data may be identified during the formal specification stage without inducing major drawbacks in the development process. On the other hand management, subscription and user data should have been defined in an earlier stage since an incomplete or erroneous definition of these data structures may result to significant modifications during the implementation phase thus causing severe delays service development and deployment. Therefore it is imperative that a detailed description of (ii) and (iii) exists prior to the service's formal specification.

The location of each SDT is determined by the location of the corresponding Service Logic Program function. As a general rule, aiming at the minimization of data transfers between the various network nodes, SDTs are located at the same network node where the respective Service Logic is executed.

4 FORMAL SERVICE DESCRIPTION

The stage of formal service description attempts to combine requirements defined within the previous stages and produce a solid service description that is understandable by both the service provider and the service developer and "freeze" the specification process. The use of SDL for this purpose is suggested because SDL is an international standard tailored for the description of telecommunication systems and in case a SCSE does not exist then additional tools can be used for verification and simulation purposes.

There are various approaches towards the representation of a telecommunication service via SDL mainly based on the possible uses of such a description. In our case the SDL specification meant to produce a detailed presentation the service logic from the telecom point of view instead of the software engineering point of view while combining of both the DFP and GFP service functionality. In the context of this paper SDL is not used as an implementation language therefore its code generation and simulation/validation facilities will not be used. Nevertheless the proposed system schematics remain aligned with the recommendations described in (ITU-T , Z.100).

Each IN service is represented by the SDL *system* structure. This way each IN service is described in an independent self-contained manner. The network elements involved in service logic execution are represented by the SDL *block* structure. These structures may be further decomposed to objects in the sub-block level if necessary. However decomposition into several layers may only be necessary for complex services or for groups of services heavily interacting with each other.

The connection between the various network elements is represented by SDL *channels.* Messages exchanged between IN network elements are represented by the SDL *signal* structure. Each service stage, described in the prose description, is represented by an SDL process. Service stages that may be activated within the scope another stage are represented by SDL *procedures.* Procedures are also used to group pieces of SDL code that are frequently repeated in various points of a service e.g. the ConnectUsertoIP procedure. At each block or sub-block, the interfaces and attributes of each object should are defined accompanied by textural comments relating to the function to be performed.

4.1 VoD service description - scripts approach

VoD service functionality can be distributed between the B-SCP and the B-IP in a number of ways. The approach presented in the following figures assumes that Service Provider Selection, Authentication-Authorisation and Type of Content Selection stages are performed in the B-IP. These operations have been realised as scripts and are completely independent entities which handle all possible service logic outcome internally. Their only relation to the B-SCP is that they are activated by it and that they are obliged to notify script termination by returning an appropriate code. After successful completion of script execution Address Translation is performed in the B-SCP and the B-SCP instructs the B-SSP to connect the user to the VS. Upon successful connection to the VS the SLP terminates.

The proposed functionality distribution results in relocating the SDTs to the network element that handles the respective database operation. The Service Providers, User Profiles, Type of Content SDTs have now been moved to the B-IP. The Routing SDTs remain in the B-SCP. An overview of the system can be seen in Figure 7.

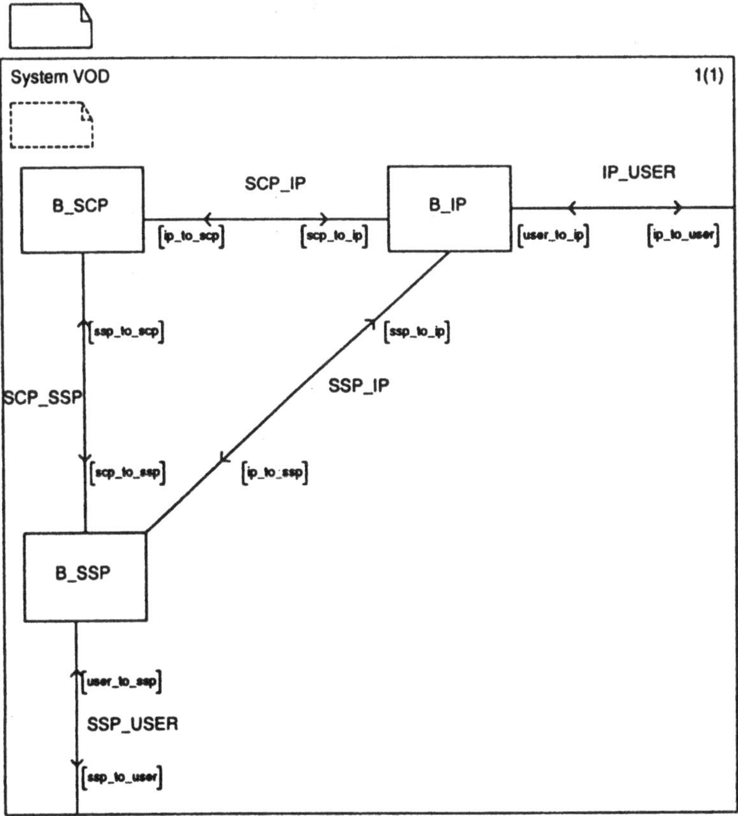

Figure 7 VoD service overview in SDL (scripts approach).

The service logic in the B-SCP is included in the Service_Logic_Program process. The portion of this process regarding the Service Provider Selection is presented in Figure 8.

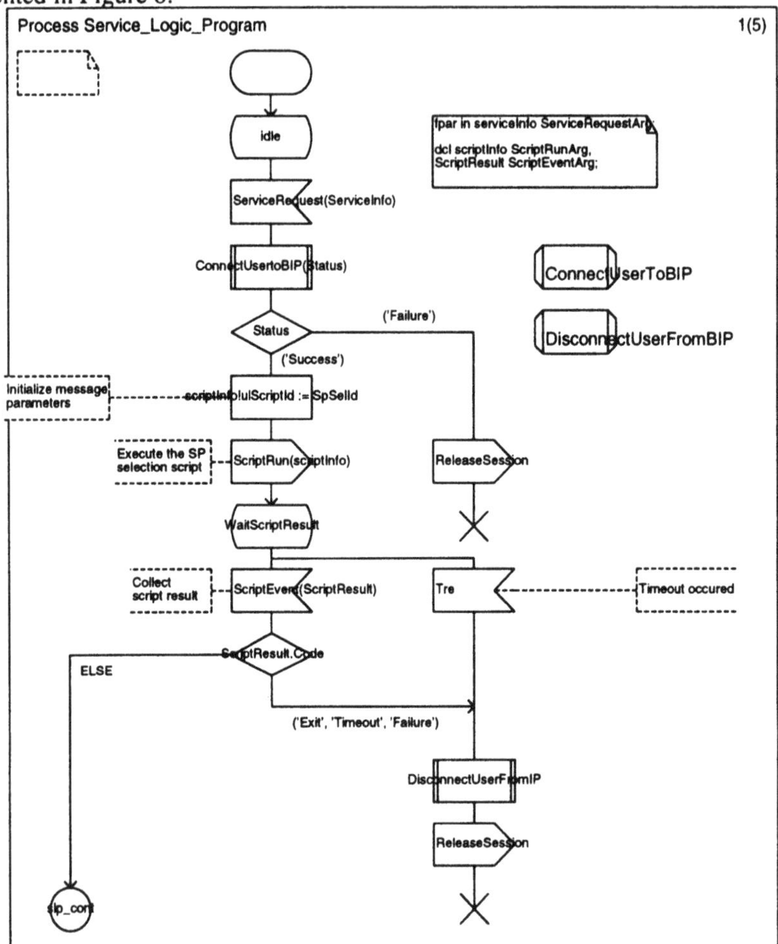

Figure 8 VoD Service Provider Selection in SDL (scripts approach).

The general structure of the corresponding B-IP service logic is depicted in Figure 9. The ScriptManager process awaits an activation message from the B-SCP. Upon receipt it executes the corresponding script. Notice that since scripts are called from inside a process they are realised as procedures.

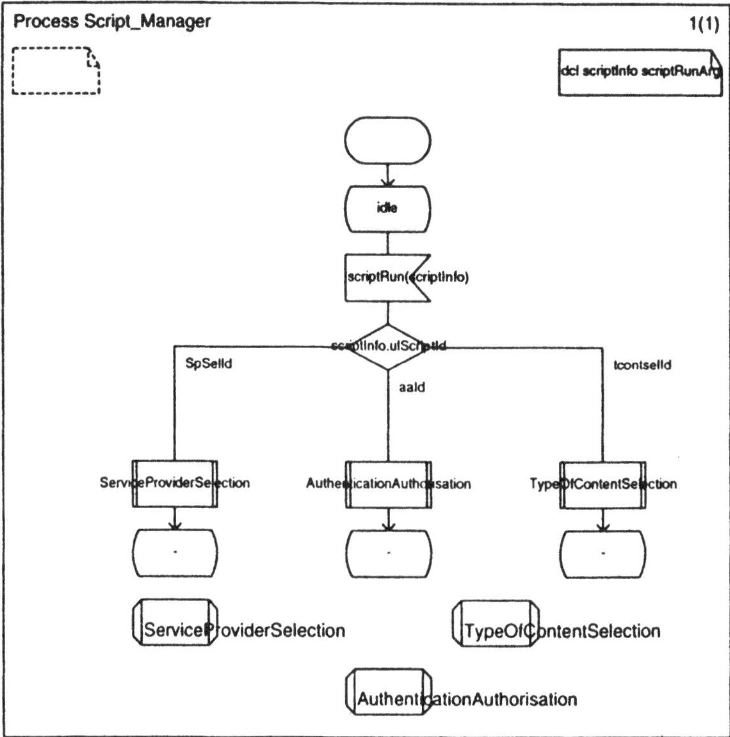

Figure 9 Description of the VoD B-IP Service Logic in SDL.

4.2 B-VC service description

The B-VC has been described as a "hybrid" service since it is not 100% IN compatible. The system overview diagram is identical to that of Figure 7. The Conference Creation process has been selected as a typical example of B-VC service logic and is described in figures 10, 11 and 12.

The Conference Creation process is invoked when a user dials the appropriate IN number. A conference creation request is issued and the following procedure is activated : The User dials the IN number indicating that he wishes to be added to the conference. Initially the service logic checks whether the user is an authorised one or not. If the user is indeed authorised then the B-SCP requests from the B-SSP to connect the user to the B-IP.

The B-IP is the network element that will undertake the role of correlating the conferee connections during the lifetime of an active conference. If the connection is successful then a user - IP dialogue takes place by which the profile of the conference to be created is determined. At the same time the B-SCP waits a notification message from the B-IP.

If the notification message from the B-IP arrives in time then the service logic requests from the B-IP to lock the conferences database and create an entry for the requested conference. The B-IP attempts to execute the request then responds by returning a status code. If the conference record has been created successfully then the B-SCP updates the local copy of the database. The B-SCP then requests from the B-IP to unlock the conference database. The B-IP once more attempts to perform the requested action, returns a status code and the service instance is terminated.

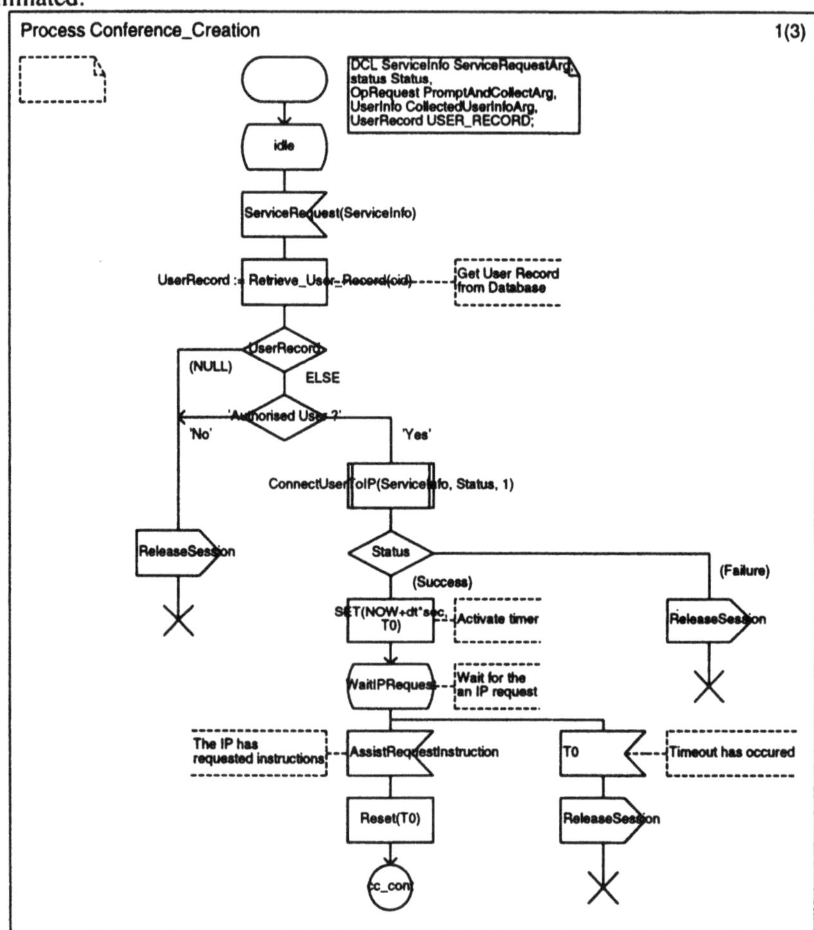

Figure 10 B-VC service Conference Creation SDL description (page 1).

The strategies used demonstrate the flexibility of the IN architecture and can be understood by consulting the SDL schematic. First of all, the application parts that handle user to service interaction remain almost intact when the service is ported to the new environment since the B-IP is used as a message router based on the existing UNI protocol. The call correlation needed for complex multi-user services (like the B-VC service) is taken care of by the B-IP and this approach results to slight modifications with respect to the initial version of the application. Also the use of the twin databases scheme compensates for the lack of record locking facilities in the B-SCP. In the majority of the existing scenarios only identifiers need to be transferred between the B-SCP and the B-IP.

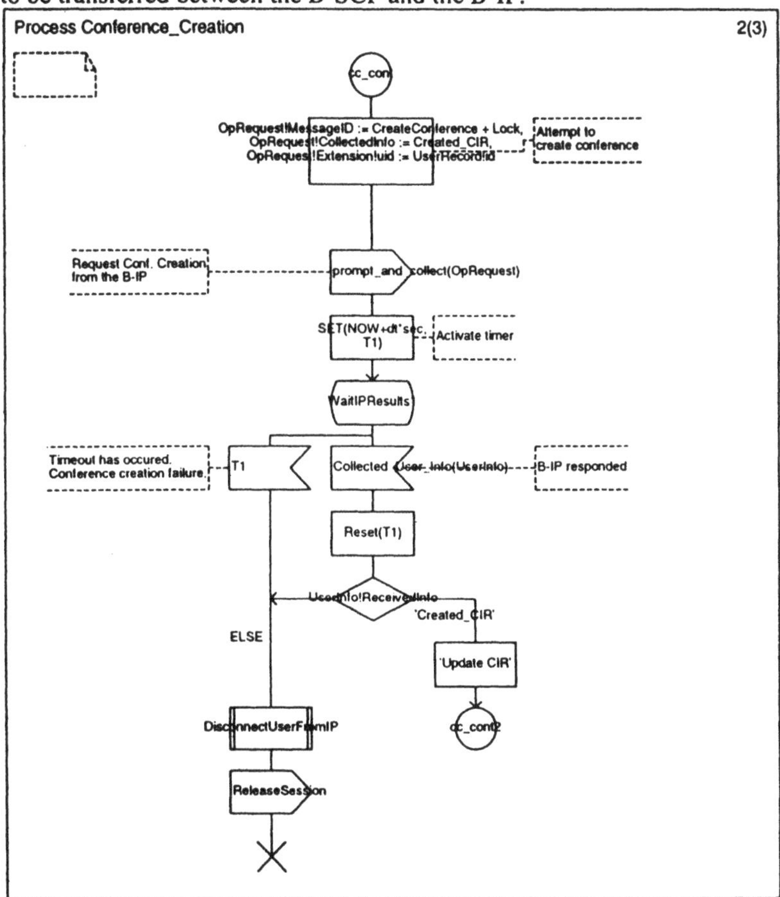

Figure 11 B-VC service Conference Creation SDL description (page 2).

Finally the *PromptAndCollect* as well as the *CollectedUserInfo* B-INAP messages have been extended so as to accommodate the B-SCP/B-IP communication. More specifically, the *MessageID* and *CollectedInfo* field of the *PromptAndCollect* message have been extended in order to carry the requested B-IP operation. An extra field, namely *Extension*, has been added divided into the *CIR*, *UIR*, *CID* and *UID* fields. These fields contain, whenever is necessary, the Conference Information Record, User Information Record, Conference Identifier and User Identifier respectively. Apart from user input the *ReceivedInfo* sub-field of the *UserInfo* field of the *CollectedUserInfo* message is also carrying B-IP responses and success/failure codes.

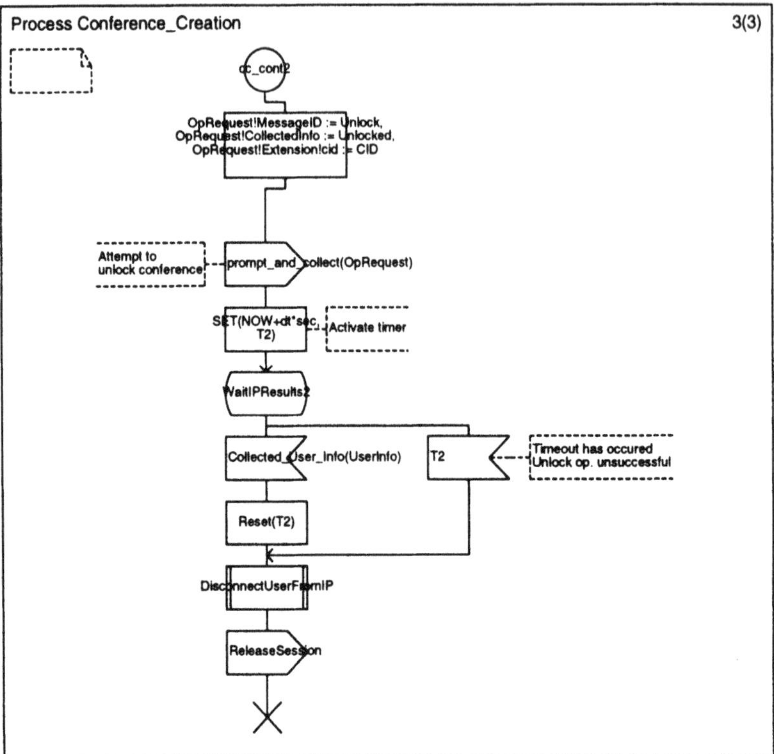

Figure 12 B-VC service Conference Creation SDL description (page 3).

Such an approach, no matter how flexible, presents certain disadvantages: The number of messages exchanged between the B-SCP and the B-IP is high, transfer of database records between the various network nodes is not completely avoided and the SLP is obliged to perform extensive check of the B-IP return codes. Nevertheless, compared to the cost of rewriting extensive parts of the existing code in order for the application to be ported to a different telecommunication architecture, these compromises seem justified.

5 SERVICE DESIGN

This section deals with the actual development of the SLP as well as the simulation of the service which are the next design stages after the solidification of the formal specification. There are a few SCSEs available in the market. This paper presents a generic broadband SCSE which is loosely based on (GPT, 1996). Although the only standardised building element for an IN service is the SIB, the majority of SCSE providers prefer to equip their tools with a proprietary set of building elements generally referred to as Icons. Nevertheless, similar design principles are used since IN services, in this case, consist of appropriately initialised Icons chained together.

A typical SCSE consists of the following components:

Designer: This module is equipped with a powerful graphical environment that allows the developer to connect a series of Icons in order to form a Service.

Version Manager: This module is equipped with a software engineering tool that allows the developer to keep track of the various service versions.

Compiler: This module is responsible for validating the existing service design and, if no errors are found, translate it into a high level language (usually C/C++).

Simulator: This module acts as a service switching point simulator based on the compiler produced code and allows the developer to model user behaviour by interacting with the service via a graphical interface. All relevant messages and errors are logged for debugging purposes.

A service is created by constructing a service picture on the Designer. Each such service picture consists of Icons joined by links. Each Icon encompasses a unique piece of functionality within the service. The starting point of each service is an Init Icon. On the other hand the service may terminate due to a variety of conditions therefore multiple terminating points are allowed denoted by respective Terminate Icons. Icons may produce results which denote the outcome of the operation performed by that Icon. These values can be stored in service variables. The user usually identifies such variables by a meaningful name. Apart from user defined variables, system pre-defined variables also exist. These pre-defined variables contain service related values i.e. the service trigger. The user may adapt an Icon's functionality to a specific service's needs by modifying the values of a set of Icon attributes known as Properties. The execution of the Service Logic always starts from the Init Icon and then follows the link to a next Icon depending on the result produced by the currently executed Icon. Icons performing a specific function can be grouped together in a special type of Icon called the Composite Icon. Composite Icons may contain other Composite Icons thus providing additional levels of navigation within the service picture. The service picture is completed with the definition of a set of Service Data Tables. These tables contain the run-time data which control the functionality of some of the Icons.

The transition from the formal description of the service to the creation environment requires a mapping procedure from SDL structures to Icons. This is necessary because the SDL specification includes characteristics of the DFP which in a high level design are transparent to the developer. A more detailed analysis of the problem can be found in (Bosco, 1994). Some general considerations regarding this transition are the following : (a) the identification of service functions that can be expressed as composite icons or as independent SLPs. The use of composite Icons makes the SLP more readable and therefore simpler to maintain, (b) the number of database transactions and logical comparisons to be performed during a service session. Forcing the service logic to perform a large number of unnecessary time consuming functions can severely affect performance and (c) the handling of exception conditions. Provision should be made for the handling of exception conditions that have been identified in the service requirements as well as usual programming exception conditions such as time-outs or failure to perform certain database transactions.

A proposed mapping of this type, aimed at the accommodation of the VoD and BVC service, is presented in the following list:

Init : This Icon initiates a service logic program. It defines whether the service is triggered by the calling or the called party's directory number.

Announce_Collect : This Icon handles the pair of *PlayAndCollect* and *CollectedUserInfo* messages. It asks the B-IP to play the requested message and returns the user's response or in case of an error propagates an exception condition.

Script: This Icon handles the pair of *ScriptRun* and *ScriptEvent* messages. It asks the B-IP to execute the requested script and returns the script's result.

BearerOp : This Icon handles messages related to parties and bearers joining an existing session such as *JoinPartyAndBearerToSession*, *ReleaseBearer* etc. It returns the status of the operation.

Algorithm : This Icon performs variable related operations such as assign, increase, decrease, add, append etc. on a single variable.

Database : This Icon performs database transactions such as retrieve, write etc. on a single SDT and returns the result.

Condition : This Icon performs logical comparisons between values, variables etc. If the selected condition triggers then the Service Logic Program follows the leg occupied by the Condition Icon

Terminate : This Icon issues a *ReleaseSession* message and terminates the SLP.

5.1 Icon based description of the VOD service - scripts approach

An image of the Service Provider Selection stage of the VOD service is presented in Figure 13. Each time user to service interaction must be performed the B-SCP demands from the B-IP the execution of the relevant script which contains the service logic code for the requested operation. This is done by sending a *ScriptRun* message from the B-SCP to the B-IP. The B-SCP then waits until an answer from the B-IP arrives, via a *ScriptEvent*, which should contain either the user's input or an error code.

The service image consists of just 7 Icons plus the relevant data tables. It is evident that the processing load on the B-SCP is significantly reduced compared to the case where we would be forced to include the entire SLP in the B-SCP. Another important factor which affects the performance an IN service is the number of database transactions which are performed during a service session. In this case a number of these operations has also been moved to the B-IP thus reducing even more the demand for processing power from the B-SCP.

1. **Init** : This Icon receives the *ServiceRequest* message. It defines that the service is triggered by the calling directory number.
2. **Script** : This Icon is used by the B-SCP in order to connect the user to the B-IP, then instruct the B-IP to execute the Service Providers Selection script and finally to receive the script result.

3. **Condition** : The occurrence of a failure to connect the user to the B-IP with respect to the previous operation is checked by this Icon. If such a situation arises then the SLP follows this leg.
4. **Terminate** : The session is terminated because of the failure that has occurred.
5. **Condition** : This Icon compares the script's result against the 'Success' code. If the selection has been carried out successfully then the SLP follows this leg and moves on to the next service stage.
6. **BearerOp** : The B-SCP instructs the B-SSP to disconnect the user from the B-IP.
7. **Terminate** : The session is terminated because the script did not return a 'Success' code.

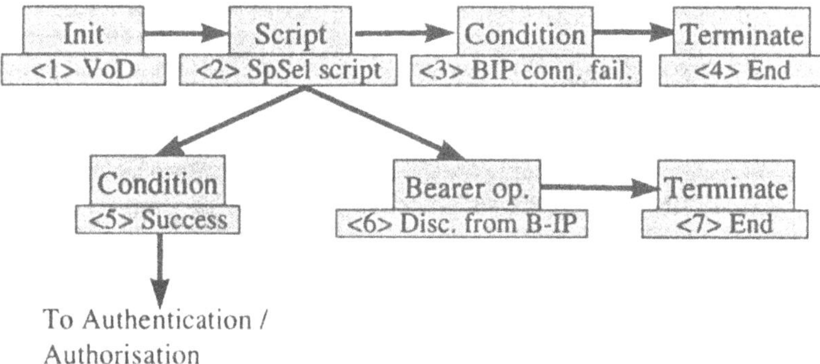

Figure 13 VoD Service Provider Selection description with Icons (scripts approach).

5.2 Icon based description of the B-VC service

An image of the B-VC service is presented in Figure 14. More specifically the Conference Creation procedure is examined.

1. **Init** : This is the starting point of the Conference Creation process
2. **Database** : The B-SCP searches the local service database in order to determine if the calling user is authorised.
3. **Condition** : The status of the database operation is checked for 'user record not found'. If such a status is returned then the SLP follows this leg.
4. **Terminate** : The session is terminated due to the failure of the database operation.
5. **Announce_Collect** : The B-SCP attempts to set-up a temporary User / B-IP connection then issues a *PromptAndCollect* message to the B-IP containing a create and lock conference command.
6. **Condition** : The status of the attempted connection is checked. If a failure has occurred then the SLP follows this leg.

7. **Terminate** : The session is terminated because of the failure that occurred.
8. **Database** : The new conference record is created in the copy of the conference database that resides in the B-SCP.
9. **Announce_Collect** : The B-SCP issues a *PromptAndCollect* message to the B-IP containing an unlock conference command.
10. **Condition** : The status of the previous operation is checked for any exception condition. If an exception has indeed occurred then the SLP follows this leg.
11. **BearerOp** : The B-SCP instructs the B-SSP to disconnect the user from the B-IP.
12. **Terminate** : The Create Conference session is terminated.

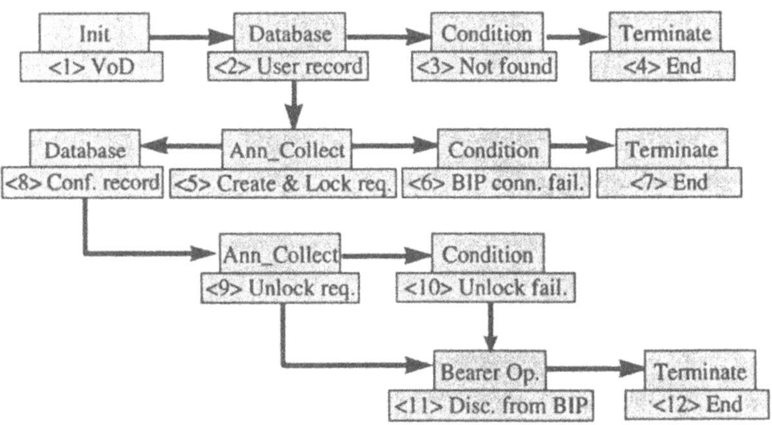

Figure 14 B-VC Conference Creation description with Icons.

6 CONCLUSIONS

In this paper we have proposed a complete methodology for the specification and design of typical IN based interactive multimedia services. This methodology is based on the GFP and DFP of the INCM and guarantees the disassociation of service provision from the network signalling capabilities. All stages of the service development process have been addressed and particular emphasis has been put to selected parts of the Service Logic for two IN services presented in detail by means of SDL diagrams and SCSE Icons. The proposed methodology has also been compared to other existing approaches in the field. Overall the service design approach is shown to be flexible enough to accommodate the requirements of a wide set of interactive multimedia services ranging from novel IN services to existing services migrating from other environments.

The authors are currently engaged in the design and implementation of broadband IN-based services, that will be deployed in a European field trial demonstration over an ATM-based infrastructure.

7 ACKNOWLEDGMENT

This work has been partially funded by the ACTS project INSIGNIA (IN and B-ISDN Signalling Integration on ATM platforms). The opinions appearing are those of the authors and not necessarily of the other members of the consortium.

8 REFERENCES

Bosco G. P., F. Faraci F., (1994) Advanced intelligent network service laboratory, *Canadian Journal of Electrical and Computer Engineering*, January 1994.

Brandt H., Tittel C., Todorova P. (1997) Broadband Video Conference in an Integrated IN / B-ISDN Architecture, to be presented in NOC'97, Antwerp, Belgium, June 17-19 1997.

Doza Z. M., Lakhani H. A., Schraffnit T. L. (1990) A modular approach to intelligent networks: Telecom Canada's perspective, Proceedings of the 10th International Conference on Computer Communication, New Delhi India, 4-9 Nov. 1990.

GPT LIMITED UK (1996) GAIN 300 Inventor User Guide for release 304.2.

ITU-T Recommendation. I.210. Principles of Telecommunications services supported by an ISDN and the means to describe them.

ITU-T Recommendation Q.1201. Principles of Intelligent Network Architecture.

Thörner J. (1994) Intelligent Networks. Artech House, Boston, London.

ITU-T Recommendation Q.1213. Global Functional Plane for Intelligent Network CS-1.

ITU-T Recommendation Q1228.

ITU-T Recommendation Z.100. SLD Methodology Guidelines, Appendices I and II.

Kelly B., Crowther M., King J., Mason R., DeLapeyre J. (1995) Service validation and testing, Proceedings of Third International Workshop on Feature interactions in Telecommunication Software Systems, Kyoto Japan, 11-13 Oct. 1995.

Niitsu Y., Mizuno O., Okamoto M. (1992) Computer-aided stepwise service creation environment for intelligent network, Proceedings of SUPERCOMM/ICC'92, Chicago USA, 14-18 June 1992.

Nyeng A., Møller-Pedersen B. (1993) Approaches to the specification of Intelligent Network Services in SDL-92, in *SDL'93 : Using Objects*, Elsevier Science Publishers B. V.

Olsen A., Nørbœk B (1995) Using SDL for Targeting Services to CORBA, Proceedings IS&N '95, Heraclion, Greece, 16-20 October 1995 .
Vezzoli L., Lorenzini L. (1996) Intelligent Mobile Video on Demand, Proceedings ICIN '96, Bordeaux , France, 25-28 November 1996.

9 BIOGRAPHY

George N. Prezerakos was born in Athens, Greece. He received the Dipl. - Ing. Degree from the National Technical University of Athens (NTUA), Athens, Greece in 1993 in electrical and computer engineering. Since 1993 he is a Ph.D. candidate in NTUA and research associate of the Telecommunications Laboratory performing research in the area of Intelligent Networks, Service Engineering and Fuzzy Logic systems. His research interests are in the fields of service design and control for broadband networks. He has several publications in the above areas. He has participated in several European Union ACTS projects and is currently involved in the INSIGNIA AC068 project. Mr. Prezerakos is a member of the Technical Chamber of Greece.

Iakovos S. Venieris was born in Naxos, Greece. He received the Dipl. - Ing. degree from the University of Patras, Greece in 1988, and the Ph.D. degree from the National Technical University of Athens (NTUA), Athens, Greece, in 1990, all in electrical and computer engineering. From 1994 he is an Assistant Professor in the Electrical and Computer Engineering Department of NTUA. His research interests are in the fields of B-ISDN, signalling, resource scheduling and allocation for network management, modelling, performance evaluation and queueing theory. He has over sixty publications in the above areas. Dr. Venieris has been exposed to standardisation body work and has participated in several European Union and national projects dealing with B-ISDN protocols, Intelligent Networks, ATM switching and access techniques. Dr. Venieris is a member of IEEE and the Technical Chamber of Greece.

22

Point-to-multipoint call modelling for IN/B-ISDN integration.[1]

M. Listanti(*), S.Salsano(**)
INFOCOM Dept., University of Roma "La Sapienza"
Via Eudossiana 18 - 00184 Roma - ITALY
(*) Phone: +39 6 44585458 Fax: +39 6 4873300
e-mail: marco@infocom.ing.uniroma1.it
(**) Phone: +39 6 20410029 Fax: +39 6 20410037
e-mail: salsano@coritel.it

Abstract

This paper deals with integration of IN and B-ISDN for the support of new sophisticated multimedia multipoint services. A survey of results of the ACTS INSIGNIA project is given, successively some enhancements of the INSIGNIA architecture in order to integrate advanced B-ISDN capability are discussed. In particular, the impact of point-to-multipoint on the IN call modelling is considered and the needed enhancements of the Basic Call State Model are presented. Moreover, the evolution of the IN *Service Switching Functions* (SSF) entity and of the interface with the IN *Service Control Function* (SCF) entity is investigated. Finally an experimental test-bed developed in the framework of the CORITEL IBIS project is described. This test bed aims at validating, with reference to the control-plane, the main features of the proposed architecture.

Keywords

IN, B-ISDN, call modelling, point-to-multipoint

---

[1] This work has been carried out within the CORITEL laboratory in the frame of a joint research project between industry and university.

Intelligent Networks and Intelligence in Networks D. Gaiti (Ed.)
Published by Chapman & Hall

1 INTRODUCTION

The introduction of ATM technology will permit the B-ISDN to support new and greatly advanced services. Suitable functional architectures and protocols which can support these services with the desired flexibility need to be deployed. The Intelligent Network (IN) concept seems very suitable for this purpose. Some reasons push towards the IN B-ISDN integration:

- IN allows a fast and flexible definition and development of services by means of independent, normalised and reusable, modular elements (Service Independent Building Block - SIB);
- IN infrastructure can be utilised to provide supplementary services in a broadband environment so avoiding to define dedicated ad-hoc protocols;
- IN could guarantee service portability and personalization capabilities in a broadband environment.

This approach has been proposed in some papers [1,2] and is the main purpose of an ad-hoc ACTS projects named INSIGNIA.

In this paper we start with a survey of current results of INSIGNIA project; we next propose some enhancements of the INSIGNIA architecture in order to support advanced B-ISDN capability, i.e. point to multipoint calls. In particular, the impact of point-to-multipoint on the IN call modelling is considered and the needed enhancements of the Basic Call State Model (BCSM) are discussed. Moreover, the evolution of the IN Service Switching Functions (SSF) entity and of the interface with the IN Service Control Function (SCF) entity is investigated.

Finally a test-bed developed in the framework of the CORITEL IBIS project is described. This simple test bed demonstrates, with reference to the control-plane, the main features of the proposed architecture.

In Sec.2, basic assumptions of the INSIGNIA project are reported. In Sec. 3, operation of point-to-multipoint call are summarised together with the main requirements for IN intervention. Enhancements of the BCSM for modelling of the point-to-multipoint calls are discussed in Sec. 4, whereas Secs. 5 and 6 are devoted to the handling of the SCP initiated calls and to the discussion of the new information flows between SCF and SSF, respectively. Finally, Secs. 7 and 8 deal with a brief presentation of IBIS, the experimental test-bed developed in CORITEL for validation of control procedures arising from IN/B-ISDN integration.

2 THE INSIGNIA APPROACH

The main objective of the INSIGNIA project is to define, to implement and to demonstrate an advanced architecture integrating IN and B-ISDN signalling. Two field trials are planned for the demonstration (respectively in the mid '97 and in the 2nd half of '98), so the project has been split in two phases with increasing capabilities. The trials will use the ATM Pan-European pilot network to interconnect broadband islands located at the German, Italian and Spanish national hosts. In this section we will first mention the services considered in the INSIGNIA project and then we will give an overview of the technical approach, which represents the starting point for the proposals contained in this work.

2.1 INSIGNIA services

Three services have been chosen for the trial demonstration: Interactive Multimedia Retrieval (IMR), Broadband Video Conference (B-VC), and Broadband Virtual Private Network [3].

The IMR is a generalisation of the "Video on Demand" service and provides the user the means to select a multimedia application and to retrieve an audio-video information stored in information centres. The information is sent on demand and can be retrieved and controlled on an individual basis. The IN will provide a brokering facility among different service providers, will perform authentication and authorisation and will control the setup and the release of the connections between the user and the different servers.

The B-VC service consists of a real-time conferencing in which both audio and video can be exchanged among a group of users via the B-ISDN. The exchange of data (images, documents) is also possible. The IN will control the whole set of connections required to allow these multi-point to multi-point flows, will keep the information about the global call/service configuration and will support the conference management functionality.

The B-VPN service will offer virtual private network functionality like private numbering plans, control of access and egress authorisation etc. The B-VPN can be seen more as a "network" service, rather than a service directly offered to end users, and can be combined with other services.

2.2 INSIGNIA functional architecture

The functional architecture developed by INSIGNIA [4] is an extension of the well known IN architecture. Four control domains have been envisaged (see Figure 1):

- *Service control domain*: contains the overall control of the IN service, which is carried out by the Service Logic in the Service Control Function (SCF).
- *Session control domain*: this is a new concept proposed by INSIGNIA to represent the association of a set of calls and connections to provide a suitable topology for the realisation of an IN service. The session view is handled at the Service Switching Function level and represents the capabilities that can be offered by the network to the control of service logic.

- *Call control domain*: this domain includes the call control functionalities in a B-ISDN and their interaction with the IN architecture. It will be included in the IN Call Control Function together with the Connection control domain.
- *Connection control domain*: this domain includes the B-ISDN functionalities for the control of bearer connections (bc) and their interaction with the IN architecture.

The role of the IN has been extended far beyond the traditional support of supplementary services. In the INSIGNIA architecture the IN service logic decides the topology of calls / connections needed to provide a service instance, instructs the network to realise this configuration and controls the status of the different connections. The session concept is the main tool for this kind of sophisticated IN control of network resources.

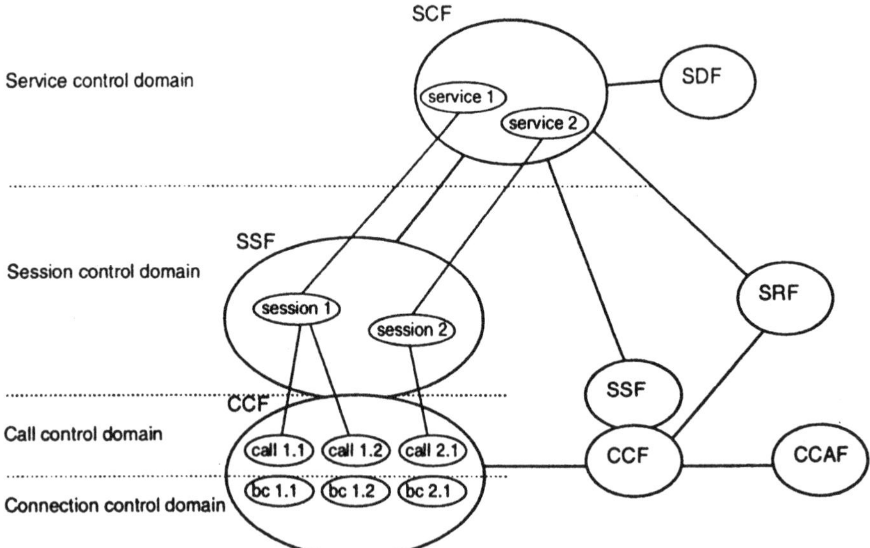

Figure 1 Functional Architecture and Control Domains.

The session model represents a complex configuration of call/connections, as perceived by the IN. This model gives a common view shared between SSF and SCF of the underlying network activities. The INSIGNIA session model is reported in Figure 2.

The session object model is constituted by: *Parties* which represent the users and the "virtual party" SCP; *Bearer Connections* which represent the B-ISDN connections; *Legs* which represent the link of a party to a *Bearer Connection*.

The set of information flows on the SSF-SCF interface is based on this model: the SCF can ask to create or remove objects (i.e. *Parties*, *Bearer Connections*), the SSF reports any information in terms of these object and their states. The SSF also maps the requests of the SCF into requests for the B-ISDN network in terms of basic call/connections. In Table 1 the list of the information flows defined by

INSIGNIA for the first phase of the project is reported. A brief explanation of the flows is provided hereafter.

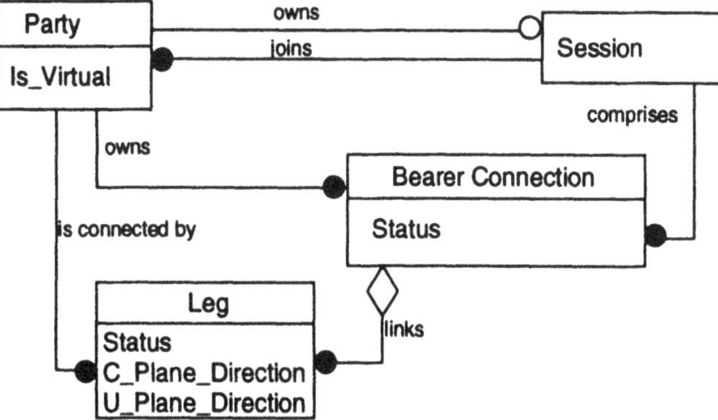

Figure 2 INSIGNIA session object model.

A *Service request* is sent by the SSF to the SCF to invoke an IN service, typically as a consequence of a trigger coming from call processing (e.g. a called party number is an IN number). An instance of the session is created in the SSF; it will last for the lifetime of the service relationship with the SCF. The *Request Report SSM change* allows the SCF to require the report of a possible future change of an object status. For example, these changes will happen when a connection has been successfully setup or has been released. The SSF will send a *Report SSM change* when the status change takes place. The remaining flows allow the SCF to build and to tear down the required connection topology, sending the requests to the SSF in terms of session objects. For example, *Add Bearer to session* contains a couple of existing *Party* objects as parameters and will be mapped by the SSF in the setup of a call/connection between the two corresponding users.

Table 1 Information flows at the SSF-SCF interface

Information flow	*Direction*
Service request	SSF → SCF
Request report SSM change	SCF → SSF
Report SSM change	SSF → SCF
Join party to session & link leg to bearer	SCF → SSF
Join party & bearer to session	" "
Add Parties & bearer to session	" "
Add bearer to session	" "
Drop Session	" "
Drop Party	" "
Release Bearer	" "

As outlined above, the SSF maps the requests coming from the SCF into requests for the B-ISDN call/connection processing. A typical case is the setup of a call between two parties. Therefore a core feature of INSIGNIA architecture is the "SCP initiated call setup". The concept is similar to "third party call setup" which is proposed for future capability set of the B-ISDN, where the third party is represented by the SCP, i.e. by the IN service logic. The main assumption in the specification of this feature has been not to modify the B-ISDN signalling at the UNI and the NNI. The defined solution consists in the use of two independent calls (outgoing from the node) and in a proper modification of the call handling within the node. This enhanced call handling will correlate the signalling messages, will dialogue with IN service logic, and will control the through-connection of the user plane links.

It is worth spending some words on the relation between the INSIGNIA session model and he evolution of B-ISDN capability. To cope with the availability of equipment for the trials the INSIGNIA assumption on B-ISDN capability has been mainly limited to the "Signalling Capability Set 1" i.e. point to point moon-connection calls. However the proposed model is really open to future evolution. Two different approaches can support this evolution. In some cases, the enhancements of B-ISDN could be hidden to IN service logic and handled at the SSF level, where the mapping between the session domain and the connection domain is performed. In other cases, the session model can be easily enhanced with the adding of new object and/or new attributes to offer the new capabilities to the IN service logic control. This last approach will be followed for the introduction of the B-ISDN point-to-multipoint call into the INSIGNIA architecture, as will be described in section 5.

3 BASIC POINT-TO-MULTIPOINT OPERATIONS AND REQUIREMENTS FOR IN INTERVENTION

A point-to-multipoint call/connection allows the distribution of an unidirectional flow of data from one source, the root party, to a set of sinks, the leaf parties. In Figure 3 a general example of a point-to-multipoint call is depicted, the multicasting is performed in the local exchanges 1 and 2 and in the transit exchange. The basic point-to-point call at the User Network Interface (UNI) is specified by the ITU-T recommendation Q.2931. The recommendation Q.2971 extends the Q.2931 functionality for the support of the point-to-multipoint call/connection. Messages and information elements of the Q.2971 are an extension of those ones described in the Q.2931. The point to multipoint calls are initiated by the root by sending a SETUP message in which the point-to-multipoint configuration is specified in the Broadband Bearer Capabilities information element. This message also contains the Endpoint Reference information element which is used to distinguish the different remote parties. The root party can send ADD PARTY messages to add further leaves and DROP PARTY messages to remove a party from the call. A leaf party can only drop itself from the call, but cannot join itself to a point-to-multipoint call. The call can be explicitly torn down by the root by sending a RELEASE message, which releases all the leaves. At the Network Node Interface (NNI) the point-to-multipoint calls are specified by the ITU recommendation Q.2721.1 It supports the same procedures defined for the UNI, obviously mapping the UNI messages into NNI messages. The Q.2722.1 allows the use of the same connection (i.e. Virtual Circuit) at the NNI for the user plane flow when the route towards two or more leaf parties is the same.

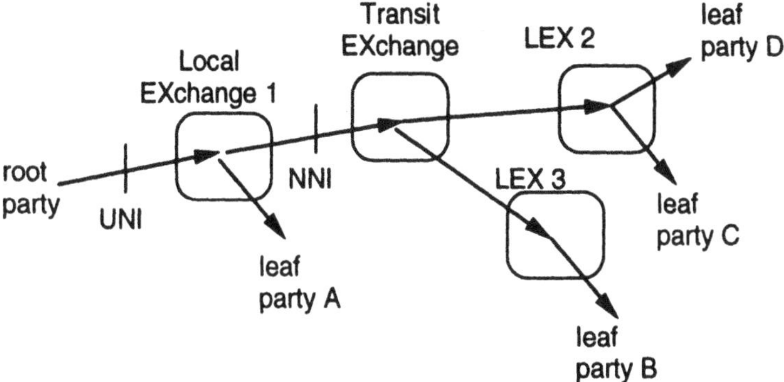

Figure 3 Example point-to-multipoint call/connection configuration

Let us consider now for what services we could benefit from IN support along with point-to-multipoint calls. A first simple case is the extension of some IN based supplementary services, like number translation services and reverse charging services to point-to-multipoint. The number translation services could be extended to point-to-multipoint calls with a one-to-many translation feature: a single called party number contained in a SETUP or ADD PARTY message could trigger IN service logic which could add a predefined set of leaves to the point to multipoint call. Broadband Virtual Private Network services could be extended to support point-to-multipoint with features like access control and private numbering planes. Finally a large set of services based on the INSIGNIA concepts could benefit from the adoption of the point-to-multipoint. On one hand, services like B-VC already considered in the INSIGNIA project could be realised in a more efficient way by using point to multipoint connections. On the other hand, distributive services with centralised control which have not been included in the INSIGNIA could be defined using the session concepts and the point-to-multipoint connections. To give an example, by means of IN control we could handle requests coming from users that want to receive an information flow which is being distributed (for example a TV channel a TV-distribution service, or a specific lesson in a Distance Learning service).

3.1 Requirements for B-ISDN point-to-multipoint call modelling in IN

The call processing and signalling activities of the switching network are modelled in the IN architecture by means of the so called Basic Call State Model (BCSM). The BCSM is a tool for representing Call Control Function (CCF) activities which can be monitored and controlled by the IN service logic.

The first requirement for an IN call model for a point-to-multipoint call is therefore to allow the control of the following features in a *basic* point-to-multipoint call (i.e. initiated by the root using Q.2971 UNI signalling):

- Call Setup (e.g. detection of an IN Called Party Number)
- Party Addition (e.g. detection of an IN Called Party Number)
- Party Answer (detection of the remote party answer)
- Call Release (detection of the release of the call)
- Party Release (detection of the release of a remote party).

Following the INSIGNIA approach for IN initiated operation, the additional requirements for an IN call model are to support:

- SCP initiated Party Addition (addition of parties to an already established pmp call on behalf of the IN)
- SCP initiated IN point-to-multipoint Call Establishment (establishment of a point-to-multipoint configuration on behalf of the IN)

4 BASIC CALL STATE MODEL (BCSM) FOR POINT-TO-MULTIPOINT CALL

The available IN standards describe the call model for a point-to-point call with a single connection, as suitable for POTS and N-ISDN network. The advances in the capability of the B-ISDN imply a more advanced modelling. The requirements coming from the multi-connection calls and from the point to multipoint calls lead to the proposals of layered call models [5]. The INSIGNIA project has developed a call model which is compatible to multi-connection (even if this capability has not been used in the field trials for practical reasons). In this section we will describe this model and propose the enhancements for the support of point-to-multipoint connections.

The INSIGNIA project has proposed a Basic Call State Model for IN and B-ISDN integration which is composed of two finite state machines, the "Call Control Manager" and the "Bearer Connection Control Manager". The former takes care of the modelling of the "call" related aspects while the latter takes care of the aspects related to the bearer connection. If we consider the evolution of the signalling toward the multiconnection, this modelling choice is future proof. Using only basic B-ISDN point-to-point call (i.e. supported by B-ISDN Signalling Capability Set 1) the call and the bearer are always in an one-to-one relationship, so that the two finite state machine are tightly coupled. When the a basic call is established a couple of "CCM" and "BCCM" are instanced to follow the evolution of the call/connection. This redundancy is a characteristic of the conceptual model, but does not introduces redundancies (and inefficiency) in the actual implementation. In fact for the modelling of a simple point-to-point call the Detection Points can be armed only at one level (typically at the CCM level), as it is specified in the IN Capability Set 1. The two levels model will be fully exploited when the multi-connection call will be available at the B-ISDN level: a "CCM" will represent the state of the call while a set of "BCCM" will be instanced to represent the evolution of the different connections. While in the traditional IN modelling the BCSM is different for the originating and terminating side, the INSIGNIA project has proposed to use an unified BCSM which can be used on either side, as well as for the SCP initiated calls. However, in the following discussion on point-to-multipoint BCSM we can consider all the state machines as originating.

The INSIGNIA modelling needs to be extended for the support of the point-to-multipoint call in order to describe the evolution of the call and of the different parties. In a point-to-multipoint call there is a set of parties which can evolve independently, making it not feasible to control them within a single state machine. The proposed solution foresees to use the defined CCM and BCCM and to add a state machine representing each remote party, called "Party Control Manager". Figure 4 and Figure 5 show the state machines for Call Control Manager and Bearer Connection Control Manager as specified by INSIGNIA, Figure 6 shows the proposed Party Control Manager.

Call Control Manager

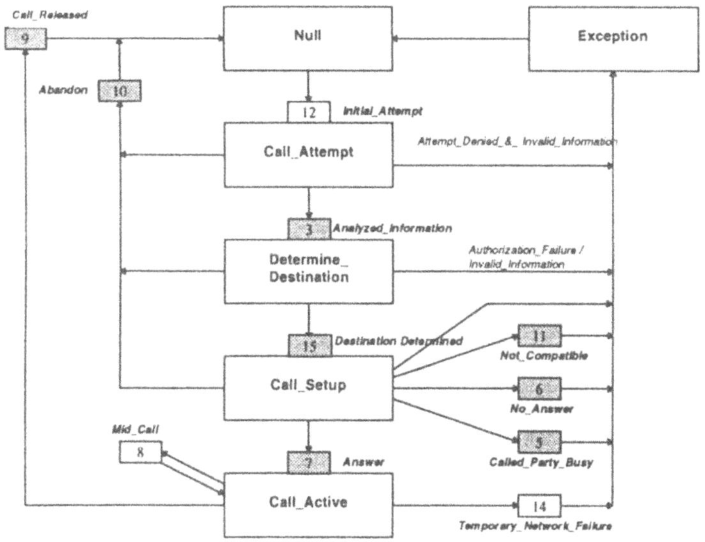

Figure 4 Finite state machine for the Call Control Manager

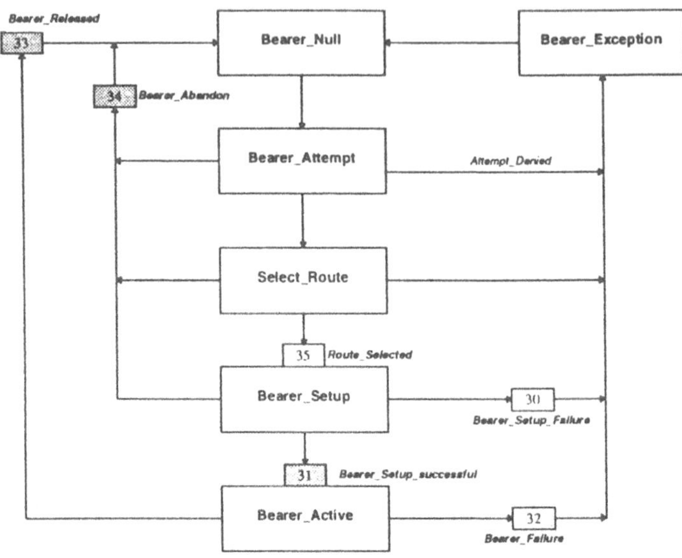

Figure 5 Finite state machine for the Bearer Connection Control Manager

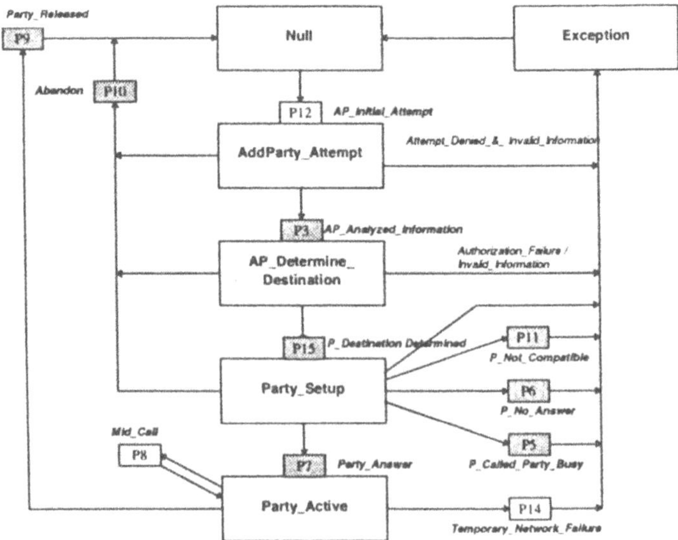

Figure 6 Finite state machine for the Party Control Manager

We will show how to use the proposed call modelling to control both a "traditional" point to multipoint call and the new features which are added in an IN integrated architecture i.e. the adding of parties on behalf of the IN and the SCP initiated point to multipoint. Let us describe the model behaviour analysing the setup of a traditional point to multipoint (i.e. setup by the root). As soon as the setup indication for a point to multipoint call is received, a PCM is instanced and will evolve in parallel with the CCM/BCCM couple which is instanced as in the point-to-point case. The CCM represents the call state while the PCM represents the state of the first remote party. The CCM is in the PIC "Call Attempt", the BCCM is in the PIC "Bearer Attempt", while the PCM is in the PIC "Add Party Attempt". When the first party answers the call, the three state machines will respectively go in the Call Active, Bearer Active and Party Active PIC. The remote parties that will be successively connected are monitored by new instances of the Party Control Manager, as shown in Figure 7. No Bearer Connection Control Manager has been added below the Party Control Manager, because only mono-connection point-to-multipoint calls are envisaged.

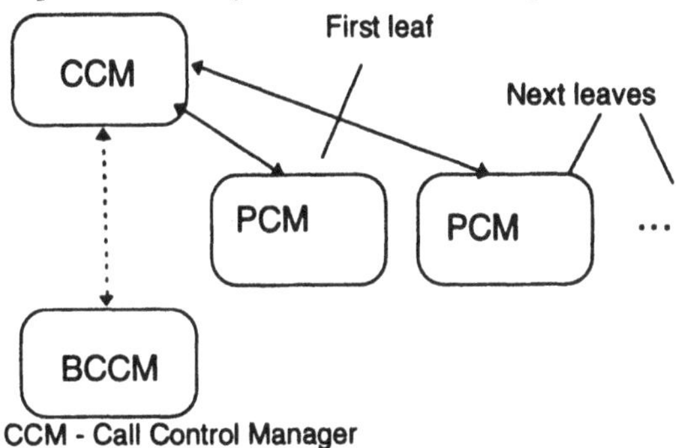

Figure 7: BCSM instances for the control of a point-to-multipoint call

The detection points (DP) in the PCM can be armed according with the service logic requirements. A complete description of the PICs, DP and possible transitions is beyond the scope of this paper[2]. We will give some examples of the use of the most important DPs in the PCM to show the capability of the model. Let us consider the DP "Add Party Attempt" which is encountered when the root sends an ADD PARTY message. If it is needed to monitor each adding of a new party, to allow an IN based access control service or accounting service, this DP will be armed to report each attempt, with an interruption of call processing for the access control service or with a simple notification for the accounting service. It could be needed to monitor whether the ADD PARTY message contains a

[2] For a complete description of INSIGNIA BCSMs (CCM and BCCM) see [4]. The PCM is quite similar to CCM.

called party number which requires IN intervention (for example a number translation service), so the "Add Party Attempt" DP will be armed with a suitable criteria.

The DP "Party Answer", together with the DPs "P_No_Answer", "P_Called_Party_Busy", allow the service logic to monitor the result of the setup phase, while the DP "Party released" allow the service logic to monitor the release of a party.

All the above detection points can be armed independently for each leaf. For example in a given service one could want to monitor only the status of a subset of the parties which are mandatory without bothering the service logic with the status of the other parties.

The detection points in the Call Control Manager allow to monitor the state of the whole call: for example the DP "Call Released", if armed, can detect the release of the whole call requested by the root party.

5 ADDING OF NEW PARTIES AND SCP INITIATED POINT-TO-MULTIPOINT CALLS

Two additional features have been introduced in this integrated architecture: i) the adding of new parties on behalf of the IN, ii) the SCP initiated point-to-multipoint call. The introduction of these two features implies a new BCSM modelling and the adding of new capabilities in the call handling inside the nodes, with minimal impact on the signalling. The proposed approach to extend the capability of the B-ISDN signalling is similar to the INSIGNIA approach for SCP initiated point-to-point calls described in section 2.

For the adding of parties on behalf of the IN, the call handler for point-to-multipoint has to be modified to receive requests from the IN and to control the signalling toward the leaf party on the outgoing UNI or NNI link. The adding of these parties will not be communicated to the root at the signalling level because the Q.2971 procedures do not allow it. The modified call handler will also intercept signalling messages from the leaves (e.g. DROP PARTY messages) which cannot be reported to the root. As far as the BCSM modelling is concerned, the parties which are added on behalf of the IN service logic will be modelled by instances of Party Control Manager as if they were added by the root. Therefore all the above described features of the PCM model also apply to this parties, allowing the IN control.

The SCP initiated point-to-multipoint call setup is supported via enhancements of the call handling functionality, without modification of signalling. As at the UNI a node can not setup a point-to-multipoint call toward a root party, a point-to-point call is established to support an unidirectional connection from the root to the node, then an independent (with respect to B-ISDN signalling) point-to-multipoint call towards the leaf parties is setup. As in the point-to-point case, the modified call handler will correlate the signalling messages, will dialogue with IN service logic, and will control the through-connection of the user plane links. In this case the adding of new parties will be performed only by IN, as the root is not even aware at the signalling level to be part of a point-to-multipoint call. The two steps for the setup of an IN initiated point-to-multipoint call are depicted in Figure 8. The thin arrows show the control plane relationships (the direction represents the party who receive the setup) while the thick arrows show the user plane links (the direction represent the flow of data).

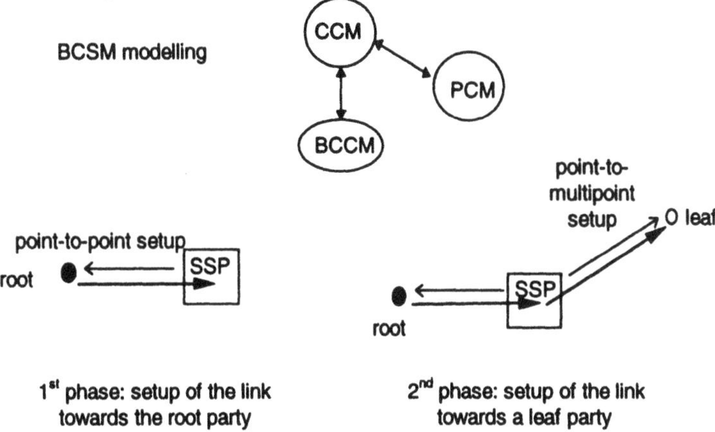

Figure 8: Setup of a SCP initiated point-to-multipoint call

In the BCSM modelling, the leaf parties will be represented by the PCMs, with the usual capabilities to control the result of the party setup, to monitor the release of the parties etc.

Due to the particular handling of the SCP initiated point-to-multipoint calls the CCM represents only the status of the root party. The CCM will go in the active state when the root has answered the call, and will reflect the status of this link, for example notifying a release coming from the root. The reason for this modelling is that it could be allowed to have an active link toward the root with no leaf party connected. This is different to the traditional point-to-multipoint where the call can be in the active state if at least one leaf party is connected. For example, broadcast services could require this capability to have always data flow ready to be distributed to user requiring it.

6 SESSION AND INAP INFORMATION FLOW ADVANCES

The session model developed by the INSIGNIA project needs to be slightly enhanced to support the point-to-multipoint calls. The *Bearer Connection* object will be extended to support a set of more than two *Legs*. A new attribute "*Configuration*" is added to the bearer connection object with possible values

"*point-to-point*" and "*point-to-multipoint*". The *Leg* objects will represent the root and the set of leaves which compose a point-to-multipoint calls. The *Leg* objects are therefore used to reflect the state of the leaf parties. The detection points monitored at the Party Control Manager level will cause object state changes in the *Leg* objects within the session. The service logic can request the monitoring of these state changes with the ***Request Report SSM change*** info flow as explained in section 2. There is no substantial difference at the session level in the handling of *Leg* objects for "root initiated" or "SCP initiated" point-to-multipoint calls.
The set of information flows for the support of point-to-multipoint has been extended with two new flows as reported in Table 2:

Table 2 New SSF-SCF information flows for the support of point-to-multipoint

Information flow	*Direction*
Add point-to-multipoint bearer	SCF → SSF
Join parties to point-to-multipoint bearer	SCF → SSF

The *Add point-to-multipoint bearer* info flow allows the service logic to establish a SCP initiated point-to-multipoint call providing the root party and the list of leaf parties to be connected. A *Bearer Connection* object will be created with the *Configuration* attribute set to "*point-to-multipoint*", the *Party* objects will be created if the parties does not still exist in the session, one *Leg* object for each party will be created to represent the link with the *Bearer Connection*. The *Join parties to point-to-multipoint bearer* info flow allows the service logic to add a set of new leaf parties to a point-to-multipoint (both "root initiated" and "SCP initiated") call. An existing *Bearer Connection* object is provided in the message, while the rules for creating *Party* and *Leg* objects are the same described above.

7 TEST BED FOR THE PROPOSED MODELLING

The proposed modelling has been implemented in a test bed running in a local area network, in the context of a CORITEL project called IBIS (Implementation of integrated B-ISDN and IN Signalling). Only control aspects have been considered in this test bed. The functionalities of the different network elements have been described with the SDL language and implemented using the Telelogic SDT. The reference functional architecture is reported in Figure 9. At the UNI a suitable subset of the recommendation for point-to-point (Q.2931) and point-to-multipoint (Q.2971) has been implemented realising the protocol state machines for the user side and the network side of UNI. These machines send and process the signalling messages on the UNI and offer a primitive based interface towards the switch call handling processes (i1). A call handler has been developed within the SSP to control a set of UNIs. This call handler controls the basic point-to-point and point-to-multipoint calls and integrates the BCSM functionality to allow the interaction with IN, acting as the CCF. An internal interface towards the SSF has been defined (i2) starting from INSIGNIA specifications. The SSF realises the session model and is capable to dialogue with the SCF using the information flows presented in the paper (interface i3). Finally a "dummy" SCF has been developed to complete the test-bed environment. This SCF can send and receive a predefined sequence of information flow to test the overall functionality.

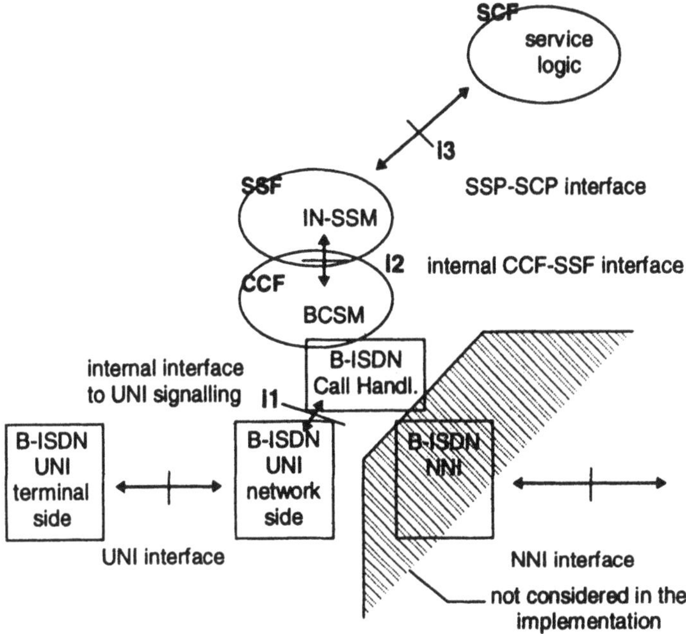

Figure 9 Reference functional architecture for the test bed implementation

The software architecture of the test bed is shown in Figure 10. A set of stand-alone applications for the different users and one application for the SSP have been developed. The UNI messages among these applications are formatted according to recommendation and are exchanged using socket interfaces provided by the UNIX operating system. The internal interfaces i1, i2, i3 within the Network Application are based on the exchange of SDL signals.

8 MESSAGE SEQUENCE CHART FOR A SAMPLE SCENARIO

In this section we provide a scenario to highlight some features of the proposed architecture. User A requires a point-to-multipoint call providing an "IN" called party number which triggers IN involvement. We assume that the IN service consists in the adding of a set of leaf parties, and in the monitoring that all the required party are connected. A Message Sequence Chart output from the test-bed simulation is reported for this sample scenario in Figure 11 (only parties B and C are added in this simplified scenario). All signals internal to SSF, CCF and UNI machines have been removed from the MSC showing only the messages on the i1, i2, i3 and all the signals parameters have been removed.

On the interface i1 the primitives from and to the UNI signalling machines are shown. The first primitive is the setup indication coming from the UNI connected to user A. On the interface i2 the CCF reports the Detection Points to the SSF, the SSF requests the CCF to arm the DPs, to complete a call, to add a new call. On the interface i3 the SSF-SCF information flows are reported.

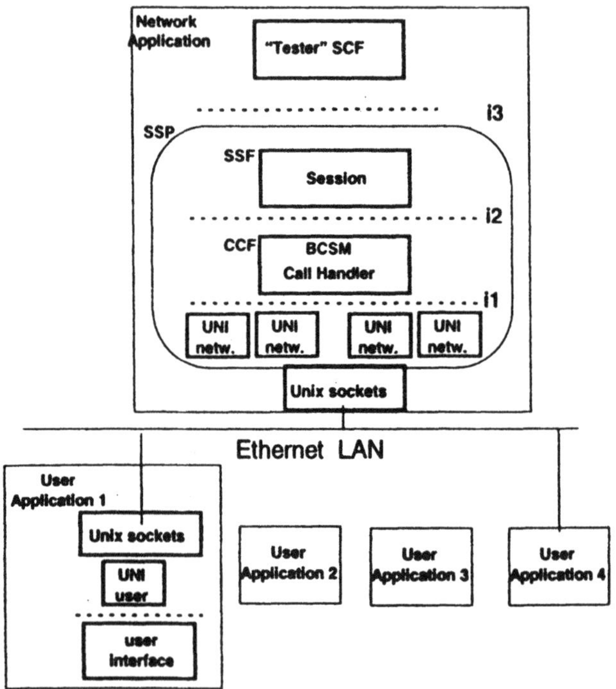

Figure 10: Architecture of the test-bed

9 CONCLUSIONS

In this paper we have presented the INSIGNIA approach for IN and B-ISDN integration and its extension towards the introduction of point-to-multipoint calls. We have proven that the INSIGNIA architecture is open to the evolution of network capability. We have considered the impact of point-to-multipoint in the Call Control Function proposing the needed enhancements to Basic Call Modelling, in the SSF showing the enhancements to the Session model, and in the SSF-SCF interface proposing new information flows to be added to this interface. The proposed architecture has been implemented in a simple test bed.

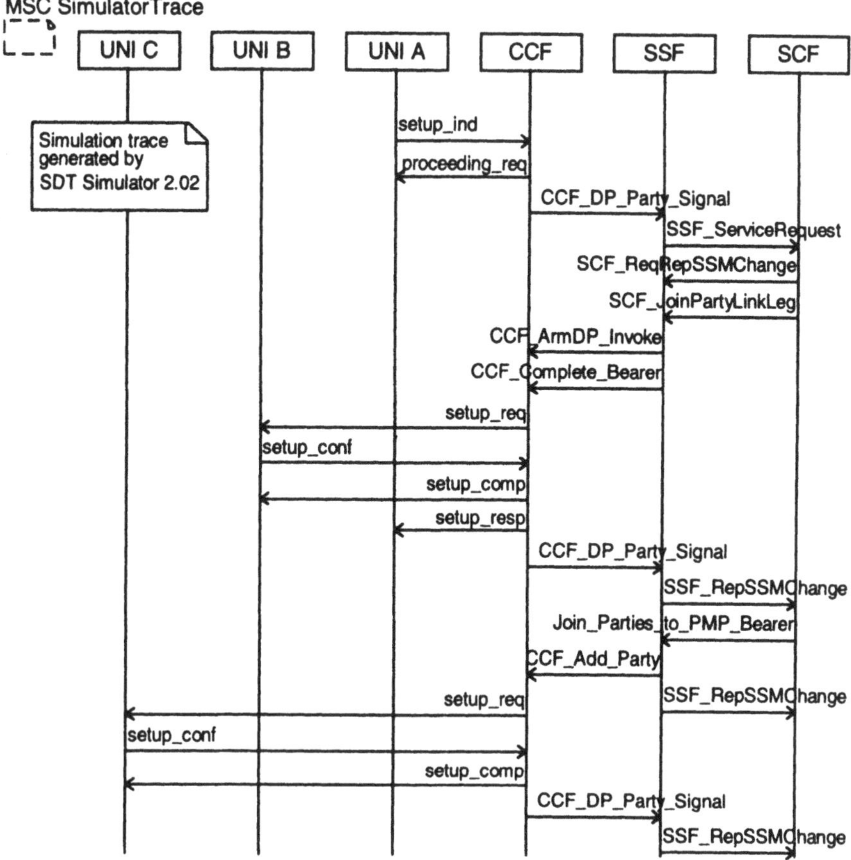

Figure 11 Message Sequence Chart for an "IN" point-to-multipoint call

10 REFERENCES

[1] Y. Bretecher, B. Vilain "The Intelligent Network in a Broadband context", *ISS'95*, Berlin, April 1995, pp. 340-344.

[2] S.Corti, L.Cipriani, S.Salsano "B-ISDN architectural evolution towards the integration with Intelligent Network" - *ICC '96*, Dallas, June 1996, pp. 947-951.

[3] ACTS project INSIGNIA deliverable "Second trial: Description of the selected services".

[4] INSIGNIA deliverable "First trial: Functions and Architecture specification".

[5] V.Carmagnola, F.Cuomo, M.Ferretti "A Layered Approach for IN Call Modelling for the Support of Multimedia Services in a B-ISDN Environment" - ICC '96, Dallas, June 1996.

BIOGRAPHIES

Marco Listanti received his Dr. Eng. degree in Electronics Engineering from the University "La Sapienza" of Roma in 1980. He joined the Fondazione Ugo Bordoni in 1981, where has been leader of the TLC network architecture group until 1991. In November 1991 he joined the University of Roma, where he is currently an Associate Professor in Switching Systems. He also holds lectures at the University of Roma "Tor Vergata" on Communications Networks. His current research interests focus on multimedia broadband communications, high throughput switching architectures and integration between the Intelligent Network and the B-ISDN.

Stefano Salsano was born in Rome in 1969. He received his degree with honours in electronic engineering from University of Rome "Tor Vergata" in 1994, with a thesis on evaluation of signalling load in a IN based PCS environment. Then he has been with CORITEL, a research institute on telecommunications, as a scholarship holder. Now he is a Ph.D. student at the INFOCOM department, University of Rome "La Sapienza". Currently, his research interest include architectures and signalling protocols for broadband networks, focusing on the integration of the B-ISDN with Intelligent Network.

PART NINE

New Trends

23

Application management by actors for SNMP

Bernard Kaddour and Michel Beigbeder
Ecole des Mines de Saint-Etienne
158, cours Fauriel,
42023 Saint-Etienne cedex 2
France
Tel: (+33) 4 77 42 01 74 Fax: (+33) 4 77 42 66 66
kaddour@emse.fr, mbeig@emse.fr

Abstract

This document focuses on management of application resources. Starting from the *message bus* design, our original approach is based on *active objects*. It provides a dynamic management scheme allowing evolutive and reusable management functions. Despite important differences with standard managenent frameworks, our management design is integrated into existing network management protocols, and so it provides application management capabilities to existing tools.

Keywords

Message bus, actors, interfaces, evolutivity, MIB integration

1 INTRODUCTION

To reduce the time and cost of application development, *Integrated Environments* (Reiss 1990) or brokers (O.M.G. 1991) (Brockschmidt 1995) were designed. They allow to build new applications by aggregation of existing software components communicating with themselves. Likeness with network entities appears at first glance.

The increasing complexity and sophistication of network services required dedicated network management tools and protocols, it will — soon — be the same for the applications.

Network management platforms have been largely available since the standardization of network management. Nevertheless, some of their characteristics are limitative. Centralization is the first one, only *managers* are able to execute complex management operations. Secondly, these platforms are restricted to manage hardware network components and not communicating applications. These limitations compel network management platforms to use specific administration functions that other platforms can't reuse.

Intelligent Networks and Intelligence in Networks D. Gaiti (Ed.)
Published by Chapman & Hall

We will describe an application modelization based on active objects and will use it for application management. We will emphasize evolutivity needs in application management which network management doesn't provide.

2 APPLICATION MANAGEMENT

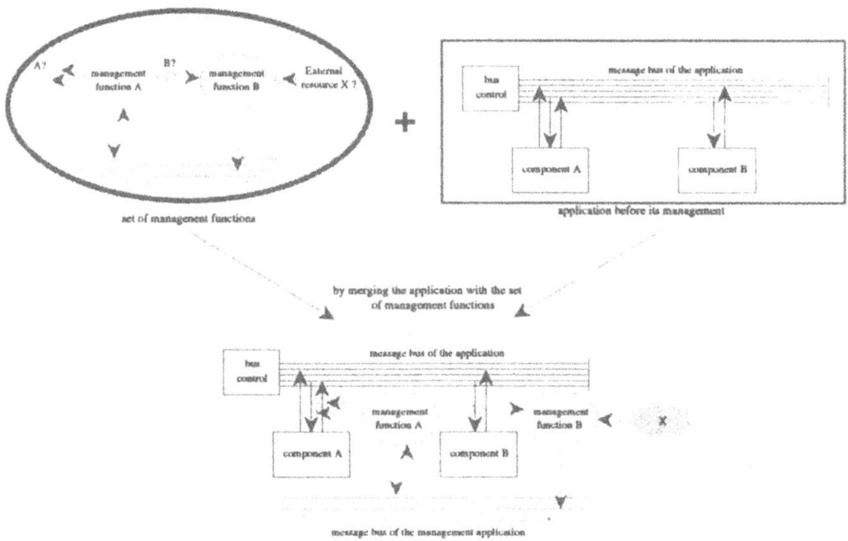

Figure 1 Example of an application management achieved by cooperating management functions

Application management is concerned with the optimization of the *service per cost* ratio, even when the application runs under slightly disturbed working conditions. Main points are:

quality of service: Checking the fulfilment of the declared services. This is achieved by monitoring sensible parts of the application.

adaptability: Customizing current services to fulfill other application requirements. For example an interpersonal mail message exchange service can be used to partially provide file transfer system facilities (Rollin 1986).

optimization of the use of resources: disks, network throughput, etc.

So, application management concerns appear close to usual network management ones.

Network management frameworks (ISO 1989) (Case, Fedor & al. 1990) based upon a passive object representation of the entities to manage is actually mainly concerned with physical components. Meanwhile, these management standards induce some limitations that application management have to bypass, such as centralization in management platforms.

A new approach for management *TINA* (Chapman, Dupy & Nilson 1995) lastly appears. We will differ from it mainly by the fact that we don't want to depict another management platform but rather to allow processing capabilities for management, taking into account basic protocols aspects. From this point of view, our approach draws closer to the *JMAPI* * spirit.

2.1 Message bus and management

Integrated Environments used for new application development are classified in families (Boyer 1994) depending on their underlying design. Nevertheless, one of these design is actually largely available from manufacturers, and it provides flexibility and genericity: the *message bus.*

A message bus acts as a server where every client registers with the Software Communication Group it belongs to. At any time, a client may indicate the message types it expects to receive and to process, then the message bus handles messages and routes them to clients (Cf. upper right part of Figure 1).

The message bus model enables management to operate on the application as a whole, or on its components only. So, the application management is no longer centralized: management functions dynamically link with the components they want to interact with. Moreover, management functions are not limited to collect data, and can be parts of a complete distributed management application (Cf. Figure 1).

3 ACTIVE OBJECT APPROACH

With the *passive* object oriented model, network entities are hardwired *templates* and their management is operated by platform dependant supervision services. When new managed entities are inserted, new templates with new specific management entities are to be (re)written. This scheme can't gracefully take into account the dynamic and autonomous aspects of the applications we want to manage. The *actor* (or *active object*) model (Hewitt 1977, Agha 1986) seems to be the most suitable for our purpose. Moreover, it allows unification of managed and management applications, providing an homogeneous framework. Lastly, the *description* of these entities enters in this framework.

Two points need some explanations to make our point of view accept-

*http://java.sun.com/products/JavaManagement/

able: *i)* We have to bypass some burdens of the actor calculus model, for example the unification in the extreme which doesn't facilitate the model use (Venkatasubramanian & Talcott 1993), *ii)* We have to take into account existing software and existing management frameworks. In particular, arrangements are necessary to draw closer to, and finally merge with, the current network management architecture.

We will introduce three kinds of entities to address our main points of § 2: *interfaces*, *activities* and *contexts*.

3.1 Interfaces

Interfaces play a descriptive role part in our application management system. They describe the operations any interface conformant actor must support, as*ASN-1 templates* do in *SNMP* or *CMIP*. However, as the expected management entities have to operate between themselves and with managed entities, an interface integrates the methods that a conformant actor renders to the community and the services it requires. Interface finally draws closer to *typed active objects* (Nierstrasz 1993).

Interfaces differ from typed active objects by the set of standardized operations an interface responds to. These operations give interfaces capabilities to manage version numbers or to combine between themselves to describe new *families* of actors.

Roughly speaking, an interface is composed of the set of the typed variables — according to SNMP allowed types. and the set of the method signatures for each one of the states that a conformant actor may enter.

An interface example will be the action table an entity has to respond to to be conformant with the *editor* notion of company *X*. For example *Apple* defines an *editor* as a program responding to a set of *Apple Events*.

Interfaces of a special kind, called *translation* interfaces, ensure that any actor conformant to a translation interface may adapt some elements — under some restrictive conditions — to be conformant to another interface (Kaddour & Beigbeder 1996).

Our design thus differs from the usual network management scheme which needs a tree of classes (or types) and a tree of instanciations, the former containing abstract representations of managed objects, the latter containing managed objects. Our approach needs a single tree which contains management entity descriptions, management entities, managed entities, and managed entity descriptions where entities descriptions are represented by interfaces.

3.2 Activities

Most of our management entities are *activities*.

The original *activity* concept has first been introduced in the *Computer Supported Co-operative Work* framework (Danielsen, Pankoke & al. 1986) (Brun 1987). We will continue to use this term although its meaning has deeply been altered.

Main parts of an activity are:

- *roles*: We distinguish external roles corresponding to resources that other third parties may provide to the activity from internal roles corresponding to sub-activities of the current activity. Both are described by means of references to interfaces.
- *constraints* and *preferences*. They are the combination of logical conditions based upon the events the activity can receive. They associate an *internal tool* to be executed when they are verified. The loading of a particular character set font as a new incomer conforming to an editor interface is such an example.
- *internal tools*: It is a set of functions embedded in the activity for it's own needs. These tools, usually inactive, can be triggered at any time by the arrival of a new element (via a preference e.g.) or by needs of the activity. Particular tools are the *incoming* or *outgoing filters* acting upon messages received or emitted by the activity and *variables filters* (Cf § a).
- *the main body of the activity* made of *methods* the activity responds to and the set of its private *variables*. Security policy to apply for each received message or termination of the activity are known methods that every activity must implement or delegate.
- *set of attributes* from which the activity can be designated. E.g. an edition activity can specify an `octet string` attribute `file` which is the name of the file it proceeds with.

This structure of the activity enables both the description of applications build as communication components that we want to manage, and the description of management applications.

It is the activity responsibility to report to the system management the interface or set of services it can respond to.

So, an activity can be seen as an actor solely composed of a set of sub-activities, variables and methods that can be called for particular processings, but also has a set of elements mainly composed of filtering functions appliable to messages. The former vision is suited to the applications to manage, the latter to the management applications. Both of them are unified under the activity concepts.

(a) Wrappers

Particular activities are *wrappers*. They acts as *gateways* between the management system and the real world we have to interact with. From the system point of view, they represent real world applications when these one don't naturally support the mechanisms required to be managed.

The manner a wrapper interacts with the software it represents is highly software dependent and cannot be exactly specified. This is the same kind of problem found in usual network management between a managed object and its management agent.

Finally, we emphasize that management functions are obtained by means of input, output or variables filters tied to wrappers as depicted by Figure 2.

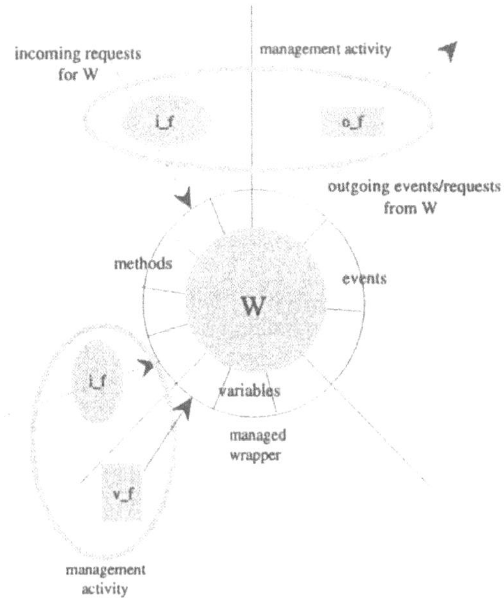

Figure 2 A wrapper with activities of management by means of filters

3.3 Contexts

The execution of any activity takes place in a dedicated context. This context represents the *environment* in which the activity operates. Taking into account the different pieces an activity is compound of, its associated context conceptually contains:

- *attributes* from which this particular instance of the activity can be designated. Some of these attributes directly come from the activity description, others, such as the set of provided services are dynamically obtained.
- a *reception port* that all the messages sent to the activity have to pass through. The port acts as a security manager (or a forwarder to a security delegate).
- the *sons-context* of the context attached to the considered activity. These are execution instances of internal sub-activities or of external resources required by the activity, provided by the management system.
- *constraints* and *preferences* which have tasks close to that of filters. The main difference is that the former proceed on incoming and outgoing activities, whereas the latter proceed on messages.
- *filters*, — incoming, outgoing and variables — registered or in execution.

(a) Filters

Incoming (outgoing) filters are lightweight processes that can receive the messages sent to (emitted by) the activity. They can notify the arrival (departure) of a message to a delegate, read, write and modify the message.

To be considered as active, a filter has to register itself to the management system.

The format of registration and the main structure of filters are standardized. At registration time, the filter provides the required privilege (notification, read or write access) and the t-uple set (*address-identification of the originator*, *method's name*, *arguments*) characterizing the incoming messages the filter wants the system to notify it.

Each part of this set may describe one or several elements. For example, (*"user=bk".cambur.emse.fr*, *m0* OR *m1*, *ANY*) is interested by messages coming from the context identified as *"user=bk".cambur.emse.fr*, calling the method *m0* or *m1*, regardless of the arguments.

From theses pieces of information, the management system either provides message manipulation functions or refuses the filter's registration.

The fact that the signature of a method has been split between its name and its arguments enables us to construct the tree of the potentially activable filters for the context.

The walk through the tree of filters is then accomplished for each received message, according to the originator's address-identification in the first stage, according to the method's name called in the second stage and finally according to the arguments in the last stage.

For each of theses stages, we search a node of the tree matching the processed message in the corresponding level. If such a node is found, firstly the filter registered with a writing/modifying privilege is spawn, thus, if after the processing of the message by this filter the node found still matchs the message, the reading and notifying registered filters are simultaneously spawn whereas the next stage begins.

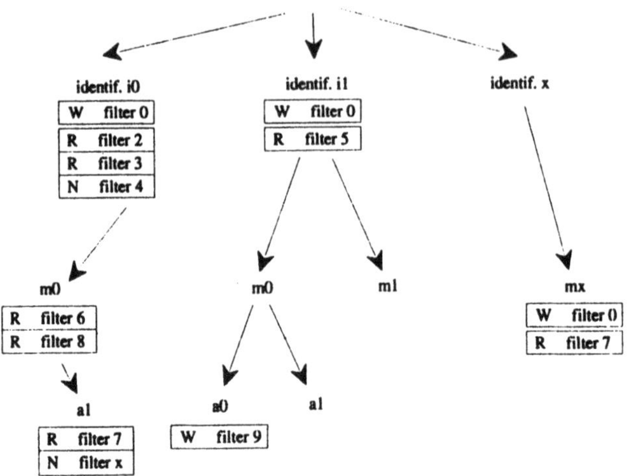

Figure 3 The tree of filters

Based upon the structure of filters, the tree obtained allows an efficient forwarding of the messages across the filters.

This is only after being processed by the activated filters that the message is finally delivered to the activity of the context — assuming that no spawned filters has stopped the forwarding process.

We note that each node of the tree contains at most one filter registered with write privilege for a given context, because allowing the registration of several filters with write privilege for the same node will lead to consider the set of activable filters as a graph, where loops may appear. Preventing any troubles from such loops would overload the system and slow down the walk-trough process having regard to the small system improvement. This "one writer constraint" applies only in a given context.

It is important to note that the particular forwarding mechanism induced by the way filters are registered and act does not conflict with existing communication protocols.

The way outgoing filters act is sensibly the same.

Variables filters are not interested in the way messages are exchanged, but they have to monitor some inner aspects of an activity. They achieve this goal by registering *expressions* made of variables with which the activity is described, for which they want to be notified as soon as they appear to be true.

Monitoring a variable value (that may be modified without any method call) needs control on the run-time or the interpreter of the language used by the application.

The variable filters act upon variables of simple or complex types. Special keys have been introduced for variables of complex types such as *SEQUENCE* and *SEQUENCE OF* to distinguish if an expression is interested in the modification of the variable (e.g. destruction of an element in a *SEQUENCE OF* variable) or in the modification of one of its component.

3.4 The layout of the contexts

A *context* represents the *environment* in which the activity is executed.

So, the activity behavior is customized to the environment it is diped in according to its needs and to the available tools the *system management* can find or build from the interfaces information.

Without more information, the context of a new activity is placed in the context of the activity which requires the activation. This can be overriden by placement specification.

This mechanism is used to manage applications. For example, the management of an application `b` is achieved by spawning a management activity `a` — mainly made of filters and functions — and the system is told to place the context of `a` as an over-context of the context attached to `b`.

As a consequence, contexts appear as stacked upon each others, almost in the same manner protocols do (Venkatasubramanian & Talcott 1993).

Precisely, the set of contexts is built as a tree. From the object model point of view, a major difference appears between activities and contexts. Activities act as autonomous entities without class or inheritance mechanism. They draw closer to *prototypes* (Lieberman 1986): note that each activity initiator is the kernel of the management system which acts as the default delegate. So, by the layout of the delegates (Stein 1987), at run time the contexts use a mechanism similar to the usual inheritance. Data or services are successively searched in the upper layers of the caller context.

(a) The session

We have to take care in using incoming (outgoing) filters.

The interface of the couple (*filter*, *main activity body*) may present to the outer community is not the same has the one of the activity (this is a way adaptability or evolutivity is achieved). This may lead to some troubles or incoherences. For example with the following scenario:

— A context `c` asks the system for an entity compatible with the interface `i0`. The system provides the entity `i`.

— A writer filter modifies the interface of `i` to interface `i1`.

`c`'s knowledge of `i` is then wrong. This kind of mistakes comes from the stateless nature of the management system. Rather than systematically freezing the attendees (which will disable us to address one of the major point stated in § 2), better seems to preserve the nature of the system but to add the *session* notion. When a session is required by a context, the system either

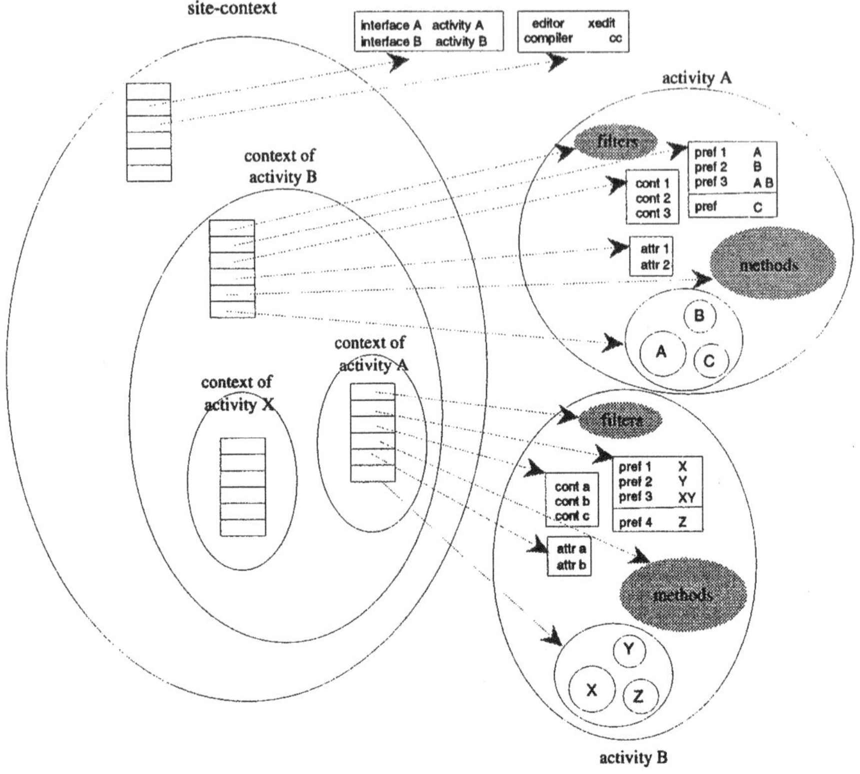

Figure 4 The layout of contexts and links with activities

ensures that the vision the context has will be stable as it will temporally freeze branchs of the tree of contexts, or at least notify the context about modifications that could not be avoided, as for example an exit of `i`.

A session may sometime disables — as long it has not been held down — the execution of attendees (the registration of filter with write privilege e.g.).

(b) Some particular contexts

Finally, to take into account existing computing, two kinds of contexts has been added: *user-contexts* and *site-contexts*.

A user-context includes all the contexts which belong to a given user. Its interest resides in the contribution offered to the security management.

The site-context enables to group the contexts present on a site/computer. While conceptually artificial, it takes into account the real world constraints.

- A context is generally tied to a computer, even if sometimes some of it sub-contexts may execute remotely.

- basic resources are provided by the operating system of the computer (network, access rights, files, ...). Operating systems are generally centralized, in spite of the emergence of distributed operating systems.
- as previously described, management induces particularities in the forwarding of messages. The site-context enables the use of existing network protocols.
  The specific part of our management approach is implemented in this site-context.

It is in the site-context that *translation* capabilities or that the description of services provided by the actors are registered.

4 THE KERNEL OF MANAGEMENT SYSTEM

The kernel of the management system (*kMS*) is used to implement and represent the management system on a computer. It corresponds to the services that the site-context must provide and to the basic services of the management system. *kMS* implements for a site the set of methods that the execution of an activity may require, such as communications, printing capabilities, etc.

Moreover, as representing the site-context, the kMS provides a way for activities that doesn't implement mandatory methods (security methods e.g.) to delegate them to it.

It's worth noting that the kMS has a global vision over the contexts of the site. This makes the kMS the manager of all the site available resources (with their interfaces) that activities may ask for.

More generally, kMS ensures coherence of the contexts in the site and it is in charge to interact with major external components such as languages interpreters or SNMP.

5 A SIMPLE EXAMPLE

In this example we assume that user `U` asks the kMS to provide a tool with editing capabilities, i.e. that is compatible with the editor interface:

```
<implement os:system>
filename: octet string
open
save
printerToUse(octet string)
print(octet string)
...
```

The kMS then locally searches for a registered activity having an interface

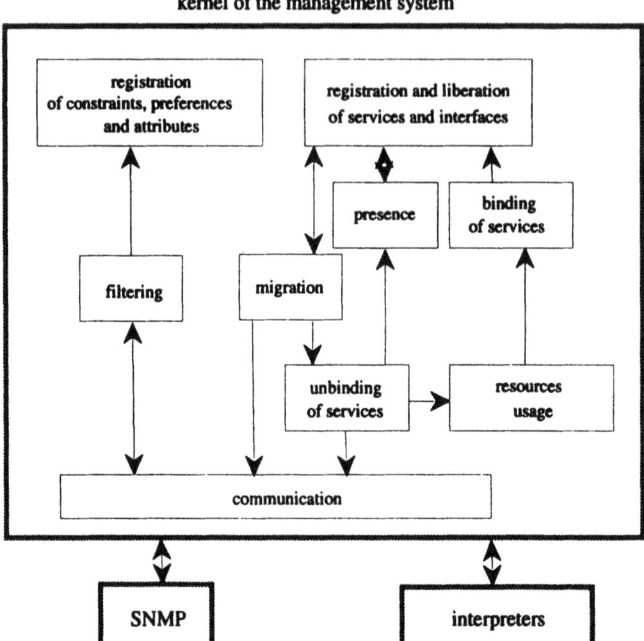

Figure 5 Major components of the kMS

conformant with the editor interface. An activity locally known by the kMS to conform to an editor/compiler/linker interface, thus including the editor interface, can be selected.

The arrival of the editing context triggers a set of management functions. One of them will set the printer to use in this context.

This is done by the triplet: **(from: ANY, method: enter, arg=editor interface)** tied to the function:

```
send("printerToUse", "my-favorite-printer")
```

We will present three management functions for the printer. The first one is initiated by the user of the editor, the other two by the owner of the printer, comparable to the only authorized manager in traditional management schemes: we will assume that the printer belongs to `root` in the rest of this section.

Firstly, we notice that the printer `my-favorite-printer` can be managed according to its known interface:

```
paper: boolean
state: integer // -1:error, 0:ready, 1:busy, 2:not responding
force
```

We assume that the user management function is in fact pain-relieving and will translate its data into a standard two columns Postscript form.

This will be achieved by the introduction of a management function acting by the mean of an output filter which translates the text data to be printed in the required form:

```
filter: (Editor of U, "print", ANY)
code: process(msg) {
        data = getArguments(1, msg);
        ps_data = enscript2rGh(data);
        out(msgHeader, msgMethod, ps_data);
        }
```

This management function is created in the context of `root`, the owner of the printer, as depicted in Figure 6.

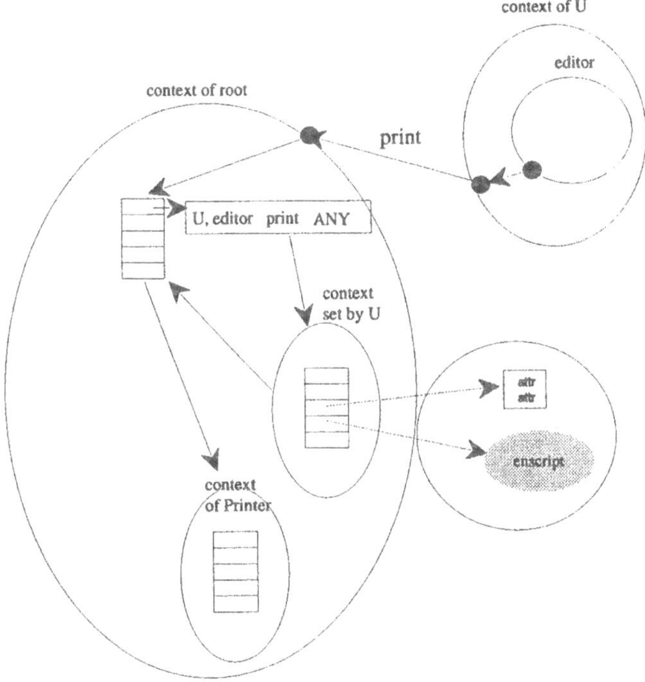

Figure 6 Contexts state after insertion of the user `U` management function

So, anyone can use the management system for its own needs according to its privileges. But, simultaneously, other management functions can coexist around the printer context: for example, management functions introduced by the owner of the printer.

Let's consider two of them. The first one monitors the requests sent to the printer and logs them; the second one automatically solves the paper size trouble (A4 paper *versus* US legal paper), forcing the printing with the actual paper.

The monitoring function is a filter put by `root` around the printer, defined by the triplet `(from=ANY, method="print", arg=ANY)`. The function attached to this filter will in turn locate the sender of the message and displays its name on the administrator's console or logs it in a file.

This function, initiated by the owner of the printer is put in a low level context around the context of the managed printer.

It can be noticed that, because the context of the printer is diped in the printer owner context, a kind of priority between management functions is implicitly induced: highest priorities for the system and the owner of the application, lowest priorities for other users.

This way, the monitoring function is placed closer to the context of the printer than the user management function (Cf. Figure 7).

The management function in charge of recovering paper size troubles acts in a different way. Let's assume that this dysfunction is not notified by an event (which would then be catched by a management output filter function), and that we are faced to an interface in which such a trouble is only notified by the setting of the variable `printerError` to `PAPERSIZE_ERROR`.

In such a realistic scheme, the paper size management function is achieved with a *variable filter*, this filter checks the condition:

```
printerError == PAPERSIZE_ERROR
```

and triggers the `force` operation when it becomes true.

In this example, we showed that the management allows to automatize the recover of the cumbersome paper size trouble; whereas incoming requests are monitored and any user may put a processing function for it's own convenience.

6 INTEGRATION INTO SNMP

As we want our management system to operate upon existing tools, it is important to incorporate a prototype into the popular SNMP framework. Integration under CMIP would be very similar and SNMP is preferred to SNMPv2, far less popular. Integration under SNMP is achieved by *Smux* (Rose 1991) protocol capabilities and is based on a complete ASN-1 description of the kMS, and as a consequence of the different entities presented in § 3.

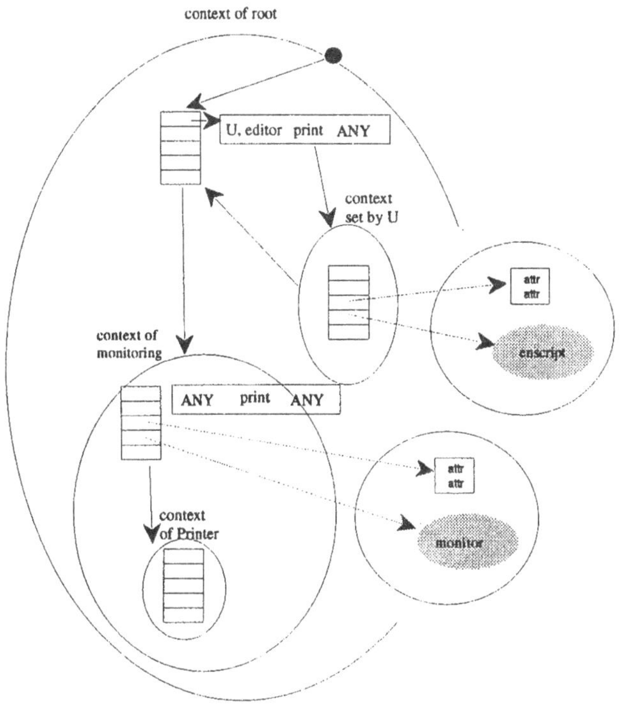

Figure 7 Contexts state after insertion of the monitoring management function

The obtention of the kMS mib isn't a straightforward process. It needs to use both complex indirections (Waldbusser 1991) and multi-types entries (Case & Levi 1993).

Though this description deals with kMS entities, it doesn't solve the interface aspects. Interfaces describe variables and method signatures that entities support. As long as this kind of description is usually achieved using the TYPE-OBJECT macro, interfaces appear to compete with this macro: we could call them *virtual MIBs*.

To be coherent with SMI and SNMP, object identifiers (*OBJ-IDs*) tied to variables and methods described by an interface must be MIB conformant and accessible for clients:

— kMS translate* variables to their equivalent ASN-1 representations, and methods to SNMP groups, according to the SNMP naming policy. From the

*This scheme can be altered as we can explicitely associate OBJ-IDs to variables or method's signatures.

mib point of view, the resulting object identifiers are always set to constant locations, relatively to the context.

— Clients have to know the virtual mib built from the interface, as this information is necessary to properly encode or decode SNMP operation arguments. This process is dynamic and can only be determinated at run time. For each interface OBJ-ID of the virtual mib, the Mib-manager sends a client-specific SNMP-trap from which the client updates its mib knowledge. Figure 8 shows the interaction between the Mib manager and kMS.

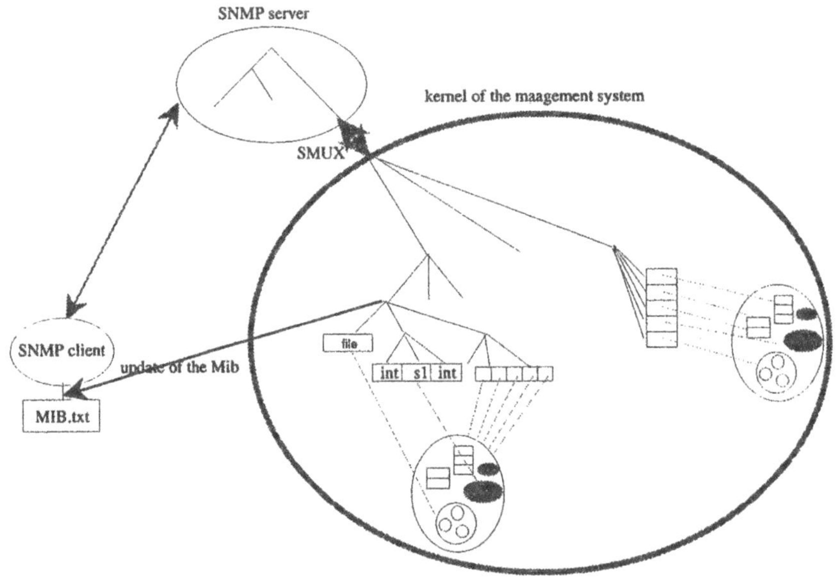

Figure 8 Integration with SNMP

From the Mib-manager point of view, kMS appears as a proprietary mib interacting with Smux, whereas kMS creates for any SNMP-client a context by which the client can interact over the whole management system.

Integration in SNMP gives the human administrator several possibilities to manage applications:

- by building new management functions or activating already existing ones (under both SNMP and kMS control security access),
- by calling over the network a complete management package: the packed management functions will first obey the administrator context environment constraints and then start the application management.

7 CONCLUSION

Although network management is nowadays world widely available, software application management is still under development.

From the basically *Integrated environments* architecture scheme, we demonstrated that applications modelized from active objects provide an homogeneous framework containing both management entities and their description. The system introduced appears to be evolutive and customizable while the frozen *MIB* notion has been reconsidered.

In spite of differences between applications and network management, opportunities offered by standardized management protocols has enabled the application management system to be integrated within existing network management tools.

REFERENCES

Agha, G. (1986), *Actors: a model of concurrent computation in distributed systems*, MIT Press, Cambridge Mass.

Boyer, F. (1994), Coordination entre outils dans un environnement intégré de développement de logiciels, PhD thesis, Bull-Imag et Université J.Fourier.

Brockschmidt, K. (1995), *Inside OLE, 2nd edition*, Microsoft Press.

Brun, P. (1987), Conférence répartie en mode messagerie, PhD thesis, Ecole des Mines et Université de St-Etienne.

Case, J., Fedor, M. & al. (1990), Simple network management protocol (SNMP), Technical report, IAB.

Case, J. & Levi, D. (1993), SNMP mid-level-manager MIB, Technical report, SNMP Research, Inc.

Chapman, M., Dupy, F. & Nilson, G. (1995), 'Overview of the telecommunications information networking architecture', *Tina'95* .

Danielsen, T., Pankoke, U. & al. (1986), 'The amigo project: advanced group communication model for computer-based communication environment', *CSCW 86 proceedings* .

Hewitt, C. (1977), 'Viewing control as patterns of passing messages', *Artificial Intelligence* .

ISO (1989), Information processing systems, open systems interconnection, Technical Report 7498-4, ISO management framework.

Kaddour, B. & Beigbeder, M. (1996), 'Application management by active objects', *Ecoop, workshop on network management* .

Lieberman, H. (1986), 'Using prototypical objects to implement shared behavior in object oriented systems', *OOPSLA* .

Nierstrasz, O. (1993), 'Regular types for active objects', *OOPSLA 93* .

O.M.G. (1991), The common object request broker: Architecture and specification, Technical report, Object Management Group.

Reiss, S. (1990), 'Connecting tools using message passing in the field environment', *IEEE software* .

Rollin, F. (1986), Transfert de fichiers en mode messagerie, PhD thesis, Ecole des Mines et Université de St-Etienne.

Rose, M. (1991), SNMP MUX protocol and MIB, Technical report, IAB.

Stein, L. (1987), 'Delegation is inheritance', *OOPSLA* .

Venkatasubramanian, N. & Talcott, C. (1993), A meta-architecture for distributed ressource management, Technical report, Univerty of Illinois - Stanford University.

Waldbusser, S. (1991), Remote network monitoring management information base, Technical report, IAB.

24

A study of Specialized Resource Function mapping alternatives for Integrated IN/B-ISDN architectures

G. T. Kolyvas, S. E. Polykalas, I. S. Venieris
Electrical & Computer Engineering Department
National Technical University of Athens
9 Heroon Polytechniou Str., 157 73 Zographou, Athens, Greece
Phone (30) 1-772 2551 Fax. (30) 1- 772 2534
e_mail: ivenieri@cc.ece.ntua.gr

Abstract

The introduction of Intelligent Network (IN) functionality to broadband networks with conventional signalling systems allows the fast and future safe provision of advanced multimedia services. Since novel services will require intense interactions with the network resulting in the exchange of a high number of control messages, the distribution of IN functional entities to network elements becomes a dominant factor in the overall system performance. In this paper we analyze the functions required for an integrated IN/B-ISDN architecture and develop a set of models for representing protocols and IN functional entities. Our purpose is to identify the system bottlenecks and to evaluate alternatives for functional to physical entity mapping that allow the most efficient operation of the system. Emphasis is given to the Specialized Resource Function entity location.

Keywords

Intelligent Networks, Intelligent Peripheral, functionality mapping, performance evaluation

Intelligent Networks and Intelligence in Networks D. Gaiti (Ed.)
Published by Chapman & Hall

1 INTRODUCTION

The Intelligent Network (IN) concept provides a flexible and modular methodology for the description and specification design and implementation of complex multimedia services. Services are created by establishing relations among Service Independent Functions in a manner that guarantees a high degree of transparency with respect to both the service implementation and the underlying physical network infrastructure. This flexibility allows network operators to upgrade their systems easily and in a cost effective fashion by taking advantage of the ability to allocate IN functionality and resources within the network without restrictions.
A tentative task in the design of an IN-based architecture is the distribution of IN functions to physical entities. In principle a physical entity is a functional group which can include service, interconnect and communications functions. A physical entity may provide the entire set of functions or a subset of them. IN functions inside a physical entity are organised into functional entities. A functional entity can be present in more than one physical entities but it cannot be split among multiple physical entities.
In this paper we investigate alternatives for the mapping of IN functional to physical entities for the case of an integrated IN/B-ISDN architecture (Hussmann, 1995), (Wu, 1995). The IN functional entities that participate in the exchange and process of the control information related to the request and provision of an IN service are the Call Control Function (CCF), the Service Switching Function (SSF) which identifies IN calls and triggers the service logic in the Service Control Function (SCF), the Specialized Resource Function (SRF) which manages the communication between the user and the IN, and the Service Data Function (SDF) containing service and call related data. The physical entities of the IN/B-ISDN network are the Broadband Service Switching Point (B-SSP) which is a typical ATM switch enhanced with the ability to recognize IN service requests and to communicate with IN entities and the B-Service Control Point (B-SCP) which provides the IN service related functionality. While CCF and SSF are always located in the B-SSP and SCF in the B-SCP, the SRF can be found either in an integrated B-SSP or in a separate B-Intelligent Peripheral (B-IP). Similarly the SDF can be located either in the B-SCP or in a separate B-Service Data Point (B-SDP). The location of these functional entities is an important issue with an impact on the architecture, topology and scalability of the IN/B-ISDN system.
Apart from the IN functional entities, the physical entities should also contain appropriate signalling protocols enabling the establishment and release of bearer connections for IN service calls. In the IN/B-ISDN system under study, the signalling protocols are those currently standardized for B-ISDN, that is the Q.2931 protocol in the UNI (ITU-T, Q.2931) and the B-ISUP (B-ISDN User Part) in the NNI (ITU-T, Q.2761).

The purpose of this paper is to provide performance driven guidelines for the design of IN based broadband networks. Similar work has been performed in the framework of Signalling System No 7 (SS7) and B-ISDN signalling protocols (Bafutto, 1994), (Lazar, 1994), (Veeraraghavan, 1995), (Veeraraghavan), (Willmann, 1990), (Xou, 1994), (La Porta, 1993) notwithstanding that in our case the integrated service facilities and the employment of IN capabilities necessitate more complex user-to-network and network-to-network transaction models (Hussmann, 1995). Our study undertakes issues related to the scalability of the IN broadband network by investigating and comparing alternatives for the mapping of SRF to physical entities. Since our emphasis is mainly placed on the quantitative than the qualitative analysis, we develop a set of models for evaluating the performance of the system in terms of the maximum number of admitted calls and the call set up delay. Despite the many alternatives for distributing functional entities to physical entities, the IN communication protocols (i.e. B-Intelligent Network Application Part - B-INAP (ITU-T, Q.1218)) and the functionality of the functional entities are almost stable or at least on their way of standardization. Therefore modeling of the functional entities can be performed independently of their location and furthermore the physical entity model can be derived as a combination of the standalone functional entities models.
The paper is organized as follows: In Section 2 we present the alternatives for the mapping of functional to physical entities and the resulting network architectures of an IN-based B-ISDN which are evaluated in the rest of the paper. Section 3 includes a set of detailed models developed to accurately describe functional entities and signalling protocols. The interaction among physical entities as well as the sequence of events in the functional entities are defined in Section 4 for a typical Broadband Video on Demand (B-VoD) call establishment and release. The performance results of Section 5 are discussed and evaluated giving input to a number of conclusions regarding system design options summarized in Section 6.

2 MAPPING OF IN FUNCTIONAL ENTITIES TO NETWORK PHYSICAL ENTITIES

The generic network configuration model of the IN-based B-ISDN signalling system contains all those physical entities that contribute to the establishment and provision of an IN service (ITU-T, Q.1214). These entities are the user terminal (e.g. a set top box or an ATM PC), the B-SSP, the B-SCP and the service provider which in the case of an interactive B-VoD service is the Video Server (VS). The B-SSP can be an integrated B-SSP in which case it includes not only the CCF and SSF functional entities but also the SRF, or a simple B-SSP. In the latter case a B-IP is required to provide the necessary specialized resources to the user. The emerging alternatives for the generic network configuration with respect to the location of the SRF functional entity are illustrated in Figure 1. In alternative A the path between the user terminal and the VS is shown to involve an integrated B-SSP,

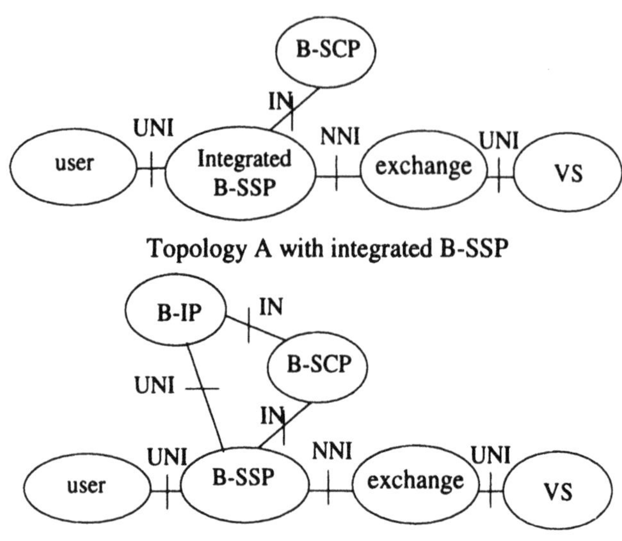

Mapping of Functional Entities to Physical Entities

Figure 1 Alternatives for an IN-based B-ISDN network configuration

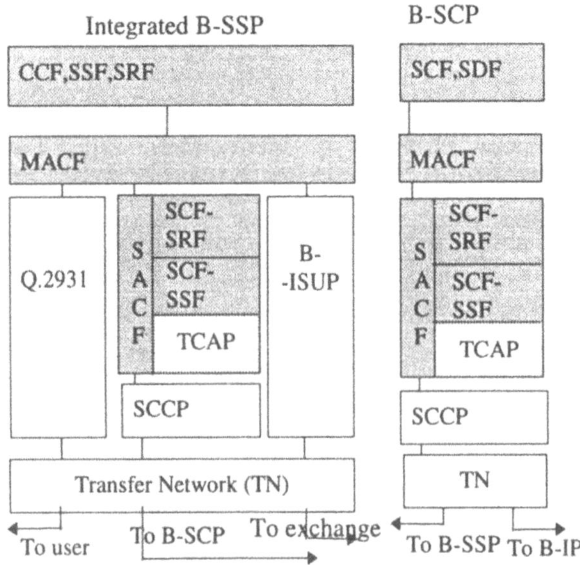

Figure 2 Protocol stacks for alternative A.

a B-SCP and an exchange. In alternative B, the B-SSP is not integrated however a B-IP is now present. The interface between the user terminal and the B-SSP is a

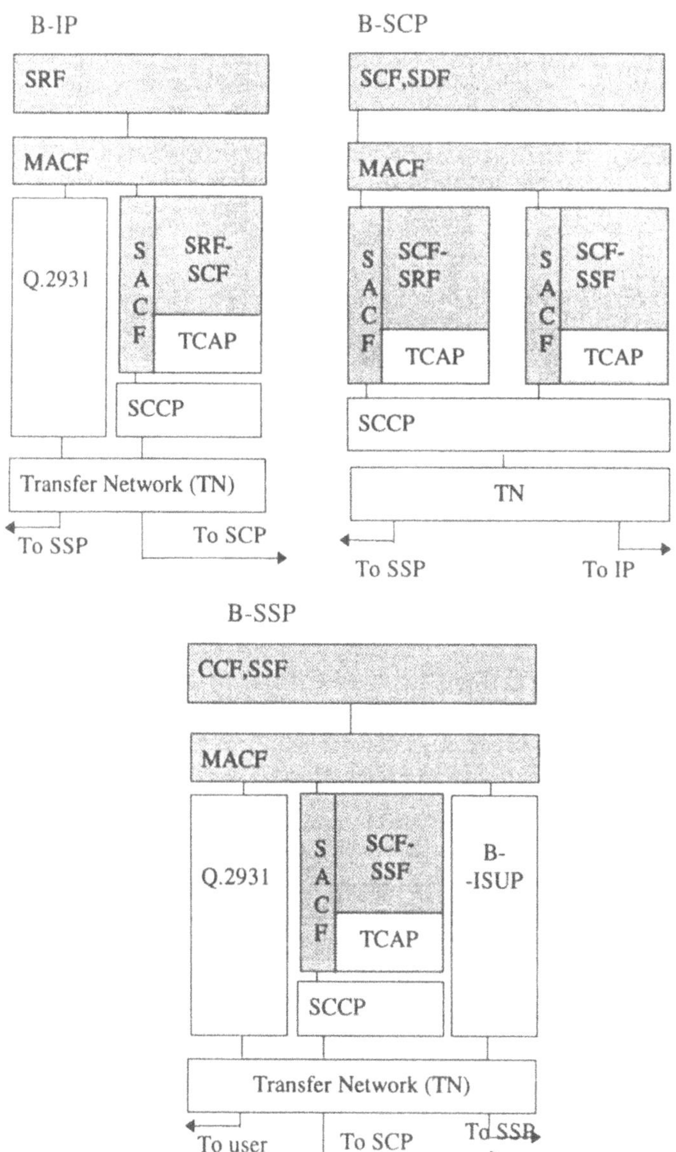

Figure 3 Protocol stacks for alternative B.

broadband UNI with Q.2931, Signalling ATM Adaptation Layer (S-AAL) (ITU-T, Q.1200), and ATM protocols and between the B-SSP and the exchange a broadband NNI with B-ISUP and Message Transfer Part 3 (MTP-3) (ITU-T, Q.701) over S-AAL protocols . The B-SCP is connected to the B-SSP through an IN interface supporting B-INAP operations (ITU-T, Q.1218) at the upper level and

Transaction Capability Application Part (TCAP) (ITU-T, Q.771) and Signalling Connection Control Part (SCCP) protocols (ITU-T, Q.711) at the lower level lying over the transfer network. In alternative B the user is connected to the B-IP through the B-SSP with a UNI protocol and the B-IP to the B-SCP through an IN interface with the same stack as the one of the B-SCP. The detailed protocol stacks of the physical entities are illustrated in Figures 2 and 3 for alternatives A and B respectively.

3 FUNCTIONAL ENTITY AND SIGNALLING PROTOCOL MODELS

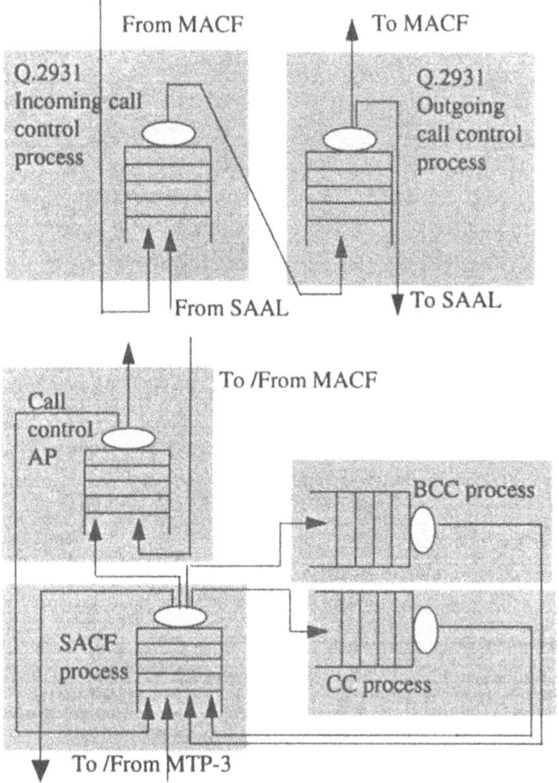

Figure 4 Q.2931/B-ISUP Models.

Since the focus of this paper is on the upper signalling and IN protocol layers, the transfer network is not modeled in detail; i.e., only the protocol overhead added in each layer is taken into account to determine the number of cells a signalling message is segmented into, while for each of the functional entities and the upper signalling protocols that are involved in a call set up and release phase of an IN service, a model is developed. The model includes the protocol layer functions, as well as the information flow among protocols and the protocol internal functions. The servers of each queue illustrated in Figures 4-7 represent the processes activated in each functional entity or protocol. We assume that a single processor serves the entire functional entity or protocol and that time sharing among processes is exercised by a scheme of priorities.

Q.2931 Model. The Q.2931 model is illustrated in Figure 4. The call/connection processing control has been divided in two processes, the incoming and outgoing call/connection process.

B-ISUP model. On account of the fact that in our study we focus on the IN functionality and performance, we have assumed that IN and signalling messages pass transparently over the network transfer part. Therefore we are not interested in compatibility and maintenance functions of the B-ISUP but only in the call and bearer connection control functions. So, the model of Figure 4 consists of the BCC, CC ASEs, the SACF and the call control AP. When the SACF receives a message, it distributes information to ASEs according to the protocol rules. The output from the ASEs is received by the SACF which forwards an appropriate message to the application process or to the underlying MTP-3 protocol layer.

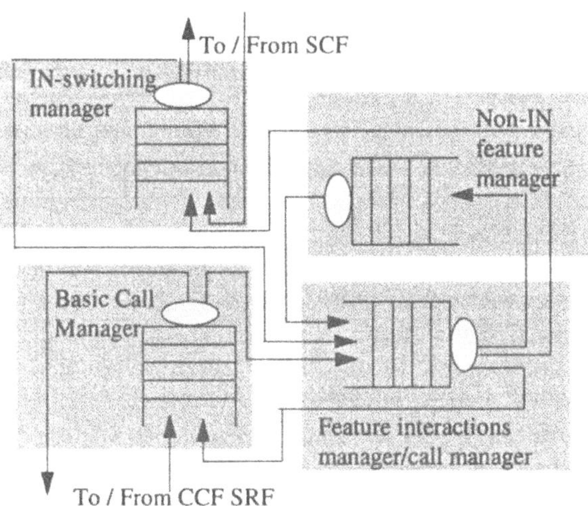

Figure 5 CCF/SSF Model.

CCF/SSF Model. The CCF/SSF Model of Figure 5 consists of the Basic Call Manager (BCM), the Feature Interactions Manager/Call Manager (FIM/CM), the Non-IN Feature Manager (NIFM), and the IN-Switching Manager (IN-SM).

The BCM detects basic call and connection control events that can lead to the invocation of IN service logic instances or should be reported to active IN service logic instances. The IN-SM interacts with the SCF in the course of providing IN service features to users. It detects IN call/connection processing events that should

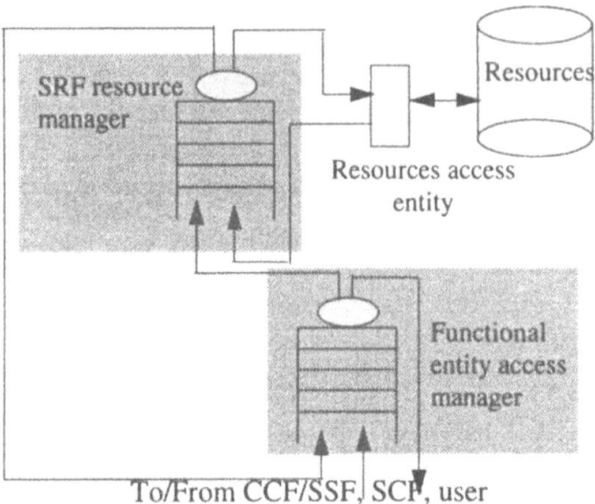

Figure 6 SRF Model.

be reported to active IN service logic instances. The FIM-CM provides mechanisms to support multiple concurrent instances of IN service logic instances and non-IN service logic instances on a single call. The NIFM executes the non-IN service logic instance.

SRF Model. The SRF model of Figure 6 consists of two components: the Functional Entity Access Manager (FEAM) which provides the necessary functionality to exchange information with other functional entities and the SRF Resource Manager SRF-RM which manages resources contained in the SRF.

SCF Model. The SCF model of Figure 7 consists of five sub-models and two libraries. These are the Functional Entity Access Manager (FEAM), the Service Logic Program Manager (SLPM), the Service Logic Execution Manager (SLEM), the Functional Routine Manager (FRM), the SCF Data Access Manager (SCF-DAM), the Functional Entity Access Manager (FEAM) and the Service Logic Program (SLP) and Functional Routine (FR) Libraries. The FEAM provides the necessary functionality to exchange information with other functional entities and interacts with all the other service managers inside the SCF model. The SLPM manages the reception and distribution function of Service Logic Programs (SLPs) from other entities. The FRM is used for reception and distribution of functional routines to functional routine library via the library access entity. The SCF-DAM provides the functionality to storage, management and access of shared and persistent information in the SCF and the functionality to access remote information in SDFs. It interacts with the SLEM to provides these functionality. The SLEM handles and controls the total service logic execution and interacts with SCF-DAM. It also has access to SLP and FR libraries via the corresponding access entities in order to support the service logic execution.

SDF Model. The SDF model consists of two components the Functional Entity Access Manager (FEAM) which provides the necessary functionality to exchange information with other functional entities and the SDF Data Manager (SDF-DM)

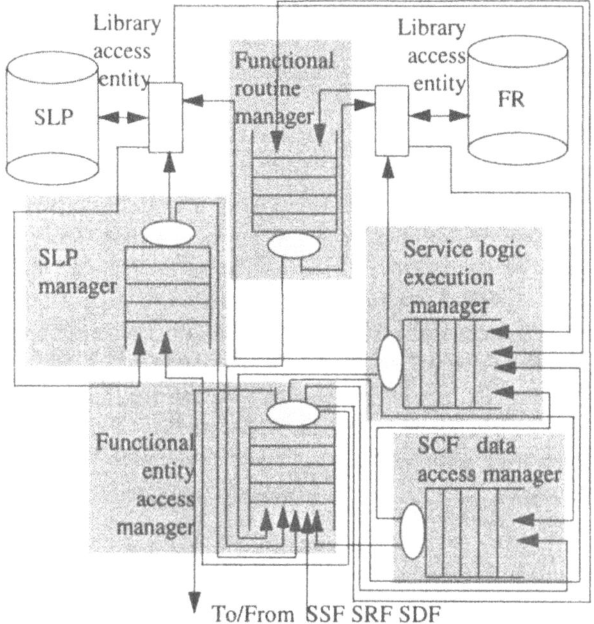

Figure 7 SCF Model.

which provides the necessary functionality to manage data contained in the SDF. It is modeled analogously to the SRF model (Figure 6).

4 MESSAGE FLOWS AND WORKLOAD DEFINITION

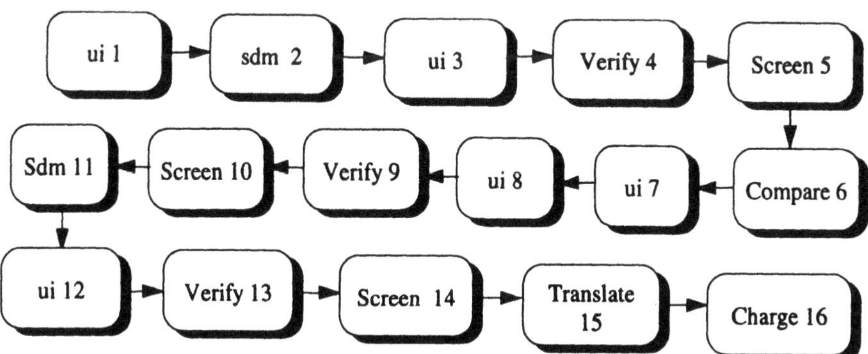

Figure 8 Global Service Logic for valid user's selections for B-VoD service.

The information flows among protocols and functional entities define the workload of the models presented so far. For simple signalling protocols that support a restricted number of well known services the information flows can be easily

defined. The IN capability of the signalling network allows for services with very different characteristics in terms of protocol and functional entities interactions and the task of providing the detailed message flows becomes more difficult as this should be performed separately for each service.
Using the Global Functional Model (GFM) (ITU-T, Q.1203) we develop the Global Service Logic (GSL) of a typical B-VoD service from which the information flow among the functional entities of the system is derived. Initially the user is connected to a SRF in order to select a VS. Upon selection the connection is released and the user is connected to the VS for content selection. The process of the VS selection is shown by SIBs ui-1 to ui-7 in Figure 8, while the content selection by the remaining SIBs. In sequence, service control is passed to the Basic Call Process of the SSF which issues a B-ISUP IAM (Initial Address Message) to the VS to establish a connection between the user and the VS for video delivery. In the B-VoD service example the B-SCP orders the B-SSP to establish one connection between the user and the B-IP and two connections between the user and the VS, one for the controlling the video play and one for receiving video.

5 PERFORMANCE RESULTS

5.1 System Parameters

The models presented in Section 3 can be used to obtain performance results either by analysis or simulation. Analytical models are based on the aggregation and decomposition principle: Each protocol layer of a stack is studied with an individual model. The aggregation of individual results leads to the estimation of the system performance. To obtain analytical solutions the Poisson assumption is usually employed (see for example developments in (Bafutto, 1994), (Veeraraghavan), (Willmann, 1990), (Bafutto, 1992), (Bafutto, 1993), (Ghosal, 1995)). Along this line arrivals at each protocol are modeled as Poisson. In the following we use the M/G/1 model with feedback and non-preemptive service priorities (Simon, 1984), (Paterok, 1989). The simulation programs were run on a Sun 20 workstation with a Sun 4.1.4 OS. A total of 250 secs of system time has been simulated which corresponds to 25,000 calls for the maximum call rate. For lower call rates the simulated system time was in the order of 1,000 s. The total CPU time to obtain all results was about four hours.
Two types of services are considered in our performance evaluation study, that is a simple telephony service requiring no IN functionality and a typical IN-based B-VoD service which makes use of the IN functions in the manner described in Section 4. Traffic scenarios consist of mixed traffic of the aforementioned services; i.e. 85% of telephony and 15% of B-VoD. The maximum traffic load considered is equal to 80% of the Busy Hour Call Attempts (BHCA) of one exchange measured in the Singapore national SS7 network (Lazar, 1994). In the analysis external arrivals are modeled as Poisson for each protocol model while in the simulation this

assumption is only used for user initiated external call arrivals at the B-SSP (Bafutto, 1994), (Willmann, 1990), (Smith, 1994), (Lekkou). For the B-VoD service we assume movies with a mean length of 110 minutes (Ghafir, 1994). Users either watch the whole movie (i.e. duration time of the call equal to 110 minutes) or stop the movie 5 minutes after their selection. Therefore the B-VoD duration (*d*) in the simulation follows a constant distribution with d=110 min with probability p_1=0.85 and d=5 min with probability p_2=0.15. The duration of telephony follows a mixture of two normal distributions on logarithmic time scale, as described below:

$$F(t) = \beta \cdot F_1(t) + (1-\beta)F_2(t) \quad (1)$$

Realistic values for the parameters of the distribution in (1) are given in (Bolotin, 1994):. mean call duration 150 sec, $\beta = 0.4$, $\mu_1 = 1.31$, $\sigma_1 = 0.33$, $\mu_2 = 2.11$, $\sigma_2 = 0.5$.

Table 1 Process time T (ms), process priority ps

SCF			*BISUP*			*SSF/CCF*		
proc	*T(ms)*	*ps*	*proc*	*T(ms)*	*ps*	*proc*	*T(ms)*	*ps*
FEAM	0.3	1	SACF	0.3	4	BCM	0.5	3
SLEM	1.5	2	BCC	1.0	2	FIM	1.0	2
DAM	0.5	5	CC	0.5	3	INSM	1.0	1
SLP_L	0.5	3	AP	0.5	1			
FRL	0.5	4						

Table 2 Process time T (ms), process priority ps

SCF			*SRF*			*SDF*		
proc	*T(ms)*	*ps*	*proc*	*T(ms)*	*ps*	*proc*	*T(ms)*	*ps*
Inc	0.15	2	FEAM	0.3	2	FEAM	0.3	2
Outg.	0.25	1	RM	0.5	1	DM	0.5	1

In both analytical model and simulation we assume constant service times. The service times per protocol process and the process priority within a functional

entity or protocol appear in Tables 1 and 2. The priorities of Tables 1 and 2 are defined according to the following rules: The internal process with the higher utilization that is crossed by multiple itineraries is always allocated the higher priority. If there is no process with the above features two cases are distinguished: if there are more than one processes that accepts external messages the process with the lower utilization due to external arrivals is allocated the higher priority. If there is only one process that accepts external messages the process with the lower utilization is allocated the higher priority. The B-ISUP processing times were defined using as input the values of (Veeraraghavan, 1995) for the time a message type spends in the entire protocol. Taking into account the nature of the specific processes activated when a message type enters the protocol machine, the protocol type has been decomposed into the process time components of Tables 1 and 2. The Q.2931, CCF/SSF, SCF, SRF and SDF processing times have been defined according to the functions of each process using input from (Veeraraghavan). The message transfer delay between different network elements has been calculated as the time required to transmit the mean number of cells, a Q.2931, B-ISUP and B-INAP signalling message is translated into, in a 1.5 Mbps signalling channel (Veeraraghavan, 1995). The mean message length is calculated for all involving signalling and IN protocols and it is equal to two ATM cells, including the overhead of the underlying transfer protocols. The inter-message delay of successive user or server generated messages is assumed to be 100 ms.
The metric used to capture the performance of the signalling system is the mean delay per protocol layer, functional and physical entity as well as the end-to-end mean set up delay; i.e., the time between a set-up message is issued by a user to the time a video channel is established from the VS to the user for B-VoD, and to the time a connect message is received by the user for telephony. Two sets of results are presented. The first captures the performance of signalling protocols and IN functional entities. The second set of results presents delays per signalling and/or IN network element as well as end-to-end delays. Both alternatives regarding the location of the SRF location are considered.

5.2 Protocol and functional entity delay

In Figures 9 and 10 the B-SSP, B-IP and exchange Q2931 mean delay is shown. We see that the Q.2931 delay is almost the same in the exchange (Figure 10) for both alternatives, while in the B-SSP the delay is slightly higher for alternative B. The reason is that the Q.2931 protocol is also activated for the communication between the B-SSP and the B-IP.
In Figures 11 and 12 the B-SSP, and the exchange B-ISUP mean delay is shown. Since the number of messages handled by these protocols is the same for both alternatives, the B-ISUP delay is kept almost stable.

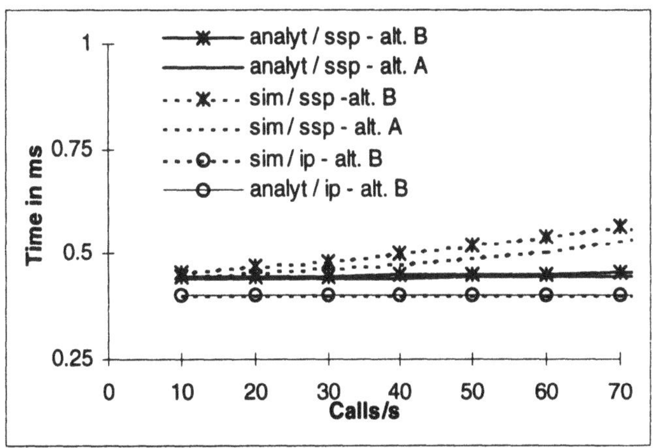

Figure 9 B-SSP / B-IP Q.2931 mean delay.

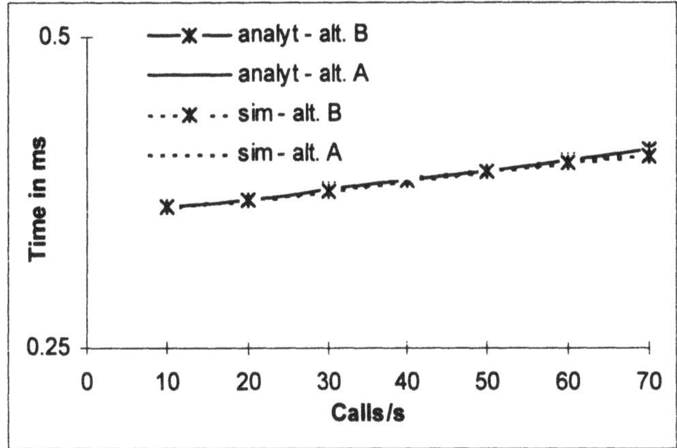

Figure 10 exchange Q.2931 mean delay.

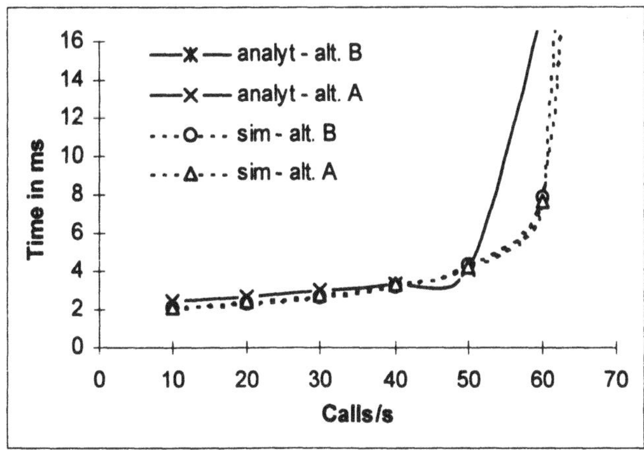

Figure 11 B-SSP B-ISUP mean delay.

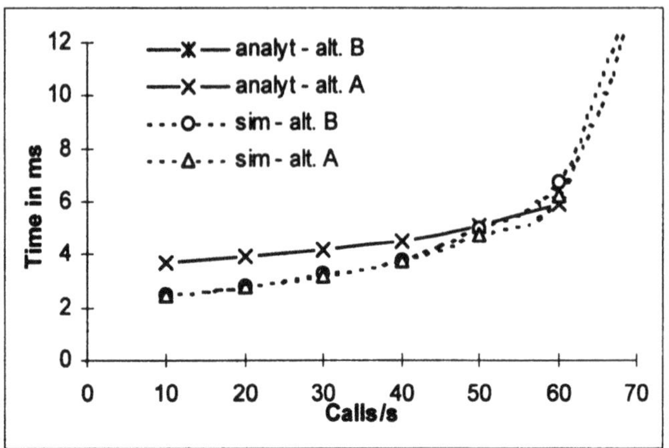

Figure 12 exchange B-ISUP mean delay.

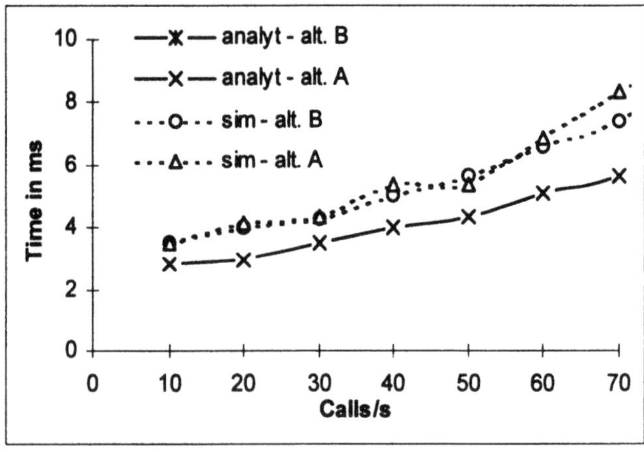

Figure 13 B-SCF mean delay.

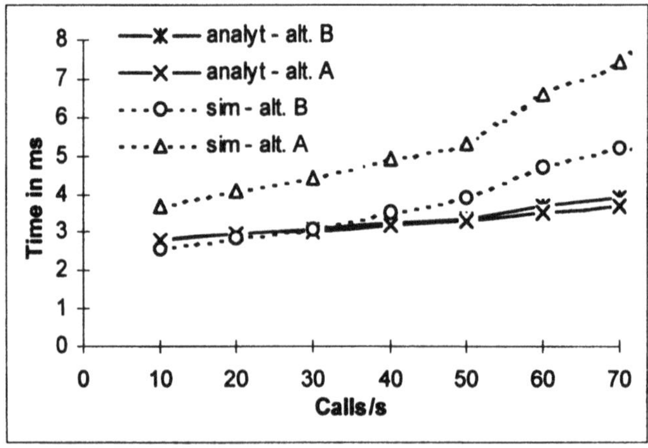

Figure 14 B-CCF/SSF mean delay.

In Figure 13 the B-SCF mean delay is illustrated. Again the delay is the same in both alternatives, while the differences between the analytical and simulation results are due to the correlated nature of the IN messages arrived at the B-SCF. The Poisson assumption adopted in the analysis cannot accurately represent the IN message arrivals.

In Figure14 the B-CCF/SSF mean delay is shown. Again the correlated nature of the IN messages arrived at the B-SSF justify the differences between simulation and analysis. We see that in simulation alternative B presents lower delay. This can be explained by consulting the message flow diagrams. In alternative B, messages entering the B-SSF present higher interarrival times while in alternative A arrivals appear more bursty. These differences can not be derived from the analysis where we assume Poisson arrivals.

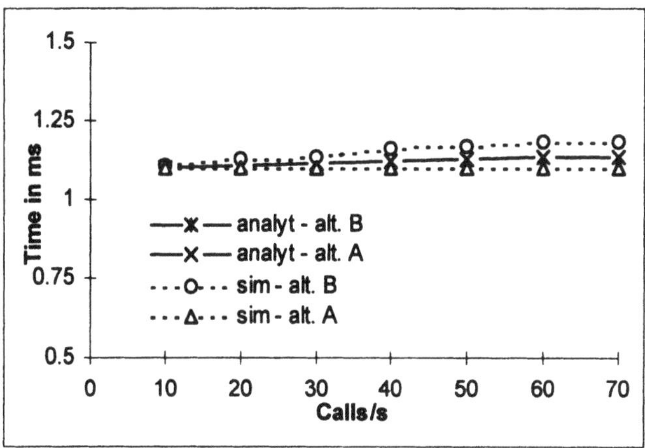

Figure 15 B-SRF mean delay.

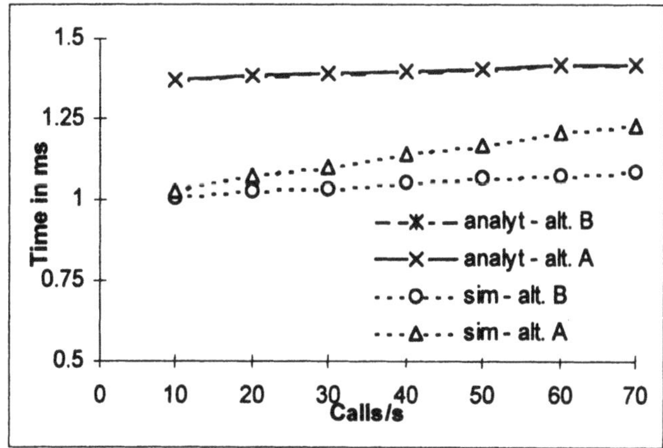

Figure 16 B-SDF mean delay.

In Figure 15 the SRF mean delay is illustrated. We see that for both alternatives the delay is the same, since the load of the functional entity does not change. The same holds also for the SDF mean delay in Figure 16.
From the above figures it becomes apparent that the delay of protocols and functional entities do not vary with alternative A and B. Also we can see that the B-ISUP protocol determines the maximum number of calls that can be processed by the network. Therefore, while the SRF can serve more than 70 calls/s, the B-ISUP protocol of the B-SSP restricts this number to 60 calls/s. This means that the same SRF can be used to serve more than one B-SSPs with acceptable performance which becomes possible only in alternative B.

5.3 Physical entity and end-to-end delay

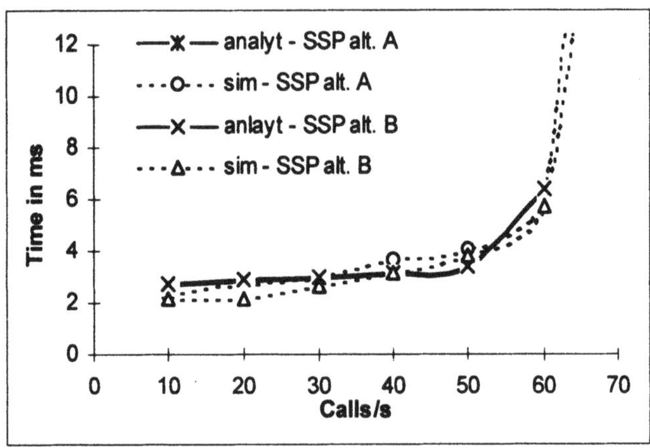

Figure 17 B-SSP mean delay.

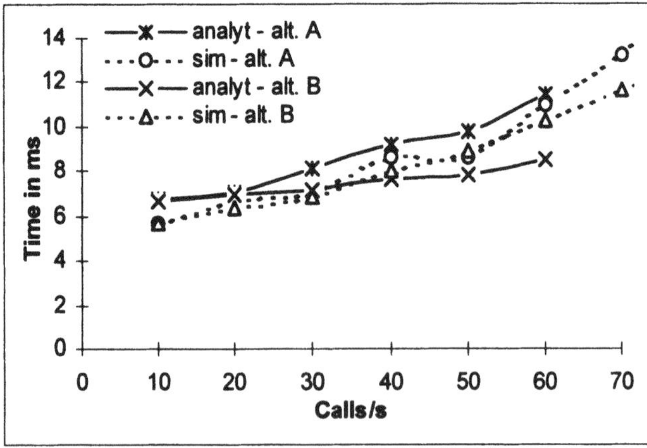

Figure 18 B-SCP mean delay.

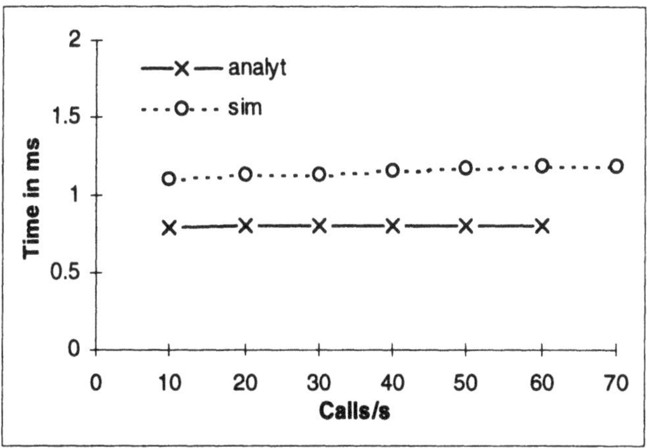

Figure 19 B-IP mean delay.

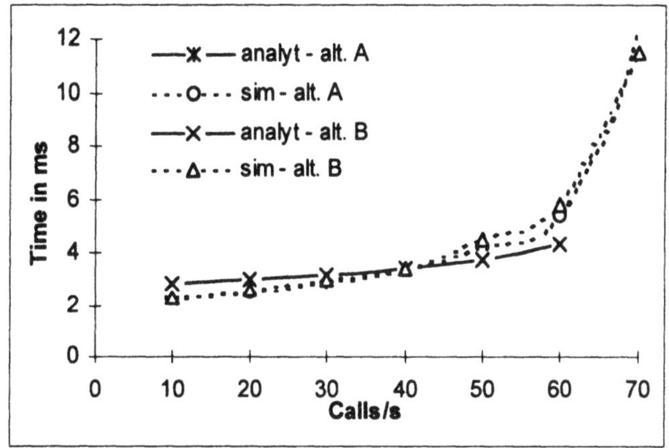

Figure 20 exchange mean delay.

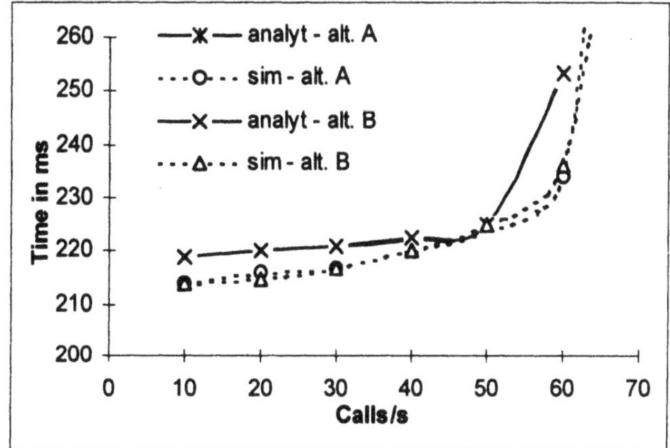

Figure 21 Telephony mean set-up delay.

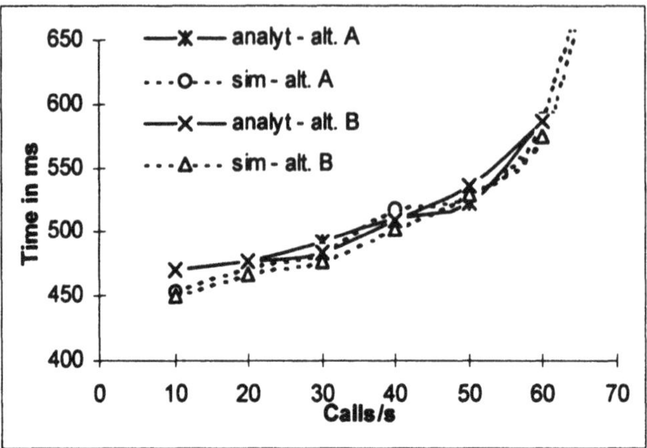

Figure 22 B-VoD mean set-up delay.

The remarks made for the functional entities also hold for the physical entities, where we can see that the delay is almost the same for both alternatives (see Figures 17-20). The B-IP mean delay is much lower than the B-SSP low, which further justifies the remark that the B-IP can support a considerably higher number of calls than the integrated B-SSP. We can also see that at the physical entity level the differences between results obtained by aggregating analytically calculated delay components and simulation become less intense and especially for the B-SSP which is located closer to the user and the exchange which does not process IN messages. Similar remarks can be made by consulting Figures 21 and 22 where we present the set-up delay for telephony and B-VoD respectively.

5.4 B-IP Maximum number of supported calls

In Figure 23 we plot the mean delay of a standalone B-IP corresponding to alternative B for different loads. As we have seen a B-SSP integrated or not can support up to 60 calls/s. Only 9 calls/s are B-VoD calls and are processed by the SRF. As shown in Figure 23 the B-IP can support up to 160 B-VoD calls/s which means that about 16 B-SSPs can use the same B-IP with acceptable performance. It is interesting to notice that even in the case where the processing times of the B-IP functional entities and protocols increase 10 times (*Tx10*), the B-IP can still support more calls than a B-SSP. This is shown in Figure 24 where we find that the calls supported by the B-IP extends to 19 B-VoD calls/s which is almost double than the corresponding number of the B-SSP.

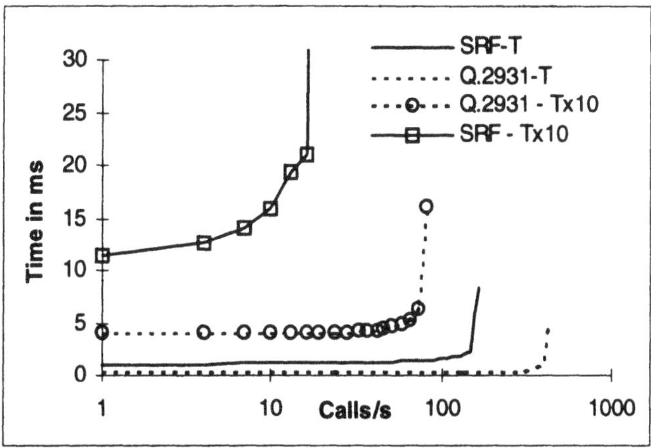

Figure 23 SRF, B-IP Q.2931 mean delay.

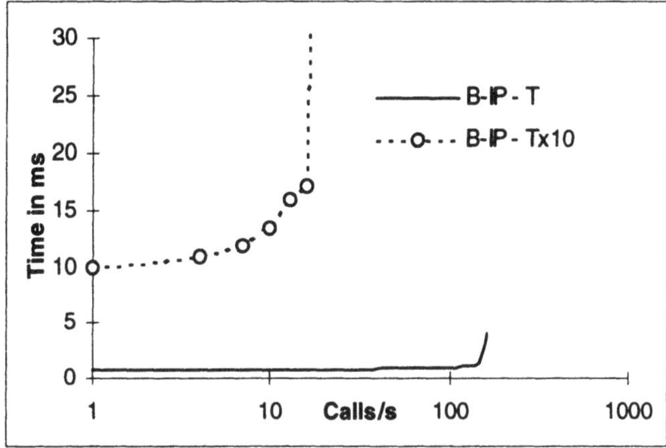

Figure 24 B-IP mean delay.

6 CONCLUSIONS

Several architectural issues of an IN/B-ISDN integrated system have been investigated in this paper from a performance viewpoint. To do so, a set of models for each functional entity and upper layer signalling protocols has been developed and information flows have been derived using the GSL methodology. The models are general enough to be used for other related performance studies. In our case the models have been used to capture the performance of all entities, functional or physical, involved in the establishment and release of an IN service call and to identify the most heavy loaded processes that constitute the system bottleneck. Special emphasis has been put on the location of the SRF for which two alternatives have been investigated. Our results have shown that for one B-SSP the performance of the system is almost stable independently of whether the SRF is embedded into an integrated and therefore more complex B-SSP or located in a standalone B-IP connected with a simpler B-SSP. Since the B-ISUP protocol inside the B-SSP is the one that determines the overall number of supported calls, the B-IP alternative becomes more advantageous as a single standalone B-IP can serve multiple non integrated and therefore less complex B-SSPs. The authors are currently engaged in the development of a B-IP which will be part of an integrated IN/B-ISDN transnational european broadband network built to realise multimedia IN services.

7 ACKNOWLEDGEMENT

This work was partially funded by the European Union Advanced Communication Technologies and Services (ACTS) Project INSIGNIA (IN and B-ISDN Signalling Integration on ATM Platforms) (INSIGNIA). The opinions appearing in this paper are those of the authors and not necessarily of the other members of the project consortium. The authors wish to express their gratitude to all members of the consortium for fruitful technical discussions.

8 REFERENCES

Bafutto, M., Kuehn, P. J. and Willmann, G. (1994) Capacity and Performance Analysis of Signaling Networks in Multivendor Environments. *IEEE J. Select. Areas Commun*, Vol. 12, No. 3, 490-500.

Hussmann, H., Straten, G.v.d., Theimer, Th. and Totzke, J. (1995) An IN-based Implementation of Interactive Video Service. *Proceedings of ICC'95*, Seattle.

Lazar, A.A., Tseng, K.H., Lim, K.S. and Choe, W. (1994) A Scalable and Reusable Emulator for Evaluating the Performance of SS7 Networks. *IEEE J. Select. Areas Commun.*, Vol. 12, No. 3.

Veeraraghavan, M., La Porta, T.F., and Lai, W.S. (1995) An Alternative Approach to Call/Connection Control in Broadband Switching Systems. *IEEE Commun. Mag.*, 90-96.

Veeraraghavan, M., Choudhury, G., and Kshirsagar, M. ( ) Implementation and Analysis of PCC (Parallel Connection Control), submitted for presentation.

Willmann, G., Kuhn, P.J., (1990) Performance Modeling of Signaling System No.7. *IEEE Commun. Mag.*, Vol. 28, No. 7, 44-56.

Bafutto, M., Kuhn, P.J. (1992) Capacity and Performance Analysis for Signaling Networks Supporting UPT. *Proceedings of Eighth ITC Specialist Seminar on Universal Personal Telecommunication,* Santa Margherita Ligure (Genova), Italy, Sess. VII, Paper 1, pp. 201-213.

Hou, X., Kalogeropoulos, N.D., Lekkou, M.E., Niemegeers, I.G., and Venieris, I.S. (1994) A Methodological Approach to B-ISDN Signaling Performance. *Int.J. of Commun.Sys.*, Special Issue: Signaling Protocols and Services for Broadband ATM Networks, Vol. 7, No. 2, 97-111.

Simon, B. (1984) Priority Queues with Feedback. *J. ACM*, Vol. 31, No. 1.
ITU-T, Rec. Q.2761-4, Broadband Integrated Services Digital Network User Part (BISUP), 1994.
ITU-T, Rec. Q.2931, Broadband Integrated Services Digital Network (B-ISDN). Digital Subscriber Signalling No.2 (DSS 2). User Network Interface Layer 3 Specification for Call/Connection Control, 1994.
ITU-T, Rec. Q1203, Intelligent Network Global Functional Plane Architecture, 1993.
ITU-T, Rec. Q1213, Global Functional Plane for Intelligent Network CS-1, 1993.
ITU-T, Rec. Q1214, Distributed Functional Plane for Intelligent Network CS-1, 1993.
ITU-T, Rec. Q1218, Interface Recommendations for Intelligent Network CS-1, 1993.
ITU-T, Rec. Q2100-30, B-ISDN Signalling ATM Adaptation Layer, 1994.
ITU-T, Rec. Q771-5, Signalling System No.7 - Transaction Capabilities (TCAP), 1993.
ITU-T, Rec. Q701, Functional description of the Message Transfer Part (MTP) of Signalling System No.7.
ITU-T, Rec. Q711-4, Signalling System No.7 - Signalling Connection Control Part (SCCP).
Smith, D. (1994) Effects of Feedback Delay on the Performance of the Transfer-Controlled Procedure in Controlling CCS Network Overloads. *IEEE J. Select. Areas Commun.*, Vol. 12, No.3.
Lekkou, M. and Venieris, I.S. A Workload Model for Performance Evaluation of Multimedia Signalling Systems. Accepted for publication in *Computer Communications*.
Bafutto, M. (1993) A Modelling Approach for the Intelligent Network Application Protocol. *Proceedings of the ITC Regional Seminar on Teletraffic Challenges for Developing Countries,* Brasilia, Brazil, 61-70.
Paterok, M. and Fisher, O. (1989) Feedback Queues with Preemption Distances Priorities. *ACM Sigmetrics Performance Evaluation Review,* Vol. 17, No. 1, 136-145.
La Porta, T.F. and Veeraraghavan, M. (1993) Evaluation of Broadband UNI Signaling Protocol Techniques. *Journal of High Speed Networks*, 2(3).
Ghafir, H. and Chadwich, H. (1994) Multimedia Servers - Design and Performance. *Proceedings of Globecom '94*, USA.
Bolotin, V. (1994) Modelling Call Holding Time Distributions for CCS Network Design and Performance Analysis. *IEEE J. Select. Areas Commun.*, Vol. 12, No.3, 433-438.
INSIGNIA project description (URL:http://www.fokus.gmd.de /nthp/ insignia/ entry.html).
Wu, T.-H., Yoshikai, N. and Fujii, H. (1995) ATM Signalling Transport Network Architectures and Analysis. *IEEE Commun. Mag.*.

Ghosal, D., Lakshman, T.V. and Huang, Y. (1995) Parallel Architectures for Processing High Speed Network Signalling Protocols. *IEEE/ACM Trans. Netw.*, Vol. 3, No. 6.

9 BIOGRAPHY

George T. Kolyvas was born in Corfu, Greece, in 1970. He received the Dipl.-Ing. degree from the Electrical Engineering Department of the University of Patras, Greece in 1993. He is currently a Ph.D. candidate in the Electrical and Computer Engineering Department of the National Technical University of Athens (NTUA), Athens, Greece. Mr. Kolyvas is a research assistant in the Telecommunications Laboratory of NTUA performing research in the area of B-ISDN access networks, signalling, multimedia service design, Intelligent Network technology, performance evaluation, modeling and queueing theory. He has participated in several European Union projects and is currently involved in the INSIGNIA AC068 project. Mr. Kolyvas has received several national awards for the entire five years of his undergraduate study. He is a member of IEEE and the Technical Chamber of Greece.

Spyros E. Polykalas was born in Kefalonia, Greece, in 1971. He received the Dipl. -Ing. Degree from the Electrical Engineering Department of the University of Patras, Greece in 1994. Since 1994 he is a Ph.D. candidate in the Electrical and Computer Engineering Department of the National Technical University of Athens (NTUA), Athens, Greece and research associate of the Telecommunications Laboratory. His research interests are in the area of signalling, Intelligent Networks, Personal Communications, performance evaluation and modeling. He has participated in several European Union ACTS projects and is currently involved in the INSIGNIA AC068 project. He has received several national awards for the entire five years of his undergraduate study. Mr. Polykalas is a member of IEEE and the Technical Chamber of Greece.

Iakovos S. Venieris was born in Naxos, Greece. He received the Dipl. -Ing. degree from the University of Patras, Greece in 1988, and the Ph.D. degree from the National Technical University of Athens (NTUA), Athens, Greece, in 1990, all in electrical and computer engineering. From 1994 he is an Assistant Professor in the Electrical and Computer Engineering Department of NTUA. His research interests are in the fields of B-ISDN, signalling, resource scheduling and allocation for network management, modeling, performance evaluation and queueing theory. He has over sixty publications in the above areas. Dr. Venieris has been exposed to standardisation body work and has participated in several European Union and national projects dealing with B-ISDN protocols, Intelligent Networks, ATM switching and access techniques. Dr. Venieris is a member of IEEE and the Technical Chamber of Greece.

25

A real-time database for future telecommunication services

T. Niklander, J. Kiviniemi and K. Raatikainen
University of Helsinki, Department of Computer Science
P.O. Box 26 (Teollisuuskatu 23), FIN-00014 University of Helsinki, Finland.
Telephone: +358 9 7084 {4235,4427,4243}.
Fax: +358 9 7084 4441. E-mail: {tiina.niklander, jukka.kiviniemi,kimmo.raatikainen}@cs.Helsinki.FI

Abstract

Future telecommunication services will extensively exploit database technology. The persistent and temporal information needed in operations and management of the telecommunication networks and services will be in databases. The current Intelligent Network (IN) Recommendations of ITU-T imply that real-time transaction processing capabilities should be provided. Telecommunications Management Network (TMN) and Telecommunications Information Networking Architecture (TINA) are object oriented. An ideal database system supporting various telecommunication applications should be a fault-tolerant distributed real-time object-oriented database system.

The most challenging issue in designing a real-time transaction processing system for telecommunications is the handling of transactions in three categories having very different characteristics. A telecommunications database system should be able to support short but voluminous simple read transactions, long but voluminous simple updating transactions, and a few very long complex updating transactions in the same real-time database system.

Keywords

Real-time transactions, fault-tolerance, concurrency control and scheduling

Intelligent Networks and Intelligence in Networks D. Gaiti (Ed.)
Published by Chapman & Hall

1 INTRODUCTION

Databases will already in the near future have a central role in telecommunications networks. The information needed in operations and management of the nets will be collected into a logically uniform database. The world-wide nature of telecommunications prescribes that the only possibility to obtain the logical uniformity is the co-operation of autonomous databases.

In the research projects Darfin and RODAIN we have examined database needs in telecommunications. Based on our results and experience the most important features will be the real-time and object-orientation. Real-time transactions are really needed in telecommunications. In telecommunications we will need both soft transactions that may continue their execution after deadline but with a reduced lower priority and firm transactions that are terminated when their deadline expires. We do not believe that hard transactions will be used in near future because systems supporting hard transactions are too expensive for open telecommunication markets.

The RODAIN database architecture is a real-time, object-oriented, fault-tolerant, and distributed database management system. The RODAIN is designed to fulfil the requirements of a telecommunications database systems. The requirements are derived from the most important telecommunications standards including Intelligent Network (IN), Telecommunications Management Network (TMN), and Telecommunication Information Networking Architecture (TINA). The requirements of the telecommunications database architectures originate in the following areas: real-time access to data, fault tolerance, distribution, object orientation, efficiency, flexibility, multiple interfaces, and compatibility (Raatikainen 1997; Taina *et al.* 1996b, 1997).

The most challenging issue in designing a real-time transaction processing system for telecommunications is the handling of transactions in three categories having very different characteristics. A telecommunications database system should be able to support short but voluminous simple read transactions, long but voluminous simple updating transactions, and a few very long complex updating transactions in the same real-time database system. The RODAIN Database (Taina *et al.* 1996b) is designed to meet those constraints. In RODAIN the object-oriented approach was chosen because a special purpose object model for real-time transactions (Kiviniemi *et al.* 1996) can be used to provide the information needed in the concurrency control and real-time scheduling of heterogeneous transactions.

The rest of the paper is organised as follows. In Section 2 we briefly summarise the RODAIN database architecture. The process structure of the RODAIN Database Management System is presented in Section 3. In Section 4 we describe how transactions are processed in the RODAIN Database. In Section 5 we discuss some aspects of fault-tolerance in the RODAIN Database.

2 RODAIN DATABASE ARCHITECTURE

The RODAIN database architecture is a real-time, object-oriented, distributed, and fault-tolerant architecture of a database management system designed for telecommunications. Below we briefly summarise the essentials of the architecture while a detailed description can be found in Taina *et al.* (1996a-c).

A RODAIN Database consists of a set of autonomous RODAIN Database Nodes that interact with each other. Each database node may communicate with one or more applications, and an application may communicate with one or more database nodes. A RODAIN Database Node consists of Database Primary Node, Database Mirror Node, and Reliable Secondary Storage Subsystem (Figure 1). The primary and mirror node are identical having a set of subsystems:

- User Request Interpreter Subsystem (URIS),
- Distributed Database Subsystem (DDBS),
- Fault-Tolerance and Recovery Subsystem (FTRS),
- Watchdog Subsystem (WDS), and
- Object-Oriented Database Management Subsystem (OO-DBMS).

User Request Interpreter Subsystem

A database management system to be used in telecommunications must support several interfaces to the database including CS-1/CS-2 INAP, CMIP, CORBA, TINA. User Request Interpreter Subsystems translate various interfaces into a common connection language. Each URIS takes care of one specific interface. The URIS on the Primary Node is active. On the Mirror Node the URIS is passive.

Distributed Database Subsystem

A RODAIN Database Node may either be used as a stand-alone system or in co-operation with the other autonomous RODAIN Database Nodes. The database co-operation management in the Database Primary Node is left to the Distributed Database Subsystem. The Distributed Database Subsystem on Mirror Node is passive.

Fault-Tolerance and Recovery Subsystem

The subsystem controls communication between the Database Primary Node and the Database Mirror Node. It also co-operates with the Watchdog Subsystem to support fault-tolerance.

The FTRS on Primary Node handles transaction logs and recovery data. It takes care of saving transaction logs either into the Mirror Node or into the Secondary Storage Subsystem. Since the database only contains committed data, the FTRS only needs to handle redo logs.

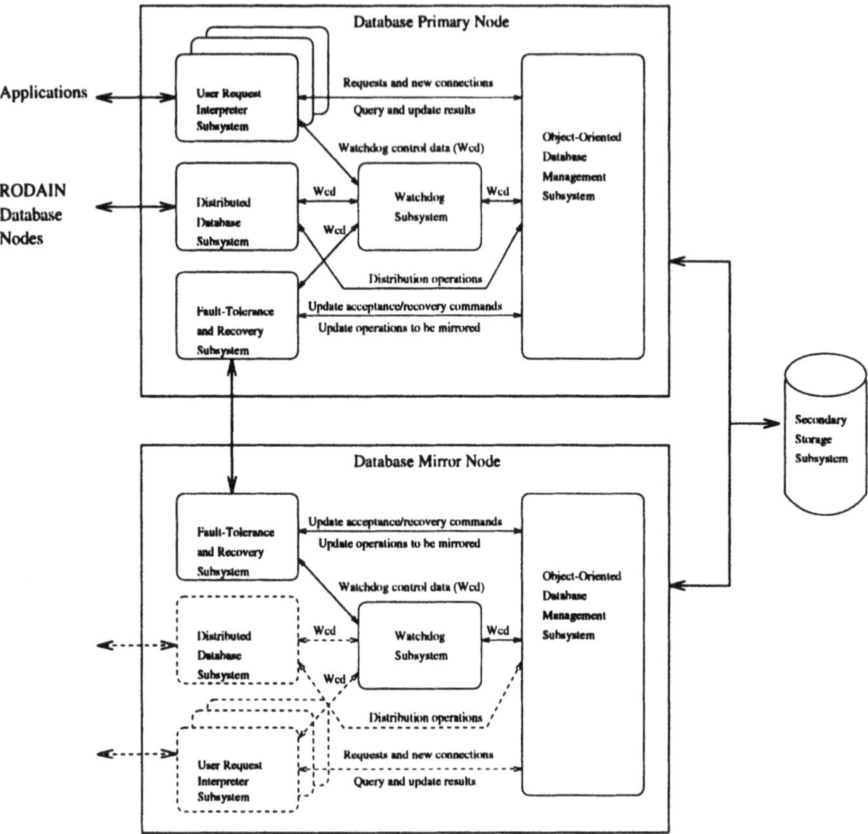

Figure 1 RODAIN database node.

The FTRS on the Mirror Node receives the logs from the FTRS on the Primary Node. It saves the logs into the Secondary Storage Subsystem and sends the corresponding update instructions to the OO-DBMS on the Mirror Node. The FTRS on the Mirror Node also receives the recovery data from the Primary Node and passes it to the local OO-DBMS.

Watchdog Subsystem
The subsystem watches over the other running subsystems locally on both Primary and Mirror Node. It communicates with the other subsystems to state the current node status. Upon a failure it restores the node. The Watchdog Subsystem notices when a system is down and starts a recovery process.

Object-Oriented Database Management Subsystem
The OO-DBMS is the main component of a RODAIN Database Node both on Primary Node and on Mirror Node. It maintains databases, real-time constraints, integrity, and concurrency control. It offers object storing, querying, and

transaction services for the URISes and the DDBS. The OO-DBMS consists of a set of database processes that use database services to resolve requests from other subsystems and of a set of manager services that implement database functionality.

3 OBJECT-ORIENTED DATABASE MANAGEMENT SUBSYSTEM IN RODAIN

The Object-Oriented Database Management Subsystem (OO-DBMS) implements the functionality of the RODAIN database. It offers object storing, querying, and transaction services for User Request Interpreter Subsystem, which communicates with an application outside RODAIN Database Node.

Transactions are executed in the Database Primary Node. The Database Mirror Node does not accept incoming transactions. When running as the Database Primary Node the node is either in the normal primary mode or in the transient mode. The key difference between the two modes is in the way how the transaction log is handled.

Processes in a RODAIN Node are induced from different sources. The sources include operating system, network communication system, database processes, and executing transactions. Processes induced by the RODAIN Database system are divided into priority levels. Database services other than transactions have usually a fixed priority. The Transaction Processes have a priority area, in which their priorities can vary. The priority of a Transaction Process depends on the deadline, importance, and other properties of the transaction. The priority can (and usually does) change during the runtime of the transaction.

The processes in the Database Primary Node are depicted in Figure 2 using a formalism of an extended DARTS software design method (Gomaa 1984) for real-time system. Below we briefly summarise the basic concepts of processes that are relevant when transactions are processed.

Runtime Transaction Controller

The Runtime Transaction Controller (RTC) accepts new transaction requests from applications. The RTC allocates one Transaction Process from the pool of Transaction Processes to serve the incoming transaction. Based on the attribute values of the transaction instance the RTC assigns a priority to the Transaction Process. The Runtime Transaction Controller can deny an incoming transaction request in an overload situation.

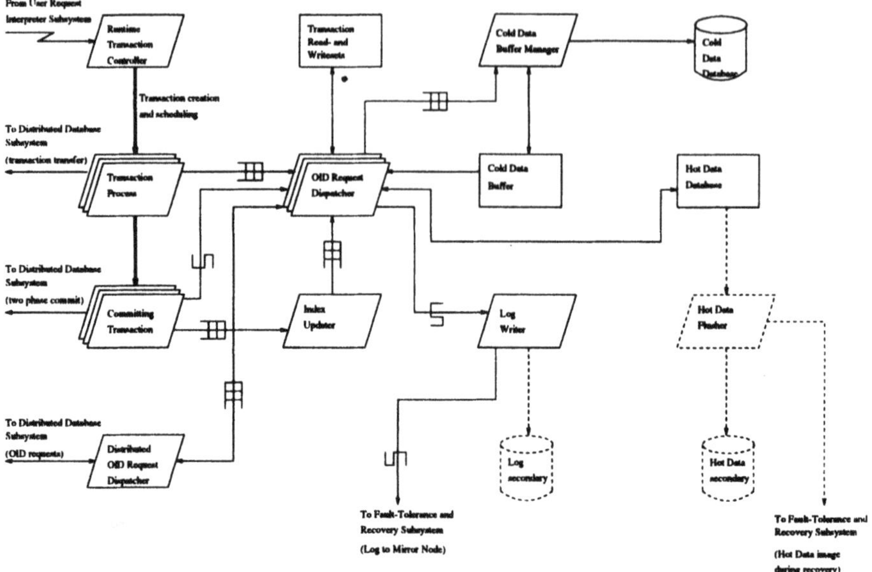

Figure 2 Processes in RODAIN Database Primary Node.

The Runtime Transaction Controller is also responsible for participating in transaction scheduling. Transaction scheduling is done by modifying the priority of each Transaction Process. The RTC adjusts the priorities of each transaction based on the selected scheduling policy. When a transaction is aborted and restarted due to concurrency control policy, the transaction is restarted in the same Transaction Process.

The Runtime Transaction Controller also handles transactions that have missed their deadlines. According to the over-deadline handling scheme, which is a mandatory attribute of any real-time transaction in the RODAIN data model (Kiviniemi *et al.* 1996), the RTC either aborts the transaction or lets it run with a lowered priority and importance. In both cases, the originator of the transaction is notified about the missed deadline.

Transaction Processes

A Transaction Process is invoked to handle requests sent by an application. A request is either a request to access an object or an invocation of method in an object (method call). Transaction Processes are permanent processes that are allocated to execute transactions. When a transaction is completed, the Transaction Process that carried out the execution of the transaction is returned into the pool of free Transaction Processes. When a transaction is aborted and restarted due to concurrency control, the same Transaction Process is used.

A Transaction Process offers the functionality specified in the RODAIN data model as well as query optimisation and usage of indices in queries. The object methods are executed in the memory space of the Transaction Process.

OID Request Dispatchers

An OID Request Dispatcher is a process that receives OID read and write requests from Transaction Processes and executes them. When a Transaction Process performs a request to access an object, the request is placed into the request queue. One OID Request Dispatcher process gets the request from the queue. When a request is completed, a result message is sent back through a buffered communication channel. Therefore, the requesting Transaction Process can decide, whether it waits for the completion of one request or whether it sends multiple requests into the queue before waiting a completion.

An OID Request Dispatcher offers services for reading and (pre)writing an object, and for validating and committing a transaction. A data accessing method depends on whether the requested object belongs to the hot data or to the cold data. When the accessed object is in the hot data, the OID Request Dispatcher computes its direct physical address in the main memory database and performs the operation. When the accessed object is in the cold data, the OID Request Dispatcher first tries to access data in the cold data buffer. If the object is not in the buffer, the request is forwarded to the Cold Data Buffer Manager. When an object is accessed, the readset or writeset of the requesting transaction is updated.

All OID Request Dispatcher processes are installed during the startup of the database. The number of processes is specified as an initialisation parameter of the RODAIN Database.

Committing Transactions

A Committing Transaction is a Transaction Process that has entered the commit phase. The Committing Transactions have the same functionality as Transaction Processes but each Committing Transaction has a higher priority than any Transaction Process. A Committing Transaction performs the validation of the transaction commit using the readset and the writeset of the transaction. If the validation is successful, all modified objects are written into the database and the transaction is committed. If the concurrency control detects a conflict, at least one transaction is aborted and restarted.

Cold Data Buffer Manager

The Cold Data Buffer Manager (CDBM) receives read and write requests to the cold data from the OID Request Dispatcher. Since a read request sent to the CDBM can not be resolved from the Cold Data Buffer, the request is resolved from the Secondary Storage Subsystem. A write request causes the written object to be pinned into the Cold Data Buffer. In the case of transaction commit, the modified objects are written into the Secondary Storage Subsystem and unpinned before the commit is accepted.

When the Cold Data Buffer is full, the CDBM makes free space by removing some objects from the buffer. The pinned objects are the last ones to be removed, since they need to be written into a temporary disk file. When ever possible the objects to be removed are selected from the set of unpinned objects. A priority-LRU method (Carey *et al.* 1989) is used in the selection.

Log Writer

The Log Writer handles log write commands. When the Database Primary Node is in the normal primary mode, the requests are passed to the Mirror Node. When the Database Primary Node is in the transient mode, the log write requests are forwarded to the Secondary Storage Subsystem. In both cases the write process is synchronous. Thus, a log write operation is finished when it is guaranteed that the entry is permanently stored either into the Mirror Node or into the Secondary Storage Subsystem.

Hot Data Flusher

The Hot Data Flusher writes the contents of the main memory database into the Secondary Storage Subsystem. This process is used in the Primary Node only when the node is in the transient mode.

4 TRANSACTION PROCESSING IN RODAIN

As mentioned in the Introduction, a database used in telecommunications meets three different types of transactions. Firstly, the short queries are used to retrieve information about characteristics of the called subscriber and the calling telephone line. These transactions have real-time requirements but strict serializability is usually not needed. Secondly, a telecommunications database is often a subject to transactions that update information of a single subscriber. Thirdly, the large TMN transactions are used to update large number of records. These transactions do not have real-time requirements but they have strict atomicity and isolation requirements. The challenge is that all the three transaction types must be scheduled in a single database but the scheduling requirements are conflicting. Therefore, we have paid special attention to overcome transaction scheduling problems in the RODAIN database system.

In RODAIN the scheduling and concurrency control exploits the real-time properties available in the RODAIN data model. Below we highlight the essentials in the RODAIN data model, transaction scheduling and concurrency control, and in overload management. All these aspects are key issues in developing a real-time database system (Yu *et al.* 1994).

4.1 Real-time properties in RODAIN data model

In the RODAIN data model each transaction has the properties **deadline** and **deadline_type**. The **deadline** property indicates the time before which the transaction should commit. The granularity and time model for deadlines are not specified in the data model. The **deadline_type** property specifies how a transaction is treated when the deadline expires. In RODAIN the alternatives of the treatment are firm, soft, and none.

When a transaction is started, it is timestamped with the start time of the transaction. An application can also specify the **expected_execution_time** property for the transaction. If the value of **expected_execution_time** is not specified in the transaction, then a weighted average of past instances is used. The granularity and time model in the **expected_execution_time** property is the same as in the **deadline** property. The **expected_execution_time** property can be changed during the execution.

In scheduling the following properties are also taken into account:

- **transaction_importance**,
- **deadline_expiration_action**, and
- **late_transaction_importance**.

The **transaction_importance** property specifies the relative importance of the transaction in respect to other transactions in the system. The **deadline_expiration_action** property specifies which actions are to be taken when the deadline expires. This property is currently an implicit one because its value depends on the value of the **deadline_type** property. Possible values are abort and continue. If the value is abort, the transaction is terminated when the deadline expires. If the value is continue, the execution is continued with a lowered priority (see Kao *et al.* 1995). The new priority value is derived from the value of the **late_transaction_importance** property.

The goal of real-time scheduling is to maximize the number of transactions that complete before their deadlines. However, this is not always possible. In these overload situations transactions having low values of the **transaction_importance** property are sacrificed in favor of those having high values. This is the concept of overload resolution policy used in the RODAIN database. The RODAIN database has also an overload prevention policy that controls the creation of new instances of transactions.

In the RODAIN model transactions have the **isolation_level** property that defines the correctness criterion sufficient for the transaction. This criterion specifies which level of correctness is needed when the transaction is executed. The isolation level of transaction is compared to the isolation level of accessed objects and the stringiest level is used. Since each transaction is individually treated, every transaction accessing the same object will receive at least the specified correctness level.

The `transaction_behavior` property indicates how a transaction is going to access data in the database. The RODAIN database model introduces all the three transaction behaviours described in Ramamritham (1993):

1. A read-only transaction reads data from a database and does not make any updates.
2. A write-only transaction collects data from the outer world and writes it into the database.
3. A read-write transaction reads data from a database, updates it, and stores it back to a database.

The `transaction_behavior` property guarantees that operations violating the behaviour will raise an exception that aborts the transaction. The default behavior of transaction is a read-write transaction.

4.2 Basic principles of scheduling and concurrency control

In our prototype implementation we are experimenting with a two level scheduling algorithm. The upper level is used to provide a reasonable fairness between different types of transactions. The lower level is used to maximise the number of transactions completed in time.

When a transaction arrives into the system, it is assigned into one of the following three groups: 1) short real-time transactions, 2) long real-time transactions, and 3) non real-time transactions. The groups correspond to the three transaction types common in telecommunications. The assignment is based on the following three properties: `deadline_type`, `expected_execution_time`, and `transaction_behavior`. Each group gets a predefined fraction (system parameter) of available cpu time in a round robin fashion. Actually, we have different fractions for low, medium, and high system load.

In the group of non real-time transactions the scheduling policy is round robin with a relatively long time slice. In the two groups of real-time transactions we use a weighted least slack time first scheduling. The weight is based on the `deadline_type` and `transaction_importance` properties. In the group of short real-time transactions the scheduling is non pre-emptive. In the group of long real-time transactions the scheduling is pre-emptive in the sense that when the priority order of two transactions changes, the running transaction is switched. The scheduler calculates the switch time beforehand and uses a threshold to prevent the so called "continuous process switch" phenomenon.

As the concurrency control algorithm we use our own modification of the OCC-TI algorithm (Son *et al.* 1992, Lee *et al.* 1993). The modifications take into account the correction criterion (the `isolation_level` property), the `transaction_importance` property, and the remaining slack time of conflicting transactions. In concurrency control our main worry is read-write conflicts because write-write conflicts are rare in telecommunication applications.

We use two basic techniques that are derived from the application semantics in telecommunication. The massive updates, which are primarily used in service management, are carried out as non real-time transactions. They create new versions of the objects that become valid in the future. Features of active databases supported in RODAIN are tailored to trigger massive new current version updates. The read-write conflicts between the simple queries and updates are removed by using the so called τ-serializability introduced in Raatikainen *et al.* (1995) as the correctness criterion. The principal idea in the τ-serializability is to allow transactions to read (slightly) old data.

Suppose that the transaction *a* has read the object **x** at time t_a and that the transaction *b* has committed an update of **x** at time t_b, $t_a < t_b$. Further, suppose that *a* tries to commit at time t_c, $t_b < t_c$. In the τ-serializability the validation of *a* fails only if $t_a+\min(\tau_x,\tau_a) < t_b$ or $t_b+\min(\tau_x,\tau_b) < t_c$, where τ_a, τ_b, and τ_x are the τ-values of transaction *a*, transaction *b*, and object **x**, respectively. The τ-value specifies how long a time an old value is useful after an update.

4.3 Overload Management

The overload policy defines how the RODAIN Database Primary Node behaves when its load temporarily exceeds its processing capacity. In an overload situation all transactions can not meet their deadlines. Thus, the system must make some decisions either to prevent overloads beforehand or to resolve overload situation when it occurs.

An overload situation can be prevented by controlling the number of executing Transaction Processes and OID Request Dispatchers. In the RODAIN Database the Runtime Transaction Controller can deny new transaction requests. In this case the request originator is notified. Another way used in the RODAIN to prevent overload situations is the control for the number of running OID Request Dispatchers. In this case transactions are accepted but their execution is delayed due to queuing OID Request Dispatcher resources. The number of Transaction Processes and the number of OID Request Dispatchers are system-wide parameters used in tuning the database performance.

In addition to the preventive overload control the RODAIN Database also exploits an observative overload policy in overload situations. When too many transactions have missed their deadline during the monitoring interval, the system load is decreased by aborting transactions that impart lower value to the system.

5 FAULT-TOLERANCE IN RODAIN

The requirement of high availability has lead us to design RODAIN Database Node so that it remains, at least partially, functional even if only one functional node operates normally. If all hardware nodes have failed, then the systems availability requirement is also violated. However, the recovery from the Secondary Storage Subsystem (SSS) turns the database into a consistent state but a few committed transactions might be lost.

The RODAIN Database, consisting of two functional nodes (the Primary Node and the Mirror Node), can currently tolerate a failure. If the system had more Mirror Nodes, then it would remain functional even it all but one node fail.

When both nodes are functional, one node (Primary Node) is active and executes the transactions. The other node (Mirror Node) is passive. The mirror only maintains its own copy of main-memory database according to information received from the primary.

Currently our failure model is based on the assumption that the whole node fails. We also assume that the communication link between the Primary Node and the Mirror Node does not fail alone. In the RODAIN system this assumption is not unrealistic since the nodes are connected through two physically separate communication paths.

5.1 Operations when both nodes functional

The Primary Node executes all arriving transactions. It uses deferred writes with optimistic scheduling just to avoid operations due to aborted transactions. The rollback in the RODAIN Database is very simple: just to remove the data structures of aborted transaction. Some cleanup operations are needed in the data structures used by concurrency control but those operations are the same as after a transaction has successfully committed.

The fault-tolerance in RODAIN is achieved by sending transaction logs including the commit log to the Mirror Node. The idea of using separate node or processor for log handling is not new; see e.g. Levy *et al.* (1992) and Lehman *et al.* (1987). In a traditional database system the logs are stored in stable memory like disk before transaction is allowed to commit. In RODAIN we assume that the Mirror Node is stable. This means that a transaction may commit when its log has arrived into the Mirror Node.

The Mirror Node uses the log to update its own database. It also stores the log to reliable disk subsystem (Secondary Storage Subsystem, SSS). If both nodes fail at the same time, our fault-tolerance assumptions are violated. However, the logs stored on the SSS guarantee that almost all committed transactions have their data maintained in the RODAIN system.

In order to make the recovery fast, the Mirror Node also makes periodic copies of its database image into the SSS. This copy is used to reduce the number of log records needed to be processed when the failed node is recovering. Checkpointing is used to mark the creation of image in the log. Our checkpointing scheme is similar to the one presented in Jagadish *et al.* (1993).

Since we make the checkpoints from a copy of the database, it never contains any uncommitted data. Therefore, we do not need any undo operation in RODAIN.

5.2 Operations when one node fails

The operations when a node fails are slightly different depending on which one of the functional nodes failed. If the passive Mirror Node fails, then the active Primary Node has to start saving transaction logs directly into stable memory. This guarantees that a huge amount of committed data will not be lost if also the active Primary Node fails.

If the active Primary Node fails, the operations are little more complex because the Mirror Node has to change its functionality to new Primary Node. First of all, the mirror updates its own copy of the main-memory database using the unprocessed logs. At the same time all non-active subsystems are activated. After both steps have been completed, the mirror can start to act as the new active Primary Node.

Currently, we loose the active transactions during this role switch. However, the amount of lost transactions can be reduced if the User Request Interpreter Subsystems in the Mirror Node maintain list of uncompleted transactions. The new active node could restart transactions that are feasible and assumed to be able to finish before deadline. The co-operation between the URISes in the two nodes is the way how fault-tolerance can be further increased in RODAIN. We have decided not to support transaction migration since we assume that most failures are due to hardware (or operating system) problems.

5.3 Operations when only one node is functional

The only functional node is always an active Primary Node in transient mode. It executes transactions and saves logs directly to the SSS. This makes the transaction commit slower but the data is not totally lost if also this node fails. However, the commit procedure can be speed up by using the so called group commit mechanism.

If the failed node remains unavailable for a long period, the Primary Node may have to also make a full copy of its main-memory database to the SSS, just to make the recovery of the other node faster.

5.4 Operations when failed node recovers

The functional active Primary Node maintains its state in transient mode until the recovering new Mirror Node informs its presence. The Primary Node then changes its state back to normal mode.

The recovering node first loads the latest database image. Then it will process all the stored log records to update the database. When the recovering node is "up-to-date", it informs the Primary Node that it is ready to serve as the Mirror Node. The Primary Node can then stop storing of logs into the SSS and start sending them to Mirror Node for further processing.

The time when the recovering node may inform its presence is not unique. The earliest possible point is when the recovering node has loaded the image and the latest possible one is when the recovering node has processed all the logs. It should, however, be noticed that there may always be new log records to be processed because the active Primary Node is writing new ones unless the system is idle. Therefore, the passive recovering Mirror Node should take the responsibility of log handling even if it has not yet processed all available log records.

5.5 Transaction commit in details

Transaction commit is the critical point in achieving fault-tolerance in database. When transaction commits, all of its logs are sent to the Mirror Node and stored to stable memory in the Secondary Storage Subsystem.

We need to consider only updating transactions since the log contains only redo operations with after images. Read-only transactions do not change the state of the database which implies that they do not produce log entries.

During the transaction commit phase the executing transaction process makes all the changes permanent into the database. The commit is allowed only if the transaction does not conflict with other transactions. The transaction commit is finished only when the logs are stored into the Mirror Node or directly into the SSS. Since the transactions are (τ-)serialised in their commit order, the Mirror Node can use the commit order as the order in which it updates its copy of the database. Therefore, the Mirror Node should use the simple "FIFO - one transaction at a time" scheduling when updating its own database.

The last log record of each transaction received by the mirror contains only the commit operation. This fact is used in synchronisation so that the OID Request Dispatcher waits for its processing. The Fault-Tolerance and Recovery Subsystem (FTRS) on the Primary Node sends to the FTRS on the Mirror Node all log records of a transaction. When the FTRS on the Mirror Node has received all the log records related to a transaction, which is indicated by the commit record, the FTRS on the Mirror Node sends an acknowledgement to the FTRS on the Primary Node.

The FTRS on the Primary Node does not destroy log records until the FTRS on the Mirror Node has acknowledged them. The FTRS on the Mirror Node sends this acknowledgement message only when it has saved the log into the SSS. This extra storing is used to avoid loosing logs of committed transactions in the case of a Mirror Node failure.

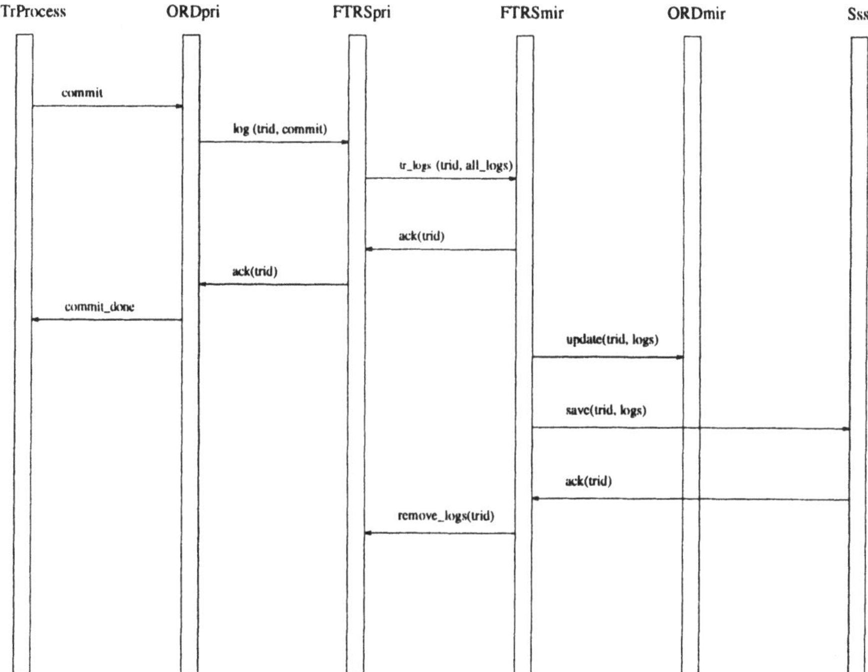

Figure 3 Message sequence chart in the commit phase

Concurrently with storing the log, the FTRS on the Mirror Node also updates its own copy of the database. The log records on the Mirror Node are removed when both the update and the storing has been done. The update and storing can be done in any order.

Should the Mirror Node fail, the FTRS on the Primary Node would save all log records that are still in its buffers. If the Primary Node fails, all the log records that are not yet sent to Mirror Node are lost. However, these records are from transactions that are not yet committed and, therefore, the changes can be lost without violating the consistency of the database.

Figure 3 shows the messages and their timings sent during the commit phase between the functional entities in the Primary and Mirror Node.

6 SUMMARY

We have described the RODAIN Database architecture and main parts of its prototype implementation. The RODAIN Database architecture is designed to meet the challenge of future telecommunication systems including Intelligent

Networks, Telecommunications Management Network, Telecommunication Information Networking Architecture.

In order to fulfil the requirements of the next generation telecommunications systems, the database architecture must be fault-tolerant and support real-time transactions with explicit deadlines. The internals of the RODAIN DBMS described are designed to meet the requirements of telecommunications applications including real-time access to data, fault tolerance, distribution, object orientation, efficiency, flexibility, multiple interfaces, and compatibility with telecommunications practices. The requirements are, in some extent, conflicting. Therefore, the RODAIN Database is based on trade-offs; novel and innovative solutions are used only when old and exercised methods are found to be insufficient.

In the RODAIN data model we defined real-time objects and real-time characteristics. The additional characteristics were designed so that the original ODMG-93 model (Cattell 1994) is a true subset of the extended model. The motivation for the extensions was to provide the real-time scheduler and concurrency controller enough knowledge to overcome the problems due to heterogeneous transaction lengths that are met in telecommunication applications. Availability of RODAIN is achieved through using a database mirror. The mirror is also used for log processing, which reduces load in the primary database node and shortens the commit times of transactions.

7 ACKNOWLEDGEMENTS

This work has been carried out in the research project RODAIN (1995-) funded by the Finnish Technology Development Center (TEKES) together with Nokia Telecommunications, Solid Information Technology, and Telecom Finland. The authors want to thank Pasi Porkka, Juha Taina, and Martti Tienari from the Department of Computer Science in the University of Helsinki for the fruitful discussions and valuable comments during the research. The industrial partners (Kyösti Laiho and Artturi Tarjanne from Solid, Jussi Ollikainen, Tapani Karttunen and Jari Vänttinen from Telecom Finland, Juha Lipiäinen, Simo Lähdesmäki and Petri Nuuttila from Nokia Telecommunications) have provided useful information and feedback comments during the project.

8 REFERENCES

Carey, M.J., Jauhari, R. and Livny, M. (1989) Priority in DBMS Resource Scheduling, in *Proceedings of the 15th Very Large DataBase Conference*, 397-410, Morgan Kaufmann, San Mateo, Calif.

Cattell, R.G.G. (ed.) (1994) *The Object Database Standard: ODMG-93*. Morgan Kauffmann, San Francisco, Calif.

Gomaa, H. (1984) A Software Design Methods for Real-Time Systems. *Communications of the ACM*, **27**, 9, 938-49.

Jagadish, H.V., Silberschatz, A. and Sudarshan, S. (1993) Recovering from Main-Memory Lapses, in *Proceedings of the 19th Very Large DataBase Conference*, 391–404, Morgan Kaufmann, San Mateo.

Kao, B. and Garcia-Molina, H. (1995) An Overview of Real-Time Database Systems, in *Advances in Real-Time Systems* (ed. S.H. Son), 463-86, Prentice-Hall.

Kiviniemi, J. and Raatikainen, K.E.E. (1996) *Object-Oriented Data Model for Telecommunications*. Technical Report C-1996-75, Department of Computer Science, University of Helsinki, Finland.

Lee, J. and Son, S.H. (1993) Using Dynamic Adjustment of Serialization Order for Real-Time Database Systems, in *Proceedings of Real-Time Systems Symposium*, 66-75, IEEE Computer Society.

Lehman, T.J. and Carey, M.J. (1987) A Recovery Algorithm for A High-Performance Memory-Resident Database System, in *Proceedings of ACM SIGMOD 1987 Annual Conference*, 104–17, ACM SIGMOD.

Levy, E. and Silberschatz, A. (1992) Incremental Recovery in Main Memory Database Systems. *IEEE Transactions on Knowledge and Data Engineering*, **4**, 6, 529–40.

Porkka, P. and Raatikainen, K.E.E. (1997) CORBA access to telecommunications databases, in *Intelligent Networks and Intelligence in Networks* (ed. D. Gaiti), Chapman & Hall, London.

Raatikainen, K.E.E. (1997) Real-Time Dtabases in Telecommunications, in *Real-Time Database Systems: Issues and Applications* (ed. A. Bestavros *et al.*), Kluwer.

Raatikainen, K.E.E., Karttunen, T., Martikainen, O. and Taina, J. (1995) Evaluation of Database Architectures for Intelligent Networks, in *Proceeding of Telecom95 Technical Summit*, Vol. 2, 549-53, ITU, Geneva, Switzerland.

Ramamritham, K. (1993) Real-Time Databases. *Distributed and Parallel Databases*, **1**, 199-226.

Son, S.H., Lee, J.and Lee, Y. (1992) Hybrid Protocols Using Dynamic Adjustment of Serialization Order for Real-Time Concurrency Control. *The Journal of Real-Time Systems*, **4**, 2, 269-76.

Taina, J. and Raatikainen, K.E.E. (1996a) Design Issues and Experimental Database Architecture for Telecommunications, in *Intelligent Networks and New Technologies* (ed. J. Nørgaard and V.B. Iversen), 121–39, Chapman & Hall, London.

Taina, J. and Raatikainen, K.E.E. (1996b) Experimental real-time object-oriented database architecture for intelligent networks. *Journal of Engineering Intelligent Systems*, **4**, 3, 57–63.

Taina, J. and Raatikainen, K.E.E. (1996c) RODAIN: A Real-Time Object-Orinted Database System for Telecommunications, in *Proceedings of the*

DART'96 Workshop (ed. N. Soparkar and K. Ramamritham), 12–5, University of Massachusetts.

Taina, J. and Raatikainen, K.E.E. (1997) Database usage and requirements in intelligent networks, in *Intelligent Networks and Intelligence in Networks* (ed. D. Gaiti), Chapman & Hall, London.

Yu, P.S., Wu, K.-L. and Son, S.H. (1994) On Real-Time Databases: Concurrency Control and Scheduling. *Proceedings of the IEEE*, **82**, 1, 140-57.

8 BIOGRAPHY

Tiina Niklander received her M.Sc. degree in computer science from the University of Helsinki, in 1993. She is currently a Ph.D. student in computer science at the University of Helsinki and a researcher in the RODAIN project. Her research interests include fault-tolerance and real-time databases.

Jukka Kiviniemi is completing his M.Sc. studies in computer science at the University of Helsinki. He is currently a research assistant in the RODAIN project. His research interests include real-time and distributed databases, and real-time systems.

Kimmo Raatikainen received the Ph.D. degree in computer science from the University of Helsinki, in 1990. He is currently an associate professor in computer science at the University of Helsinki. He is a member of ACM, IEEE (Communications and Computer Societies), and IFIP TC6 Special Interest Group of Intelligent Networks. His research interests include nomadic computing, telecommunications software architectures, and real-time databases.

PART TEN

Performance

26

Performance issues in Intelligent Networks

T. Jensen
Telenor Research and Development,
P.O.Box 83, N-2007 Kjeller, Norway
Tel. +47 63 84 88 39
Fax. +47 63 81 00 76
E-mail: terje.jensen@fou.telenor.no

Abstract

Intelligent Networks used as basis for an increasing number of services places more emphasis on the corresponding performance issues. Although ensuring sufficient service quality has been essential for most network operators, diversified customers and services together with growing competition request for effective utilisation of the network elements. A number of aspects have to be considered in order to maintain an effective operational network. In this paper, issues related to deployment of Intelligent Networks, including relevant services and sizing of network elements, characterisation of services and interconnect are treated.

Keywords

Intelligent Network, performance, dimensioning

Intelligent Networks and Intelligence in Networks D. Gaiti (Ed.)
Published by Chapman & Hall

1 INTRODUCTION

Variants and usage of services based on Intelligent Network (IN) solutions grow steadily. The complexity, measured in terms of number of processing steps and devices involved for handling a call, does also seem to increase. Although one of the arguments for describing the IN concept was to ease service administration, e.g. (Q.12xx), the additional processing, signalling and usage of devices, may lead to that bottlenecks arise. In addition, patterns of service usage could further result in potential problems in certain portions of an IN.

Utilisation of network elements and resulting service quality would depend on the principles applied for deploying an IN. Two examples are overlay networks and integrated solutions. Although applying different philosophies for rolling out the network elements, similar questions with respect to performance are met. Such questions are given for a holistic view as well as for more specific aspects. A number of publications have been issued on these questions, like (Ramaswami, 1995) and (Pandya, 1994) for overall descriptions. Response times and related performance issues for querying data bases and personal communications have also been treated in papers, like (Demounem, 1992), (Saito, 1994), (Kwiatkowski, 1995). Corresponding analyses of the signalling network have also been carried out, e.g. (Bafutto, 1994). Other issues have also been examined. From an operational point of view, the relevant network elements and service logic/data must work together in a holistic sense. The presence of a number of actors involved in service handling could clutter the picture of determining the better ways of implementing services. In particular, when the different actors are not co-ordinated, appropriate mechanisms should be incorporated in the network solution.

One of the main objectives of this paper is to describe performance issues to be considered in relation to deployment of INs. Several questions arise during the belonging activities. The nature of these questions depends on the environment in which an actor is situated. As the resulting performance is tightly coupled with the dimensioning process, input data and scopes for carrying out dimensioning are treated in Section 2. Some specific issues of network elements are described in Section 3 outlining potential bottlenecks and studies to be undertaken. However, observing the performance from the users' point of view, a complete implementation should be examined. This also includes characterising services and service demands as presented in Section 4. Topics resulting from the presence of multiple actors are treated in Section 5.

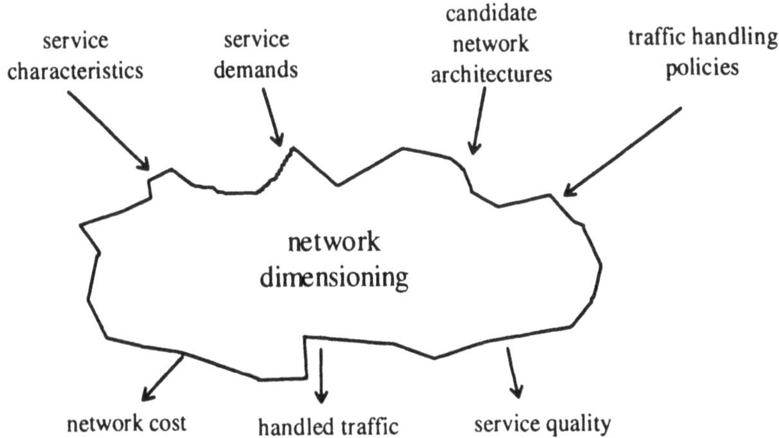

Figure 1 Potential input and output data for a dimensioning process

2 DIMENSIONING PROCESSES

The scopes for dimensioning an IN varies from establishing a network in a greenfield area to re-calculating the concerned parameters after changing the service demands. In addition, management activities are included in the performance studies. Commonly, different approaches are defined for the different scopes, natural as the possible means that can be undertaken vary. For a greenfield area, an optimisation problem can be formulated, like to minimise the cost of deploying a network when handling a set of service demands while meeting a set of requirements. In principle, the process can be illustrated as in Figure 1.

Characterising the services includes describing the network resources used by a service invocation. That is, load implied on the circuit switched connections, signalling links, processing elements and other relevant devices. The adequate service quality requirements are to be stated as well. Demand patterns for the different service must be given. Typically, these are related to a number of reference periods, leading to some mixtures of service usage. As the different customer groups often use different service variants, these variants could have peak demands at noncoinciding time periods. When the service variants are invoked and the user behaviour influence the load on network resources, identifying the time period resulting in highest load on a set of resources may be involved. Carrying out the examinations for several time periods are therefore important.
Candidate network structures have to be specified. For several scopes, however, the network structure is given (one candidate only). For studies of greenfield

areas, candidate locations of network elements including links will be specified. At some locations network elements could be already installed. Such aspects must be incorporated in the procedure allowing for flexibility in the configurations that can be considered. The candidate locations have to be given for all types of network elements considered, like SSPs, IPs, STPs, SCPs and SDPs. In addition, a number of combinations of the functional entities as well as equipment from different vendors could be taken into account.

Traffic handling candidates include routing and load control policies. Different sets of candidates could be given for the different service variants. These could allow for introducing priorities for some services and customers. Potential policies for traffic handling differ for the different portions on an IN. Although each of these could be studied in detail, reaching holistic profitable solutions are requested.

Output from the activity is a description of the network solution. The results include the cost of the network, traffic handled and the corresponding service quality. In addition, more specific data can be given, like utilisation of certain network elements and requirements for available storage devices.

Depending on the flexibility and current equipment in place, different scopes could be relevant as seen from a network operator's point of view, ref. Figure 2. Naturally, all of these scopes may not be of interest for all operators. The axis named time scale/flexibility indicates how much of the network is assumed to be given. Often, there is a correspondence between the time scale and the flexibility. For instance, in a long term solution, more possible candidates could be allowed. The axis named accuracy indicates the level of detail usually considered during the evaluations.

As indicated in Figure 2, when the flexibility increases, less accuracy may be considered. One aspect of this is that measurements and detailed information can be obtained for an existing network. For a greenfield study, however, more coarse descriptions are usually considered.

Dimensioning a network, the topology could be given. Then, finding capacities of the network elements and the relevant links is requested. All the input and output data outlined above may not be relevant for every case that is faced and approach that is used.

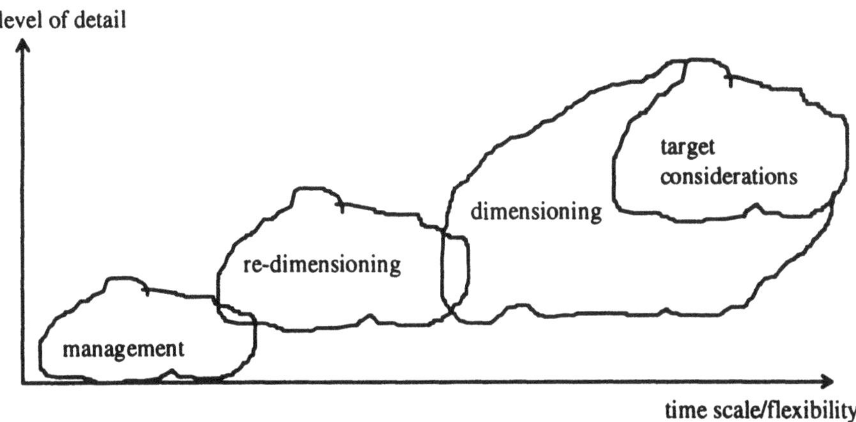

Figure 2 Scopes of network view

The IN-related part of the network can be divided into at least two portions: the circuit switched network and the signalling network. For dimensioning the circuit switched part, traditional methods can be applied. However, for certain service implementations special phenomena should be considered. A number of legs have been identified, e.g. involving the use of IP. Different holding times for the different portions could also be present. In addition, for some service calls, only a connection between a user and an SSP/IP is established. That is, a second user may not be involved. Typically, these aspects are considered when the traffic matrices are established.

Similar comments can be attached when dimensioning the signalling network. The lengths of signalling messages can be different implying that allowed arrival rates may be lower compared to other applications of the signalling protocols. Specified mechanisms for load control could also influence the characteristics of service implementations. However, it is questionable whether the load control should be considered during dimensioning or if these mechanisms can be introduced afterwards to ensure that specific measures are reached.

When locations and capacities of these parts are considered as variables, an optimisation problem could be formulated. In case an estimate of the network cost is to be minimised, this could be calculated as the sum of costs for elements and connections when their corresponding capacities are considered. Main constraints to be fulfilled could be derived from the service quality requirements.

The network dimensioning is usually performed for a large portion of a network where the capacities of most nodes and link/circuit sets are subject to changes.

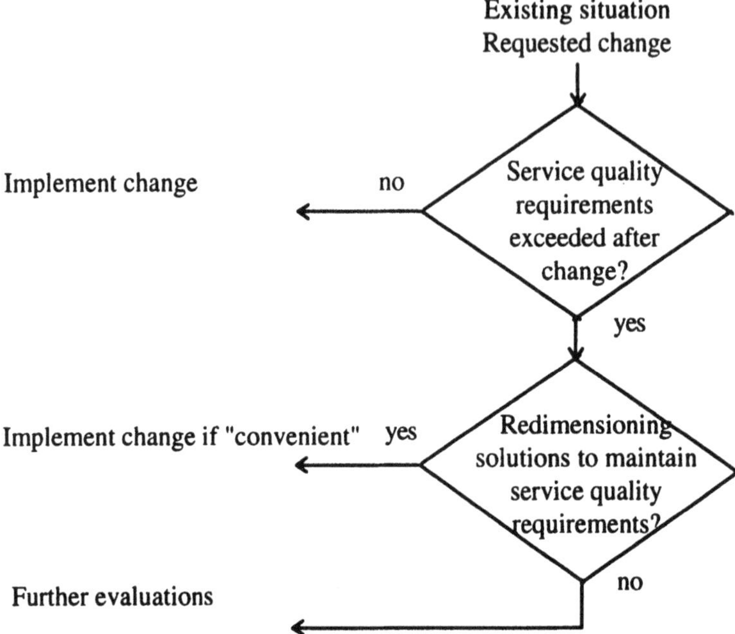

Figure 3 Redimensioning procedure

In a shorter time scope, like when a new IN-based service is introduced or the demand for an existing IN-based service is changed, another approach could be applied. In this procedure, the revised service demand can be added to the demand of an existing network in order to check whether or not this network is able to handle this demand satisfactorily. In case the answer is affirmative, the procedure is ended. Otherwise, a bottleneck is to be identified and measures undertaken to resolve this bottleneck. The procedure is iterated until no more bottlenecks are found. In some cases, major changes could be needed to resolve the congestion. Then, the dimensioning procedure could be started implying that more equipment may be needed, the change of service demand is postponed or service quality reduction could be expected. This procedure is illustrated in Figure 3, based on the description found in (E.734).

In case specific means have to be undertaken in order to maintain the service quality, the corresponding cost could be estimated in order to decide whether or not the activities should be carried out.

The management scope refers to mechanisms implemented which take care of traffic handling in the operational state. Examples of such mechanisms are load control and failure protection.

For all these scopes, elaborating adequate performance models and analyses are fundamental. In particular, performing sensitivity studies on selected groups of input data are requested in order to identify the critical factors. Then, these factors could be modelled more accurately and followed more closely.

3 NETWORK ELEMENTS

Dimensioning a network element, similar input data as for the network dimensioning processes can be identified:

- Load described by arrival process for each class, usage of resources and corresponding service times.
- Characteristics of components used to implement the network element. Both hardware and software architectures must be given. In addition, mapping of software blocks onto the hardware units have to be described. This may also describe candidate policies for handling the load.
- Requirements to be fulfilled, e.g. given by thresholds for delays and blocking probabilities.

For each type of network element, a suitable algorithm taking these input data and finding the following output data should be described:

- Number of units for each type of hardware component. In case these are grouped, differing in functionality or accessibility, the corresponding grouping must also be given.
- Resulting performance for each class.
- Resulting element cost for the network element.
- Service demand that is handled for each class.

A number of scopes for dimensioning a network element could be relevant. For instance, estimating resulting performance for an element when the load is given could be one task. At the other end, optimising the design of the element, e.g. minimising its cost for a mixture of loads could also be carried out. For a network operator, these scopes may differ for the different elements as some of them are tightly integrated with other functions, like an SSF, while others could even be implemented based on specifications from the operator.

The performance models relevant for the different network elements must capture the role played by the element. For instance, related to an STP, signalling load including processing of signalling messages has to be considered. For an SSP, both signalling load and load related to circuit switched connections have to be included. This is also influenced by whether or not the IN-based service handling is integrated or not with other services. In the former case, additional load resulting from IN-related traffic could be considered in the performance studies. However, when the situation for IN-based services is examined, any other services may be modelled as an additional class.

Which hardware and software architectures that are used for an element have to be reflected in the model. This may strongly influence which component that may become the bottleneck. Such a bottleneck, however, may depend on the mixture of classes that is assumed.

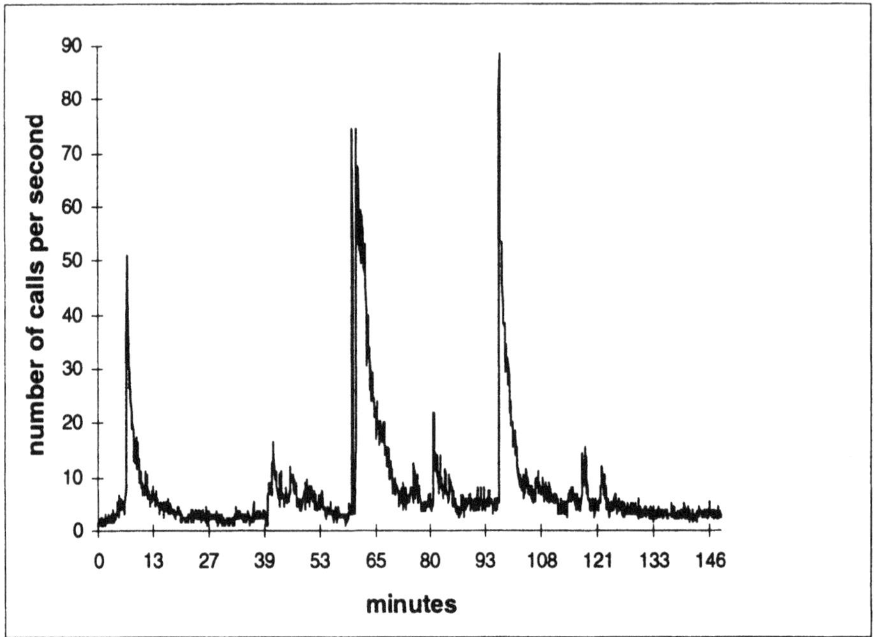

Figure 4 Mass calling situation

Related to IPs and SNs (or SRFs in general), specific concerns on how the load is distributed on the device groups should be taken. In particular, if specialised devices are present, their capacities should be tuned according to the mixture of loads foreseen.

In addition, aspects of the management system could be of concern for performance studies. In case users may access their own profiles through this system, examinations of the load and corresponding performance variables should be undertaken.

4 SERVICE CHARACTERISTICS

Characterising services includes the task of estimating the arrival processes and the sets of network resources requested for every class of service. A suitable division into classes has to be made, balancing the trade-off between having a intractable number of classes and sufficient level to assess the specific characteristics. Based on the assumed usage of services, the arrival processes might be given as Poissonian or not. The former could be used when there is no correlation between the different users. However, for some services, a common event could trigger the service invocation. One example of such a phenomenon is the mass calling service as illustrated in Figure 4. From these measurements, instants when the directory number was announced can clearly be identified.

Capturing parameter values for the arrival processes, a reference period has often been chosen. As the demand patterns for the different services change during the day, a number of reference periods could be used. A simple case could be to select one period for the working hours and another period for the evening period. The former may be related to mostly business users while the latter to mostly private users. Finding penetration and usage of the different services for the different market segments could be undertaken in order to better describe the market.

Values for traffic interests describing which directory number series that have been used describe the flow of traffic loads in the network. In particular, distribution of the load on the legs after SSPs could be derived, although this may also be influenced by the service implementation, like time dependent routing.

As basis for network dimensioning traffic matrices are often elaborated. These matrices should take into account the network elements into where the functional entities have been mapped. Matrices both for circuit switched portion and signalling portion could be used. Relationships between values in these matrices could be identified, e.g. derived from a description of the service. One example is that number of messages exchanged between an SSP and an SCP could be found from examining the path through the service script. In case the script path may vary depending on the user's behaviour, adequate information must be added.

Requirements for the service quality are either stated as blocking or as delays (E.724). Delays can be estimated by applying queueing network models. For certain cases, additional models could be requested. Estimates for delay and blocking are required for networks and individual elements. In addition, as mass calling services can be based on IN, transient studies of blocking due to abrupt changes of the service demand are requested, e.g., see (Jormakka 1995).

Currently, most requirements are given as seen from the users' point of view. When IN-based services are considered, these requirements could be given for the additional delay/blocking implied by using the IN concept. For several services, however, current implementations may not exist or several options could exist. Different approaches for defining values of service quality parameters could be examined. One way is to decompose the chain of elements which interactions need for handling the corresponding call. The resulting values could then be estimated by proper additions and/or multiplications of the components involved. Corresponding estimates for each of the components must also be found which is in line with describing a reference connection and allocating the service quality degradation to the sections involved. Requirements for each network element must be stated by identifying relevant contributions to the resulting service quality.

Load control both for individual network elements and for networks should also be included. Proper mechanisms, ways of deciding values or parameters and effect of the load control mechanisms must be treated. In principle, the traffic load can be limited by introducing mechanisms in several places in the network, like in the circuit switched part, in SSPs and in SCPs. A specific objective to be achieved by applying load control is to ensure fairness between services as well as to reserve capacity for certain services (e.g., emergency services). In addition, load control applied for mass calling services should be included.

Measurement schemes for IN-based services must be described. As far as possible, existing measurement methods should be applied, like measurements of circuit switched traffic, number/length of signalling messages and processing loads. The introduction of additional functional entities, like SCF (Service Control Function) and SRF (Specialised Resource Function), requires the definition of additional measurements both of service usage and network performance.

The service demands as appearing from the networks' point of view, are derived from the users' interest although influenced by a range of circumstantial factors. The service quality and charges are also two factors having impact on these transformations. Network cost could be used as basis for deciding the charges (cost-based charges), although other principles could also be applied. The cost of the network is found after dimensioning, taking the assumed service demands into account. The service quality variables can also be estimated. Other inputs are needed for those calculations, as described in Section 2. The service quality and cost could be fed back in order to estimate service demands. In case no changes of service demands result, the task is finished, while changes invites for recalculating the network solution. In principle this could be regarded as an outer iteration loop. The iterations are continued until the convergence criteria are met. Naturally, this could be a tedious activity depending on the dimension of the problem and the rate of convergence. In addition, convergence may not be guaranteed. However, a major challenge is to describe the relationships between service demands and uses' interests and to capture values for the other effects. To a certain extent historical observations could be applied, but new services and new environments may limit the validity of those observations. Then, simple relationships could be used in order to gain insight into the dynamics and expressiveness of the model. The more important issue is also to identify factors on which the outcome is more sensible to. That is, factors strongly influencing the results. Then, these factors could be further detailed in order to increase the accuracy and the understanding.

Interface identity

performance variable/meassure	traffic condition	performance threshold	reaction pattern	measurement scheme

Figure 5 Potential content of interconnect agreement related to an interface with corresponding content

5 MULTI ACTOR CONSIDERATIONS

Operating telecommunication networks have long traditions for interworking. That is, it should be possible to establish connections between users in networks managed by different organisations. Interconnect agreements must be described correspondingly. Although generic agreements could be proposed, the interfaces in relation to INs have different characteristics which should be reflected in the corresponding contract. Typically, such an agreement covers several issues, like legal, financial and technical. Some of the technical ones will be treated in the following.

An agreement should include aspects like the conditions for operation, how to assess these conditions and actions to be taken in case agreed levels on any of the conditions are exceeded. Naturally, the particularities on interfaces have to be considered when describing these aspects. For instance, delays may be more essential on signalling relationships while blocking probabilities are used for circuit switched connections. In the general case, both variables describing delays and variables describing blocking are relevant.

Interfaces could be identified horizontally and vertically. Horizontal means interconnecting network domains at the same functional level, e.g., between two exchanges. Vertical means connecting different levels in a functional view or a network architecture view. An example is connections between SCPs and SDPs. Functional relationships would exist between the different network elements. In addition, interfaces could be present without separate physical elements, like when service logic/data are executed on a platform provided by another actor. That is, an interface may be more diffuse than a physical link between network elements. Naturally, when interfaces are incorporated in an element, assessing the conditions may become more involved unless external equipment can be used.

Deciding thresholds for performance variables, the load conditions for when these are valid must be described, see Figure 5.

In addition, an actor would also like to know the characteristics of the loads at the ingress points. For instance, loads with higher variability or having sever correlation may influence the network such that the performance is significantly worse compared to situations where such effects are not present. Therefore, descriptions of traffic characteristics should also be given. Alternatively, counteracts could be taken if the offered traffic load deviates from the characteristics. It might be tempting to either avoid such situations or making the relevant traffic flows confirm with the better characteristics (e.g., by applying shaping). Naturally, if the situation is such that no significant reduction of performance is foreseen, the traffic flow could be treated as it is. This may, in one way, seem similar to a "best effort" manner of treating the traffic load and could be stated as such in a contract. In that way the thresholds in the agreement may be regarded as minimum values which commonly are met and where higher values can be found when the network states allow for it.

Naturally, the actor will usually be the only instance having a complete view of the network state. In order to limit any disturbances following a network condition, it is a sound principle to choke the relevant traffic flows at the edges of the network. Considering interconnects, this means that suitable mechanisms should be present in the network elements associated with the ingress points.

Often, having described the conditions to appear on an interface, belonging measurements schemes are identified. Values for variables of the arrival processes, service mixture and the resulting performance are to be captured. As for every measurement, decision of when, where and what to measure must be made. That is, topics like time and duration, interface/location and events have to be specified. These are measurements which may be carried out by both parties of an interface. It must also be decided whether or not continuous measurements are to be performed. As measuring could be regarded as sampling, it is to be agreed upon if terms in a contract can be questioned based on a single measurement period or if a number of measurement periods have to be done of which several indicate that the terms can be questioned before the contract is renegotiated or other means are applied. This is also seen as a trade-off between the time for reactions (responsiveness of a scheme) and the effort needed for preparing for and carrying out the reactions.

In addition, measures treating sudden changes in the arrival processes must be present. Load control is an example of such quick response measures. Which measures to apply for an interface should also be stated in the interconnect contract. A number of measures, operating on a range of times scales, may be thought of.

Load control implying rejecting or delaying calls is considered as a feature utilised during operation. One of the purposes may be to avoid that a single group of services/call types seizes too large fraction of the capacity leading to degradation of the quality for other services/call types. This may be particularly relevant when mass calling services are introduced.

However, mass calling services could also mean that specific means should be taken by the neighbouring operators. One potential solution is that the dialled number is recognised as a mass calling type in those network domains as well, and the operators co-operate in order to collect the results, e.g., in case of televoting. Another potential solution is that the neighbouring operators recognise these calls and may be allowed to throttle a certain fraction (stated in the contract). It may, however, happen that directory numbers not belonging to the predefined mass calling series are announced leading to mass calling situations towards these numbers. To cater for such circumstances, appropriate load control schemes have to be applied on the basis of directory number series. In case information about application of directory numbers is not exchanged between actors, such means could be needed.

Another example where load control between operators may be requested is when an operator chooses to reroute calls to other domains through a network not prepared for that situation. This may happen when the more direct connection is not available (e.g. the circuit group is disconnected because of failure). Although accounting rules may treat this situation by introducing financial compensations, using measures for not degrading the service quality for the remaining services could be more fruitful in order to keep ones reputation.

Ensuring availability and successful calls for calls originated in a network domain and destined for other domains, is also an issue. In particular, as the users may require explanations and possible compensations by the operator/provider dealing with the originating side. Therefore, an interconnect agreement has to incorporate such cases as well. That is, on the call level both outgoing and incoming situations must be considered and the view of both parties must be taken on.

6 CONCLUSIONS

Effective utilisation of the involved equipment related to IN implies that methods for service quality calculations and network planning are needed. In particular, additional elements and potential service demand patterns may request that methods currently applied for telecommunication networks should be revisited. Most operators seem to base their future service portfolios on solutions similar to INs. Having appropriate methods covering the issues raised in this paper will therefore be essential.

Handling the IN-based services implies more signalling and processing. In order to carry out the performance evaluations, service demands have to be characterised, meaning that the resource usage of a call and the users' requests for calls are described. Commonly, an IN is integrated with networks also dealing with non-IN-based services. Specific phenomena associated with IN-based services in the circuit switched network, the signalling network and the network elements should be examined.

As more customers are basing their businesses on available telecommunication services, utilising proper mechanisms for achieving dependable solutions which at the same time are cost effective will also be an issue of specific interest. In particular, as more actors can result in higher competition, providing services with appropriate level of service quality will be essential. More actors, may also mean that more interconnect arrangements are needed. These interconnections should have agreements associated which also cover service quality issues.

REFERENCES

Bafutto, M.; Kühn, P.J. and Willmann, G. (1994) Capacity and Performance Analysis of Signaling Networks in Multivendor Environments. *IEEE JSAC.* Vol. 12, no. 3, 490-500.

Demounem, L. and Arai, H. (1992) A Performance Evaluation of an Integrated Control and OAM Information Transport Network with Distributed Database Architectures. *IEICE Trans. Commun.* E75-B, no. 12, 1315-1326.

E.724; ITU-T recommendation E.724: GOS parameters and target GOS objectives for IN-based services.

E. 734; ITU-T recommendation E.734: Methods for allocating and dimensioning Intelligent Network (IN) resources.

Jormakka, J. (1995) Calculation of blocking probability in televoting. *12th Nordic Teletraffic Seminar.* Helsinki, 97-107.

Kwiatkowski, M. (1995) Performance modelling of UPT networks. *ICUPC'95.* Tokyo, 543-547.

Pandya, R. (1994) Emerging Standards for PCS Traffic Performance. *ICUPC'94.* San Diego, CA, 581-585.

Q.12xx; ITU-T recommendation series Q.1200: Intelligent Network recommendation.

Ramaswami, V. (1995) The essential role of traffic performance analysis in Intelligent Networks. *Globecom'95.* Singapore, 1254-1259.

Saito, H. and Asaka T. (1994) Traffic aspect of personal telecommunications in intelligent networks. *Computer Networks and ISDN Systems*, 26, 1089-1099.

PART ELEVEN

Mobile, Intelligent Agents

27

Intelligent Agents for a Mobile Network Manager (MNM)

Akhil Sahai[†], *Christine Morin*[†], *Stéphane Billiart*[‡]
†*INRIA*
‡ *BULL*
IRISA, Campus Universitaire de Beaulieu
35042 Rennes Cedex (France)
{asahai, cmorin, billiart}@irisa.fr

Abstract

MAGENTA (Mobile AGENT for Administration) is our mobile agent environment for network management. The MAGENTA environment is being developed under the action Astrolog* which is a highly dynamic and decentralized management system meant for the management of Astrolab, a distributed system comprising of heterogeneous machines running varied operating systems connected by a LAN. The MAGENTA environment enables the introduction of a unique idea of a Mobile Network Manager(MNM).

Keywords

Mobile Agents, Mobile Computing, Network Management, SNMP, Java

1 INTRODUCTION

The research project Astrolog intends to design a management environment for the Astrolab environment. The Astrolab environment comprises of a variety of machines running different Operating systems like PCs (executing Win3.1, Win95, WinNT, Linux, NetBSD) and many variants of POSIX environment. Astrolog introduces the concept of a simple, portable, light-weight and cost-effective manager for management of our local network. The manager being light-weight and portable can be executed from either a static computer or a mobile computer. The manager operating from a mobile computer is termed a Mobile Network Manager (MNM).

Under the action astrolog we are implementing the MAGENTA (Mobile AGENT for Administration) environment to enable the functioning of the

*Part of this work is being carried out under the GIE-DYADE collaboration between INRIA and BULL.

Intelligent Networks and Intelligence in Networks D. Gaiti (Ed.)
Published by Chapman & Hall

MNM and to decentralize network management functions. The MAGENTA environment is highly generic in nature and can be utilized for the administration of any kind of services including information retrieval, electronic commerce and data mining.

In this paper, we present the network management architecture of Astrolog and describe the design and implementation of the MNM. We also present the MAGENTA environment and also describe, how it is utilized to enable the functioning of the MNM. The rest of the paper is structured as follows. The subsequent section provides an overview of the mobile agents. This, is followed by an overview of network management systems.Section 4 presents an overview of the Astrolog architecture. Section 5 presents the MAGENTA environment. This is followed by the implementation details before concluding.

2 OVERVIEW OF INTELLIGENT MOBILE AGENTS

In lieu of the client-server paradigm which has not been able to cope with the various kinds of demands put on it, the mobile agent based computing approach has been propounded as the possible approach to the next generation computing (Colin *et al.* 1995). With the rapid proliferation of available data and its sources the users have been increasingly finding it difficult to obtain, analyze and utilize the available data in a coherent manner. the agent based computing has thus been proposed as a solution to lessen the burden of the users. The agent based computing has also been shown to be more effective in the case of partially connected computing.

In the weaker notion of agency an agent has been variously described as an autonomous program acting on behalf of the user and working under constraints predetermined by the user in order to accomplish a task or as an assistant of a user delegated to perform activities autonomously in order to lessen his responsibilities. Of late, the term agent has been increasingly used and hence it lacks a coherent description. An effort has been made in (Jennings, Wooldridge 1994) to study the hallmarks of agent-hood. The hallmarks have been put down namely as autonomy, social ability, responsiveness and proactiveness. The agents available are numerous and differ substantially in their functionality and performance. In (Beale *et al.* 1994), an effort to classify the various types of available agents has been made. The various types of agents have been classified as user agents, agent guides, autonomous agents, symbiotic and cooperative agents, anthropomorphic agents, agents for multi-agent systems, and agents for agent-oriented programming.

In the stronger notion of agency the agents along with the above mentioned capabilities are intended to possess human like qualities and behaviour, specially in the field of AI. The agents are endowed with notions like knowledge, belief, intention and obligation (Reilly, Bates 1995). The agents in some cases have ***mental states*** and sometimes are given human like visualization (Maes 1994).

Mobile agents have been proposed for various applications like electronic commerce, desktop applications, information retrieval, data-mining, messaging, user interface and network management. In the case of network management, they have been proposed for Telecommunication management Network (TMN) as in (Magedanz *et al.* 1996) and as generalized scripted and delegated agents for management in (Goldzmith, Yemini 1995). In (Goldzmith, Yemini 1995) the mobile agents are sent to remote sites where they are incorporated into the local network management program and are used for intelligent tasks like MIB (Management Information Base) filtering. These are mostly one hop agents and they are used to avoid transfer of data over the network and to execute management logic close to the remote site. However, these agents are not generic and are not portable. In (Krause 1997) the mobile agents are used to ameliorate the service scalability problem inherent in Intelligent Networks. They intend to utilize the mobile agent technology to provide telecommunication services instantly and to be customized directly at the locations where the intelligence is needed. CyberAgents (CyberAgent. 1997) are being sold as a commercial product and are intended for simple network management configuration applications.

Some agent implementations have been proposed and carried out (Gray 1995) (Johansen *et al.* 1995) (Telescript. 1996). The mobile agents we utilize are however generalized and highly portable in nature and are attuned particularly to the needs of working in a constrained and fallible environment thus enabling the development of an MNM. In MAGENTA environment mobile agents are programs that can move through a network under their own control migrating from host to host and interacting with other agents and resources on each of the hosts. This is thus an extension to the client/server model in which the client and server exchange messages during execution. Mobile agents are an effective paradigm for distributed computing and are particularly attractive for partially connected computing.

3 OVERVIEW OF NETWORK MANAGEMENT SYSTEMS

Network management systems essentially have the functionality of network monitoring and network control. Network monitoring is concerned with monitoring the state of the network without interference. While network control involves active participation and interference in the state of the network.

The network-monitoring portion of network-management is concerned with observing and analyzing the status of the network to be managed. Network monitoring is an essential aspect of automated network management. The information to be gathered includes static information, related to the configuration, dynamic information related to events in the network and statistical information, summarized from dynamic information. It also involves identification of faults and determining the reasons of the fault and taking remedial actions. It also involves proactive response to an impending fault and minimization and containment of the fault.

Network control is concerned with changing the variable values of various components of the network and causing those components to perform predefined actions. The area of configuration control encompasses a variety of functions relating to the configuration of network and computing elements. These include initialization, maintenance, and shutdown of individual components and logical subsystems. In the area of security control, the responsibility of the network management system is to coordinate and control the security mechanisms built into the configuration of networks and systems under its management control. These security mechanisms are intended to protect user and system resources, including the network management system itself.

A network management system contains four types of components: Network Management Stations (NMSs), agents running on managed nodes, management protocols, and management information. An NMS uses the management protocol to communicate with agents running on the managed nodes. The information communicated between the NMS and agents is defined by a Management Information Base (MIB). The management standards that have emerged are the Simple Network Management Protocol (SNMP) and the OSI management system which utilizes the Common Management Information Protocol (CMIP)(Warrier, Besaw. 1989). SNMP is simpler and more concise in comparison to CMIP which is more elaborate and provides many more functionalities.

Astrolog utilizes SNMP in keeping with its intention of being light-weight and simple. The SNMP protocol includes the following capabilities mainly,

- *Get*: enables the management station to retrieve the value of objects from the agent;
- *Set*: enables the management station to set the value of objects at the agent;
- *Trap*: enables an agent to notify the management station of significant events.

The prevalent architectures of network management systems are

- Centralized network management. A single centralized manager overlooks the management. It queries the network components on a timely basis to determine the health of the network. In this case, there is a centralized database located at the site of the manager which stores and provides the information about the network components.

- Hierarchical network management. A central manager is aided by a set of subordinate managers. The subordinate managers take off some of the responsibilities of the central manager. The central manager performs the role of overall manager and has the centralized database. The subordinate managers in turn manage their domains.
- Peer network management. A set of network managers manage the different domains of the network with timely interaction amongst them. Each of the peer managers have a database and thus the information stored is partitioned and to an extent replicated.
- Fully distributed network management. A totally distributed management architecture in which every agent shares the responsibility of management. The managers have information which pertains to their domain and thus the overall information is highly partitioned.

4 ASTROLOG OVERVIEW

Astrolog (Sahai *et al.* 1997(1))(Sahai *et al.* 1997(2)) is our management platform for managing our local research platform called Astrolab which comprises of heterogeneous machines running several different operating systems connected by LAN. Thus, it was necessary for us to have a light-weight, portable and cost-effective manager. The idea was not only to make a light and simple manager for our local platform but also to introduce new ideas in the realm of network management.

The design of Astrolog is highly modular in nature. This modularity enables the development of a light-weight *manager* which can be executed from a mobile computer. In Astrolog, there is a provision of multiple managers which are designed to be portable and can run from a variety of machines over the network in a client-server mode or in the mobile agent mode or sometimes utilizing both. These managers communicate with one or multiple *servers*(depending on the size of the network) running on sites containing databases. The databases are populated by respective discovery daemons which gather information about the network components and store them in the database. These values are updated timely by obtaining SNMP values from the SNMP agents running on the managed machines. Another daemon obtains the required information from the database or directly from the agents located at the managed system components, as and when requested by the managers. As compared to a typical centralized management system in which the centralized manager comprises of the GUI, the management applications

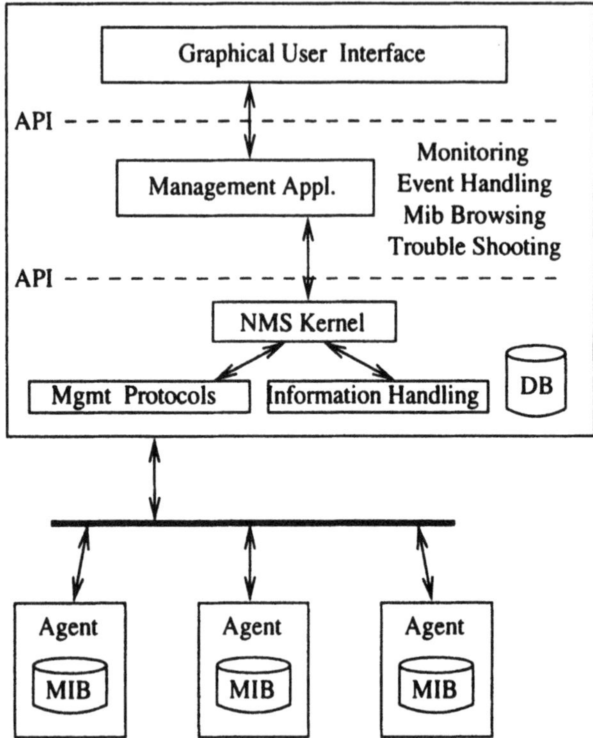

Figure 1 A typical centralized Network Management System

and the NMS kernel along with the database as shown in Figure 1, Astrolog is divided into light-weight managers comprising of the GUI and the management applications like MIB browsing and monitoring and a mechanism for connecting to the server and obtaining the required management information. The other part comprises of the NMS kernel (code which acts as the counterpart of the applications on the manager side and daemons), the database (DB) and a communication mechanism to interact with the managers, which in turn acts as the management server. There can be multiple managers querying one or more management servers. The managers can either exist on the same site as the server or can also exist at a different site and can query the server over the network as shown in Figure 2.

What facilitates the flexibility of the architecture is that the network managers are light-weight and thus there can be multiple interchangeable managers. We are utilizing this light-weightedness of the manager to build MNMs. Now-a-days in the event of a crisis the system administrator is informed by the management system through a pager message. One of the recourse left to the administrator is to rush to the central management station. In case of the absence of the system administrator in the proximity of the centralized

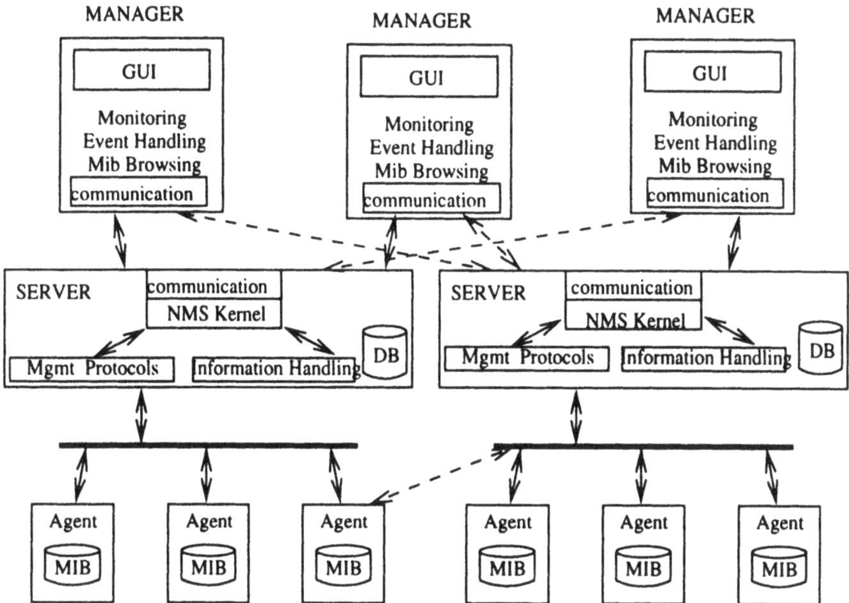

Figure 2 Astrolog Network Management System

management station, the system administrator is unaware of exact diagnostic information about the cause of the crisis and is thus extremely difficult for the administrator to undertake important decisions in case of a network breakdown. In case of a large network, there can be more than one administrators and it is sometimes essential to seek the opinion of more than one administrators at the same time. Also there is an increasing trend towards wireless networks and which according to us require a wireless network manager, thus we consider that there is an ample need and usefulness of MNMs . MNMs we propose are managers that run on portable computers which can either run in the tethered mode using a PPP/SLIP mechanism or can run on a roaming wireless computer (Gray *et al.* 1996). Our design takes care of both the situations.

What distinguishes these mobile computers are the extreme constraints on the link available to them. The links have serious bandwidth constraints, have high latency and are prone to sudden failures such as when a signal from a cellular modem is blocked by an obstacle. The computer may be forced to use different transmission channels depending on its physical location. Finally depending on the nature of the transmission channel, the computer may be assigned a different network address each time it connects. Both wireless networks and phone lines are orders of magnitude more constrained than traditional LANs (Oracle. 1995) as shown in Table 1 and in Table 2. Table 1

Table 1 Comparison of Networks (from (Oracle. 1995))

Networks	*BW (Kbps)*	*Latency (secs)*
Wireless WAN	2K-9	4-10
Modem	2.4K-28.8	0.2-0.5
LAN	5K-10K	0.0005-0.002

Table 2 Comparison for 50 round trips (from (Oracle. 1995))

Networks	*Latency (secs)*	*Response time (secs)*
Wireless WAN	4	200
Modem	0.3	15.0
LAN	0.002	0.1

shows the dramatic discrepancies between bandwidth (kilobytes per second) and the network round trip times (latency) of the media.

Normally a client-server paradigm is utilized for most of the distributed computation. Considering a client-server application which exchanges approximately fifty messages, the Table. 2 shows how that application fares over a LAN, a phone line, and a wireless network.

The mobile computer thus has a highly constrained and fallible link and has limited battery storage capacity. Because of these reasons a mobile computer is more attuned to partially connected computing. The mobile agent paradigm provides this facility of partially connected computing and also the capability of performing functions inspite of intermittent connections. Thus mobile agent paradigm is suitable for the implementation of the MNMs. In order to enable the MNMs we are developing our own mobile agent environment called MAGENTA (Mobile AGENT for Administration). We also utilize the environment for decentralizing certain network management functions.

For implementing this scheme of MNMs, we model an indirect interaction. There is thus a concept of a static proxy in our design. One of the existing static managers is allocated to each portable computer to act as a proxy. The proxy acts as an intermediary between the portable computer and the server. The agent emanating from the portable computer on reaching the proxy conveys the requests to the proxy. The proxy tries to get the information from the server. In case the operation is successfully carried out, the agent before going back to the portable computer checks whether it is still connected. In case the proxy is not able to provide the information to the agent, it can either move to the server site or to the site of SNMP agents to obtain the

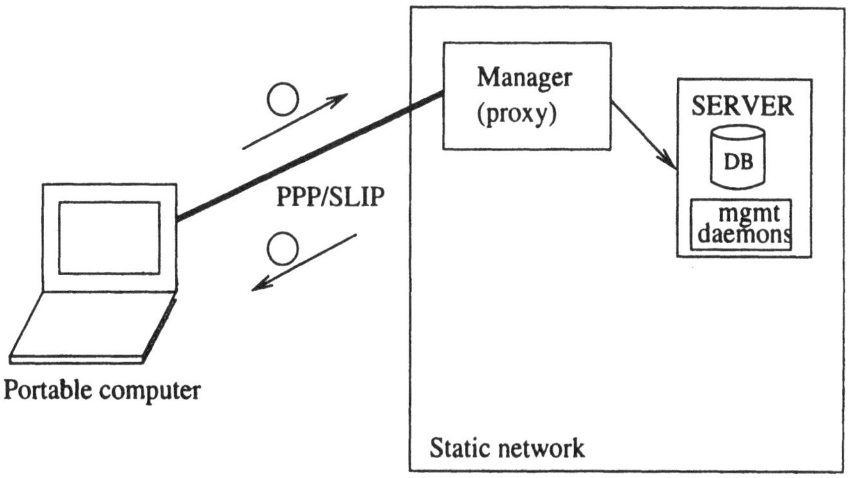

Figure 3 The MNM in tethered mode

necessary information. If the portable computer is connected it goes back to the portable computer otherwise the agent waits for the portable computer to connect again. The agents thus reduce the continuous usage of the highly constrained link and also take care of it fallibility. The tethered mode of operation is straightforward as depicted in Figure 3. In the tethered mode the portable is connected to the static network through a PPP/SLIP mechanism and the mobile manager runs on the portable which sends mobile agents to retrieve the required information from time to time. These agents collect the information and either return back immediately if the portable remains connected otherwise they wait and return back as soon as the portable is connected back.

The wireless mode of operation needs to be explained in detail. Normally in the area of wireless computing the total domain is divided into cells. Each of the cells have a Mobile Support Station (MSS) of their own. The responsibility of serving the Mobile Host (MH) as it moves from one cell to another cell changes from one MSS to another (Bakre, Badrinath. 1994)(Markku *et al.* 1995). The utilization of a static proxy serves us in good stead. The mobile agent as launched by the portable computer (MH) goes to the proxy which in turn obtains the required information. In the meanwhile if the MH moves to a new cell the new MSS is informed by the MH to retrieve the agent waiting at the proxy with the results. The proxy then delivers the agent at the new location of MH as shown in the Figure 4.

5 MAGENTA ENVIRONMENT

MAGENTA (Mobile AGENT for Administration) is our local mobile agent en-

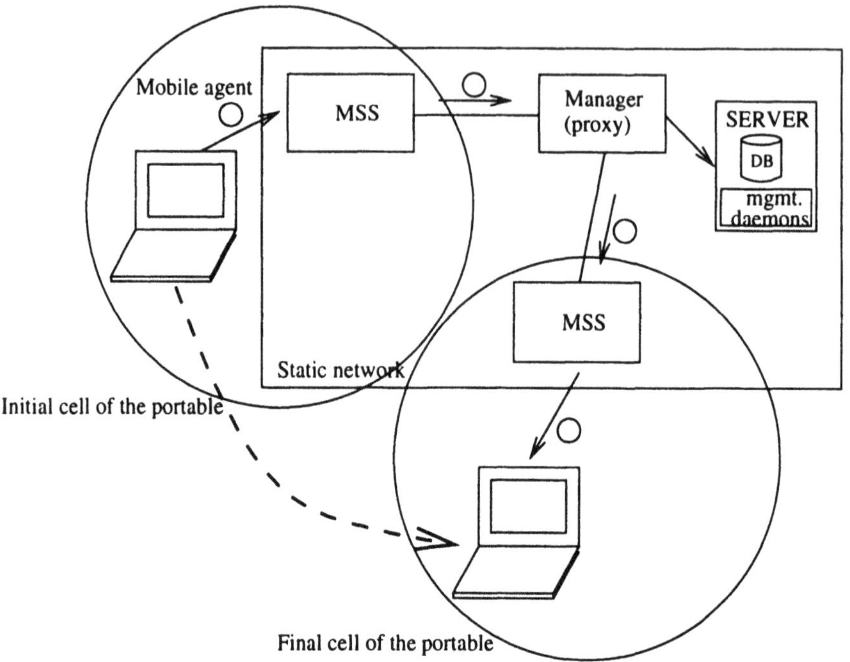

Figure 4 The MNM in wireless mode

vironment written in Java. The MAGENTA environment essentially comprises of the lieus and agents. The lieus are sites which provide the functionality of sending, receiving and executing the agents and of allowing the agents to access the local resources, if necessary as shown in Figure 5. Lieus can exist independently as in the case of network elements supporting SNMP agents and the network management server(s) but are integrated with the network managers on the network elements where the managers exist. Agents are mobile code which move from one lieu to another and perform a goal-directed behaviour. They exhibit the characteristics of autonomy, mobility, social ability, reactivity and proactiveness. The agents are autonomous as they exhibit control over their state and actions as they *move* from one lieu to another. They are reactive as they react to the changes in the environment and alter their behaviour accordingly. They are proactive because they take the initiative and have a predefined *purpose*. They are socially able as they can *meet* other agents.

In our environment mobile agents are autonomous programs and perform a predefined task and interact with the available resources in the optimum manner. An agent interacts with the resources that are available on the lieu where it executes its task. For security reasons, an access control is introduced: the agents are not given direct access to system resources and the access to any resource is always predefined and controllable by the lieu. Every agent carries a permit which identifies the agent and the origin of it. These permits determine the priority and the range of functionality of the agent. The MAGENTA environment provides autonomy to the agent by providing it the capability of operating without direct human intervention, they can utilize the *move* primitive to move to a destination without human intervention. The agents can change their itinerary by using a *decide* primitive. They exhibit social ability, interact with other agents and pass information amongst themselves through *notes*. They are reactive because they perceive their environment and respond to them in a timely fashion for example they have *decide* primitive to decide their itinerary depending on the availability of services at a lieu. They are proactive because they exhibit goal-directed behaviour by taking initiative. Each agent is provided with a *purpose* and they perform actions to fulfill the *purpose*.

In our case an agent can move from one lieu to another, thus occupying different lieus at different times, but only one lieu at time, i.e they cannot be fragmented. An agent moves to other destination by utilizing *move* instruction. This instruction can appear at arbitrary points, and once the instruction is called, the agent is transmitted to the destination machine with its state. The lieus handle all transmission details, including the possibility of the destination machine being disconnected.

In order to provide the knowledge of available services to the agent we utilize *backward learning*. An agent carries its own history, that is, the identifier of the sender that has launched it, the identifier of the lieus on which the agent has been and the services that the agent has used on each. So, when an agent arrives on a lieu, the lieu can read the agent's history and learns which are some services that the lieus, which the agent comes from, perform. Therefore, the lieu updates a list called *other service list*. This technique is utilized to update the already available information at the lieu given to them initially. If a lieu has no information about a service, the lieu gives the agent a list of lieus from which the agent can choose to go to and get the required information.

So, the logical state of the lieu in our environment comprises of:

- The list of available services "other service list".
- The list of it's own services, the "own service list" with all services that the lieu performs.
- The state of all the running agents.
- The list of all lieus which are up and working.

while the logical state of the agent comprises of:

- Purpose: The intention of the agent.
- Services Done: it is the agent's history. It can be null if the agent hasn't completed. This information is necessary for the backward learning.

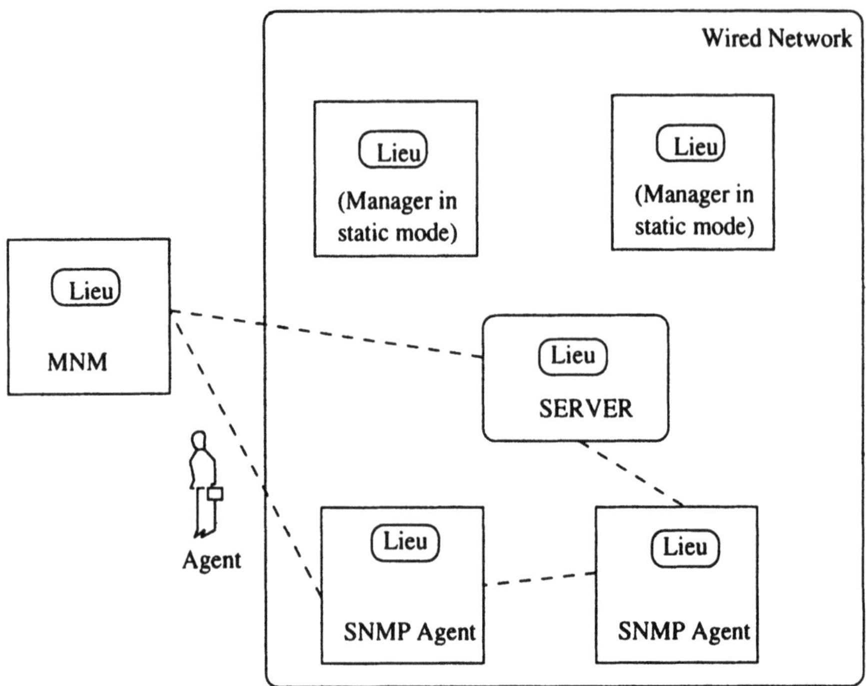

Figure 5 Utilization of mobile agents for network management in MAGENTA environment

- Next Service List: it can hold 0, 1, or more elements. The list carries the services that the agent hasn't accomplished yet.
- Sender: it is the address of the sender lieu which has launched the mobile agent. It is necessary to allow the agent to go back;
- Folder: In this the agent carries the results and responses.
- Permit: It is used to authenticate the sender lieu of the mobile agent, to control the resources and functions access.
- Note: In case there is a note to be passed to other agents.

The design of MAGENTA environment, thus is highly generic in nature and can be utilized for the administration of different services like data mining, electronic commerce and obviously network management.

6 IMPLEMENTATION

The Astrolog action as detailed above comprises of the managers and the servers. The implementation of manager and server is underway. A skeletal manager and server having limited functionality have been implemented. The server part comprises of a database, a communication mechanism, a network management system kernel which also comprises of a discovery daemon. The discovery daemon discovers the devices and populates the database. The NMS kernel also comprises of daemon which queries the SNMP agents executing on SNMP capable devices to know their status and stores the information in the database. The manager comprises of the GUI, the applications and a mechanism to access the information from the server. The managers operate in static or dynamic mode depending on their mode of communication which is either utilization of client-server mechanism or utilization of mobile agent technology respectively.

The implementation of MAGENTA environment is nearing completion. A small agent demonstrator has been implemented. The MAGENTA environment is written in Java and utilizes Java Object Serialization of JDK1.1.1. The agents are Java classes which migrate between the lieus which are integrated with the managers.

Java (Gosling, McGilton. 1995) was chosen for implementation of MNM and MAGENTA because it is architecturally neutral. It was intended to have multiple managers accessing the server from a variety of platforms, thus only the local managers needed to be platform-independent. It was a necessity in our case because Astrolab is a heterogeneous system. Java is also object-oriented and dynamically extensible and thus suitable for writing mobile agents. Java also provides the capability of native methods to access the local operating system and thus is ideally suited for obtaining system information. Because of these reasons Java has been recently used for network management applications like MIB browsing (AdventNet. 1997). Java also provides the capability of deriving meaningful meta-variables from the available SNMP variables to the local managers enabling them to monitor the local domains more effectively. The local managers are thus capable of providing the system users and the system administrator an easily portable network and system visualization and management platform. The managers connect to the management servers over the network through a high-level protocol or by utilizing mobile agents.

7 CONCLUSION

Astrolog contributes significantly to the utilization of mobile agents in the domain of network management. It introduces the unique concept of Mobile Network Manager (MNM) which would be extremely useful in the near future because of proliferation of wireless networks. It also furthers the cause of the utilization of mobile agents for resource constrained portable computers and as an essential mode of usage in the case of partially connected computing. It introduces the concept of a simple, portable, cost-effective, light-weight and mobile manager. It also introduces the generic MAGENTA environment for administration.

We intend to utilize MAGENTA environment for decentralizing most of the network management functions in the static mode of operation of the manager also. An elaborate study of the appropriateness of the mobile agent paradigm and the client-server paradigm for different network management functionalities is envisaged.

REFERENCES

AdventNet (1997) Advent NetMonitor *Fabricated by Advent Network Management Inc.*, http://www.adventnet.com.

Bakre, A. and Badrinath, B.R. (1994) I-TCP: Indirect TCP for Mobile Hosts *Technical Report DCS-TR-314, Department of Computer Science, Rutgers University, 1994.*

Beale, R. and Wood, A. (1994) Agent Based Interaction.*In People and Computers IX: Proceedings of HCI'94, Glasgow, UK, August 1994* 239-245.

Case, J. Fedor, M. Schoffstall. M, and Davin, J. (1990) A Simple Network Management Protocol (SNMP) *RFC 1157.*

Colin, G. and Harrison et al. (1995) Mobile Agents: Are they a good idea? *IBM T.J. Watson Research Center Technical Report, 1995.*

CyberAgent (1997) Agent applications *Fabricated by FTP Software*, http://www.ftp.com/product/.

Goldzmith, G. and Yemini, Y. (1995) Decentralizing Control and Intelligence in Network Management. *In the Proc. of 4th International Symposium on Integrated Network Management, Santa Barbara, CA, 1995.*

Gosling, J. and McGilton, H. (1995) The Java Language Environment: A White paper *Technical Report, Sun Microsystems, 1995.*

Gray, R. Kotz, D. Nog, S. Rus,D. Cybenko, G. (1996) Mobile Agents for Mobile Computing *Technical report PCS-TR96-285, Department of Computer Science, Dartmouth College, hanover, 1996.*

Gray , R.S. (1995) Agent Tcl: Alpha Release 1.1, 1995. *Available at http://www.cs.dartmouth.edu/ rgray/transportable.html.*

Jennings, N. and Wooldridge, M. (1994) Software Agents. *IEE Review, January 1994*, 17-20.

Johansen, D. Renesse, R.V. and Schneider, F.B.(1995) An Introduction to TACOMA Distributed System *Technical report CS-95-23, Department of Computer Science, Institute of Mathematical and Physical Sciences, University of Tromso.*, http://www.cs.uit.no/DOS/Tacoma/.

Maes, P. (1994) Agents that reduce work and information overload *Communications of the ACM, 37(7):31-40, 1994 .*

Magedanz, T. Rothermel, K. and Krause, S. (1996) Intelligent Agents: An Emerging technology for Next Generation Telecommunications *INFO-*

COM 96, USA, March 24-28, 1996.

Kraus, S. (1997) MAGNA-A DPE-based Platform for Mobile Agents in Electronic Service Markets.*Submission for ISADA '97-The Third International Symposium on Autonomous Decentralized Systems, 9-11 April 1997, Berlin, Germany.*

Markku, Kojo. Alanko, Timo. Liljeberg, Mika. and Raatikainen, Kimmo. (1995) Enhanced Communication Services for Mobile TCP/IP Networking *Technical Report C-1995-15, Deptt. of Computer Science, University of Helsinki.*

Oracle. (1995) Oracle White Paper: Oracle Mobile Agents *Technical Report , August, 1995.*

Reilly, S. and Joseph, W.B. (1995) Natural negotiation for Believable Agents *Technical report CMU-CS-95-164, School of Computer Science, Carnegie Mellon University, 1995.*

Rose, M. and McCloghrie, K. (1990) Structure and Identification of Management Information for TCP/IP-based internets (SMI) *RFC 1155.*

Sahai, A. Billiart, S. and Morin, C. (1997(1)) Astrolog: A distributed and dynamic environment for network and system management.*In the Proc. of 1st European Information Infrastructure User Conference, Stuttgart, Germany, Feb. 1997*, http://www.irisa.fr/solidor/doc/pub97.html.

Sahai, A. Billiart, S. and Morin, C. (1997(2)) A portable and mobile manager for distributed system management.*In the Proc. of Third Joint Conferenceon Information Sciences, Raleigh, USA, Mar. 1997*, http://www.irisa.fr/solidor/doc/pub97.html.

Stallings. SNMP, SNMPv2 and CMIP: The practical guide to network management standards. *Addison-Wesley publication, 1994.*

Telscript (1996) Telescript at General Magic Inc. *Information available at http://www.genmagic.com/Telescript/index.html.*

Warrier, U. and Besaw, L. (1989) The Common Management Information Services and Protocols over TCP/IP (CMOT) *RFC 1095.*

28

Deploying IN Services in a Mobile Environment

D. Haran

Comverse Network Systems

170 Crossways Park Drive, Woodbury , New York 11797 USA
Tel: (516) 677-7200, Fax: (516) 677-7355
E-mail danny_haran@comverse.com

Abstract

Introducing new IN services into mobile networks presents new challenges with respect to the integration of IN Service Nodes into a mobile environment. This paper examines the issues which are involved in routing calls to and from the Service Node, for both Originating and Terminating IN services, in centralised and distributed system configurations. The paper highlights the inherent difficulties associated with subscriber mobility, and present solutions for the various cases.

Keywords

Service Node, SN, Mobile Networks, IN Services

1. INTRODUCTION

This paper presents a method by which IN services can be seamlessly deployed in a mobile environment, through a Service Node (SN) solution. It introduces the difficulties in getting the calls to the SN, on one hand, and reaching the Mobile Station (MS), on the other hand, without requiring software changes in the network components. Finally, the paper presents possible solutions available with the TRILOGUE INfinity IP/SN.

2. IN SERVICES ON A SERVICE NODE

Most subscriber value-added services, which are referred to as IN services, have one common characteristic - they are all "calling services". In other words, they deal with making or receiving telephone calls in a way that brings an added value to the subscriber. The service can affect the way the call is initiated or terminated, how it is billed, etc.

Typical examples for *terminating* IN services are Personal Number Service and Call Screening. Common *originating* IN services are Pre-Paid Service, Voice Activated Dialing and Virtual Private Network.

Such IN services can be implemented in several ways, regardless of whether the network has full IN infrastructure or not. In a pre-IN network, IN services are often deployed on a Service Node, which provides all the necessary ingredients, including service logic, switching and voice resources. A self contained SN, such as the TRILOGUE INfinity IP/SN, can deploy IN services even if the telephone network is not yet IN compliant.

When deploying IN services on an SN, all calls must flow through the SN, at least for the call setup phase. The network switches need a way to get calls to the SN, and the SN must be able to deliver the calls to their final destination. This raises several interesting issues, especially in a mobile environment, where mobile subscribers may be "connected" to any of the network switches, depending on their current location.

3. CALL PROCESSING IN A MOBILE NETWORK

3.1. Mobile Network Architecture

In order to discuss the issues of using an SN in a mobile network, it is important to fully understand the way *regular* calls are processed and routed by the network, and introduce some of the key concepts and entities used in mobile networks.

The following schematic diagram shows the basic components of a mobile network, with two switches (MSCs - Mobile Switching Centers), and a mobile subscriber connected to one of the switches through a base station.

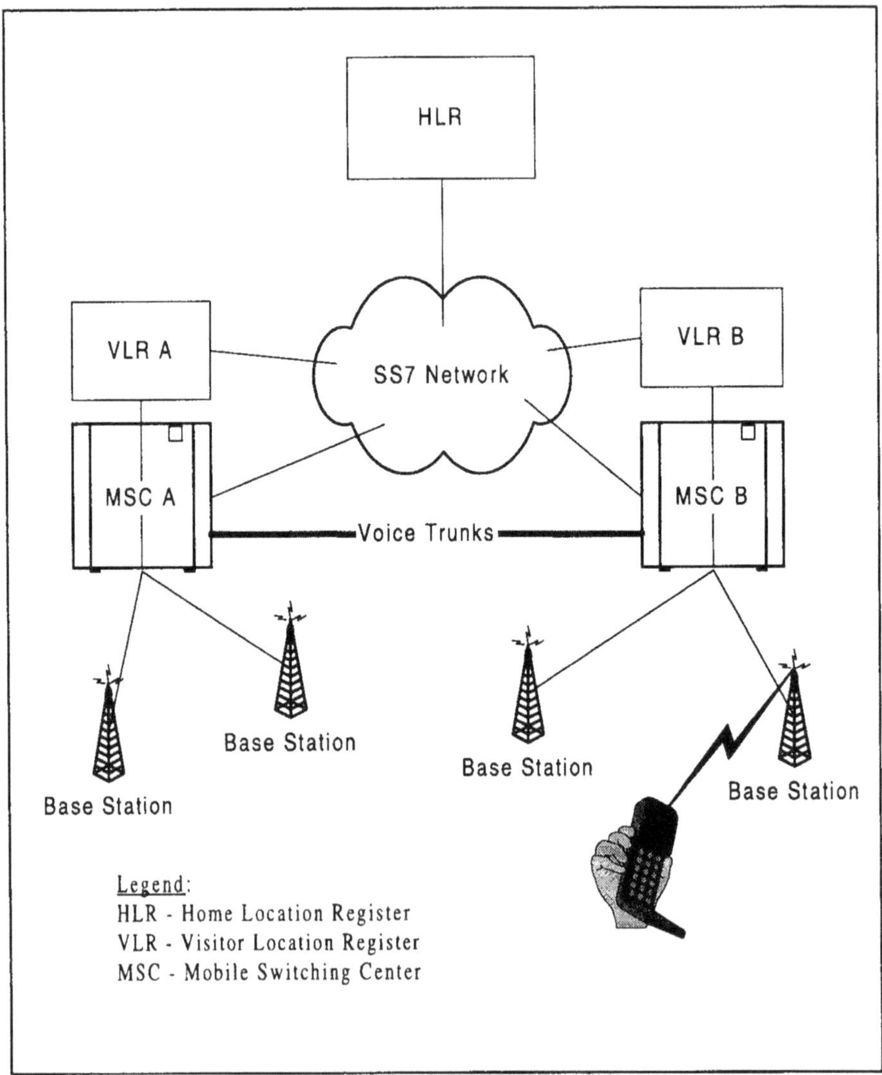

Figure 1 - Mobile Network Entities

The diagram is very schematic, and does not show other systems used for management, authentication, etc. The following systems are shown:

- **MSC - Mobile Switching Center**. This is the switch within the mobile network. Two MSCs are shown, but a network can contain any number of

MSCs, depending on its size and geographical disparity. Some of the MSCs may be also used as gateways to the fixed network.

- **Base Stations**. These are the cellular stations, which handle the wireless communication with the mobile subscribers. Each base station can represent one or multiple cells in the cellular network. In the diagram, only two are shown for each MSC; in reality, one MSC may be connected to dozens or even hundreds of base stations, depending on the area which must be covered by the MSC, cell sizes, etc.
- **HLR - Home Location Register**. A centralized database of mobile subscribers. One or several HLRs may be used in one mobile network. The HLR stores the subscribers profile, for example their call forwarding options. Most important, the HLR keeps track of the current location of each mobile subscriber, that is, through which MSC the subscriber can be reached.
- **VLR - Visitor Location Register**. This is a local database for each MSC, where all the mobile subscribers who are currently reachable through the MSC are listed. Whenever a mobile subscriber turns on his handset, or moves into range of one of the MSC base stations, he is registered in the VLR. In addition, the VLR queries the HLR for the subscriber profile, for future use.

Obviously, the main difference between a fixed network and a mobile network, is the mobility of the subscribers. Unlike fixed network subscribers, which are permanently associated with a specific Central Office switch, a mobile subscriber may move around (roam) between areas covered by different MSCs. So the process of routing a call to a mobile subscriber is more complex, and requires knowing (or finding out) through which MSC the subscriber can be reached at any time.

Before describing the process of calling a mobile subscriber, two additional terms need to be defined. The specific terms used are taken from the GSM network, and may have other names in other network types.

- **MSISDN** (Mobile Station ISDN) Number- This is, simply, the mobile subscriber telephone number. It can contain up to 16 digits (including the area code), and varies in length depending on the home country numbering plan. The MSISDN number is associated with the mobile handset, or, in GSM, the SIM card. It is not changed when the subscriber moves from one MSC to another.
- **MSRN** (Mobile Subscriber Roaming Number). This is a temporary number assigned to each visiting subscriber by the VLR, which is associated with each MSC. The MSRN is uniquely associated with an MSC/VLR, and is used for routing calls within the network. The idea is to allow the network switches use conventional call switching techniques, which are based on analyzing the Dialed Number. While the MSISDN number cannot be used that way (as it does not imply anything on the target MSC, where the subscriber can be found), the MSRN can be analyzed for routing purposes, since it is linked to

the visiting MSC/VLR, not with the subscriber. The allocation of the MSRN, and the association between the MSRN and the MSISDN numbers is local to each VLR.

3.2. Routing Call to Mobile Subscribers

The following diagram shows the messages exchanged between the various network entities in order to get a call to a Mobile Station (MS), who happens to be in an area covered by MSC B (refer to Fig. 1). The call originates in MSC A, which is referred to as the Gateway MSC (GMSC) for that call. MSC B is called the Visiting MSC (VMSC). The call could have been initiated by another mobile subscriber registered on MSC A, or from a fixed network telephone, assuming that MSC A is also the PSTN gateway. The base station, where the MS is actually connected, and the MS itself are not shown, for simplicity.

The diagram shows two scenarios. The first one takes place when the MS registers at MSC B, for instance after turning on the handset. After establishing a radio connection with one of MSC B's base stations, the MS is registered at VLR B, which also notifies the HLR of the new location of the MS. The HLR, in response, will send several fields of the MS profile back to VLR B, where they will be later used if necessary.

The second scenario shows a call for the MS, which arrives at MSC A. The origin of the call is not relevant for the search of the MS. MSC A issues a query to the HLR, asking for an MSRN of the MS. The HLR, knowing that the MS is visiting MSC B, will prompt VLR B for that MSRN, and will return that MSRN to MSC A. Now, MSC A can apply standard routing techniques, based on the MSRN, to select the proper trunk group leading to MSC B, and finally to the MS.

The diagram does not try to follow the call setup all the way through. There may be many different scenarios, depending on whether the MS was busy, or did not answer, on forwarding options, etc. If, for instance, the call needs to be forwarded to another MSISDN number, then MSC B will start the process all over again, so it can route the call to its final destination.

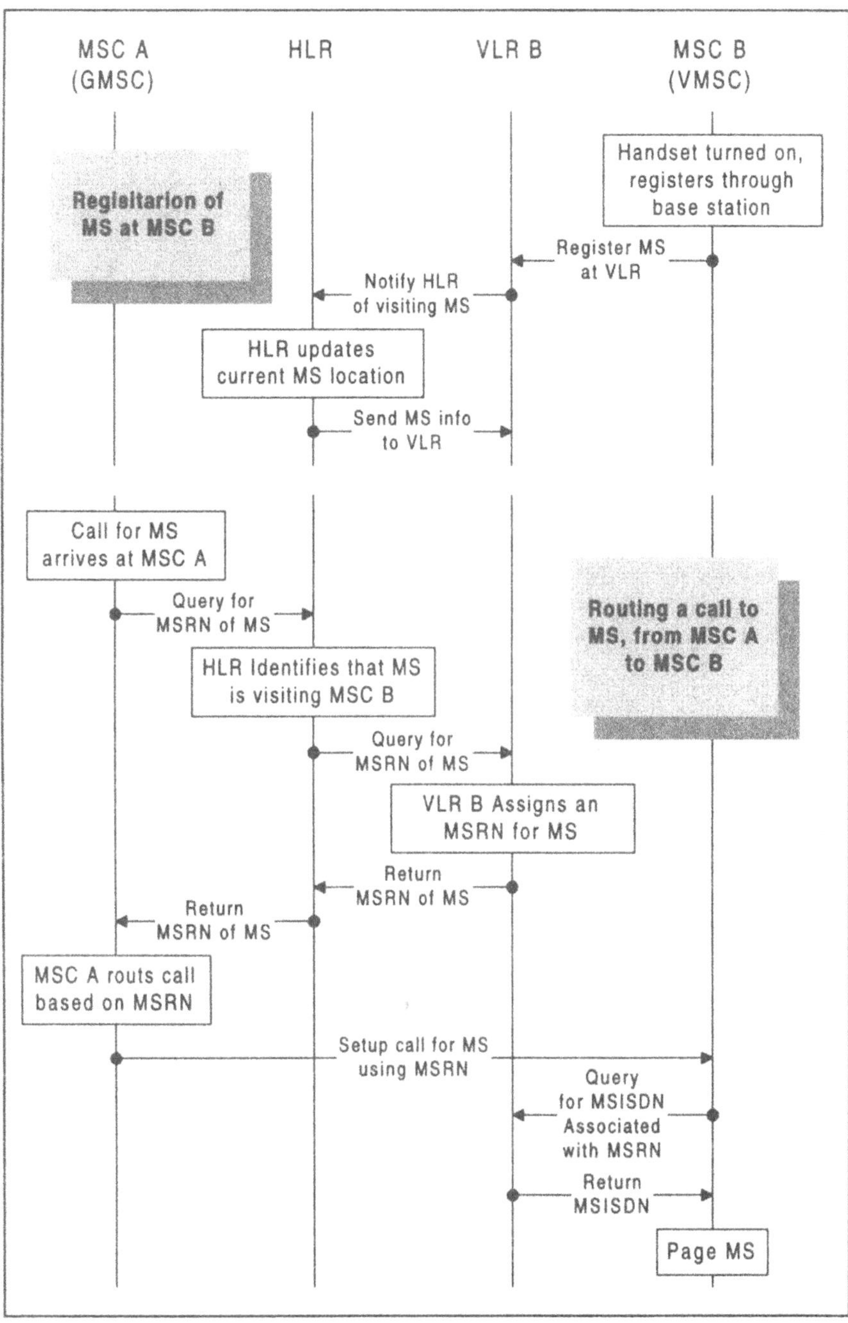

Figure 2 - Routing Calls to a Mobile Subscriber

3.2. Service Nodes - the Additional Complexity

The problems and issues related to deploying service nodes in a mobile network, which are the main topic of this paper, can be attributed to several factors:

- Some services require that all originating or terminating calls for *particular* subscribers are routed through a service node. MSCs were not built to *selectively* route calls to a destination other than the dialed number itself. Deciding how to handle each call is a complex task.
- If more than one SN is involved, then the issue of which SN should be selected to provide a specific service for a given subscriber could also be problematic. The HLR was not designed to provide routing information for anything but mobile subscribers, so if MSCs need routing assistance for locating the proper SN, there may be a need in another HLR-like solution for that purpose.
- Some calls directed to an MSISDN number must reach an SN. Other calls, especially those generated by the SN, need to get to the mobile handset. This could result in loops, and may require significant attention to accomplish.
- Originating service calls may present special problems, as they require processing based on the *calling* party number, which is, again, a task MSCs are not optimized to handle.

The following sections deal in greater detail with these and other issues, and present the solutions, which are available with the Comverse TRILOGUE INfinity IP/SN system.

4. GETTING CALLS TO THE SERVICE NODE

In order for the network switches to route calls to the SN, a three-step process is required:

- Identifying that a particular call needs to be delivered to the SN. This is different for originating and terminating services.
- Translating the Dialed Number (DN) of the call to a value can be routed to the SN. The new DN may be a special prefix followed by the subscriber MSISDN number. This step may not be required, if the call was made to a special access code.
- Routing the call to the SN, using standard call routing techniques. This is possible if the previous stage set the DN to a value which leads to a proper routing tree, which is associated with the SN.

4.1. Originating Services

Originating IN services include Pre-Paid Services (PPS) and Virtual Private Network (VPN). In these services, each call originated by the mobile subscriber must, first of all, get to the SN for processing. Other services, such as Voice Activated Dialing (VAD) require that the subscriber dial some short code in order to access the service.

Whenever the subscriber tries to make an outgoing call, the call is processed by the local MSC covering the area where the subscriber is presently situated. This MSC is known as the Visiting MSC (VMSC) for the mobile subscriber.

In order to identify that this call must be sent to the SN, the VMSC must route the call based on the identity of the *caller* (the "A number"), which in this case is represented by the subscriber's MSISDN number. Clearly, the dialed number (the "B number") cannot be used for routing to the SN in services such as PPS or VPN, since any number may be dialed.

The VMSC may decide that a call needs to be processed by the SN in one of several ways:

- Based on the A number, if it is within a predefined number range. This requires that all the telephone numbers associated with a particular service form one or several contiguous number blocks. This requirement is often not acceptable for network operators, since it means that the mobile subscriber has to *change his number* when subscribing to a new service. In addition, the subscriber is also limited in the number of services he can subscribe to, due to potentially conflicting number ranges.
- Through an HLR interrogation operation, the VMSC can query if the given subscriber has a predefined flag set, representing the IN originating service. If the flag is set, the call needs to be delivered to the SN. The query makes use of the Send Routing Information (SRI) MAP message. Note that this solution requires that a free field is available for that purpose in the HLR subscriber profile.
- Based on the dialed number, if it is equal to a specific access number to that service. That method may be used in VAD, but is not pertinent for VPN and PPS.

Note that this processing only relates to calls, which are *originated* at the VMSC, directly from the mobile handset. Any other calls, coming over other trunk groups, from other switches or networks, are not subject to this processing.

4.2. Terminating Services

In terminating IN services, such as Personal Number Service (PNS), the MSC decides whether a call needs to be transferred to the SN based on the dialed number (the "B number"). The calling number is not relevant, since the call may be originated from any telephone, mobile or not.

The MSC may use one of the following methods to make the decision:

- If the dialed number is within a predefined number block, which is all dedicated to the service. This may not always be applicable, since in many cases mobile subscribers should be able to subscribe to the service without having to change their number.
- Using HLR interrogation, and expecting a special flag in a reserved field of the subscriber profile.

4.3. Routing the Call to the Service Node

Once the decision has been made to transfer the call to the SN, both for originating and terminating services, then routing the call to the SN is done using regular switch routing techniques, as explained below.

The call is sent to the SN either through a dedicated trunk group, or by changing the dialed number to a specific predefined number which is associated with the SN and the specific service. The network MSCs are programmed to route this number to the SN, even if they do not have a direct connection to it.

Regardless of the method used, it is crucial that the SN receives both the original A and B numbers, so it can process the call properly. Also, there must be an indication of the exact *service* being requested. This may be implied by the predefined number used to access the SN, or through any other IAM message field. However, if the network cannot identify (or cannot deliver) the exact service required, the SN can still identify the service based on the subscriber profile stored in the SN. Alternatively, the SN can query a remote subscriber profile, for instance, through HLR interrogation.

Note that in a distributed environment, where multiple service nodes provide the service, routing the call to the right SN may be quite complex. The issue of distributed solutions is discussed in section 7 below.

5. CALLING THE MOBILE SUBSCRIBER

Once the call has reached the SN, it is processed according to the service, the subscriber profile and the call parameters. Often, the SN needs to make an outgoing call, resembling the original call in many ways. Getting this call through the network is the tricky part of deploying IN services in mobile networks.

For instance, in a PNS scenario, the SN may wish to deliver the incoming call to the mobile subscriber, based on the PNS subscriber profile. The problem is that the PNS number is usually the *same number* as the mobile number (the MSISDN number), so unless some measures are taken, the network may bounce that call back to the SN, creating infinite loops. There must be a way for the mobile network to differentiate calls coming from the SN and calls coming from any other origin, even if they are trying to reach the same number.

There are two ways in which the SN and the mobile network can handle the situation, avoiding potential loops:

- By initiating all calls from the SN to the MSC on a dedicated trunk group, and thus guiding the switch to handle the call arriving on this trunk group in a different manner than what is described above. Hence, for such calls, the MSC does not check if the dialed number refers to any terminating service such as PNS, but rather, handles the call in the standard way, just like any call directed to a mobile subscriber. One problem with this approach is that it may require dividing the trunk group leading from the SN to the MSC into several smaller trunk groups, each dedicated for a specific service and use.
- By issuing calls from the SN to the network using an *MSRN number* rather than the MSISDN number. The TRILOGUE INfinity IP/SN can interrogate the HLR, using the SRI message, and route the call based on the returned MSRN number. The call will be handled in a totally different manner because now it is routed by the network based on the MSRN and not the MSISDN number, effectively eliminating infinite loops.

The second solution provides a smoother integration of the SN with the mobile network, by not imposing any dedicated trunk groups from the SN to one or several MSCs. It utilizes the TRILOGUE INfinity IP/SN HLR Interrogation capability, making the SN tightly integrated into the mobile network.

6. COMPLETING ORIGINATING SERVICE CALLS

In an IN originating service, such as Pre-Paid Service (PPS), the SN issues the outgoing call "on behalf" of the mobile subscriber, either to another mobile subscriber or to a PSTN number. Here, in order to maintain features such as CLI display, the SN needs to initiate the call with the same A number as the original call, which is the PPS subscriber MSISDN number. Here also, there is a potential problem of infinite loops, if the network cannot differentiate between the call from the SN and the call coming from the mobile handset. The potential problem is that the MSC will look at the A number and find out that it relates to a PPS subscriber, and thus route the call back to the SN.

There are two ways, in which the SN outgoing call can be distinguished from a call originating from the mobile handset:

- The best way is to have the switches only refer to the A number on calls *coming directly from mobile subscribers*, that is, from trunk groups connecting the MSC to its base stations. That way, only the originating MSC will ever look at the A number and will check if this call has to be transferred to the SN. Other MSCs, which may be transferring the call to the SN will not do any A number processing. Similarly, calls originated at the SN will not be subject to any such IN originating service processing.

- If, for some reason, the above method cannot be used, there is always the possibility of using another A number when making the outgoing call from the SN. That is, the SN will use its *own* predefined number in the Calling Party Number (CGPN) field. This special number is not configured on the network as a subscriber to an IN originating service, hence it is not subject to any originating service processing, and the call is handled and routed as a regular telephone call.

  The one clear disadvantage of this method is the fact that the real subscriber MSISDN number is not used as the Calling Party Number, which can affect other value added services normally available to the *recipient* of the call, such as CLI Display, Call Back, or any CLI-based Screening.

7. DISTRIBUTED MULTI-NODE NETWORKS

The issue of routing calls to an SN is even more complicated in a distributed environment, where there are multiple service nodes performing one or several services. Under these conditions, the MSC has to find out, on a per call basis, the correct service node identity, depending both on the subscriber ID and the service requested.

The problem of routing calls to multiple systems exists even in non-calling services, such as Voice Mail (VM). There are several cases where a distributed multi-node solution is deployed in a network:

- The network is very large, and a single platform cannot service all the subscribers.
- The network is geographically dispersed, and using several local platforms is more cost-effective than using one large central system.
- Existing systems cannot be expanded to provide additional capacity, and another system, sometimes of a new vendor, is added to service new subscribers.

7.1. Voice Mail Call Routing

A special case, which can use the existing mobile network forwarding mechanism to do routing, is for Voice Mail (VM) *message deposit* calls, where calls are conditionally forwarded to the VM system based on busy or no-answer states.

The forwarding number is temporarily stored at the VLR, after it has been downloaded from the HLR when the subscriber registered at the VMSC. Hence, when the VMSC fails to deliver the call to the mobile subscriber, it uses the forwarding number to send the call to the VM system. Potentially, the forwarding number can be individually specified for each subscriber, so that each subscriber can be assigned a forwarding number corresponding to the VM system where his mailbox is stored.

In most networks, using the busy/no-answer forwarding numbers for VM usually results in restricting any subscriber self modification of these numbers. Hence, when subscribing to VM, subscribers lose their busy/no-answer forwarding options. Only unconditional call forwarding can be used by VM subscribers.

Unlike message deposit, *Message retrieval* may be handled in one of two ways:

- The subscriber may call his own number, resulting in a busy condition, hence the call is *forwarded* to the VM system in the same way a guest call is. In fact, some VM systems cannot even tell that this is a subscriber message retrieval call, until the subscriber performs a login procedure, e.g., by pressing "*" followed by his password. More sophisticated VM systems, such as the TRILOGUE INfinity, can identify that the calling number is identical to the subscriber ID number, and start a message retrieval session with no explicit login process.
- The common solution is for the subscriber to dial an access *short code* to enter his mailbox. The VMSC should identify this short code and transfer the call to the correct VM system. In this case, since the busy/no-answer states do not apply, no forwarding takes place, and the VMSC must use "A Number" routing, as described above. Getting to the right VM system is more complex, since the forwarding number cannot be used.

Since most mobile network operators require that a short code be used to retrieve VM messages, the call forwarding mechanism cannot provide a satisfactory solution for accessing multiple VM systems. Alternative methods for getting calls to the right VM system are described below.

7.2. Getting to the Right Node

In most cases where multiple systems are deployed, doing either Voice Mail or other services, the easy and straightforward way to find the right node for each subscriber, is to use predefined *number ranges*. Under this scheme, every platform is associated with a predefined MSISDN number range (e.g., 10,000 numbers). Every call related to a subscriber whose number falls within this range is routed to the specific node.

Actual routing usually requires the addition of a specific *prefix* to the MSISDN number, so that the call is routed to the appropriate SN, and not to the actual subscriber. Different prefixes are used for different service node types (e.g., one for VM and another for PNS). For message deposits, the routing prefixes are usually part of the HLR call forwarding fields, which contain both the prefix and the MSISDN number. For message retrieval using a short code, the prefix is inserted to the Called Party Number by the routing tree used for that short code, depending on the MSISDN number range.

The advantages of the number range method is its simplicity, and its suitability for switch routing. This is, essentially, the way *all* calls are routed. It is also local to the switch, requiring no more than the correct setting of the routing tables, and use of standard GSM call forwarding mechanisms.

Yet, that simplicity is also the drawback of the number range solution. It allows no flexibility at the single subscriber level. It is not possible to allocate subscribers to platforms based on any other parameter except their MSISDN number. Worse than that, it is impossible to move a single subscriber from one platform to another without changing its MSISDN number, which is generally unacceptable.

The ability to allocate single subscribers to specific service nodes is very important to network operators. The issue is often raised when the operator introduces a new platform, with additional service features, and wishes to allow subscribers to upgrade their service to include the new features without changing their number. Another case is when an old system reaches its capacity limit, and new subscribers must be allocated to a new one, regardless of their MSISDN number.

The only way an MSC can tell where to route a call on a *per-subscriber basis* (except for call forwarding), is by issuing a *query* to an external database, and receiving the correct Service Node ID in the response message. The query parameter must include the subscriber MSISDN number as well as an indication of the required service, since separate services may be deployed on different service nodes.

A routing database may be queried by the MSC in one of several ways, explained below. Note, this database may be the actual network HLR or any other network-wide "SCP-like" entity, which the switches query when they need the routing information.

7.2.1. HLR Interrogation

The network HLR cannot always be used for getting the proper SN routing information, since in many networks it will only accept simple MSISDN-based routing queries, which result in the MSRN of the *mobile subscriber* (handset) - and not any service node routing information. In other networks, the MSISDN number contains a special part (e.g., two digits), which can be used to identify a specific service query, using the regular Send Routing Information (SRI) MAP message.

If the MSC can indeed query the HLR for the MSRN by providing a special service query indicator, the HLR interprets this query as related to the *service node* rather than the mobile handset. The HLR can then request the MSRN from a designated TRILOGUE INfinity system, which has the whole routing database, and functions as a pseudo VLR for that purpose. Just like the HLR queries regular VLRs for mobile subscribers MSRN, using the PRN (Provide Routing Number) MAP message, the same is done regarding the TRILOGUE INfinity "VLR".

Note that the TRILOGUE INfinity "VLR" can hold the routing information for every subscriber in the network, including those subscribers which have their mailboxes on other VM systems, of any type (TRILOGUE INfinity or other).

7.2.2. MAP Query

If the HLR cannot be used for this task, because of inherent limitations, then another network-wide database must be deployed to serve that need.

The MSC may issue a MAP SRI message to that database, with the subscriber MSISDN number *and* an indication of the required service (e.g., as a prefix) in the B number field. The return value may be an MSRN used to route the call to the SN, or, in fact, *any number* which can be used by the switch for routing.

Note that the SRI message may be inappropriate in the case of A number routing, since several types of MSCs cannot place the A number in the "B number" field of the SRI message. So, for instance, if a Voice Mail subscriber calls to retrieve his messages using a fixed short code such as "*123", then the SRI message can only have the original B number, that is "*123", which makes the query useless.

7.2.3. INAP Query

When MAP messages cannot be used due to limitations of the SRI message and how it is used, a more advanced INAP query mechanism may be applied in a similar way.

The MSC issues an *InitialDP* INAP message, which contains both the A & B numbers, as well as the *service key* field, which identifies the service to which the query is related.

The database looks at the subscriber's profile and responses with the *Connect* INAP message. The *Connect* message includes the Destination Routing Address field, which is usually an MSRN, which uniquely identifies the appropriate SN.

7.3. Distributed INfinity - The "No Routing" Solution

The TRILOGUE INfinity distributed architecture offers another innovative solution for the problem of routing calls to several service nodes.

With Distributed INfinity (DIN), all the TRILOGUE INfinity nodes are connected via high bandwidth data communication links, creating a service node cluster. Each call, reaching any SN, may be handled by that SN, even if the subscriber profile or mailbox resides on another TRILOGUE INfinity system.

For VM, a distributed session is established between the *local* system front-end unit (MMU) and the subscriber *home* system back-end unit (MSU). Thus, voice may be recorded or played over the distributed data network, allowing ubiquitous access to any mailbox from any node.

For IN services, the situation is normally simpler, since all that is required is for the local service node to query the home service node *once* for the subscriber profile, so it can serve this subscriber.

The following diagram shows three TRILOGUE INfinity systems, interconnected via an inter-site network, connected to three network MSCs.

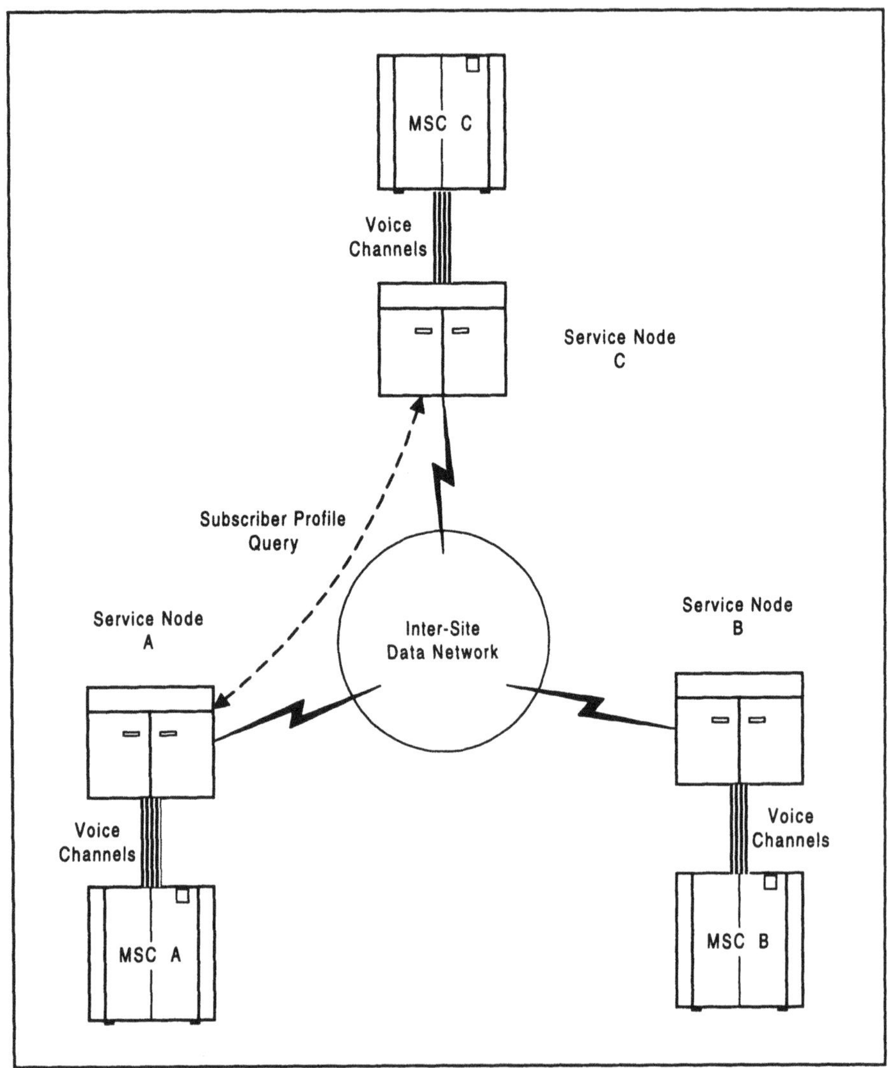

Figure 3 - Distributed INfinity Configuration

A typical scenario would be a call reaching MSC "A", which needs to be processed by a specific IN service. Once MSC "A" identifies that the call needs to be routed to an SN, it always forwards the call to the closest SN, which is SN "A".

If the subscriber profile resides on SN "A", then the call is processed locally. However, if the profile is not found in SN "A" database, the SN performs the following steps:

- SN "A" issues an "Address Resolution" query to the DIN network, looking for the SN which holds the subscriber record related to the service being provided.
- Once a response is received (assuming it is SN "C"), "A" queries "C" for the subscriber record. In fact, only the subscriber profile fields which are necessary for processing the call are sent back in response.
- SN "A" continues to process the call, based on the retrieved profile.
- Once the call is completed, SN "A" may need to update "C" with respect to possible changes in the profile (e.g., decrement the remaining balance in a Pre-Paid service).

Note that Voice Mail calls are handled differently, since a distributed voice session is established between the local system and the subscriber "home" system.

Note that by having a Distributed INfinity solution, the multi-node routing issue is, in fact, eliminated. As shown in the figure, each MSC may be connected to one of the nodes, and route all calls to that node, knowing they can be processed by that node regardless of whether the subscriber really has his account on that node, or not. In other words, each MSC is only aware on one service node, where it routes all calls where some service is required.

Clearly, such a "no routing" multi-node solution is only possible for a homogeneous architecture, where only TRILOGUE INfinity systems are deployed, and where they are all connected in one Distributed INfinity cluster.

INDEX OF CONTRIBUTORS

KEYWORD INDEX

GPSR Compliance
The European Union's (EU) General Product Safety Regulation (GPSR) is a set of rules that requires consumer products to be safe and our obligations to ensure this.

If you have any concerns about our products, you can contact us on

ProductSafety@springernature.com

In case Publisher is established outside the EU, the EU authorized representative is:

Springer Nature Customer Service Center GmbH
Europaplatz 3
69115 Heidelberg, Germany

www.ingramcontent.com/pod-product-compliance
Ingram Content Group UK Ltd.
Pitfield, Milton Keynes, MK11 3LW, UK
UKHW012145240726
13966UKWH00001B/152

* 9 7 8 1 4 7 5 7 5 5 4 2 8 *